Contemporary Authors®

ISSN 0010-7468

Contemporary

Authors®

A Bio-Bibliographical Guide to Current Writers in Fiction, General Nonfiction, Poetry, Journalism, Drama, Motion Pictures, Television, and Other Fields

volume 255

THOMSON

GALE

Detroit • New York • San Francisco • New Haven, Conn. • Waterville, Maine • London

THOMSON
GALE

TM

Contemporary Authors, Vol. 255

Project Editor
Amy Elisabeth Fuller

Editorial
Michelle Kazensky, Lisa Kumar, Mary Ruby, Rob Russell, Amanda Sams

Permissions
Margaret Gaston-Chamberlain, Lisa Kinkade, Tracie Richardson

Imaging and Multimedia
Lezlie Light

Composition and Electronic Capture
Gary Oudersluys

Manufacturing
Drew Kalasky

LIBRARY OF CONGRESS CATALOG CARD NUMBER 62-52046

ISBN-13: 978-0-7876-7884-5
ISBN-10: 0-7876-7884-8
ISSN 0010-7468

This title is also available as an e-book.
ISBN-13: 978-1-4144-2904-5
ISBN-10: 1-4144-2904-5
Contact your Thomson Gale sales representative for ordering information.

Printed in the United States of America
10 9 8 7 6 5 4 3 2 1

Contents

Indexing note: All *Contemporary Authors* entries are indexed in the *Contemporary Authors* cumulative index, which is published separately and distributed twice a year.

As always, the most recent Contemporary Authors cumulative index continues to be the user's guide to the location of an individual author's listing.

Preface

Contemporary Authors (*CA*) provides information on approximately 130,000 writers in a wide range of media, including:

- Current writers of fiction, nonfiction, poetry, and drama whose works have been issued by commercial publishers, risk publishers, or university presses (authors whose books have been published only by known vanity or author-subsidized firms are ordinarily not included)

- Prominent print and broadcast journalists, editors, syndicated cartoonists, graphic novelists, screenwriters, television scriptwriters, and other media people

- Notable international authors

- Literary greats of the early twentieth century whose works are popular in today's high school and college curriculums and continue to elicit critical attention

A *CA* listing entails no charge or obligation. Authors are included on the basis of the above criteria and their interest to *CA* users. Sources of potential listees include trade periodicals, publishers' catalogs, librarians, and other users of the series.

How to Get the Most out of *CA*: Use the Index

The key to locating an author's most recent entry is the *CA* cumulative index, which is published separately and distributed twice a year. It provides access to *all* entries in *CA* and *Contemporary Authors New Revision Series* (*CANR*). Always consult the latest index to find an author's most recent entry.

For the convenience of users, the *CA* cumulative index also includes references to all entries in these Thomson Gale literary series: *Authors and Artists for Young Adults, Authors in the News, Bestsellers, Black Literature Criticism, Black Literature Criticism Supplement, Black Writers, Children's Literature Review, Concise Dictionary of American Literary Biography, Concise Dictionary of British Literary Biography, Contemporary Authors Autobiography Series, Contemporary Authors Bibliographical Series, Contemporary Dramatists, Contemporary Literary Criticism, Contemporary Novelists, Contemporary Poets, Contemporary Popular Writers, Contemporary Southern Writers, Contemporary Women Poets, Dictionary of Literary Biography, Dictionary of Literary Biography Documentary Series, Dictionary of Literary Biography Yearbook, DISCovering Authors, DISCovering Authors: British, DISCovering Authors: Canadian, DISCovering Authors: Modules* (including modules for Dramatists, Most-Studied Authors, Multicultural Authors, Novelists, Poets, and Popular/Genre Authors), *DISCovering Authors 3.0, Drama Criticism, Drama for Students, Feminist Writers, Hispanic Literature Criticism, Hispanic Writers, Junior DISCovering Authors, Major Authors and Illustrators for Children and Young Adults, Major 20th-Century Writers, Native North American Literature, Novels for Students, Poetry Criticism, Poetry for Students, Short Stories for Students, Short Story Criticism, Something about the Author, Something about the Author Autobiography Series, St. James Guide to Children's Writers, St. James Guide to Crime & Mystery Writers, St. James Guide to Fantasy Writers, St. James Guide to Horror, Ghost & Gothic Writers, St. James Guide to Science Fiction Writers, St. James Guide to Young Adult Writers, Twentieth-Century Literary Criticism, 20th Century Romance and Historical Writers, World Literature Criticism*, and *Yesterday's Authors of Books for Children*.

A Sample Index Entry:

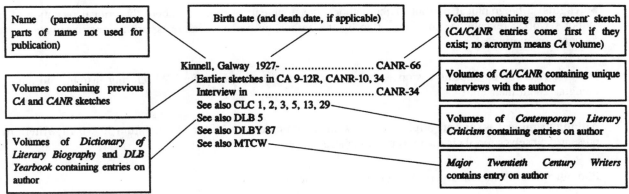

How Are Entries Compiled?

The editors make every effort to secure new information directly from the authors; listees' responses to our questionnaires and query letters provide most of the information featured in *CA*. For deceased writers, or those who fail to reply to requests for data, we consult other reliable biographical sources, such as those indexed in Thomson Gale's *Biography and Genealogy Master Index,* and bibliographical sources, including *National Union Catalog, LC MARC,* and *British National Bibliography.* Further details come from published interviews, feature stories, and book reviews, as well as information supplied by the authors' publishers and agents.

An asterisk (*) at the end of a sketch indicates that the listing has been compiled from secondary sources believed to be reliable but has not been personally verified for this edition by the author sketched.

What Kinds of Information Does An Entry Provide?

Sketches in *CA* contain the following biographical and bibliographical information:

- **Entry heading:** the most complete form of author's name, plus any pseudonyms or name variations used for writing

- **Personal information:** author's date and place of birth, family data, ethnicity, educational background, political and religious affiliations, and hobbies and leisure interests

- **Addresses:** author's home, office, or agent's addresses, plus e-mail and fax numbers, as available

- **Career summary:** name of employer, position, and dates held for each career post; resume of other vocational achievements; military service

- **Membership information:** professional, civic, and other association memberships and any official posts held

- **Awards and honors:** military and civic citations, major prizes and nominations, fellowships, grants, and honorary degrees

- **Writings:** a comprehensive, chronological list of titles, publishers, dates of original publication and revised editions, and production information for plays, television scripts, and screenplays

- **Adaptations:** a list of films, plays, and other media which have been adapted from the author's work

- **Work in progress:** current or planned projects, with dates of completion and/or publication, and expected publisher, when known

- **Sidelights:** a biographical portrait of the author's development; information about the critical reception of the author's works; revealing comments, often by the author, on personal interests, aspirations, motivations, and thoughts on writing

- **Interview:** a one-on-one discussion with authors conducted especially for *CA*, offering insight into authors' thoughts about their craft

- **Autobiographical essay:** an original essay written by noted authors for *CA*, a forum in which writers may present themselves, on their own terms, to their audience

- **Photographs:** portraits and personal photographs of notable authors

- **Biographical and critical sources:** a list of books and periodicals in which additional information on an author's life and/or writings appears

- **Obituary Notices** in *CA* provide date and place of birth as well as death information about authors whose full-length sketches appeared in the series before their deaths. The entries also summarize the authors' careers and writings and list other sources of biographical and death information.

Related Titles in the *CA* Series

Contemporary Authors Autobiography Series complements *CA* original and revised volumes with specially commissioned autobiographical essays by important current authors, illustrated with personal photographs they provide. Common topics include their motivations for writing, the people and experiences that shaped their careers, the rewards they derive from their work, and their impressions of the current literary scene.

Contemporary Authors Bibliographical Series surveys writings by and about important American authors since World War II. Each volume concentrates on a specific genre and features approximately ten writers; entries list works written by and about the author and contain a bibliographical essay discussing the merits and deficiencies of major critical and scholarly studies in detail.

Available in Electronic Formats

GaleNet. *CA* is available on a subscription basis through GaleNet, an online information resource that features an easy-to-use end-user interface, powerful search capabilities, and ease of access through the World-Wide Web. For more information, call 1-800-877-GALE.

Licensing. *CA* is available for licensing. The complete database is provided in a fielded format and is deliverable on such media as disk, CD-ROM, or tape. For more information, contact Thomson Gale's Business Development Group at 1-800-877-GALE, or visit us on our website at www.galegroup.com/bizdev.

Suggestions Are Welcome

The editors welcome comments and suggestions from users on any aspect of the *CA* series. If readers would like to recommend authors for inclusion in future volumes of the series, they are cordially invited to write the Editors at *Contemporary Authors*, Thomson Gale, 27500 Drake Rd., Farmington Hills, MI 48331-3535; or call at 1-248-699-4253; or fax at 1-248-699-8054.

Contemporary Authors Product Advisory Board

The editors of *Contemporary Authors* are dedicated to maintaining a high standard of excellence by publishing comprehensive, accurate, and highly readable entries on a wide array of writers. In addition to the quality of the content, the editors take pride in the graphic design of the series, which is intended to be orderly yet inviting, allowing readers to utilize the pages of *CA* easily and with efficiency. Despite the longevity of the *CA* print series, and the success of its format, we are mindful that the vitality of a literary reference product is dependent on its ability to serve its users over time. As literature, and attitudes about literature, constantly evolve, so do the reference needs of students, teachers, scholars, journalists, researchers, and book club members. To be certain that we continue to keep pace with the expectations of our customers, the editors of *CA* listen carefully to their comments regarding the value, utility, and quality of the series. Librarians, who have firsthand knowledge of the needs of library users, are a valuable resource for us. The *Contemporary Authors* Product Advisory Board, made up of school, public, and academic librarians, is a forum to promote focused feedback about *CA* on a regular basis. The six-member advisory board includes the following individuals, whom the editors wish to thank for sharing their expertise:

- **Anne M. Christensen,** Librarian II, Phoenix Public Library, Phoenix, Arizona.

- **Barbara C. Chumard,** Reference/Adult Services Librarian, Middletown Thrall Library, Middletown, New York.

- **Eva M. Davis,** Youth Department Manager, Ann Arbor District Library, Ann Arbor, Michigan.

- **Adam Janowski, Jr.,** Library Media Specialist, Naples High School Library Media Center, Naples, Florida.

- **Robert Reginald,** Head of Technical Services and Collection Development, California State University, San Bernadino, California.

- **Stephen Weiner,** Director, Maynard Public Library, Maynard, Massachusetts.

International Advisory Board

Well-represented among the 120,000 author entries published in *Contemporary Authors* are sketches on notable writers from many non-English-speaking countries. The primary criteria for inclusion of such authors has traditionally been the publication of at least one title in English, either as an original work or as a translation. However, the editors of *Contemporary Authors* came to observe that many important international writers were being overlooked due to a strict adherence to our inclusion criteria. In addition, writers who were publishing in languages other than English were not being covered in the traditional sources we used for identifying new listees. Intent on increasing our coverage of international authors, including those who write only in their native language and have not been translated into English, the editors enlisted the aid of a board of advisors, each of whom is an expert on the literature of a particular country or region. Among the countries we focused attention on are Mexico, Puerto Rico, Germany, Luxembourg, Belgium, the Netherlands, Norway, Sweden, Denmark, Finland, Taiwan, Singapore, Spain, Italy, South Africa, Israel, and Japan, as well as England, Scotland, Wales, Ireland, Australia, and New Zealand. The sixteen-member advisory board includes the following individuals, whom the editors wish to thank for sharing their expertise:

- **Lowell A. Bangerter,** Professor of German, University of Wyoming, Laramie, Wyoming.

- **Nancy E. Berg,** Associate Professor of Hebrew and Comparative Literature, Washington University, St. Louis, Missouri.

- **Frances Devlin-Glass,** Associate Professor, School of Literary and Communication Studies, Deakin University, Burwood, Victoria, Australia.

- **David William Foster,** Regent's Professor of Spanish, Interdisciplinary Humanities, and Women's Studies, Arizona State University, Tempe, Arizona.

- **Hosea Hirata,** Director of the Japanese Program, Associate Professor of Japanese, Tufts University, Medford, Massachusetts.

- **Jack Kolbert,** Professor Emeritus of French Literature, Susquehanna University, Selinsgrove, Pennsylvania.

- **Mark Libin,** Professor, University of Manitoba, Winnipeg, Manitoba, Canada.

- **C. S. Lim,** Professor, University of Malaya, Kuala Lumpur, Malaysia.

- **Eloy E. Merino,** Assistant Professor of Spanish, Northern Illinois University, DeKalb, Illinois.

- **Linda M. Rodríguez Guglielmoni,** Associate Professor, University of Puerto Rico—Mayagüez, Puerto Rico.

- **Sven Hakon Rossel,** Professor and Chair of Scandinavian Studies, University of Vienna, Vienna, Austria.

- **Steven R. Serafin,** Director, Writing Center, Hunter College of the City University of New York, New York City.

- **David Smyth,** Lecturer in Thai, School of Oriental and African Studies, University of London, England.

- **Ismail S. Talib,** Senior Lecturer, Department of English Language and Literature, National University of Singapore, Singapore.

- **Dionisio Viscarri,** Assistant Professor, Ohio State University, Columbus, Ohio.

- **Mark Williams,** Associate Professor, English Department, University of Canterbury, Christchurch, New Zealand.

CA Numbering System and Volume Update Chart

Occasionally questions arise about the *CA* numbering system and which volumes, if any, can be discarded. Despite numbers like "29-32R," "97-100" and "255," the entire *CA* print series consists of only 342 physical volumes with the publication of *CA* Volume 255. The following charts note changes in the numbering system and cover design, and indicate which volumes are essential for the most complete, up-to-date coverage.

CA First Revision

- 1-4R through 41-44R (11 books)
  Cover: Brown with black and gold trim.
  There will be no further First Revision volumes because revised entries are now being handled exclusively through the more efficient *New Revision Series* mentioned below.

CA Original Volumes

- 45-48 through 97-100 (14 books)
  Cover: Brown with black and gold trim.
  101 through 255 (155 books)
  Cover: Blue and black with orange bands.
  The same as previous *CA* original volumes but with a new, simplified numbering system and new cover design.

CA Permanent Series

- *CAP*-1 and *CAP*-2 (2 books)
  Cover: Brown with red and gold trim.
  There will be no further Permanent Series volumes because revised entries are now being handled exclusively through the more efficient *New Revision Series* mentioned below.

CA New Revision Series

- CANR-1 through CANR-160 (160 books)
  Cover: Blue and black with green bands.
  Includes only sketches requiring significant changes; **sketches are taken from any previously published CA, CAP, or CANR volume.**

If You Have:	You May Discard:
CA First Revision Volumes 1-4R through 41-44R and *CA Permanent Series* Volumes 1 and 2	*CA* Original Volumes 1, 2, 3, 4 Volumes 5-6 through 41-44
CA Original Volumes 45-48 through 97-100 and 101 through 255	**NONE:** These volumes will not be superseded by corresponding revised volumes. Individual entries from these and all other volumes appearing in the left column of this chart may be revised and included in the various volumes of the *New Revision Series*.
CA New Revision Series Volumes *CANR*-1 through *CANR*-160	**NONE:** The *New Revision Series* does not replace any single volume of *CA*. Instead, volumes of *CANR* include entries from many previous *CA* series volumes. All *New Revision Series* volumes must be retained for full coverage.

A Sampling of Authors and Media People
Featured in This Volume

James Bradley

With the publication of his first book, *Flags of Our Fathers,* Bradley became a best-selling author. Written with Ron Powers, the biography traces the lives of six U.S. soldiers immortalized in the famous photograph that shows them raising an American flag on the island of Iwo Jima during World War II. One of the soldiers was Bradley's father, who received a Navy Cross for bravery. *Flags of Our Fathers* was adapted for a 2006 feature film directed by Clint Eastwood and starring Ryan Phillippe. Bradley's other works include *Flyboys: A True Story of Courage.*

Anne Fleming

Fleming is an award-winning author and educator who has taught at universities throughout her native Canada. As a lesbian and a writer, Fleming balances the expectations that the literary world has for "queer writers" with her desire to write evocative fiction that does not necessarily serve as a showcase for lesbian theory or homosexual stereotypes. Noted for her skill with language and story, Fleming has won the Canadian National Award for fiction. Her books include *Pool-Hopping and Other Stories* and the novel *Anomaly.*

Paulo Lins

A native of Rio de Janeiro, Brazil, Lins is a poet, novelist, and screenwriter. His 1997 novel *Cidade de Deus,* later published in English as *City of God,* paints a graphic portrait of life in the *favelas,* or slums, of Brazil. Named after the crime-plagued housing project where Lins grew up, *City of God* chronicles the lives of the myriad gangsters who vie for control of the city's drug dens. In 2002 the book was adapted into the critically-acclaimed, award-winning movie of the same title.

Max

Max, a pseudonym for artist and illustrator Francesc Capdevila Gisbert, is a pioneering figure in Spain's underground comics scene. He first came to prominence in the 1970s as a member of El Rrollo, an artists' collective, and as cofounder of *El Víbora,* an edgy, independent comics journal. Max published his first collection, *Gustavo Contra la Actividad del Radio,* in 1981, and four years later he published *Peter Pank,* the first of three volumes featuring the anarchic title character.

Paula Poundstone

Poundstone is a stand-up comedian who has appeared on television and in comedy clubs across the country. A panelist on the National Public Radio show *Wait Wait Don't Tell Me!,* she has received an Emmy Award for her work on the Public Broadcasting Service series *Life & Times,* and an American Comedy Award for best female stand-up comedian. In 2001 Poundstone was arrested for driving under the influence of alcohol with her children in the car. Though her three adopted children were returned to her full custody in late 2002, she ultimately lost the right to care for her foster children. Poundstone has incorporated her struggles into her comedy routines and writing, including her memoir *There's Nothing in This Book That I Meant to Say.*

Giuliana Sgrena

Italian journalist Sgrena was working in Baghdad as a war correspondent when she was kidnapped by armed gunmen in February of 2005. She was released after a month, but on her way to the airport, U.S. soldiers who were part of the security detail for American diplomat John Negroponte fired upon Sgrena and her escorts. Shrapnel entered her shoulder and one of the agents protecting her was killed. Sgrena relates her experiences in *Friendly Fire: The Remarkable Story of a Journalist Kidnapped in Iraq, Rescued by an Italian Secret Service Agent, and Shot by U.S. Forces.*

Ersi Sotiropoulos

Born in Patras, Greece, Sotiropoulos studied philosophy and cultural anthropology in Florence, Italy, before going on to become a writer, poet, and screenwriter. She is the author of numerous books in Greek, as well as scripts for film and television. In 2000 her novel *Zigzag through the Bitter Orange Trees,* translated into English by Peter Green, won both the National Literature Prize of Greece and the Book Critics' Award.

Jerry Springer

Talk-show host Springer has become an American institution and a touchstone in debates about morality in modern popular culture. Springer was elected mayor of Cincinnati, Ohio, in 1977, where he made a point of serving the interest of average citizens. After losing his bid for the Ohio governorship, Springer became a journalist for a Cincinnati television station, where he won an Emmy for his investigative reporting. Though his talk show began as an extension of his "serious" journalism, after three years of low ratings, *The Jerry Springer Show* revamped itself into a carnival of camp, complete with chair-throwing, hair-pulling brawls. While the show has many detractors, it has remained popular for over a decade, and to some critics, it presents a welcome counterbalance to polished, middle-class programming. Springer charts his career in his memoir, *Jerry Springer: Ringmaster.*

A

ADKINS, David
See SINBAD

*   *   *

AIDAN, Pamela
   [A pseudonym]
   (Pamela Mogen)

PERSONAL: Divorced; married second husband; children: (first marriage) three; stepchildren: three. *Education:* Millersville University of Pennsylvania, B.S.; University of Illinois at Urbana-Champaign, M.L.S.

ADDRESSES: Office—Wytherngate Press, Inc., P.O. Box 3134, Coeur d'Alene, ID 83816. *E-mail*—pamela_aidan@hotmail.com.

CAREER: Worked as a librarian for more than thirty years; currently a director of a library in Liberty Lake, WA; Wytherngate Press, Coeur d'Alene, ID, owner.

WRITINGS:

"FITZWILLIAM DARCY, GENTLEMAN" TRILOGY

An Assembly Such as This, Wytherngate Press (Atlanta, GA), 2003, reprinted, Touchstone/Simon & Schuster (New York, NY), 2006.

Duty and Desire, Wytherngate Press (Coeur d'Alene, ID), 2004, reprinted, Touchstone/Simon & Schuster (New York, NY), 2006.
These Three Remain, Wytherngate Press (Coeur d'Alene, ID), 2005, reprinted, Touchstone/Simon & Schuster (New York, NY), 2007.

SIDELIGHTS: A librarian by profession, Pamela Aidan became an author when she penned a trilogy based on a Jane Austen character from *Pride and Prejudice,* Fitzwilliam Darcy. Originally, she published the "Fitzwilliam Darcy, Gentleman" trilogy through a company she created, Wytherngate Press, but they were later reprinted by the Touchstone imprint at Simon & Schuster. The books tell the same story as *Pride and Prejudice,* focusing on Darcy and his growing love for Elizabeth Bennet. Aidan, who strives to mimic the same tone and writing style that is characteristic of Austen's book, adds to the story by including new characters and adding insights into Darcy's inner emotions and personality. "Her original contributions . . . ," as Kathy Piehl noted in a *Library Journal* review of the first installment of the trilogy, *An Assembly Such as This,* "infuse humor into the plot and reveal Darcy's humanity." "Austen fans will relish the tale's retelling from Darcy's perspective as well as new characters," concluded *Booklist* reviewer Patty Engelmann of the same book.

In the second novel of the trilogy, *Duty and Desire,* Aidan follows Darcy through a period of time in which he was absent in the original Austen story. Darcy has left the *Pride and Prejudice* setting of Netherfield to visit his sister and becomes involved in an unusual mystery, which is solved with the help of his intelligent valet, Fletcher. "Plenty of period detail, witty dialogue, humor . . . and elements of the gothic will keep readers entertained," according to Mary Ellen Quinn in *Booklist*. A *Publishers Weekly* contributor praised Aidan for, "instead of imitating Austen, convincingly makes Darcy's story her own." Aidan concludes her trilogy with *These Three Remain*.

Aidan told *CA:* "Many years ago when I was in junior high, a friend of mine, who was as enamored with the original broadcasts of the television program *Star Trek* as I was, suggested that we write our own *Star Trek* stories. I took up the challenge and penned a 100-page script that only she ever saw. I treasured the surge of creative energy that I felt at the time but took the practical route of professional librarianship, which has resulted in a very satisfying career. But thirty-five years later, I decided that it was the time to make a serious attempt to write. I had intended to write children's books. The veer into Austen and novels for adults was unexpected and my success a wonderful surprise.

"At this point in my writing, Jane Austen and Georgette Heyer have been the main influences. As I leave that genre for other sorts of writing, that will change. What will not change is the generous influence of my husband, who is my best critic and coach. Although I would not wish to be categorized as a 'Christian writer,' I find that my writing is motivated by the struggle for influence of mercy, hope, and love in our everyday life and culture.

"Since I have 'traipsed after Jane' for most of my writing to this point, I have yet to develop a writing process. I have found that the best preparation for writing is to have a firm grasp on the characters of my protagonists and the historical context of my story, then make a cup of tea, retreat to a quiet, softly lit area, and listen to some music. Then it is just a matter of starting to type.

"The most surprising thing I have learned is that there are times when the characters take over and the writing is easy and sweet—I find myself riding a rhythm different than anything I've ever experienced.

"My favorite book of mine is *Duty and Desire*, the second book in the trilogy, because it is my own creation rather than the other side of events in *Pride and Prejudice*. In it I could flesh out my ideas, create characters, and otherwise stretch my writing wings.

"My purpose in writing the trilogy was to answer a question: Who is Fitzwilliam Darcy, and how and why did he change? As I disclosed the struggles of this much admired literary character, I began hearing from readers since the very first chapters were posted online in 1997. Most expressed that I have made Austen's story fuller or more understandable, and as a result, they have come to appreciate her work more and been encouraged to read the rest of her oeuvre. This is high praise! Others have written that my books have helped them through difficult times in their lives, providing an island of peace and pleasure. What more could a writer hope for?"

BIOGRAPHICAL AND CRITICAL SOURCES:

PERIODICALS

Booklist, May 1, 2006, Patty Engelmann, review of *An Assembly Such as This*, p. 69; September 1, 2006, Mary Ellen Quinn, review of *Duty and Desire*, p. 53; December 14, 2006, Mary Ellen Quinn, review of *These Three Remain*, p. 20.
Kirkus Reviews, May 1, 2006, review of *An Assembly Such as This*, p. 423.
Library Journal, May 1, 2006, Kathy Piehl, review of *An Assembly Such as This*, p. 74; September 1, 2006, Kathy Piehl, review of *Duty and Desire*, p. 132.
Publishers Weekly, June 5, 2006, review of *Duty and Desire*, p. 28; November 13, 2006, review of *These Three Remain*.

ONLINE

Jane Austen Centre Web site, http://www.janeausten.co.uk/ (November 24, 2006), reviews of *An Assembly Such as This* and *Duty and Desire*.
Literature Classics.com, http://www.literatureclassics.com/ (November 24, 2006), review of *An Assembly Such as This*.
Wytherngate Press Web site, http://www.wytherngate press.com (November 24, 2006), brief biography of Pamela Aidan.

*   *   *

ALBA, Ben 1957-

PERSONAL: Born 1957. *Education:* DePaul University, B.S.; Loyola University (Chicago, IL), J.D.

ADDRESSES: *Office*—College of Law, DePaul University, 25 E. Jackson Blvd., Chicago, IL 60604. *E-mail*—balba@depaul.edu.

CAREER: Loyola University School of Law, Chicago, IL, instructor; William J. Sneckenberg & Associates (now Sneckenberg, Thompson & Brody), Chicago, attorney; DePaul University College of Law, Chicago, legal writing instructor and director of the bar passage program.

WRITINGS:

Inventing Late Night: Steve Allen and the Original Tonight Show, Prometheus Books (Amherst, NY), 2005.

SIDELIGHTS: Ben Alba is an attorney who studies the life and talent of one of the most versatile television entertainers of all time in *Inventing Late Night: Steve Allen and the Original Tonight Show.* In 1954 Allen brought to the small screen a format that entranced a nation and featured entertainers such as Carl Reiner, Sid Caesar, Steve Lawrence, Groucho Marx, Bud Abbott, and Lou Costello. His regulars included Don Knotts, Tom Poston, Louis Nye, Bill Dana, and his wife, actress Jayne Meadows. It was a program that replaced the test pattern and expanded viewing hours so that other shows soon followed. Comedy was a big part of the show, as was music. Allen, a pianist, performed and also invited jazz greats, including Buddy Rich and Thelonious Monk, and others such as classical pianist Van Cliburn and composer Leonard Bernstein. His comedy skits included his "Question Man," in which he provided the question to an answer, and "Meeting of the Minds," in which historical figures engaged in spirited discussions. Allen's use of visuals have been imitated by many comedians and talk show hosts ever since.

In a *Weekly Standard* review of *Inventing Late Night,* Stefan Kanfer wrote: "Looking back, Allen observed, 'I seem to have stumbled in at the right time in history, where a man who owns a combination of fairly mediocre abilities and wears a clean shirt can do well in a particular medium. A hundred years ago, I'd probably have been an unsuccessful writer.' This modesty was both legitimate and false. He might well have failed in the creative arts a century before. But his abilities were far from commonplace. . . . As Ben Alba indicates in this lively hagiography, Allen drove himself hard, and never settled for the safe mediocrity of network programming."

In a *Daily Variety* review, Steven Gaydos noted that the National Broadcasting Company (NBC), the network that aired the show, destroyed most of the kinescopes of the original programs. Therefore, he noted: "This is one more reason to look into Alba's merry tribute and get the feel of what latenight was like in more innocent times, when the brilliant Mr. Allen was having a blast 'inventing' on the fly what has become a multibillion-dollar industry."

BIOGRAPHICAL AND CRITICAL SOURCES:

PERIODICALS

Booklist, October 1, 2005, Mike Tribby, review of *Inventing Late Night: Steve Allen and the Original Tonight Show,* p. 13.
Daily Variety, November 17, 2005, Steven Gaydos, review of *Inventing Late Night,* p. A12.
Weekly Standard, December 5, 2005, Stefan Kanfer, review of *Inventing Late Night.*

ONLINE

DePaul University College of Law Web site, http://www.law.depaul.edu/ (February 2, 2007), brief biography.

* * *

ALBERTYN, Dorothy
    See BLACK, Dorothy

* * *

ALLAHYARI, Rebecca A.
    See ALLAHYARI, Rebecca Anne

* * *

ALLAHYARI, Rebecca Anne 1963-
    (Rebecca A. Allahyari)

PERSONAL: Born 1963. *Education:* University of California, Davis, Ph.D.

ADDRESSES: Office—School for Advanced Research, P.O. Box 2188, Santa Fe, NM 87504-2188. *E-mail*—allahyari@sarsf.org.

CAREER: Writer, educator, and qualitative sociologist. School for Advanced Research, Santa Fe, NM, staff scholar. University of California, Santa Barbara, visiting professor of sociology and religious studies, 2002. Has taught women's studies and American studies at the University of Maryland and has also taught at Georgetown University.

AWARDS, HONORS: Spencer Foundation research grant.

WRITINGS:

Visions of Charity: Volunteer Workers and Moral Community, University of California Press (Berkeley, CA), 2000.

Contributor to periodicals.

SIDELIGHTS: Rebecca Anne Allahyari is a qualitative sociologist whose research focuses on "understandings of the sacred" and how these understandings are applied in "everyday practice and politics," commented a biographer on the *School for Advanced Research* Web site. This interest in the commingling of the sacred and the practical needs of everyday life is reflected in her book, *Visions of Charity: Volunteer Workers and Moral Community.* This book "makes an important contribution to understanding how faith-based organizations function," commented a reviewer in the *Journal of Sociology & Social Welfare.* "More importantly," the reviewer continued, "her analysis of their different approaches to the problem of homelessness provides helpful insights into the potential of faith based organizations to address social needs."

In the book, Allahyari closely analyzes volunteer activity at two distinct charitable organizations based in Sacramento, California: the Salvation Army and the Catholic-based Loaves and Fishes. Both of these charities are involved in providing assistance and food for the poor and homeless, but each approaches its mission with a different philosophical, practical, and moral concept. Allahyari focuses her analysis on the volunteers who are directly involved in the day-to-day as-

sistance activities and on what this type of volunteerism means for those who participate. She notes how volunteers for Loaves and Fishes were predominantly white, middle-class females, whereas Salvation Army workers were largely working-class minority males from other Salvation Army shelters or from Alternative Sentencing programs. She explores how Loaves and Fishes functions more from a core belief in compassion, altruism, and simple giving, whereas the Salvation Army stresses rehabilitation, recovery, and acquisition of independence through discipline and work. Allahyari also considers issues of race, class, community, and gender as they exist within the context of social services. Much of her analysis is concerned with the "moral selving" of the volunteers, the process whereby volunteers work to advance themselves as more spiritual individuals. "The sophistication of Allahyari's examination of the social foundations of moral community shines in her attention to how practical problems faced by charity staff members affected organizational practices of visions of charity," commented Cheryl Carpenter in *Social Forces.* A reviewer in the *Journal of Community Health* called Allahyari's book a "very well-crafted and stimulating volume that will be of great interest" to persons involved in charitable activities with the homeless, the impoverished, and the needy. Carpenter named it "a significant contribution to the sociology of charity, social welfare, and volunteerism."

BIOGRAPHICAL AND CRITICAL SOURCES:

PERIODICALS

Journal of Community Health, February, 2002, review of *Visions of Charity: Volunteer Workers and Moral Community,* p. 76.
Journal of Sociology & Social Welfare, December, 2001, review of *Visions of Charity,* p. 230.
Sacramento News and Review, December 6, 2001, Matt Raymond, review of *Visions of Charity.*
Social Forces, December, 2001, Cheryl Carpenter, review of *Visions of Charity,* p. 743; March, 2002, Cheryl Carpenter, review of *Visions of Charity,* p. 1125.
Sojourners, May, 2001, Jim Wallis, review of *Visions of Charity,* p. 55.

ONLINE

School for Advanced Research Web site, http://www.sarweb.org/ (January 22, 2007), biography of Rebecca Anne Allahyari.

University of California, Santa Barbara Web site, http://www.ucsb.edu/ (March 26, 2002), "Emotions and Morality of Charity to Be Compared at UCSB Affiliates Spirituality, Culture Discussion."

* * *

ALLEN, Brooke 1956-

PERSONAL: Born 1956; daughter of Lewis M. (a theatrical producer and film producer) and Jay Presson Allen (a playwright and screenwriter); married Peter Aaron (an architectural photographer), September 8, 1992. *Education:* University of Virginia, B.A., 1979; Columbia University, M.A., Ph.D., 1993.

CAREER: Writer and literary critic. Served as managing editor of *Grand Street* magazine.

WRITINGS:

Twentieth-Century Attitudes: Literary Powers in Uncertain Times, Ivan R. Dee (Chicago, IL), 2003.
(Author of introduction and notes) Sinclair Lewis, *Main Street,* consulting editorial direction by George Stade, Barnes & Noble (New York, NY), 2003.
Artistic License: Three Centuries of Good Writing and Bad Behavior, Ivan R. Dee (Chicago, IL), 2004.
Moral Minority: Our Skeptical Founding Fathers, Ivan R. Dee (Chicago, IL), 2006.

Contributor to periodicals, including the *New York Times Book Review, New Criterion,* and *Atlantic Monthly.*

SIDELIGHTS: Writer and literary critic Brooke Allen has authored books of literary criticism and also written about the early religious beliefs of America's founding fathers. In *Twentieth-Century Attitudes: Literary Powers in Uncertain Times,* Allen presents a series of essays profiling twentieth-century writers such as Colette, Virginia Woolf, H.G. Wells, Edith Wharton, Henry James, James Baldwin, Grace Paley, and others. Writing in *Booklist,* Donna Seaman noted that the author "eschews an excessively text-oriented approach and writes out of passion and with panache."

Library Journal contributor Charles C. Nash wrote that "Allen brings forth a wealth of information to support her argument that the last century produced 'a wide variety of odd attitudes.'"

Artistic License: Three Centuries of Good Writing and Bad Behavior is another collection of literary essays that combines biography and criticism to delve into the lives and works of famous authors who were also known for their dysfunctional and often painful lives. Allen includes essays on a wide range of authors, from Laurence Sterne, Hans Christian Andersen, and Bram Stoker to Sinclair Lewis and William Saroyan. Seaman, writing again in *Booklist,* called the collection "saucy and shrewd," adding that Allen "matches literary erudition with a lithe yet pithy writing style." A *Kirkus Reviews* contributor referred to *Artistic License* as "bold criticism from a knowledgeable, bright writer who would rather declare than question, speculate, or wonder." Robin Imhof wrote in the *Library Journal* that "Allen's essays both entertain and illuminate."

Allen turns her attention from literary criticism to political and religious matters in *Moral Minority: Our Skeptical Founding Fathers.* Focusing on the religious beliefs of Benjamin Franklin, George Washington, John Adams, Thomas Jefferson, James Madison, and Alexander Hamilton, Allen presents her case that none were devout Christians, some were agnostics, and nearly all of them stressed the importance of the separation of church and state and the need to keep religion out of politics. Writing in the *Weekly Standard,* Christopher Hitchens commented that Allen "is especially interesting on the extent to which the Founders felt obliged to keep their doubts on religion to themselves." Hitchens also noted: "In a first-class closing chapter on the intellectual and scientific world that shaped the Framers, Allen discusses the wide influence then exerted by great humanist thinkers like Hume, Shaftesbury, Bolingbroke, Locke, and Voltaire." In a review in the *Library Journal,* D.L. Davey wrote that the author "explicitly warns that the Enlightened ideals on which this country was founded are now under grave threat." George F. Will commented in the *New York Times:* "Her conviction is well documented, exuberantly argued and quite persuasive." A *Kirkus Reviews* contributor referred to *Moral Minority* as "substantial and scholarly."

BIOGRAPHICAL AND CRITICAL SOURCES:

PERIODICALS

Booklist, September 15, 2003, Donna Seaman, review of *Twentieth-Century Attitudes: Literary Powers in Uncertain Times,* p. 193; September 15, 2004, Donna Seaman, review of *Artistic License: Three Centuries of Good Writing and Bad Behavior,* p. 193.

Kirkus Reviews, July 1, 2004, review of *Artistic License,* p. 609; June 15, 2006, review of *Moral Minority: Our Skeptical Founding Fathers,* p. 607.

Library Journal, August, 2003, Charles C. Nash, review of *Twentieth-Century Attitudes,* p. 81; August, 2004, Robin Imhof, review of *Artistic License,* p. 75; August 1, 2006, D.L. Davey, "Q&A: Brooke Allen," p. 100; August 1, 2006, D.L. Davey, review of *Moral Minority,* p. 100.

New York Times, September 13, 1992, "Weddings; Brooke Allen, Peter Aaron"; October 22, 2006, George F. Will, review of *Moral Minority.*

Reference & Research Book News, November, 2006, review of *Moral Minority.*

Weekly Standard, December 11, 2006, Christopher Hitchens, review of *Moral Minority.*

ONLINE

EnterStageRight.com, http://www.enterstageright.com/ (April 11, 2005), Bernard Chapin, "Interview with Brooke Allen."

*   *   *

ALLEY, Richard B.

PERSONAL: Education: Ohio State University, B.Sc. (summa cum laude), 1980, M.Sc., 1983; University of Wisconsin-Madison, Ph.D., 1987.

ADDRESSES: Office—Department of Geosciences, Pennsylvania State University, 503 Deike Bldg., University Park, PA 16802; fax: 814-863-7823. *E-mail*—ralley@essc.psu.edu.

CAREER: Writer and educator. Pennsylvania State University, University Park, PA, assistant professor, 1988-92, associate professor, 1992-96, professor, 1996—, Evan Pugh Professor of Geosciences, 2000—. Guest on television and radio programs, including *Nova* and *Earth and Sky.*

AWARDS, HONORS: Seligman Crystal, International Glaciological Society; Louis Agassiz Medal, European Geosciences Union Cryospheric Section; fellowship, American Geophysical Union; Horton Award, American Geophysical Union Hydrology Section; Don J. Easterbrook Award, Geological Society of America Quaternary Geology and Geomorphology Division; David and Lucile Packard Foundation Fellowship for Science and Engineering; Gary C. Comer Abrupt Climate Change Mentorship; Presidential Young Investigator Award; Wilson Teaching Award, College of Earth and Mineral Sciences, Pennsylvania State University; Mitchell Innovative Teaching Award, College of Earth and Mineral Sciences, Pennsylvania State University; Faculty Scholar Medal in Science, Pennsylvania State University.

WRITINGS:

The Two-Mile Time Machine: Ice Cores, Abrupt Climate Change, and Our Future, Princeton University Press (Princeton, NJ), 2000.
(With Robert A. Bindschadler) *The West Antarctic Ice Sheet: Behavior and Environment,* American Geophysical Union (Washington, DC), 2001.

Contributor to journals, including *Philosophical Transactions of the Royal Society of London, Quaternary Science Reviews, Annual Review of Earth and Planetary Sciences, Paleoceanography, Journal of Glaciology, Geology, Science,* and *Nature.*

SIDELIGHTS: Richard B. Alley is a professor of geosciences at Pennsylvania State University, where he specializes in glaciology, the study of ice sheet stability, and the investigation of ancient climatology as represented in ice cores. Alley is a scientist whose "contributions to the ice core, sea-level, and climate communities have been exceptional," stated Samuel C. Colbeck of the Earth and Environmental Systems Institute in the citation for Alley's 1996 Horton Award.

In *The Two-Mile Time Machine: Ice Cores, Abrupt Climate Change, and Our Future,* Alley presents detailed research findings derived from the study of two-mile-long ice cores drilled and extracted from the ice covering Greenland. These cylindrical cores offered Alley and other scientists access to more than 110,000 years of uninterrupted climatic information, sealed within the ice. Alley also describes the Greenland expeditions themselves, offers a primer on the use of ice cores to examine climate history, and details the methodologies used to collect and analyze the ice cores.

Some of Alley's findings were unexpected, even alarming, especially in terms of current controversies surrounding global warming and abrupt climate change. He discovered, for example, that the last ice age ended not in a gradual decline over decades or centuries, but sharply and quickly within a three-year period. He notes that throughout the history represented in the ice cores, global climate has been much colder than the relatively mild temperatures experienced during the time period during which modern humans developed. The relatively warm and stable climate of the last 10,000 years, Alley contends, is not the norm. He identifies factors that contribute to climate change, including continental drift, wind patterns, the concentration of greenhouse gases in the atmosphere, and changes in warmth and patterns of the ocean currents. Alley concludes that global climate has, does, and likely will again change abruptly and with little warning. Though not alarmist in his predictions, Alley suggests that climatic disaster is inevitable, whether precipitated by man-made influences or by natural factors that have been in play for millennia. Ultimately, he concludes that "proceeding as if humanity could affect climate change is only prudent," noted Ray Olson in *Booklist*. A *Publishers Weekly* reviewer called Alley's book a "brilliant combination of scientific thriller, memoir and environmental science" that "provides instructive glimpses into our climatic past and global future." Olson concluded by calling the study "wonderfully accessible, information-packed science reading."

BIOGRAPHICAL AND CRITICAL SOURCES:

PERIODICALS

Booklist, October 15, 2000, Ray Olson, review of *The Two-Mile Time Machine: Ice Cores, Abrupt Climate Change, and Our Future*, p. 397.
Publishers Weekly, October 30, 2000, review of *The Two-Mile Time Machine*, p. 57.
Science News, August 31, 2002, review of *The Two-Mile Time Machine*, p. 143.
Weatherwise, November-December, 2001, Stanley David Gedzelman, review of *The Two-Mile Time Machine*, p. 50.

ONLINE

Earth and Environmental Systems Institute Web site, http://www.eesi.psu.edu/ (January 22, 2007), Samuel C. Colbeck, "Citation for Richard B. Alley: Horton Award, 1996."

Pennsylvania State University Department of Geosciences Web site, http://www.geosc.psu.edu/ (January 22, 2007), curriculum vitae of Richard B. Alley.

*　　*　　*

ALVIC, Philis

PERSONAL: Education: School of the Art Institute of Chicago, B.A.E., 1964; graduate study at Winthrop College.

ADDRESSES: Home—Lexington, KY. *E-mail*—philis@philisalvic.info.

CAREER: Professional artist with studio in Lexington, KY; writer and speaker on weaving techniques and the history of weaving in Southern Appalachia. Complex Weavers Newsletter, editorial coordinator, 1980-84; The Guild Record, Kentucky Guild of Artists and Craftsmen, editor, 1990-94. *Exhibitions:* Has exhibited original artworks in more than two hundred juried, invitational, and solo shows in the United States and has served as curator of exhibits in Kentucky and Michigan.

MEMBER: Kentucky Guild of Artists and Craftsmen, Kentucky Craft Marketing, Kentucky Museum of Art and Craft.

AWARDS, HONORS: Certificate of excellence, Handweavers Guild of America 1976; Alden B. Dow Creativity Fellowship, Alden B. Dow Creativity Center, 1987; Al Smith Fellowship, Kentucky Arts Council, 1993; grants from Kentucky Foundation for Women, 1995, Appalachian Community Development Association, Appalachian Center of Berea College, McKissick Museum of the University of South Carolina, Lexington Arts and Cultural Council, American Crafts Council, arts councils in North Carolina and Kentucky, and humanities councils in five states, including Tennessee, North Carolina, and Kentucky.

WRITINGS:

(Editor) *Crafts of Armenia,* International Executive Service Corps [Armenia], 2003.

Weavers of the Southern Highlands, University Press of Kentucky (Lexington, KY), 2003.

PAMPHLETS

Weavers of the Southern Highlands: The Early Years in Gatlinburg, 1991.
Weavers of the Southern Highlands: Penland, 1992.
The Weaving Room of Crossnore School, Inc., 1998.

Also author of other pamphlets. Contributor to books, including *American Folklore: An Encyclopedia,* edited by Jan Harold Brunvard, Garland Publishing (New York, NY), 1996, and *Encyclopedia of Appalachia,* edited by Rudy Abramson and Jean Haskell, University of Tennessee Press (Knoxville, TN), 2006. Author of column, "Notes of a Pattern Weaver," *Shuttle, Spindle, and Dyepot,* 1982-84, and *The Weavers Journal,* 1984-87. Contributor to periodicals, including *Art across Kentucky, Art Papers,* and *Dialogue.*

SIDELIGHTS: Philis Alvic is a textile artist and a specialist on early twentieth-century weaving in the southern Appalachians. Her book *Weavers of the Southern Highlands* explores the history of the weaving centers that were founded and run as part of a larger social movement that aimed to provide meaningful employment for Appalachian women, while also helping them to preserve their unique regional artworks. Some of the documentation Alvic used to prepare her text has been donated to the Wilson Library of the University of North Carolina, Chapel Hill. In her book, she gives histories of various weaving centers, their financial histories and marketing approaches, and the cultural conflicts that arose there. *Library Journal* critic Eloise R. Hitchcock called it "well researched" and of value to historical collections.

Alvic told *CA:* "I first started writing magazine articles about technical weaving subjects as a way to publicize my own work. In 1988, I attended the Hambidge Center in Rabun Gap, Georgia, for an artist retreat. I discovered the weaving of Mary Hambidge and wanted other people to know about her. That writing led me to research weavers throughout Appalachia and finally to write *Weavers of the Southern Highlands.* Even though it is written to stand up to scholarly scrutiny, I hope that people without Ph.D.s will find these stories of energetic, courageous women engaging.

"The University Press of Kentucky has offered me a contract for a crafts development book that draws on my experiences from international consulting on crafts marketing and product design. Again I am writing a book that I wanted to read, but did not find in the marketplace.

"I write to convey ideas and contribute to an accessible body of knowledge. I strive to present concepts clearly and concisely. I prefer to [let the readers make] value judgements based on materials that I have collected."

BIOGRAPHICAL AND CRITICAL SOURCES:

PERIODICALS

Journal of Southern History, August, 2004, Eileen Boris, review of *Weavers of the Southern Highlands,* p. 709.
Library Journal, March 15, 2003, Eloise R. Hitchcock, review of *Weavers of the Southern Highlands,* p. 79.

ONLINE

Library of the University of North Carolina Web site, http://www.lib.unc.edu/ (December 12, 2006), biographical information about Philis Alvic.

*   *   *

ANDERS, Lou

PERSONAL: Married; children. *Education:* Studied theatre in college. *Hobbies and other interests:* Science fiction, fantasy, books, cinema, karate.

ADDRESSES: *Home and office*—Birmingham, AL. *Office*—Pyr, 59 John Glenn Dr., Amherst, NY 14228-2197.

CAREER: Editor, author, and journalist. Titan Publishing Group, Los Angeles liaison; Bookface.com, executive editor, 2000; *Argosy* magazine, senior editor, 2003-04; Prometheus Books, editorial director of Pyr imprint.

WRITINGS:

The Making of Star Trek: First Contact, Titan Books (London, England), 1996.
(Editor) *Live without a Net* (stories), ROC (New York, NY), 2003.
(Editor) *Projections: Science Fiction in Literature and Film* (essays), ROC (New York, NY), 2006.
(Editor) *Futureshocks,* ROC (New York, NY), 2006.
(Editor) *Fast Forward 1: Future Fiction from the Cutting Edge,* Pyr (New York, NY), 2007.

Contributor to anthologies, including *Strange Pleasures,* Prime Books, 2003; *Science Fiction and Fantasy: Themes, Works, and Wonders,* Greenwood Press, 2005; *So Say We All: Collected Thoughts and Opinions on Battlestar Galactica,* Benbella Books, 2006; *The Man from Krypton: A Closer Look at Superman,* Benbella Books, 2006; and *Webslinger: SF and Comic Writers on Your Friendly Neighborhood Spider-Man,* Benbella Books, 2007. Contributor to periodicals, including *Publishers Weekly, Believer, Dreamwatch, Star Trek Monthly, Star Wars Monthly, Babylon 5,* and *Manga Max.*

Articles and stories have been translated into several languages, including Danish, German, French, Italian, and Greek.

SIDELIGHTS: An editor, writer, and journalist, Lou Anders is also a well-known advocate of intelligent, creative, and literate science fiction. In addition to compiling SF anthologies collecting both short stories and essays, he serves as editorial director of Pyr, an imprint of Prometheus Books that is devoted to cutting-edge science fiction and fantasy. In addition to his editorial work, Anders has contributed numerous stories and nonfiction articles to both print and online publications, and several of his works have appeared in anthologies. One of his more unusual collections, *Projections: Science Fiction in Literature and Film* brings together the thoughts of such respected writers as Catherine Asaro, John Clute, Michael Moorcock, and Jonathan Lethem with regard to the history, social and cultural impact, and future of speculative fiction.

One of several fiction anthologies that benefits from Anders' editorship, *Futureshocks* showcases contributions from a variety of new writers together with genre veterans such as Mike Resnick, Harry Turtledove, and

Caitlin R. Kearnan. It presents readers with a collection of sixteen science fiction stories that contemplate the future and what would happen given certain scientific and technological advances. The collection displays a wide variety of hypothetical situations that are allowed to play out, including a world where thanks to a new drug, people no longer have the need to sleep; in another story an overly enthused professor changes the past in order to try to help the Native American population from being decimated by European explorers, but contrary to his high hopes the change in history yields disastrous results.

In an interview with Rick Kleffel for *Agony* online, Anders described the overarching theme of *Futureshocks* as a focus on the "new fears and cultural transitions arising from biological, sociological, technological or environmental change. Science fiction is often called the literature of estrangement and distinguished from the other genres by its refusal to make the reader too comfortable," he added, "and I wanted to explore that for its own sake." Reflecting on that focus, Lesley Farmer wrote in a *Kliatt* review that the stories in *Futureshocks* "are not really shocking or gruesome. Rather, they are 'high concept' ruminations about possible dark futures" that feature "both new and seasoned award-winning SF authors, so the writing is high quality." In a review for *Booklist,* Carl Hayes commented that because Anders "wisely limits the selections . . . to extrapolating inventive scenarios from today's more disquieting trends," the "entertaining and thought-provoking stories" included in *Futureshocks* "are just unsettling enough that readers may want to spread out reading them over several sittings."

In his interview with Kleffel, Anders discussed his experiences in the publishing world, particularly as it related to his role as executive editor of Pyr. Discussing what he looks for in prospective manuscripts, he noted that he makes a special effort to appeal to readers of traditional "hard" science fiction: fiction that focuses on technology. "I think there is at least one faction of the science fiction community that believes and bemoans the idea that science fiction is losing its grounding in science," Anders noted, adding that this group is one "that I'm very much interested in reaching" through Pyr. "I want my fiction smart whether that's scientifically smart or literarily smart," the editor noted of the books he selects for publication. "I want my science fiction and my fantasy to stimulate, to educate, to elucidate, to provoke and instigate."

BIOGRAPHICAL AND CRITICAL SOURCES:

PERIODICALS

Booklist, January 1, 2006, Carl Hays, review of *Futureshocks,* p. 73.
California Bookwatch, June, 2006, review of *Futureshocks.*
Kliatt, May, 2006, Lesley Farmer, review of *Futureshocks,* p. 22.
Publishers Weekly, June 30, 2003, review of *Live without a Net,* p. 62; November 21, 2005, review of *Futureshocks,* p. 32.

ONLINE

Agony Column Online, http://trashotron.com/ (April 18, 2004), Rick Kleffel, interview with Anders.
Eternal Night, http://www.eternalnight.co.uk/ (January 20, 2007), interview with Anders.
Lou Anders Home Page, http://www.louanders.com (January 20, 2007).*

*   *   *

ANDERSON, Cynthia 1945-

PERSONAL: Born March 2, 1945, in Joplin, MO; daughter of Robert George (a heavy-duty truck dealer) and Mary Elizabeth (a homemaker) Smith; married Michael Ferrell Anderson, June 12, 1965 (divorced, March, 1976); children: Colin Michael, Nathan Ferrell. *Ethnicity:* "White." *Education:* Attended William Woods College, University of Missouri at Columbia, University of Missouri at Kansas City, and University of Kansas; earned B.A., 1967, M.S., 1980, and administration certification. *Politics:* Republican. *Religion:* Episcopalian.

ADDRESSES: Home—Fairway, KS. *E-mail*—cyndeeanderson@sbcglobal.net.

CAREER: Shawnee Mission School District, Shawnee Mission, KS, worked as librarian, elementary school principal, director of media and services, and associate superintendent, between 1978 and 2005; Linworth Publishing, Inc., Worthington, OH, editor, 2005—. Kansas Exemplary Educator Network, member, 1994-2005; consultant in education and library information management.

MEMBER: American Library Association, American Association of School Librarians, Kansas Association of School Librarians.

AWARDS, HONORS: National Educator Award, Milken Family Foundation, 1994; Broadcast Media Award for television, International Reading Association, 2003; named distinguished library media specialist, Kansas Association of School Librarians, 2005.

WRITINGS:

Write Grants, Get Money, Linworth Publishing (Worthington, OH), 2002.
District Library Administration: A Big Picture Approach, Linworth Publishing (Worthington, OH), 2005.

SIDELIGHTS: Cynthia Anderson told *CA:* "Literacy, libraries, and learning form the keystone of our democracy. Today, more than ever before, it is critical that we use our resources to build literacy, to build and staff libraries, and to foster learning. School districts are scrounging for dollars while the expectations for student learning climb skyward. Grant writing is a critical skill for educators and librarians, and yet the skill or art of grant writing is not part of pre-service education. I wrote *Write Grants, Get Money* to help educators get their slice of grant funds for their students. Those grant dollars can make a huge different to student learning.

"I am an avid reader. I read both fiction and nonfiction and am usually reading five or six books at once. I feel a little desperate if I don't have a really good book near me at all times. I listen to audiobooks in the car and while walking. Writers learn by reading, so I believe in reading the masters. The more you write, the better writer you become."

BIOGRAPHICAL AND CRITICAL SOURCES:

PERIODICALS

Booklist, November, 2005, Esther Sinofsky, review of *District Library Administration: A Big Picture Approach,* p. 77.

Book Report, March-April, 2002, Esther Sinofsky, review of *Write Grants, Get Money,* p. 69.
Colorado Libraries, summer, 2003, Carol Krismann, review of *Write Grants, Get Money,* p. 41.
Library Talk, March-April, 2002, Esther Sinofsky, review of *Write Grants, Get Money,* p. 58.
School Library Journal, April, 2002, Mary Lankford, review of *Write Grants, Get Money.*
VOYA, October, 2003, Deborah L. Dubois, review of *Write Grants, Get Money,* p. 342.

*   *   *

ANDERSON, Warren R.

PERSONAL: Male.

ADDRESSES: Home—Aloha, OR.

CAREER: Author.

WRITINGS:

Mastering the Craft of Smoking Food, Burford Books (Springfield, NJ), 2006.

SIDELIGHTS: Warren R. Anderson is a longtime enthusiast of the art of smoking food—that is, preserving meats using burning wood under controlled conditions. It can be a difficult technique for people to master, and if it is not done correctly the food can spoil and cause illness if eaten. Therefore, Anderson provides readers with meticulous details on how to preserve meat in this manner in his *Mastering the Craft of Smoking Food.* For some reviewers, his great attention to detail goes overboard. For instance, a *Publishers Weekly* contributor felt that the book "suffers from an excess of explanation," and sometimes Anderson's recipe descriptions can go on for pages. The critic found the second part of the book, with its information on brining and curing meats, "more enticing." A critic for *The Smoke Ring* online was puzzled by the *Publisher Weekly* reviewer's complaint, praising Anderson's book as "probably the most complete, detailed book available on smoking food" that will be useful for anyone who is "serious about smoked food." A writer for *Chef Talk* online admitted

that *Mastering the Craft of Smoking Food* is "definitely not for everyone," but added that for those who are serious about smoking meats for themselves at home then it is "a must have book."

BIOGRAPHICAL AND CRITICAL SOURCES:

PERIODICALS

Internet Bookwatch, May, 2006, review of *Mastering the Craft of Smoking Food.*
Publishers Weekly, February 27, 2006, review of *Mastering the Craft of Smoking Food,* p. 53.

ONLINE

Chef Talk, http://www.cheftalk.com/ (November 25, 2006), "Backyard Creations—A Review of Two Cookbooks," review of *Mastering the Craft of Smoking Food.*
Smoke Ring, http://www.thesmokering.com/ (November 25, 2006), review of *Mastering the Craft of Smoking Food.*

*   *   *

**ANTHONY, Robert N. 1916-2006
(Robert Newton Anthony)**

OBITUARY NOTICE— See index for *CA* sketch: Born September 6, 1916, in Orange, MA; died December 1, 2006, in Hanover, NH. Accountant, educator, and author. Anthony was a former Harvard professor whose accomplishments included improving accounting practices in the U.S. military and making the discipline of accounting more comprehensible and interesting to both students and businesspeople. After completing his B.A. at Colby College in 1938 and a master's degree in business administration at Harvard in 1942, he served in the U.S. Navy during World War II. Anthony then returned to his studies at Harvard, where he received his D.C.S. in 1952. He joined the Harvard faculty and was promoted to Ross Graham Walker Professor of Management Control in 1963. Anthony would teach at Harvard for the rest of his academic career, retiring in 1982; however, from 1965 to 1968 he worked as secretary comptroller for the

U.S. Department of Defense. Secretary of Defense Robert S. McNamara had specifically requested Anthony's services in order to bring accounting practices in line among the five military branches in an effort to curtail wasteful spending. Anthony is credited with establishing procedures that made it far easier to track down inappropriate expenses. He received the Distinguished Public Service Medal from the Defense Department for his work. As a teacher and author, Anthony was widely praised by students, colleagues, and business executives for making the field of accounting more palatable and intellectually engaging. In this way, he contributed greatly to making the discipline a more appreciated part of doing business. Among the over two dozen books he wrote or cowrote are *Management Accounting: Text and Cases* (1956; 11th edition, 2004), *Essentials of Accounting* (1964; 8th edition, 2003), *Accounting Principles* (1965; 7th edition, 1995), *Management Control of Nonprofit Organizations* (1975; 7th edition, 2003), and *Management Control Systems* (11th edition, 2004). His other more recent titles include *Financial Accounting in Nonbusiness Organizations* (1978), *Tell It Like It Was* (1983), *Future Directions for Financial Accounting* (1984), *The New Corporate Director* (1986), *The Management Control Function* (1988), *Should Business and Nonbusiness Accounting Be Different?* (1989), and *Rethinking the Rules of Financial Accounting* (2003). He also created the computer software title *Teach Yourself the Essentials of Accounting* (1999). After retiring from teaching, Anthony worked as the town auditor of Waterville Valley, New Hampshire, for ten years. A former president of the American Accounting Association, he was inducted into the Accounting Hall of Fame.

OBITUARIES AND OTHER SOURCES:

PERIODICALS

New York Times, December 18, 2006, p. A25.

*   *   *

ANTHONY, Robert Newton
    See ANTHONY, Robert N.

*   *   *

ARNOLD, Nathalie
    See KÖENINGS, N.S.

ARTHUR, Wallace 1952-

PERSONAL: Born 1952, in Belfast, Northern Ireland. *Education:* Attended Campbell College (Belfast, Northern Ireland); Queen's University (Belfast, Northern Ireland); New University of Ulster (now University of Ulster), B.Sc.; University of Nottingham, Ph.D., 1977.

ADDRESSES: Office—Department of Zoology, National University of Ireland, Galway, University Rd., Galway, Ireland; fax: 00 353 91 750526. *E-mail*—wallace.arthur@nuigalway.ie.

CAREER: Writer, educator, theoretical biologist, and zoologist. National University of Ireland, Galway, professor of zoology and head of department, 2004—. Held academic positions at the University of Sussex, University of Liverpool, University of Sunderland, and Harvard University.

WRITINGS:

Mechanisms of Morphological Evolution: A Combined Genetic, Developmental, and Ecological Approach, Wiley (New York, NY), 1984.
The Niche in Competition and Evolution, Wiley (New York, NY), 1987.
Theories of Life: Darwin, Mendel, and Beyond, Penguin Books (New York, NY), 1987.
A Theory of the Evolution of Development, Wiley (New York, NY), 1988.
The Green Machine: Ecology and the Balance of Nature, Blackwell (Cambridge, MA), 1990.
The Origin of Animal Body Plans: A Study in Evolutionary Developmental Biology, Cambridge University Press (New York, NY), 1997.
Biased Embryos and Evolution, Cambridge University Press (New York, NY), 2004.
Creatures of Accident: The Rise of the Animal Kingdom, Hill & Wang (New York, NY), 2006.

Contributor to journals, including *National Review of Genetics, BioEssays, Evolution & Development, Evolutionary Development, Current Biology, Heredity,* and *Nature. Evolution and Development,* founding editor.

SIDELIGHTS: A theoretical biologist and zoologist at the National University of Ireland in Galway, author Wallace Arthur works in the relatively new and growing area of evolutionary development. This field of evolutionary science suggests that development is the cause of evolutionary change—that is, for an organism to be appreciably different from its progenitors, it must somehow change the way it develops. This developmental change therefore leads to evolutionary change. In *A Theory of the Evolution of Development,* Arthur explores this concept of evolutionary development, establishing a hierarchical model of the development of organisms and identifying those areas where change takes place. These hierarchical controls of development have a genetic basis, and in this work, Arthur "provides the most coherent statement of this viewpoint and has best explored its implications," commented Gary Freeman in *BioScience.* Arthur, Freeman noted, "has gone to a great deal of trouble to present his ideas clearly and to explore their implications." Freeman concluded that *A Theory of the Evolution of Development* "should be required reading for every molecular biologist who sets out to explain evolution."

With *Creatures of Accident: The Rise of the Animal Kingdom,* Arthur considers in greater depth the methods and mechanisms by which living organisms change and evolve. Underlying Arthur's book is an argument against the concept of intelligent design, the theory that suggests that, since life is so complex, it must have been the result of an intelligent force that designed and balanced all the elements. Arthur explains clearly and in depth how even the most complex organisms and living systems could have resulted from the occurrence of numerous random genetic accidents. He notes that evolution does not strictly occur along axes of either great diversity or deep complexity, but instead exists in a continuum between diversity and complexity. Complex living creatures can arise through entirely natural processes, and Arthur's book "makes this case through a series of easily intelligible, chatty chapters," commented a reviewer in *Publishers Weekly.* He traces the steps whereby organisms became complex, from the earliest mutations that allowed cells to clump together and create a multicellular organism, to the mutations that changed shapes from round to bilateral, creating a left and right and a front and rear, to the evolutionary changes that allowed organisms to better interact with their environments. "Arthur's precision about the process of evolution will benefit serious students of the topic," remarked *Booklist* reviewer Gilbert Taylor.

A *Kirkus Reviews* critic called the book "a short, reader-friendly discourse on the accidental rise of creatures great and small—emphasis on accidental."

BIOGRAPHICAL AND CRITICAL SOURCES:

PERIODICALS

BioScience, September, 1989, Gary Freeman, review of *A Theory of the Evolution of Development,* p. 568.
Booklist, September 1, 2006, Gilbert Taylor, review of *Creatures of Accident: The Rise of the Animal Kingdom,* p. 30.
Kirkus Reviews, June 15, 2006, review of *Creatures of Accident,* p. 607.
Publishers Weekly, June 5, 2006, review of *Creatures of Accident,* p. 51.
Quarterly Review of Biology, June, 2005, W.J. Dickinson, review of *Biased Embryos and Evolution,* p. 244.
Science News, October 21, 2006, review of *Creatures of Accident,* p. 271.

ONLINE

American Scientist Online, http://www.americanscientist.org; (January 22, 2007), "Scientists' Nightstand: The Bookshelf Talks with Wallace Arthur."
Creatures of Accident Web site, http://www.creaturesofaccident.com/ (January 22, 2007), interview with Wallace Arthur.
National University of Ireland, Galway, Department of Zoology Web site, http://www.nuigalway.ie/zoology/ (January 22, 2007), curriculum vitae of Wallace Arthur.*

*   *   *

ASHFORD, Lindsay
   See ASHFORD, Lindsay Jayne

*   *   *

ASHFORD, Lindsay Jayne
   (Lindsay Ashford)

PERSONAL: *Education:* Queen's College, Cambridge University, M.S.

ADDRESSES: *E-mail*—post@lindsayashford.co.uk

CAREER: Writer and novelist. Former television journalist with the British Broadcasting Corporation (BBC).

WRITINGS:

"MEGAN RHYS" MYSTERY NOVELS

Frozen, Honno (Dinas Powys, Wales), 2003, St. Martin's Minotaur/Thomas Dunne Books (New York, NY), 2006.
Strange Blood, Honno (Dinas Powys, Wales), 2005.
Death Studies, Honno (Dinas Powys, Wales), 2006.

SIDELIGHTS: Mystery novelist Lindsay Jayne Ashford is a former television journalist with the British Broadcasting Corporation (BBC). A resident of Wales, she was the first woman to graduate from Queens' College, Cambridge University, with a master's degree in criminology. Ashford puts this criminological training to use in *Frozen,* the first book in her "Megan Rhys" series of mystery novels. Rhys is a university professor, forensic psychologist, and criminal profiler based in Birmingham, England. When several prostitutes are found murdered in the Birmingham/Wolverhampton area of Britain's West Midlands, similar DNA evidence is discovered in each case. Rhys is called in by Detective Superintendent Leverton to assemble a profile of what looks more and more like a serial killer. Complicating the matter is the fact that two distinct blood types have been found on some of the victims. The possibility arises of two killers, one of which could be a cop gone bad. After Rhys assembles her profile, however, her results are all but ignored by the police, who are focused on the person they already think is the killer. To Rhys's frustration,

Leverton selectively applies only those parts of her profile that advance his own agenda in the case. As the criminal investigation mounts, developments in Megan's personal life threaten to distract her. Someone is constantly entering and leaving her house without her knowledge or permission and leaving subtle threats against her. She struggles against the pain of separation from her philandering husband, even while cultivating newfound interest in graduate student and Dutch police officer Patrick van Zeller. When more murders occur, Rhys realizes that she must convince Leverton and the police to act quickly on the profile she provided them or face the real possibility of many more killings.

"Megan is a likable, complex character," remarked Sue O'Brien, writing in *Booklist,* and "the fast-paced story keeps the reader involved." A *Kirkus Reviews* critic commented that "the intriguing heroine's complicated debut can be hard to follow but is well worth the effort."

BIOGRAPHICAL AND CRITICAL SOURCES:

PERIODICALS

Booklist, August 1, 2006, Sue O'Brien, review of *Frozen,* p. 45.
Kirkus Reviews, June 15, 2006, review of *Frozen,* p. 602.
Publishers Weekly, June 12, 2006, review of *Frozen,* p. 34.

ONLINE

Fantastic Fiction Web site, http://www.fantasticfiction. co.uk/ (January 22, 2007), bibliography of Lindsay Jayne Ashford.
NewMysteryReader.com, http://www.newmystery reader.com/ (January 22, 2007), Susan Illis, review of *Frozen.**

B

BAEHR, Theodore 1946-

PERSONAL: Born May 31, 1946, in New York, NY; son of I.E. Theodore Baehr (an actor) and Evelyn Peirce (an actress); married Liliana Milani (an architect), February 18, 1975; children: Theodore, James, Robert, Evelyn. *Education:* Dartmouth College, B.A. (with high honors); New York University, J.D.; Institute of Theology at Cathedral of St. John the Divine, seminarian; Belhaven College, H.H.D.; also attended University of Munich, Cambridge University, University of Bordeaux, and University of Toulouse. *Religion:* Christian.

ADDRESSES: Home—Camarillo, CA. *E-mail*—ted@tedbaehr.com.

CAREER: During early career, worked as an actor and attorney; City University of New York, former director of the Television Center; former president, Episcopal Radio-Television Foundation, beginning 1979; founder and chair, Christian Film and Television Commission, 1983—; editor and publisher, *Movieguide,* 1985—; founding chair, Good News Communications Ministry. Executive producer, "The Power," exhibit, World's Fair; executive producer and host of PBS series *Perspectives: War and Peace.* Founder of the Episcopal "Communicate" Workshops. Member of board of advisors for numerous organizations, including Religious Heritage of America, National Religious Broadcasters, Mastering Life, Mission America, National Council on Bible Curriculum in Public Schools, National Council of Churches Communications Board, National Broadcast Day of Prayer, Independent Christian Churches International, Campus Renewal Ministries, American Theater of Actors, and Theological Summit Conference.

MEMBER: United Seniors Association, National Academy of Television Arts and Sciences, National Religious Broadcasters, Council for National Policy, National Press Club.

AWARDS, HONORS: Eagle Award, Western National Religious Broadcasters; Educational Policy Conference Award; TV 38 Hope Award; five Angel Awards for Excellence in Media; Chicago Intercom Silver Plaque; Wilbur Award; three awards from Southern California Motion Picture Council; President's Award, ICVA/ICCM; Religious Heritage of America Faith and Freedom Award; Covenant Award, Radio Television Commission of the Southern Baptist Convention; Hollywood Anti-Pornography Coalition Award; Knights of Columbus Gold Plaque; Emmy Award nomination, for work on PBS series *Perspectives: War and Peace.*

WRITINGS:

NONFICTION

Getting the Word Out: How to Communicate the Gospel in Today's World, Harper & Row (New York, NY), 1986.
(With Bruce W. Grimes and Lisa Ann Rice) *Movie and Video Guide for Christian Families,* T. Nelson (Nashville, TN), 1987.

The Christian Family Guide to Movies and Video, two volumes, Wolgemuth & Hyatt (Brentwood, TN), 1989.

The Media-Wise Family, Chariot Victor (Colorado Springs, CO), 1998.

(With Tom Snyder) *Frodo and Harry: The Lord of the Rings versus Harry Potter,* Crossway Press (Wheaton, IL), 2003.

(With Tom Snyder) *What Can We Watch Tonight? A Family Guide to Movies: Movies Released since 1990,* Zondervan (Grand Rapids, MI), 2003.

(Editor, with Susan Wales) *Faith in God and Generals: An Anthology of Faith, Hope, and Love in the American Civil War,* Broadman & Holman (Nashville, TN), 2003.

So You Want to Be in Pictures? A Christian Resource for "Making It" in Hollywood, Broadman & Holman (Nashville, TN), 2005.

(Editor, with son James Baehr) *Narnia Beckons: C.S. Lewis's "The Lion, the Witch, and the Wardrobe" and Beyond,* illustrated by Angela West, Broadman & Holman (Nashville, TN), 2005.

(With Pat Boone) *The Culture-Wise Family,* Regal Books (Ventura, CA), 2007.

(With Susan Wales and Ken Wales) *The Amazing Grace of Freedom: The Inspiring Faith of William Wilberforce, the Slaves' Champion,* New Leaf Press (Green Forest, AR), 2007.

Also author of *Hollywood's Reel of Fortune: A Winning Strategy to Redeem the Entertainment Industry,* Coral Ridge Ministries, and *Television and Reality,* ERTVF. Contributor to anthologies, including *Religion and Prime Time Television,* Praeger (Westport, CT), 1997; *Advocacy Groups and the Entertainment Industry,* Praeger (Westport, CT), 2000; and *God Stories,* Starburst Publishers (Lancaster, PA), 1999. Contributor to periodicals, including *USA Today, Los Angeles Times, Washington Post, Hollywood Reporter,* and *U.S. News and World Report.* Author of nationally syndicated column.

SIDELIGHTS: Theodore Baehr's writing, media work, and lecturing focus on the impact of the media on audiences, and on teaching audiences to use good judgment when selecting movies and other forms of entertainment. As the founder and chair of the Christian Film and Television Commission, Theodore Baehr is an international spokesman for Christian values in entertainment. The periodical he publishes, *Movieguide,* and some of his books provide lists of films and television programs that Baehr has screened for language, sexual themes, and violence, as well as for the overall world view they present.

Baehr is the son of I.E. Theodore Baehr, also known as Robert "Tex" Allen, a well-known star of western movies, who was an actor on stage and television as well. Baehr's mother, Evelyn Peirce, was also a successful actor. As he grew up in New York, Baehr followed in his parents' footsteps and worked on stage, in movies, and on television. He studied in England, Germany, and France, and graduated with honors from Dartmouth College before going on to earn a law degree from New York University. In 1975, Baehr began reading the Bible at a friend's suggestion. His life changed dramatically as a result, and he decided to attend the seminary at the Institute of Theology at the Cathedral of St. John the Divine. He began to form the concepts that would eventually take shape as the Christian Film and Television Commission. The mission of this organization is to serve as a liaison between movie studio executives and audiences who are seeking wholesome family entertainment.

In *What Can We Watch Tonight? A Family Guide to Movies: Movies Released since 1990,* Baehr and collaborator Tom Snyder use the system found in the *Movieguide* to analyze and rate movies according to a Christian perspective. The first four chapters supply background information on how movies are perceived by children and adults, suggestions for viewing with discernment, and an explanation of the criteria used to rate the films. The bulk of the volume is given over to movie reviews, arranged alphabetically and by year; several lists summarize the worst, the best for children, and the best for adults. Reviewing *What Can We Watch Tonight?* for *Practical Homeschooling,* Mary Pride remarked: "I just wish the book was bigger and had even more movies in it!" In another review for *Practical Homeschooling,* Pride recommended *The Media-Wise Family,* a "very readable book" about learning how to choose good entertainment and how to teach children to do the same.

Baehr and his son James collaborated on the essay collection *Narnia Beckons: C.S. Lewis's "The Lion, the Witch and the Wardrobe" and Beyond,* which analyzes C.S. Lewis, his work, and his influence on modern culture. Lewis's "Narnia" books are rich with Christian symbolism, and the Baehrs' book offers "many fascinating glimpses" into the success of this series, according to William F. Jasper in the *New American.* Jasper added that *Narnia Beckons* also functions on another level as "a family album and picture book."

In a work not related to the media, *Faith in God and Generals: An Anthology of Faith, Hope, and Love in the American Civil War,* Baehr and coeditor Susan Wales collected material that illustrates the importance of religion in the lives of those who fought the Civil War. Stonewall Jackson, Robert E. Lee, William Rosecrans, George McClellan and many others are featured. It is an "attractive, accessible" book well-suited for young adult readers, according to Roland Green in *Booklist.*

BIOGRAPHICAL AND CRITICAL SOURCES:

PERIODICALS

Booklist, January 1, 2003, Roland Green, review of *Faith in God and Generals: An Anthology of Faith, Hope, and Love in the American Civil War,* p. 810.
Practical Homeschooling, January-February, 2004, Mary Pride, review of *The Media-wise Family* and *What Can We Watch Tonight? A Family Guide to Movies: Movies Released since 1990,* p. 37.
New American, December 12, 2005, William F. Jasper, review of *Narnia Beckons: C.S. Lewis's "The Lion, the Witch and the Wardrobe" and Beyond,* p. 22.

ONLINE

Mediawise Family, http://mediawisefamily.com/ (December 23, 2006), biographical information on Theodore Baehr.

*   *   *

BAGWELL, James E. 1941-

PERSONAL: Born March 16, 1941, in Plains, GA; son of Henry Lafayette and Floy Bagwell; married Cynthia Baker, June 8, 1980; children: James Bradford, Victoria Floy. *Education:* University of Georgia, B.S. Ed., 1963; Georgia Southern University, M.A., 1967; University of Southern Mississippi, Ph.D., 1978.

ADDRESSES: Home—Plains, GA. *Office*—Department of History, Georgia Southwestern State University, 800 Georgia Southwestern State University Dr., Americus, GA 31709-4379.

CAREER: Georgia Southwestern State University, Americus, professor of history, beginning 1967, associate professor of history, beginning 2000, professor of history, beginning 2002.

WRITINGS:

Rice Gold: James Hamilton Couper and Plantation Life on the Georgia Coast, Mercer University Press (Macon, GA), 2000.

Also author of a history of Sumter County, GA, and a history of the mayors of Plains, GA, 1997.

BIOGRAPHICAL AND CRITICAL SOURCES:

PERIODICALS

Journal of American History, March, 2001, Shearer Davis Bowman, review of *Rice Gold: James Hamilton Couper and Plantation Life on the Georgia Coast,* p. 1477.
Journal of Southern History, November, 2001, Jeffrey Robert Young, review of *Rice Gold,* p. 842.*

*   *   *

BAILEY, Anne J. 1944-

PERSONAL: Born August 7, 1944, in Cleburne, TX; divorced; children: two. *Education:* University of Texas, B.A., 1982; Texas Christian University, M.A., 1984, Ph.D., 1987.

ADDRESSES: Office—Department of History, Georgia College & State University, Box 47, Milledgeville, GA 31061. *E-mail*—anne.bailey@gcsu.edu.

CAREER: Historian, educator, and writer. Georgia College & State University, Milledgeville, history professor, 1997—. Previously served on the faculty at

Tarrant County Junior College, Fort Worth, TX, 1984-87; Texas Tech University, Lubbock, 1987-88; Georgia Southern University, Statesboro, 1988-93; University of Arkansas, Fayetteville, 1993-97.

MEMBER: Georgia Historical Association, Historical Society, Society of Civil War Historians, Society of Military Historians, Arkansas Historical Association, East Texas Historical Association, Georgia Association of Historians, Southern Historical Association, St. George Tucker Society, Southern Association of Women Historians.

AWARDS, HONORS: Barnett fellow, 1986-87; grant from the Georgia Southern College, 1988, 1993-94; Andrew J. Mellon research stipend, 1995; Richard Barksdale Harwell Book Award, Civil War Round Table of Atlanta, GA, 2001; Grady McWhiney Award of Merit, Civil War Round Table of Dallas, TX, 2005.

WRITINGS:

Between the Enemy and Texas: Parsons's Texas Cavalry in the Civil War, Texas Christian University Press (Fort Worth, TX), 1989.

Texans in the Confederate Cavalry, under the general editorship of Grady McWhiney, Ryan Place Publishers (Fort Worth, TX), 1995.

(With Walter J. Fraser, Jr.) *Portraits of Conflict: A Photographic History of Georgia in the Civil War,* foreword by the general editors, Bobby Roberts and Carl Moneyhon, University of Arkansas Press (Fayetteville, AR), 1996.

(Editor and contributor, with Daniel E. Sutherland) *Civil War Arkansas: Beyond Battles and Leaders,* University of Arkansas Press (Fayetteville, AR), 2000.

The Chessboard of War: Sherman and Hood in the Autumn Campaigns of 1864, University of Nebraska Press (Lincoln, NE), 2000.

War and Ruin: William T. Sherman and the Savannah Campaign, Scholarly Resources (Wilmington, DE), 2003.

(Editor) *In the Saddle with the Texans: Day-by-Day with Parsons's Cavalry Brigade, 1862-1865,* McWhiney Foundation Press, McMurry University (Abilene, TX), 2004.

Invisible Southerners: Ethnicity in the Civil War, University of Georgia Press (Athens, GA), 2006.

Contributor to books, including *The Confederate General,* edited by William C. Davis, National Historical Society, 1991; *Western Horse Tales,* edited by Don Worcester, Wordware Publishing, 1994; *Lone Star Blue and Gray: Essays on Texas in the Civil War,* edited by Ralph A. Wooster, Texas State Historical Association, 1995; *The American Civil War: A Handbook of Literature and Research,* edited by Steven E. Woodworth, Greenwood Press, 1996; *Valor and Lace: The Roles of Confederate Women, 1861-1865,* Mauriel Phillips Joslyn, Southern Heritage Press (Murfreesboro, TN), 1996; *Southern Families at War: Loyalty and Conflict in the Civil War South,* edited by Catherine Clinton, Oxford University Press (New York, NY), 2000; *Enemies of the Country: New Perspectives on Unionists in the Civil War South,* edited by John C. Inscoe and Robert C. Kenzer, University of Georgia Press, 2001; *Black Soldiers in Blue: African American Troops in the Civil War Era,* edited by John David Smith, University of North Carolina Press, 2002; and *Black Flag over Dixie: Racial Atrocities and Reprisals in the Civil War,* edited by Gregory J.W. Urwin, Southern Illinois University Press, 2004. Contributor to encyclopedias, including *Encyclopedia of the Confederacy,* edited by Richard N. Current, Simon & Schuster (New York, NY), 1993. Editor of the *Georgia Historical Quarterly.*

SIDELIGHTS: Anne J. Bailey, a historian with a special interest in the American Civil War and military history, has written several books focusing on these topics. Bailey collaborated with Walter J. Fraser, Jr., to write *Portraits of Conflict: A Photographic History of Georgia in the Civil War.* Through 260 photographs and explanatory text, the authors present a look at Georgia during the Civil War that includes women and families, architecture, fortifications, military prisons, soldiers, factories, and towns. "The accompanying text provides a fast-paced narrative that identifies each image and places it in context with events," wrote W. Todd Groce in *Civil War History.* Todd went on to note: "Professors Bailey and Fraser have made a major contribution by presenting the first comprehensive photographic examination of the Civil War in Georgia—and they have done it in a way that is both informative and pleasurable to read."

In *The Chessboard of War: Sherman and Hood in the Autumn Campaigns of 1864,* Bailey focuses on Civil War battles that took place in Georgia and Tennessee by chronicling William T. Sherman's March to the Sea and John Bell Hood's fighting in Tennessee. Among the topics Bailey covers are the role of black soldiers in the campaigns, their efforts to prove themselves, and both the Northern and Southern soldiers' resentment of them. "Her writing is crisp and clear as she considers questions of military strategy and leadership and issues of politics and race," wrote Lesley J. Gordon in the *Journal of Southern History.*

Bailey returns to Sherman's march through the South in *War and Ruin: William T. Sherman and the Savannah Campaign.* The author discusses in depth Sherman's decision to allow his troops to freely plunder and pillage as they battled through the South. She focuses primarily on his ransacking of Savannah and provides a look at the city and its society prior to Sherman's invasion and as the South began to lose the war. Writing in the *Journal of Southern History,* James H. Birdseye noted: "Bailey examines the strategic situation in very clear terms and does a great deal to dispel the popular belief that Sherman's march was an easy triumph with little risk and no chance of failure."

Bailey served as coeditor with Daniel E. Sutherland of *Civil War Arkansas: Beyond Battles and Leaders.* Bailey also contributed one of the book's eleven essays, which cover topics such as individual historical figures, the role of geography in Arkansas's involvement in the war, and the abuse of Arkansas property and farms as Union soldiers marched through the state. Michael B. Dougan, writing in the *Journal of Southern History,* noted that "scholars should . . . welcome this collection . . . that supposedly represent the 'new' Civil War history."

As editor of *In the Saddle with the Texans: Day-by-Day with Parsons's Cavalry Brigade, 1862-1865,* Bailey presents various communications among officers in regard to the Texas cavalry's Parsons's Brigade during the Civil War. Bailey also provides an introduction and extensive footnotes. An *Internet Bookwatch* contributor noted that the many primary references provide "an up-close and personal look Texas cavalry life."

BIOGRAPHICAL AND CRITICAL SOURCES:

PERIODICALS

Civil War History, September, 1998, W. Todd Groce, review of *Portraits of Conflict: A Photographic History of Georgia in the Civil War,* p. 238.

Internet Bookwatch, February, 2005, review of *In the Saddle with the Texans: Day-by-Day with Parsons's Cavalry Brigade, 1862-1865.*

Journal of Southern History, November, 2001, Michael B. Dougan, review of *Civil War Arkansas: Beyond Battles and Leaders,* p. 872; February, 2002, Lesley J. Gordon, review of *The Chessboard of War: Sherman and Hood in the Autumn Campaigns of 1864,* p. 184; February, 2004, James H. Birdseye, review of *War and Ruin: Sherman and Hood in the Autumn Campaigns of 1864,* p. 161; November, 2005, Brady Lee Hutchison, review of *In the Saddle with the Texans,* p. 968.

Wisconsin Bookwatch, February, 2005, review of *In the Saddle with the Texans.*

*　　　*　　　*

BAILEY, Gauvin Alexander

PERSONAL: Education: Trinity College at the University of Toronto, B.A., 1989; Harvard University, Ph.D., 1996.

ADDRESSES: Office—Department of Theology, Boston College, 21 Campanella Way, Rm. 349, Chestnut Hill, MA 02467; fax: 617-552-0794. *E-mail*—gauvin.bailey.1@bc.edu.

CAREER: Writer, art historian, curator, and educator. Clark University, Worcester, MA, assistant professor, 1997-2003, associate professor of Renaissance and Baroque art, 2003-06; Boston College, Chestnut Hill, MA, associate professor of the history of art and religion, 2006—. Boston University, Luce Visiting Professor in Scripture and the Visual Arts, 2006. Conducts graduate seminars in art and religion at Weston Jesuit School of Theology. Curator of museum exhibitions on Renaissance, Baroque, and Asian art, including *Saints and Sinners: Art and Culture in Caravaggio's Italy,* McMullen Museum of Art, Boston, College, 1999; *Baroque: vision jésuite du Tintoret à Rubens,* Musée des Beaux-Arts de Caen, 2003; and *Hope and Healing: Painting in Italy in a Time of Plague, 1500-1800,* Worcester Art Museum, 2005.

AWARDS, HONORS: Hanna Kiel Fellowship, Harvard University Center for Italian Renaissance Studies, 2000-01; Rome Prize, American Academy of Rome,

2000-01 (declined); Robert Lehman Foundation research grant, Renaissance Society of America, 2000, 2003; and National Endowment for the Humanities grant, 2004, 2004-05.

WRITINGS:

(With Lisa Bolombek and Robert B. Mason) *Tamerlane's Tableware: A New Approach to Chinoiserie Ceramics of Fifteenth- and Sixteenth-Century Iran,* Mazda Publishers in association with the Royal Ontario Museum (Costa Mesa, CA), 1996.

The Jesuits and the Grand Mogul: Renaissance Art at the Imperial Court of India, 1580-1630 (exhibition catalogue), Freer Gallery of Art, Arthur M. Sackler Gallery, Smithsonian Institution (Washington, DC), 1998.

Art on the Jesuit Missions in Asia and Latin America, 1542-1773, University of Toronto Press (Toronto, Ontario, Canada), 1999.

Between Renaissance and Baroque: Jesuit Art in Rome, 1565-1610, University of Toronto Press (Toronto, Ontario, Canada), 2003.

Ignazio e l'arte dei gesuiti, edited by Giovanni Sale, Jaca Book (Milan, Italy), 2003, published as *The Jesuits and the Arts, 1540-1773,* edited by John W. O'Malley and Gauvin Alexander Bailey, St. Joseph's University Press (Philadelphia, PA), 2005.

Art of Colonial Latin America, Phaidon (New York, NY), 2005.

(With Pamela M. Jones and Franco Mormando) *Hope and Healing: Painting in Italy in a Time of Plague, 1500-1800,* Worcester Art Museum (Worcester, MA), 2005.

Contributor to books, including *Fundaciones jesuiticas en Iberoamerica,* Luisa Elena Alcala, Ediciones El Viso (Madrid, Spain), 2002; *Oxford Encyclopedia of the Enlightenment,* Oxford University Press (New York, NY), 2003; *The Chinese Face of Jesus Christ II,* edited by Roman Malek, Sankt Augustin, 2003; *Encounters: The Meeting of Asia and Europe, 1500-1800,* edited by Anna Jackson and Amin Jaffer, Victoria and Albert Museum (London, England), 2004; *The Jesuits II,* edited by John W. O'Malley and others, University of Toronto Press (Toronto, Ontario, Canada), 2006; and *Tesoros/Reasures/Tesouros: The Arts in Latin America, 1492-1820,* edited by Joseph J. Rishel, Philadelphia Museum of Art (Philadelphia, PA) and Yale University Press (New Haven, CT), 2006.

Contributor to journals, including *Archivum Historicum Societatis Iesu, Apollo, Renaissance Quarterly, Catholic Historical Review,* and *Oriental Art.*

SIDELIGHTS: Gauvin Alexander Bailey is a scholar of the "intersection of art and Catholicism in the Renaissance and Baroque eras, especially in Italy, Latin America, and Asia," noted a biographer on the Boston College Department of Theology Web site, with a specialty in the "arts patronage of the Society of Jesus" (the Jesuits). Bailey explores this topic in a number of his books. In *Art on the Jesuit Missions in Asia and Latin America, 1542-1773,* Bailey considers how Jesuits "effectively utilized images of all kinds in their mission to educate Catholics," and how these educational activities were conducted outside of Europe, commented Claire Farago in the *Renaissance Quarterly.* He looks specifically at missions in Japan, China, Mughal India, and Paraguay. In Japan, Christian art was accepted and even became an influence on Japanese painting, Farago noted. In China, however, the realistic Christian artwork was rejected. In Mughal India, locals had already adopted many Christian images and subjects, and the Jesuits had to encourage the Indians to adopt a different interpretation of the meaning of those images. Jesuit missions in Paraguay adopted local art and sculpture styles to help bring their religious message to local populations.

Between Renaissance and Baroque: Jesuit Art in Rome, 1565-1610 contains Bailey's scholarly examination of pre-Baroque Jesuit art in Rome, and how it came to involve the Jesuits in later Counter-Reformation art. He "argues that much Jesuit art deserves a second look, not only because the Jesuits themselves were deeply concerned with images and their efficacy in religious devotion, but also because of the inherent interest of the objects themselves," commented Ian Verstegen in the *Canadian Journal of History.* Verstegen asserted that Bailey's book "will now be the standard source on the subject" of early Jesuit art.

In *The Jesuits and the Arts, 1540-1773,* Bailey and coeditor John W. O'Malley assemble "the first comprehensive survey of the worldwide artistic enterprise of the early Society of Jesus," remarked James Martin in *America.* The contributors cover a wide variety of topics, including Jesuit architecture, theater, and music; Jesuit influence on Italian Renaissance and Baroque painting; Jesuit artistic and architectural heritage in Latin America; and Jesuit influences on art in Asia and North America. "By any measure," Martin stated, "this new volume is brilliantly conceived, consistently fascinating and absolutely gorgeous to look at."

BIOGRAPHICAL AND CRITICAL SOURCES:

PERIODICALS

America, December 5, 2005, James Martin, "Jesuit Arts: A New Book on Art and the Society of Jesus," review of *The Jesuits and the Arts, 1540-1773,* p. 16.

Canadian Journal of History, April, 2005, Ian Verstegen, review of *Between Renaissance and Baroque: Jesuit Art in Rome, 1565-1610,* p. 90.

Reference & Research Book News, February, 2006, review of *The Jesuits and the Arts, 1540-1773.*

Renaissance Quarterly, spring, 2002, Claire Farago, review of *Art on the Jesuit Missions in Asia and Latin America, 1542-1773,* p. 319.

ONLINE

Boston College Department of Theology Web site, http://www.bc.edu/schools/cas/theology/ (December 22, 2007), biography of Gauvin Alexander Bailey.*

*   *   *

BAINGANA, Doreen

PERSONAL: Daughter of Neri (a physician) and Erina (a human resources professional and Permanent Secretary of the Public Service Commission, Uganda) Baingana. *Education:* Makerere University, Kampala, Uganda, J.D.; University of Maryland, M.F.A.; attended the American University, Washington, DC.

ADDRESSES: Home—U.S. *E-mail*—dbaing@yahoo. com.

CAREER: Writer, educator, short-story writer, broadcaster, and lawyer. Ugandan Embassy, Rome, Italy, former administrative assistant; Voice of America, Washington, DC, former broadcaster. University of Maryland, College Park, writer-in-residence, 2005; Summer Literary Festival, Nairobi, Kenya, member of faculty, 2005. Conducts creative writing workshops and seminars.

MEMBER: FEMRITE (a Ugandan women writers association).

AWARDS, HONORS: Artist Grant, District of Columbia Commission of the Arts and Humanities, 2002; Associated Writing Programs (AWP) Award for Short Fiction, 2003; Washington Independent Writers Fiction Prize, 2004; Caine Prize in African Writing nomination, 2004 and 2005; Bread Loaf Writers Conference scholarship, 2004; Key West Writers Seminar scholarship, 2004; Fairbanks International Fellowship to Bread Loaf Writers Conference, 2005; Commonwealth Writers' Prize for the Best First Book Award in the Africa Region, 2006, for *Tropical Fish: Stories out of Entebbe.*

WRITINGS:

Tropical Fish: Stories out of Entebbe, University of Massachusetts Press (Amherst, MA), 2005.

Contributor to periodicals, including *Sun Magazine, African American Review, Callaloo, Glimmer Train, Crab Orchard Review, Chelsea, New Vision, Monitor* (Uganda), and the *Guardian.* Author of monthly column for *African Woman,* a Ugandan magazine.

SIDELIGHTS: Ugandan author Doreen Baingana originally studied international law at Makerere University, in Kampala, Uganda, and expected to embark on a career as a lawyer. Concurrent with her legal studies, she also took fiction and poetry classes, she told Jane Musoke-Nteyafas in an interview on *UGPulse.com.* "The workshops were the most thrilling thing I had ever done, while the law classes were dull and uninspiring," she remarked to Musoke-Nteyafas. "I realized that I did not have a passion for legal work, but had a passion for writing. Making a lot of money has never been important to me. Alas! I felt that I could use my skills better by trying to change hearts and minds through fiction and creative nonfiction, than by trying to improve legal systems."

Baingana's debut collection, *Tropical Fish: Stories out of Entebbe,* is a series of linked stories that tell the story of three Ugandan sisters living in the aftermath of the brutal Idi Amin dictatorship of the 1970s. "What Doreen Baingana brilliantly evokes here is the experience of growing up in the wake of [Amin's] regime, in Uganda's former colonial capital of Entebbe," commented reviewer Michael Upchurch in the *Seattle Times.* Christine Mugisha is the youngest of the three sisters. Patti is a devout, born-again Christian, while Rosa is more worldly and interested in earthly pleasures. Christine's attitudes fall somewhere between those two extremes. The sisters' father, a senior bank executive, dies of alcoholism as the family's situation deteriorates in the failing post-Amin Uganda. Thereafter, the sisters and their mother struggle to maintain themselves. The stories shed light on the nature of life in Uganda while tackling difficult issues such as AIDS, poverty, food shortages, and governmental abuses. "A Thank-You Note" is constructed as a letter from Rosa to an ex-lover, recounting her battle with AIDS. "Lost in Los Angeles" contrasts Christine's experiences of racism in the United States with those she faced in Uganda. The title story tells of Christine's uninspired affair with an older white man who courts her with the influence of his money. "Baingana's richly detailed stories are lush with cultural commentary," remarked a *Publishers Weekly* reviewer. Reviewer Angela Nampewo, writing in the *Monitor,* called the collection a "brilliantly written, touching, and very honest book." Baingana's "fiction debut is compelling and very human," commented Joanna M. Burkhardt in the *Library Journal.*

BIOGRAPHICAL AND CRITICAL SOURCES:

PERIODICALS

Accra Mail (Accra, Ghana), February 14, 2006, "Ghanaian Wins Book Prize."

Asia Africa Intelligence Wire, August 30, 2005, David Kaiza, "African Writing Still Not at Ease."

Kirkus Reviews, June 1, 2006, review of *Tropical Fish: Stories out of Entebbe,* p. 531.

Library Journal, July 1, 2006, Joanna M. Burkhardt, review of *Tropical Fish,* p. 61.

Monitor (Uganda), April 16, 2006, Angela Nampewo, "Baingana: From Lawyer to Award-Winning Writer," profile of Doreen Baingana; April 16,

2006, Angela Nampewo, "*Tropical Fish* is about Aspirations," review of *Tropical Fish;* April 24, 2006, Gaaki Kigambo, "Baingana Launches *Tropical Fish.*"

Publishers Weekly, May 1, 2006, review of *Tropical Fish,* p. 31.

Seattle Times, October 4, 2006, Michael Upchurch, review of *Tropical Fish.*

Washington Post, February 24, 2005, "Off the Page," transcript of online chat with Doreen Baingana.

ONLINE

UGPulse.com, http://www.ugpulse.com/ (August 14, 2006), Jane Musoke-Nteyafas, "1 on 1 with Multiple Award-Winning Ugandan Writer Doreen Baingana," interview with Doreen Baingana.*

*   *   *

BAKKER, R. Scott 1967-

PERSONAL: Born February 2, 1967, in Simcoe, Ontario, Canada; son of a tobacco sharecropper. *Education:* University of Western Ontario, B.A., M.A.; graduate study at Vanderbilt University.

ADDRESSES: Home—London, Ontario, Canada.

CAREER: Writer. Scholar of ancient languages and philosophy.

AWARDS, HONORS: Social Sciences and Humanities Research Council Fellowship.

WRITINGS:

"PRINCE OF NOTHING" TRILOGY; FANTASY NOVELS

The Darkness That Comes Before, Penguin Books Canada (Toronto, Ontario, Canada), 2003.

The Warrior-Prophet, Overlook Press (Woodstock, NY), 2005.

The Thousandfold Thought, Overlook Press (Woodstock, NY), 2006.

SIDELIGHTS: R. Scott Bakker's "Prince of Nothing" trilogy is a dark fantasy that runs much deeper than many works in that genre, according to numerous critics. The story is set in a world called Earwa, where a highly diverse population is caught up in a holy war triggered by the prophet Maithanet. Drusas Achamian, a sorcerer, is the character who pulls together the many plotlines of the story. A *Publishers Weekly* reviewer, commenting on the first book in the series, *The Darkness That Comes Before,* identified Bakker as a worthy successor to the great fantasy writer J.R.R. Tolkien, and praised the author for his "willingness to take chances and avoid the usual genre cliches." In a *Publishers Weekly* review of the second book in the trilogy, *The Warrior-Prophet,* a critic called the series "daringly unconventional," yet noted that beneath all the elaborate fantasy, the story works because it is an "all-too-human tale of love, hatred and justice." The concluding book, *The Thousandfold Thought,* sees Earwa on the brink of an apocalypse, while the sorcerer Drusas faces personal betrayal. It is a "shattering climax" to the trilogy, according to a *Publishers Weekly* reviewer, who added that the three books together form "a work of unforgettable power."

BIOGRAPHICAL AND CRITICAL SOURCES:

PERIODICALS

Bookseller, December 9, 2005, review of *The Thousandfold Thought* and *The Warrior Prophet,* p. 34.
Library Journal, April 15, 2004, Jackie Cassada, review of *The Darkness That Comes Before,* p. 128.
Publishers Weekly, May 24, 2004, review of *The Darkness That Comes Before,* p. 49; December 6, 2004, review of *The Warrior-Prophet,* p. 48; December 19, 2005, review of *The Thousandfold Thought,* p. 46.

ONLINE

R. Scott Bakker's Home Page, http://www.princeof nothing.com (December 21, 2006).*

*   *   *

BANY-WINTERS, Lisa 1968-

PERSONAL: Born April 15, 1968, in Hamilton, OH; daughter of John (a jazz bass player) and Nancy (a laboratory technician) Bany; married Brian Winters (a naturalist), August 28, 1993; children: Michaela, Carlin. *Education:* Attended Wright State University, 1986-87; Columbia College, Chicago, IL, B.A., 1990. *Religion:* Unitarian-Universalist.

ADDRESSES: Home—Glenview, IL. *E-mail*—banywinters@sbcglobal.net.

CAREER: Emanon Theatre Company, Chicago, IL, founder and managing director, 1984-2000; Northlight Theatre, Skokie, IL, academy director, 1998-2007. Skokie Jewish Community Center, educator and administrator, 1990-98; Second City Northwest, instructor, 1993-95; theater producer, director, performer, and consultant.

MEMBER: Women's Club of Evanston (board member, 2005-06).

AWARDS, HONORS: Parents' Choice Award for Excellence in Education and selection among top ten arts book of the year, *Chicago Tribune,* both 1998, for *On Stage: Theatre Games and Activities for Kids.*

WRITINGS:

On Stage: Theatre Games and Activities for Kids, Chicago Review Press (Chicago, IL), 1997.
Show Time: Music, Dance, and Drama Activities for Kids, Chicago Review Press (Chicago, IL), 2000.
Funny Bones: Comedy Games and Activities for Kids, Chicago Review Press (Chicago, IL), 2003.
Family Fun Nights, Chicago Review Press (Chicago, IL), 2006.

Contributor to encyclopedias.

The book *On Stage* was translated into German.

SIDELIGHTS: Lisa Bany-Winters told *CA:* "I was lucky because I never had to look for a publisher. My publisher was looking for someone to write a book on theater games and came to me as a drama teacher. I had never thought to write a book, but when the opportunity presented itself, I quickly embraced it. Writing *On Stage: Theatre Games and Activities for Kids* was like a thesis for me. I wrote all I had learned and all I was teaching about theater to young people. The other books have come about more as I had developed my theater programs, and most recently since I have had my own family to play with.

"I try to write how I teach—clear and accessible to kids, without ever talking down to them. I hope my enthusiasm and love for kids, games, and the performing arts comes through in my books."

BIOGRAPHICAL AND CRITICAL SOURCES:

PERIODICALS

School Library Journal, December, 2002, Cynde Suite, review of *Funny Bones: Comedy Games and Activities for Kids,* p. 153.

*   *   *

BARBERA, Joe 1911-2006
(Joseph Roland Barbera)

OBITUARY NOTICE— See index for *CA* sketch: Born March 24, 1911, in New York, NY; died December 18, 2006, in Los Angeles, CA. Animator, producer, director, and author. Along with longtime partner William Hanna, Barbera was an Oscar- and Emmy-winning producer and director of television cartoons ranging from *The Flintstones* and *Tom and Jerry* to *The Smurfs* and *The Powerpuff Girls.* Originally contemplating a career in banking, he graduated from the American Institute of Banking and also attended the Pratt Institute. The financial world did not maintain its appeal for him, however, and after two years as a bank clerk Barbera left to explore play writing, drawing, and amateur boxing. His life would change forever when *Collier's* magazine accepted one of his cartoons. Encouraged by this, he unsuccessfully tried to obtain work at Walt Disney Studios. Instead, Van Beuren Studios hired him in 1932. The studio went bankrupt during the Depression, and Barbera worked for Terrytoons before being hired by Metro-Goldwyn-Mayer in 1937. It was here that he met Hanna, and the two found they complemented each other's skills well: Hanna was talented in characterization and comic timing, while Barbera had the artistic

talent and was a good gag writer. They initially collaborated on an animated adaptation of the *Katzenjammer Kids* comic strip before creating their own film short, *Puss Gets the Boot,* in 1940. The short earned them their first Academy Award nomination.*Puss Gets the Boot,* featured characters Jasper the cat and Jinx the mouse who would later be rewritten as Tom and Jerry. Hanna and Barbera would continue to produce *Tom and Jerry* cartoons into the mid-1950s, earning seven Oscars and six more Oscar nominations. The team was put in charge of MGM's animation department in 1955, but it proved to be a short run. Two years later, the division was closed. The two animators decided to concentrate on their already established H-B Enterprises, which they founded to produce animated commercials. Hanna and Barbera would go on to turn it into a television cartoon factory. Renamed Hanna-Barbera Productions, the studio would be the first company to produce prime-time television cartoon series. Beginning with 1957's *The Ruff & Reddy Show,* Barbera and Hanna would go on to create such favorites as *The Huckleberry Hound Show, The Flintstones, The Jetsons,* and *Scooby-Doo.* By the 1960s and 1970s, Hanna-Barbera cartoons were omnipresent on American television, and shows such as *The Flintstones* regularly made the top-rated listings and were popular among both children and adults. Keeping up with the times, they continued their success through the 1980s and 1990s with such shows as *Space Ghost, The Super-Powers Team, The Smurfs,* and *The Powerpuff Girls.* Also praised for their full-length movie adaptation of E.B. White's classic children's book, *Charlotte's Web* (1973), which won an Annie Award, the team would run independently until 1990. Purchased by Turner Broadcasting that year, they were later incorporated into the Warner Brothers media conglomerate. In his later years, Barbera primarily worked as an executive producer, though he still sometimes wrote cartoons. One of his last contributions was the 2005 Tom and Jerry cartoon, *The KarateGuard,* his last cartoon featuring the cat and mouse and the first one he had written since 1960. Frequently credited with making television cartoons a mainstay of American entertainment, Barbera inspired many animators to follow in his footsteps. Among his other awards are seven Emmys, a Golden Globe Award, the Humanitas Prize, and the Governor's Award from the National Academy of Television Arts and Sciences. Barbera recorded his story in his autobiography, *My Life in 'Toons: From Flatbush to Bedrock in under a Century* (1994).

OBITUARIES AND OTHER SOURCES:

BOOKS

Barbera, Joe, and Alan Axelrod, *My Life in 'Toons: From Flatbush to Bedrock in under a Century,* Turner (Atlanta, GA), 1994.

PERIODICALS

Chicago Tribune, December 19, 2006, Section 2, p. 10.
New York Times, December 19, 2006, p. C15; December 22, 2006, p. A2.
Times (London, England), December 20, 2006, p. 58.
Washington Post, December 19, 2006, p. B7.

* * *

BARBERA, Joseph Roland
    See BARBERA, Joe

* * *

BARONE, Sam

PERSONAL: Born in New York, NY. *Education:* Manhattan College, B.S., 1965.

ADDRESSES: Home—Scottsdale, AZ. *E-mail*—info@sambarone.com.

CAREER: Writer, novelist, software designer, and software developer. *Military service:* Served in the U.S. Marine Corps.

AWARDS, HONORS: Arizona Authors Association Literary contest, first place, 2006, for *Dawn of Empire.*

WRITINGS:

Dawn of Empire, William Morrow (New York, NY), 2006.

SIDELIGHTS: After a thirty-year career in software development, Sam Barone retired in 1999 to pursue his love of writing. His first project after retirement took the form of a science fiction novel. However, "after a few months, I began having recurring dreams about an ancient warrior, drafted by a small village to defend it from an oncoming barbarian invasion," he stated on his home page. "The dreams would not go away, and started becoming more and more detailed, more and more real to me." "To get the story out of my head, I decided to write a chapter, knowing there's nothing like actual work to make you lose interest," Barone continued. The story, far from dissipating after his tentative first efforts, grew into Barone's debut novel, *Dawn of Empire.* Set in the lush lands of Mesopotamia in the fourth century A.D., the book tells the story of the people of Orak, an agricultural village of more than 2,000 residents, and the proto-city's siege by a horde of barbarians intent on its destruction. Situated in the fertile valley of the Tigris and Euphrates rivers, Orak is a prosperous and peaceful town. Around them lurks the constant threat of the barbarous Alur Meriki clan, a group of barbarians that regularly raids agricultural settlements along the Tigris to capture slaves and steal supplies for the clan's warriors. When the residents of Orak learn that the Alur Meriki has targeted them for a raid, they hurriedly rise to form their own defense. The village leader, Nicar, chooses former barbarian Eskkar as the city's war leader, relying on the warrior to devise a defense that will turn away the marauding Alur Meriki. Eskkar is given a teenage slave girl, Trella, as a companion, and together the two form a personal and martial partnership. Eskkar directs that a wall of fireproof brick be constructed around the city, and hurriedly works to train both men and women in archery and other combat arts. As preparations are made, weapons forged, and training conducted, the relationship between Eskkar and Trella deepens, and the two eventually marry. A *Kirkus Reviews* critic called the novel "a Bronze Age historical romance with brains as well as brawn, ripe for a sequel." A *Publishers Weekly* writer concluded: "Equal parts history lesson, love story, and war saga, Barone's first historical will have readers turning pages."

BIOGRAPHICAL AND CRITICAL SOURCES:

PERIODICALS

Kirkus Reviews, June 16, 2006, review of *Dawn of Empire,* p. 587.

Library Journal, July 1, 2006, Jane Henriksen Baird, review of *Dawn of Empire,* p. 61.

Publishers Weekly, May 22, 2006, review of *Dawn of Empire,* p. 30.

ONLINE

Sam Barone Home Page, http://www.sambarone.com (January 22, 2007).*

*   *   *

BARRON, James 1954-
(James Turman Barron)

PERSONAL: Born December 25, 1954, in Washington, DC; son of James Pressley and Leirona Faith Barron; married Jane-Iris Farhi, April 1, 1995. *Education:* Princeton University, B.A., 1977. *Religion:* Methodist. *Hobbies and other interests:* Playing the piano.

ADDRESSES: Home—New York, NY. *Office*—New York Times Company, 229 W. 43rd St., New York, NY 10036.

CAREER: New York Times, New York, NY, copy person, 1977-78, research assistant, 1978-79, reporter, 1979—, acting editor of Living section, 1996-97, author of "Public Lives" column, 1998-2001, author of "Boldface Names" column, 2001-02; WQXR-FM, New York, NY, broadcast correspondent, 1987; WQEW-AM, New York, NY, broadcast correspondent, 1992-98.

MEMBER: Deadline Club (vice president, 1995-99), Princeton Club.

WRITINGS:

(And narrator) *Page One* (television documentary), Discovery Times Channel, 2005.

Piano: The Making of a Steinway Concert Grand, Times Books (New York, NY), 2006.

Also contributor to books.

SIDELIGHTS: A longtime reporter and columnist for the *New York Times,* James Barron used a series of articles he wrote for the newspaper as the basis for his first book, *Piano: The Making of a Steinway Concert Grand.* Barron is himself an amateur pianist, so he had a natural interest in his subject. The center of the book is the story of a single piano as it makes its way, over eleven months, from a pile of wooden planks to the finished instrument ready for its debut at a concert hall at the hands of a master musician. Interspersed with this journey is information about the Steinway company itself and interviews with the people who assemble the pianos and run the company. Reviewing the book in the *Los Angeles Times,* Robert Lloyd felt that, although *Piano* contains interesting information, the author's reportorial style distances the reader from the subject, making it seem less personal. As Lloyd pointed out, Barron, as a pianist, could easily have expressed a more personal view of what it is like to play one of the most famous instruments in the world, yet the author remains objective. "Even as he doggedly anthropomorphizes his subject," related Lloyd, "he is never able to bring his protagonist alive. As a conscientious reporter, he has taken himself out of the picture and, although this may be good newspaper style, it doesn't work here." The critic noted that the "historical passages are largely well told," though the author relies on secondary sources for this information, and concluded that "there's much of interest here, nevertheless, in this sometimes surprising tale of the humble beginnings of a musical aristocrat." Barry Zaslow, writing for *Library Journal,* was more appreciative of Barron's efforts, calling *Piano* "an informative and amusing" work that has a "flowing style and [conveys] evident affection for the material."

BIOGRAPHICAL AND CRITICAL SOURCES:

PERIODICALS

Booklist, August 1, 2006, Donna Chavez, review of *Piano: The Making of a Steinway Concert Grand,* p. 24.

Library Journal, June 15, 2006, Barry Zaslow, review of *Piano,* p. 70.

Los Angeles Times, September 17, 2006, Robert Lloyd, "A Book in 88 Keys," review of *Piano.*

Reference & Research Book News, November, 2006, review of *Piano.**

BARRON, James Turman
   See BARRON, James

*   *   *

BARTOY, Mitchell

PERSONAL: Married; children: two. *Education:* Wayne State University, B.A., M.A.

ADDRESSES: Home—Troy, MI. *E-mail*—mitch@ mitchellbartoy.com.

CAREER: Author.

WRITINGS:

"PETE CAUDILL" SERIES; CRIME NOVELS

The Devil's Own Rag Doll, St. Martin's Minotaur (New York, NY), 2005.
The Devil's Only Friend, St. Martin's Minotaur (New York, NY), 2006.

SIDELIGHTS: Mitchell Bartoy debuted his noir crime series in 2005 with *The Devil's Own Rag Doll.* A native of Detroit, the author sets his stories in that city but goes back in time to the 1940s. It is a time of racial tensions, police corruption, and worries about the war; into this setting Bartoy places Pete Caudill, a flawed police detective who has lost two fingers and an eye in an accident and, thus, is not able to enlist in the military. In the first novel, Caudill is assigned to find the killer of a teenager who was the daughter of a prominent Detroit industrialist. In the second novel, *The Devil's Only Friend,* Caudill has quit the force but becomes an investigator again after a friend asks him to find out who killed his sister. Bartoy fills his stories with dark images, a complex and at times unsympathetic hero, and language that reminded some critics of Mickey Spillane's stories. The overall impression of many reviewers was that Bartoy's fiction is uneven but promising in quality. "The depth and sincerity that shine through Bartoy's sometimes overheated prose make this a promising debut," stated a *Kirkus Reviews* contributor about *The Devil's Own Rag Doll.* "The writing is lean and tight, invoking the period as much through style as through the descriptions of places and events," observed Dana King in the *Mystery Reader.* "Its occasional lapses into Spillane-esque purple prose can be explained as representing the period, jarring only in comparison to the matter of factness which surrounds it," King continued.

Discussing the second installment in the series, a *Kirkus Reviews* writer concluded: "The ultra-dark noir sometimes gets lost in its brooding, but Caudill keeps the pages turning." Although a *Publishers Weekly* contributor perceived a "lack of narrative drive" to *The Devil's Only Friend,* the critic felt the author "provides a moving, frighteningly real view of WWII-era Detroit."

BIOGRAPHICAL AND CRITICAL SOURCES:

PERIODICALS

Booklist, September 1, 2005, Bill Ott, review of *The Devil's Own Rag Doll,* p. 67; October 1, 2006, Wes Lukowsky, review of *The Devil's Only Friend,* p. 39.
Kirkus Reviews, August 1, 2005, review of *The Devil's Own Rag Doll,* p. 817; September 15, 2006, review of *The Devil's Only Friend,* p. 930.
Publishers Weekly, August 29, 2005, review of *The Devil's Own Rag Doll,* p. 36; September 25, 2006, review of *The Devil's Only Friend,* p. 48.

ONLINE

Mitchell Bartoy Home Page, http://mitchellbartoy.com (January 7, 2007).
New Mystery Reader, http://www.newmysteryreader. com/ (January 7, 2007), Dana King and Robin Thomas, review of *The Devil's Own Rag Doll.**

*   *   *

BASCOM, Tim 1961-

PERSONAL: Born 1961; son of a physician and missionary father and missionary mother; married; children: two sons. *Education:* University of Iowa, M.F.A.

ADDRESSES: Home—Newton, IA. Office—DMACC—Newton Polytechnic, 600 N. 2nd Ave., Newton, IA 50208. E-mail—tpbascom@dmacc.edu.

CAREER: Des Moines Area Community College, Des Moines, IA, teacher.

AWARDS, HONORS: Editor Prize, *Missouri Review,* Editor Prize, *Florida Review,* both for excerpt from *Chameleon Days: An American Boyhood in Ethiopia;* Katharine Bakeless Nason Prize for nonfiction, Bread Loaf Writer's Conference, 2005, for *Chameleon Days.*

WRITINGS:

Squatters' Rites (novel), New Day Publishers (Quezon City, Philippines), 1990.
The Comfort Trap: Spiritual Dangers of the Convenience Culture (nonfiction), InterVarsity Press (Downers Grove, IL), 1993.
Chameleon Days: An American Boyhood in Ethiopia (memoir), Houghton Mifflin (Boston, MA), 2006.

Author of poems and essays. Contributor to anthology *The Best American Travel Writing,* 2005. Poems have appeared in periodicals, including *Christian Century, The Other Side, Wapsipinicon Almanac,* and *Sojourners.*

SIDELIGHTS: A graduate of the University of Iowa Writer's Workshop, Tim Bascom has published essays and poetry. He has also written the novel *Squatters' Rites,* a story set in a Manila slum, and *The Comfort Trap: Spiritual Dangers of the Convenience Culture,* which takes a critical look at the practice of Christianity in America. More recently, however, Bascom received considerable attention for his memoir, *Chameleon Days: An American Boyhood in Ethiopia.*

The son of medical missionaries, Bascom spent much of his childhood growing up in Ethiopia during the time of Emperor Haile Selassie. Having parents who were very preoccupied with their Christian missionary work was difficult for the young Bascom, and in *Chameleon Days* he relates how he and his two brothers tried to cope with their constantly changing circumstances. Bascom was the middle child, and he often was alone because his older brother was sent to

boarding school first and his younger brother was too little to spend play time with. Bascom spent considerable time exploring the wildlife of the country, and he made a pet out of a chameleon. He was later sent to boarding school, too, but when Ethiopia was thrown into political unrest and violent student protests ensued, his parents gathered up their children and returned to America.

Critics of *Chameleon Days* found the author's work to be a rich portrayal of the times and setting. Although *Entertainment Weekly* reviewer Gilbert Cruz believed that the novel "would have benefited from more context" about the political situation in Ethiopia, a *Kirkus Reviews* contributor declared it a "stirring tribute to a turbulent, beautifully evoked era." "Nostalgic but not overwrought," according to a *Publishers Weekly* critic, the work has "gently captured [a] place in time."

BIOGRAPHICAL AND CRITICAL SOURCES:

BOOKS

Bascom, Tim, *Chameleon Days: An American Boyhood in Ethiopia,* Houghton Mifflin (Boston, MA), 2006.

PERIODICALS

Entertainment Weekly, June 16, 2006, Gilbert Cruz, review of *Chameleon Days,* p. 81.
Kirkus Reviews, May 1, 2006, review of *Chameleon Days,* p. 443.
Kliatt, September, 2006, Patricia Moore, review of *Chameleon Days,* p. 39.
Publishers Weekly, April 24, 2006, review of *Chameleon Days,* p. 49.

*   *   *

BASE, Ron

PERSONAL: Male.

ADDRESSES: Home—Montreal, Quebec, Canada.

CAREER: Writer, novelist, screenwriter, movie critic, magazine writer, and journalist. Worked as a reporter for the *Toronto Star.*

WRITINGS:

Matinee Idol, Doubleday (Garden City, NY), 1985.
Foreign Object, Doubleday (New York, NY), 1986.
The Movies of the Eighties, Macdonald (London, England), 1990.
"If the Other Guy Isn't Jack Nicholson, I've Got the Part": Hollywood Tales of Big Breaks, Bad Luck, and Box-Office Magic, Contemporary Books (Chicago, IL), 1994.
Starring Roles: How Movie Stardom in Hollywood Is Won and Lost, Stoddart (Toronto, Ontario, Canada), 1994.
Magic Man (novel), Thomas Dunne Books (New York, NY), 2006.

SCREENPLAYS

(With Lawrence Dane) *Heavenly Bodies,* Moviecorp VIII, 1984.
White Light, Brightstar Pictures, 1991.
(With Olivier Austen and Hugo Pratt) *Jesuit Joe,* Duckster Productions, 1991.
(And producer) *First Degree,* Incorporated Television Company (ITC), 1996.
(With Michael Stokes) *Press Run,* Avalanche Home Entertainment, 1999.
Cover Story, Aladdin Entertainment, 2002.
(With Anne Ray-Wendling and Heidrun Schleef) *The Last Sign,* Transfilm, 2002.
(With Valerio Manfredi and Rospo Pallenberg) *Memoirs of Hadrian,* Rai Cinemafiction, 2007.

Also author of episode of television series *Night Heat,* Columbia Broadcasting System (CBS), 1985.

SIDELIGHTS: Ron Base is a screenwriter, journalist, and movie critic. Several of Base's nonfiction works focus on film and, in particular, the effects of casting decisions on the lasting fame of both movie and actor. In *"If the Other Guy Isn't Jack Nicholson, I've Got the Part": Hollywood Tales of Big Breaks, Bad Luck, and Box-Office Magic,* Base describes how chance, whim, and off-the-cuff decisions have made some stars and movies famous while denying others the chance in the limelight. Humphrey Bogart's tough-guy movie career was propelled by the fact that contemporary star George Raft turned down several roles that then went to Bogart. The well-publicized search for the perfect actress to play Scarlett O'Hara in *Gone with the Wind* was less a concession to careful selection and more of a result of indecision on the part of director David O. Selznick. Base notes that offers and acceptances of parts in movies have had as much impact on stars' and films' enduring fame as have technical superiority or excellent scriptwriting. Base's "eminently readable and informative film history imparts valuable insight into the workings" of Hollywood's casting and star-making apparatus, noted Mike Tribby in *Booklist.*

A more mythic Hollywood forms the backdrop for Base's novel *Magic Man.* The time is the late 1920s, and sound is the new innovation in moviemaking, all the better to help Americans forget the woes of ongoing Prohibition. Into this setting steps Brae Orrack, a dapper Scotsman on a quest for something that will save his life, but which, he is told, cannot be found: true love. Orrack is a "magic man," cursed by his equally magical father to perish unless he can find that elusive true love. His one trick, turning stones into bees, seems ridiculous and useless, but it has so far served him well through some difficult situations. Convinced by his cousin that true love can be found in Hollywood, Orrack arrives, clad in a tuxedo, and immediately begins his search. His efforts bring him into contact with many of Hollywood's greats of the time, including Gary Cooper, Clara Bow, and George Raft. Friend and neighbor Lily helps Orrack secure a job when his rent money runs low, putting him in position as a bodyguard/nursemaid for a womanizing Gary Cooper. When Orrack meets adventurous mountaineer Nell Devereaux, he believes he has found the true love he seeks. His efforts to woo her are complicated by Cooper, who also falls for the woman, and by Devereaux's jealous Cuban suitor, dictator Gerardo Machado. When Machado abducts Nell and takes her to Cuba, Orrack sets out in determined pursuit, which will lead to further encounters with gangsters, gamblers, and hired killers. "Base works his own magic as he crisply choreographs the entrances and exits of his large cast" in his "delicious tongue-in-cheek debut," remarked a *Kirkus Reviews* critic. "There's something for everyone: humor, mystery, suspense, nostalgia and, of course, a little magic," commented a reviewer in *Publishers Weekly.*

BIOGRAPHICAL AND CRITICAL SOURCES:

PERIODICALS

Booklist, October 15, 1994, Mike Tribby, review of *"If the Other Guy Isn't Jack Nicholson, I've Got the Part": Hollywood Tales of Big Breaks, Bad Luck, and Box-Office Magic,* p. 389.
Entertainment Weekly, August 11, 2006, Gilbert Cruz, review of *Magic Man,* p. 73.
Kirkus Reviews, June 1, 2006, review of *Magic Man,* p. 532.
Publishers Weekly, May 1, 2006, review of *Magic Man,* p. 33.

ONLINE

Hour.ca, http://www.hour.ca/ (July 6, 2006), M.J. Stone, "Movie Magic," review of *Magic Man.*
Internet Movie Database, http://www.imdb.com/ (January 22, 2007), filmography of Ron Base.
Ron Base Home Page, http://www.ronbase.com (January 22, 2007).*

* * *

BATISTA, Paul A. 1948-

PERSONAL: Born December 9, 1948, in Milford, MA. *Education:* Bowdoin College, A.B., 1970 (magna cum laude); Cornell University, J.D., 1974.

ADDRESSES: Office—Paul A. Batista Law Firm, 26 Broadway, Ste. 1900, New York, NY 10004.

CAREER: Lawyer. Works as a criminal litigator in New York, NY. Guest commentator, Court TV, 1996—.

WRITINGS:

Civil RICO Practice Manual, Wiley Law Publications (New York, NY), 1987, 2nd edition, 1997.
Death's Witness (crime novel), Sourcebooks Landmark (Naperville, IL), 2006.

Contributor to periodicals, including the *New York Times, Securities Regulation Law Journal, Wall Street Journal, National Law Journal, New York Law Journal,* and *Delaware Journal of Corporate Law.*

SIDELIGHTS: A criminal attorney based in New York City, Paul A. Batista knew what he was writing about when he penned his debut crime thriller, *Death's Witness.* The story involves police corruption, money laundering, fraud, and, of course, murder. Julie Perini finds herself a widow when her lawyer husband, Tom, is shot while jogging in Central Park. He had been defending accused mobster Sy Klein at the time, and so foul play is naturally suspected. Julie has no training as a detective, but when she decides to return to her former career as a journalist, she initiates her own investigation. Little does she know that the Federal Bureau of Investigation (FBI) agent she has been consulting for help is the man who put out the hit on Tom, and as she digs deeper, Julie becomes the next target in a novel Mary Ann Smyth called "a thriller that is not to be missed" in her *BookLoons* review. A *Kirkus Reviews* critic had some reservations, remarking: "With the exception of some engrossing scenes of complex legal maneuvering, Batista's fiction debut is fairly ordinary and predictable." Other reviewers were more impressed, however. Although a *Publishers Weekly* contributor felt the story's conclusion was wrapped up a little too neatly, the critic concluded that the author is "guilty of delivering not only sharp courtroom drama but steamy romantic escapism as well," and Bruce Tierney, writing on *BookPage,* declared *Death's Witness* to be "an outstanding debut novel."

BIOGRAPHICAL AND CRITICAL SOURCES:

PERIODICALS

Kirkus Reviews, August 1, 2006, review of *Death's Witness,* p. 736.
Publishers Weekly, August 7, 2006, review of *Death's Witness,* p. 34.
Reference & Research Book News, November, 2005, review of second edition of *Civil RICO Practice Manual.*

ONLINE

BookLoons, http://www.bookloons.com/ (January 6, 2007), Mary Ann Smyth, review of *Death's Witness.*

BookPage, http://www.bookpage.com/ (January 6, 2007), Bruce Tierney, review of *Death's Witness.**

*   *   *

BAUDE, Dawn-Michelle 1959-

PERSONAL: Born 1959. *Education:* New College of California, M.A., 1987; Mills College, M.F.A., 1989; Université de Paris IV, Sorbonne, D.E.A., 1997; University of Illinois-Chicago, Ph.D., 2003.

ADDRESSES: E-mail—info@dawnmichellebaude. com.

CAREER: Poet, writer, educator, and consultant. Université de Paris, France, visiting assistant professor, 1989-93; Bard College Year-Abroad, Lacoste, France, assistant professor, 1998-2001; American University of Beirut, Beirut, Lebanon, visiting professor, 1999-2000; American University of Paris, Paris, France, assistant professor, Alexandria University, Alexandria, Egypt, adjunct professor, 2004, assistant professor, 2006—. Also communications consultant to private industry, including IBM International, 1999—; freelance journalist for Condé Nast publications, 1992-2000; and guest editor for *Van Gogh's Ear,* 2007.

AWARDS, HONORS: Senior Fulbright Award in creative writing, 2005-06.

WRITINGS:

The Book of One Hand, Laincourt Press (Paris, France), 1998.
The Beirut Poems, Skanky Possum Editions (Austin, TX), 2001.
reConnaître: Curt Asker (exhibition catalogue), Réunion des Musées Nationaux (Paris, France), 2001.
Sunday, Signum Editions (Paris, France), 2002.
Egypt, Post-Apollo Press (Sausalito, CA), 2002.
Through a Membrane/Clouds (e-book), GONG (Portland, OR), 2006.
The Flying House: Poems 1996-2006, Free Verse/Parlor Press (North Carolina), 2007.

Also author of numerous chapbooks, including *The Tropologue, A Week in the Life of the Marines, The Anatolian Tapestry,* and *Graffiot Exquis.* Contributor of poetry reviews and literary criticism to periodicals, including *American Book Review, San Francisco Chronicle, Verse, Rain Taxi, Poetry Flash,* and *Chicago Review.*

SIDELIGHTS: Dawn-Michelle Baude is a widely traveled poet and critic who has lived in France, Egypt, Greece, Belgium, and Lebanon and has also made extended visits to Jordan, Kenya, Uganda, and Zaire. With degrees from Mills College and the Sorbonne, Baude has supported herself by teaching, and she has also undertaken research projects such as her 1993-94 exploration of the Karnak Temple in Luxor, Egypt. Her poetry reflects this deep engagement with other cultures while also demonstrating "daring flights of . . . poetic imagination," to quote Nina Zivancevic in an *American Book Review* piece. Zivancevic also noted that Baude "is real, and she cuts deep as she punctures the slices of reality, here and there, and lets it bleed, after which it can never recover nor be the same, nor can the reader." A *Publishers Weekly* contributor commended *Egypt* for its "gusto" and "musical combinations of language."

BIOGRAPHICAL AND CRITICAL SOURCES:

PERIODICALS

American Book Review, March-April, 2003, Nina Zivancevic, review of *The Beirut Poems* and *Egypt,* pp. 23-24.
Publishers Weekly, September 3, 2001, review of *Egypt,* p. 85.

ONLINE

Accepted.com, http://www.accepted.com/ (March 15, 2004), "Editor Profile."
American University of Paris Web site, http://www.aup.fr/ (December 31, 2006), faculty profile of author.
Dawn-Michelle Baude Home Page, http://www.dawn michellebaude.com (December 31, 2006).

*   *   *

BAYARD, Louis

PERSONAL: Born in Albuquerque, NM; children: two sons. *Education:* Princeton University, B.A.; Northwestern University, M.A.

ADDRESSES: Home—Washington, DC. *Agent*—Christopher Schelling, Ralph Vicinanza Ltd., 303 W. 18th St., New York, NY 10011. *E-mail*—contact@louisbayard.com.

CAREER: Writer, book reviewer, journalist. Worked as a congressional press secretary, a communications director, and a speechwriter.

AWARDS, HONORS: Nominee, Outstanding Newspaper Article, Gay and Lesbian Alliance against Defamation, for *Washington Post Magazine* article, "Two Men and a Baby"; Notable Book, *New York Times,* and 10 Best Books for 2003, *People* magazine, for *Mr. Timothy;* Top 10 Historical Fiction Audiobooks, *Booklist,* 2004, for *Mr. Timothy.*

WRITINGS:

NOVELS

Fool's Errand, Alyson Books (Los Angeles, CA), 1999.
Endangered Species, Alyson Books (Los Angeles, CA), 2001.
Mr. Timothy, HarperCollins (New York, NY), 2003.
The Pale Blue Eye, HarperCollins (New York, NY), 2006.

Contributor of articles to periodicals and online publications, including the *New York Times, Washington Post, Washington DC City Paper, Ms., Salon.com,* and *Nerve.com.* Contributor to anthologies, including *The Worst Noel,* HarperCollins, *Maybe Baby,* HarperCollins, and *101 Damnations,* St. Martin's Press.

ADAPTATIONS: Mr. Timothy was adapted for audiobook, BBC/Sound, 2004; *The Pale Blue Eye* was adapted for audiobook, BBC.

SIDELIGHTS: Louis Bayard is a journalist and novelist whose fiction ranges from light, contemporary tales of gay men in Washington DC, to dark historical reconstructions, including *Mr. Timothy* and *The Pale Blue Eye.* Bayard's first novel, *Fool's Errand,* features thirty-ish Patrick Beaton who is looking for love in Washington, DC. The object of his desires is Scottie, a man he met only briefly; or, in fact, did he? Patrick

begins to wonder if the meeting was real or simply in his mind. *Library Journal* reviewer Christopher Koranowsky called this debut novel "darkly comic," and concluded that it was a "pleasant read for all audiences." *Lambda Book Report* reviewer Bill Mann similarly praised Bayard's "considerable skill with dialogue," while a contributor for *Publishers Weekly* found *Fool's Errand* both "accomplished," and "a witty romantic comedy." A similar humorous tone informs Bayard's second novel, *Endangered Species,* in which a gay man, Nick Broome, decides to do something about the fact that his family line will die off with his generation. With siblings who do not procreate, Nick takes it on himself to continue the family line with comic consequences. A *Publishers Weekly* contributor felt this was a "well-crafted" work, and that Bayard manages to inform the reader "about the force that drives procreation." *Booklist* writer Whitney Scott felt "Bayard's gently touching humor helps the novel stay the course," and Peter Marcus, writing in the *Gay & Lesbian Review* recommended the novel as a "mostly pleasurable reading experience."

Bayard provides a change of pace with his next two novels, both set in the nineteenth century. *Mr. Timothy* is an "inventive updating" of the *Christmas Carol* by Charles Dickens, according to *Booklist* contributor Bill Ott. The reader finds Tiny Tim now in his twenties and residing in a brothel, where he teaches the ladies how to read. His aimless life takes sudden direction, however, when he tackles a child porn ring in an attempt to save a young girl he has befriended. Though Ott felt the "transition from character study to historical thriller is a bit awkward," he went on to call the work "first-rate entertainment." Similar positive remarks came from many critics. Reviewing the novel in *Bookreporter.com,* Kate Ayers found it a "combination of droll wit, sidelong glances at 19th-century London and headlong suspense." For *Bookseller* contributor Lizzie Ludlow it was a "disturbing thriller," while *Entertainment Weekly* contributor Rebecca Ascher-Walsh thought it was a "fabulous Victorian mystery." Likewise, a *Publishers Weekly* reviewer felt *Mr. Timothy* was "an audacious and triumphant entertainment," and Bella Stande, writing in *People* called the same work a "dazzling blend of literary fiction and white-knuckle thriller."

In *The Pale Blue Eye,* Bayard concocts a mystery in which the young Edgar Allan Poe plays detective. Poe, a cadet at West Point in 1830, helps a retired New York

City detective solve a grisly murder at the school. *Library Journal* reviewer Jo Ann Vicarel noted that the novel was "charmed by a skillful and lyrical writing style and the intrigue of West Point." Further praise came from *Salon.com* contributor Laura Miller, who felt the novel was a "a fond, often funny, but also unvarnished portrait of the real Poe." Miller also commended "Bayard's prose [which] flows like silk, weightless but enveloping, and never shows its seams." For a *Kirkus Reviews* critic *The Pale Blue Eye* was a "literary tour de force," and a reviewer for *Publishers Weekly* found it "an intense and gripping novel."

BIOGRAPHICAL AND CRITICAL SOURCES:

PERIODICALS

Booklist, April 1, 2001, Whitney Scott, review of *Endangered Species,* p. 1446; November 15, 2003, Bill Ott, review of *Mr. Timothy,* p. 579; May 15, 2004, Joyce Saricks, "Top 10 Historical Fiction Audiobooks," p. 1637.

Bookseller, June 17, 2005, Lizzie Ludlow, review of *Mr. Timothy,* p. 13.

Entertainment Weekly, October 31, 2003, Rebecca Ascher-Walsh, review of *Mr. Timothy,* p. 79; May 26, 2006, "That's So Raven," review of *The Pale Blue Eye,* p. 108.

Gay & Lesbian Review, July, 2001, Peter Marcus, review of *Endangered Species,* p. 40.

Kirkus Reviews, September 15, 2003, review of *Mr. Timothy,* p. 1138; May 1, 2006, review of *The Pale Blue Eye,* p. 424.

Lambda Book Report, July-August, 1999, Bill Mann, review of *Fool's Errand,* p. 18.

Library Journal, January, 2000, Christopher Koranowsky, review of *Fool's Errand,* p. 200; August, 2003, Barbara Love, review of *Mr. Timothy,* p. 127; May 1, 2006, Jo Ann Vicarel, review of *The Pale Blue Eye,* p. 67.

People, December 1, 2003, Bella Stande, review of *Mr. Timothy,* p. 49.

Publishers Weekly, May 17, 1999, review of *Fool's Errand,* p. 57; April 2, 2001, review of *Endangered Species,* p. 39; September 15, 2003, review of *Mr. Timothy,* p. 40; April 10, 2006, review of *The Pale Blue Eye,* p. 43.

Spectator, December 11, 2004, Sophie Lewis, review of *Mr. Timothy,* p. 44.

ONLINE

Bookreporter.com, http://www.bookreporter.com/ (November 13, 2006), Kate Ayers, review of *Mr. Timothy.*

HarperCollins Web site, http://www.harpercollins.com/ (November 13, 2006), "Louis Bayard."

Louis Bayard Home Page, http://www.louisbayard.com (November 13, 2006).

Metro Weekly Online, http://www.metroweekly.com/ (May 25, 2006), Thomas Avila, review of *The Pale Blue Eye.*

Pop Matters, http://www.popmatters.com/ (February 24, 2004), Claire Zulkey, review of *Mr. Timothy.*

Salon.com, http://www.salon.com/ (June 19, 2006), Laura Miller, review of *The Pale Blue Eye.*

*   *   *

BEATTY, Jan 1952-

PERSONAL: Born 1952.

ADDRESSES: Office—Department of English, University of Pittsburgh, Pittsburgh, PA 15260. *E-mail*—beattyjp@carlow.edu.

CAREER: University of Pittsburgh, Pittsburgh, PA, part-time instructor in English and creative writing; Carlow University, Pittsburgh, writing instructor, interim director of the creative writing program, 2006—. Has also worked as social worker, teacher in maximum security prisons, waitress, welfare caseworker, rape counselor, and nurse's aide. Host and producer, *Prosody* (radio show), WYEP-FM, Pittsburgh.

AWARDS, HONORS: Pablo Neruda Prize, 1990; Agnes Lynch Starrett Poetry Prize, University of Pittsburgh Press, 1994, for *Mad River;* State Street Press chapbook prize, 1995, for *Ravenous;* Creative Achievement Award, Pittsburgh Cultural Trust, 2000; two fellowships from Pennsylvania Council on the Arts.

WRITINGS:

Mad River (poetry), University of Pittsburgh Press (Pittsburgh, PA), 1995.

Ravenous (poetry chapbook), State Street Press Chapbooks (Brockport, NY), 1995.
Boneshaker (poetry), University of Pittsburgh Press (Pittsburgh, PA), 2002.

Contributor to poetry anthologies published by University of Illinois Press, Kent State University Press, and University of Iowa Press. Contributor of poetry to periodicals, including *Indiana Review, Witness,* and *The Journal.*

SIDELIGHTS: Although Jan Beatty has stated that her poetry is not autobiographical, its voice is forged from the experiences of people living, loving, working, and wondering in the city of Pittsburgh, Pennsylvania. Beatty has herself spent much of her life there and has held a wide variety of jobs that inform her work, from counseling rape victims and teaching in maximum security prisons to working tables in diners and hamburger joints. Beatty's observations on life neither flinch from its difficult moments nor do they mince words. As Lauren McCollum put it in the *American Book Review,* Beatty's poetry "is out for blood, hunting after truth despite all consequences." McCollum also noted that the author's work "poses emotional and intellectual challenges to its reader, and it is utterly, brutally honest."

Beatty's first three collections of poetry have all garnered praise. *Ravenous* won the 1995 State Street Press chapbook prize, and both *Mad River* and *Boneshaker* drew warm reviews. *Booklist* contributor Elizabeth Millard wrote of *Mad River:* "To dive into Beatty's river is to discover a universe of possibilities," and a *Publishers Weekly* reviewer called the work "deeply visceral and sensory." In the *Pittsburgh Post-Gazette,* Mary Gannon found *Boneshaker* to be "rife with the high-stakes and rhythmic velocity of an urgent message." Gannon added that Beatty's poems "appeal to the heart and the ear. . . . But it is the search for one's bearing in the world accompanied by the impulse to strike out against all that is wrong in it that makes this collection so exhilarating."

BIOGRAPHICAL AND CRITICAL SOURCES:

PERIODICALS

American Book Review, March-April, 2003, Lauren McCollum, review of *Boneshaker,* p. 19.

Belles Lettres: A Review of Books by Women, January, 1996, Phebe Davidson, review of *Ravenous,* p. 37.
Booklist, September 1, 1995, Elizabeth Millard, review of *Mad River,* p. 32.
Pittsburgh Post-Gazette, April 7, 2002, Mary Gannon, review of *Boneshaker.*
Publishers Weekly, August 28, 1995, review of *Mad River,* p. 108.*

*   *   *

BEEBER, Steven Lee

PERSONAL: Male.

CAREER: Writer, journalist, editor, and musician.

WRITINGS:

The Heebie-Jeebies at CBGB's: A Secret History of Jewish Punk, Chicago Review Press (Chicago, IL), 2006.
(Editor) *Awake: A Reader for the Sleepless,* Soft Skull Press (Brooklyn, NY), 2007.

Contributor to periodicals, including *Paris Review, Fiction Bridge, Spin, Mojo, Maxim, Details, Rain Taxi, Playboy.com, Conduit,* and the *New York Times.*

SIDELIGHTS: Steven Lee Beeber is a writer and editor who also plays saxophone and worked with bands such as the Chowder Shouters, a gospel-punk bank in Atlanta, Georgia. He is a frequent contributor to a variety of magazines and is the editor of *Awake: A Reader for the Sleepless,* an anthology featuring fiction, comics, essays, poetry, found texts, and other material for insomniac readers.

In *The Heebie-Jeebies at CBGB's: A Secret History of Jewish Punk,* Beeber reconsiders the origins of punk rock, the rebellious musical genre of the mid-1970s characterized by Mohawk haircuts, safety-pin piercings, and defiant attitudes. Beeber challenges the conventional theories of punk's origins in England and instead asserts that it developed from the efforts of Jewish performers, club owners, and producers in New York and America. "Beeber discloses that prime movers in creating, supporting, and popularizing punk were Jews," noted Benjamin Segedin in *Booklist*. Based on more than 125 interviews with musicians and other sources, the book identifies a Jewish lineage for punk that begins with irreverent comic Lenny Bruce and continues through some of the genre's most influential participants, including Lou Reed, Joey and Tommy Ramone, Chris Stein of Blondie, and the Beastie Boys. Beeber also finds it significant that one of the most influential and iconic music clubs of the time, the storied CBGB's, was owned by a Jewish man, Hilly Kristal. Beeber assembles dozens of "interesting biographical sketches of the preeminent Jewish punks, rather astutely placing the punk rockers among the pantheon of Jewish entertainers," observed a *Publishers Weekly* reviewer.

Beeber also addresses one of punk rock's most controversial aspects: the embracing of Nazi imagery and symbolism. He finds this behavior to be in no way an endorsement of Nazism, but is instead a means of removing the power from these symbols through overexaggerated acceptance. Nazi symbols not only fed punk rock's inherent need for rebellion, but also expressed "the intention of disrespecting Nazism by mocking the "failed seriousness" of these same symbols," commented Sam Jemielity in *Playboy*. "So songs such as the Dictators' 'Master Race Rock' or the Ramones' 'Blitzkrieg Bop' are not disrespectful of Jews, but a joke—perhaps unsophisticated and in poor taste—mocking Nazism," Jemielity stated.

"With equal parts spirit and scholarship, Beeber succeeds in placing this still-influential music within a broader historical and cultural context, and assures that punk's 'secret history' is a secret no more," concluded Reneé Graham in the *Boston Globe*. *Library Journal* contributor Matthew Moyer commented that "strong writing and even stronger subject matter keep one enthralled" with Beeber's historical account.

BIOGRAPHICAL AND CRITICAL SOURCES:

PERIODICALS

Booklist, September 15, 2006, Benjamin Segedin, review of *The Heebie-Jeebies at CBGB's: A Secret History of Jewish Punk*, p. 14.
Boston Globe, December 4, 2006, Renée Graham, "Author Thoroughly Examines the Jewish Roots of Punk Rock," review of *The Heebie-Jeebies at CBGB's*.

Library Journal, September 1, 2006, Matthew Moyer, review of *The Heebie-Jeebies at CBGB's*, p. 147.
Phoenix (Boston, MA), November 1, 2006, Ian Sands, "Who You Callin' a Punk?," review of *The Heebie-Jeebies at CBGB's*.
Playboy, October 26, 2006, Same Jemielity, review of *The Heebie-Jeebies at CBGB's*.
Publishers Weekly, July 31, 2006, review of *The Heebie-Jeebies at CBGB's*, p. 63.

ONLINE

Forward.com, http://www.forward.com/ (September 22, 2006), Alexander Gelfand, "Blitzkrieg Flop," review of *The Heebie-Jeebies at CBGB's*.
FrontStreetReviews.com, http://www.frontstreetreviews.com/ (January 22, 2007), Susan Helene Gottfried, review of *The Heebie-Jeebies at CBGB's*.
Steven Lee Beeber Home Page, http://www.jewpunk.com (January 22, 2007).*

* * *

BEHRENS, Peter

PERSONAL: Born in Montreal, Quebec, Canada. *Education:* Attended Lower Canada College, Concordia University, and McGill University.

ADDRESSES: Home—Brooklin, ME, and Los Angeles, CA. *Agent*—Sarah Burnes, The Gernert Company, 136 E. 57th St., New York, NY 10022; Lynn Pleshette, The Lynn Pleshette Agency, 2700 N. Beachwood, Los Angeles, CA 90068. *E-mail*—himself@peterbehrens.org.

CAREER: Writer, novelist, screenwriter, and short-story writer.

MEMBER: Writers Guild of America (West), Writers Guild of Canada.

AWARDS, HONORS: Governor-General's Award for fiction, Canada, 2006, for *The Law of Dreams;* Wallace Stegner fellow in creative writing, Stanford University; Fine Arts Work Center fellow, Provincetown, MA.

WRITINGS:

Night Driving (short stories), Macmillan of Canada (Toronto, Ontario, Canada), 1987.
The Law of Dreams (novel), Steerforth Press (Hanover, NH), 2006.

Contributor to anthologies, including *Second Impressions,* compiled by John Metcalf, Oberon (Ottawa, Ontario, Canada), 1981; *Best Canadian Stories 1978,* edited by John Metcalf and Clark Blaise, 1978; *Best Canadian Stories 1979,* edited by John Metcalf and Clark Blaise, 1979; and *Stories of Quebec,* Oberon Press (Ottawa, Ontario, Canada), 1980. Contributor to periodicals, including *Atlantic Monthly, National Post, Globe and Mail, Walrus, Tin House,* and *Maisonneuve.*

SIDELIGHTS: In his debut novel, *The Law of Dreams,* screenwriter and author Peter Behrens presents "a fearsome story of such prolonged agony and unquenchable spirit that you can't escape till the final page abandons you to astonished silence," remarked *Washington Post Book World* reviewer Ron Charles. The protagonist of the novel, Fergus O'Brien, "endures abuses and deprivations that would make a lesser man feral, but there's a native decency in him, a natural grace that renders his decision to survive all the more agonizing," Charles commented. O'Brien is the teenage son of a tenant farmer family in Ireland during the Great Famine of 1847, when a blight wiped out the majority of the potato crop that the Irish tenant farmers subsisted on. Hunger and disease swept through the country. The O'Brien family resists eviction from their farm, even though they have been hit hard by the blight. Typhus has killed Fergus's younger sisters and, as his parents lie ill from the disease, their cabin is set afire with them still inside it. In what is seen as an act of generosity, Fergus's landlord arranges for him to be sent to a workhouse, where the boy joins a gang of violent juvenile outlaws, the Bog Boys, led by the tough and tenacious female, Luke, with whom Fergus falls in love. He joins the group for a deadly raid on his former landlord's farm, then heads to Dublin and Liverpool, where he nearly settles into a luxurious life as a male prostitute. Working as a laborer on the railroad, Fergus falls for Molly, the innkeeper's wife, and heads out with her for Canada and America, where he intends to become a horse trader. Their plans for a new life in the new world are thwarted by fate and by betrayal as Fergus's tenacity and will to survive is tested anew.

With his book, Behrens has "fashioned a paean to the strength of the human spirit that illuminates a piece of history," stated Michele Leber in *Booklist.* "If the novel were judged solely on the language, precise and poetic in a way that cuts into the heart like a razor, no one could deny Behrens' brilliance," commented Juliet Walters in the *Montreal Mirror.* The novel must also be judged on the quality of the story, Walters noted, adding that "it's worth pointing out that Behrens can also spin a wild yarn. *The Law of Dreams* is a novel with as much craft as art, an adventure tale as epic and gripping as a modern Dickens."

BIOGRAPHICAL AND CRITICAL SOURCES:

PERIODICALS

America's Intelligence Wire, November 21, 2006, Jeanine Aversa, "Peter Behrens Grabs Top Literature Award in Canada for *The Law of Dreams.*"
Booklist, August 1, 2006, Michele Leber, review of *The Law of Dreams,* p. 36.
Bookseller, July 28, 2006, "Canongate's *Law of Dreams* Garners International Interest," p. 13.
Kirkus Reviews, June 15, 2006, review of *The Law of Dreams,* p. 587.
Library Journal, June 1, 2006, Maureen Neville, review of *The Law of Dreams,* p. 104.
Montreal Mirror, August 31-September 6, 2006, Juliet Waters, "Feast of Famine," review of *The Law of Dreams.*
New York Times Book Review, December 10, 2006, Kevin Baker, "The Coffin Ships," review of *The Law of Dreams.*
Publishers Weekly, May 22, 2006, review of *The Law of Dreams,* p. 27.
Washington Post Book World, September 1, 2006, Ron Charles, "The Famished Road," review of *The Law of Dreams.*

ONLINE

Peter Behrens' Home Page, http://www.peterbehrens.org (January 22, 2007).
Resource News International, November 21, 2006, "Canadian Entertainment at a Glance," review of *The Law of Dreams.*
The Law of Dreams Web site, http://www.thelawofdreams.com/ (January 22, 2007).

BELL, Gabrielle

PERSONAL: Born in London, England. *Education:* Attended San Francisco Community College.

ADDRESSES: Home—Brooklyn, NY. *E-mail*—gabriellabell90@yahoo.com.

CAREER: Writer and cartoonist. Has worked at a soap store, for the census bureau, as a nude model, art teacher to children, and as a jewelry assembler.

AWARDS, HONORS: Most Outstanding Minicomic, 2003, for comic in the "Lucky" series; Ignatz Award.

WRITINGS:

COMICS

Book of Insomnia: Comics (self-published), Gabrielle Bell, 1998.
Book of Ordinary Things (self-published), Gabrielle Bell, 2002.
When I'm Old and Other Stories, Alternative Comics (Gainesville, FL), 2003.
Lucky, Drawn & Quarterly (Montreal, Quebec, Canada), 2006.

Also author of *Book of Sleep, Book of Black,* and *Book of Lies.* Contributor to numerous anthologies, including *Hi-Horse Omnibus, Volume 1,* Alternative Comics, 2004; *Horror Classics: Graphic Classics, Volume Ten,* Eureka Productions, 2004; *Kramers Ergot; Bogus Dead; Scheherezade;* and *Orchid.* Contributor to periodicals, including *Stereoscomic, Bogus Dead, Orchid,* and *Shout!* magazine.

SIDELIGHTS: Gabrielle Bell is a comics artist, writer, and creator of a minicomics series that includes the self-published titles *Book of Insomnia: Comics, Book of Sleep, Book of Black, Book of Lies* and *Book of Ordinary Things.* "The pieces are a versatile mix in both content and genre, ranging from dreams and fantasies to more didactic parables, as well as straightforward autobio," wrote a contributor to the *QuickDraw* Web site. The contributor went on to note: "As her characters find unexpected consequences to their actions and attitudes, Bell's work explores the hidden connections in our everyday lives, much like the theorem that bears her name."

When I'm Old and Other Stories is a collection of many of Bell's previously self-published minicomics. In addition to her autobiographical stories, Bell inserts herself into fantastic tales in which she imagines herself as a fifty-foot woman or an eccentric old lady living on the streets. In a fantasy tale, Bell writes of a young girl who wants to commit suicide but who ends up killing something else instead with each attempt to do away with herself. Bell also adapts stories written by Herman Hesse and D.H. Lawrence and presents a story based on the film *Repulsion* by Roman Polanski. Writing in *Booklist,* Gordon Flagg commented that "it is exciting to watch her emerging talent tackle all sorts of subject matter." *Library Journal* contributor Steve Raiteri wrote that "this diverse collection shows her broad range of styles."

In her collection *Lucky,* Bell presents autobiographical and fantasy-based short comics, most of which were previously serialized on the *Serializer.net* Web site. For example, a former resident of San Francisco, Bell presents a comic detailing her hunt for an apartment when she moves to Brooklyn and her bout of depression when she has to earn money working as a nude model. She also relates her experience with teaching two young French boys who are strictly interested in drawings featuring sex.

In his review of *Lucky* in the *Boston Globe,* Matthew Shaer wrote: "There's a vague spiritual malaise, the feeling that everything could be better, if only given the chance." Shaer went on to note: "In stark black-and-white frames, four to a page, it tracks the progress of a young artist struggling for professional and emotional traction in a city already clogged with people like her. Bell is lost, but she can't find time to get found." Francisca Goldsmith, writing in *Booklist,* noted that Bell's stories "are palpably real and eloquently understated, with neither a wasted word nor an extra line." A *Kirkus Reviews* contributor wrote: "These slice-of-life, matter-of-fact (and occasionally fantasy) strips sustain a wry, bittersweet humor and disarming warmth." A reviewer writing in *Publishers Weekly* called the collection "completely engrossing" and a "sophisticated, nuanced pleasure."

BIOGRAPHICAL AND CRITICAL SOURCES:

BOOKS

Bell, Gabrielle, *Lucky,* Drawn & Quarterly (Montreal, Quebec, Canada), 2006.

PERIODICALS

Booklist, July, 2003, Gordon Flagg, review of *When I'm Old and Other Stories,* p. 1855; August 1, 2006, Francisca Goldsmith, review of *Lucky,* p. 59.
Boston Globe, November 25, 2006, Matthew Shaer, review of *Lucky.*
Kirkus Reviews, June 15, 2006, review of *Lucky,* p. 608.
Library Journal, September 1, 2003, Steve Raiteri, review of *When I'm Old and Other Stories,* p. 138.
Publishers Weekly, August 14, 2006, review of *Lucky,* p. 186.

ONLINE

Comics Reporter, http://www.comicsreporter.com/ (November 5, 2007), Tom Spurgeon, "A Short Interview with Gabrielle Bell."
Drawn & Quarterly Web site, http://www.drawnandquarterly.com/ (January 11, 2007), brief biography of author.
Graphic Classics, http://www.graphicclassics.com/ (January 12, 2007), brief biography of author.
Indyworld.com, http://www.indyworld.com/ (January 11, 2007), discusses *When I'm Old and Other Stories.*
Lambiek.net, http://lambiek.net/ (January 11, 2007), brief profile of author.
QuickDraw, http://www.qdcomic.com/ (January 12, 2007), "Bell's Theorems," profile of author.
Withitgirl.com, http://www.withitgirl.com/ (January 11, 2007), Sandy Olkowski, "Interview with Gabrielle Bell."*

* * *

BELOZERSKAYA, Marina 1966-

PERSONAL: Born 1966, in Moscow, Russia; married to a museum curator. *Education:* University of California, Berkeley, B.A., 1987; University of Chicago, M.A., 1992, Ph.D., 1997.

ADDRESSES: Home—Los Angeles, CA. *Office*—J. Paul Getty Museum, 1200 Getty Center Dr., Los Angeles, CA 90049-1679. *Agent*—Lippincott Massie McQuilkin, 80 5th Ave., Ste. 1101, New York, NY 10011.

CAREER: Writer and art historian. Hellenic College, Brookline, MA, lecturer, 1996; Boston University, Boston, MA, lecturer, 1996, 1998-99; Harvard University, Cambridge, MA, teaching assistant, 1997-99; Tufts University, Boston, teaching assistant, 1999. Agora Museum, Athens, Greece, assistant manager, 1988-89; participated in excavations in Corinth, Greece, 1989, and Rome, Italy, 1990; American Academy in Rome, Rome, Italy, visiting scholar, 1989-90.

AWARDS, HONORS: Dean's travel grant, University of Chicago, 1994; Mellon fellowship in humanistic studies, 1991-96; Samuel H. Kress Foundation dissertation fellowship, 1996-97; College Art Association/Kress Foundation travel grant, 1998; certificate of distinction in teaching, Harvard University, 1997 and 1998; Frieda L. Miller fellow, Bunting Institute, Radcliffe College/Harvard University, 1999-2000; Dean's fellow, Bunting Fellowship Program, Radcliffe College/Harvard University, 2000-2001; Samuel H. Kress Foundation publication grant, 2001; Millard Meiss publication grant, College Art Association, 2001; Bogliasco fellowship, Liguria Study Center for the Arts and Humanities, 2002.

WRITINGS:

Rethinking the Renaissance: Burgundian Arts across Europe, Cambridge University Press (New York, NY), 2002.
(With Kenneth Lapatin) *Ancient Greece: Art, Architecture, and History,* J. Paul Getty Museum (Los Angeles, CA), 2004.
Luxury Arts of the Renaissance, J. Paul Getty Museum (Los Angeles, CA), 2005.
The Medici Giraffe: And Other Tales of Exotic Animals and Power, (New York, NY), 2006.

Contributor to books, including *Antiquity and Its Interpreters,* Cambridge University Press (New York, NY), 2000; *The Folio Society Book of the Hundred Greatest*

Portraits, edited by Martin Bailey, 2004; and *Portraits of Exotic Animals in Eighteenth-Century France,* edited by Mary Morton, J. Paul Getty Museum (Los Angeles, CA), 2007. Contributor to periodicals, including *Journal of Early Modern History* and *Source: Notes in the History of Art.*

SIDELIGHTS: Art historian Marina Belozerskaya is the author of a number of works of nonfiction, including *Rethinking the Renaissance: Burgundian Arts across Europe* and *The Medici Giraffe: And Other Tales of Exotic Animals and Power.* In *Rethinking the Renaissance,* the author examines the influence of paintings, textiles, architecture, music, and sculpture from the Burgundian Netherlands and "argues for a complete reappraisal of the phenomenon known as the Renaissance," observed *Art Bulletin* contributor Julien Chapuis. According to Anne Simonson, writing in the *Renaissance Quarterly,* "Belozerskaya's excellent introduction to a fifteenth century dominated by a Burgundian, not Florentine, aesthetic is sure to renew investigation of the once-familiar and should help convince general and specialist readers alike of the need to adopt more international and pluralist perspectives."

In *Ancient Greece: Art, Architecture, and History,* Belozerskaya and coauthor Kenneth Lapatin focus on Greek culture from the Minoan era to the Hellenistic period. In the words of *Bryn Mawr Classical Review* critic Fiona Greenland, the authors "have produced a book on Greek material culture that is rich in illustration, stimulating in discussion, and clear in its organization of information." *Luxury Arts of the Renaissance* focuses on the jewel-studded goldwork, engraved armor, rich tapestries, and other objects that reflected social status during the fifteenth and sixteenth centuries. Belozerskaya also devotes a chapter to the spectacular productions of the period, "which discusses the combined effect of ceremonial parades, elaborate and costly table settings and clothes, rich food with exotic ingredients, and music on the guests a Renaissance prince or merchant wanted to impress," wrote a critic in the *Architectural Science Review.* Containing more than 200 illustrations, the work constitutes "a beautiful object in its own right and is readable and well documented" as well, noted *Library Journal* reviewer Nancy Mactague.

The Medici Giraffe is "a lively account of how exotic animals have helped further the political ends of princes and potentates, from the Ptolemys to Chair-

man Mao," wrote a *Kirkus Reviews* contributor. In the work, Belozerskaya recounts the stories of King Rudolf II of Bohemia (1575) and Holy Roman Emperor (1576-1612), who allowed a lion to roam freely throughout his castle; Lorenzo de' Medici, the Italian prince who offered his pet giraffe as proof of his family's prestige; and newspaper magnate William Randolph Hearst, who populated his estate at San Simeon, California, with buffalo, kangaroo, and tapirs. *New York Times Book Review* critic William Grimes stated that the author "proclaims a lofty theme in *The Medici Giraffe*: the relationship between political power and exotic animals. What she actually delivers is an unconnected series of historical essays devoted to strange and wonderful animals, and the great men who lusted after them. The whole is less than the sum of its parts." Other reviewers were more complimentary. *Library Journal* critic Edell M. Schaefer called Belozerskaya "talented" and described the book as a mixture of "unique and little-known historical facts . . . that never fail to keep the reader interested." Ingrid D. Rowland, writing in the *American Scholar,* praised the author's ability to accurately portray humankind's relationship to the natural environment. "As *The Medici Giraffe* shows in telling detail," Rowland commented, "the power of human institutions and human engineering has always worked against a background of powers greater still, embodied for us by creatures whose strangeness, perfection, and uncanny independence have always beggared our imagination."

BIOGRAPHICAL AND CRITICAL SOURCES:

PERIODICALS

American Scholar, autumn, 2006, Ingrid D. Rowland, "Peaceable Kingdom," review of *The Medici Giraffe: And Other Tales of Exotic Animals and Power,* p. 133.
Architectural Science Review, March, 2006, "What the Luxury Art Objects in Renaissance Palaces Meant to Their Owners," review of *Luxury Arts of the Renaissance,* p. 106.
Art Bulletin, September, 2004, Julien Chapuis, "The Donor's Image," review of *Rethinking the Renaissance: Burgundian Arts across Europe,* p. 599.
Booklist, July 1, 2006, Nancy Bent, review of *The Medici Giraffe,* p. 17.
Bryn Mawr Classical Review, December 1, 2004, Fiona Greenland, review of *Ancient Greece: Art, Architecture, and History,* p. 144.

California Bookwatch, October, 2006, review of *The Medici Giraffe.*

Entertainment Weekly, August 25, 2006, Wook Kim, review of *The Medici Giraffe,* p. 89.

Kirkus Reviews, June 1, 2006, review of *The Medici Giraffe,* p. 553.

Library Journal, February 1, 2006, Nancy Mactague, review of *Luxury Arts of the Renaissance,* p. 75; August 1, 2006, Edell M. Schaefer, review of *The Medici Giraffe,* p. 116.

New York Times Book Review, August 25, 2006, William Grimes, "Where Wild Things Are Perks of Power," review of *The Medici Giraffe.*

Renaissance Quarterly, summer, 2004, Anne Simonson, review of *Rethinking the Renaissance,* p. 671

ONLINE

Hatchette Book Group Web site, http://www.twbookmark.com/ (February 4, 2007), "Marina Belozerskaya."*

*   *   *

BENN, James R.

PERSONAL: Married Deborah Mandel (a psychotherapist); children: two sons. *Education:* Graduated from University of Connecticut; Southern Connecticut State University, M.L.S.

ADDRESSES: Home—Hadlyme, CT. *Agent*—Barbara Braun, Barbara Braun Associates, Inc., 104 5th Ave., 7th Fl., New York, NY 10011. *E-mail*—jrb@jamesrbenn.com.

CAREER: Writer, novelist, and librarian. Works in educational technology field.

MEMBER: American Library Association, Mystery Writers of America, Authors Guild.

WRITINGS:

(Editor) *Genealogical and Local History Resources in New London County Libraries,* compiled by Susan Fraile, Southeastern Connecticut Library Association (Groton, CT), 1982.

Desperate Ground (novel), Quiet Storm Publishers (Martinsburg, WV), 2004.

Billy Boyle: A World War II Mystery (novel), Soho Press (New York, NY), 2006.

The First Wave: A Billy Boyle World War II Mystery (novel), Soho Press (New York, NY), 2007.

SIDELIGHTS: James R. Benn is a librarian and novelist whose career has revolved around books since his first job as a library page at age fifteen, he commented in an interview in *Library Journal.* Becoming a novelist is another step in Benn's lifetime journey devoted to words and books. "Writing has brought my career full circle, back to books as the basis of what I love doing," Benn commented in the *Library Journal* interview.

Billy Boyle: A World War II Mystery tells the story of the eponymous title character, a police officer in Boston during World War II. A good cop from a long line of peace officers, Billy is taken by the patriotic fervor of the time and decides to enlist in the army. From the beginning of his stint, Billy's luck is favorable. His mother makes use of a propitious family connection with General Eisenhower (a distant relative Billy calls "Uncle Ike") to ensure her son receives a safe, favorable, noncombat assignment. Billy is soon tasked by "Uncle Ike" to bring his detective skills to bear and ferret out a spy operating within Allied circles in London and Norway. The spy jeopardizes Allied plans to force the Nazis out of Norway through the invasion code-named Operation Jupiter. Billy joins a special team of military personnel assigned the task of keeping the King of Norway and other dignitaries apprised of the status of Operation Jupiter. The death of one of the men suspected of being the spy, diplomat Knut Birkeland, attracts Billy's attention. At first, Birkeland's death appears to be suicide by leap from a high window—the man even leaves behind a suicide note. However, as Billy investigates, the death begins to look more like murder. *Booklist* reviewer Bill Ott noted that the story's "action builds to a suspenseful climax, and there is even a hint of moral ambiguity in the wrap-up." A *Kirkus Reviews* critic commented that Benn "crafts a crackling good adventure, with much flavorsome period color, and an acceptable whodunit."

BIOGRAPHICAL AND CRITICAL SOURCES:

PERIODICALS

Booklist, August 1, 2006, Bill Ott, review of *Billy Boyle: A World War II Mystery,* p. 46.

Kirkus Reviews, June 1, 2006, review of *Billy Boyle,* p. 546.

Library Journal, July 1, 2006, "Three Questions for a Librarian Who Writes," p. 15.

Publishers Weekly, June 26, 2006, review of *Billy Boyle,* p. 34.

ONLINE

James R. Benn's Home Page, http://www.jamesrbenn. com (January 22, 2007).

* * *

BENNION, Janet 1964-

PERSONAL: Born October 2, 1964, in Salt Lake City, UT; daughter of Colin (a teacher) and Sergene (a teacher) Bennion; married John Potter (an artist), July 8, 2001; children: Liza Cannon, Frances Cannon. *Ethnicity:* "Caucasian." *Education:* Utah State University, B.J.; Portland State University, M.A.; University of Utah, Ph.D. *Politics:* Democrat.

ADDRESSES: Home—Saint Johnsbury, VT. *Office*—Lyndon State College, Lyndonville, VT 05851.

CAREER: Lyndon State College, Lyndonville, VT, associate professor of anthropology.

WRITINGS:

Women of Principle: Female Networking in Contemporary Mormon Polygyny, Oxford University Press (New York, NY), 1998.

Desert Patriarchy: Mormon and Mennonite Communities in the Chihuahua Valley, University of Arizona Press (Tucson, AZ), 2004.

* * *

BERTON, Kathleen
See MURRELL, Kathleen Berton

BÉRUBÉ, Michael 1961-

PERSONAL: Born September 26, 1961, in New York, NY; married Janet Lyon (a literature and women's studies professor); children: Nick, James. *Education:* Columbia University, B.A.; University of Virginia, M.A., Ph.D., 1989.

ADDRESSES: Office—Department of English, Pennsylvania State University, 230 Burrowes Bldg., University Park, PA 16802. *E-mail*—mfb12@psu.edu.

CAREER: University of Illinois, Urbana-Champaign, assistant professor, 1989-93, associate professor, 1993-96, professor, 1996-2001, director of Illinois Program for Research in the Humanities, 1997-2001; Pennsylvania State University, University Park, Paterno Family Professor in Literature, 2001—, codirector of disability studies program, 2004—.

MEMBER: Modern Language Association (member of executive council, 2002-05), American Association of University Professors (member of national council, 2005—; member of executive committee, 2006—), National Council of Teachers of English (chair of Public Language Committee, 2006—).

AWARDS, HONORS: National Endowment for the Humanities Summer Stipend, 1990; Humanities Released Time Fellowship, University of Illinois Research Board, 1990-91, 1996-97; honorable mention in *Best American Essays,* 1994, for "Life as We Know It"; Notable Books of the Year list, *New York Times,* for *Life as We Know It: A Father, a Family, and an Exceptional Child;* University of Illinois Incomplete List of Excellent Teachers, 1990-97, 1999, 2000; University Scholar, University of Illinois; National Humanities Center fellow (Assad Meymandi Fellowship), 2006.

WRITINGS:

Marginal Forces/Cultural Centers: Tolson, Pynchon, and the Politics of the Canon, Cornell University Press (Ithaca, NY), 1992.

Public Access: Literary Theory and American Cultural Politics, Verso (New York, NY), 1994.

(Editor, with Cary Nelson) *Higher Education under Fire: Politics, Economics, and the Crisis of the Humanities,* Routledge (New York, NY), 1995.

Life as We Know It: A Father, a Family, and an Exceptional Child, Pantheon Books (New York, NY), 1996.

The Employment of English: Theory, Jobs, and the Future of Literary Studies, New York University Press (New York, NY), 1998.

(Editor) *The Aesthetics of Cultural Studies,* Blackwell (Malden, MA), 2005.

Rhetorical Occasions: Essays on Humans and the Humanities, University of North Carolina Press (Chapel Hill, NC), 2006.

What's Liberal about the Liberal Arts? Classroom Politics and "Bias" in Higher Education, W.W. Norton (New York, NY), 2006.

Also author of the blog *Le Blogue Bérubé,* 2004-07. Contributor to periodicals, including the *Nation, New York Times Magazine, Dissent, Harper's,* and the *New Yorker.* Member of editorial boards, including for *Comparative Literature Studies, Contemporary Literature, Electronic Book Review, Iowa Journal of Cultural Studies, Journal of Aesthetic Education, Journal of Sport and Social Issues, Minnesota Review, Modern Fiction Studies, Pedagogy, Postmodern Culture, Twentieth-Century Literature,* and *Symploke.*

SIDELIGHTS: Called an "academic whiz-kid" by a *Publishers Weekly* reviewer, Michael Bérubé is an English professor who has written widely, persuasively, and popularly in repudiation of the conservative critique of academia. In books such as *Public Access: Literary Theory and American Cultural Politics, Higher Education under Fire: Politics, Economics, and the Crisis of the Humanities,* and the 2006 work *What's Liberal about the Liberal Arts? Classroom Politics and "Bias" in Higher Education,* Bérubé has attempted to answer right-wing criticisms of the supposedly leftist-liberal bias in the nation's universities. He deals with topics ranging from political correctness to multiculturalism and fostering the spirit of open inquiry. Additionally, in his 1996 book, *Life as We Know It: A Father, a Family, and an Exceptional Child,* Bérubé presents an account of the first years of his son Jamie, who was born with Down syndrome.

With his *Public Access,* Bérubé provides eleven essays that answer conservative critics of what they consider liberal academia. In this work the self-professed liberal progressive Bérubé admonishes other liberals to join in the debate and not leave the field to the polemics of think tanks and conservative spokespeople. A contributor for *Publishers Weekly* felt that the author's "research is breathtaking and persuasive" in this collection. Reviewing the same work in *World Literature Today,* David S. Gross found it "most interesting" and "well-documented."

In *Higher Education under Fire,* Bérubé "offers a complex, nuanced diagnosis of the threats and opportunities confronting a vital but troubled American institution," according to *Booklist* contributor Mary Carroll. The book, edited by Bérubé and Cary Nelson, presents essays offered at a 1993 conference and includes both liberal and conservative perspectives on the problems facing higher education. For Susan Talburt, writing in the *Journal of Higher Education,* the "volume serves as a call to academics to engage in analysis and activism in order to reshape discourses surrounding higher education." Talburt further noted: "The editors describe the book as a combination of the theoretical and the practical that stands as a corrective to misconceptions about university life," and went on to conclude that "one of the chief strengths of this collection is the implicit and explicit dialogic mode across themes, a mode that challenges the reader to put his or her assumptions into play and to reflect on conflicting analyses and their implications for action."

In the same vein, Bérubé's *What's Liberal about the Liberal Arts?* provides "a discussion of so-called liberal academic bias that effectively dismembers the charges of the right-wing of a bias reflected in America's classrooms," according to a contributor for *Talking Dog* online. Bérubé explained some of the reasoning for *What's Liberal about the Liberal Arts?* in his *Talking Dog* interview: "The fact that liberals outnumber conservatives on campus—by a ratio of roughly 2.6 to 1—is indisputable. What the culture-war right derives from this fact, however, are two highly disputable conclusions: one, that the ratio can be explained only by active collusion among liberals . . . [and] two, that this preponderance of campus liberals actively discriminates against conservative students as well as potential conservative colleagues." Bérubé answers both charges in his work, noting the dearth of well-trained conservatives in certain fields, such as the sciences, and also by criticizing the anecdotal nature of much of the evidence given for the second charge. Vanessa Bush, reviewing *What's*

Liberal about the Liberal Arts? in *Booklist,* found it "a passionate appeal for preserving the best notions of the liberal-arts education." Likewise, Scott Walter, writing in *Library Journal,* felt "Bérubé provides an effective liberal counterpoint to the conservative criticism of schools."

Bérubé's 1996 title, *Life as We Know It,* is a social critique of another sort. Inspired by his second son's struggle with Down syndrome, Bérubé penned a book that was part memoir of the trials of raising a child with such special needs, as well as an examination of society's reaction to such handicapped individuals. *New York Times Book Review* contributor Beverly Lowry commented that "Bérubé digs deep and wide. Trying to decipher how it is we came to think the way we do, he scans Darwinism, deconstruction, social constructionism, eugenics." Lowry praised this work for its challenging premises: "Like all books of philosophical investigation, this one means to question more than to answer, to prick our minds and imaginations," concluding that *Life as We Know It* is "an astonishingly good book, important, literate and ferociously articulated." A *Publishers Weekly* contributor also had praise for the same work, remarking on its "impassioned reportage," and further reporting that Bérubé "frames advocacy and righteous anger with wry humor." Harold Isbell observed in *Commonweal* that Bérubé also "embarks on a provocative analysis of the pro-life, pro-choice controversy, a discussion which produces difficult questions and few if any easy answers." Writing in the *Nation,* Nancy Mairs commented that Bérubé "uses his formidable intellectual skills . . . not merely to narrate in engaging detail the story of his son James . . . , but to explore the medical, social and political implications of being the disabled 'other' in the United States today." For Mairs, *Life as We Know It* "is a book that needed to be written, asking hard questions that must be asked."

BIOGRAPHICAL AND CRITICAL SOURCES:

BOOKS

Bérubé, Michael, *Life as We Know It: A Father, a Family, and an Exceptional Child,* Pantheon Books (New York, NY), 1996.

PERIODICALS

Booklist, December 1, 1994, Mary Carroll, review of *Higher Education under Fire: Politics, Economics, and the Crisis of the Humanities,* p. 639;

September 15, 2006, Vanessa Bush, review of *What's Liberal about the Liberal Arts? Classroom Politics and "Bias" in Higher Education,* p. 81.

Chronicle of Higher Education, February 17, 2006, Jennifer Jacobson, "Dangerous Minds."

College Literature, fall, 2001, Kathleen McCormick, "Finding Hope in the Humanities," review of *The Employment of English: Theory, Jobs, and the Future of Literary Study,* p. 129.

Commonweal, Harold Isbell, April 25, 1997, review of *Life as We Know It,* p. 27.

Contemporary Literature, summer, 1994, Bruce Robbins, review of *Marginal Forces/Cultural Centers: Tolson, Pynchon, and the Politics of the Canon,* p. 365.

Journal of English and Germanic Philology, January, 1994, Russell J. Reising, review of *Marginal Forces/Cultural Centers,* p. 150.

Journal of Higher Education, January-February, 1997, Susan Talburt, review of *Higher Education under Fire,* p. 106.

Kirkus Reviews, August 1, 1996, review of *Life as We Know It,* p. 1112.

Library Journal, September 15, 2006, Scott Walter, review of *What's Liberal about the Liberal Arts?,* p. 70.

Nation, October 28, 1996, Nancy Mairs, review of *Life as We Know It,* p. 30.

New York Times Book Review, October 27, 1996, Beverly Lowry, "We Can Handle This," review of *Life as We Know It,* p. 22; September 10, 2006, Alan Wolfe, "Defending the Ph.D.'s," review of *What's Liberal about the Liberal Arts?,* p. 13.

Publishers Weekly, January 13, 1994, review of *Public Access: Literary Theory and American Cultural Politics,* p. 59; August 26, 1996, review of *Life as We Know It,* p. 82; August 7, 2006, review of *What's Liberal about the Liberal Arts?,* p. 48.

World Literature Today, spring, 1995, David S. Gross, review of *Public Access,* p. 446.

ONLINE

Penn State English Department Web site, http://english.la.psu.edu/ (December 11, 2006), brief biography of Michael Bérubé.

Salon.com, http://www.salon.com/ (October 26, 1998), Michele Tepper, "The Maturing of Michael Bérubé."

Talking Dog, http://thetalkingdog.com/ (November 27, 2006), "TD Blog Interview with Michael Bérubé."

BISBORT, Alan 1953-

PERSONAL: Born 1953.

CAREER: Library of Congress, Washington, DC, writer, editor, researcher.

WRITINGS:

Kansas America (poetry), Chancey Town Press (Chapel Hill, NC), 1977.

(With Parke Puterbaugh) *Life Is a Beach: A Vacationer's Guide to the East Coast,* McGraw-Hill (New York, NY), 1985.

(With Parke Puterbaugh) *Life Is a Beach: A Vacationer's Guide to the West Coast,* McGraw-Hill (New York, NY), 1988.

The White Rabbit and Other Delights: East Totem West, a Hippie Company, 1967-1969, Pomegranate Artbooks (San Francisco, CA), 1996.

Sunday Afternoon, Looking for the Car: The Aberrant Art of Barry Kite, Pomegranate (Rohnert Park, CA), 1997.

(Author of captions, with Sarah Day) Edward S. Curtis, *Heart of the Circle: Photographs of Native American Women,* edited by Sarah Day, introduction by Pat Durkin, Pomegranate Artbooks (San Francisco, CA), 1997.

(With Parke Puterbaugh) *Groovy, Man: A Trip through the Psychedelic Years,* introduction by Howard Kaylan, General Publishers (Los Angeles, CA), 1998.

Charles Bragg, the Works!: A Retrospective, Pomegranate Artbooks (San Francisco, CA), 1999.

(With Parke Puterbaugh) *Rhino's Psychedelic Trip,* introduction by Howard Kaylan, Miller Freeman Books (San Francisco, CA), 2000.

(With Linda Barrett Osborne) *The Nation's Library: The Library of Congress, Washington, DC,* Library of Congress/Scala Publishers (Washington, DC), 2000.

(Compiler) *Famous Last Words: Apt Observations, Pleas, Curses, Benedictions, Sour Notes, Bon Mots, and Insights from People on the Brink of Departure,* Pomegranate (San Francisco, CA), 2001.

"When You Read This, They Will Have Killed Me": The Life and Redemption of Caryl Chessman, Whose Execution Shook America, Carroll & Graf (New York, NY), 2006.

(With Parke Puterbaugh) *Moon Florida Beaches: The Best Places to Swim, Play, Eat, and Stay* ("Foghorn Outdoors Florida Beaches" series), Avalon Travel Publishers (Emeryville, CA), 2006.

Also author, with Parke Puterbaugh, of other titles in the "Foghorn Outdoors Florida Beaches" series, including *Foghorn Outdoors California Beaches,* 3rd edition, Avalon Travel Publishers (Emeryville, CA). Author of blog *Alan Bisbort's Blog—The Smirking Chimp.* Coauthor of annual "Literary Companions" series. Contributor to periodicals, including *Advocate, Hit List, New York Times, Washington Post,* and *Rolling Stone.*

SIDELIGHTS: A longtime researcher and writer at the Library of Congress, Alan Bisbort has written about cultural and countercultural affairs since the early 1970s. Often collaborating with his former college roommate, Parke Puterbaugh, Bisbort has also created numerous guides to the beaches of the United States, focusing on Florida and California. In the 1998 title *Groovy, Man: A Trip through the Psychedelic Years,* written with Puterbaugh, Bisbort presents a profile of the 1960s. The authors examine all aspects of the counterculture, from music to film, comics, fashion, and media. Illustrated with over two hundred photographs from the era, *Groovy, Man* "captures the decade of mind-blowing reform in social mores," according to *Library Journal* reviewer Eric C. Shoaf.

Bisbort captures the feel of an earlier decade in his 2006 title, *"When You Read This, They Will Have Killed Me": The Life and Redemption of Caryl Chessman, Whose Execution Shook America.* Chessman, the so-called Los Angeles "Red-Light Bandit," was convicted and sentenced to death in California in 1948 in a case that challenged the morality of the death penalty nationwide. Chessman, a career criminal who always denied his guilt, was convicted of robbing couples in parked cars and of raping some of the female victims. Kidnapping charges in association with these crimes were the tipping point for capital charges. Spending the next twelve years on Death Row, Chessman wrote about his own life and his transformation in prison, most notably in his memoir *Cell 2455.* By the time of his execution, Chessman had become the focus of the death penalty debate. Reviewing *"When You Read This, They Will Have Killed Me"* in the *San Diego Union-Tribune,* Emily Schmall found the work "engaging," and commended Bisbort's writing. She noted that the author "neatly dichotomizes Chessman's life as he moved from rebel to author—and from condemned to redeemed." Further praise came from a *Publishers Weekly* contributor who observed: "Chessman's story loses none of its haunting power, and Bisbort's retelling reaffirms its significance in America's quest for social justice."

BIOGRAPHICAL AND CRITICAL SOURCES:

PERIODICALS

Booklist, October 1, 2006, Vernon Ford, review of *"When You Read This, They Will Have Killed Me": The Life and Redemption of Caryl Chessman, Whose Execution Shook America,* p. 7.
Library Journal, September 15, 1998, Eric C. Shoaf, review of *Groovy, Man: A Trip through the Psychedelic Years,* p. 100; February 1, 2001, Thomas F. O'Connor, review of *The Nation's Library: The Library of Congress, Washington, DC,* p. 130.
Publishers Weekly, August 9, 1999, "Bragging Rights," p. 249; August 7, 2006, review of *"When You Read This, They Will Have Killed Me,"* p. 44.
San Diego Union-Tribune, October 22, 2006, Emily Schmall, review of *"When You Read This, They Will Have Killed Me."*

ONLINE

Foghorn Web site, http://www.foghorn.com/ (December 11, 2006), brief biography of Alan Bisbort.
Gadfly Online, http://www.gadflyonline.com/ (December 11, 2006), "Gadfly Contributors: Alan Bisbort."*

* * *

BISHOP, Edward
    See BISHOP, Ted

* * *

BISHOP, Edward L.
    See BISHOP, Ted

BISHOP, E.L.
    See BISHOP, Ted

* * *

BISHOP, Ted
    (E.L. Bishop, Edward Bishop, Edward L. Bishop)

PERSONAL: Education: University of Alberta, B.A.; Queen's University, M.A., Ph.D.

ADDRESSES: Home—Edmonton, Alberta, Canada. *Office*—Department of English, University of Alberta, 3-5 Humanities Ctr., Edmonton, Alberta T6G 2E1, Canada. *E-mail*—edward.bishop@ualberta.ca.

CAREER: University of Alberta, Edmonton, Alberta, Canada, professor of English.

AWARDS, HONORS: Best Motorcycle Book, Motorcycle Awards of Excellence, City of Edmonton Book Award, Province of Alberta Wilfred Eggleston Award, Governor-General's Literary Awards finalist, all 2005, all for *Riding with Rilke: Reflections on Motorcycles and Books.*

WRITINGS:

(As Edward Bishop) *A Virginia Woolf Chronology,* G.K. Hall (Boston, MA), 1989.
(As Edward Bishop) *Virginia Woolf,* St. Martin's Press (New York, NY), 1991.
(Editor and transcriber, as Edward L. Bishop) Virginia Woolf, *Jacob's Room: The Holograph Draft: Based on the Holograph Manuscript in the Henry W. and Albert A. Berg Collection of English and American Literature at the New York Public Library,* Pace University Press (New York, NY), 1998.
(Editor, as Edward L. Bishop) Virginia Woolf, *Jacob's Room,* Blackwell Publishers (Malden, MA), 2004.
(As Ted Bishop) *Riding with Rilke: Reflections on Motorcycles and Books,* Penguin Canada (Toronto, Canada), 2005, W.W. Norton (New York, NY), 2006.

Contributor to periodicals, including *Cycle Canada, Enroute, Prairie Fire, Rider,* and *Word Carving.*

SIDELIGHTS: Ted Bishop is a Canadian professor of English who has specialized in writers such as Virginia Woolf, James Joyce, and other modernists. His 2006 book, *Riding with Rilke: Reflections on Motorcycles and Books,* is a popular departure from his usual academic writings, blending Bishop's own love of riding motorcycles with his knowledge of literature. The book was written during Bishop's convalescence from a motorcycle accident, and it chronicles a road trip he took from his hometown in Edmonton, Alberta, to Austin, Texas. Part memoir and part literary discussion, *Riding with Rilke* is, according to *Booklist* critic David Pitt, a "joyful book, a celebration of intellectual pursuit and carefree exploration," as well as a "one-of-a-kind treat." Similarly, a *Publishers Weekly* reviewer termed it an "easygoing, romantic memoir infused with joie de vivre." Writing in Toronto's *Globe and Mail,* Ira Nadel noted that *Riding with Rilke* blends "travelogue, autobiography and literary history with the art of motorcycle maintenance." Mark Alan Williams, writing in *Library Journal,* voiced a similar opinion, calling *Riding with Rilke* "an unusual combination of literature and travelog but one that ultimately works and is an enjoyable read."

BIOGRAPHICAL AND CRITICAL SOURCES:

BOOKS

Bishop, Ted, *Riding with Rilke: Reflections on Motorcycles and Books,* W.W. Norton (New York, NY), 2006.

PERIODICALS

Biography, winter, 2006, Ira Nadel, review of *Riding with Rilke: Reflections on Motorcycles and Books,* p. 200.

Booklist, September 1, 2006, David Pitt, review of *Riding with Rilke,* p. 43.

Globe and Mail (Toronto, Ontario, Canada), October 1, 2005, Ira Nadel, review of *Riding with Rilke,* p. D16.

Library Journal, November 1, 2006, Mark Alan Williams, review of *Riding with Rilke,* p. 76.

Playboy, January, 2006, Amy Loyd, review of *Riding with Rilke,* p. 34.

Publishers Weekly, August 7, 2006, review of *Riding with Rilke,* p. 48.

ONLINE

Austin Chronicle Online, http://www.austinchronicle. com/ (November 10, 2006), Jess Sauer, review of *Riding with Rilke.*

College Quarterly Online, http://www.senecac.on.ca/ (December 11, 2006), Howard A. Doughty, review of *Riding with Rilke.*

Doing "It" Weekly, http://www.blogto.com/ (December 11, 2006), "Interview # 1: Ted Bishop."

FFWD Weekly, http://www.ffwdweekly.com/ (November 17, 2005), Roberta McDonald, "The Professor and the Motorcycle."

International Journal of Motorcycle Studies Online, http://ijms.nova.edu/ (December 11, 2006), review of *Riding with Rilke.*

Penguin Canada Online, http://www.penguin.ca/ (December 11, 2006), brief biography of Ted Bishop.

University of Alberta English Department Web site, http://www.humanities.ualberta.ca/english/ (December 11, 2006), faculty profile of E.L. Bishop.

*   *   *

BITSUI, Sherwin 1975-

PERSONAL: Born 1975, in Fort Defiance, AZ. *Education:* Institute of American Indian Arts, A.F.A., 1999; attended University of Arizona.

ADDRESSES: Home—Tucson, AZ.

CAREER: Poet.

AWARDS, HONORS: Truman Capote Creative Writing Fellowship, 1999; Lannan Foundation Literary Residency Fellowship; Individual Poet Grant, Witter Bynner Foundation for Poetry, 2000-01; Whiting Writers' Award, 2006.

WRITINGS:

Shapeshift (poetry), University of Arizona Press (Tucson, AZ), 2003.

Contributor of poetry to periodicals, including *American Poet, Iowa Review, Frank, Red Ink,* and *Lit Magazine,* and to the anthology *Legitimate Dangers: American Poets of the New Century.*

SIDELIGHTS: Poet Sherwin Bitsui is a Native American, a member of the Bitter Water clan of the Diné, or Navajo. An active participant in the culture and the ceremonies of his tribe, Bitsui composes poetry, as Arthur Sze noted on *Poetry.org,* that "struggles with the tension between Diné and English, between the desire to restore a balance with the natural world and the recognition of how ineluctable the forces of twentieth century technology are." Sze continued: "In struggling to reconcile these opposing forces, [Bitsui's] poems and prose poems enact a personal ceremony." According to Frances Sjoberg, literary director of the University of Arizona Poetry Center, as quoted in the *AZ Daily Star,* Bitsui's "aesthetic reflects a new direction in Native American poetry."

Bitsui's 2003 verse collection, *Shapeshift,* is a work characterized by its use of carefully chosen language and its novel look at Native American life in the twenty-first century. The poems in this book range from the historical, such as "1868," to the edgy modern tone of "Is This What I Deserve: A White Anthropologist Sitting beside Me at a Winter Ceremony?" Greg Gagnon, writing in the *American Indian Quarterly,* praised the "vibrant renderings of [Bitsui's] Dine (Navajo) foundations, combined with an urban Indian's spin on life off-reservation" in this debut collection. Gagnon went on to commend the "evocative choice of words used to convey a unique perspective beautifully." Writing in *BellaOnline.com,* Deborah Adams felt that the thirty-three poems in this collection express the "dry lack of spirituality among interactions between the Indian and those who are not."

BIOGRAPHICAL AND CRITICAL SOURCES:

PERIODICALS

American Indian Quarterly, winter-spring, 2005, Greg Gagnon, review of *Shapeshift,* p. 295.

AZ Daily Star (Tucson, AZ), November 10, 2006, Doug Kreutz, "Master of Words."
Publishers Weekly, October 30, 2006, "The Whiting Winners," p. 6.

ONLINE

BellaOnline.com, http://www.bellaonline.com/ (December 11, 2006), Deborah Adams, review of *Shapeshift.*
Poets.org, http://www.poets.org/ (December 11, 2006), Arthur Sze, "Emerging Poet: On Sherwin Bitsui."
Sherwin Bitsui Home Page, http://www.bitsui.com (December 11, 2006).

*   *   *

BIZONY, Piers

PERSONAL: Male.

CAREER: Science writer, publicist, television producer, and exhibition organizer.

AWARDS, HONORS: Shortlist, NASA/Eugene M. Emme Award for Astronautical Writing, 1998, for *The Rivers of Mars: Searching for the Cosmic Origins of Life.*

WRITINGS:

NONFICTION

Island in the Sky: Building the International Space Station, Aurum Press (London, England), 1996.
The Rivers of Mars: Searching for the Cosmic Origins of Life, Aurum Press (London, England), 1997, revised edition published as *The Exploration of Mars: Searching for the Cosmic Origins of Life,* Aurum Press (London, England), 1998.
(With Jamie Doran) *Starman: The Truth behind the Legend of Yuri Gagarin,* Bloomsbury (London, England), 1998.
2001: Filming the Future, Aurum Press (London, England), 2000.

Digital Domain: The Leading Edge of Visual Effects, Billboard Books (New York, NY), 2001.

Invisible Worlds: Exploring the Unseen, Weidenfeld & Nicolson (London, England), 2004.

The Man Who Ran the Moon: James E. Webb and the Secret History of Project Apollo, Thunder's Mouth Press (New York, NY), 2006.

Space 50, Collins (London, England), 2006.

Contributor of science articles to periodicals.

ADAPTATIONS: *Starman: The Truth behind the Legend of Yuri Gagarin* was adapted for a BBC Television production.

SIDELIGHTS: British science writer Piers Bizony specializes in works about space for the layman and technical reader alike. His first book, the 1996 *Island in the Sky: Building the International Space Station,* is a "well-written introduction to the technical and political history of the International Space Station," according to a reviewer for *SpaceViews.* In the award-winning *The Rivers of Mars: Searching for the Cosmic Origins of Life,* Bizony, inspired by the 1996 announcement of the discovery of life forms in a Martian meteorite, "looks at the history of our studies of Mars, with particular attention to the suite of Viking experiments designed to detect life," as another reviewer for *SpaceViews* wrote. Bizony also provides accompanying text for the 2004 work *Invisible Worlds: Exploring the Unseen,* a "collection of stunning images," according to *Geographic* reviewer Ivo Grigorov. Such images range from the cellular level to galactic patterns, and are not normally visible to the unaided eye. Grigorov went on to comment that Bizony's writing "makes complex science enjoyable and informative."

With *The Man Who Ran the Moon: James E. Webb and the Secret History of Project Apollo,* Bizony looks at the years from 1961 to 1968 when Webb presided over the National Aeronautics and Space Agency (NASA), setting on track a lunar landing in the summer of 1968. Indeed, it is Bizony's contention that Webb was largely responsible for the United States winning the space race for such a landing with the Russians. A critic for *Kirkus Reviews* found this book a "fascinating look at how politics and science intersected in the glory years of NASA." Similar praise

came from *Booklist* contributor Taylor Gilbert, who noted that the "prosaic side of space exploration . . . is insightfully illustrated" by *The Man Who Ran the Moon.*

BIOGRAPHICAL AND CRITICAL SOURCES:

PERIODICALS

Booklist, May 1, 2006, Gilbert Taylor, review of *The Man Who Ran the Moon: James E. Webb and the Secret History of Project Apollo,* p. 60.

Geographical, August, 2004, Ivo Grigorov, review of *Invisible Worlds: Exploring the Unseen,* p. 94.

Kirkus Reviews, April 15, 2006, review of *The Man Who Ran the Moon,* p. 387.

Library Journal, July 11, 2006, Nancy R. Curtis, review of *The Man Who Ran the Moon,* p. 103.

ONLINE

acftv.com, http://www.acftv.com/ (November 15, 2006), "Piers Bizony: Author/Producer."

Space Show, http://www.thespaceshow.com/ (November 15, 2006), "Piers Bizony."

SpaceViews, http://www.seds.org/spaceviews/ (May, 1997), review of *The Rivers of Mars: Searching for the Origins of Cosmic Life,* and *Island in the Sky: Building the International Space Station.**

*   *   *

BLACH, Peter Jost
    See BLAKE, Peter

*   *   *

BLACK, Dorothy 1914-2006
    (Dorothy Albertyn, Kitty Black)

OBITUARY NOTICE— See index for *CA* sketch: Born April 30, 1914, in Johannesburg, South Africa; died December 26, 2006. Agent, translator, and author. One of the most respected theatrical agents in Britain, Black was an influential figure in West End productions who worked with such prominent actors as John

Gielgud and Margaret Rutherford, and playwrights such as Christopher Fry, Arthur Miller, and Jean Cocteau. She got her start at the H.M. Tennent agency in London, the most prominent agency in the country. Hired as a secretary in 1937, she worked her way up to assistant administrator of the nonprofit branch of Tennent's called the Company of Four. She helped run the Lyric Theatre in Hammersmith for eight years before leaving Tennent in 1953. Black then became a full-time agent. She worked for Curtis Brown for the remainder of the 1950s, then for Granada Television from 1961 to 1963. During the mid-1960s she was in the drama department for Associated-Rediffusion. Her last working years were spent at London's MacOwan Theatre, where she was house manager from 1976 to 1986. In addition to working closely with actors, writers, and directors, Black was herself an active translator of plays. Under the pseudonym Kitty Black, she adapted works by Jean-Paul Sartre, Fritz Hochwälder, Georges Simenon, Jean Anouilh, and others. She also penned three original plays: *The Prince of Bohemia* (1942), *Landslide* (1943), written with David Peel, and *The Singing Dolphin* (1963), written with Beverley Cross.

OBITUARIES AND OTHER SOURCES:

BOOKS

Black, Dorothy, *Upper Circle, a Theatrical Chronicle,* Methuen (London, England), 1984.

PERIODICALS

Times (London, England), January 12, 2007, p. 61.

*   *   *

BLACK, Kitty
    See BLACK, Dorothy

*   *   *

BLAKE, Peter 1920-2006
    (Peter Jost Blach)

OBITUARY NOTICE— See index for *CA* sketch: Born September 20, 1920, in Berlin, Germany; died of complications from a respiratory infection, December 5, 2006, in Branford, CT. Architect, editor, educator,

and author. A leading adherent to the modernist school of architecture, Blake designed dozens of buildings, published influential books, and was a longtime professor at the Catholic University of America. Born to a Jewish family in Berlin, he was forced to immigrate to England in 1933 after the Nazi Party came to power. Here he graduated from the University of London with a degree in mathematics in 1938; he then studied for a year at the Regent Street Polytechnic School of Architecture. A scholarship led him to study architecture at the University of Pennsylvania, where he studied under Louis Kahn. Blake graduated in 1941, and would go on to earn a second degree in architecture from the Pratt Institute in 1949. During the years before World War II, Blake wrote for *Architectural Forum.* He enlisted in the U.S. Army in 1943 and assigned to Intelligence in Europe; notably, Blake was to return to his native Berlin in 1945 as one of the first troops to occupy the city with the collapse of the Third Reich. During his time in the army, too, he became a U.S. citizen and changed his surname from Blach to Blake. He left the military in 1947 and moved to New York City, where he made friends with artist Jackson Pollack, who would help influence his concepts of modern architecture. The Museum of Modern Art hired Blake in 1948 to work in its department of architecture and design. Two years later, he returned to *Architectural Forum,* rising from associate editor in 1950 to managing editor in 1961, and heading the magazine as editor in chief from 1964 to 1972. When the magazine folded, he founded *Architectural Plus,* which only survived for three years. Meanwhile, however, Blake was actively working as an architect. He was a partner in the firm Peter Blake & Julian Neski in the late 1950s and of James Blake & Peter Blake from 1964 to 1971. During these years, he designed such structures as the Pin Wheel House in Long Island and a theater at Vanderbilt University. As an architect, Blake favored simple, clean lines and functionality. Like such other prominent modernist architects as Mies van der Rohe, he felt that architecture should be used to facilitate better living through good design. He related his ideas in such important books as *The Master Builders: Le Corbusier, Mies van der Rohe, Frank Lloyd Wright* (1960) and *God's Own Junkyard: The Planned Deterioration of America's Landscape* (1964). During his later years, Blake was chair of the Boston Architectural Center from 1975 to 1979, and a professor and chair of the department of architecture and planning at the Catholic University of America from 1979 until his 1991 retirement. Among his many other publications are *The New Forces* (1971), *Our Housing Mess, and*

What Can Be Done about It (1974), and *Form Follows Fiasco: Why Modern Architecture Hasn't Worked* (1977).

OBITUARIES AND OTHER SOURCES:

BOOKS

Blake, Peter, *No Place Like Utopia: Modern Architecture and the Company We Kept,* Knopf (New York, NY), 1993.
Contemporary Architects, 3rd edition, St. James Press (Detroit, MI), 1994.

PERIODICALS

New York Times, December 6, 2006, p. A21; December 22, 2006, p. A2.
Washington Post, December 7, 2006, p. B7.

*　　*　　*

BLOCK, Robert 1960-

PERSONAL: Born 1960. *Hobbies and other interests:* Guitars, motorcycles, and Labrador retrievers.

ADDRESSES: Home—Washington, DC. *Office*—c/o Wall Street Journal, 200 Liberty St., New York, NY 10281. *E-mail*—bobby.block@wsj.com.

CAREER: Journalist. Reuters, London, England, 1982-90, began as Mexico correspondent, became El Salvador bureau chief and global reporter; *Independent,* London, England, assistant foreign editor, 1990-92, chief foreign correspondent, 1992-95, Africa correspondent, 1995; *Sunday Times,* London, reporter, 1995-97; *Wall Street Journal,* Washington, DC, Africa correspondent, 1997-2003, homeland security correspondent, 2003—.

AWARDS, HONORS: Foreign Media Award, British Overseas Correspondents Association, 1996; Amnesty International Award, 1996, for human rights reporting; Pulitzer Prize (with staff members of *Wall Street Journal*), 2002, for breaking news; Elizabeth Neuffer

Award, 2004, for reporting about United Nations peacekeeping operations; Excellence in Reporting Award, Society of Publishers in Asia, 2005, for coverage of Asian tsunami; President's Award, New Jersey Deputy Fire Chiefs Association, 2006; Health Braintrust Leadership Award in Print Journalism, Congressional Black Caucus, 2006.

WRITINGS:

(With Christopher Cooper) *Disaster: Hurricane Katrina and the Failure of Homeland Security,* Times Books (New York, NY), 2006.

Contributor to *New York Review of Books,* 1993-96.

ADAPTATIONS: Home Box Office has acquired the rights to *Disaster.*

SIDELIGHTS: Wall Street Journal reporters Robert Block and Christopher Cooper are the authors of *Disaster: Hurricane Katrina and the Failure of Homeland Security,* an examination of the U.S. government's response to the devastating storm that struck the Gulf Coast on August 29, 2005, killing more than 1,000 people and leaving hundreds of thousands homeless. In the work, Block and Cooper contend that Hurricane Katrina exposed major weaknesses in the federal government's ability to cope with natural disasters, and that many of the problems faced by the government were a direct result of policies that reduced funding to the Federal Emergency Management Agency and transferred much of its authority to the Department of Homeland Security. "The authors' exhaustively researched account slogs through the intricacies of this bureaucratic nightmare," wrote a contributor in *Publishers Weekly.* Block and Cooper also note that years of neglect by the Army Corps of Engineers and local officials left the levees and floodwalls of New Orleans vulnerable to storm surges, resulting in catastrophic breaches of the system when Katrina made landfall. An estimated eighty percent of the city was flooded. "*Disaster* is likely the best in-depth contemporary analysis we are going to get—and it does that job quite admirably," noted *Washington Post* critic Stephen Flynn. "Given that future catastrophes are inevitable, this book is a call to arms to demand a far more competent federal emergency response than Washington has been willing to provide."

BIOGRAPHICAL AND CRITICAL SOURCES:

PERIODICALS

Publishers Weekly, July 24, 2006, review of *Disaster: Hurricane Katrina and the Failure of Homeland Security,* p. 53.

Reference & Research Book News, November, 2006, review of *Disaster.*

Washington Post, October 31, 2006, Stephen Flynn, "Ignoring One Threat for Another," review of *Disaster,* p. C2.

ONLINE

Blogcritics Magazine Web site, http://blogcritics.org/ (September 22, 2006), Dominick Evans, review of *Disaster.**

*   *   *

BOLT, Rodney

PERSONAL: Male.

ADDRESSES: Home—Amsterdam, Netherlands. *Agent*—David Miller, Rogersm Coleridge, and White, 20 Powis Mews, London W12 9QE, England.

CAREER: Writer. Former theater director in London, England.

WRITINGS:

Amsterdam (travel guide), Globe Pequot Press (Chester, CT), 1992, 2nd edition published as *Amsterdam, Rotterdam, Leiden and the Hague: Art History, Walks, Hotels, Cafés, Shops, Markets, Day Trips,* Cadogan (London, England), 1997, 3rd edition published as *Amsterdam,* Cadogan (London, England), 2000.

Germany (travel guide), Globe Pequot Press (Old Saybrook, CT), 1993.

Bavaria (travel guide), Globe Pequot Press (Old Saybrook, CT), 1995.

Madeira (travel guide), Cadogan (London, England), 1995, revised edition published as *Madeira & Porto Santo,* 1999.

The Xenophobe's Guide to the Dutch, Ravette (Horsham, England), 1995.

(With Paul Rubens) *Amsterdam* (children's travel guide), Cadogan (London, England), 2000.

History Play: The Lives and Afterlife of Christopher Marlowe (speculative biography), HarperCollins (London, England), 2004, Bloomsbury (New York, NY), 2005.

The Librettist of Venice: The Remarkable Life of Lorenzo Da Ponte, Mozart's Poet, Casanova's Friend, and Italian Opera's Impresario in America, Bloomsbury (New York, NY), 2006, published as *Lorenzo da Ponte: The Adventures of Mozart's Librettist in the Old and New Worlds,* Bloomsbury (London, England), 2006.

SIDELIGHTS: Rodney Bolt is the author of numerous travel guides and of two well-received biographies. His *History Play: The Lives and Afterlife of Christopher Marlowe* is, according to a *Kirkus Reviews* critic, a "lively, speculative biography." Bolt postulates a Marlowe who is not only a great playwright, but also a secret agent for the anti-Catholic spymaster of Queen Elizabeth I. However, when Marlowe himself was tempted by Catholicism and also uncovered a plot to overthrow the queen from among her advisors, he was marked for death. History records Christopher Marlowe dying in a tavern brawl before the age of thirty; Bolt, however, has him escaping death and roaming Europe for years, sending back his coded plays to the man he, Marlowe, had hired to be his stand-in: William Shakespeare. Thus, as Bolt has it, Shakespeare's plays were all written by Marlowe, which would explain the use of foreign languages and the foreign settings, knowledge of which some literary critics have felt Shakespeare did not personally possess. The *Kirkus Reviews* critic went on to call *History Play* a "grand entertainment for literary sleuths." *Entertainment Weekly* contributor Adam B. Vary similarly observed that Bolt's speculations were "all in good fun." Further praise came from *Library Journal* reviewer William D. Walsh, who called *History Play* an "audacious and entertaining work."

Less speculative is Bolt's 2006 biography, *The Librettist of Venice: The Remarkable Life of Lorenzo Da Ponte, Mozart's Poet, Casanova's Friend, and Italian*

Opera's Impresario in America. In fact, the subject of the biography led such an interesting life that there was little need for speculative embroidery in this title. Da Ponte was a womanizing priest in Italy and friend of Casanova who was expelled from Venice. Then he came to Vienna, where he became librettist for three of Mozart's operas, *The Marriage of Figaro, Don Giovanni,* and *Cosi fan Tutte.* Da Ponte thereafter moved to London, where he married. He ended up in the United States, pursuing a varied life as a grocer, professor of Italian at New York's Columbia University, and a promoter of opera. Barry Zaslow, writing in *Library Journal,* felt that the author's "scholarship is well documented but appears at odds with his highly charged style," making the target audience unclear. A similar criticism came from *New York Times* critic Charles McGrath, who observed that the book was written "in a somewhat operatic style, with a weakness for metaphors that are either clichéd or . . . just plain odd." However, McGrath went on to note that *The Librettist of Venice* is a "remarkable yarn." Megan Marshall, writing for the *New York Times Book Review,* agreed, calling the author a "masterly scene-setter," and the book "irresistible reading, even for those who prefer Italy's olives to its opera."

BIOGRAPHICAL AND CRITICAL SOURCES:

PERIODICALS

Booklist, June 1, 2006, Alan Hirsch, review of *The Librettist of Venice: The Remarkable Life of Lorenzo Da Ponte, Mozart's Poet, Casanova's Friend, and Italian Opera's Impresario in America,* p. 24.
Contemporary Review, January, 2005, review of *History Play: The Lives and Afterlife of Christopher Marlowe,* p. 61.
Entertainment Weekly, September 2, 2005, Adam B. Vary, review of *History Play,* p. 85.
Kirkus Reviews, July 15, 2005, review of *History Play,* p. 772; May 1, 2006, review of *The Librettist of Venice,* p. 444.
Library Journal, August 1, 2005, William D. Walsh, review of *History Play,* p. 84; May 15, 2006, Barry Zaslow, review of *The Librettist of Venice,* p. 102.
New York Times, July 21, 2006, Charles McGrath, "A Maestro of Second Acts, in Opera and in Life," review of *The Librettist of Venice,* p. E32.

New York Times Book Review, July 30, 2006, Megan Marshall, review of *The Librettist of Venice.*
Observer (London, England), July 23, 2006, review of *Lorenzo da Ponte: The Adventures of Mozart's Librettist in the Old and New Worlds.*
Opera News, October, 2006, Joanne Sydney Lessner, review of *The Librettist of Venice,* p. 77.
Publishers Weekly, April 17, 2006, review of *The Librettist of Venice,* p. 174.
Reference & Research Book News, November, 2005, review of *History Play;* November, 2006, review of *The Librettist of Venice.*
Washington Post, July 16, 2006, Jonathan Keats, review of *The Librettist of Venice.*

ONLINE

Bloomsbury USA Web site, http://www.bloomsburyusa.com/ (December 11, 2006), brief biography of Rodney Bolt.

*   *   *

BONADUCE, Danny 1959-
(Dante Daniel Bonaduce)

PERSONAL: Last name pronounced "*bon*-uh-*doo*-chee"; born August 13, 1959, in Broomall, PA; son of Joseph (a writer) and Betty (a freelance writer) Bonaduce; married Setsuko Hattori, c. 1985 (divorced, 1988); married, 1989; wife's name Gretchen (an actress); children: (second marriage) Countess Isabella Michaela, Count Dante Jean-Michel Valentino.

ADDRESSES: Agent—William Morris Agency, 151 S. El Camino Dr., Beverly Hills, CA 90212.

CAREER: Actor, radio broadcaster, game show host, disc jockey, and writer. Actor in television series, including (as Danny Partridge) *The Partridge Family,* American Broadcasting Companies (ABC), 1970-74; (as voice of Danny) *Goober and the Ghost Chasers* (animated), ABC, 1973-75; (as voice of Danny Partridge) *The Partridge Family: 2200 A.D.* (animated), Columbia Broadcasting System (CBS), 1974-75; (as host) *Danny!,* syndicated, 1995; (as narrator) *Bellbottoms to Boogie Shoes: The 70's,* 2001; (as cohost) *The Other Half,* syndicated, 2001—; and (as himself), *Breaking Bonaduce*, VH1, c. 2005; also host of *Starface* (game show), GSN, 2006—; also appeared (as voice) in *Fred Flintstone and Friends* (animated). Actor in television movies, including (as Millard Kensington) *Murder on Flight 502*, ABC, 1975. Actor in television pilots, including (as Danny Partridge) *A Knight in Shining Armor*, ABC, 1971; (as boy at museum) *Call Holme*, National Broadcasting Company (NBC), 1972, then CBS, 1984; (as Franklin) *Honest Al's A-OK Used Car and Trailer Rental Tigers*, syndicated, 1978.

Appeared in television specials, including *Thanksgiving Reunion with The Partridge Family and My Three Sons*, ABC, 1977; *The Lost Youth of Hollywood*, NBC, 1991; *Hardcore TV*, Home Box Office (HBO), 1993; (as himself) *Child Stars: Their Story*, 2000; (as himself) *Intimate Portrait: Shirley Jones*, 2001; (as himself) *Celebrity Boxing*, 2002; (as himself) *The 2002 Blockbuster Hollywood Christmas Spectacular*, 2002; and (as himself) *We Are Family*, 2003. Narrator and executive consultant for the television movie *Come On, Get Happy: The Partridge Family Story*, 1999. Guest star on television shows, including *Mayberry R.F.D.*, *Bewitched*, *CHiPs*, *The Ben Stiller Show*, *That 70's Show*, *Who Wants to Be a Millionaire*, *The Drew Carey Show*, *That 70's Show*, and many others.

Actor in films, including (as voice of Avery Arable) *Charlotte's Web* (animated; also known as *E.B. White's Charlotte's Web*), Paramount, 1973; (as Robertson) *Baker's Hawk*, Doty/Dayton, 1976; (as Kootz) *Corvette Summer* (also known as *The Hot One*), United Artists, 1978; (as Richie) *H.O.T.S.* (also known as *T & A Academy*), Derio, 1979; (as John; also stunt coordinator) *Deadly Intruder* (also known as *The Deadly Intruder*), 1985; (as Doug) *America's Deadliest Home Video*, 1993; (as himself) *Dickie Roberts: Former Child Star*, 2003; and (as Roscoe) *Firedog*, 2005. Recorded the track "59th Street Bridge Song" for *Hollywood Hi-Fi*, Brunswick Records, 1996.

Host or cohost of radio shows, including a late-night show for WEGX-FM, Philadelphia, PA, c. 1989 and c. 1991; a show for KKFR, Phoenix, AZ, c. 1990; a midday show for WLUP, Chicago, IL, c. 1992-96; a morning show for WKQI-FM, Detroit, MI, 1996-c. 1998; a morning show for WBIX-FM, New York, NY, 1998-99; *The Jamie and Danny Show*, 98.7 Star FM, Los Angeles, CA, beginning 1999; and *Adam Carolla Show*, CBS Radio, 2007—; also hosted the syndicated, two-minute *The Hollywood Report* radio program, United Stations Radio Network.

WRITINGS:

Random Acts of Badness: My Story (autobiography), Hyperion (New York, NY), 2001.

SIDELIGHTS: Danny Bonaduce first became a star as the red-headed, freckle-faced boy Danny Partridge on the hit television series *The Partridge Family* in the early 1970s. He had a few film roles after the show ended in 1974, but by the time he turned twenty-one he had already spent all of the money he made. By the 1980s Bonaduce was in a lot of trouble, particularly with substance abuse, as he explains in his autobiography, *Random Acts of Badness: My Story*. The former-child-star-gone-bad story is not an uncommon one, but Bonaduce distances himself from his fellow former child actors and actresses who blame all of their adult problems on Hollywood. "Show business had not ruined our lives," he wrote in *Random Acts of Badness*. "We had."

Bonaduce's mother knocked on his door one day, at the height of his crack cocaine addiction, and told him, "It's important that you know that I love you, because you're going to die really soon. And as your mother, I want to know that the last thing I told you before you died, was I love you," as Bonaduce remembered the conversation in an interview on the *C'mon Get Happy* Web site. Bonaduce realized that she was right, and that scared him into trying to turn his life around. He moved in with his mother, who had moved back to his native Philadelphia, and got a job as a late-night radio host with a Philadelphia radio station. A few years later, Bonaduce took a job with a radio station in Phoenix. There, he met his wife Gretchen, whom he married seven hours after their first blind date. Bonaduce credits her with making him kick his drug habit once and for all, even at times sleeping in the driveway behind his car so he couldn't drive away to meet his dealer. "I married a strong, decent woman who was going to break her back making a man of me, and did. And God bless her for it," Bonaduce told an interviewer from the *Houston Chronicle*. Once Bonaduce was finally sober, his career turned around. He moved out of late-night radio into highly rated morning shows, got his own television talk show, and became part of the popular daytime television talk show *The Other Half,* which featured four men (including actors Dick Clark and Mario Lopez) in a studio trying to explain the male world view to women.

Bonaduce writes openly about his problems in *Random Acts of Badness,* but "his wit and humor help blunt the otherwise depressing topics of drug addiction," Jon Humbert wrote in the *Rocky Mountain News.* "He's a good-natured guide who never falls into self-pity," wrote a *Publishers Weekly* contributor. However, the book isn't all about the down side of Bonaduce's life. *Booklist* contributor Mike Tribby appreciated Bonaduce's chapter about his televised 1994 boxing match with another former child star, singer Donny Osmond, which sprang from an extended trash-talking episode that started in their shared Chicago health club and spread to radio. Bonaduce won using what he admits was a cheap trick: he was aware that Osmond got bloody noses very easily, so he continually aimed for Osmond's nose. "Does show-biz autobio get any better than this?," Tribby wrote.

BIOGRAPHICAL AND CRITICAL SOURCES:

BOOKS

Bonaduce, Danny, *Random Acts of Badness: My Story,* Hyperion (New York, NY), 2001.

PERIODICALS

Billboard, October 24, 1994, Phyllis Stark, interview with Bonaduce, pp. 97-98; February 21, 1998, Chuck Taylor, "An Eager Bonaduce Hits New York," pp. 69-70.
Booklist, October 15, 2001, Mike Tribby, review of *Random Acts of Badness,* pp. 366-367.
Broadcasting & Cable, October 10, 1994, "Raising the New Generation of Talk Talent," pp. 36-38.
Daily Herald (Arlington Heights, IL), November 29, 2001, Joel Reese, "Star(?) Trek: Former Bad Boy Danny Bonaduce Takes a Stroll down Michigan Avenue," p. 1.
Daily News (Los Angeles, CA), September 15, 1999, Fred Shuster, review of *The Jamie and Danny Show,* p. L5; November 13, 1999, Fred Shuster,

interview with Bonaduce, p. L3, David Kronke, review of *Come On, Get Happy: The Partridge Family Story,* p. L3.
Entertainment Weekly, April 28, 1995, J.R. Taylor, review of *America's Deadliest Home Video,* p. 73; September 15, 1995, Lisa Milbrand, review of *Danny!,* p. 55; September 29, 1995, Ken Tucker, review of *Danny!,* p. 44; November 16, 2001, review of *Random Acts of Badness,* p. 168.
Knight Ridder/Tribune News Service, November 21, 2001, John Smyntek, review of *Random Acts of Badness,* p. K0124.
Muscle & Fitness, September, 2005, Jeanine Detz, "Little Big Guy," interview with author, p. 40.
New York Times, July 16, 1995, Elizabeth Kolbert, interview with Bonaduce, p. H24.
People, April 25, 1994, Toby Kahn, "Danny Bonaduce," p. 75; February 27, 1989, Tom Cunneff, "Spinning Off His Partridge Past, Danny Bonaduce Rocks Philly as a Raunchy Midnight Deejay," pp. 97-99; March 26, 1990, William Plummer, "Dual Drug Busts Turn a Painful Spotlight on Two Children of Hollywood," pp. 51-52.
Philadelphia Magazine, September, 2001, Richard Rys, interview with Bonaduce, p. 25.
Plain Dealer (Cleveland, OH), November 13, 1999, Mark Dawidziak, interview with Bonaduce, p. 6E; November 28, 2001, Andrea Simakis, review of *Random Acts of Badness,* p. E5.
Publishers Weekly, August 13, 2001, review of *Random Acts of Badness,* p. 293.
Rocky Mountain News (Denver, CO), November 9, 2001, Jon Humbert, review of *Random Acts of Badness,* p. 28D.
Rolling Stone, September 10, 1987, Deborah Mitchell, "Where Are They Now? Danny Bonaduce," p. 58.
Sports Illustrated, January 31, 1994, "A Danny-Donnybrook," pp. 11-12.
TV Guide, October 14, 1995, Jane Marion, "Food for Talk," pp. 29-31.

ONLINE

C'mon Get Happy!: The Unofficial Home Page of "The Partridge Family," http://www.cmongethappy.com/ (October 30, 2000), interview with author.
Internet Movie Database, http://www.imdb.com/ (February 27, 2004), "Danny Bonaduce."

NNDB.com, http://www.nndb.com/ (January 17, 2007), biography of author.*

*   *   *

BONADUCE, Dante Daniel
   See BONADUCE, Danny

*   *   *

BONILLA, Juan 1966-

PERSONAL: Born 1966, in Jerez, Spain.

ADDRESSES: Home—Sevilla, Spain. *E-mail*—juanbonillaweb@yahoo.es.

CAREER: Writer, poet, journalist. *El Mundo,* columnist.

AWARDS, HONORS: Luis Cernuda de Poesía Prize, 1992; Biblioteca Breve Prize, 2003, for *The Nubian Prince.*

WRITINGS:

El que apaga la luz (short stories), Pre-Textos (Valencia, Spain), 1994.
Partes de guerra (poetry), Pre-Textos (Valencia, Spain), 1994.
Yo soy, yo eres, yo es (novella), Ediciones Imperdonables (Málaga, Spain), 1995.
Nadie conoce a nadie (novel), Ediciones B (Barcelona, Spain), 1996.
Cansados de estar muertos (novel), Espasa (Madrid, Spain), 1998.
La compañía de los solitarios (short stories), Pre-Textos (Valencia, Spain), 1999.
La noche del Skylab (short stories), Espasa Calpe (Madrid, Spain), 2000.
El Belvedere (poetry), Pre-Textos (Valencia, Spain), 2002.
Los príncipes nubios (novel), Seix Barral (Barcelona, Spain), 2003, translation by Esther Allen published as *The Nubian Prince*, Metropolitan Books (New York, NY), 2006.

El estadio de Mármol (short stories), Editoral Seix Barral (Barcelona, Spain), 2005.
Buzón Vacío (poems), 2006.

Also translator (from English to Spanish) of *Boyhood* by J.M. Coetzee and of poems by A.E. Housman.

ADAPTATIONS: Nadie conoce a nadie was adapted for a feature film, 1999.

SIDELIGHTS: Spanish journalist and writer Juan Bonilla is the author of numerous novels, short story and poetry collections, as well as nonfiction books of essays. His award-winning 2003 novel, *Los príncipes nubios,* was translated and published in English in 2006 as *The Nubian Prince,* earning a good deal of critical acclaim.

The Nubian Prince is a work in which the "international sex trade becomes the unlikely source of an ironic metamorphosis," according to a *Kirkus Reviews* critic. The novel is narrated by Moises Froissard, a twenty-two-year-old artist and former humanitarian worker from Seville who becomes a talent scout for an organization, Club Olympus, which poses as a relief organization. In reality, it is a recruiting agency for prostitutes for the wealthy around the world. Thus, famines and floods are good times for Club Olympus, for they produce refugees and displaced persons. It is Moises's job to find the most attractive of these and recruit them. Now Moises is sent by the Club's director, Carmen, to find the Nubian Prince, a prizefighter and a perfect African specimen. Along the way, the callow Moises develops a conscience, which complicates his mission. The *Kirkus Reviews* critic concluded, "Not exactly effortlessly readable, but a skillful treatment of its unusual and tricky subject." Similarly, a *Publishers Weekly* contributor found the novel "bittersweet," and *Booklist* writer Hazel Rochman called it an "intimate first-person narrative." *Library Journal* contributor Stephen Morrow had further praise for the "irreverent, self-absorbed tone that keeps this novel unexpectedly lighthearted, though it easily could have been tragic."

BIOGRAPHICAL AND CRITICAL SOURCES:

PERIODICALS

Booklist, June 1, 2006, Hazel Rochman, review of *The Nubian Prince,* p. 33.

Clarín Revista de Nueva Literatura, February, 2003, Javier Garcia Rodriguez, "Juan Bonilla: Maneras de vivir."

Kirkus Reviews, May 15, 2006, review of *The Nubian Prince,* p. 477.

Library Journal, June 1, 2006, Stephen Morrow, review of *The Nubian Prince,* p. 106.

Publishers Weekly, May 29, 2006, review of *The Nubian Prince,* p. 37.

ONLINE

Barcelona Review, http://www.barcelonareview.com/ (November 16, 2006), "Juan Bonilla."

Catedra Miguel Delibes, http://www.catedramdelibes.com/ (November 16, 2006), "Juan Bonilla."

Holtzbrinck Publishers Web site, http://www.holtzbrinckus.com/ (November 16, 2006), "Juan Bonilla."

Juan Bonilla Home Page, http://es.geocities.com/juanbonillaweb (November 16, 2006).

[Sketch reviewed by Webmaster, Natalia Zarco.]

*   *   *

BOUILLIER, Grégoire 1960-

PERSONAL: Born 1960, in Tizi-Ouzou, Great Kabylia, Algeria.

ADDRESSES: Home—Paris, France.

CAREER: Painter and writer.

AWARDS, HONORS: Prix de Flore, 2002, for *Rapport sur moi.*

WRITINGS:

MEMOIRS

Rapport sur moi (title means "Report on Myself"), Allia (Paris, France), 2002.

L'invité mystère, Allia (Paris, France), 2004, translation by Lorin Stein published as *The Mystery Guest: An Account,* Farrar, Straus & Giroux (New York, NY), 2006.

Contributor to *L'Infini, NRV,* and *New York Times Magazine.*

SIDELIGHTS: Paris-based writer Grégoire Bouillier is the author of *Rapport sur moi,* an award-winning memoir, and *The Mystery Guest: An Account,* "an ostensibly autobiographical novella that is charmingly absurd, gently metafictional, and gloriously French," noted *Booklist* critic Brendan Driscoll. In *The Mystery Guest,* Bouillier receives a phone call from the woman who left him, without explanation, years before. Instead of discussing her abrupt departure, she invites him to serve as the "mystery guest" at a birthday party for her husband's best friend, the artist Sophie Calle. The bewildered narrator accepts the invitation but is overwhelmed by suspicion and self-doubt as he deliberates endlessly on the caller's motivations. "Anyone whose anxieties tend to buzz in the ear, creating a din that makes it impossible to act unselfconsciously, will enjoy this slim volume," noted Emily Bobrow in the *New York Observer.* "Mr. Bouillier is looking back and poking fun at himself, but the events are captured with a raw immediacy, making his parade of humiliations feel fresh and profound."

The Mystery Guest received strong critical acclaim. Bouillier's "text is brilliantly entertaining and at times hilarious," Regan McMahon stated in the *San Francisco Chronicle.* "His biting observations have the ring of truth, whether he's berating himself in his gloomy apartment, where for the longest time he refuses to change the lightbulb (a metaphor for the extinguished relationship) or mocking the celebrity artistic and literary elite he finds at the party." According to Erica Wagner, writing in the *New York Times Book Review,* "This memoir—which is shot through with references to the literature that Bouillier loves, to Ulysses and to 'Ulysses' and to Virginia Woolf—gives shape to the question of 'meaning,' whether it's illusory, whether that matters at all."

"We're always hearing that truth is stranger than fiction, and yet it's amazing how many books act as if nothing happened and keep telling stories that can't hold a candle to reality," Bouillier told Yann Nicol in the *Brooklyn Rail.* "When it's this continual tendency of truth—to keep being stranger than fiction—that is the very essence of the novelistic. And in everything I've written I've tried to capture this novelistic effect."

BIOGRAPHICAL AND CRITICAL SOURCES:

BOOKS

Bouillier, Grégoire, *Rapport sur moi,* Allia (Paris, France), 2002.

Bouillier, Grégoire, *L'invité mystère,* Allia (Paris, France), 2004, translation by Lorin Stein published as *The Mystery Guest: An Account,* Farrar, Straus & Giroux (New York, NY), 2006.

PERIODICALS

Booklist, October 15, 2006, Brendan Driscoll, review of *The Mystery Guest,* p. 27.

Kirkus Reviews, June 15, 2006, review of *The Mystery Guest,* p. 609.

Library Journal, October 15, 2006, Ali Houissa, review of *The Mystery Guest,* p. 59.

New York Times Magazine, October 15, 2006, Grégoire Bouillier, "Meanings of Origin," p. 88.

New York Observer, August 28, 2006, Emily Bobrow, "A Mortifying Turtleneck No Cure for Heartache," review of *The Mystery Guest,* p. 13; November 6, 2006, Sheelah Kolhatkar, "Who's *Le Plus Chaud?* French Emo-Memoirist Grégoire Bouillier," p. 1.

New York Times Book Review, September 17, 2006, Erica Wagner, "The Birthday Party," review of *The Mystery Guest,* p. 8.

Publishers Weekly, July 17, 2006, review of *The Mystery Guest,* p. 149.

San Francisco Chronicle, September 10, 2006, Regan McMahon, "She Wants Him Back—As a Party Guest," review of *The Mystery Guest,* p. M1.

ONLINE

Brooklyn Rail Online, http://brooklynrail.org/ (September, 2006), Yann Nicol, "Experiential Lit: Grégoire Bouillier with Yann Nicol, translated by Violaine Huisman and Lorin Stein."

Time Out New York Online, http://www.timeout.com/newyork/ (August 24-30, 2006), Michael Miller, review of *The Mystery Guest.**

* * *

BOYLE, Dan 1959-

PERSONAL: Born October 18, 1959, in Tacoma, WA; son of Raymond (a certified public accountant) and Marilyn (a realtor) Boyle. *Ethnicity:* "Irish." *Education:* Western Washington University, B.A., 1982. *Politics:* Democrat. *Religion:* Roman Catholic.

ADDRESSES: Home—Burbank, CA. *Office*—Providence Health System, 501 S. Buena Vista St., Burbank, CA 91505. *E-mail*—sheltiesx3@charter.net.

CAREER: Writer.

WRITINGS:

Huddle (novel), Haworth Press (New York, NY), 2003.

Housecleaning (novel), Haworth Press (New York, NY), 2007.

SIDELIGHTS: Dan Boyle told *CA:* "I love novels of ideas, and my second novel stemmed from my interest in scientists who search for God by searching the universe. *Housecleaning* is about a Cal Tech physicist trying to understand the meaning of life through a unified theory of the universe known as string theory. He takes a sabbatical to Washington State to care for his mother, who is dying of a strange form of dementia, in which she falls back in time all the way back to the Big Bang.

"I've been writing since I was a little kid, writing from my top bunk bed. My first attempt was a story called 'Fourteen Dogs on a Vacation.' I was first influenced by the power of the novel as a freshman in college when I began reading French, German, and Russian novelists, especially Tolstoy, Lermontov, and Dostoevsky. [Now] I get up early in the morning, have a double shot of espresso, and start writing. I find it's best for me to work without an outline at first. An outline becomes cumbersome for me and does not allow my characters to live and breathe. I need to go where my characters take me.

"I want my novels to make people think, to realize that all those thoughts in their heads that they never share with others are shared by others."

*   *   *

BRADLEY, James 1954-

PERSONAL: Born 1954, in WI; son of John (a funeral director) and Betty Bradley; married twice (divorced). *Education:* University of Wisconsin, graduated. *Hobbies and other interests:* Reading history, discovering exotic cuisine, cliff diving, SCUBA diving, golfing, skiing.

ADDRESSES: Home—Rye, NY. *Agent*—Wayne Kabak, William Morris Agency, 1325 Avenue of the Americas, New York, NY 10019. *E-mail*—info@ jamesbradley.com.

CAREER: Writer and speaker. Producer of corporate films; founder and president, James Bradley Peace Foundation.

WRITINGS:

(With Ron Powers) *Flags of Our Fathers,* Bantam (New York, NY), 2000, paperback edition with a new afterword by the author, Bantam Books (New York, NY), 2006.
(With others) *What If? 2: Eminent Historians Imagine What Might Have Been: Essays,* edited by Robert Cowley, Putnam (New York, NY), 2001, published as *More What If? Eminent Historians Imagine What Might Have Been,* Macmillan (London, England), 2002.
Flyboys: A True Story of Courage, Little, Brown (New York, NY), 2003.

ADAPTATIONS: Flags of Our Fathers was adapted for a feature film by Clint Eastwood, 2006; a printed edition for young readers was also adapted by Michael French as *Flags of Our Fathers: Heroes of Iwo Jima,*

Delacorte Press (New York, NY), 2001. *Flyboys: A True Story of Courage,* was adapted for audio by Time Warner Audiobooks, 2004.

SIDELIGHTS: James Bradley became a best-selling author with the publication of his nonfiction book *Flags of Our Fathers,* written with Ron Powers. The book traces the lives of the six American soldiers who were immortalized in the famous photograph of them raising a flag on the island of Iwo Jima during World War II. One of those soldiers was Bradley's father. Though a small, seemingly insignificant island in the Pacific, Iwo Jima was crucial to the American effort against Japan in World War II, and the battle to gain control of it was one of the most horrific of the war. Fighting went on for over a month, with huge losses on both sides. The photograph of Bradley's father and the others raising a flag was not really the moment of victory, but a seemingly random incident during the Iwo Jima campaign. Yet the photograph became a powerful tool for bolstering the war effort in the United States. Three of the flag-raisers were subsequently killed on Iwo Jima, but the survivors were used for public relations and helped raise millions of dollars in war bond sales. The fame was difficult to handle, and two of the survivors went to early graves after leading unhappy lives. "Doc" Bradley, the author's father, went on to live a seemingly normal life in which the war was seldom mentioned. Yet despite his outward calm, the war veteran cried in his sleep for years after his discharge, and his family discovered the Navy Cross for bravery tucked away in his belongings. He had never told anyone that he had been awarded this honor.

Flags of Our Fathers is "a riveting read that deals with every detail of the photograph, its composition, the biographies of the men, what heroism is, and the dubious blessings of fame," noted Gilbert Taylor in his *Booklist* review. The author's detailed description of the battle for Iwo Jima is told "vividly, often with horrifying verisimilitude," reported Gregory Orfalea in the *National Review.* That the book works on several levels was confirmed by Gary Pounder, a reviewer for *Aerospace Power Journal,* who wrote: "This is a remarkable book, richly detailed and extraordinarily moving." He further credited *Flags of Our Fathers* with "brilliantly conveying both the sweep of war and the individual struggles of soldiers locked in its grip." Yet another aspect of the book was pointed out by William D. Bushnell in *Library Journal,* who stated that

Flags of Our Fathers is "more than just a history of a famous battle"; it is also "a poignant and fitting tribute to a loving father."

The Pacific during World War II was again the theme of Bradley's next book, *Flyboys: A True Story of Courage*. In it he focused on nine pilots who were gunned down off the Japanese-held island of Chichi Jima. One of the nine escaped and later became president of the United States: George H.W. Bush. The other eight were captured and eventually executed. Bradley took the same approach to the story as he had in *Flags of Our Fathers*, looking at each man's life in detail from early youth on into his term of military service. *Booklist* reviewer Gilbert Taylor warned that there are "many brutally graphic passages" about the torture inflicted on the captive airmen, "which may prove too daunting for some readers," but also credited the author with handling the horrific details of the story "sensitively." Janet Maslin, reviewing *Flyboys* in the *New York Times*, was less appreciative of Bradley's graphic account, writing: "Much of this account has a B-movie luridness that cheapens the events described, even if the details are accurate." A *Publishers Weekly* reviewer found the author's attempt to create a sweeping picture of not only the pilots, but of their respective cultures, to be overly ambitious; yet, the critic commented that "when the book keeps its eye on the aviators . . . it is as compelling as its predecessor."

BIOGRAPHICAL AND CRITICAL SOURCES:

PERIODICALS

Aerospace Power Journal, spring, 2001, Gary Pounder, review of *Flags of Our Fathers*, p. 112.

American History, June, 2000, Dominic Caraccilo, review of *Flags of Our Fathers*, p. 67.

Book, November-December, 2003, Eric Wargo, review of *Flyboys: A True Story of Courage*, p. 76.

Booklist, March 1, 2000, Gilbert Taylor, review of *Flags of Our Fathers*, p. 1147; August, 2003, Gilbert Taylor, review of *Flyboys*, p. 1922.

Book Report, November-December, 2001, Joan Chezem, review of *Flags of Our Fathers*, p. 75.

Entertainment Weekly, October 3, 2003, Benjamin Svetkey, review of *Flyboys*, pp. 78-79.

Journal of Military History, April, 2001, Merrill L. Bartlett, review of *Flags of Our Fathers*, p. 554.

Kirkus Reviews, August 1, 2003, review of *Flyboys*, p. 998.

Kliatt, January, 2005, Raymond Puffer, review of *Flyboys*, p. 32.

Library Journal, March 15, 2000, William D. Bushnell, review of *Flags of Our Fathers*, p. 102; September 15, 2003, Edwin B. Burgess, review of *Flyboys*, p. 68.

M2 Best Books, October 24, 2003, review of *Flyboys*.

Military Law Review, June, 2001, W.G. Perez, review of *Flags of Our Fathers*, pp. 227-234.

Military Review, September-October, 2004, Robert J. Rielly, review of *Flyboys*, p. 115.

National Review, July 3, 2000, Gregory Orfalea, review of *Flags of Our Fathers*.

Naval War College Review, spring, 2001, Tom Fedyszyn, review of *Flags of Our Fathers*, 149.

Newsweek, May 29, 2000, Kenneth Auchincloss, review of *Flags of Our Fathers*, p. 68.

New York Times, May 3, 2000, Richard Bernstein, review of *Flags of Our Fathers*, p. E9; October 23, 2003, Janet Maslin, review of *Flyboys*, p. E8.

Parameters, winter, 2000, Vince Goulding, review of *Flags of Our Fathers*, p. 151.

People, May 29, 2000, "Saluting the Flag: James Bradley Unfurls the Story behind Old Glory's Raising on Iwo Jima," p. 87.

Philadelphia Daily News, October 20, 2006, Gary Thompson, "Author's Dad Was Silent about Iwo."

Philadelphia Inquirer, July 11, 2000, Sandy Bauers, review of *Flags of Our Fathers*.

Publishers Weekly, May 8, 2000, review of *Flags of Our Fathers*, p. 216; May 7, 2001, "Indelible Images," p. 249; June 16, 2003, review of *Flags of Our Fathers*, p. 74; August 11, 2003, review of *Flyboys*, p. 273; December 22, 2003, "A Job Well Done," p. 10.

School Library Journal, May, 2001, Andrew Medlar, review of *Flags of Our Fathers*, p. 162.

Time, June 12, 2000, R.Z. Sheppard, review of *Flags of Our Fathers*, p. 84.

Sewanee Review, fall, 2000, Clay Lewis, review of *Flags of Our Fathers*, p. 124.

Washington Post Book World, June 18, 2000, Richard Harwood, review of *Flags of Our Fathers*, p. 9.

ONLINE

James Bradley Home Page, http://www.jamesbradley.com (December 11, 2006).

BRANDÃO, Ignácio de Loyola 1936-

PERSONAL: Born July 31, 1936, in Araraquara, São Paulo, Brazil; son of Antonio Maria (accountant) and Rosário Lopes Brandão. *Education:* Attended college.

CAREER: Writer, screenwriter, and journalist. Contributor to newspaper *Estado,* São Paulo, Brazil. Began career writing film reviews.

AWARDS, HONORS: Brasilia Prize, for *Zero;* Jabuti Prize, 2000.

WRITINGS:

Depois do sol; contos, Editora Brasiliense (São Paulo, Brazil), 1965.

Bebel que a cidade comeu; romance, Editora Brasiliense (São Paulo, Brazil), 1968, reprinted, Global (São Paulo, Brazil), 1986.

Cadeiras proibidas: contos, Edicoes Simbolo (São Paulo, Brazil), 1976, revised edition, Editora Codecri (Rio de Janeiro, Brazil), 1979.

Dentes ao sol: ou, A destruição da catedral, Editora Brasilia/Rio (Rio de Janeiro, Brazil), 1976.

Pega ele, silêncio: contos, Edicoes Simbolo (São Paulo, Brazil), 1976.

Cães danados, edited by André Carvalho; illustrations by Joyce Brandão, Editora Comunicacao (Belo Horizonte, Brazil), 1977.

Cuba de Fidel: viagem à ilha proibida (travel; title means "Cuba of Fidel: Trip to the Forbidden Island"), Livraria Cultura Editora (São Paulo, Brazil), 1978.

Não veras pais nenhum: memorial descritivo, Codecri (Rio de Janeiro, Brazil), 1981, published as *And Still the Earth,* Avon Books (New York, NY), 1985.

(With Vallandro Keating) *E gol (torcida amiga, boa tarde),* Palavra e Imagem Editora (São Paulo, Brazil), 1982.

Cabeças de segunda-feira, Codecri (Rio de Janeiro, Brazil), 1983.

Zero (novel), translated by Ellen Watson, Avon Books (New York, NY), 1983, reprinted with an introduction by Thomas Colchie, Dalkey Archive Press (Normal, IL), 2004.

O Verde violentou o muro: visões e alucinações alemãs, Global Editora (São Paulo, Brazil), 1984, 13th edition, revised, 2002.

O Beijo não vem da boca, Global (São Paulo, Brazil), 1985.

O Presente é o futuro: manifesto verde, 2nd edition, Editora Ground (São Paulo, Brazil), 1985.

O ganhador: romance, Global Editora (São Paulo, Brazil), 1987.

(Author of text) Lily Sverner e Andre Boccato, *Fragmentos de uma paisagem urbana,* (title means "Fragments of an Urban Landscape"), Sver & Boccato Editores (São Paulo, Brazil), 1988.

(Author of text) Eduardo Castanho, *Paulista, símbolo da cidade,* Banco Itau (São Paulo, Brazil), 1990.

Ignácio de Loyola Brandão (short stories), selected by Deonísio da Silva, Global (São Paulo, Brazil), 1993.

Olhos de banco: Avelino A. Vieira, DBA-Dorea Books and Art (Curitiba, Brazil), 1993.

(Author of text) *Teatro Municipal de São Paulo: grandes momentos,* photographs by Rômulo Fialdini and Cristiano Mascaro, illustrations by Roberto Stickel, DBA-Dorea Books and Art (São Paulo, Brazil), 1993.

(Author of text) *Luz no êxtase: vitrais e vitralistas no Brasil* (title means "Light on Ecstasy: Brazil's Stained Glass Windows and Artists"), photographs by Ary Diesendruck, Dorea Books and Art (São Paulo, Brazil), 1994.

O anjo do adeus: sacanas honestos jogam limpo jogos sujos, Global Editora (São Paulo, Brazil), 1995.

(Author of text) *Itaú, 50 anos,* DBA-Dorea Books and Art (São Paulo, Brazil), 1995.

Oficina de sonhos: Américo Emílio Romi, aventuras de um pioneiro, photographs by Claudio Edinger, Dorea Books and Art (São Paulo, Brazil), 1996.

(Author of text) *Santa Marina, um futuro transparente: 100 anos,* photographs by Romulo Fialdini, Dorea Books and Art (São Paulo, Brazil), 1996.

(Author of text) *Fundação Armando Alvares Penteado, FAAP, 1947-1997,* photographs by Romulo Fialdini, design by Victor Burton, DBA (São Paulo, Brazil), 1997.

(Author of text) *SESC, 50 anos,* DBA (São Paulo, Brazil), 1997.

Veia bailarina, Global Editora (São Paulo, Brazil), 1997.

(With Rodolpho Telarolli) *Addio bel campanile: a saga dos Lupo,* Global Editora (São Paulo, Brazil), 1998.

(Author of text) *Energia em evolução: COMGÁS, a Companhia de Gás de São Paulo,* photographs by Romul Fialdini, Dorea Books and Art (São Paulo, Brazil), 1998.

Universidade do Coração: 100 anos de história, Dezembro Editorial (São Paulo, Brazil), 1998.

(Author of text) *Bolsa de Valores de São Paulo: 110 anos,* DBA (São Paulo, Brazil), 1999.

Camargo Corrêa 60 anos (title means "Camargo Corrêa: 60 Years"), research by Hildegard Herbold, DBA (São Paulo, Brazil), 1999.

O Homem que odiava a segunda-feira: as aventuras possíveis, 2nd edition, Global Editora (São Paulo, Brazil), 1999.

(With Deonísio Silva) *Villares 80 Years,* DBA (São Paulo, Brazil), 1999.

Club Athletico Paulistano: corpo e alma de um clube centenário, DBA (São Paulo, Brazil), 2000.

(Author of text) *Crônicas da vida lindeira = Cronicas of people and dams,* (title means "Chronicles of People and Dams"), photographs by Eduardo Simães, Luciano Candisani, and Romulo Fialdini, DBA (São Paulo, Brazil), 2001.

(Author of text) *Dutra 50 anos: quatro séculos em cinco horas,* photographs by Luciano Candisani, DBA (São Paulo, Brazil), 2001.

O Anônimo célebre: reality romance, 2nd edition, Global Editora (São Paulo, Brazil), 2002.

(Author of text) *A Embaixada do Brasil em Lisboa,* photographs by Valentino Fialdini, Dezembro Editorial (São Paulo, Brazil), 2002.

Pinheiro Neto Advogados: 60 Years, Dezembro Editorial (São Paulo, Brazil), 2002.

(Author of text) *Leite de Rosas: uma história,* photographs by Romulo Fialdini, DBA (São Paulo, Brazil), 2003.

Romi-Isetta: o pequeno pioneir, DBA (São Paulo, Brazil), 2004.

A Última viagem de Borges: duas possibilidades de encenação, Global Editora (São Paulo, Brazil), 2005.

Also author of screenplays for films, including *Bebel, Garota Propaganda* (based on his short story *"Bebel Que a Cidade Comeu"*), 1968; *Anuska, Manequim e Mulher* (based on his short story *"Ascensão ao Mundo de Anuska"*), 1968; *Obscenidades,* 1986; *Urbania,* 2001. Contributor to books, including *Ação,* Atual Editora (São Paulo, Brazil), 1989; author of introduction to *Bodas de sangue,* by Gregorio Gruber, Best Editora (São Paulo, Brazil), 1986.

SIDELIGHTS: Ignácio de Loyola Brandão is a Brazilian writer and novelist whose novel *Zero* was initially banned in his own country and subsequently published in Italy. The novel revolves around an exterminator who finds humans to be approximately on the same level as the pests he exterminates. However, as the protagonist deals with a seemingly unending bureaucracy, the reader becomes aware of the author's "artful juxtaposition of seemingly unrelated information" to attack the Brazilian dictatorship, as noted by Ruth Doughterty in the *Library Journal.* In his novel *And Still the Earth,* Brandão presents a nightmarish vision of São Paulo, Brazil, as an overpopulated city that has even further widened the gap between its rich and poor inhabitants. Depicting dead bodies dumped in rivers and constant battles between the police and the criminal underworld, Brandão presents a futuristic vision in which environmental degradation has led to only the rich being able to afford "real" plants and food and water being strictly rationed to the poor. The novel's protagonist, Souze, a blacklisted former history professor, guides the reader through a walled-off city and a country under strict control of militarists who have auctioned off its northern states as residencies for foreigners. "Despite the very Brazilian flavor of Mr. Brandão's writing and concerns . . . , *And Still the Earth* makes compelling reading for foreigners," wrote Larry Rohter in the *New York Times Book Review.* "The conditions he describes and the grim future he foresees for his city may also await Lagos, Calcutta, Shanghai and Mexico City."

BIOGRAPHICAL AND CRITICAL SOURCES:

PERIODICALS

Library Journal, October 1, 1983, Ruth Doughterty, review of *And Still the Earth,* p. 1888.

New York Times Book Review, September 29, 1985, Larry Rohter, review of *Zero.*

ONLINE

Brazilmax.com, http://www.brazilmax.com/ (January 17, 2007), biography of author.

International Movie Database, http://www.imdb.com/ (January 17, 2007), information on author's film work.

Releituras, http://www.releituras.com/ (January 17, 2007), biography of author.*

*   *   *

BRINK, Elisabeth 1956-
(Elisabeth Panttaja Brink)

PERSONAL: Born 1956; married (divorced); remarried; children: a son and a daughter. *Education:* Graduated from Brown University; Brandeis University, Ph.D., 1993.

ADDRESSES: Home—Newburyport, MA. *Agent*—Maria Carvainis, Maria Carvainis Agency, 1350 Avenue of the Americas, Ste. 2905, New York, NY 10019. *E-mail*—Elisabeth@elisabethbrink.com.

CAREER: Writer, editor, and educator. Worked as an editor at *Cricket, the Magazine for Children;* has taught writing and literature at Harvard University, Tufts University, and Boston College. Previously worked as a technical editor, a high-tech marketing director, a product manager, an advertising copywriter, and a halfway-house counselor.

AWARDS, HONORS: Pushcart Prize nomination for short stories; fellowships in Prague and St. Petersburg; Fellowship for Graduate Research on Women.

WRITINGS:

Save Your Own (novel), Houghton Mifflin (Boston, MA), 2006.

Essays and short stories have appeared in periodicals, including the *Vermont Literary Review, Gettysburg Review, Alaska Quarterly Review, Manoa, Fiddlehead,* and *Orchid.*

SIDELIGHTS: Known as a short-story writer, Elisabeth Brink turned to the novel to tell the story of Harvard Divinity School graduate student Gillian Cormier-Brandenburg. *Save Your Own* recounts Gillian's experience as a supervisor of recovering addicts, a position she takes so she can obtain conversion narratives for her dissertation on the secular conversion experience. The homely and sexually inexperienced Gillian soon finds herself as night manager at Responsibility House, where she oversees a dozen recovering female addicts. Before long, she finds that she wants more out of her charges than their conversion stories; she also wants them to approve of her and perhaps help her lose her virginity. In addition, she finds herself becoming attracted to Janet, a tough resident who rides a motorcycle. "Brink has crafted an original heroine in Gillian, a half-pint, over-educated neurotic who finds the courage to let her heart override her overworked brain," wrote a *Kirkus Reviews* contributor. A *Publishers Weekly* contributor referred to *Save Your Own* as a "sweet, well-premised . . . debut novel," adding that "Gillian's repetitive moral posturing presents questions that are compelling." Another reviewer writing in *Publishers Weekly* commented that "Gillian is well developed as a narrator." Caroline Leavitt, Porter Shreve, and Josh Emmons, writing in *People,* called the novel "funny [and] engaging."

BIOGRAPHICAL AND CRITICAL SOURCES:

PERIODICALS

Kirkus Reviews, April 15, 2006, review of *Save Your Own,* p. 365.
People, July 24, 2006, Caroline Leavitt, Porter Shreve, and Josh Emmons, review of *Save Your Own,* p. 43.
Publishers Weekly, January 16, 2006, review of *Save Your Own,* p. 33; March 13, 2006, review of *Save Your Own,* p. 35.

ONLINE

Elisabeth Brink Home Page, http://www.elisabeth brink.com (October 30, 2006).

*   *   *

BRINK, Elisabeth Panttaja
See BRINK, Elisabeth

*   *   *

BROWN, Aaron 1956-

PERSONAL: Born 1956, in Seattle, WA; married Deborah Pastor (a portfolio manager), 1987; children: Jacob and Aviva. *Education:* Graduated from Harvard University; University of Chicago, M.B.A. *Hobbies and other interests:* Swimming, sailing, hiking, biking.

ADDRESSES: Home—New York, NY. *E-mail*—Aaron. Brown@PrivateerAM.com.

CAREER: Investment banker, financial manager, and writer. Morgan Stanley, New York, NY, executive director of risk management. Worked for Prudential Insurance, Newark, NJ, and Lepercq, de Neuflize, New York, became head of Mortgage Securities, ending 1988; later taught finance at Fordham University, New York, and Yeshiva University, New York; later worked for JP Morgan, Rabobank, and Citigroup. Serves on the editorial board of the Global Association of Risk Professionals. Also ran the Allied Owners Action Fund.

MEMBER: National Book Critics Circle

WRITINGS:

The Poker Face of Wall Street, John Wiley (Hoboken, NJ), 2006.

Columnist for *Wilmott Magazine.* Has contributed chapters to professional books on poker and finance.

SIDELIGHTS: Aaron Brown is an investment expert, poker player, and author of *The Poker Face of Wall Street.* In his book, Brown writes about playing poker but focuses on Wall Street and investing. The reason for discussing poker and investments is that Brown believes the two have a lot in common. For example, he writes about how playing poker can help train someone not only in risk evaluation but also in how to accept the risks inherent in investing. Brown offers advice that applies both to poker and investing, such as how to do your homework and aiming for success. He also relates the "pot" in poker to investing and writes that neither the poker player or the investor should become so "pot committed" that they don't know when to fold. The author also writes about the important personal assets that can lead the poker player and investor to accept losses and still play the game. Writing in *Business Week,* Peter Coy noted: "*The Poker Face of Wall Street* is a sprawling, idiosyncratic, and sometimes poker-obsessed book filled with nuggets about American history and finance." Coy went on to write that it is the author's "quirkiness that makes this book special." In a review

in *Publishers Weekly,* a contributor noted that the author's "model is instantly graspable, but so contrary to . . . conventional wisdom . . . that it may well spark debate." D. Murali, writing in the *Hindu Business Line,* commented: "Ideal read to cool off with before the market opens on Monday."

Brown told *CA:* "It has been a lifelong dream of mine to write a book. I don't mean to make my living by writing, or to express some specific ideas, just to write one book. Like any good dream, it turned out to be much harder than I thought, much different than I thought, but just as rewarding as I thought.

"I started out by learning and doing some things that could serve as the basis of a good book and by writing a lot of magazine articles and stories. When I got good enough to pound out a competent 2,500-word article in a day, I figured I could do a 100,000-word book in three months with little trouble. That [reasoning] is completely mistaken, because it ignores the links within the material. I could have written forty essays in three months without trouble, but to express an idea worth 100,000 words requires weaving together many threads. The number of connections increases with the square of the length, so the 100,000-word book is 1,600 times as hard as a 2,500-word article and should take about five years.

"I somehow finished it in three months anyway (because I'd been thinking about it for much longer than five years), eventually writing 220,000 words, then cutting it down to 90,000. I later discovered that this is very common for first-time authors. At the beginning, you can't imagine filling the book, so you start writing any drivel to fill the pages. Some of that drivel turns out to be much better than the stuff you meant to write about. It needs strict editing, but a book begins to emerge naturally from the process. Of course it's nothing like the book you started out to write.

"I was very gratified to sell 15,000 copies immediately, enough for the publisher to bring it out in hardcover, then see it settle down to moderately robust sales. My fear was that no one would buy it, so I would never know if it was any good. Even a couple thousand sales would have been enough so that if it didn't take off, I would know it had its chance and lost. I could live with that, but not with the book never having a chance. I didn't try to write a book that everyone would like. It was more important to me that people will still be reading it ten years from now.

"I used to gag a bit when writers thanked their families and copyeditors and friends, but I no longer have that reaction. One of the best parts of writing a book is the help you get from family, friends, and strangers, and you need every bit of that help.

"I recommend the experience. If you think you have a book in you, you should write it. Don't do it to get rich or famous, do it for the book."

BIOGRAPHICAL AND CRITICAL SOURCES:

BOOKS

Brown, Aaron, *The Poker Face of Wall Street*, John Wiley (Hoboken, NJ), 2006.

PERIODICALS

Business Week, June 5, 2006, Peter Coy, review of *The Poker Face of Wall Street*, p. 134.
Global Investor, June, 2006, Claire Milhench, "Dealer's Choice," profile of author, p. 14.
Hindu Business Line, May 27, 2006, D. Murali, review of *The Poker Face of Wall Street*.
Publishers Weekly, March 6, 2006, review of *The Poker Face of Wall Street*.

ONLINE

Aaron Brown Home Page, http://www.eraider.com/index.php (November 15, 2006).

*   *   *

BROWN, James 1933(?)-2006
(James Joe Brown, Jr.)

OBITUARY NOTICE— See index for *CA* sketch: Born May 3, 1933 (some sources say June 17, 1928, or May 3, 1928), in Barnwell, SC; died of heart failure, December 25, 2006, in Atlanta, GA. Singer, entertainer, and author. Widely revered as the "Godfather of Soul," Brown exerted a profound influence on American music that ranged from rock and funk to hip-hop and rap. Entering the world under humble circumstances, he was abandoned by his parents when he was four years old. Relatives took him in, but the young Brown found himself in trouble on the streets. He was sent to reform school for breaking into cars, but his life turned around when he met Bobby Byrd. Byrd took Brown under his wing and invited him to join his group, the Gospel Starlighters. Brown was in his element, and soon became the group's leader. Renamed the Famous Flames in 1956, the group switched from gospel to R&B and signed a contract with King Records. Their first hit, "Please, Please, Please," made it to the Top Ten list that year. Other hits followed, and by the early 1960s Brown had become a hugely successful solo performer. His 1963 album, *James Brown Live at the Apollo*, was a musical landmark that still reverberates today. By this time, Brown had honed his style, which emphasized rhythms over melodies. His arrangements made not only drums, but also wind and string instruments into rhythm sections, all complimented by his passionate lyrics which were used not only in expressive vocals but also to direct the musicians in often improvised performances. Brown was clearly interested more in creating dynamic, innovative sounds than he was in becoming a pop icon. He achieved popularity nonetheless with songs such as "Papa's Got a Brand New Bag," which was a Grammy Award winner, "Get Up I Feel Like Being a Sex Machine," and "I Got You (I Feel Good)." His 1968 song "Say It Loud—I'm Black and I'm Proud" was adopted as a rallying cry during the civil rights movement. After enjoying a height in popularity from the 1960s through the mid-1970s, Brown was somewhat overshadowed by the rise of disco music. Nevertheless, he never faded from the scene completely. His rhythms and musical arrangements would influence disco, hip-hop, and rap, and Brown continued to perform through his last years. An interruption to his career came in 1988 when he was arrested on charges of assault and resisting police officers. Asserting his innocence, Brown nevertheless served three years in prison; he was officially pardoned in 2003 after being released in 1991. Another setback happened in 1998, when an addiction to painkillers put him in the hospital. Also called the hardest-working performer of his time, Brown could put on energetic stage performances even when he reached his seventies. Over his long career, his records went gold forty-four times; he won his second Grammy in 1986 for "Living in America," was inducted into the Rock 'n' Roll Hall of Fame in 1986, and received a lifetime achievement award from the American Music Awards in 1992, among other honors.

His autobiography, *James Brown: The Godfather of Soul,* was first published in 1986.

OBITUARIES AND OTHER SOURCES:

BOOKS

Brown, James, and Bruce Tucker, *James Brown: The Godfather of Soul,* revised edition, Thunder's Mouth Press (New York, NY), 1990.
Contemporary Black Biography, Volume 15, Thomson Gale (Detroit, MI), 1997.
Contemporary Musicians, Volume 16, Thomson Gale (Detroit, MI), 1996.
Contemporary Theatre, Film, and Television, Volume 35, Thomson Gale (Detroit, MI), 2001.
Dictionary of Twentieth Century Culture,, Volume 5: *African American Culture,* Thomson Gale (Detroit, MI), 1996.

PERIODICALS

Chicago Tribune, December 26, 2006, Section 1, pp. 1, 4.
New York Times, December 26, 2006, pp. A1, C16; December 27, 2006, p. A2.
Times (London, England), December 26, 2006, p. 68.
Washington Post, December 26, 2006, pp. A1, A12.

*　　*　　*

BROWN, James Joe, Jr.
　　See BROWN, James

*　　*　　*

BROWNE, Sylvia 1936-

PERSONAL: Born October 19, 1936, in Kansas City, MO; daughter of Bill Shoemaker; children: Paul and Christopher. *Education:* Roman Catholic College, Kansas City, MO, M.A.

ADDRESSES: Office—Sylvia Browne Corporation, 1700 Winchester Blvd., Ste. 100, Campbell, CA 95008.

CAREER: Psychic, spiritual teacher, and author. Sylvia Browne Corporation, Campbell, CA, president; Society of Novus Spiritus, Campbell, CA, founder.

WRITINGS:

(With Antoinette May) *My Guide, Myself: The Psychic Odyssey of Sylvia Browne,* New American Library (New York, NY), 1990.
(With Antoinette May) *Adventures of a Psychic: The Fascinating and Inspiring True-Life Story of One of America's Most Successful Clairvoyants,* Hay House (Carlsbad, CA), 1998.
Angels and Spirit Guides: How to Call upon Your Angels and Spirit Guide for Help (sound recording), Hay House Audio (Carlsbad, CA), 1999.
(With Lindsay Harrison) *The Other Side and Back: A Psychic's Guide to Our World and Beyond,* Dutton (New York, NY), 1999.
Sylvia Browne's Tools for Life (sound recording), Hay House (Carlsbad, CA), 2000.
Soul's Perfection, Hay House (Carlsbad, CA), 2000.
The Other Side of Life (sound recording), Hay House Audio (Carlsbad, CA), 2000.
Meditations, Hay House (Carlsbad, CA), 2000.
Life on the Other Side: A Psychic's Tour of the Afterlife, Dutton (New York, NY), 2000.
God Creation and the Tools for Life, Hay House (Carlsbad, CA), 2000.
(With Lindsay Harrison) *Blessings from the Other Side: Wisdom and Comfort from the Afterlife for This Life,* Dutton (New York, NY), 2000.
Astrology through a Psychic's Eyes, Hay House (Carlsbad, CA), 2000.
(With Lindsay Harrison) *Past Lives, Future Healing: A Psychic Reveals the Secrets of Good Health and Great Relationships,* Dutton (New York, NY), 2001.
The Nature of Good and Evil, Hay House (Carlsbad, CA), 2001.
(With Nancy Dufresne) *A Journal of Love and Healing: Transcending Grief,* Hay House (Carlsbad, CA), 2001.
(With Lindsay Harrison) *Sylvia Browne's Book of Dreams,* Dutton (New York, NY), 2002.
Prayers, Hay House (Carlsbad, CA), 2002.
Conversations with the Other Side, Hay House (Carlsbad, CA), 2002.
Sylvia Browne's Book of Angels, Dutton (New York, NY), 2003.

(With Lindsay Harrison) *Visits from the Afterlife: The Truth about Hauntings, Spirits, and Reunions with Lost Loved Ones,* Dutton (New York, NY), 2003.

Contacting Your Spirit Guide, Hay House (Carlsbad, CA), 2003.

Sylvia Browne's Lessons for Life, Hay House (Carlsbad, CA), 2004.

Mother God: The Feminine Principle to Our Creator, Hay House (Carlsbad, CA), 2004.

Prophecy: What the Future Holds for You, Dutton (New York, NY), 2004.

Angels, Guides & Ghosts (sound recording), Hay House (Carlsbad, CA), 2004.

A Day in the Life of a Spirit Guide, Hay House (Carlsbad, CA), 2005.

(With Lindsay Harrison) *Phenomenon: Everything You Need to Know about the Paranormal,* Dutton (New York, NY), 2005.

Secrets & Mysteries of the World, Hay House (Carlsbad, CA), 2005.

(With Kat Shehata) *Animals on the Other Side,* Angel Bea (Cincinnati, OH), 2005.

The Mystical Life of Jesus: An Uncommon Perspective on the Life of Christ, Dutton (New York, NY), 2006.

If You Could See What I See: The Tenets of Novus Spiritus, Hay House (Carlsbad, CA), 2006.

Exploring the Levels of Creation, Hay House (Carlsbad, CA), 2006.

Light a Candle, Angel Bea (Cincinnati, OH), 2006.

(With Lindsay Harrison) *Insight: Case Files from the Psychic World,* Dutton (New York, NY), 2006.

Spiritual Connections: How to Find Spirituality throughout All the Relationships in Your Life, Hay House (Carlsbad, CA), 2007.

Secret Societies—And How They Affect Our Lives Today, Hay House (Carlsbad, CA), 2007.

Father God: Co-Creator to Mother God, Hay House (Carlsbad, CA), 2007.

ADAPTATIONS: Author's books have been adapted for audio, including *Life on the Other Side,* High-Bridge (St. Paul, MN), 2000; *Blessings from the Other Side,* Simon & Schuster Audio, 2001; *Past Lives, Future Healing,* HighBridge (St. Paul, MN), 2001; and *Contacting Your Spirit Guide,* Hay House (Carlsbad, CA), 2005.

SIDELIGHTS: Sylvia Browne is known as one of the most famous spiritual teachers and psychics in the United States. She is the best-selling author of a number of books about her own psychic abilities, the world of psychic phenomena, and spiritual philosophy. Browne has touched a chord with fans and readers and is a publishing phenomenon in the area of new age and psychic teachings.

Browne quotes her spirit guide Francine in *The Other Side and Back: A Psychic's Guide to Our World and Beyond.* The focus is on the intricacies of life and the spirit life with an emphasis on the age-old issues of why we are born, what our purpose is, and what happens after death. The author addresses more than forty major life themes overall, with advice on overcoming fears, and daily affirmations that people can make to improve their lives. She also makes predictions. Ilene Cooper, writing in *Booklist,* noted the author's "cheerful, down-to-earth attitude about her gift and the state of our souls." Referring to the book as a "comprehensive manual on living a spiritual life," a *Publishers Weekly* contributor commented that it offers "ample fare for readers with a taste for comfortable excursions to the other side."

Life on the Other Side: A Psychic's Tour of the Afterlife has been compared to a spiritual travel guide by some reviewers. The author describes the afterlife, for example, providing details about buildings, concert halls, schools, and libraries. She also writes about how to get to heaven and discusses concepts such as reincarnation. Cooper, writing again in *Booklist,* commented: "For believers, . . . Browne offers a comforting view of the other side." A *Publishers Weekly* reviewer called the book "a well-written and entertaining cultural bellwether."

In *Contacting Your Spirit Guide,* Browne writes about her own life and how to recognize and contact spirit guides. A *Bookwatch* contributor recommended the book for "personal Metaphysical Studies reading lists." *Prophecy: What the Future Holds for You* examines the role of prophecy in modern-day life and its historic role in mainstream religions such as Christianity and Islam, as well as in Native American religions and other beliefs. The author profiles prophets old and new and writes of her own prophecies. She also makes many predictions concerning the future of science, technology, and medicine. "In the end, all readers, even those skeptical of specific forecasts, can applaud the author for her strong spirituality," wrote a *Publishers Weekly* contributor.

BIOGRAPHICAL AND CRITICAL SOURCES:

BOOKS

Encyclopedia of Occultism and Parapsychology, 5th edition, Thomson Gale, 2001.

PERIODICALS

Booklist, July, 1999, Ilene Cooper, review of *The Other Side and Back: A Psychic's Guide to Our World and Beyond,* p. 1898; May 15, 2000, review of *Life on the Other Side: A Psychic's Tour of the Afterlife,* p. 1698.

Bookwatch, February, 2006, review of *Contacting Your Spirit Guide.*

PR Newswire, November 10, 2003, "World Renowned Psychic Sylvia Browne Explores the Spirit World in Indianapolis."

Publishers Weekly, May 10, 1999, John F. Baker, "Beyond the Grave," p. 25; June 28, 1999, review of *The Other Side and Back,* p. 66; June 19, 2000, review of *Life on the Other Side,* p. 70; July 5, 2004, review of *Prophecy: What the Future Holds for You,* p. 50; August 9, 2004, Daisy Maryles, "Browne's Future Is Rosy," p. 120.

ONLINE

43People.com, http://www.43people.com/ (December 17, 2006), brief profile of Sylvia Browne.

Sylvia Browne Home Page, http://www.sylvia.org/home/index.cfm (December 17, 2006).

[Sketch reviewed by agent, Bonnie Solow.]

*   *   *

BUCKLEY-ARCHER, Linda

PERSONAL: Born in Sussex, England; married; children: two. *Education:* Undergraduate degree; studied for a doctorate at London University.

ADDRESSES: Home—London, England.

CAREER: Has worked as a freelance journalist for the London *Independent* and other newspapers, and as a French teacher.

WRITINGS:

Gideon the Cutpurse: Being the First Part of the Gideon Trilogy (novel; for children), Simon & Schuster Books for Young Readers (New York, NY), 2006.

Also author of radio scripts, including *Gideon the Cutpurse, Pearls in the Tate, One Night in White Satin,* and *Brief Encounters.*

ADAPTATIONS: Gideon the Cutpurse was adapted as an audiobook, Simon & Schuster, 2006.

SIDELIGHTS: Linda Buckley-Archer initially intended her first children's novel, *Gideon the Cutpurse: Being the First Part of the Gideon Trilogy,* to be a radio play; but her children's enthusiastic response to readings in progress led her to develop it as a novel. The time travel story takes Peter and Kate, two modern-day twelve-year-olds, back to 1763 England via a mishap with an antigravity device being developed by Kate's father. Fortunately, the device went back in time with them. As a result, Peter and Kate have high hopes of returning to their own time, until the machine is stolen by the nefarious thief known as the Tar Man. Gideon, a former thief, helps the two children track down the Tar Man as the children's parents frantically search for them. "Readers will be eager for the sequel to this exciting time travel adventure," asserted Paula Rohrlick in *Kliatt.* Jennifer Mattson, writing in *Booklist,* commented that the author proves herself skilled at portraying "the pistol-waving encounters with highwaymen and chases through London's underbelly." Melissa Moore concluded in *School Library Journal* that "this novel is a rare gem."

BIOGRAPHICAL AND CRITICAL SOURCES:

PERIODICALS

Booklist, August 1, 2006, Jennifer Mattson, review of *Gideon the Cutpurse: Being the First Part of the Gideon Trilogy,* p. 63.

Bookseller, June 3, 2005, "Global Children's Deal for Simon & Schuster," p. 13; April 21, 2006, "DVD Trailer for *Gideon,*" p. 10.

Kirkus Reviews, June 1, 2006, review of *Gideon the Cutpurse,* p. 569.

Kliatt, September, 2006, Paula Rohrlick, review of *Gideon the Cutpurse,* p. 8.

Publishers Weekly, June 19, 2006, review of *Gideon the Cutpurse,* p. 63.

School Library Journal, July, 2006, Melissa Moore, review of *Gideon the Cutpurse,* p. 97; October, 2006, review of *Gideon the Cutpurse,* p. S58.

ONLINE

Authortrek.com, http://www.authortrek.com/ (December 17, 2006), brief profile of Linda Buckley-Archer.

BookLoons.com, http://www.bookloons.com/ (December 17, 2006), Hilary Williamson, review of *Gideon the Cutpurse.*

Gideon Trilogy, http://www.thegideontrilogy.com (December 17, 2006).

London Times Online, http://www.timesonline.co.uk/ (December 17, 2006), Amanda Craig, review of *Gideon the Cutpurse.*

*   *   *

BUMGARNER, John R. 1912-

(John Reed Bumgarner)

PERSONAL: Born January 30, 1912, in Lansing, NC; son of J.L.A. (a minister) and Margaret P. (a homemaker) Bumgarner; married August 30, 1947; wife's name Evelyn S. (a homemaker); children: John Reed, Jr., Evelyn Lyn. *Education:* Lincoln Memorial University, B.A.; Medical College of Virginia, M.D. *Politics:* Republican. *Religion:* Methodist.

ADDRESSES: Home—Greensboro, NC.

CAREER: Wesley Long Hospital, Greensboro, NC, cardiologist and head of cardiology department, 1954-73. Affiliate of American Board of Cardiology and American Board of Internal Medicine. *Military*

service: U.S. Army, Medical Corps, 1942-45, including time as Japanese prisoner of war; became major; received Bronze Star.

MEMBER: Young Men's Christian Association, Kiwanis.

WRITINGS:

Health of the Presidents: The 41 U.S. Presidents through 1993 from a Physician's Point of View, McFarland (Jefferson, NC), 1994.

Parade of the Dead: A U.S. Army Physician's Memoir of Imprisonment by the Japanese, 1942-1945, illustrated by Doris B. Hayes, McFarland (Jefferson, NC), 1995.

Sarah Childress Polk: A Biography of the Remarkable First Lady, McFarland (Jefferson, NC), 1997.

Life in the Methodist Parsonage, Vantage Press (New York, NY), 2000.

*   *   *

BUMGARNER, John Reed
    See BUMGARNER, John R.

*   *   *

BURNETT, John F.

PERSONAL: Married, wife's name Virginia (a professor); children: three. *Education:* University of Texas Austin, B.A., 1978.

ADDRESSES: Home—Austin, TX. *Office*—National Public Radio, 635 Massachusetts Ave., N.W., Washington, DC 20001.

CAREER: Journalist. Reporter for newspapers in Texas, 1979-83; United Press International, Guatemala City, Guatemala, reporter, 1983-86; National Public Radio, Washington, DC, southwest correspondent, 1986-2004, national desk correspondent, 2004—. Poynter Institute for Media Studies, faculty member, 1997 and 2002, and ethics fellow, 2006.

AWARDS, HONORS: Ford Foundation grant, 1997; silver prize, New York Festivals, for radio documentary "The Oil Century"; National Headliner Award, 2003, for investigative reporting; Alfred I. duPont-Columbia University Award, 2003, for coverage of Iraq war; Edward R. Murrow Award, Radio-Television News Directors Association, 2004, for investigative reporting.

WRITINGS:

Uncivilized Beasts and Shameless Hellions: Travels with an NPR Correspondent, Rodale (Emmaus, PA), 2006.

SIDELIGHTS: John F. Burnett, a National Public Radio (NPR) reporter based in Austin, Texas, is the author of *Uncivilized Beasts and Shameless Hellions: Travels with an NPR Correspondent.* In the work, Burnett chronicles his thirty-year career as a newsman, during which he witnessed atrocities committed during a Guatemalan uprising, investigated abuse in the American crop insurance system, reported on the 1993 federal government raid on the Branch Davidian compound in Texas, attended a "Death to America" rally in Peshawar, Pakistan, after 9/11, and served as an embedded reporter with the First Marine Division during the 2003 invasion of Iraq. In a section on the Hurricane Katrina disaster, he addresses the role of the journalist as "detached chronicler," writing, "Purists argue that journalists should never participate in a story—period. We bear witness to history; we don't step into it. But it's not that simple. We don't leave our humanity at home when we cover a disaster. Anytime I, as a journalist, record a person in misery and then walk away, I feel like the photographer who queasily described his role, saying, 'We came to take our trophies and left.' There's something unbecoming about that behavior, particularly if we can offer a small kindness without neglecting our job." According to a critic in *Publishers Weekly,* "This absorbing review of newsworthy events and intriguing people by an award-winning reporter is also a subtle manual about journalism."

BIOGRAPHICAL AND CRITICAL SOURCES:

BOOKS

Burnett, John F., *Uncivilized Beasts and Shameless Hellions: Travels with an NPR Correspondent,* Rodale (Emmaus, PA), 2006.

PERIODICALS

Publishers Weekly, July 24, 2006, review of *Uncivilized Beasts and Shameless Hellions,* p. 52.
Texas Monthly, September, 2006, Mike Shea, review of *Uncivilized Beasts and Shameless Hellions,* p. 60.

ONLINE

Written Voices Podcasts, http://writtenvoices.com/ (February 10, 2007), "John F. Burnett."*

*   *   *

BUSCH, Eberhard 1937-

PERSONAL: Born August 22, 1937, in Witten, Germany; son of Johannes (a pastor) and Margarete (a musician) Busch; married Beate H. Blum (a pastor), November 25, 1967; children: Emanuel, Christian, Sara, Nathanael. *Education:* Studied at institutions in Wuppertal, Göttingen, Heidelberg, and Münster, Germany, and Basel, Switzerland.

ADDRESSES: Home—Friedland, Germany. *Office*—Platz der Göttingen Sieben 2, D-37073 Göttingen, Germany. *E-mail*—ebusch@gwdg.de.

CAREER: Pastor of Reformed church in Uerkheim, Switzerland, 1969-86; University of Göttingen, Göttingen, Germany, professor of Reformed theology, 1986-2002, professor emeritus, 2002—, director of Karl Barth Research Center, 1986—. Princeton Theological Seminary, Warfield Lecturer, 2004; Campbell scholar in Decatur, GA; guest lecturer in the United States, 1985, and in Romania, Switzerland, Japan, Canada, Italy, and the Netherlands. Member of synod, Reformed Church, 1990-2006, and Evangelical Church in Deutschland, 1990-2002.

AWARDS, HONORS: Honorary doctorates from institutions in Romania and Hungary.

WRITINGS:

Pfarrer Dr. Wilhelm Busch: Ein Pietist in der Kaiserzeit, Schriftenmissions-Verlag (Gladbeck, Germany), 1969.

Karl Barths Lebenslauf: Nach seinen Briefen und autobiograph. Texten, Kaiser (Munich, Germany), 1975, translation by John Bowden published as *Karl Barth: His Life from Letters and Autobiographical Texts,* Fortress Press (Philadelphia, PA), 1976.

Freiheit und Autorität: Das Generationenproblem in der Sicht des alten Barth, Theologischer Verlag (Zurich, Switzerland), 1976.

Karl Barth und die Pietisten: d. Pietismuskritik d. jungen Karl Barth und ihre Erwiderung, Kaiser (Munich, Germany), 1978, translation by Daniel W. Bloesch published as *Karl Barth and the Pietists: The Young Karl Barth's Critique of Pietism and Its Response,* InterVarsity Press (Downers Grove, IL), 2004.

Juden und Christen im Schatten des Dritten Reiches: Ansätze zu e. Kritik d. Antisemitismus in d. Zeit d. Bekennenden Kirche, Kaiser (Munich, Germany), 1979.

(With Hinrich Stoevesandt) *Der Zug am Glockenseil: Vom Weg und Wirken Karl Barths,* Theologischer Verlag (Zurich, Switzerland), 1982.

Unter dem Bogen des einen Bundes: Karl Barth und die Juden 1933-1945, Neukirchener (Neukirchen-Vluyn, Germany), 1996.

(Editor) Karl Barth, *Gespräche, 1964-1968,* Theologischer Verlag (Zurich, Switzerland), 1997.

Grosse Leidenschaft: Einführung in die Theologie Karl Barths, Kaiser (Gütersloh, Germany), 1998, translation by Geoffrey W. Bromiley published as *The Great Passion: An Introduction to Karl Barth's Theology,* William B. Eerdmans Publishing (Grand Rapids, MI), 2004.

(Editor and contributor) *Reformationstag 1933: Dokumente der Begegnung Karl Barths mit dem Pfarrernotbund in Berlin,* Theologischer Verlag (Zurich, Switzerland), 1998.

(Editor) *Reformierte Bekenntnisschriften,* Neukirchener (Neukirchen-Vluyn, Germany), 2002.

(Editor) Karl Barth, *Briefe des Jahres 1933,* Theologischer Verlag (Zurich, Switzerland), 2004.

SIDELIGHTS: Eberhard Busch told *CA* that the focus of his research and writing is "the beginnings, the history, and the present situation of the Reformed and Presbyterian churches, and their theology; especially research on the theology of Karl Barth in Basel."

BIOGRAPHICAL AND CRITICAL SOURCES:

BOOKS

Dahling-Sander, Christoph, Margin Ernst, and Georg Plasger, editors, *Herausgeforderte Kirche: An-*

stösse, Wege, Perspektiven; Eberhard Busch zum 60. Geburtstag, Foedus (Wuppertal, Germany), 1997.

ONLINE

Eberhard Busch Home Page, http://www.gwdg.de/~ebusch/welcome.htm (December 23, 2006).

*   *   *

BUSHWELLER, Sarah 1977(?)-
(Sarah H.W. Bushweller, Libby Street, a joint pseudonym)

PERSONAL: Born c. 1977; daughter of Brian (in politics) and P. Raquel ("Rocky") Bushweller; married. *Education:* Graduated from University of Pittsburgh.

ADDRESSES: Home—New York, NY. *E-mail*—libby@libbystreet.com.

CAREER: Writer and novelist. Advertising executive at a pharmaceutical marketing firm.

WRITINGS:

WITH EMILY S. MORRIS UNDER JOINT PSEUDONYM LIBBY STREET

Happiness Sold Separately, Downtown Press (New York, NY), 2005.
Accidental It Girl, Downtown Press (New York, NY), 2006.

Authors' works have been translated into German and Dutch.

SIDELIGHTS: Sarah Bushweller and Emily S. Morris are the writing duo behind the chick-lit pseudonym of Libby Street. Bushweller, an advertising executive in New York, NY, and Morris, who holds a master's degree in screenwriting from Ohio University, have been the best of friends since they first met as preschoolers in a residential neighborhood of Dover, Delaware. In adulthood, their friendship evolved into a creative writing partnership that has resulted in two well-received books.

In their first novel, *Happiness Sold Separately,* main character Ryan Hadley watches her friends' lives thrive and prosper professionally, personally, and romantically, while her own boring existence seems to be taking her nowhere, except to a dead-end job in data entry and back home to a tiny, cramped apartment. She is still feeling the emotional toll of her breakup with Charlie, her ex-boyfriend and first love, who left four years earlier to take a job at a record company. Worse, Ryan feels she is becoming more and more peripheral to her friends' lives. Will's band has just scored a record contract, Audrey is busy with a promotion at work, and Veronica is assembling a career-making deal for her firm. To jolt herself into taking action, Ryan assembles "The Plan," a fifty-item list of things she has always wanted to do and desires she has never had the chance to fulfill. The items on the list range from the routine and easy, such as brush and floss every day, to the practical but difficult, such as get out of debt, to the fanciful and unlikely, such as become queen of an island nation. Still, the motivation of her list is undeniable, and Ryan's plan begins to show results. Her plans are unexpectedly derailed with Charlie's sudden reappearance in her life, as band manager for her friend Will. "Ryan's efforts to find herself will strike a chord with younger women," commented Aleksandra Kostovski in *Booklist.*

Photographer Sadie Price, the protagonist of *Accidental It Girl,* is a member of the often-reviled but equally sought-after paparazzi, those specialist photographers whose candid shots of celebrities and screen stars sell tabloids by the millions. The life of a celebrity photographer is not easy. Sadie must dodge her subjects' anger and sneak about in difficult terrain in search of the perfect shot. Still, she feels her work has its place in the world, and it certainly affords her ample financial reward. When one of her photographic subjects takes a keen interest in Sadie and in turning her paparazzi intensity back on herself, she begins to question whether she has made a good career choice after all. After she takes some questionable photos of Hollywood actor Ethan Wyatt, pictures that cause him considerable personal and professional grief, he decides that he will take his revenge on the photographer that caused him so much trouble. Suddenly, the tables are turned, and Sadie becomes the subject of Ethan's determined efforts to catch her in an unguarded moment. Her life is jolted when a picture of her appears in the tabloids, suggesting that she is dating a particular movie star, and causing her colleagues and other photographers to focus their attention on her. Sadie is not dating any actor, and the photograph of her and the actor simply depicts an unfortunate suggestion of involvement between them. The turn of events makes her realize what her professional work has done to the people who appear in her photos. Realizing that Ethan Wyatt is the paparazzo behind the pictures causes her to further question her ethics and career. Bushweller and Morris have "collaborated to create a singular, spirited voice," remarked Kostovski.

BIOGRAPHICAL AND CRITICAL SOURCES:

PERIODICALS

Booklist, June 1, 2005, review of *Happiness Sold Separately,* p. 1757; September 15, 2006, Aleksandra Kostovski, review of *Accidental It Girl,* p. 29.
Delaware State News, June 14, 2004, Jenna Kania, "Dover Natives a Novel Pair," profile of Sarah Bushweller and Emily S. Morris.
News Journal (Wilmington, DE), December 7, 2004, Christopher Yasiejko, "Dover Friends Always Finish Each Other's Thoughts, Decide to Write a Book," profile of Sarah Bushweller and Emily S. Morris.

ONLINE

Book Fetish, http://www.bookfetish.org/ (January 22, 2007), Vivian Whipp, review of *Accidental It Girl.*
BookLoons, http://www.bookloons.com/ (January 22, 2007), Tarah Schaeffer, review of *Happiness Sold Separately;* Kim Atchue-Cusella, review of *Accidental It Girl.*
ChickLitGurrl Web log, http://chicklitgurrl.blogspot.com/ (November, 2006), profile of Sarah Bushweller and Emily S. Morris.
Fallen Angel Reviews, http://www.fallenangelreviews.com/ (January 22, 2007), review of *Accidental It Girl.*
Libby Street's Home Page, http://www.libbystreet.com (January 22, 2007).*

BUSHWELLER, Sarah H.W.
See BUSHWELLER, Sarah

*   *   *

BUZBEE, Lewis 1957-

PERSONAL: Born 1957, in CA; married; children: Maddy. *Education:* Warren Wilson College, Asheville, NC, M.F.A.

ADDRESSES: Home—San Francisco, CA. *Office*—University of San Francisco, Master of Fine Arts in Writing Program, 2130 Fulton St., San Francisco, CA 94117-1080; fax: 415-422-6996. *E-mail*—buzbee@usfca.edu.

CAREER: Writer and educator. Chronicle Books, CA, sales rep, beginning 1986; University of San Francisco, Master of Fine Arts in Writing Program, San Francisco, CA, adjunct professor of writing, 2000—. Previously worked in the bookstores Upstart Crow, San Jose, CA, and Printers Inc., Palo Alto, CA, manager.

WRITINGS:

Fliegelman's Desire (novel), Ballantine Books (New York, NY), 1990.
After the Gold Rush: Stories, Tupelo Press (Dorset, VT), 2004.
The Yellow-Lighted Bookshop: A Memoir, a History, Graywolf Press (St. Paul, MN), 2006.

Contributor to periodicals, including *Harper's, Paris Review, Gentleman's Quarterly, New York Times Book Review, Black Warrior Review,* and *ZYZZYVA;* contributor to *Best American Poetry 1995.*

SIDELIGHTS: Lewis Buzbee is a writer whose first novel, *Fliegelman's Desire,* tells the story of a disenfranchised man whose perpetual longings lead him to quit his job and go to work in a bookstore. Once there he meets Mimi, who, like Fliegelman, lives a life of vague, unfulfilled desires. When the two begin an affair, it sends their lives into a bizarre direction. A *Publishers Weekly* contributor noted that the author "has a playful imagination and a charming way of animating the ordinary."

Like Fliegelman from *Fliegelman's Desire,* Buzbee also worked in bookstores and recounts his love of books in *The Yellow-Lighted Bookshop: A Memoir, a History.* The author tells of his first fascination with books as an elementary student and his time working as a bookseller's rep. He also delves into the history of bookmaking and bookselling from ancient to modern times. Allison Block, writing in *Booklist,* noted: "Both anecdotal and eloquent, *The Yellow-Lighted Bookshop* is a tribute to those who crave the cozy confines of a bookshop." A *Publishers Weekly* contributor commented that the author writes about "everything one would want to know about the modern business of bookselling." A contributor to the *Shapiro UGLi Booktalk* blog wrote: "This charmingly honest memoir is a garden of personal joy and celebration where a book geek's sensibilities and appreciation for the history of books and bookstores blossom in full color."

Buzbee told *CA:* "A book report my sophomore year in high school [was what first got me interested in writing]. A cousin suggested *The Grapes of Wrath,* and when I finished the first chapter of that, I started my first short story."

In response to the question "What kind of effect do you hope your books will have?" Buzbee said: "I suppose what I'd want most is what books have given me—a sense of the power of the written word and all the pleasure that comes with that, and a strong urge to get out of the reading chair and become engaged in the world. If someday I can write a book that's strong and clear enough to get a teenager more engaged in the world, then I'll be very happy."

BIOGRAPHICAL AND CRITICAL SOURCES:

BOOKS

Buzbee, Lewis, *The Yellow-Lighted Bookshop: A Memoir, a History,* Graywolf Press (St. Paul, MN), 2006.

PERIODICALS

Booklist, June 1, 2006, Allison Block, review of *The Yellow-Lighted Bookshop,* p. 20.

Publishers Weekly, April 17, 2006, Penny Kaganoff, review of *Fliegelman's Desire,* p. 184; April 17, 2006, review of *The Yellow-Lighted Bookshop,* p. 184.

ONLINE

After the MFA, http://afterthemfa.com/ (November 16, 2006), "A Post-MFA Done Good: Interview with Lewis Buzbee."
Booksmith Bookstore Blog, http://booksmith.blogspot. com/ (November 16, 2006), brief profile of author.
Shapiro UGLi Booktalk Blog, http://mblog.lib.umich. edu/UGLread/ (November 16, 2006), review of *The Yellow-Lighted Bookshop.*
The Book's the Thing Blog, http://blogs.nsls.info/ thebook/ (August 31, 2006), "An Interview with Lewis Buzbee, *Author of The Yellow-Lighted Bookshop*"; (November 16, 2006), review of *The Yellow-Lighted Bookshop.*
Tupelo Press Web site, https://www.tupelopress.org/ (November 16, 2006), brief profile of author.
University of San Francisco College of Arts and Sciences Web site, http://artsci.usfca.edu/ (November 16, 2006), faculty profile of author.

*　*　*

BYERS, A. Martin 1937-

PERSONAL: Born 1937, in Thunder Bay, Ontario, Canada. *Education:* McGill University, B.A., 1966, M.A., 1969; State University of New York at Albany, Ph.D., 1987.

ADDRESSES: Home—Montreal, Quebec, Canada. *Office*—Department of Anthropology, Stephen Leacock Bldg., McGill University, 855 Sherbrooke St. W., Montreal, Quebec H3A 2T7, Canada. *E-mail*—a. byers@mcgill.ca.

CAREER: McGill University, Montreal, Quebec, Canada, research affiliate of the anthropology department.

WRITINGS:

Ohio Hopewell Episode: Paradigm Lost and Para- digm Gained, University of Akron Press (Akron, OH), 2004.

Cahokia: A World Renewal Cult Heterarchy, University Press of Florida (Gainesville, FL), 2006.

*　*　*

BYRD, Lee Merrill

PERSONAL: Born in NJ; married Bobby Byrd (a publisher and author); children: two sons, one daughter.

ADDRESSES: Office—Cinco Puntos Press, 701 Texas, El Paso, TX 79901.

CAREER: During early career, worked as a technical writer at Fort Bliss, TX; El Paso Natural Gas, El Paso, TX, magazine editor for three years; Cinco Puntos Press, El Paso, cofounder, copublisher, senior editor, and president, 1985—.

AWARDS, HONORS: Southwest Book Award, Border Regional Library Association, 1993, for outstanding achievement in bringing national recognition to their regional literature; Southwest Book Award and Stephen F. Turner Award, Texas Institute of Letters, 1993, for *My Sister Disappears;* Dobie-Paisano Fellowship, 1997; Skipping Stones Honor Book Award, Southwest Book Award, Paterson Poetry Center Prize, and Teddy Award from the Texas Writers League, all 2003, all for *The Treasure on Gold Street;* Cultural Freedom Fellowship, Lannan Foundation, 2005; American Book Award, for excellence in publishing; inducted into the Latino Literary Hall of Fame; five National Endowment for the Arts publishing grants; three Texas Commission for the Arts grants; two grants from Fideicomiso para la Cultura de México y Estados Unidos, funded by the Belles Artes and the Rockefeller Foundation.

WRITINGS:

My Sister Disappears: Stories and a Novella, Southern Methodist University Press (Dallas, TX), 1993.
The Treasure on Gold Street = El tesoro en la Calle Oro: A Neighborhood Story in English and Spanish (bilingual children's picture book), illustrated by Antonio Castro L., translated by Sharon Franco, Cinco Puntos Press (El Paso, TX), 2003.

Lover Boy = Juanito el cariñoso (bilingual counting book for children), illustrated by Francisco Delgado, Cinco Puntos Press (El Paso, TX), 2005.

Riley's Fire (novel), Algonquin Books of Chapel Hill (Chapel Hill, NC), 2006.

SIDELIGHTS: Lee Merrill Byrd is the founder, with her husband, Bobby Byrd, of Cinco Puntos Press, which specializes in publishing the multicultural literatures of the American Southwest. She is also the author of fiction for children and adults. In *My Sister Disappears: Stories and a Novella,* the author "paints disturbingly realistic pictures of the pain and beauty of difficult family situations," according to David Cline in *Booklist.* Cline also declared the stories "remarkably beautiful." Byrd's title story is about the breakdown of a girl named Emily, who is getting ready to go to the prom. Byrd returns to Emily again in the collection's novella. The author, whose own two children suffered serious burns, also writes of badly burned children and their families in two other tales. A *Publishers Weekly* contributor reported that "Byrd has a plain style that lays bare the quirks inherent in family relationships." Kathy J. Whitson further commented in *Studies in Short Fiction:* "The strength of the volume may be that it forces us to examine the unthinkable and the unpleasant, as Byrd shows us images that make us instantly turn away in a revulsion that diminishes us until we consent to take a second, more compassionate look."

In her first novel, *Riley's Fire,* Byrd writes of young Riley Martin, who ends up in a burn clinic after playing with matches and gasoline. With burns covering nearly two-thirds of his body, Riley finds himself trying to cope in a new world of fellow burn victims and distraught parents. Writing in the *State,* Claudia Smith Brinson felt that "*Riley's Fire* is a near-perfect novel, elegantly compressed, deep in heart and spirit, miraculously true to a young voice and a child's truth." Brinson added: "Among the book's many strengths is its remorseless portrayal of Riley's mom. She is heartbroken and crazed in her grief." Debbie Bogenschutz commented in the *Library Journal* that the author "does a beautiful job of inhabiting the mind of a seven-year-old boy." Marta Segal Block, writing in *Booklist,* observed that there is a "seductive dreamlike quality to both Riley and the book," while *Texas Monthly* contributor Mike Shea called *Riley's Fire* a "singularly powerful book."

Byrd has also written two bilingual children's books: *The Treasure on Gold Street = El tesoro en la Calle Oro: A Neighborhood Story in English and Spanish* and *Lover Boy = Juanito el cariñoso. Lover Boy* is a counting book featuring a young boy who likes to give kisses, from one for his big sister to two for his dad, and three for his mother. The story then follows the boy as he goes on to other kissing encounters. *School Library Journal* critic Maria Otero-Boisvert called the story "tender" and enjoyed the "enthusiastic text." A *Kirkus Reviews* contributor referred to *Lover Boy* as "a winning story of love of family and friends," while a *Children's Bookwatch* reviewer deemed the book a "fun and entertaining guide to counting."

The Treasure on Gold Street features Hannah, who narrates the story about her friendship with Isabel, a mentally disabled woman. Young and innocent, Hannah sees her friend as maintaining her childlike view of the world while Hannah's friend Erica, who is a little older than Hannah, maintains a more reserved attitude toward Isabel. "Cast as narrative, it is actually a work of sociology based on the lives of Byrd's family and neighbors," according to a *Kirkus Reviews* contributor, who also noted that *The Treasure on Gold Street*'s length and the subject matter make it a book that is best read to children and then discussed later. *School Library Journal* contributor Ann Welton concluded: "This is at once a sensitive treatment of the mentally challenged and a celebration of the real-life Isabel."

BIOGRAPHICAL AND CRITICAL SOURCES:

PERIODICALS

Austin Chronicle, June 9, 2006, Melanie Haupt, review of *Riley's Fire.*

Booklist, December 15, 1993, David Cline, review of *My Sister Disappears: Stories and a Novella,* p. 737; January 1, 1994, David Cline, review of *My Sister Disappears,* p. 804; April 1, 2006, Marta Segal Block, review of *Riley's Fire,* p. 18.

Children's Bookwatch, July, 2006, review of *Lover Boy = Juanito el cariñoso*

Kirkus Reviews, November 1, 2003, review of *The Treasure on Gold Street = El tesoro en la Calle Oro: A Neighborhood Story in English and Spanish,* p. 1309; March 15, 2006, review of *Lover Boy,* p. 287.

Library Journal, February 1, 2006, Debbie Bogenschutz, review of *Riley's Fire,* p. 69.

Publishers Weekly, October 25, 1993, review of *My Sister Disappears,* p. 57.

School Library Journal, December, 2003, Ann Welton, review of *The Treasure on Gold Street,* p. 142; June, 2006, Maria Otero-Boisvert, review of *Lover Boy,* p. 142.

State (Columbia, SC), June 14, 2006, Claudia Smith Brinson, review of *Riley's Fire.*

Studies in Short Fiction, spring, 1996, Kathy J. Whitson, review of *My Sister Disappears,* p. 298.

Texas Monthly, May, 2006, Mike Shea, review of *Riley's Fire,* p. 54.

ONLINE

Cinco Puntos Press Web site, http://www.cincopuntos. com/ (December 18, 2006), brief profile of Lee Merrill Byrd.

Lannan Foundation Web site, http://www.lannan.org/ (December 18, 2006), brief profile of Lee Merrill Byrd.

Planeta.com, http://www.planeta.com/ (December 18, 2006), Soll Sussman, "Cinco Puntos," interview with Lee Merrill Byrd.

C

CALLAHAN, Tom

PERSONAL: Male.

ADDRESSES: Office—Golf Digest, 20 Westport Rd., P.O. Box 850, Wilton, CT 06897. *Agent*—David Black, David Black Literary Agency, 156 5th Ave., Ste. 608, New York, NY 10010. *E-mail*—callahan@ golfdigest.com.

CAREER: Journalist. *Golf Digest,* Wilton, CT, columnist. Has worked as a reporter for the *San Diego Union, U.S. News & World Report, Washington Post, Newsweek,* and the *National,* and as a senior writer for *Time.*

AWARDS, HONORS: National Headliner Award.

WRITINGS:

NONFICTION

(With Dave Kindred) *Around the World in Eighteen Holes,* Doubleday (New York, NY), 1994.
In Search of Tiger: A Journey through Golf with Tiger Woods, Crown (New York, NY), 2003.
The Bases Were Loaded (And So Was I): Up Close and Personal with the Greatest Names in Sports, Crown (New York, NY), 2004.
Dancin' with Sonny Liston, Mainstream Publishing (Edinburgh, Scotland), 2005.

Johnny U: The Life and Times of John Unitas, Crown (New York, NY), 2006.

SIDELIGHTS: Tom Callahan, a former reporter with the *National* and the *Washington Post,* is the author of a number of sports biographies, including *In Search of Tiger: A Journey through Golf with Tiger Woods* and *Johnny U: The Life and Times of John Unitas.* A longtime columnist for *Golf Digest,* Callahan published his first book, *Around the World in Eighteen Holes,* in 1994 with coauthor Dave Kindred. In the work, the authors chronicle their 37,319-mile journey to play eighteen holes of golf on eighteen of the world's most exotic courses. Their adventure, beginning at St. Andrews in Scotland and ending at Augusta National Golf Club in Georgia, took them to Iceland, Scotland, Russia, Nepal, and Singapore, among other nations. "In less talented hands, the book could have been a self-absorbed slog," wrote David Ellis in *People.* Rather, the book is "an engaging, . . . insightful read." In the words of *Booklist* contributor Bill Ott, "Anyone who has dreamed of the ultimate golf vacation will savor each page of this fantasy come to life."

Callahan profiles golfing phenomenon Tiger Woods in *In Search of Tiger,* "a comprehensive examination of the man, his talent, his competition and the world of professional golf," according to a *Publishers Weekly* reviewer. The author traces Woods's professional career, including his victories in major tournaments, and pays special attention to the golfer's relationship with his father. *In Search of Tiger* received mixed reviews, with several critics noting that Woods, a famously guarded individual, makes a difficult subject for a biography. In *Booklist* Gilbert Taylor remarked that "Callahan's assemblage of anecdote and conversation is more a sequence of digressions than an unfolding narrative," and a *Kirkus Reviews* contributor observed that, despite the author's efforts, Woods "continues to be a pleasant and graceful cipher." *Sports Illustrated* reviewer Jeff Silverman, on the other hand, felt that Callahan "seems to be in search of larger game than even the most prized golfer in the universe, and it is the perspective he picks up along the way that makes his book more than just another recap of Woods's accomplishments." Writing in the *New York Times Book Review,* Charles Salzburg called the work "a loving appreciation of golf and those who play it, using the otherworldly Tiger Woods as the standard against whom all other golfers will be forever judged."

Hall of Fame quarterback John Unitas is the subject of *Johnny U,* a legend of the early decades of the National Football League, as well as "a look at the nature of the sport in his day," a *Publishers Weekly* critic stated. Unitas, a native of Pittsburgh who was cut by his hometown Steelers during his rookie year, eventually played eighteen seasons and led the Baltimore Colts to three National Football League championships. According to *Washington Post Book World* critic Jonathan Yardley, the author "graciously and gracefully pays Unitas the tribute due him without lapsing into sentimentality." Callahan's stories describe the world Unitas inhabited, "providing insight into this cool, collected leader who inspired his teammates and epitomized what it was to be a professional football player during the game's halcyon days," remarked a *Kirkus Reviews* critic.

BIOGRAPHICAL AND CRITICAL SOURCES:

PERIODICALS

Booklist, June 1, 1994, Bill Ott, review of *Around the World in Eighteen Holes,* p. 1757; January 1, 2003, Gilbert Taylor, review of *In Search of Tiger: A Journey through Golf with Tiger Woods,* p. 831.

Entertainment Weekly, April 30, 2004, Warren Cohen, review of *The Bases Were Loaded (And So Was I): Up Close and Personal with the Greatest Names in Sports,* p. 170.

Kirkus Reviews, January 1, 2003, review of *In Search of Tiger,* p. 33; June 15, 2006, review of *Johnny U: The Life and Times of John Unitas,* p. 610.

Library Journal, January 1, 2003, William O. Scheeren, review of *In Search of Tiger,* p. 123; September 1, 2006, John Maxymuk, review of *Johnny U,* p. 154.

New York Times Book Review, April 27, 2003, Charles Salzberg, "Books in Brief: Nonfiction," review of *In Search of Tiger.*

People, July 11, 1994, David Ellis, review of *Around the World in Eighteen Holes,* p. 26; June 16, 2003, review of *In Search of Tiger,* p. 66.

Post-Gazette (Pittsburgh, PA), September 3, 2006, Allen Barra, "How Quarterback Went from Steelers Reject to NFL Legend," review of *Johnny U.*

Publishers Weekly, May 16, 1994, review of *Around the World in Eighteen Holes,* p. 57; February 17, 2003, review of *In Search of Tiger,* p. 64; July 31, 2006, review of *Johnny U,* p. 63.

Sports Illustrated, May 5, 2003, Jeff Silverman, "Still Searching," review of *In Search of Tiger,* p. G19.

Washington Post Book World, October 22, 2006, Jonathan Yardley, "How a Legendary Athlete Became the Heart of His Team—and of His City," review of *Johnny U,* p. 2.

ONLINE

Blogcritics Magazine Web site, http://blogcritics.org/ (January 6, 2007), Tim Gebhart, review of *Johnny U.**

* * *

CALLO, Joseph
 See CALLO, Joseph F.

* * *

CALLO, Joseph F. 1929-
 (Joseph Callo, Joseph Francis Callo)

PERSONAL: Born December 16, 1929, in New York, NY; son of Joseph Francis and Mary Ellen Callo; married Susan Catherine Jones, June 10, 1952 (divorced, November, 1978); married Sally Chin McElwreath (senior vice president of utility/energy company), March 17, 1979; children: (first marriage) Joseph Francis III, James D., Mary Ellen, Kathleen E., Patricia A.; (second marriage) Robert Joseph McElwreath (stepson). *Education:* Yale University, B.A., 1952.

ADDRESSES: Home—New York, NY. *E-mail*—jfc1952@aol.com.

CAREER: Marketing executive, writer, and educator. Joseph F. Callo Inc., New York, NY, account executive, 1952-58; Potts-Woodbury Inc., New York, NY, vice president and director, 1958-60; Callo & Carroll Inc., New York, NY, president, 1960-74; Callo Berger Albanese Inc., chairman of the board of directors and creative director, 1974-75; National Broadcasting Company, Inc. (NBC), and Public Broadcasting Service (PBS), television producer, 1976-78; Albert Frank/FCB. Inc., New York, NY, executive vice president, 1978-81; Grey Advertising, senior vice president, 1981-83; Muir Cornelius Moore, Inc., senior vice president, 1983-84. Also St. John's University, New York, NY, adjunct associate professor of communication arts, 1965-78; United States Navy, member of marketing review group, 1973-74; and National Maritime Historical Society, board of advisors. *Military service:* U.S. Navy; retired from Naval Reserve as Rear Admiral.

MEMBER: Society of Nautical Research (Great Britain), Surface Navy Association (founding president of greater New York chapter), The Naval Club (London, England), Yale Club of New York.

AWARDS, HONORS: George Foster Peabody Broadcasting Award, for work as line producer on the NBC-TV prime-time special *Tut: The Boy King;* Telly Award for script for *The Second Life of 20 West Ninth*; Samuel Eliot Morison Award, Naval Order of the United States, for *John Paul Jones: America's First Sea Warrior;* Author of the Year, *Naval History* magazine, 1998.

WRITINGS:

(As Joseph Callo) *Legacy of Leadership: Lessons from Admiral Lord Nelson,* Hellgate Press (Central Point, OR), 1999.

Nelson Speaks: Admiral Lord Nelson in His Own Words, Naval Institute Press (Annapolis, MD), 2001.

Nelson in the Caribbean: The Hero Emerges, 1784-1787, Naval Institute Press (Annapolis, MD), 2003.

(With Alastair Wilson) *Who's Who in Naval History: From 1550 to the Present,* Routledge (New York, NY), 2004.

(As Joseph Callo) *John Paul Jones: America's First Sea Warrior,* Naval Institute Press (Annapolis, MD), 2006.

Also author of the script for *The Second Life of 20 West Ninth,* PBS and the History Channel; contributor to periodicals, including *Naval History, U.S. Naval Institute Proceedings, New York Post, Sea History, Yale Free Press, Kansas City Business Journal,* and *Canadian Yachting.*

SIDELIGHTS: Joseph F. Callo served in the U.S. Navy and the Naval Reserve and has written several historical books about prominent naval leaders, including three books about Admiral Lord Nelson. In *Nelson in the Caribbean: The Hero Emerges, 1784-1787,* Callo analyzes three years in the life of the famous British admiral. The focus is unusual in that it reflects on Nelson's time as a young Royal Navy captain in the Caribbean, during which he was beset more by administrative problems rather than wartime heroics. Carolyn S. Knapp, writing in the *Historian,* commented that the author "is convinced that the course of his subject's life was determined by the Caribbean experiences." Knapp added: "The result is an accessible and enjoyable work." *U.S. Naval Institute Proceedings* contributor Richard Seamon wrote that the author "manages to show how the geopolitics of the time, the Royal Navy's internal politics, and even Nelson's colorful love life combined to mould the character of the man."

John Paul Jones: America's First Sea Warrior focuses on the first and perhaps still best-known American naval hero, whose sarcophagus rests in the U.S. Naval Academy Chapel. In his biography, Callo presents Jones as the epitome of naval officers as he recounts his youth, successes, and failures. The author also includes tactical and strategic commentary on sea battles. Writing in the *U.S. Naval Institute Proceedings,* William M. Fowler, Jr., commented that the "biography challenges us once again to reflect on this officer and the cause for which he fought." A *Seacoast-NH.com* contributor wrote: "While others have described Jones as egomaniacal, reckless or even possibly suffering from a bipolar personality disorder, Callo sees a driven, but admirable, even a visionary, figure."

BIOGRAPHICAL AND CRITICAL SOURCES:

PERIODICALS

Historian, winter, 2004, Carolyn S. Knapp, review of *Nelson in the Caribbean: The Hero Emerges, 1784-1787,* p. 864.

U.S. Naval Institute Proceedings, January, 2003, Richard Seamon, review of *Nelson in the Caribbean,* p. 102; April, 2006, William M. Fowler, Jr., review of *John Paul Jones: America's First Sea Warrior,* pp. 84-85.

ONLINE

Joseph Callo Home Page, http://www.josephcallo.com (November 16, 2006).
SeacoastNH.com, http://seacoastnh.com/ (November 16, 2006), review of *John Paul Jones.*
U.S. Naval Institute Web site, http://www.usni.org/ (November 16, 2006), profile of author.

* * *

CALLO, Joseph Francis
    See CALLO, Joseph F.

* * *

CARDOZA, Anthony L. 1947-

PERSONAL: Born January 31, 1947, in Berkeley, CA; married, 1989; children: one. *Education:* Princeton University, Ph.D.

ADDRESSES: Office—History Department, Loyola University, Chicago, 6525 N. Sheridan Rd., Chicago, IL, 60626. *E-mail*—acardoz@luc.edu.

CAREER: Historian, educator, and writer. Loyola University, Chicago, IL, professor of history.

AWARDS, HONORS: Howard R. Marraro prize, American Historical Association, 1998.

WRITINGS:

Agrarian Elites and Italian Fascism: The Province of Bologna, 1901-1926, Princeton University Press (Princeton, NJ), 1982.
Aristocrats in Bourgeois Italy: The Piedmontese Nobility, 1861-1930, Cambridge University Press (New York, NY), 1997.
Patrizi in un Mondo Plebeio, Donzelli Editore (Rome, Italy), 1999.
Benito Mussolini: The First Fascist, Pearson Longman (New York, NY), 2006.
(With Geoffrey Symcox) *La Storia di Torino* (title means "The History of Turin"), Einaudi (Turin, Italy), 2006.

Contributor to scholarly journals, including *Journal of Modern History* and *European History Quarterly.*

SIDELIGHTS: Anthony L. Cardoza is an historian who specializes in modern Italian social and political history. In his book *Agrarian Elites and Italian Fascism: The Province of Bologna, 1901-1926,* Cardoza writes about the varieties of fascism and fascism's development in local and regional areas. Focusing on both the culture and the economy of the era, the author "portrays the dynamic, development of agriculture and commerce, labor and politics, finance and journalism," according to *History Teacher* contributor James A. Young. Writing that the book is "bound to become a classic of its genre," Young also noted that the author "has fashioned a highly useful instrument for the better understanding of history on several levels." F.M. Snowden wrote in the *English Historical Review* that the author "analyses the violent reaction of landlords and commercial farmers in Bologna province to the subversive challenge presented by the unionization of farmworkers and sharecroppers." Noting that "Cardoza's work fills an important gap in the field," Snowden went on to write: "Cardoza's work is original . . . in the wealth of new material he presents in a sound and workmanlike book." In a review in the *American Historical Review,* Donald Howard Bell noted that the author "has written a study that in some respects supplies a benchmark for future investigations."

Aristocrats in Bourgeois Italy: The Piedmontese Nobility, 1861-1930 focuses on the growing influence of industrialization and democratic views on the Piedmontese nobility from the late middle ages to the Risorgimento era in Italy. The author discusses the nobility's slide from political and social influence, their adaptability to change, and their plans for survival. Charles L. Bertrand, writing in the *Canadian Journal of History,* commented: "The author's view contrasts sharply with the perceived wisdom that the story of the nobility in the nineteenth century is one of slow, but inevitable, amalgamation with the bourgeoisie. Cardoza demonstrates convincingly that the Piedmontese nobility continued to inculcate aristocratic values in their children into the twentieth century." Writing in the *Journal of Social History,* Raymond Grew noted that the author is able to "present his careful research on the Piedmontese nobility as a case study with broader implications for Italian social and political history." Grew added: "The research is remarkable in extent and care. Because the number of cases is necessarily small, Cardoza eschews elaborate statistical manipulations, relying primarily on percentages. Individual readers may in some instances choose to give a slightly different emphasis to the patterns Cardoza uncovers, but his basic claims appear irrefutable." *History: Review of New Books* contributor Andrew Rolle wrote that the author "has produced a splendid account of an important component of Italian life." Rolle also pointed out: "No other book in English covers this topic." A contributor to the *Historian* wrote that *Aristocrats in Bourgeois Italy* "has been praised as a major contribution to our understanding of both the Italian and wider European nobility."

BIOGRAPHICAL AND CRITICAL SOURCES:

PERIODICALS

American Historical Review, February, 1984, Donald Howard Bell, review of *Agrarian Elites and Italian Fascism: The Province of Bologna, 1901-1926,* pp. 160-162.
Canadian Journal of History, April, 1999, Charles L. Bertrand, review of *Aristocrats in Bourgeois Italy: The Piedmontese Nobility, 1861-1930,* p. 112.
English Historical Review, October, 1985, F.M. Snowden, review of *Agrarian Elites and Italian Fascism,* pp. 932-933.
Historian, winter, 2000, review of *Aristocrats in Bourgeois Italy,* p. 376.
History: Review of New Books, spring, 1999, Andrew Rolle, review of *Aristocrats in Bourgeois Italy,* p. 123.
History Teacher, February, 1984, James A. Young, review of *Agrarian Elites and Italian Fascism,* pp. 310-311.
Journal of Modern History, June, 2000, David Laven, review of *Aristocrats in Bourgeois Italy,* p. 547.
Journal of Social History, winter, 1999, Raymond Grew, review of *Aristocrats in Bourgeois Italy,* p. 507.

ONLINE

American Historical Association Web site, http://www.historians.org/ (November 17, 2006), information on Howard R. Marraro Prize in Italian History.
Loyola University Chicago Web site, http://www.luc.edu/ (November 17, 2006), faculty profile of author.

*   *   *

CARTER, Brian S. 1957-

PERSONAL: Born April 12, 1957, in La Mesa, CA; son of Arthur Robert (in U.S. Navy) and Dolores (a homemaker) Carter; married Angela Powell (a nurse), June 4, 2005; children: Sean, Yvonne, Jacquelyn, Rebecca Ewing. *Ethnicity:* "Caucasian." *Education:* Attended U.S. Coast Guard Academy, 1975-76; David Lipscomb College, B.S., 1979; University of Tennessee, M.D., 1983. *Religion:* Christian. *Hobbies and other interests:* Running, reading, music, fly fishing.

ADDRESSES: Home—Nashville, TN. *Office*—Vanderbilt Children's Hospital, Vanderbilt University, 11111 Doctor's Office Tower, Nashville, TN 37232-9544. *E-mail*—brian.carter@vanderbilt.edu.

CAREER: U.S. Army, Medical Corps, 1983-96, leaving service as lieutenant colonel; Medical College of Georgia, Augusta, associate professor, 1996-99; Vanderbilt University, Nashville, TN, professor of pediatrics, 1999—. University of Colorado, Denver, assistant professor, 1991-94. *Military service:* U.S. Army Reserve, 1979-83; received Bronze Star and Meritorious Service Medal.

MEMBER: American Academy of Pediatrics, National Perinatal Association, American Society for Bioethics and Humanities, Southern Society for Pediatric Research.

AWARDS, HONORS: Research support from National Hospice and Palliative Care Organization, 2003.

WRITINGS:

Palliative Care for Infants, Children, and Adolescents: A Practical Handbook, Johns Hopkins University Press (Baltimore, MD), 2004.

SIDELIGHTS: Brian S. Carter told *CA* that his writing is inspired by "my experiences in dealing with critically ill children and their parents."

* * *

CELANI, David P. 1946-

PERSONAL: Born June 6, 1946, in Englewood, NJ; son of Pasquale (a mechanical engineer) and Maude (a homemaker) Celani; married, 1968; wife's name Veronica H. (a state commissioner of social welfare). *Education:* Rutgers University, B.A., 1968; University of Vermont, M.A., 1972, Ph.D., 1974. *Hobbies and other interests:* Kayaking, skiing, auto racing.

ADDRESSES: Home—Jericho, VT. *E-mail*—celani1@ adelphia.net.

CAREER: Licensed psychologist in private practice in Burlington and South Burlington, VT, 1975-2001. Member of adjunct faulty, University of Vermont, 1978-84, and St. Michael's College, 1986-92; Onion River Educational Network, presenter of workshops for mental health professionals.

MEMBER: Sports Car Club of America.

WRITINGS:

The Treatment of the Borderline Patient: Applying Fairbairns Object Relations Theory in the Clinical Setting, International Universities Press (Madison, CT), 1993.
The Illusion of Love: Why the Battered Woman Returns to Her Abuser, Columbia University Press (New York, NY), 1994.

Leaving Home: The Art of Separating from Your Difficult Family, Columbia University Press (New York, NY), 2004.

Contributor to periodicals, including *American Journal of Psychoanalysis.*

* * *

CHAMBERLIN, E.R. 1926-2006
  (Eric Russell Chamberlin)

OBITUARY NOTICE— See index for *CA* sketch: Born May 25, 1926, in Kingston, Jamaica; died December 8, 2006. Historian and author. Chamberlin was the author of numerous popular history books ranging from ancient Rome to twentieth-century Britain. Although he was born in Jamaica, he returned to England with his father during the Great Depression. Chamberlin dropped out of school when he was fourteen and became an apprentice leather dresser. When he was old enough, he eagerly left this work behind to enlist in the Royal Navy in 1944. He served in the military until 1947 and then found work at the Norwich Public Library. It was here that his real education began, and Chamberlin took advantage of his vocation by reading history texts avidly. He later also worked at the Holborn Public Library and then for the book division at Readers' Digest. His first book, *The Count of Virtue: Giangaleazzo Visconti, Duke of Milan,* was released in 1965. This would be followed by thirty more books over the next three decades. Among these are *The Bad Popes* (1969), *The Sack of Rome* (1979), *The Nineteenth Century* (1983), *The Emperor, Charlemagne* (1986), and *The Tower of London: An Illustrated History* (1989). Also active in historical preservation projects, Chamberlin helped rescue the Guildford Institute building from destruction in 1982 and had a monument to Admiral Horatio Nelson constructed on Mt. Etna in Italy. For the former endeavor, Chamberlin was recognized with an honorary degree from the University of Surrey in 1982.

OBITUARIES AND OTHER SOURCES:

PERIODICALS

Times (London, England), January 26, 2007, p. 69.

CHAMBERLIN, Eric Russell
See CHAMBERLIN, E.R.

*   *   *

CHILDS, Mark C. 1959-

PERSONAL: Born June, 1959, in Roseville, CA. *Education:* Massachusetts Institute of Technology, B.S., 1981; University of Oregon, M.Arch., 1983; University of Washington, Seattle, M.P.A., 1991.

ADDRESSES: Home—Albuquerque, NM. *Office*—School of Architecture and Planning, University of New Mexico, Albuquerque, NM 87131. *E-mail*—mchilds@unm.edu.

CAREER: Arrowstreet, Boston, MA, intern architect, 1979, 1980; ARC Architects, Seattle, WA, project architect, 1984-89; King County Parks and Planning, Seattle, urban design planner, 1991-93; Southwest Land Research, Albuquerque, NM, urban design planner, 1995-96; Mark C. Childs Design Consultant, principal, 1996—. University of New Mexico, associate professor of architecture and planning, affiliated faculty of Landscape Architecture Program, 2002—, director of Design and Planning Assistance Center, 2002-06, founder and director of Town Design Certificate Program, 2004—; academic lecturer in the United States, England, Cyprus, and Greece; conference participant and public speaker. 1000 Friends of New Mexico, charter member, 1995—; Institute for Civic Arts and Public Space, Albuquerque, founder and president, 1996-2001; Alliance for Green Development, member of steering committee, 2000-02; New Mexico Trust for Public Land, member of advisory board, 2000—; Cornerstones, board member, 2002—.

AWARDS, HONORS: Boit Prize for poetry, Massachusetts Institute of Technology, 1980; Heritage Preservation Award (with Anthony Anella), State of New Mexico, 1999, for *Never Say Goodbye: The Albuquerque Rephotography Project;* Innovation in Planning/Historic Preservation Award, New Mexico chapter, American Planning Association, 2002, and Charter Award, Congress for New Urbanism, 2003, both for Doña Ana Plaza Plan; senior Fulbright scholar in Cyprus, 2005; National Council of Architectural Registration Boards Prize, 2006.

WRITINGS:

(And photographer) *Parking Spaces: A Design, Implementation, and Use Manual for Architects, Planners, and Engineers,* McGraw-Hill (New York, NY), 1999.
(With Anthony Anella) *Never Say Goodbye: The Albuquerque Rephotography Project* (originally published in *Albuquerque Tribune*), Albuquerque Museum (Albuquerque, NM), 2000.
(And photographer) *Squares: A Public Place Design Guide for Urbanists,* University of New Mexico Press (Albuquerque, NM), 2004.

Contributor to books, including *La Puerta: Doorway to the Academy,* Kendall-Hunt (Dubuque, IA), 1997; *Architectural Design Portable Handbook,* edited by Andy Pressman, McGraw-Hill (New York, NY), 2001; and *Time Saver Standards for Urban Design,* edited by Don Watson, McGraw-Hill, 2003. Contributor to periodicals, including *Urban Design International, Designer/Builder, Utne Reader, Fine Homebuilding, Planning, New Pacific,* and *Journal of Urban Design.*

Childs's first book was also published in Chinese.

*   *   *

CHRISTIE, Ann Philippa
See PEARCE, Philippa

*   *   *

CLAUDEL, Philippe 1962-

PERSONAL: Born 1962. *Education:* Attended college.

CAREER: Author. Previously worked as a teacher of handicapped children, at the prison of Nancy, France, and at the University of Nancy.

AWARDS, HONORS: Prix Renaudot, 2005, for *Les Âmes grises.*

WRITINGS:

Meuse l'oubli, Éditions Balland (France), 1999.

Le café d'excelsior, Éditions la Dragonne (Nancy, France), 1999.

Barrio Flores: petite chronique des oubliés, photographs by Jean-Michel Marchetti, Dragonne (Nancy, France), 2000.

Quelques uns des cent regrets (title means "Sum of the Hundred Regrets"), Éditions Balland (France), 2000.

J'abandonne (title means "I Give Up"), Éditions Originale Balland (France), 2000.

Au revoir Monsieur Friant (essay), Éditions Phileas Fogg (France), 2001.

Le bruit des trousseaux, 2001.

Sur le bout des doigts (screenplay), 2002.

Nos si proches orient, Éditions National Géographique (France), 2002.

Les âmes grises, Éditions Stock (France), 2003, translated by Adriana Hunter as *Grey Souls,* Weidenfeld & Nicolson (London, England), 2005, translated by Hoyt Rogers as *By a Slow River,* Knopf (New York, NY) 2006.

Trois petites histoires de jouets (title means "Three Small Stories of Toys"), Éditions Virgile (France), 2003.

Les petites mécaniques: nouvelles, Mercure de France (Paris, France), 2003.

Les petite fille de monsieur Linh (novel; title means "Mr. Linh's Little Girl"), Mercure de France (Paris, France), 2005.

Les Âmes grises (screenplay), 2005.

Also author of *Mirbaela,* Éditions Aencrages. Contributor to *Vu de la lune: nouvelles optimists,* Gallimard (Paris, France), 2005.

ADAPTATIONS: Grey Souls was adapted for film, Epithete Films, c. 2005.

SIDELIGHTS: Philippe Claudel is a French writer who became a novelist after working for a time as a teacher. His novel *Les âmes grises* was published in England as *Grey Souls* and in the United States as *By a Slow River.* The narrator of this story tells the of a young girl whose body is found in a river during World War I. She has been strangled, and before long a man is arrested and then executed for the crime. The narrator, a retired French policeman, is reinvestigating the crime some twenty years later and once again looks into the lives of those involved, from lawyers and judges to a schoolteacher who has hung herself.

"The mystery that propels this story is not the question of who strangled a little girl, but the deeper, universal mystery of human existence," reflected a *Kirkus Reviews* contributor. "Psychologically complex, elegantly written and tightly plotted, this is far from your average policier," observed a *Publishers Weekly* writer. Terrence Rafferty commented in the *New York Times:* "This is a book that hits the ground brooding." Rafferty added: "The narrator's flowing style . . . lulls and reassures, swaddles the reader in Gallic worldliness."

BIOGRAPHICAL AND CRITICAL SOURCES:

PERIODICALS

Booklist, April 15, 2006, Brad Hooper, review of *By a Slow River,* p. 38.

Entertainment Weekly, June 16, 2006, Jennifer Reese, review of *By a Slow River,* p. 81.

Financial Times, July 23, 2005, review of *Grey Souls,* p. 33.

First Things: A Monthly Journal of Religion and Public Life, December, 2006, review of *By a Slow River,* p. 57.

Kirkus Reviews, May 15, 2006, review of *By a Slow River,* p. 480.

New York Times, July 2, 2006, Terrence Rafferty, review of *By a Slow River.*

Publishers Weekly, March 20, 2006, review of *By a Slow River,* p. 33.

ONLINE

Calou, http://perso.orange.fr/calounet/ (December 21, 2006), brief biography of Philippe Claudel.

Internet Movie Database, http://www.imdb.com/ (December 21, 2006), information on Philippe Claudel's film work.

London Telegraph Web site, http://www.telegraph.co.uk/ (May 29, 2005), review of *Grey Souls.*

*   *   *

CONLON, Christopher 1962-

PERSONAL: Born August 7, 1962. *Education:* Humboldt State University, B.A.; University of Maryland, M.A.

ADDRESSES: Home—Silver Spring, MD. *Office*—The Nora School, 955 Sligo Ave., Silver Spring, MD 20910. *E-mail*—WEHSconlon@aol.com.

CAREER: Poet, writer, and educator. Nora School (formerly the Washington Ethical High School), Silver Spring, MD, teacher, 1995—. Peace Corps Volunteer, Botswana, 1988-90.

AWARDS, HONORS: Peace Corps Poetry Prize for *Gilbert and Garbo in Love: A Romance in Poems;* Pushcart Prize nomination for *What There Is.*

WRITINGS:

Saying Secrets: American Stories (short stories), Writers Club Press, 2000.
A Stained Dawn: Poems about Africa, Mango Biscuit Press (Silver Spring, MD), 2001.
What There Is (poetry), Argonne Hotel Press (Washington, DC), 2002.
Gilbert and Garbo in Love: A Romance in Poems, Word Works (Washington, DC), 2003.
(Editor) *Filet of Sohl: The Classic Scripts and Stories of Jerry Sohl,* BearManor Media (Boalsburg, PA), 2003.
The Weeping Time: Elegy in Three Voices (poetry), Argonne House Books (Washington, DC), 2004.
(Editor) *The Twilight Zone Scripts of Jerry Sohl,* Bear-Manor Media (Boalsburg, PA), 2004.
(Editor) *Poe's Lighthouse: All New Collaborations with Edgar Allan Poe,* Cemetery Dance Publications (Forest Hill, MD), 2006.
Thundershowers at Dusk: Gothic Stories, introduction by Gary A. Braunbeck, Rock Village Publishing (Middleborough, MA), 2006.

Also author of novella, "The Wild Track," issue #9 of the online literary journal *The King's English.* Contributor of poetry to periodicals, including *Santa Barbara Review, Wind, Poet Lore,* and *America;* contributor of fiction to literary journals, including *The Long Story* and to anthologies, including *Masques V;* contributor of nonfiction to periodicals, including *Poets & Writers* and *Filmfax* and to collections, including *September 11, 2001: American Writers Respond,* Etruscan Press.

SIDELIGHTS: Christopher Conlon writes poetry and fiction. In *Saying Secrets: American Stories,* the author presents five stories in which young people suffer physical pains and/or mental torments. For example, in "The Map of the World," a black girl finds herself in a hospital after being raped and burned by racists. She makes friends with another burn victim, who, like her, no longer has an identifying racial skin color. Karl Luntta, writing on the *Peace Corps Writers* Web site, commented: "Early on in *Saying Secrets,* it is evident that Christopher Conlon is—in the best tradition of writers of any genre—an honest writer."

Conlon writes poetry about Botswana, where he was stationed in the Peace Corps, in his book *A Stained Dawn: Poems about Africa.* "To his credit, Conlon steers away from the confessional road it might have been convenient to take with such material," wrote Ann Neelon on the *Peace Corps Writers* Web site.

In *Gilbert and Garbo in Love: A Romance in Poems,* the author presents a fictionalized portrayal of the lives of silent-film stars John Gilbert and Greta Garbo. "This is a tour de force for author Christopher Conlon," wrote Grace Cavalieri on the *Montserrat Review* Web site. Cavalieri went on to note the author's "mastery of form for each poem," adding: "The poet writes narrative poems, lyric poems, scenes, and meditations all within the story's frame." Tony Zurlo, writing on the *Peace Corps Writers* Web site, noted that "narrative skill and lyrical imagination coalesce" in the collection of poems.

The Weeping Time: Elegy in Three Voices is a story about the Civil War and slavery in poetry form. It begins with Georgian Pierce Butler setting free his slaves and follows Butler, his British actress wife, and a slave named Jack in a story that *Peace Corps Writers* Web site contributor Ann Neelon compared to *Gone with the Wind.* Neelon wrote: "Ultimately, the strength of *The Weeping Time* lies in its commitment to the bigness of the story, to giving us Pierce and Fanny and Jack in cinemascope." In his 2006 collection *Thundershowers at Dusk: Gothic Stories,* Conlon presents five stories about loss, yearning, and past ghosts. "Each tale is dark, and exposes the pit of what is deep inside us, yet isn't shared," wrote Christina Francine Whitcher on *Yet Another Book Review Site.*

Conlon has also served as editor of several books, including *Poe's Lighthouse: All New Collaborations with Edgar Allan Poe,* which features twenty-three stories based on fragments of the tale started by Edgar

Allan Poe and reworked and completed by other writers. "If you're a fan of Poe, or of any of his collaborators . . . then *Poe's Lighthouse* is well worth your time," wrote Martina Bexte on the *BookLoons* Web site. Benjamin Boulden, writing on the *SFReader.com* Web site, commented: "The better of the stories tend to lean away from Poe's narration and tell their own stories; they are the visions of their modern author's rather than a revamped 'what would Poe have written?' version."

BIOGRAPHICAL AND CRITICAL SOURCES:

PERIODICALS

Publishers Weekly, February 22, 2006, review of *Poe's Lighthouse: All New Collaborations with Edgar Allan Poe.*

ONLINE

BookLoons, http://www.bookloons.com/ (November 20, 2006), Martina Bexte, review of *Poe's Lighthouse.*
Christopher Conlon Home Page, http://christopher conlon.com (November 20, 2006).
Gazette.net, http://gazette.net/ (July 18, 2003), Ellyn Wexler, "Silver Screen Legends Give Author Golden Opportunity."
Montserrat Review, http://www.themontserratreview. com/ (November 20, 2006), Grace Cavalieri, review of *Gilbert and Garbo in Love: A Romance in Poems.*
Peace Corps Writers, http://www.peacecorpswriters. org/ (November 20, 2006), Ann Neelon, reviews of *The Weeping Time: Elegy in Three Voices* and *A Stained Dawn: Poems about Africa;* Tony Zurlo, review of *Gilbert and Garbo In Love;* Karl Luntta, review of *Saying Secrets: American Stories.*
SFReader.com, http://www.sfreader.com/ (November 20, 2006), Benjamin Boulden, review of *Poe's Lighthouse.*
Sidereality, http://www.sidereality.com/ (November 20, 2006), Gilbert Wesley Purdy, review of *Gilbert and Garbo in Love.*
Yet Another Book Review Site, http://www. yetanotherbookreview.com/ (November 20, 2006), Christina Francine Whitcher, reviews of *Thundershowers at Dusk: Gothic Stories* and *Poe's Lighthouse.*

COOPER, Christopher 1961-

PERSONAL: Born 1961; married; children: one son.

ADDRESSES: Home—Washington, D.C. *Office*—c/o Wall Street Journal, 200 Liberty St., New York, NY 10281. *E-mail*—christopher.cooper@wsj.com.

CAREER: Journalist. *New Orleans Times-Picayune,* New Orleans, LA, staff writer, until 1998; *Wall Street Journal,* New York, NY, began as staff reporter, became national political correspondent, 1998—.

AWARDS, HONORS: President's Award, New Jersey Deputy Fire Chiefs Association, 2006; Health Braintrust Leadership Award in Print Journalism, Congressional Black Caucus, 2006.

WRITINGS:

(With Robert Block) *Disaster: Hurricane Katrina and the Failure of Homeland Security,* Times Books (New York, NY), 2006.

ADAPTATIONS: Home Box Office has acquired the rights to *Disaster.*

SIDELIGHTS: For *Sidelights,* see BLOCK, Robert.

BIOGRAPHICAL AND CRITICAL SOURCES:

PERIODICALS

Publishers Weekly, July 24, 2006, review of *Disaster: Hurricane Katrina and the Failure of Homeland Security,* p. 53.
Reference & Research Book News, November, 2006, review of *Disaster.*
Washington Post, October 31, 2006, Stephen Flynn, "Ignoring One Threat for Another," review of *Disaster,* p. C2.

ONLINE

Blogcritics Magazine Web site, http://blogcritics.org/ (September 22, 20006), Dominick Evans, review of *Disaster.**

CRANE, Dan 1971-
(Björn Türoque)

PERSONAL: Born 1971.

ADDRESSES: Home—New York, NY. *E-mail*—rockstar@aireoke.com

CAREER: Writer and musician. Former software producer.

WRITINGS:

(As Björn Türoque) *To Air Is Human: One Man's Quest to Become the World's Greatest Air Guitarist,* Riverhead Books (New York, NY), 2006.

Contributor to *Esquire, Slate,* the *New York Times,* and the *Los Angeles Times.*

SIDELIGHTS: A software producer turned freelance writer, Dan Crane became infatuated in his early thirties with the highly theatrical performance of air guitar. He created an alter ego named Björn Türoque and took to the competitive air-guitar circuit, over the next three years garnering a number of high finishes. Türoque earned notoriety as an air guitarist for a number of television performances, a role in the 2006 documentary *Air Guitar Nation,* and a string of prominent second-place finishes at international competitions. Crane chronicled his journey from "there" musician (he plays the guitar in a faux French rock band) to air-guitar rock star in *To Air Is Human: One Man's Quest to Become the World's Greatest Air Guitarist,* written as Türoque. The memoir also explores the activity's cultural impact and the reasons why competitions draw large numbers of participants and fans. A *Publishers Weekly* reviewer noted the book's "hilarious detail," commenting that Crane "easily and accurately captures the telling elements of what is uniquely a visual event." In an article for *Kirkus Reviews,* a contributor described *To Air Is Human* as an "absurd yet contemplative chronicle that will charm anyone who believes in rocking hard with a guitar—or with nothing at all."

BIOGRAPHICAL AND CRITICAL SOURCES:

BOOKS

Crane, Dan (As Björn Türoque), *To Air Is Human: One Man's Quest to Become the World's Greatest Air Guitarist,* Riverhead Books (New York, NY), 2006.

PERIODICALS

Kirkus Reviews, June 1, 2006, review of *To Air Is Human,* p. 565.
Publishers Weekly, July 17, 2006, review of *To Air Is Human,* p. 154.

ONLINE

Dan Crane Home Page, http://www.dancrane.com (March 12, 2007).
Björn Türoque Home Page, http://www.bjornturoque. com (January 16, 2007).

*   *   *

CREECH, Morri 1970-

PERSONAL: Born 1970, in Moncks Corner, SC; children: Hattie. *Education:* Attended Winthrop University, 1995; McNeese State University, M.F.A.

ADDRESSES: Home—Lake Charles, LA. *Office*—McNeese State University, Kaufman Hall, Lake Charles, LA 70609.

CAREER: Poet and educator. McNeese State University, Lake Charles, LA, faculty member.

AWARDS, HONORS: Ruth Lilly fellow, the Poetry Foundation, 1997; Louisiana Arts Prize literature fellowship, 1998; Wick Poetry Prize for first books, Kent State University, 2000, for *Paper Cathedrals;* Anthony Hecht Poetry Prize, Waywiser Press, 2005, for *Field Knowledge.*

WRITINGS:

Paper Cathedrals (poetry), Kent State University Press (Kent, OH), 2001.
Field Knowledge (poetry), Waywiser Press (Baltimore, MD), 2006.

Work has been published in periodicals, such as *Poetry, Southern Review, Missouri Review, Sewanee Review, New Criterion, Crazyhorse,* and *Tar River.* Contributed poetry to *Listening to the Earth,* photographs by Robert ParkeHarrison, 21st Editions (South Dennis, MA), 2004.

SIDELIGHTS: Morri Creech was born in the South Carolina town of Moncks Corner and was educated at Winthrop University and McNeese State University. As a graduate student in creative writing at McNeese, he became the school's first recipient of the Ruth Lilly Poetry fellowship, a national competition underwritten by the Poetry Foundation. Creech's work has been widely published in noted poetry journals such as *Poetry* and *New Criterion,* and he has since published two award-winning collections of his poetry. His first collection, *Paper Cathedrals,* was awarded the Wick Poetry Prize, which included publication of the poems by Kent State University Press.

Field Knowledge was selected from over 360 entries to earn Creech the inaugural Anthony Hecht Poetry Prize in 2005. Callie Siskel commented in a *New Criterion* review that Creech has "set the bar high" for subsequent applicants. She went on to declare: "Creech weaves form into the delicate description of raw, Southern landscapes. . . . He makes the reader question his own past and the facility with which it can be restored." In a review for *Booklist,* Ray Olson remarked: "There is a use of the European poetic tradition that is as gratifying and profound as it is assured. This man's good."

BIOGRAPHICAL AND CRITICAL SOURCES:

PERIODICALS

Booklist, September 15, 2006, Ray Olson, review of *Field Knowledge,* p. 17.
New Criterion, November, 2006, Callie Siskel, review of *Field Knowledge,* p. 79.

ONLINE

McNeese State University Master of Fine Arts Program Web site, http://www.mfa.mcneese.edu/ (January 16, 2007), faculty profile.*

*   *   *

CRIMI, Carolyn 1959-

PERSONAL: Born December 28, 1959, in Long Island, NY; married Alfonso Segreti. *Education:* Lake Forest College, B.A., 1982; Vermont College, M.F.A., 2000. *Hobbies and other interests:* Eating chocolate, watching *I Love Lucy* reruns, being outdoors, reading, drawing, napping with her dog Emerson.

ADDRESSES: Home and office—Evanston, IL. *E-mail*—crims@aol.com.

CAREER: Writer. Teaches courses on children's writing.

MEMBER: Society of Children's Book Writers and Illustrators (Illinois chapter).

AWARDS, HONORS: Best of the Best selection, Chicago Public Library, 1999, Kentucky Bluegrass Award for Best Picture Book, 2001, and Midland Author's Best Children's Fiction award runner-up, all for *Don't Need Friends;* Read-Aloud Books Too Good to Miss selection, Association for Indiana Media Educators, 2005, for *Henry and the Buccaneer Bunnies.*

WRITINGS:

PICTURE BOOKS

Outside, Inside, illustrated by Linnea Asplind Riley, Simon & Schuster (New York, NY), 1995.
Don't Need Friends, illustrated by Lynn Munsinger, Doubleday (New York, NY), 1999.
Tessa's Tip-Tapping Toes, illustrated by Marsha Gray Carrington, Scholastic (New York, NY), 2002.
Get Busy, Beaver!, illustrated by Janie Bynum, Orchard (New York, NY), 2004.
Boris and Bella, illustrated by Gris Grimly, Harcourt (Orlando, FL), 2004.
Henry and the Buccaneer Bunnies, illustrated by John Manders, Candlewick (Cambridge, MA), 2005.
The Louds Move In, illustrated by Regan Dunnick, Marshall Cavendish (New York, NY), 2006.

OTHER

Kidding around Chicago: What to Do, Where to Go, and How to Have Fun in Chicago, J. Muir (Santa Fe, NM), 1998.
Ribbee Dibbee Doo, illustrated by Barry Gott, Women's Board of Ravinia Festival (Highland Park, IL), 2003.

Contributor of short fiction to *Highlights for Children*. Author, under house pseudonym R.L. Stine, of two novels in "Ghosts of Fear Street" series. Also author, with Andrea Beaty and Julia Durango, of *Three Silly Chicks* blog at www.threesillychicks.com.

SIDELIGHTS: Carolyn Crimi always knew she wanted to write children's books, and as a child she got a head start on this dream by giving original, self-illustrated stories to family members as gifts. As an author, Crimi is best known for creating silly picture books that feature characters ranging from a grouchy rat and dancing mouse to a gang of buccaneer bunnies. "I love writing humorous stories the most, I suppose because I find them easier to write," Crimi told Cynthia Leitich Smith in an interview on Smith's *Cynsations* Web site.

Crimi's first published children's book, *Outside, Inside,* finds a young girl comparing the cozy world inside her home to the rainy day outside her window. "Rainy days were my sanctuary," Crimi recalled to Smith. "I could stay inside without being pushed out the door. I still love rainy days for this reason." According to a critic for *Publishers Weekly,* "Crimi's inventive use of language adds lyricism and sparkle" to *Outside, Inside,* and in *Horn Book,* Lolly Robinson wrote that the "poetic text vividly evokes sounds and atmosphere."

In *Don't Need Friends,* Rat feels alone after his best friend moves away from the garbage dump. Although the grouchy rodent decides that, to avoid a similar hurt, he does not need anyone, when grumpy Dog moves in, the pair find they are two of a kind, and when Dog gets sick Rat comes to the rescue. Jennifer M. Brabander, writing in *Horn Book,* noted that Crimi successfully captures the meaning of friendship in a text that "neatly avoids sentimentality," while a *Publishers Weekly* critic dubbed *Don't Need Friends* a "slyly funny and deeply touching story."

Tessa's Tip-Tapping Toes introduces Tessa, a mouse who cannot keep from dancing, despite her mother's warnings. Fortunately, another resident of the house, a cat named Oscar, is more singer than hunter, and although he tries to muffle his yowls, his greatest wish is to sing. When cat and mouse meet, their artistic impulses enliven the entire household. Shelle Rosenfeld, reviewing *Tessa's Tip-Tapping Toes* for *Booklist,* wrote that Crimi's "bouncy, alliterative prose cel-

ebrates the joys of creative self-expression." In *Kirkus Reviews* a contributor noted the "expressive, rollicking language" used by the author, and in *Publishers Weekly* a critic praised the book's "snappy prose."

Like *Tessa's Tip-Tapping Toes, Get Busy, Beaver!* celebrates creativity. Thelonious Beaver is not interested in the work other beavers do; instead, he builds things his own way, and teaches his fellow beavers to enjoy the world around them. A *Kirkus Reviews* contributor found the book to be "a charming salute to the creative dreamers of the world," while Rachel G. Payne cited Crimi's story as "an enjoyable read-aloud with a valuable message" in her in *School Library Journal* review.

In *Boris and Bella,* a very messy monster named Bella LeGrossi lives next door to a very tidy monster named Boris Kleanitoff. The Fiendish neighbors argue endlessly, until a wild Halloween party brings them together. As a *School Library Journal* reviewer stated, Crimi's picture book serves as "a bewitching choice for libraries looking to boost their Halloween offerings."

Henry comes to the rescue of his father's rascally pirate crew in *Henry and the Buccaneer Bunnies,* a picture book that has been honored with several state award nominations. Unlike the other pirates, Henry enjoys reading, and wants to spend his time curled up and reading a book. Fortunately, when the pirate crew runs into trouble, Henry's book-learned knowledge saves the day. Todd Morning, reviewing the picture book for *Booklist,* praised the humorous illustrations by John Manders and noted that, while "a story on the joys and usefulness of reading is nothing new, . . . the funny Buccaneer Bunnies should provide some interest."

Another humorous title by Crimi focuses on a quiet neighborhood that is disrupted by noisy new neighbors. In *The Louds Move In!,* a community's quiet-loving residents are poised to complain, but when the energetic Loud family suddenly leaves, their neighbors are left wondering if quiet is all its cracked up to be. "Warmth and good humor abound in this satisfying tale," wrote a *Publishers Weekly* contributor, and Martha V. Parravano concluded in her *Horn Book* review that Crimi's "crowd pleaser has it all."

Smith asked Crimi why she writes for children. "The children's books themselves inspired me to write for children," the author answered. "I spent so many hours reading books. I remember desperately wishing that I could crawl inside them. I guess writing children's books is a way for me to do just that." As Crimi told Kelsey Kirkpatrick for the *Medill News Service,* she is more than happy with her career choice. "I'll be in the grave and still coming up with ideas. I really hope I'm still doing it when I'm ninety."

BIOGRAPHICAL AND CRITICAL SOURCES:

PERIODICALS

Booklist, June 1, 1995, Stephanie Zvirin, review of *Outside, Inside,* p. 1784; November 15, 1999, Hazel Rochman, review of *Don't Need Friends,* p. 634; March 1, 2002, Shelle Rosenfeld, review of *Tessa's Tip-Tapping Toes,* p. 1140; January 1, 2005, Ilene Cooper, review of *Boris and Bella,* p. 868; December 1, 2005, Todd Morning, review of *Henry and the Buccaneer Bunnies,* p. 52.

Bulletin of the Center for Children's Books, June, 2006, Maggie Hommel, review of *The Louds Move In!,* p. 448.

Childhood Education, winter, 2002, Liane Troy, review of *Tessa's Tip-Tapping Toes,* p. 109.

Horn Book, September-October, 1995, Lolly Robinson, review of *Outside, Inside,* p. 587; November, 1999, Jennifer M. Brabander, review of *Don't Need Friends,* p. 728; May-June, 2006, Martha V. Parravano, review of *The Louds Move In!,* p. 293.

Kirkus Reviews, January 15, 2002, review of *Tessa's Tip-Tapping Toes,* p. 102; August 15, 2004, review of *Boris and Bella,* p. 804; October 1, 2004, review of *Get Busy, Beaver!,* p. 958; September 1, 2005, review of *Henry and the Buccaneer Bunnies,* p. 971; February 15, 2006, review of *The Louds Move In!,* p. 180.

Publishers Weekly, April 17, 1995, review of *Outside, Inside,* p. 56; November 8, 1999, review of *Don't Need Friends,* p. 67; December 3, 2001, review of *Tessa's Tip-Tapping Toes,* p. 59; August 9, 2004, review of *Boris and Bella,* p. 248; March 13, 2006, review of *The Louds Move In!,* p. 64.

School Library Journal, September, 2004, Donna Cardon, review of *Boris and Bella,* p. 156; November, 2004, Rachel G. Payne, review of *Get Busy, Beaver!,* p. 96; November, 2005, Lisa S. Schindler, review of *Henry and the Buccaneer Bunnies,* p. 89; May, 2006, JoAnn Jonas, review of *The Louds Move In!,* p. 85.

ONLINE

Carolyn Crimi Home Page, http://www.carolyncrimi. com (January 10, 2007).

Cynsations, http://www.cynthialeitichsmith.com/ (September 10, 2005), Cynthia Leitich Smith, interview with Crimi.

Medill News Service http://mesh.medill.northwestern. edu/ (October 8, 2004), Kelsey Kirkpatrick, interview with Crimi.

Random House Web site, http://www.randomhouse. com/ (January 10, 2007), "Carolyn Crimi."

Society of Children's Book Writers and Illustrators: Illinois Web site, http://www.scbwi-illinois/ (January 10, 2007), "Carolyn Crimi."

* * *

CROSBY, Ellen 1953-

PERSONAL: Born 1953, in Boston, MA; married; children: three sons. *Education:* Catholic University of America, B.A.; Johns Hopkins University, M.A.

ADDRESSES: Home—VA. *Agent*—Dominick Abel, Dominick Abel Literary Agency, Inc., 146 W. 82nd St., 1B, New York, NY 10024. *E-mail*—ellen@ ellencrosby.com.

CAREER: Freelance journalist. Former foreign correspondent for ABC News Radio and former economist for the U.S. Senate.

MEMBER: International Association of Crime Writers (North American branch), Mystery Writers of America, Sisters in Crime.

WRITINGS:

Moscow Nights (novel), Piatkus (London, England), 2000.

The Merlot Murders: A Wine Country Mystery (mystery novel), Scribner (New York, NY), 2006.

The Chardonnay Charade (mystery novel), Scribner (New York, NY), 2007.

Contributor to periodicals, including the *Wall Street Journal, Christian Science Monitor,* and the *Journal* (now the *Washington Enquirer*).

SIDELIGHTS: A longtime freelance journalist, Ellen Crosby is also a mystery writer. In Crosby's second mystery, *The Merlot Murders: A Wine Country Mystery,* Lucie Montgomery gets a call while overseas in France informing her that her father has died. When she returns to Virginia, she not only finds her father's wine estate neglected but also discovers that her brother, Eli, has convinced their younger sister, Mia, to agree to sell the estate. It appears that Eli needs money to help support his wife's frivolous spending habits and that Mia is having an affair with Lucie's former lover, who was involved in the accident that killed her father. Before long, Lucie learns from her godfather that her father's death was not an accident, and she sets out to solve the crime and save the estate in the process. In a review of *The Merlot Murders* in *Publishers Weekly,* a contributor wrote: "Like a fine wine, Crosby's debut is complex and intricate." *Booklist* critic Barbara Bibel commented that the book has "an absorbing plot, rich with details on the wine industry." Calling the book "superb," in the *South Florida Sun-Sentinel,* Oline H. Cogdill added that the author "writes . . . evocatively about wine and wine-making."

BIOGRAPHICAL AND CRITICAL SOURCES:

PERIODICALS

Booklist, May 1, 2006, Barbara Bibel, review of *The Merlot Murders: A Wine Country Mystery,* p. 24.
Kirkus Reviews, May 15, 2006, review of *The Merlot Murders,* p. 496.
Publishers Weekly, June 12, 2006, review of *The Merlot Murders,* p. 33.
South Florida Sun-Sentinel (Fort Lauderdale, FL), September 27, 2006, Oline H. Cogdill, review of *The Merlot Murders.*

ONLINE

Ellen Crosby Home Page, http://www.ellencrosby.com (December 22, 2006).

CROWLEIGH, Ann
See POWER, Jo-Ann

*   *   *

CULLEN, Lisa Takeuchi

PERSONAL: Born in Kobe, Japan; married; husband's name Chris; children: Mika. *Education:* Canadian Academy International School, graduated, 1988; Rutgers College, B.A.; Columbia University Graduate School of Journalism, graduated, 1998.

ADDRESSES: Home—NJ. *E-mail*—lisa@lisacullen.com.

CAREER: Writer. *Money,* New York, NY, staff writer, 1997-2001; *Time,* New York, NY, staff writer, 2001—. Worked previously as an editor or reporter at *Financial Planning, Resident, Ladies' Home Journal,* and *Adweek.*

AWARDS, HONORS: International Reporting Project fellow to Japan, 2000; Barnes & Noble Discover Great New Writers nominee, 2006.

WRITINGS:

Remember Me: A Lively Tour of the New American Way of Death, Collins (New York, NY), 2006.

Contributor of articles to periodicals, including the *New York Times* and *Bon Appétit.* Author of the blog *Work in Progress* for *Time.*

SIDELIGHTS: Lisa Takeuchi Cullen grew up in Kobe, Japan, and moved to the United States to attend university. She joined the staff of *Money* as a writer in 1997, and has been steadily working as a journalist for some of the nation's most prominent magazines, including *Time,* and also contributes to a regular blog about the American workplace for *Time*'s Web site. In 2003 Cullen was assigned a story about how the funeral industry has been affected by the growing number of aging baby boomers. From that story came her first book, *Remember Me: A Lively Tour of the*

New American Way of Death. As part of her research, Cullen traveled around the country exploring how different cultures approach death as a celebratory process, including biodegradable burials, keepsakes such as diamonds made from cremains, and theme-based funerals. She also looked into the increasing role that Americans are taking in helping to pre-plan their own funerals. A reviewer for *Publishers Weekly* remarked that Cullen's "vivid reportage and wryly sympathetic tone feel anything but embalmed." A *Kirkus Reviews* contributor called *Remember Me* a "a fresh and funny look at what's new in funerals," concluding that Cullen is "an amiable guide, and her tour is enjoyable and enlightening."

BIOGRAPHICAL AND CRITICAL SOURCES:

PERIODICALS

Kirkus Reviews, May 15, 2006, review of *Remember Me: A Lively Tour of the New American Way of Death,* p. 504.
Publishers Weekly, May 8, 2006, review of *Remember Me,* p. 53.

ONLINE

Lisa Takeuchi Cullen Home Page, http://www.lisacullen.com (January 16, 2007).

* * *

CURTIS, Gregory 1944-
(Gregory Benson Curtis)

PERSONAL: Born December 5, 1944, in Corpus Christi, TX; son William Hall and Vivian Dorene Curtis; married Tracy Lynn Lewis, September 27, 1975; children: three daughters and a son, including Vivian Reed and Gregory. *Education:* Rice University, B.A., 1966; San Francisco State College, M.A., 1968. *Hobbies and other interests:* Horse riding, racquetball, book collecting, record collecting, and magic.

ADDRESSES: Home—Austin, TX. *E-mail*—thecavepainters@hotmail.com.

CAREER: Writer and editor. Ran printing and publishing company, San Francisco, CA, 1967-72; *Texas Monthly,* staff writer/senior editor, 1972-81, editor, 1981-2000; joined Time Inc., as editor-at-large, 2001.

MEMBER: American Association of Magazine Editors (executive committee), Headliners (Austin, TX).

WRITINGS:

Disarmed: The Story of the Venus de Milo, Knopf (New York, NY), 2003.
The Cave Painters: Probing the Mysteries of the World's First Artists, Knopf (New York, NY), 2006.

Contributor to periodicals, including *New York Times, Rolling Stone, Fortune,* and *Time.*

SIDELIGHTS: Gregory Curtis spent nearly three decades at *Texas Monthly* magazine as a writer and then as its editor before leaving in 2000. In his first book, *Disarmed: The Story of the Venus de Milo,* Curtis tells the story of the famous armless statue discovered on the island of Melos in 1820 by a French naval officer and a local farmer. In addition to writing about how the French acquired the statue for the Louvre and the origins of a fallacious story that the statue lost its arms during a battle over it between French and Turkish soldiers on a Melos beach, the author delves into the questions surrounding the statue's origins and profiles the many museum officials and art historians who have debated the statue's history. He also presents his own hypothesis of what the complete statue may have looked like and what it represented. In a frequently-asked-questions segment on the author's home page, Curtis explains that he decided to write about the statue for several reasons, including his admiration for the piece of art, the debate surrounding its creator, and the fact that no author has explored the subject for a general audience.

In a review of *Disarmed* in *Publishers Weekly,* a contributor noted the author's "sense of a good anecdote" and referred to the book as "judicious." A *Kirkus Reviews* contributor called *Disarmed* "a brisk and brilliant trot through the history of one of the world's most famous pieces of sculpture." The reviewer also referred to it as "lush, learned, and surpassingly entertaining."

In his next book, *The Cave Painters: Probing the Mysteries of the World's First Artists,* Curtis discusses the 30,000-year-old colored paintings that have been found in caves in France. He delves into their possible origins and describes the world that the artists lived in during the end of the Neanderthal era. He also probes the heated debates concerning the various theories surrounding the paintings, such as their possible creation as part of shamanistic practices and why certain animals were drawn while others that were known to exist at the time were not. "For readers who may never visit the caves, Curtis's sensitive narration gives a chance to share that encounter with mystery," wrote a *Publishers Weekly* contributor. William Alfred Kern, writing on the *PopMatters* Web site, noted that the author "brings us somewhat up to date on the scope of materials discovered and gives some tentative conclusions that reflect a consensus." Kern added: "He leaves no doubt, however, that this is merely an interim report on an area of inquiry, which may never be concluded."

BIOGRAPHICAL AND CRITICAL SOURCES:

PERIODICALS

Folio's Publishing News, November 15, 1992, Todd Brewster, "Why Is Texas Monthly the Country's Best Regional? In Two Words: Gregory Curtis," p. 32.

Kirkus Reviews, August 15, 2003, review of *Disarmed: The Story of the Venus de Milo,* p. 1055.

Mediaweek, July 3, 2000, Anne Torpey-Kemph, "Curtis to Roam over Time Inc. Titles," p. 26.

Publishers Weekly, August 25, 2003, review of *Disarmed,* p. 49; July 24, 2006, review of *The Cave Painters: Probing the Mysteries of the World's First Artists,* p. 49.

ONLINE

Gregory Curtis Home Page, http://www.gregorycurtis. com (January 17, 2007).

PopMatters, http://www.popmatters.com/ (January 17, 2007), William Alfred Kern, review of *The Cave Painters.**

*　　　*　　　*

CURTIS, Gregory Benson
See CURTIS, Gregory

CYRUS, Kurt 1954-

PERSONAL: Born August 17, 1954, in Redmond, OR; son of Warren H. and Joan F. Cyrus; married Linnea Lindberg (a precognitive creative landscaping consultant). *Education:* Lane Community College, A.S., 1985; also attended Art Center College of Design and Oregon State University. *Hobbies and other interests:* Tree farming, raising tadpoles.

CAREER: Sacred Heart General Hospital, Eugene, OR, respiratory therapist, 1984-94; writer and illustrator of children's books, 1994—.

AWARDS, HONORS: Christopher Award, for *The Mousery;* Children's Choice Award, for *Tangle Town;* list of nature books for young readers, John Burroughs Association, 2005, and book award, Pacific Northwest Booksellers Association, both for *Hotel Deep: Light Verse from Dark Water;* ALA Notable Book selection, American Library Association, and Parents' Choice Award, for *Mammoths on the Move.*

WRITINGS:

PICTURE BOOKS

Tangle Town, Farrar, Straus & Giroux (New York, NY), 1997.

Slow Train to Oxmox, Farrar, Straus & Giroux (New York, NY), 1998.

Oddhopper Opera: A Bug's Garden of Verses, Harcourt (Orlando, FL), 2001.

Hotel Deep: Light Verse from Dark Water, Harcourt (Orlando, FL), 2005.

ILLUSTRATOR:

Judith Mathews, *There's Nothing to Do-o-o!,* Harcourt (Orlando, FL), 1999.

Charlotte Pomerantz, *The Mousery,* Harcourt (Orlando, FL), 2000.

Lisa Wheeler, *Sixteen Cows,* Harcourt (Orlando, FL), 2002.

Eve Bunting, *The Bones of Fred McFee,* Harcourt (Orlando, FL), 2002.

Lisa Wheeler, *Avalanche Annie,* Harcourt (Orlando, FL), 2003.

Anne Bustard, *Buddy: The Story of Buddy Holly,* Simon & Schuster (New York, NY), 2005.

M.T. Anderson, *Whales on Stilts,* Harcourt (Orlando, FL), 2005.

M.T. Anderson, *The Clue of the Linoleum Lederhosen,* Harcourt (Orlando, FL), 2006.

Lisa Wheeler, *Mammoths on the Move,* Harcourt (Orlando, FL), 2006.

Julia Durango, *Pest Fest,* Simon & Schuster (New York, NY), 2007.

D

DALY, David J.

PERSONAL: Education: University of Virginia, B.A.; Syracuse University, M.F.A. and M.S.

ADDRESSES: Home—Syracuse, NY.

CAREER: Writer. Has held a variety of blue-collar and white- collar jobs.

WRITINGS:

The Legend of Killer Noon (novel), Green Boat Press (Manlius, NY), 1999.
Druidic Twilight (novel), Green Boat Press (Manlius, NY), 2003.
Cold Soul Demands (poetry), Green Boat Press (Manlius, NY), 2004.

SIDELIGHTS: David J. Daly's novels explore what happens when an ancient Irish warrior king and his Druid advisor become blown off course in a boat and—at the whim of a god—travel through time to modern Manhattan. In The Legend of Killer Noon, the two heroes drift into roles that suit their Celtic sensibilities: The king, Kilty Conaire O'Neill, follows his ruthless nature and seeks out the Mafia. The Druid, Sean, immerses himself in education, learning all he can about the technological advances he sees all around him. In the sequel, Druidic Twilight, Sean, now working in an office, is jolted out of the middle-class existence he has crafted for himself when he meets a young man who seems suitable as an apprentice, and who accompanies Sean on a journey from New York to Las Vegas to Los Angeles. Jackie Cassada in Library Journal described the Druid Sean as a character with "one foot in the mean streets and the other in the 'auld sod.'" Mark W. Videan in Fore-Word Reviews suggested that readers of Daly's books "will garner many fascinating insights on modern culture, as seen through ancient Irish eyes." Daly is also author of the book of poetry Cold Soul Demands.

BIOGRAPHICAL AND CRITICAL SOURCES:

PERIODICALS

Library Journal, March 15, 2003, Jackie Cassada, review of Druidic Twilight, p. 121.

ONLINE

ForeWord Reviews, http://www.forewordreviews.com/ (September 30, 2003), Mark W. Videan, review of The Legend of Killer Noon.

*   *   *

DALY, Joe 1979-

PERSONAL: Born 1979, in London, England. Education: Attended City Varsity College.

ADDRESSES: Home—Cape Town, South Africa.

CAREER: Comic book artist and writer.

WRITINGS:

COMICS

The Red Monkey: The Leaking Cello Case (graphic novel), Double Storey Books (Johannesburg, South Africa), 2003.
Scrublands (stories), Fantagraphics (Seattle, WA), 2006.

Regular contributor to *Student Life,* a South African magazine. Work has been anthologized in *Africa Comics.*

SIDELIGHTS: Born in London, England, and raised in South Africa, Joe Daly had originally intended on a career in animation. After two years of college, he decided to pursue his passion for creating comic books. The title character in *The Red Monkey: The Leaking Cello Case,* Daly's first book, is a young man named Dave who is chasing a career as a professional illustrator and is burdened with an unusual birth defect: monkey feet. In addition to dealing with the most universal of conflicts—a failed relationship, poor self-esteem, and strange neighbors—Dave becomes unintentionally embroiled in a smuggling plot. Ruby Bernard wrote in a review for the *artSMart* Web site that the book "encapsulates much of the dynamics of the generation that [Daly] hails from. In the events that lead up to the grand finale you are given a first-hand account of the dilemmas and enquiries into life that most young adults experience."

Scrublands is the first book of Daly's to be released in the United States and is a compilation of fantastical and graphic stories. "Funky, weird and wonderful," wrote a *Publishers Weekly* reviewer, who added: "Daly's surprisingly compelling collection is a fever dream of a place." *Booklist* contributor Ray Olson described the book as a "handsome, generous album." A contributor to *Creative Review* called the stories "amusing and frequently surreal."

BIOGRAPHICAL AND CRITICAL SOURCES:

PERIODICALS

Booklist, May 15, 2006, Ray Olson, review of *Scrublands,* p. 31.

Creative Review, September 4, 2006, review of *Scrublands,* p. 64.
Publishers Weekly, May 29, 2006, review of *Scrublands,* p. 43.

ONLINE

artSMart, http://www.artsmart.co.za/ (January 13, 2004), Ruby Bernard, review of *The Red Monkey: The Leaking Cello Case.*
Lambiek.net, http://lambiek.net/ (January 20, 2007), author profile.*

*   *   *

DALY, John 1966-

PERSONAL: Born April 28, 1966, in Carmichael, CA; married, 1990; wife's name Dale; married Paulette (third wife; divorced, 1997); married Sherri Miller, 2001 (marriage ended); children: Sierra Lynn, Austin, John Patrick. *Education:* Attended University of Arkansas.

ADDRESSES: Home—Cordova, TN. *Office*—John Daly Enterprises, LLC, P.O. Box 585159, Orlando, FL 32858-5159; fax: 407-841-2561.

CAREER: Golfer, businessperson, and writer. Founder of John Daly Enterprises, 2001.

AWARDS, HONORS: Winner, PGA Championship, 1991; Named PGA Tour Rookie of the Year, 1991; Winner, B.C. Open, 1992; Winner, BellSouth Classic, 1994; Winner, British Open, 1995.

WRITINGS:

(With John Andrisani) *Grip It and Rip It!,* HarperCollins (New York, NY), 1992.
(With Glen Waggoner) *My Life In and Out of the Rough: The Truth behind All That Bull**** You Think You Know about Me,* HarperCollins (New York, NY), 2006.

SIDELIGHTS: John Daly is a professional golfer who is as well known for his exploits off the golf course as for his powerful golf swing and Professional Golf Association (PGA) tournament victories, which number only a few. Although much has been written about his personal life—including his excessive drinking, womanizing, and gambling—he continues to have a huge fan following and is among the most popular players on the professional golf tour. Daly teams with writer Glen Waggoner to tell his side of the story in *My Life In and Out of the Rough: The Truth behind All That Bull**** You Think You Know about Me.* The autobiography chronicles Daly's life beginning with his youth and first efforts at playing golf at the age of four, his scholarship to the University of Arkansas, and his eventual success playing in the PGA.

The authors also delve into what many perceive as the inner demons that have prevented Daly from being one of the truly great golfers of his time. For example, he reveals that he estimates he has lost fifty million dollars gambling, a fact that astonished even him when he did research for his book and went over his tax returns. The book also addresses Daly's alcoholism and refusal to continue to undergo outside rehabilitation, choosing, instead, to address the problem himself by weaning himself off of hard liquor and drinking only beer. According to Joe Juliano, writing in the *Philadelphia Inquirer,* Daly noted at a 2006 news conference for the Exelon Invitational charity event: "I figured rehab is for quitters. I just didn't enjoy it. I tried it and I had people convincing me saying I'm this or I'm that. But when I looked in the mirror in 1999, I took myself off all the medication and my heart and my mind said, 'This is it. I'm doing this on my own.'" In an interview with *New York Times* contributor Damon Hack, Daly pointed out: "The whole book is not just about gambling, it's just life. A lot of good things, and a lot of bad things. It was kind of therapeutic talking about it."

In a review of *My Life In and Out of the Rough* in the *Europe Intelligence Wire,* Liam Kelly noted: "Daly is above all, very honest. He deals with all the issues in this book." Noting that Daly tells his story "with uncompromising self-honesty," Kelly added: "It's a sports autobiography with a difference and golf fans will be intrigued to hear John Daly's story in his own words." David S. Hauck, writing in the *Christian Science Monitor,* called the book a "blunt assessment (in blunt language) of a man-child who's trying to cast out his demons."

BIOGRAPHICAL AND CRITICAL SOURCES:

BOOKS

Daly, John, and Glen Waggoner, *My Life In and Out of the Rough: The Truth behind All That Bull**** You Think You Know about Me,* HarperCollins Publishers (New York, NY), 2006.
Notable Sports Figures, four volumes, Thomson Gale (Detroit, MI), 2004.

PERIODICALS

Christian Science Monitor, June 2, 2006, David S. Hauck, review of *My Life In and Out of the Rough.*
Europe Intelligence Wire, July 15, 2006, Liam Kelly, "Drinker, Gambler, Womaniser, but He's Still the People's Champion," review of *My Life In and Out of the Rough.*
New York Times, May 3, 2006, Damon Hack, "Daly Is an Open Book in Discussing His Gambling Habit," p. D2.
Philadelphia Inquirer, June 6, 2006, Joe Juliano, "Candor, Color: Daly Delivers: Golf's Lovable Loaf Is Still a Crowd Pleaser."
Sports Illustrated, May 15, 2006, Richard Hoffer, "Goodbye, Mr. Chips. (John Daly's Gambling)," p. 18.

ONLINE

John Daly Home Page, http://www.johndaly.com (January 18, 2007).*

*   *   *

DANIEL, Elton L.

PERSONAL: Education: University of North Carolina at Chapel Hill, B.A., 1970; University of Texas at Austin, Ph.D., 1978.

ADDRESSES: Office—Department of History, University of Hawaii, 2530 Dole St., Sakamaki Hall, Honolulu, HI 96822. *E-mail*—edaniel@hawaii.edu.

CAREER: Professor and writer. University of Hawaii, Honolulu, professor of history.

WRITINGS:

The Political and Social History of Khurasan under Abbasid Rule, 747-820, Bibliotheca Islamica (Minneapolis, MN), 1979.
(Editor and translator, with Hafez Farmayan) *A Shi'ite Pilgrimage to Mecca (1885-1886),* University of Texas Press (Austin, TX), 1990.
The History of Iran, Greenwood Press (Westport, CT), 2001.
(Editor) *Society and Culture in Qajar Iran: Studies in Honor of Hafez Farmayan,* Mazda Publishers (Costa Mesa, CA), 2002.
(With Ali Akbar Mahdi) *Culture and Customs of Iran,* Greenwood Press (Westport, CT), 2006.

Contributor to the *Journal of the Royal Asiatic Society.* Associate editor for the *Encyclopaedia Iranica.*

SIDELIGHTS: As a professor of history at the University of Hawaii, Elton L. Daniel teaches classes and conducts research in the areas of Islamic and Middle Eastern history and civilization. He has published several books on related topics, with a particular focus on Iranian history. In *The History of Iran,* for instance, Daniel covers more than 2,500 years of Iranian history, beginning with the pre-Islamic era and continuing through the turn of the twenty-first century. In a review for the *Middle East Journal,* Monica M. Ringer described the volume as "a sophisticated and comprehensive introductory survey of the history of Iran which is, at the same time, an easy read." She further remarked: "This book would serve equally well as an introduction to Iranian history and as a basic guide to understanding contemporary Iranian politics and culture."

In 2002 Daniel served as editor of a collection of works paying tribute to Hafez Farmayan, a noted historian of Iran and Islam. *Society and Culture in Qajar Iran: Studies in Honor of Hafez Farmayan* explores the history of this nineteenth-century Iranian society, including its interactions with Western and neighboring countries. Willem Floor wrote in a review of the book for the *Middle East Journal:* "Elton Daniel shows that making the pilgrimage to Mecca was more than a spiritual journey, for travel through other Muslim countries and meeting other Muslims did leave its impact. . . . Those who wish to understand better how material conditions, social values, and intellectual perspectives in Iran changed during the 19th century will be enlightened by this nicely printed book."

BIOGRAPHICAL AND CRITICAL SOURCES:

PERIODICALS

Middle East Journal, autumn, 2001, Monica M. Ringer, review of *The History of Iran,* p. 685; spring, 2003, Willem Floor, review of *Society and Culture in Qajar Iran: Studies in Honor of Hafez Farmayan,* p. 353.

ONLINE

University of Hawaii Department of History, http://www.hawaii.edu/history/ (August 8, 2006), faculty profile.*

*　　*　　*

DANIELS, Cynthia R.

PERSONAL: Education: University of Massachusetts at Amherst, Ph.D., 1984.

ADDRESSES: Office—Department of Political Science, Rutgers, State University of New Jersey, 89 George St., New Brunswick, NJ 08901. *E-mail*—crd@rci.rutgers.edu.

CAREER: Political scientist, educator and writer. Rutgers University, New Brunswick, NJ, associate professor of political science. Previously taught at Harvard University, Cambridge, MA, and the University of Hawaii.

AWARDS, HONORS: Recipient of fellowships from the Bunting Institute at Radcliffe College, the American Association of University Women, and the Woodrow Wilson Foundation.

WRITINGS:

(With Maureen Paul and Robert Rosofsky) *Family Work & Health: Survey Report Sponsored by Commonwealth of Massachusetts,* Women's Health Unit, Department of Public Health (Boston, MA), 1988.

(Editor, with Eileen Boris) *Homework: Historical and Contemporary Perspectives on Paid Labor at Home,* University of Illinois Press (Urbana, IL), 1989.

At Women's Expense: State Power and the Politics of Fetal Rights, Harvard University Press (Cambridge, MA), 1993.

(Editor) *Feminists Negotiate the State: the Politics of Domestic Violence,* University Press of America (Lanham, MD), 1997.

(Editor) *Lost Fathers: The Politics of Fatherlessness in America,* St. Martin's Press (New York, NY), 1998.

Exposing Men: The Science and Politics of Male Reproduction, Oxford University Press (New York, NY), 2006.

Contributor to periodicals, including *Policy Studies Review* and *Journal of Social History.* Contributor to books, including *Medicine Unbound: The Human Body and the Limits of Medical Interventions,* edited by R. Blank and A. Bonnicksen, Columbia University Press (New York, NY), 1993; *Feminist Frameworks: Alternative Theoretical Accounts of the Relations between Men and Women,* 3rd edition, edited by Jaggar and Rothenberg, McGraw-Hill (New York, NY), 1992; and *From Abortion to Reproductive Freedom,* edited by M. Fried, South End Press, 1990.

SIDELIGHTS: Cynthia R. Daniels is a political scientist who has written and edited books about working, family, and female and male reproductive health. Daniels served as coeditor with Eileen Boris of *Homework: Historical and Contemporary Perspectives on Paid Labor at Home.* The editors provide numerous case studies of the homework issue in the United States, beginning with a history of industrialized homework and including a discussion of how the nature of homework has changed. The essays also explore new policy issues surrounding laws concerning homework. "Most of the essays share a broad concern with the gender, race, and class dynamics surrounding homework, but they offer no consensus on

how policymakers should address the issue," wrote Ruth Milkman in the *Business History Review.* "This is a book that raises all the right questions but offers few definitive answers." Milkman added: "Indeed, scholars interested in the topic of homework in the past and present will be indebted to Boris and Daniels for years to come."

In her book *At Women's Expense: State Power and the Politics of Fetal Rights,* Daniels discusses issues of fetal rights beyond the boundaries of the abortion debate. Specifically, the author is interested in "the pregnant body to expose the inadequacy of the liberal concept of 'citizen' which is gendered male," according to Sally J. Kenney writing in the *American Political Science Review.* Kenney went on to note: "Daniels carefully examines three legal cases to challenge the ability of classical liberalism's notions of individualism, privacy, and self-determination to defend women's rights during pregnancy." The reviewer also wrote: "Her work is a major contribution to the emerging literature on this important topic."

As the editor of *Lost Fathers: The Politics of Fatherlessness in America,* the author presents carefully selected writings that present views from both the left and the right about fatherhood, focusing on the political and public debates that surround the importance of fatherhood and a strong nuclear family. Writing in *Signs,* David S. Gutterman commented that "there are great lessons to be learned from such a collection about the way ideology shapes scholarship, the construction of public policy, and the difficulty of creating conversation about such highly charged moral and political issues." Mary J. Brustman, writing in the *Library Journal,* commented that the essays provide "an interesting and multifaceted discussion."

Daniels explores threats to the male reproductive process in *Exposing Men: The Science and Politics of Male Reproduction.* In addition to discussing the issue of distorted and unfair views of men's role in the reproductive process, the author goes on to discuss the importance of good male reproductive health and myths such as the idea that men are not as vulnerable to reproductive problems as women. She also explores the role that men's reproductive health, especially as it is damaged by environmental pollutants, may play in fetal harm. Referring to the book as "intensely argued," *Chronicle of Higher Education* contributor Nina C. Ayoub wrote that "the political scientist takes a biological turn, exploring male vulnerabilities that are ignored at our peril."

BIOGRAPHICAL AND CRITICAL SOURCES:

PERIODICALS

American Political Science Review, June, 1994, Sally J. Kenney, review of *At Women's Expense: State Power and the Politics of Fetal Rights,* p. 467.

Business History Review, winter, 1989, Ruth Milkman, review of *Homework: Historical and Contemporary Perspectives on Paid Labor at Home,* p. 954.

Chronicle of Higher Education, September 15, 2006, Nina C. Ayoub, review of *Exposing Men: The Science and Politics of Male Reproduction.*

Family Matters, autumn, 1999, Carole Jean, review of *Lost Fathers: The Politics of Fatherlessness in America,* p. 81.

Library Journal, June 15, 1998, Mary Jane Brustman, review of *Lost Fathers,* p. 97.

Political Science Quarterly, fall, 1997, Joyce Gelb, "Fetal Rights, Women's Rights: Gender Equality in the Workplace," includes brief discussion of *At Women's Expense,* p. 531.

Signs, summer, 2002, David S. Gutterman, review of *Lost Fathers,* p. 1186.

Times Literary Supplement, November 13, 1998, Melanie Phillips, review of *Lost Fathers,* p. 12.

Wilson Quarterly, winter, 2005, "Seed Money," discusses article on procreative compounds coauthored by author, p. 98.

ONLINE

Living on Earth Web site, http://www.loe.org/ (November 22, 2006), "Navigating Masculinity," interview with author.

Rutgers University Political Science Web site, http://polisci.rutgers.edu/ (November 22, 2006), faculty profile of author.

*   *   *

DANNENMAIER, William D. 1930-

PERSONAL: Born 1930; married; children: eight. *Education:* Harris Teachers' College, A.B., 1952; Washington University, master's degree and Ph.D.

ADDRESSES: Home—Cumberland Furnace, TN.

CAREER: Psychologist, operations research analyst, author and newspaper columnist. Taught for twenty-five years at colleges and universities in the United States and Canada. *Military service:* U.S. Army, 1952-54, Korea, served in Fifteenth Infantry Regiment, received Combat Infantryman's Badge for service in Korea.

WRITINGS:

Mental Health, Nelson-Hall, 1978.
We Were Innocents: An Infantryman in Korea, University of Illinois Press (Urbana, IL), 1999.
Laughter and Tears: Sparks from the Furnace, Writer's Showcase Press (Lincoln, NE), 2002.

Contributor of articles to journals. Author of the blog *Sparks from the Furnace.*

SIDELIGHTS: In 1952, college graduate William D. Dannenmaier enlisted in the U.S. Army and was sent to Korea to serve with the Fifteenth Infantry Regiment in the Third Division. Originally a radioman, he used Morse code and voice to communicate with soldiers in the field and the air. After growing bored with the position, Dannenmaier volunteered for the more dangerous job of scout and went on to fight in one of the Korean Conflict's bloodiest battles. Dannenmaier returned to the United States in 1954 and went on to a long career as a educator, focusing in the area of educational and psychological testing. He completed his paid career working as a researcher for the U.S. Army, specializing in intelligence and wargaming.

More than forty years after the war ended, Dannenmaier's sister presented him with letters that he had written to her during his two-year service. Urged by family to publish them, he set to work on writing a memoir of his service in Korea. It was not an easy task: In many of the letters, Dannenmaier had deliberately lied about his locations and activities in an attempt to reassure his loved ones at home. *We Were Innocents: An Infantryman in Korea* was published in 1999 and brings to light many of the atrocities, crises, and acts of courage that occurred during this oft-forgotten conflict. B. Keith Toney remarked in a *Military History* review: "At times humorous, other times sad, the story is always gripping. Dannenmaier conveys the sense of frustration, exhaustion and, above all, the tension that is the combat soldier's constant companion."

BIOGRAPHICAL AND CRITICAL SOURCES:

PERIODICALS

Military History, June, 2000, B. Keith Toney, review of *We Were Innocents: An Infantryman in Korea,* p. 70.

ONLINE

CNN.com, http://www.cnn.com/ (June 13, 2000), "Author William Dannenmaier: 50th Anniversary of Korean War."

*   *   *

DARK, Taylor
(Taylor E. Dark, III)

PERSONAL: Education: University of California— Berkeley, B.A, 1983, M.A., 1986, Ph.D., 1993; London School of Economics, M.Sc., 1984.

ADDRESSES: Office—Department of Political Science, California State University, Los Angeles, Los Angeles, CA 90032-8226. *E-mail*—td@taylordark. com.

CAREER: Brookings Institution, Washington, DC, research fellow, 1989-90; University of California, Berkeley, lecturer, 1990-93; Kuban State University, Krasnodar, Russia, faculty fellow, 1993-95; Chernivtsi State University, Civic Education Project, Ukraine, faculty fellow, 1993-95; University of California, Irvine, visiting lecturer, 1995-96; Doshisha University, Graduate School of American Studies, Kyoto, Japan, associate professor of American politics, 1996-2004, associate dean, 1998-2004; California State University, Los Angeles, began as instructor, currently assistant professor, 2005—.

AWARDS, HONORS: University fellow, University of California, Berkeley, 1991-92.

WRITINGS:

The Unions and the Democrats: An Enduring Alliance (political science), ILR Press (Ithaca, NY), 1999, updated edition, 2001.

Contributor of scholarly articles to journals, including *Party Politics, Political Science Quarterly, Polity, Presidential Studies Quarterly, National Interest, Journal of Labor Research, Labor History, International Journal of Organization Theory and Behavior,* and *PS: Political Science and Politics.* Member of editorial board, *Doshisha American Studies,* 1998-2004, *Labor History,* 2003—.

SIDELIGHTS: In *The Unions and the Democrats: An Enduring Alliance,* political scientist Taylor Dark looks at the continually changing relationship between the Democratic Party and organized labor on the American political scene. The Democratic Party has historically received support from organized labor unions since the 1930s. However, some pundits have suggested that the conservative trend in American politics since Ronald Reagan assumed the presidency in 1981 damaged or even destroyed the relationship. Dark suggests in his study that, despite declining union membership, the relationship between labor unions and the Democrats is as strong as ever. "While private sector union membership has dwindled to less than 10 percent of the private sector labor force," declared Myron Lieberman in a review of the volume published on the Education Policy Institute's Web site, "membership in public sector unions has increased dramatically." "Public sector unions are opposed to tax limits, budgetary restraints, and anti-inflation measures that call for limits on union wage demands," Lieberman concluded. "As the book makes clear, Democratic candidates who do not support AFL-CIO positions face major difficulties in winning primary victories over union-endorsed candidates."

Dark concludes that unions and unionism still remain in the forefront of the political debate in American society. "The peculiarities of American unionism," Stephen Amberg declared in his *American Political Science Review* assessment of the book, "are at the heart of debates about American exceptionalism, the New Deal, the welfare state, interest group liberalism, and the transformations of the party system since the 1960s." "When labor operates in sync with the tide of decision-making forces, its potential influence is enlarged, but [it is] still institutionally constrained by natural barriers to translating popular will into legislative reality," *Industrial and Labor Relations Review* contributor Marick F. Masters explained. "When unions are out of sync, their power lapses, until they muster the internal change needed to achieve realignment." "Dark conceives unions as interest groups of an especially potent type, namely, those with the ability to shut down significant parts of the economy," wrote Amberg, "and his study focuses on how the leaders of the AFL-CIO plus the dozen most active federation member unions have adapted to changes in the political, economic, and ideological environment in the last 35 years."

BIOGRAPHICAL AND CRITICAL SOURCES:

PERIODICALS

American Political Science Review, March, 2000, Stephen Amberg, review of *The Unions and the Democrats: An Enduring Alliance,* p. 187.
Booklist, January 1, 1999, David Rouse, review of *The Unions and the Democrats,* p. 804.
Industrial and Labor Relations Review, April, 2000, Marick F. Masters, review of *The Unions and the Democrats,* p. 539.
Journal of Labor Research, winter, 2001, Joseph P. McGarrity, review of *The Unions and the Democrats,* p. 217.
Labor Studies Journal, fall, 2000, Robert Bruno, review of *The Unions and the Democrats,* p. 113.
Political Science Quarterly, winter, 1999, John C. Gerring, review of *The Unions and the Democrats,* p. 704.

ONLINE

Education Policy Institute, http://www.education policy.org/ (January 19, 2007), Myron Lieberman, review of *The Unions and the Democrats.*

* * *

DARK, Taylor E., III
See DARK, Taylor

* * *

DAVEY, Janet 1953-

PERSONAL: Born 1953; children: two.

ADDRESSES: Home—London, England.

CAREER: Novelist. Former teacher.

WRITINGS:

English Correspondence (novel), Chatto & Windus (London, England), 2003.
First Aid (novel), Back Bay Books (New York, NY), 2006.

SIDELIGHTS: London-based writer Janet Davey is a former teacher turned novelist. Her first novel, 2003's *English Correspondence,* tells the story of a woman stuck in a failing marriage who is forced after her father's sudden death to face the path her life has taken. The book was selected to the 2003 Orange Prize for Fiction long list. *First Aid,* Davey's first novel to be released in the United States, is also a story of family dysfunction and complex interactions. The central characters include a divorcée who is wounded physically and mentally by her boyfriend's abrupt departure and subsequently decides to move with her children to her childhood home, and her oldest child who rebels against the relocation by running away. In an article for the *New York Times Online,* Jennifer Egan described *First Aid* as a "a sharp, unsettling book that invokes a number of rich tales without exploring them directly. It has a curious power, like watching a play from a very hard chair and finding yourself in a heightened state of observation and attention." *Booklist* reviewer Emily Melton called the book an "affecting mix of thriller and literary fiction with skillfully drawn characters and expressive writing." Caroline M. Hallsworth remarked in a *Library Journal* review that Davey "peels away the layers of each character with exactitude" and has "a keen eye for the minutia of ordinary life."

BIOGRAPHICAL AND CRITICAL SOURCES:

PERIODICALS

Booklist, May 1, 2006, Emily Melton, review of *First Aid,* p. 24.
Library Journal, July 1, 2006, Caroline M. Hallsworth, review of *First Aid,* p. 64.

ONLINE

New York Times Online, http://www.nytimes.com/ (September 3, 2006), Jennifer Egan, "Dangerous Bliss," review of *First Aid.*

DAVIES, Adam 1972(?)-

PERSONAL: Born c. 1972. *Education:* Attended Kenyon College; Syracuse University, M.F.A.

ADDRESSES: Home—New York, NY.

CAREER: Writer and educator. Previously worked as an editorial assistant at Random House, New York, NY, and as an instructor of English literature and creative writing at the University of Georgia, Athens.

WRITINGS:

The Frog King: A Love Story (novel), Riverhead Books (New York, NY), 2002.
Goodbye Lemon (novel), Riverhead Books (New York, NY), 2006.

SIDELIGHTS: In his first novel, *The Frog King: A Love Story,* Adam Davies features Harry Driscoll, an editor at a publishing firm in New York City (a job that Davies once held himself). Stuck at the lower end of the company ladder and emotionally stunted, Harry not only cannot tell his coworker and girlfriend Evie that he loves her, but he is also unfaithful, pursuing an affair with a powerful editor at another publishing house. Evie tries to make the relationship work even though she is well aware of Harry's failings. Harry dreams of becoming a famous writer one day, and eventually forms an attachment to a young homeless girl, Birdie, whom he saved from a life on the streets. After Evie has had enough and leaves Harry, he comes to realize that she is really the most important thing in his life.

In a review of *The Frog King* on the *Bookreporter.com* Web site, Sarah Rachel Egelman wrote: "Davies's prose is fast paced and clever, and his dialogue is inventive." Egelman also called the novel "an original and promising debut." Gavin Quinn, writing in *Booklist,* commented that the author's "subtle observations about life . . . make for an impressive and thought-provoking work." A *Publishers Weekly* contributor referred to *The Frog King* as "intelligent and amusing."

The author's second novel, *Goodbye Lemon,* focuses on a disaffected English professor named Jack Tennant, who once dreamed of becoming a classical pianist but who, because of a family tragedy, can only review classical concerts for a paper in Atlanta. When his father suffers a stroke, Jack is convinced by his girlfriend, Hahva, to go visit his father up north and try to mend their broken relationship. Once there, Hahva finds out the depth of the family breach, which stems from the death of Jack's brother, Dex, at the age of six, and Jack's father breaking Jack's finger, thus ending his dream of attending the prestigious Juilliard School.

"Davies deftly handles a large cast of characters, but his real accomplishment is retaining our sympathy for Jack as he self-destructs," wrote David Daley of *Goodbye Lemon* on the *USA Today* Web site. Daley added that the novel "is mostly funny, evocative and emotionally true." Although a *Publishers Weekly* contributor noted that familiar scenario and plot devices of the novel, the reviewer added that the author "makes it all happen in such a fresh, smart way the conventions of this conceit are almost forgotten." The reviewer also wrote that the novel is "bitter, smart and soaked in dark humor." Jan Blodgett, writing in the *Library Journal,* commented that *Goodbye Lemon* "tenderly captures Jack's reshaping of his legacy and relationships," adding that it "is filled with compassion and humor."

BIOGRAPHICAL AND CRITICAL SOURCES:

PERIODICALS

Booklist, August, 2002, Gavin Quinn, review of *The Frog King: A Love Story,* p. 1917.
Entertainment Weekly, August 23, 2002, Troy Patterson, "Croak Monsieur: Adam Davies' Debut Novel, *The Frog King,* Offers a Precocious Peek at the Book World," p. 138.
Kirkus Reviews, June 15, 2002, review of *The Frog King,* p. 823; June 1, 2006, review of *Goodbye Lemon,* p. 534.
Library Journal, August 1, 2006, Jan Blodgett, review of *Goodbye Lemon,* p. 67.
Publishers Weekly, June 17, 2002, review of *The Frog King,* p. 39; May 8, 2006, review of *Goodbye Lemon,* p. 45; May 29, 2006, Marc Schultz, "Looking and Spilling: PW Talks with Adam Davies," p. 34.

ONLINE

Bookreporter.com, http://www.bookreporter.com/ (January 18, 2007), Sarah Rachel Egelman, review of *The Frog King.*

USA Today, http://www.usatoday.com/ (August 7, 2006), David Daley, review of *Goodbye Lemon.**

*   *   *

DAYTON, Anne

PERSONAL: Born in San Jose, CA; married, September, 2005. *Education:* Princeton University, B.A.; attended graduate school at New York University.

ADDRESSES: Home—Brooklyn, NY. *E-mail*—anne. dayton@gmail.com.

CAREER: Writer, editor, novelist. Worked as an editor for Random House and Broadway Books.

WRITINGS:

(With May Vanderbilt) *Emily Ever After,* Broadway Books (New York, NY), 2005.
(With May Vanderbilt) *Consider Lily: A Novel,* Broadway Books (New York, NY), 2006.

SIDELIGHTS: Novelists Anne Dayton and May Vanderbilt launched their successful series of Christian novels when a dinner conversation with friends revealed a deficit in the popular chick-lit genre aimed at young adult female readers. A pair of twenty-something professional women and devoted Christians, Dayton and Vanderbilt realized that traditional chick-lit fare, with its abundance of sex and sin, did not reflect their religious values. They "joked that there should be chick-lit for Christians like them, whose faith might be strong but whose single-girl imperfections loom just as large," observed a reviewer on the *Columbia News Service* Web site. In response, Dayton and Vanderbilt wrote *Emily Ever After,* a version of the biblical story of Esther in which the title character struggles to keep her Christian faith intact while living a big-city life full of distraction and temptation. The book proved to be successful not only for Dayton and Vanderbilt, but also became "one of the first Christian chick lit books to ignite a hot market of similar big sellers," the *Columbia News Service* biographer noted.

Emily Ever After follows recent college graduate Emily Hinton as she leaves her small-town California home to take on what she believes will be a glamorous editorial job in New York. The job and the move are a dream come true for Emily, who had always dreamed of working in cosmopolitan Manhattan. However, she soon discovers that the risks and temptations of big-city life are in conflict with her Christian beliefs. She makes friends at work and tries to fit in, but realizes that her new pals have wild streaks that Emily doesn't share. Christians—particularly Christian men—seem to be in short supply. To cope, she goes to church and volunteers in her Uncle Matthew's soup kitchen. When she meets Bennett Edward Wyeth III, she thinks she may have found the perfect combination of good looks, charm, and Christian identity. However, Bennett's professed purity and alleged benign motives may be a ruse concealing what he's really after. Emily must also deal with the possible rekindling of an old romance with former boyfriend Jacob, and reconcile her religious views with controversial material she encounters in the course of her job. "Frank, witty, and funny, this story succeeds in spite of its sometimes awkward reminders of Emily's Christian faith and upbringing," commented reviewer Molly Connolly in *School Library Journal.* A reviewer in *Today's Christian Woman* called Emily a "refreshingly real chick-lit heroine." Dayton and Vanderbilt's "charming offering will appeal to readers looking for a wholesome heroine navigating big-city life," remarked *Booklist* reviewer Kristine Huntley.

BIOGRAPHICAL AND CRITICAL SOURCES:

PERIODICALS

Booklist, May 1, 2005, Kristine Huntley, review of *Emily Ever After,* p. 1568.
Kirkus Reviews, April 15, 2005, review of *Emily Ever After,* p. 436; May 1, 2006, review of *Consider Lily: A Novel,* p. 425.
Publishers Weekly, May 9, 2005, review of *Emily Ever After,* p. 47.
School Library Journal, November, 2005, Molly Connally, review of *Emily Ever After,* p. 181.
Today's Christian Woman, July-August, 2005, review of *Emily Ever After,* p. 59.

ONLINE

Columbia News Service Web site, http://jscms.jrn. columbia.edu/cns/ (November 15, 2005), Jessica

Heasley, "They Love Jesus (and Cute Boys Too!)," profile of Anne Dayton and May Vanderbilt.

Daystar eStore, http://www.daystarestore.com/ (November 25, 2006), biography of Anne Dayton.

GoodGirlLit.com, http://www.goodgirllit.com/ (November 25, 2006), biography of Anne Dayton.

*   *   *

DEHART, Robyn

PERSONAL: Born in TX. Married to a university professor. *Education:* Has degree in sociology.

ADDRESSES: Home and office—Cleveland, TN. *E-mail*—robyn@robyndehart.com.

CAREER: Writer. Has held a variety of jobs, including computer software trainer, personnel recruiter, and administrative assistant.

MEMBER: Romance Writers of America.

WRITINGS:

ROMANCE NOVELS

Courting Claudia, Avon Books (New York, NY), 2005.
A Study in Scandal, Avon Books (New York, NY), 2006.
Deliciously Wicked, Avon Books (New York, NY), 2006.
Tempted at Every Turn, Avon Books (New York, NY), 2007.

SIDELIGHTS: Robyn DeHart is "one of those writers who always knew that she wanted to be a writer," as she put it on her Web site. She did not always know what type of writing she wanted to do, but she decided to try penning romance novels after reading *A Rose in Winter* by Kathleen Woodiwiss. DeHart elaborated on the appeal of romance writing in an interview with Cathy Sova for *Romance Reader,* saying: "I'm drawn to the basics of the genre. I love happy endings. And I love watching characters grow and change." She added that she likes to see a protagonist not only find love but "come into her own."

The eponymous heroine of her first novel, *Courting Claudia,* is a nineteenth-century Englishwoman who comes into her own through an unconventional career as an illustrator, her romance with a dashing newspaper editor, and her rebellion against the control of her sinister and manipulative father. Claudia, who has felt unattractive because of her plumpness, also learns that "beauty comes in all shapes and sizes," DeHart told Sova. *Romance Reader* reviewer Wendy Livingston praised DeHart's writing style as "concise" and "skillful," noting further that "the descriptions are very good and the dialogue is easy to read."

DeHart's next novel, *A Study in Scandal,* is also set in Victorian England and is the first in a series on the Ladies' Amateur Sleuth Society, a group of women who get together to discuss mysteries. When an Egyptian sculpture is stolen from the father of society founder Lady Amelia Watersfield, the outgoing Amelia joins with stoic private detective Colin Brindley to find it. As he begins to open up to her, they fall in love. "The dialogue between them can be fast and furious," related Susan Tam in the online publication *Road to Romance.* Their relationship, observed a *Publishers Weekly* critic, is "at turns competitive, comical and sexy." The *Publishers Weekly* commentator thought the novel's love scenes were better than its mystery, saying the latter "drags." Tam, though, found the book satisfying overall. "It is a great start for this series!" she remarked.

The series continues with *Deliciously Wicked,* which focuses on another woman in the Ladies' Amateur Sleuth Society, Meg Piddington. Meg, more independent than many women of her time, is assisting in the management of her family's chocolate factory when she meets Gareth, an appealing man who has just started working there. They are attracted to each other, and when he is accused of a theft—falsely—Meg and the other society members set out to find the real thief. Some critics summed up the novel as light entertainment. It "offers some chuckles and intrigue," not a "vortex of drama," reported Shannon Johnson on the Web site *Romance Reader at Heart.* Such a story, she added, is sometimes "refreshing." A *Publishers Weekly* reviewer found the romance well-done but the mystery "anemic." The critic allowed, however, that some readers "may enjoy DeHart's breezy style."

BIOGRAPHICAL AND CRITICAL SOURCES:

PERIODICALS

Publishers Weekly, February 13, 2006, review of *A Study in Scandal,* p. 67; August 7, 2006, review of *Deliciously Wicked,* p. 38.
Chicago Tribune, November 19, 2006, John Charles, review of *Deliciously Wicked.*

ONLINE

Road to Romance, http://www.roadtoromance.ca/ (February, 2006), Susan Tam, review of *A Study in Scandal.*
Robyn DeHart Home Page, http://www.robyndehart. com (December 21, 2006).
Romance Reader, http://www.theromancereader.com/ (December 21, 2006), Cathy Sova, interview with Robyn DeHart; Wendy Livingston, review of *Courting Claudia.*
Romance Reader at Heart, http://romancereaderat heart.com/ (October 6, 2006), Shannon Johnson, review of *Deliciously Wicked.*

* * *

DEVENS, Toby
(Toby D. Schwartz)

PERSONAL: Born in Brooklyn, NY; married. *Education:* American University, B.A.; New York University, M.A.

ADDRESSES: Home—MD. *E-mail*—readers@ tobydevens.com.

CAREER: Writer. *Where* magazine, New York, NY, former editor and critic; Harcourt Brace, New York, NY, former writer and senior editor; has also served as senior vice president for a network of transplant banks.

WRITINGS:

(As Toby D. Schwartz) *Mercy Lord, My Husband's in the Kitchen and Other Equal Opportunity Conversations with God,* Doubleday (New York, NY), 1982.
My Favorite Midlife Crisis (Yet) (novel), Sourcebooks (Naperville, IL), 2006.

Contributor of poetry, short fiction, and articles to periodicals, including *Reader's Digest, Family Circle, McCall's,* and *Parents.* Also contributor of medical articles to professional journals.

SIDELIGHTS: Toby Devens's debut novel, *My Favorite Midlife Crisis (Yet),* follows Dr. Gwyneth Berke, a wealthy and successful gynecologic oncologist who finds herself suddenly single at age fifty-four. After Berke's husband reveals he is gay and leaves her for another man, she divorces him and begins devoting her time to her practice and to caring for her elderly father, who suffers from Alzheimer's Disease. With the help of her two best friends, the widowed Kat and the newly single Fleur, Berke begins dating again, finding little success at first. She then falls for Simon York, a charming British doctor who sweeps her off her feet. Over time, however, York proves too good to be true, and Berke again turns to Kat and Fleur for advice and comfort. "Refreshingly, these women stick together through travails tougher than mere dating disasters," noted a contributor in *Kirkus Reviews.* According to Maria Hatton, writing in *Booklist, My Favorite Midlife Crisis (Yet)* concerns "women successful in life, in friends, and in their chosen profession, realizing what's really important as they reach middle age." Though one critic faulted Devens for addressing too many themes, *Library Journal* reviewer Lesa M. Holstine observed that the work "does cover an age group usually left out of the literary loop," and the *Kirkus Reviews* contributor believed that *My Favorite Midlife Crisis (Yet)* "still manages to get to the heart of being a 50-year-old single woman."

Devens told *CA:* "I've been writing since I was able to hold a pencil. At the age of seven, dissatisfied with Grimm's fairy tales, I revised them to suit myself. More princesses, fewer ogres. I was a teenager when the process of creative writing jelled for me. Adolescence is a tumultuous time, so the idea of creating one's own world, of having control over the destinies of one's characters, is especially enticing. Plus, I've always been a voracious reader and have a vivid imagination, which is the perfect combination for a writer.

"My work is influenced by Elizabeth George, though our writing styles are so different—hers deep and intricate, mine bright and breezy—demonstrates that good writing untangles an emotional story as well as a riveting plot. Laura Lippman, who recreates Baltimore neighborhoods so marvelously, reminds me to enrich my story with local color. And Susan Isaacs' wit inspires me to 'find the funny' in almost every situation.

"The most surprising thing I've learned, in writing as in life, is that perseverance is almost as important as talent. That, as my father used to tell me, ninety-nine percent of success in any endeavor is just showing up.

"*My Favorite Midlife Crisis (Yet)* focuses on women who take on the challenges of a particular life stage with courage and humor. I intended for it to celebrate the universal community of women who help each other through the tricky parts. If the book shows a single struggling woman that she's not alone and that what seems a daunting and depressing phase can be turned into a sometimes hilarious and most certainly enlightening adventure, I'll have accomplished what I set out to do.

"And I love to make my readers laugh."

BIOGRAPHICAL AND CRITICAL SOURCES:

PERIODICALS

Booklist, July 1, 2006, Maria Hatton, review of *My Favorite Midlife Crisis (Yet)*, p. 29.
Kirkus Reviews, June 15, 2006, review of *My Favorite Midlife Crisis (Yet)*, p. 591.
Library Journal, September 15, 2006, Lesa M. Holstine, review of *My Favorite Midlife Crisis (Yet)*, p. 47.
Publishers Weekly, May 15, 2006, review of *My Favorite Midlife Crisis (Yet)*, p. 44.

ONLINE

Toby Devens's Home Page, http://tobydevens.com (January 15, 2007).

*   *   *

DOBBS, Lou 1945-

PERSONAL: Born September 24, 1945, in Childress, TX; married Debi Segura; children: Chance, Jason, Hilary, Heather. *Education:* Degree from Harvard University, 1967. *Politics:* Republican.

ADDRESSES: Office—Cable News Network, One CNN Center, Atlanta, GA 30303.

CAREER: Broadcast journalist and writer. Worked as copy reader at *Los Angeles Times,* Los Angeles, CA, and as reporter with radio and television stations in Arizona and Washington; Cable News Network (CNN), Atlanta, GA, chief economics correspondent and *Moneyline* anchor, 1980-99, *Primenews* anchor, 1981, managing editor, business news, 1984-97, executive vice president, 1995-99, anchor and managing editor of *Lou Dobbs Tonight* (originally titled *Lou Dobbs Moneyline*), 2001—. CNNfn.com, president 1995-99. Space.com, founder, chairman, and chief executive officer, 1999-2001. Anchor of special programs for CNN. Anchor of nationally syndicated financial news radio report, *The Lou Dobbs Financial Report.* Columnist for *Money* magazine and *U.S. News and World Report.* Member of board of Society of Professional Journalists Foundation, Horatio Alger Association, National Space Foundation, and Space.com.

MEMBER: Planetary Society, Overseas Press Club, American Economic Association, National Academy of Television Arts and Sciences.

AWARDS, HONORS: George Foster Peabody Award (shared with CNN business news team), 1987, for coverage of 1987 stock market crash; Luminary Award, Business Journalism Review, 1990; Father of the Year, National Father's Day Committee, 1993; Horatio Alger Association Award for Distinguished Americans, 1999; National Space Club Media Award,

2000; Emmy Award, National Academy of Television Arts and Sciences, 2004, for "Exporting America" series of reports on Lou Dobbs Tonight; Eugene Katz Award for Excellence in the Coverage of Immigration, Center for Immigration Studies, for "Broken Borders" series of reports on Lou Dobbs Tonight; Man of the Year Award, Organization for the Rights of American Workers, 2004; George J. Kourpias Excellence in Journalism Award, International Association of Machinists and Aerospace Workers, 2004; Hugh O'Brien Youth Leadership in Media Award, Albert Schweitzer Leadership Awards, 2004; Lifetime Achievement Emmy Award, National Academy of Television Arts and Sciences, 2005, for business and financial reporting; CableAce Award, Front Page Award, New York Film Festival Award, Janus Award, and Daniel Webster Award.

WRITINGS:

NONFICTION

(With H.P. Newquist) *Space: The Next Business Frontier,* Pocket Books (New York, NY), 2001.
Exporting America: Why Corporate Greed Is Shipping American Jobs Overseas, Warner Books (New York, NY), 2004.
War on the Middle Class: How the Government, Big Business, and Special Interest Groups Are Waging War on the American Dream and How to Fight Back, Viking Press (New York, NY), 2006.

SIDELIGHTS: Lou Dobbs has long covered business and finance as a broadcast journalist, having joined the Cable News Network (CNN) on its founding in 1980 and hosted such CNN series as *Moneyline* and *Lou Dobbs Tonight.* His work has also appeared in print in such books as *Space: The Next Business Frontier,* which focuses on the commercial opportunities offered by space exploration. His interest in space is such that he left CNN for two years to launch Space.com, a multimedia company providing information about the universe. Another major interest for Dobbs is the impact of globalization, especially the outsourcing of jobs—when U.S. companies reduce employment domestically and expand it in countries where wages are lower—on the U.S. economy.

"The principal issue I have with outsourcing is that American companies . . . are killing jobs in this country and sending them overseas to provide the same

goods and services back to the U.S. economy," Dobbs told Jeff Fleischer in an interview for *Mother Jones* magazine's Web site shortly after the publication of *Exporting America: Why Corporate Greed Is Shipping American Jobs Overseas.* "I have no problem if they want to invest and create a market in India or the Philippines or wherever. That's great, but don't kill an American job and put it in the hands of someone making one-tenth as much just to send that same good or service back to the United States." Unfettered outsourcing, he continued, costs hundreds of thousands of U.S. jobs each year, puts downward pressure on wages, and will undermine environmental and labor laws.

Some commentators have noted that Dobbs, a conservative Republican, has taken what many consider the liberal position on the outsourcing issue. He remarked to Fleischer, though, that many conservatives also oppose outsourcing. When Ronald Reagan was president, he called for Japanese automakers to build factories in the United States as part of a trade policy that Dobbs characterized as "rational, balanced, reciprocal." Mary Frances Wilkens, reviewing *Exporting America* for *Booklist,* related that Dobbs thinks the solution to outsourcing will come from neither the Republicans nor the Democrats alone. He does, however, outline "sound ideas for reversing the course" in his "tightly written account," she added.

Dobbs further explores what he sees as anti-worker policies in *War on the Middle Class: How the Government, Big Business, and Special Interest Groups Are Waging War on the American Dream and How to Fight Back.* Middle-class Americans are in a precarious economic position, he says, because politicians are beholden to corporate contributors rather than to constituents, religious activists are focused on gay rights and abortion instead of Americans' standard of living, and companies are hiring illegal immigrants. His proposed remedies include taxpayer funding of political campaigns, stronger ethics rules for public officials, and tighter border control.

Several critics observed that Dobbs's viewpoints do not follow any political party line and that his writing is stimulating and challenging. A *Publishers Weekly* reviewer found that Dobbs is "a refreshingly bold thinker who refuses to be intellectually pigeon-holed." Mary Whaley, writing in *Booklist,* thought Dobbs "correctly identifies important national issues." Dermot McEvoy, who interviewed Dobbs for *Publishers*

Weekly, found him and his book to be in harmony with the nation's concerns. "Love him or hate him," McEvoy reported, "Lou Dobbs has earned America's attention."

BIOGRAPHICAL AND CRITICAL SOURCES:

BOOKS

Gale Encyclopedia of E-Commerce, Thomson Gale (Detroit, MI), 2002.

PERIODICALS

ABA Banking Journal, May, 2004, Steve Cocheo, "The Dobbs Effect," p. 32.
Booklist, October 15, 2004, Mary Frances Wilkens, review of *Exporting America: Why Corporate Greed Is Shipping American Jobs Overseas,* p. 385; October 15, 2006, Mary Whaley, review of *War on the Middle Class: How the Government, Big Business, and Special Interest Groups Are Waging War on the American Dream and How to Fight Back,* p. 22.
Daily Variety, June 10, 2003, Pamela McClintock, "'Dobbs' Revamped, Renamed, Expanded," p. 4.
Hollywood Reporter, June 10, 2003, Andrew Grossman, "CNN Redubs 'Dobbs,' Adds Two Segments," p. 8; October 18, 2005, Paul J. Gough, "Emmy: Dobbs Career Is Money," p. 6; October 11, 2006, Paul J. Gough, "CNN Features Dobbs Going into Election," p. 6.
Publishers Weekly, August 7, 2006, review of *War on the Middle Class,* p. 46; September 4, 2006, Dermot McEvoy, "The Infuriated American: Lou Dobbs's Campaign for the Middle Class," p. 30.
Securities Industry News, May 31, 2004, Carol E. Curtis, "What to Say When Lou Dobbs Calls."

ONLINE

CNN Web site, http://www.cnn.com/ (December 27, 2006), brief biography.
Mother Jones Web site, http://www.motherjones.com/ (February 7, 2005), Jeff Fleischer, "Exporting America: An Interview with Lou Dobbs."*

DOLAN, Michael T. 1975-

PERSONAL: Born November 9, 1975, in Drexel Hill, PA. *Ethnicity:* "Caucasian." *Education:* Villanova University, B.A., 1999. *Religion:* Roman Catholic.

ADDRESSES: Home—West Chester, PA. *E-mail*—mdolan@conversari.com.

CAREER: Writer.

AWARDS, HONORS: O'Meara Award, Society for the Propagation of the Faith, 2004, for a magazine article.

WRITINGS:

Walden (fiction), Conversari House (West Chester, PA), 2006.

Contributor to periodicals, including *Philadelphia Inquirer.*

*　　　*　　　*

DOOGAN, Mike

PERSONAL: Born in AK. *Education:* University of San Francisco, B.A.; University of Alaska, Anchorage, M.F.A.

ADDRESSES: Home—Anchorage, AK.

CAREER: Writer and journalist. *Anchorage Daily News,* Anchorage, AK, metro columnist, 1985-2004. Variously worked as a teamster, janitor, baggage handler, and a legislative aide.

AWARDS, HONORS: Robert L. Fish Award for short fiction.

WRITINGS:

(Editor) *How to Speak Alaskan,* illustrated by Jamie Smith, Epicenter Press (Fairbanks, AK), 1993.

Fashion Means Your Fur Hat Is Dead: A Guide to Good Manners and Social Survival in Alaska, illustrated by Dee Boyles, Epicenter Press (Fairbanks, AK), 1996.

Doogan: The Best of the Newspaper Columnist Alaskans Love to Hate, edited by Michael Carey, Epicenter Press (Kenmore, WA), 2003.

Lost Angel: A Nik Kane Alaska Mystery, Putnam (New York, NY), 2006.

SIDELIGHTS: Mike Doogan is an Alaskan-born journalist who has spent most of his life in the arctic state. Although he worked various jobs, including being a teamster, janitor, baggage handler, and a legislative aide, Doogan is a local celebrity for his nineteen-year period with the *Anchorage Daily News,* particularly in his role as the metro columnist. During his fourteen years as "the columnist Alaskans love to hate," Doogan wrote his take on Alaska and the world around it, oftentimes at political odds with the majority of the periodical's readership.

In 2006 Doogan published his first novel, *Lost Angel: A Nik Kane Alaska Mystery,* a mystery that introduces ex-detective Nik Kane. Having recently been released from prison after a wrongful conviction, the now-divorced cop starts his own private detective agency and takes a case about a girl who went missing from a religious cult in central Alaska. A critic writing in *Publishers Weekly* called the prose "engaging" and "lucid." In a *Kirkus Reviews* article, a critic noted that "this series kickoff provides a righteously appealing hero and terrific local color." Writing on the *Book-Loons* Web site, Tim Davis agreed that the characters were "finely conceived." He concluded by calling the book "a fascinating, well-written, explosive tale of deceit and danger."

BIOGRAPHICAL AND CRITICAL SOURCES:

PERIODICALS

Booklist, July 1, 2006, Connie Fletcher, review of *Lost Angel: A Nik Kane Alaska Mystery,* p. 36.
Kirkus Reviews, June 15, 2006, review of *Lost Angel,* p. 603.
Publishers Weekly, June 19, 2006, review of *Lost Angel,* p. 43.

ONLINE

BookLoons, http://www.bookloons.com/ (January 18, 2007), Tim Davis, review of *Lost Angel.*
Poynter Institute Web site, http://www.poynter.org/ (January 6, 2004), "The Exit Interview."*

* * *

DOOLITTLE, Sean 1971-

PERSONAL: Born 1971; married; children: two.

ADDRESSES: Home—Omaha, NE.

CAREER: Writer.

WRITINGS:

NOVELS

Dirt, UglyTown (Los Angeles, CA), 2001.
Burn, UglyTown (Los Angeles, CA), 2003.
Rain Dogs, Dell (New York, NY), 2005.
The Cleanup (includes excerpts from *Rain Dogs*), Dell (New York, NY), 2006.

Contributor to anthologies, including *The Year's Best Horror Stories XXII,* DAW Books, 1994; *Noirotica,* Masquerade/Rhinoceros, 1996; and *Darkside: Horror for the Next Millennium,* Penguin/ROC, 1998. Contributor to magazines, including *Cavalier, Crimewave,* and *Kinesis.*

SIDELIGHTS: Sean Doolittle has written mystery novels that some critics have characterized as being in the "hard-boiled" vein of crime fiction, with violent action, dark humor, and uncluttered prose. David Pitt, in a review of *The Cleanup* for *Booklist,* described Doolittle's novels as being "little noir gems," while David J. Montgomery, discussing *Rain Dogs* for *Mystery Ink Online,* called the author's writing style "lean and mean." Various commentators have compared Doolittle's work to that of Elmore Leonard, James M. Cain, and Jim Thompson.

Author Stephen King inspired Doolittle to write several short stories in the horror genre early in his career. "After a while I found myself trying too hard," Doolittle remarked in an interview with fellow mystery writer Victor Gischler for the Web site *Mystery Net.* Having switched to crime fiction, he noted to Gischler, "I think crime fiction seems to be really wide open in terms of what you can do (or what fits within the boundaries after you do it)."

Doolittle's first novel, *Dirt,* focuses on unscrupulous business practices at a funeral home. *Dirt,* Doolittle told Gischler, is "sort of a slacker crime novel sprinkled with industry satire." He followed it with *Burn,* in which a well-known Los Angeles fitness instructor is murdered, his body discovered by firefighters trying to put out wildfires near the city. A retired organized-crime arsonist, Andrew Kindler, becomes involved in investigating the murder. This novel led some reviewers to apply the "hard-boiled" label, while noting some unconventional aspects of the story. Terry D'Auray, critiquing for the online publication *Agony Column,* reported: "Doolittle has managed a somewhat genre-bending feat in the mystery realm— he's written a feel-good, hard-boiled mystery; all the classic hard-boiled elements are combined with a sympathetic gentleness of characterization that is wholly original." D'Auray went on to praise Doolittle's prose as "smooth and stylish," his characters as "realistic and humanistic," and his plot as "suspenseful and well-paced." In a similar vein, *South Florida Sun-Sentinel* contributor Oline H. Cogdill dubbed *Burn* "a briskly plotted, hard-boiled mystery" featuring "off-the-wall but believable characters."

Rain Dogs deals with a onetime Chicago journalist who has retreated to his Nebraska hometown to manage a campground after the death of his young daughter and the breakup of his marriage. His life in Nebraska, however, is complicated by his heavy drinking, difficult relationships, and corrupt local police. His protagonist, Tom Coleman, is "an original," observed Cogdill in the *South Florida Sun-Sentinel,* adding that the tale is "compelling." Keir Graff, writing in *Booklist,* deemed the story a "lifelike and nuanced" one that will appeal to readers who enjoy "hard-boiled fiction and classic noir." Montgomery, in *Mystery Ink Online,* complimented the "quality and authenticity of the writing."

The Cleanup is set in Omaha, Nebraska, where police officer Matthew Worth assists in a cover-up when an appealing young woman kills her violent boyfriend. Some critics found the novel a suspenseful and stylish effort. A *Publishers Weekly* contributor described it as a "tense crime drama" told in "punchy and sincere prose," commenting further that Worth is a "well-crafted read." In *Booklist,* Pitt concluded: "Noir fans will savor this one."

BIOGRAPHICAL AND CRITICAL SOURCES:

PERIODICALS

Booklist, November 15, 2005, Keir Graff, review of *Rain Dogs,* p. 29; October 1, 2006, David Pitt, review of *The Cleanup,* p. 40.
Publishers Weekly, September 11, 2006, review of *The Cleanup,* p. 40.
South Florida Sun-Sentinel, November 12, 2003, Oline H. Cogdill, review of *Burn;* June 7, 2006, Oline H. Cogdill, review of *Rain Dogs.*
New York Sun, December 6, 2006, Otto Penzler, review of *The Cleanup.*
New York Times Book Review, December 24, 2006, Marilyn Stasio, review of *The Cleanup.*

ONLINE

Agony Column, http://trashotron.com/agony/ (December 8, 2003), Terry D'Auray, review of *Burn.*
The Cleanup Web site, http://www.thecleanup.com/ (December 26, 2006).
Mystery Ink Online, http://www.mysteryinkonline.com/ (January, 2001), David J. Montgomery, review of *Rain Dogs.*
Mystery Net, http://www.mysterynet.com/ (December 26, 2006), Victor Gischler, interview with Sean Doolitte.
Mystery One Bookstore Web site, http://www.mysteryone.com/ (October 20, 2001), interview with Sean Doolittle.
Sean Doolittle Home Page, http://www.seandoolittle.com (December 26, 2006).

*   *   *

DOWD, Matthew J. 1962-

PERSONAL: Born 1962, in Detroit, MI; children: three sons. *Education:* Cardinal Newman College, graduated.

ADDRESSES: E-mail—authors@applebeesamerica. com.

CAREER: Public Strategies, Inc. (consulting firm), founding partner and president; ViaNovo (consulting firm), founding partner; cofounder of *HotSoup.com;* University of Texas, Lyndon Baines Johnson School of Public Affairs, Austin, instructor. Has worked on the staff of Senator Lloyd Bentsen; Republican National Committee, consultant; strategist for the reelection campaigns of President George W. Bush, 2004, and Governor Arnold Schwarzenegger, 2006.

AWARDS, HONORS: Named Pollster of the Year, American Association of Political Consultants.

WRITINGS:

(With Douglas B. Sosnik and Ron Fournier) *Applebee's America: How Successful Political, Business, and Religious Leaders Connect with the New American Community,* Simon & Schuster (New York, NY), 2006.

SIDELIGHTS: Matthew J. Dowd is a political consultant and, along with Douglas B. Sosnik and Ron Fournier, the author of *Applebee's America: How Successful Political, Business, and Religious Leaders Connect with the New American Community.* The writers explore similarities in the lives of successful Americans. They assert that America does not consist of "red" and "blue" states, but rather of values-based "tribes" and a large group of voters who can be swayed with the proper marketing techniques. The authors call this "life targeting." Dowd, as a former strategist for President George W. Bush, provides insights on how his campaign relied heavily on polling. Dowd and his collaborators contend that Bush defeated John Kerry because of highly focused advertising and because opinion was swayed in local communities by his followers who believed him when he told them where he stood on the issues. This strategy, they say, provides a "Gut Values Connection" that is sustainable even when voters do not fully agree. Similarly, the popularity of the Applebee's restaurant chain mentioned in the title is derived from the fact that it has created a neighborhood atmosphere.

Fournier is a political writer, and Sosnik a former advisor to President Bill Clinton, who also successfully reached out emotionally to the voters. The authors also write of the success of religious leaders, such as Rick Warren, who have created communities in mega-churches because of shared values and a need people have to belong. They demonstrate that decisions often tend to be made based on emotion rather than issues and feel that Republicans are better than Democrats at knowing who the voters are and what they want. The authors conclude, too, that the younger generation shows a great deal of promise and tends to be more optimistic, civic minded, and politically active, especially because of the power of online networking.

BIOGRAPHICAL AND CRITICAL SOURCES:

PERIODICALS

American Prospect, October, 2006, E.J. Dionne, Jr., review of *Applebee's America: How Successful Political, Business, and Religious Leaders Connect with the New American Community,* p. 52.
Booklist, September 15, 2006, Vanessa Bush, review of *Applebee's America,* p. 13.
Library Journal, September 1, 2006, Carol J. Elsen, review of *Applebee's America,* p. 158.
Publishers Weekly, July 24, 2006, review of *Applebee's America,* p. 52.
San Francisco Chronicle, September 18, 2006, Austin Considine, review of *Applebee's America.*
Washington Post, September 12, 2006, Amy Goldstein, review of *Applebee's America,* p. A21.

ONLINE

Applebee's America Web site, http://www.applebees america.com (January 11, 2007).
Think and Ask, http://www.thinkandask.com/ (September 3, 2006), review of *Applebee's America.**

*   *   *

DOWNS, Greg

PERSONAL: Married; wife's name Diane (an associate dean). *Education:* Yale University, B.A., 1993; University of Iowa Writers' Workshop, M.F.A., 1999; Northwestern University, M.A., 2003; University of Pennsylvania, Ph.D., 2006.

ADDRESSES: Home—New York, NY. *Office*—Department of History, City College of New York, 138th St. and Convent Ave., New York, NY 10031. *E-mail*—GDowns@ccny.cuny.edu.

CAREER: Writer and educator. City College of the City University of New York, assistant professor of history, 2006—. University School of Nashville, Nashville, TN, former varsity basketball coach. Worked as a newspaper editor, a reporter, and a high-school English teacher.

AWARDS, HONORS: Flannery O'Connor Award, for *Spit Baths;* James Michener/Copernicus Society of America Prize, Iowa Writer's Workshop; Josephine DeKarman Fellowship.

WRITINGS:

Spit Baths (short stories), University of Georgia Press (Athens, GA), 2006.

Contributor of short stories to periodicals, including *Glimmer Train, Greensboro Review, Black Warrior Review, Meridian, CutBank, South Dakota Review, Chicago Reader, Southeast Review, Literary Review, StorySouth, Wind, Philadelphia Stories, New Letters, Madison Review, Witness,* and *Sycamore Review.*

SIDELIGHTS: Greg Downs's debut short-story collection *Spit Baths* "offers a multifaceted and exquisite rendering of the modern (and postmodern) south, the stories' realism and detail no less effective for their imaginative, poetic depictions," observed reviewer Scott Yarbrough on *StorySouth.com.* "Living in a place where the present blurs into the past, Downs' characters are often childlike adults or precocious children who display an innocence bordering on ignorance, until a moment of sudden and bitter epiphany," commented a contributor to *SmallSpiral Notebook.com.* In the two-page short "Adam's Curse," which a *Kirkus Reviews* writer noted "demonstrates nicely the strange beauty of Downs's imagination," the nineteen-year-old protagonist watches with bemusement as his female relatives decide that they can and will live their lives without men. Meanwhile, the narrator is keenly aware of the female charms of the cheerful checkout girl at the grocery store. In "Snack

Cakes," a high-school boy is kicked out by his mother when she catches him having sex with his girlfriend. He seeks help from his grandfather, a man married six times and unsure which ex-wife he loves the best, and who has just been kicked out by wife number six. Together, grandfather and grandson consider the mysteries of women as the two visit each of the six ex-wives, dropping off boxes of the grandfather's keepsakes and mementoes for each. "Field Trip" examines the place where a young man's sexual fantasies and daydreams coincide with a school trip. The protagonist of "Ain't I a King, Too?" leaves behind some domestic strife in 1935 Kentucky. When he arrives in Shreveport, Louisiana, however, he is mistaken for recently killed Huey Long, the state's controversial, corrupt, firebrand senator. What follows is a case of mistaken identity with its own peculiar dangers. Downs's "work has a cerebral, surreal element that requires a little piecing together," remarked a *Kirkus Reviews* critic. Joey Rubin, writing for the *San Francisco Chronicle,* felt that Downs "speaks elegantly of those ugly histories, namely of racism and hatred, that we'd rather forget, and paints a hopeful portrait of the role family can play in healing those wounds." A *Publishers Weekly* contributor noted that in his writing, Downs displays a "strong sense of style and unfaltering command of his material" allowing him to "take the kinds of risks in tone and subject" that will cause readers to either love or hate the collection.

BIOGRAPHICAL AND CRITICAL SOURCES:

PERIODICALS

Kirkus Reviews, July 15, 2006, review of *Spit Baths,* p. 690.
Philadelphia Inquirer, January 21, 2007, Martha Woodall, "Realizing the Past Can Never Be Escaped."
Publishers Weekly, August 7, 2006, review of *Spit Baths,* p. 34.
San Francisco Chronicle, December 14, 2006, Joey Rubin, review of *Spit Baths,* p. F1.

ONLINE

City University of New York Department of History Web site, http://www.ccny/cuny.edu/ (December 20, 2006), biography of Greg Downs.

Greg Downs Home Page, http://www.gregdowns.net (December 20, 2006).

Greg Downs MySpace.com, http://www.myspace.com/ (December 20, 2006), profile of Greg Downs.

Litpark.com, http://www.litpark.com/ (October 28, 2006), Susan Henderson, interview with Greg Downs.

My.Tennessean.com, http://my.tennessean.com/ (November 17, 2006), Angela Patterson, "Greg Downs: USN Grad Awash in Southern Culture in *Spit Baths.*"

SmallSpiralNotebook.com, http://www.smallspiral notebook.com/ (November 16, 2006), Brendan Hughes, review of *Spit Baths.*

StorySouth.com, http://www.storysouth.com/ (August, 2006), biography of Greg Downs; (November, 2006), Scott Yarbrough, review of *Spit Baths.*

*   *   *

DRAY, Matt 1967-
(Matthew Frederick Dray)

PERSONAL: Born April 2, 1967, in Proserpine, Queensland, Australia; son of Frederick William (a sugar cane farmer) and Genevieve Amy (a homemaker) Dray. *Education:* Attended secondary school in Brisbane, Australia. *Religion:* Roman Catholic.

ADDRESSES: Home—Palm Beach, Queensland, Australia.

CAREER: Writer. Worked at many odd jobs, including work as milk deliverer, farmhand, construction laborer, fruit picker, security guard, and plant operator.

WRITINGS:

A Day at the Races (novel), Penguin (Camberwell, Victoria, Australia), 2000.

(And photographer) *Dougal the Garbage Dump Bear* (juvenile picture book), Penguin (Camberwell, Victoria, Australian), 2004, Kane/Miller Book Publishers (La Jolla, CA), 2005.

(And photographer) *Dougal and Bumble and the Long Walk Home* (juvenile picture book), Penguin (Camberwell, Victoria, Australia), 2006.

SIDELIGHTS: Matt Dray told *CA:* "*Dougal the Garbage Dump Bear* is the result of a series of incidents and accidents that occurred in the early months of 2002. Dougal was the first of more than fifty toy animals found at a garbage dump by me and my work mates, then kept there as a joke. In late March I started taking photos of them and a vague idea for a story emerged, with Dougal as the main character, but I didn't know how to begin it.

"The light-bulb moment came one day in April, after I'd had a fairly serious accident in one of the bulldozers. It had tipped over and I was sent down to the site office as a precaution in case I was injured. While I was sitting in the office feeling foolish, Neil Young's song 'Heart of Gold' came on the radio. I love that song and the first line of the book came to me. 'Dougal was a shy little bear with a heart of gold.'

"Making the best of a bad situation, I grabbed a camera, drove back to the dump site, and started taking photos of the accident scene with Dougal and his sidekick, Bumble the Bee, in the foreground giving instructions. In one morning I had a beginning and a middle; and when the company's state manager arrived for an inspection a month later and told us to get rid of the toys, I had an ending.

"All the animals stay at my place now. So I can't take too much credit; it just happened."

*   *   *

DRAY, Matthew Frederick
See DRAY, Matt

*   *   *

DR. FRANK
See PORTMAN, Frank

*   *   *

DUNN, Jancee 1966-

PERSONAL: Born 1966, in NJ; married. *Education:* Attended the University of Delaware.

ADDRESSES: Home—Brooklyn, NY. *Agent*—David McCormick, McCormick & Williams Literary Agents, 37 W. 20th St., New York, NY 10011.

CAREER: Writer, journalist, columnist, and television show host. MTV2, veejay (music video presenter and host), 1996-2001; *Good Morning America,* entertainment correspondent. Worked as a fact-checker for an advertising agency.

WRITINGS:

(Author of introduction) *The Insomniac's Handbook: A Companion for the Nocturnally Challenged,* photographs by Ben Asen, Universe Publishing (New York, NY), 2001.
But Enough about Me: A Jersey Girl's Unlikely Adventures among the Absurdly Famous (memoir), HarperCollins (New York, NY), 2006.

Rolling Stone, writer and editor, 1989—; author of sex advice column, *GQ* magazine.

Contributor to periodicals, including *New York, GQ, O: The Oprah Magazine, Vogue,* and the *New York Times.*

SIDELIGHTS: Jancee Dunn is a music journalist, columnist, and author who starred as one of the original veejays for MTV2, the all-video spin-off network of entertainment and music channel MTV. A writer for *Rolling Stone* and other magazines and newspapers, Dunn has long been both a participant and an observer in the popular entertainment industry. In *But Enough about Me: A Jersey Girl's Unlikely Adventures among the Absurdly Famous,* Dunn presents a memoir of her sometimes glamorous, sometimes stressful, but always interesting life as a music writer, reporter, and television host. In an interview with Jac Chebatoris in *Newsweek,* Dunn commented that she wrote the book in order to tell the "'stories behind the stories.' I just found myself in the most surreal situations and I thought, 'Nobody would believe this stuff.'"

A New Jersey native, Dunn attended the University of Delaware and worked as a fact-checker at an advertising agency before landing a dream job as an editorial

assistant at *Rolling Stone.* Her move to New York brought her into an unfamiliar world of parties, celebrities, men, and fame. Throughout her memoir, she "relays in self-deprecating, highly appealing fashion various autobiographical snippets as well as tricks of the trade," observed Joanne Wilkinson in *Booklist.* She relates how, when interviewing celebrities and famous musicians, her inner geek would threaten to get the better of her, but how she managed to keep her interactions professional even when the interviewee misbehaved. She describes how Brad Pitt launched into an air guitar solo during an interview; how shopping with the Olsen twins made her feel like a beast lumbering along in pursuit of the nimble young actresses; and how she considers her interview with the singular Dolly Parton to be a high point of her career. Eventually, the appeal of the high-energy party life with celebrities and musicians dimmed, and Dunn retreated closer to her family and her roots. For this reason, a *Kirkus Reviews* contributor found Dunn's memoir to be less about working in entertainment journalism and more "about becoming acquainted with, and accepting, your true self." *Entertainment Weekly* reviewer Missy Schwartz called Dunn an "irresistible narrator." A *Publishers Weekly* critic observed that the book is "tough to define, but a delight to read," and concluded: "Amusing, clever and affable, Dunn shares a satisfying memoir-turned-celebrity dish."

Dunn once told *CA:* "I have always loved to read and even when I was quite young, I thought that being a writer would be the best job in the world. I used to write books when I was around eight years old and sell them on a card table set up in my driveway. I didn't have my buyers. I had a pretty big remainders table. It didn't discourage me, though."

BIOGRAPHICAL AND CRITICAL SOURCES:

BOOKS

But Enough about Me: A Jersey Girl's Unlikely Adventures among the Absurdly Famous (memoir), HarperCollins (New York, NY), 2006.

PERIODICALS

Booklist, June 1, 2006, Joanne Wilkinson, review of *But Enough about Me,* p. 16.

Entertainment Weekly, June 2, 2006, Missy Schwartz, review of *But Enough about Me,* p. 87.

Kirkus Reviews, April 1, 2006, review of *But Enough about Me,* p. 332.

Newsweek, June 12, 2006, Jac Chebatoris, "Fast Chat: All-Star Journalist," interview with Jancee Dunn, p. 9.

Publishers Weekly, April 3, 2006, review of *But Enough about Me,* p. 56.

ONLINE

Jancee Dunn Home Page, http://janceedunn.typepad.com (December 2, 2006).

*   *   *

DYKEMAN, Wilma 1920-2006

OBITUARY NOTICE— See index for *CA* sketch: Born May 20, 1920, in Asheville, NC; died of an infection resulting from a broken hip, December 23, 2006, in Asheville, NC. Author. Well known for her fiction and nonfiction works celebrating Appalachia, Dykeman often wrote on themes concerning the environment, race relations, history, and world peace. A 1940 graduate of Northwestern University, she married poet James R. Stokely, Jr., that year. Her first book, *The French Broad* (1955), won the Thomas Wolfe Memorial Trophy, while her second, *Neither Black nor White,* was written with her husband and won the Hillman Award for best book on world peace, race relations, or civil liberties. Dykeman would go on to publish twenty books over the years. Among her other titles are *The Far Family* (1966), *Return the Innocent Earth* (1973), *Explorations* (1984), and *Haunting Memories: Echoes and Images of Tennessee's Past (Hand-tinted Photographs)* (1996). An active public speaker who continued to make appearances for years after her husband's 1977 death, Dykeman also wrote a regular column for the Knoxville *News-Sentinel.* She received an honorary doctorate from Maryville College, was named both Tennessee Conservation Writer of the Year and Tennessee Outstanding Speaker of the Year, and was declared Tennessee state historian in 1981.

OBITUARIES AND OTHER SOURCES:

PERIODICALS

Chicago Tribune, December 25, 2006, Section 3, p. 11.

New York Times, December 29, 2006, p. A23.

Washington Post, December 26, 2006, p. B4.

E

EAST, James H. 1951-

PERSONAL: Born April 25, 1951, in Barnstable, MA; son of Marjorie S. East (a professor); married January 20, 1990; wife's name Stephanie (a teacher); children: James Stephen. *Education:* Florida State University, B.A., 1975; University of North Carolina at Chapel Hill, M.A., 1980; University of North Carolina at Greensboro, Ph.D., 1991.

ADDRESSES: Home—Columbus, GA

CAREER: Brookstone School, Columbus, GA, English teacher, 1981—, and department head.

WRITINGS:

The Humane Particulars: The Collected Letters of William Carlos Williams and Kenneth Burke, University of South Carolina Press (Columbia, SC), 1993.*

*   *   *

EDWARDS, Doreen
See MADOC, Gwen

*   *   *

EDWARDS, Karen L.

PERSONAL: Female.

ADDRESSES: Office—Department of English, University of Exeter, Room 203, Queen's Bldg., The Queen's Drive, Exeter, Devon EX4 4QJ, England. *E-mail*—k.l.edwards@exeter.ac.uk.

CAREER: Writer, historian, scholar, and educator. College of New Rochelle, New Rochelle, NY, visiting assistant professor of English, 1979-80; Kenyon College, Gambier, OH, assistant professor, 1980-87, associate professor of English, 1987-92; University of Exeter, Exeter, Devon, England, lecturer, 1992-2004, senior lecturer in English, 2004—.

AWARDS, HONORS: National Endowment for the Humanities fellow, 1996-97; Audrey Lumsden Kouvel fellow, Newberry Library, 1996-97; Exeter University Research Committee grant, 1999; British Academy Overseas Conference Grant, 2005.

WRITINGS:

Milton and the Natural World: Science and Poetry in "Paradise Lost," Cambridge University Press (New York, NY), 1999.

Contributor to *Milton and the Ends of Time: Essays on the Apocalypse and the Millennium,* edited by Juliet Cummins, Cambridge University Press (New York, NY), 2003, and *A Concise Companion to Milton,* edited by Angelica Duran, Blackwell, 2006.

SIDELIGHTS: Karen L. Edwards is a senior lecturer in English at the University of Exeter in England. Her academic interests include Renaissance literature, the works of poet John Milton, and the confluence of natural history and literature. In *Milton and the Natural World: Science and Poetry in "Paradise Lost,"* Edwards explores in depth "the full extent of Milton's debt and contribution to experimental science in the seventeenth century and, in particular, to his imaginative and creative engagements with the natural world," noted Jayne Archer in the *Renaissance Journal*. Milton, according to Edwards, would have considered it his duty as a writer and intellectual to be conversant with all the learning of his time, even that which was being discredited and that which was still considered speculative. Edwards considers how this knowledge was synthesized by Milton and how it appeared within the passages of *Paradise Lost*. Reviewer Peter Harrison, writing in *Metascience,* noted that "it is the central thesis of this book that John Milton's masterpiece [*Paradise Lost*] provides evidence of its author's familiarity with current trends in natural history and of his willingness to press them into the service of his epic vision." In addition to addressing Milton's knowledge of science and his use of that knowledge in the creation of his literary works, Edwards's book also "gives a useful account of the state of natural history during the middle decades of the seventeenth century, presented in a style that is both informative and entertaining," Harrison noted.

"This is an important book, full of new scholarly information and cherished ideas," commented Sara Van Den Berg in the *Renaissance Quarterly*. "In its own terms . . . it succeeds brilliantly, not only joining but also greatly expanding upon other reevaluations of Milton's naturalism and materialism," stated Catherine Gimelli Martin in *Modern Philology*. "Karen Edwards' close readings of passages from *Paradise Lost* are clearly informed by years of research and teaching. The book is beautifully written, too, with fresh ideas vividly expressed on every page," Van Den Berg remarked. "Written with grace and clarity, Edwards's work is an education for the twenty-first-century reader," Archer concluded.

BIOGRAPHICAL AND CRITICAL SOURCES:

PERIODICALS

Metascience, March, 2002, Peter Harrison, "John Milton, Scientist," review of *Milton and the Natural World: Science and Poetry in "Paradise Lost."*

Modern Philology, November, 2001, Catherine Gimelli Martin, review of *Milton and the Natural World,* p. 299.

Renaissance Journal, June, 2001, Jayne Archer, review of *Milton and the Natural World.*

Renaissance Quarterly, spring, 2003, Sara Van Den Berg, review of *Milton and the Natural World,* p. 250.*

*   *   *

ELDRED, Tim 1965-

PERSONAL: Born June, 1965.

ADDRESSES: E-mail—timeldred@yahoo.com.

CAREER: Writer, artist, director, animator, illustrator, storyboard artist, and publisher. Director of animated television programs, including *Extreme Ghostbusters,* Columbia Pictures Television, 1997; *Dragon Tales,* Columbia TriStar Children's Television, 1999; *Heavy Gear: The Animated Series,* Adelaide Productions, Inc., 2001; *Spider-Man,* Marvel Enterprises, 2003; *Xiaolin Showdown,* Warner Bros. Television, 2004. Storyboard artist for animated features. Comic book writer and artist for such titles as *Star Blazers, Armored Trooper Votoms, Captain Harlock, Robotech* and several original series.

AWARDS, HONORS: Best Books for Young Adults selection, American Library Association, 2007, for *Grease Monkey.*

WRITINGS:

(Illustrator) Daniel Quinn, *The Man Who Grew Young,* Context Books (New York, NY), 2001.
(Author and illustrator) *Grease Monkey,* edited by Teresa Nielsen Hayden, Tor (New York, NY), 2006.

Author of documentary *Space Battleship Yamato: The Making of an Anime Legend.* Author and artist of Web comic *Star Blazers Rebirth.*

SIDELIGHTS: An artist, animation director, and illustrator in the animation field, Tim Eldred is also an accomplished comic book writer and artist. His interest in art and animation was sparked in his youth by the Japanese cartoon series *Star Blazers,* an early example of the Japanese anime genre that is currently extremely popular in the United States. He has worked on comic book versions of *Star Blazers* as well as on another popular Japanese franchise, *Robotech.* As an animation director, he has worked on cartoons in series ranging from *Dragon Tales* to *Spider-Man* to the *Xiaolin Showdown.* Eldred has also produced content for original digital video disc (DVD) productions of *Star Blazers* and *Votoms.*

Eldred is the writer and artist of *Grease Monkey,* a combination of comedy and science fiction set in a future world in which humans coexist with artificially evolved apes. In this world, an alien invasion has severely damaged the planet Earth, nearly obliterating the human race. With so few humans left to defend her, the planet is vulnerable to another attack. Unexpectedly, a race of advanced, intergalactic missionaries steps in to help, using their high technology to evolve millions of gorillas very rapidly to a level similar to that of humans. Suddenly, humans must adjust to sharing equal time with creatures they once considered beneath them on the evolutionary scale but that are stronger, faster, and at least as intelligent. The gorillas face adjustments as well as they set about to define their own civilization while defending Earth and learning to get along with their hairless brethren.

The story in *Grease Monkey* begins when young human spaceship mechanic Robin Plotnik is assigned to a mechanics detail aboard the spaceship *Fist of Earth.* He becomes the subordinate of gorilla Mac Gimbensky, whose fearsome reputation for eating people terrifies Robin. Mac and Robin work for the Barbarian Squadron, an all-female team of gorgeous combat pilots who capture Robin's youthful attention. As the story progresses, Robin learns that Mac is not a ferocious people-eater but is in fact a wise and gentle soul who becomes his protector and mentor. Mac becomes involved in an emotionally touching romance with a gorilla fleet admiral while Robin tries to court a young librarian named Kara. In the background, human and gorilla must still find ways to interact successfully with one another while the threat of renewed alien attack constantly looms over everyone.

Reviewer Jesse Karp, writing in *Booklist,* noted that the story "contains trenchant commentary on racism, politics, animal rights, dating, family, loyalty, and the importance of books." *School Library Journal* reviewer Benjamin Russell called the story "enjoyable and emotionally effective." Eldred's storytelling is "filled with gentle comedy and wise personal insights," commented a *Publishers Weekly* reviewer, who called Eldred's art "traditional in the best sense: not flashy but clear, efficient, and handsome."

Eldred once told *CA:* "I was influenced most by the books, movies, and TV shows that made strong impressions on me as a youth, such as *M*A*S*H, Star Wars, Star Blazers,* and many more. I have always found that writing becomes easiest when you develop characters with a strong individuality so that dialogue and situations suggest themselves rather than being struggled over.

"The most surprising thing I've learned about writing is how easily a good idea can be derailed once it is subjected to the scrutiny of a committee, most especially in the realm of screenwriting. This becomes especially apparent when one realizes that all the most important works of fiction tend to be the product of a single mind. *Grease Monkey* is definitely my favorite work because it most strongly represents my personal opinions and beliefs, undiluted by any committee.

"I hope for two things: first, to blur the distinctions between graphic novels (a format) and entertaining fiction (a genre), and second, to offer readers (especially younger ones) a unique view of the world that may help them to navigate through the murky waters of life."

BIOGRAPHICAL AND CRITICAL SOURCES:

PERIODICALS

Booklist, March 15, 2006, Jesse Karp, review of *Grease Monkey,* p. 55.
Publishers Weekly, March 6, 2006, review of *Grease Monkey,* p. 52.
School Library Journal, July, 2006, Benjamin Russell, review of *Grease Monkey,* p. 125.

ONLINE

Anime-cons.com, http://www.anime-cons.com/ (April 9, 2000), "Tim Eldred—Anime Convention Personality of the Week," biography of Tim Eldred.

Internet Movie Database, http://www.imdb.com/ (December 3, 2006), filmography of Tim Eldred.

Tim Eldred Home Page, http://www.greasemonkey book.com (December 3, 2006).

* * *

ELLERTON, Roger R.W. 1946-

PERSONAL: Born May 28, 1946, in Kingston, Ontario, Canada; son of William and Irene Ellerton; married Donna Boudreau (a real estate agent), August 17, 2001; children: Kimberley, Deanna, Nicholas LeBrun-Ellerton, Matthew LeBrun-Ellerton. *Ethnicity:* "Caucasian." *Education:* Carleton University, B.Sc., 1969, M.Sc., 1970; Virginia Polytechnic Institute and State University, Ph.D., 1973.

ADDRESSES: Office—Renewal Technologies, Inc., 5423 North Dr., Ottawa, Ontario K4M 1G5, Canada. *E-mail*—info@renewal.ca.

CAREER: Renewal Technologies, Inc., Ottawa, Ontario, Canada, managing partner, coach, trainer, and consultant, 1995—. Certified NLP (neuro-linguistic programming) coach and trainer, 1996—; codesigner and copresenter of audiotape series "Change at the Speed of Thought"; certified management consultant; international public speaker. Former executive of Canadian federal government; former associate professor at University of New Brunswick.

MEMBER: Canadian Association of Neuro-Linguistic Programming, Canadian Association of Management Consultants.

WRITINGS:

Live Your Dreams, Let Reality Catch Up: NLP and Common Sense for Coaches, Managers, and You, Trafford Publishing (Victoria, British Columbia, Canada), 2005.

SIDELIGHTS: Roger R.W. Ellerton told *CA:* "For over thirty years I have been helping individuals to address challenges at work and at home and get more

of what they desire in life. I am the founder and managing partner of Renewal Technologies, Inc., a company providing management of change and personal growth consulting, coaching, and training services. Participants have traveled from across Canada, the United States, and as far away as Australia, New Zealand, Brazil, Taiwan, and Japan to be in my classes.

"I hope my books will assist people to discover who they are, what they truly desire and help them find and navigate the path to achieving it. In other words, to get more out of life."

* * *

ELLIOTT, Patricia 1946-

PERSONAL: Born 1946, in London, England; married; children: two sons. *Education:* Earned M.A., 1995.

ADDRESSES: Home and office—London, England.

CAREER: Author. Teacher of children's literature at an adult education college. Formerly worked in publishing in London, England, and as a bookseller in New York, NY.

AWARDS, HONORS: Fidler Award for first novel, Branford Boase Award shortlist, and West Sussex Children's Book Award shortlist, all for *The Ice Boy; Guardian* Children's Fiction Award longlist, and Best Novel Award nomination, British Fantasy Society, both for *Murkmere.*

WRITINGS:

FANTASY NOVELS; FOR YOUNG ADULT READERS

The Ice Boy, Hodder (London, England), 2002.

Murkmere, Hodder (London, England), 2004, Little, Brown (New York, NY), 2006.

Ambergate, Hodder (London, England), 2005, Little, Brown (New York, NY), 2006.

The Night Walker, Hodder (London, England), 2007.

SIDELIGHTS: Though Patricia Elliott was born in England, she spent much of her childhood living with her family in the Far East. "While we were abroad, there was no school in the afternoons, and I would spend my free time reading," Elliott recalled on *Time Warner Bookmark.* "When I ran out of books I wrote my own in pencil, in much-smudged exercise books." Although she continued writing, Elliott spent several years working in the publishing industry and as a bookseller before her first novel, *The Ice Boy,* was published. Her more recent novels include the young-adult fantasies *Murkmere, Ambergate,* and *The Night Walker.*

Based on a Norse legend, *The Ice Boy* follows the adventures of young Edward as he searches for his father, who was lost at sea. Though unable to discover his father's fate, when Edward rescues a man from drowning, he begins to have visions of an icy land located somewhere just beyond the horizon. Praised by critics, *The Ice Boy* won the Fidler Award for a first novel and was nominated for several others literary honors.

In *Murkmere,* Elliott spins a gothic tale that focuses on the friendship between Leah, a fey girl who is the ward of the Master of Murkmere Hall, and Aggie, a villager chosen to be Leah's companion. When Aggie arrives, a bad omen, delivered by birds, accompanies her. Soon she realizes that, not only are dark things happening in the halls of Murkmere, but her employer may in fact be behind them all. Of even more concern to the girl, the faith she has practiced all her life may not be all she once assumed it to be. "There is plenty of suspense, and readers will not be able to put the book down," wrote Tasha Saecker in a review of *Murkmere* for *School Library Journal.* According to *Kliatt* contributor Claire Rosser, the book's "challenging vocabulary," Elliott's inclusion of "concepts that stretch the mind of the reader," and the novel's inclusion of "intrepid young women will win over readers." In *Kirkus Reviews,* a critic deemed the novel a "wonderfully atmospheric and moody" tale set firmly "on the border between fantasy and fiction."

Set in the same world as *Murkmere, Ambergate* is the story of Scruff, an orphan escaping a crime she committed in the city by fleeing to Murkmere Hall. Unfortunately, when the law follows her, Scruff must also flee Murkmere, only to become embroiled in a plot to assassinate the Lord Protector's son. "This is a beautiful, compelling novel," with "deftly drawn" characters and descriptions "worth a whole page of explanations," wrote Leslie Wilson in the London *Guardian.* A critic for *Bookseller* also praised Elliott's novel, describing *Ambergate* as "an intricate blend of mythology and symbolism."

As Elliott explained on *Time Warner Bookmark,* she draws on mythology, particularly Norse and Celtic myths, in her writing. The writer elaborated on the inspiration behind her novels in an essay posted on the Hachette Book Group USA Web site, writing that "all the superstitions in *Murkmere* can, in fact, be found in British folklore—I didn't have to invent anything, except the religion itself." In an online interview with the West Sussex Grid for Learning Web site, Elliott acknowledged that she always wanted to be a writer. "I started writing when I was a child because I enjoyed reading so much and wanted to create the same 'worlds' as in the books I had just read and enjoyed," she said. "Nowadays the only difference is that I create my own worlds!"

BIOGRAPHICAL AND CRITICAL SOURCES:

PERIODICALS

Booklist, January 1, 2006, Holly Koelling, review of *Murkmere,* p. 81.

Bookseller, February 18, 2005, review of *Ambergate,* p. 40.

Bulletin of the Center for Children's Books, April, 2006, Karen Coats, review of *Murkmere,* p. 350.

Horn Book, March-April, 2006, Anita L. Burkham, review of *Murkmere,* p. 187.

Guardian (London, England), April 30, 2005, Leslie Wilson, review of *Ambergate,* p. 33.

Kirkus Reviews, January 15, 2006, review of *Murkmere,* p. 83.

Kliatt, January, 2006, Claire Rosser, review of *Murkmere,* p. 7.

Publishers Weekly, February 20, 2006, review of *Murkmere,* p. 158.

School Librarian, autumn, 2004, Sarah Wilkie, review of *Murkmere,* p. 156; autumn, 2005, Griselda Greaves, review of *Ambergate,* p. 154.

School Library Journal, October, 2006, Tasha Saecker, review of *Murkmere,* p. 150.

Times (London, England), June 12, 2004, Amanda Craig, "Girls, Girls, Girls," p. 17.

ONLINE

Fantastic Fiction Web site, http://www.fantasticfiction. co.uk/ (January 11, 2007), "Patricia Elliott."

Hachette Book Group USA Web site, http://www. hachettebookgroupusa.com/ (January 11, 2007), Patricia Elliott, "The Making of Murkmere."

Society of Authors Web site, http://www.societyof authors.net/ (January 11, 2007), "Patricia Elliott."

Time Warner Bookmark, http://www.twbookmark.com/ (January 11, 2007), "Patricia Elliott."

West Sussex Grid for Learning Web site, http://wsgfl. westsussex.gov.uk/ (September 20, 2004), interview with Elliott.*

*   *   *

EMLEY, Dianne

PERSONAL: Born in Los Angeles, CA; married; husband's name Charlie. *Education:* University of California at Los Angeles, B.A., M.B.A.; attended Université de Bordeaux, France.

ADDRESSES: E-mail—dianne@dianneemley.com.

CAREER: Writer and novelist. Has worked as a department store division manager, clothing boutique buyer, egg and poultry industry marker, sales and support manager for a software company, customer service representative at the California Department of Consumer Affairs, polling place recruiter, drill press operator, and technical writer.

WRITINGS:

The First Cut, Ballantine (New York, NY), 2006.

SIDELIGHTS: Mystery novelist and crime writer Dianne Emley is the author of *The First Cut,* her debut novel featuring Nan Vining. The character of Vining originated during Emley's participation in the Pasadena Police Department's Citizen Police Academy, a twelve-week outreach program during which the police educate citizens on the role of the police and the techniques of law enforcement, Emley told an interviewer on *NewMysteryReader.com.* This experience led her to an immersion in learning about law enforcement, Emley stated, including repeated ride-alongs with patrolling officers, participation in disciplinary review boards, and close association with district attorneys and police officers. "I found the experience life-altering," Emley told the *NewMystery Reader.com* interviewer. "I came to appreciate what it means to put on that uniform and walk the streets and the pressures involved in making life-and-death instantaneous decisions that will be scrutinized by the public and media."

With this newfound clarity informing her fiction, Emley created Pasadena, California-based homicide detective and single mother Nan Vining, protagonist of *The First Cut,* the first book in a projected series of crime novels that combine thriller elements with a touch of the supernatural. Vining has just returned to work on the police force after a year-long convalescence following a near-fatal knife attack. Her injuries were so severe that she was left clinically dead for more than two minutes. Her attacker was never found or identified, but she and her daughter refer to him as T.B. Mann, short for "The Bad Man." In the wake of the assault, her self-confidence is injured. She suffers from panic attacks and struggles to make herself enter the homes of strangers. Despite her fears, she knows she has to conquer them for her sake and for her teenage daughter's sake. On Vining's first day back on the job, a beautiful LAPD vice cop, Frankie Lynde, is found dead in an upscale neighborhood, her throat cut. At the crime scene, Vining seems to hear Lynde's bloodied corpse mutter a cryptic message, which spurs her investigation. She discovers that Lynde had been involved in a kinky relationship with rich club owner John Lesley and his ex-stripper wife, Pussycat. Though Lesley is the prime suspect, he is clever enough to conceal his involvement, leaving Vining and the police with little evidence to connect him with Lynde's murder. As Lesley searches for a new victim, Vining recreates Lynde's final days, bringing her ever closer to a final showdown with the dangerous Lesley. "Nicely developed characters and genuine suspense elevate this impressive crime debut," commented a

Kirkus Reviews critic. Nanci Milone Hill, writing in the *Library Journal,* called the novel a "gripping debut page-turner" that takes a close look at the "shadier side of humanity while providing readers with a first-rate story."

BIOGRAPHICAL AND CRITICAL SOURCES:

PERIODICALS

Kirkus Reviews, June 1, 2006, review of *The First Cut,* p. 534.

Library Journal, September 1, 2006, Nanci Milone Hill, review of *The First Cut,* p. 135.

Mystery Scene, fall, 2006, Mary Welk, review of *The First Cut.*

Publishers Weekly, July 10, 2006, review of *The First Cut,* p. 52.

South Florida Sun-Sentinel, September 27, 2006, Oline H. Cogdill, review of *The First Cut.*

ONLINE

Dianne Emley Home Page, http://www.dianneemley. com (December 20, 2006).

NewMysteryReader.com, http://www.newmystery reader.com/ (December 20, 2006), interview with Dianne Emley.

* * *

ETCHESON, Nicole 1963-

PERSONAL: Born April 30, 1963, in Huntington, NY; daughter of Gerald (a naval officer) and Joy (a high school mathematics teacher) Etcheson; married Robert J. Williams, August 16, 1986; children: Robert. *Education:* Grinnell College, B.A., 1985; Indiana University, Ph.D., 1991.

ADDRESSES: Office—Ball State University, 2000 University, Muncie, IN 47306. *E-mail*—netcheson@ bsu.edu.

CAREER: Hiram College, Hiram, OH, assistant professor of history, 1991-92; University of South Dakota, Vermillion, assistant professor of history,

1992-96; University of Texas at El Paso, associate professor of history, 1996-2005; Ball State University, Muncie, IN, Alexander M. Bracken Professor of History, 2005—. South Dakota History Day, state coordinator, 1992-96; El Paso History Day, regional coordinator, 1996-2005.

WRITINGS:

The Emerging Midwest: Upland Southerners and the Political Culture of the Old Northwest, Indiana University Press (Bloomington, IN), 1996.

Bleeding Kansas: Contested Liberty in the Civil War Era, University Press of Kansas (Lawrence, KS), 2004.

Contributor to books, including *The Pursuit of Public Power: Political Culture in Ohio, 1787-1861,* edited by Jeffrey B. Brown and Andrew R.L. Cayton, Kent State University Press (Kent, OH), 1994; *Lethal Imagination: Violence and Brutality in American History,* New York University Press (New York, NY), 1999; *The American Midwest: Essays on Regional History,* edited by Andrew R.L. Cayton and Susan E. Gray, [Bloomington, IN], 2001; and *Territorial Kansas Reader,* edited by Virgil W. Dean, [Topeka, KS], 2005; and *John Brown to Bob Dole: Movers and Shakers in Kansas History,* edited by Virgil W. Dean, University Press of Kansas (Lawrence, KS), 2006. Contributor to periodicals, including *Ohio Valley History, North and South, American Nineteenth Century History, Journal of the Early Republic,* and *Kansas History.*

SIDELIGHTS: Nicole Etcheson told *CA:* "As a teacher, I've always had difficulty advising students who don't know what career they want. I've always known that I loved history, although, given the academic job market, I didn't always know I would be able to be a professional historian.

"My writing projects almost always focus on the Midwest and the Civil War. In graduate school I wanted to focus my dissertation on the much-neglected Midwest, and so my first book, *The Emerging Midwest: Upland Southerners and the Political Culture of the Old Northwest,* discussed the growth of a unique politics and society in the Midwest as migrants from

North and South forged a new kind of culture. While working on that book, I found that Midwesterners were often arguing about the situation in Bleeding Kansas, where pro-slavery and free-state settlers were waging an early version of the conflict that would lead to national civil war. The Kansas Civil War of the 1850s became the subject of my second book, *Bleeding Kansas: Contested Liberty in the Civil War Era.* I am now at work on a third book, a micro-history of the Union home front through the history of one Indiana county. Putnam County was home to both loyal Unionists, many of whom fought for the North, and antiwar Democrats, whose draft resistance unionists considered treasonous."

F

FAINARU-WADA, Mark 1965-

PERSONAL: Born 1965; married; children: two.

ADDRESSES: Office—San Francisco Chronicle, 901 Mission St., San Francisco, CA 94103. *E-mail*—mfainaru-wada@sfchronicle.com.

CAREER: Writer, journalist, and investigative reporter. *San Francisco Chronicle,* San Francisco, CA, reporter.

AWARDS, HONORS: George Polk Award, Long Island University, 2004, for sports reporting involving investigation into use of steroids in major sports; Dick Schaap Excellence in Sports Journalism Award, 2004; Journalist of the Year, Northern California Pro Chapter, Society of Professional Journalists, 2006.

WRITINGS:

(With Lance Williams) *Game of Shadows: Barry Bonds, BALCO, and the Steroids Scandal That Rocked Professional Sports,* Gotham Books (New York, NY), 2006.

SIDELIGHTS: Mark Fainaru-Wada and Lance Williams are investigative reporters with the *San Francisco Chronicle.* Their work has received wide acclaim from both peers and audiences. However, their investigations have also brought them into conflict with the American legal system. In 2006, Fainaru-Wada and Williams both faced up to eighteen months in jail for contempt of court when they refused to divulge their sources for a series of articles and a book on steroid abuse involving high-profile athletes in major-league baseball and other sports.

Fainaru-Wada, a sports journalist, and Williams, an investigative reporter, became involved in the story after a federal raid on the Bay Area Laboratory Co-Operative (BALCO), a sports nutrition company in California, and on the home of Greg Anderson, the personal trainer of baseball superstar Barry Bonds. At first, the raid appeared to stem from an IRS tax-related issue, but as Fainaru-Wada and Williams investigated, they discovered that BALCO was accused of providing illegal steroids and other performance-enhancing substances to several professional athletes. Most notable among the list of BALCO's clients was baseball slugger Bonds, whose athletic prowess saw him set new home-run records. Williams and Fainaru-Wada wrote a series of articles on the BALCO scandal, with an emphasis on Bonds's association with the company and evidence of his use of illegal steroids. Records taken from BALCO "tracked Bonds's drug protocol in extraordinary detail and revealed that he had been consuming drugs in multiple forms over several years," including two potent but undetectable designer steroids, noted Mark Starr in *Newsweek.* They found that the BALCO prosecutors, while claiming to be interested in cleaning up major league sports, carefully concealed the identities of the sports stars accused of illegal steroid use. Anderson pleaded guilty to steroids distribution and was sentenced to six months in jail. In the course of their investigation, Fainaru-Wada and Williams obtained leaked grand jury testimony which included many statements from Bonds himself.

With this grand jury testimony and material gathered from other sources, Fainaru-Wada and Williams wrote *Game of Shadows: Barry Bonds, BALCO, and the Steroids Scandal That Rocked Professional Sports*, a book covering the development and impact of the BALCO case on professional sports and on Bonds in particular. Reviewer Michiko Kakutani, writing in the *New York Times Book Review*, called the book "necessary reading for anyone concerned with the steroids era in baseball and track and field and its fallout on sports history." Following the release of *Game of Shadows*, the reporters' peers praised and defended their work. However, in May, 2006, Fainaru-Wada and Williams were served with subpoenas compelling them to reveal the confidential source that leaked Bonds's grand jury testimony to them. After failing to divulge their source, Williams and Fainaru-Wada were sentenced to up to eighteen months in jail. Both vowed to serve the time, if necessary, rather than violate their personal and journalistic ethics. Colleagues came to their defense. Steve Kettman, for example, writing in *San Francisco Magazine*, commented that with their exposure of the high levels of hypocrisy and deception in both government and professional sports, "Fainaru-Wada and Williams reminded everyone that reporting still matters."

BIOGRAPHICAL AND CRITICAL SOURCES:

PERIODICALS

Booklist, September 1, 2006, Mike Tribby, review of *Game of Shadows: Barry Bonds, BALCO, and the Steroids Scandal That Rocked Professional Sports*, p. 150.

Chicago Sun Times, March 9, 2006, Roman Modrowski, "Author Knows All about This Giant Controversy," profile of Mark Fainaru-Wada.

Entertainment Weekly, April 21, 2006, Melissa Rose Bernardo, Jeff Labrecque, and Bob Cannon, review of *Game of Shadows*, p. 77.

Hollywood Reporter, August 16, 2006, "Talk, Judges Rule," p. 3; September 22, 2006, "Facing Jail," p. 5.

New York Times Book Review, March 23, 2006, Michiko Kakutani, "Barry Bonds and Baseball's Steroids Scandal," review of *Game of Shadows*; May 7, 2006, Michael Sokolove, review of *Game of Shadows*, p. 12.

Newsweek, March 20, 2006, Mark Starr, "Bonds Gets Blasted: A Scorching New Book Boosts the Case That the Slugger's Records Were Drug-Assisted," review of *Game of Shadows*, p. 49.

Quill, October-November, 2006, "NorCal Chapter to Honor Bay Area Journalists," p. 11.

San Francisco Chronicle, February 22, 2005, Stacy Finz, "*Chronicle* Reporters Honored for Sports Steroids Coverage; Polk Award among Journalism's Highest," p. A-2; August 30, 2006, Debra J. Saunders, "Justice Department of Steroids," p. E-7; September 21, 2006, "Statement by *Chronicle* reporter Mark Fainaru-Wada"; September 21, 2006, "Statement by *Chronicle* reporter Lance Williams."

ONLINE

ABC News Web site, http://abcnews.go.com/ (September 22, 2006), Wright Thompson, "Jail for Barry Bonds Reporters: We All Lose."

Bookreporter.com, http://www.bookreporter.com/ (December 20, 2006), Ron Kaplan, review of *Game of Shadows*.

CJR Daily, http://www.cjrdaily.org/ (December 17, 2004), Susan Q. Stranahan, "Mark Fainaru-Wada on the Sports Doping Probe and Protecting Sources," interview with Mark Fainaru-Wada.

San Francisco Magazine, http://www.sanfrancisco magazine.com/ (December 20, 2006), Steve Kettmann, "Who Put the *Chron* on Steroids?," profile of Mark Fainaru-Wada and Lance Williams.

Scriptorium Web site, http://illuminate.redline6.net/ (June 20, 2006), Matthew Davis, review of *Game of Shadows*.

Truthdig.com, http://www.truthdig.com/ (June 13, 2006), James Harris, interview with Mark Fainaru-Wada.

*   *   *

FARNHAM, Barbara
  (Barbara Rearden Farnham)

PERSONAL: Education: Columbia University, Ph.D., 1991.

ADDRESSES: Office—Arnold A. Saltzman Institute of War and Peace Studies, Columbia University, 420 W. 118th St., 13th Fl., IAB, New York, NY 10027.

CAREER: Columbia University, Arnold A. Saltzman Institute of War and Peace Studies, New York, NY, senior associate, 1994—. Lecturer at Hunter College, 1989-91, and Princeton University, 1991.

AWARDS, HONORS: John M. Olin Institute for Strategic Studies postdoctoral fellow, 1992-93; Erik H. Erikson Award, International Society of Political Psychology, 2001.

WRITINGS:

(With Alexander Farnham) *Kingwood Township of Yesteryear,* Kingwood Studio Publications (Stockton, NJ), 1988.

(Editor) *Avoiding Losses/Taking Risks: Prospect Theory and International Conflict,* University of Michigan Press (Ann Arbor, MI), 1994.

Roosevelt and the Munich Crisis: A Study of Political Decision-Making, Princeton University Press (Princeton, NJ), 1997.

Contributor to books, including *Good Judgment and Foreign Policy,* edited by Stanley Renshon and Deborah Larson, Rowman & Littlefield (Lanham, MD), 2003. Contributor to journals, including *Political Psychology* and *International Studies Quarterly.*

SIDELIGHTS: Barbara Farnham is a scholar of geopolitical studies whose *Roosevelt and the Munich Crisis: A Study of Political Decision-Making* is a consideration of the ongoing controversy over Franklin Roosevelt's response to the Nazi threat in Europe. In studying Roosevelt's policy from 1936 to 1941, Farnham writes that the president used a "political approach to decision-making," but after Adolf Hitler threatened war over Czechoslovakia he took a stronger position in providing aid to the European allies. His appeasement of American isolationists, however, prevented him from actually intervening. He warned of the dangers of fascism but did not modify his stance until he clearly perceived Hitler to be a danger.

Thomas W. Zeiler wrote in *H-Net: Humanities and Social Sciences:* "Farnham's message is clear: decision-makers have to compromise in the face of resistance, but they do not give in or orchestrate quid pro quos. Instead, they try to satisfy multiple interests—which is what Roosevelt did." *History: Review of New Books* critic T. Michael Ruddy commented: "Using her theory of political decision making, Farnham effectively weaves together the diverse and contradictory aspects of Roosevelt's policy into a coherent description of a president intent on acting to address American security needs but responsive to domestic political restraints."

BIOGRAPHICAL AND CRITICAL SOURCES:

PERIODICALS

American Political Science Review, June, 1999, Stephen G. Walker, review of *Roosevelt and the Munich Crisis: A Study of Political Decision-Making,* p. 482.

History: Review of New Books, fall, 1998, T. Michael Ruddy, review of *Roosevelt and the Munich Crisis.*

Perspectives on Political Science, fall, 1998, Mark J. Rozell, review of *Roosevelt and the Munich Crisis,* p. 235.

ONLINE

Arnold A. Saltzman Institute of War and Peace Studies Web site, http://www.columbia.edu/cu/siwps/ (January 10, 2006), brief biography of Barbara Farnham.

H-Net: Humanities and Social Sciences Online, http://www.h-net.msu.edu/ (January 10, 2006), Thomas W. Zeiler, review of *Roosevelt and the Munich Crisis.**

* * *

**FARNHAM, Barbara Rearden
  See FARNHAM, Barbara**

* * *

**FARR, Dennis 1929-2006
  (Dennis Larry Ashwell Farr)**

OBITUARY NOTICE— See index for *CA* sketch: Born April 3, 1929, in Luton, Bedfordshire, England; died of a cerebral hemorrhage, December 6, 2006. Curator and author. A former director of the Birmingham

Museums and Art Gallery and the Courtauld Institute Galleries, Farr was a notable proponent of modern British art. Himself a graduate of the Courtauld Institute of Art at the University of London, he earned a B.A. there in 1950 and an M.A. in 1956. His early career, too, began at the Courtauld, where he was an assistant Witt librarian in the early 1950s. He joined the Tate Gallery in London in 1954 as an assistant keeper. Here he became a specialist in modern British artworks, culminating in the publication of two important catalogs: the coauthored *Catalogue of the Modern British School Collection* (1964) and the solo work *British Sculpture since 1945* (1965). Leaving his homeland in 1964, Farr served as curator at the Paul Mellon Collection in Washington, DC, but returned to Great Britain in 1967 to be a senior lecturer and deputy keeper at the University of Glasgow. Next, Farr was art advisor to the Calouste Gulbenkian Foundation. More significantly, however, he became director of the Birmingham Museums and Art Gallery. Farr was the director at Birmingham from 1969 to 1980, and his work in improving the collection led to his receiving an honorary doctorate from the University of Birmingham in 1981. The Courtauld Institute Galleries hired Farr as its director next, and he remained there until his 1993 retirement. As he had done in his previous position, Farr strove to improve the Courtauld's holdings; he also was instrumental in moving the collection to more spacious and well-lit accommodations at Somerset House. Such contributions led to Farr being named a Commander of the British Empire in 1991. Also the general editor of the "Clarendon Studies in the History of Art" series from 1985 to 2001, Farr continued to publish other catalogs and art books over the years. Among these are the cowritten *The Northern Landscape: Flemish, Dutch, and British Drawings from the Courtauld Collections* (1986), *The Courtauld Institute Galleries, University of London* (1990), and *Lynn Chadwick: Tate Britain Exhibition* (2003).

OBITUARIES AND OTHER SOURCES:

PERIODICALS

Times (London, England), December 21, 2006, p. 60.

*   *   *

FARR, Dennis Larry Ashwell
    See FARR, Dennis

FARRELL, Betty G. 1949-

PERSONAL: Born 1949.

ADDRESSES: Office—Pitzer College, 1050 N. Mills Ave., Claremont, CA 91711.

CAREER: Writer, sociologist, and educator. Pitzer College, Claremont, CA, professor of sociology.

WRITINGS:

Elite Families: Class and Power in Nineteenth-Century Boston, State University of New York Press (Albany, NY), 1993.
Family: The Making of an Idea, an Institution, and a Controversy in American Culture, Westview Press (Boulder, CO), 1999.

SIDELIGHTS: Betty G. Farrell is a sociologist and professor of sociology at Pitzer College in Claremont, California. Her works address issues related to family life, both modern and historical. *Elite Families: Class and Power in Nineteenth-Century Boston* looks at changes and adaptations in the Boston Brahmin families as corporations slowly took over for family proprietorships in the nineteenth century. Farrell analyzes "family strategies, class consolidation, and economic change" that challenges the notion that the rise of corporate control and decline of family management of businesses effectively removed the Boston elite from power, noted Frederic Cople Jaher in the *Journal of Interdisciplinary History.* Farrell carefully considers the structure and behavior of upper-class Boston families; the intricate family networks created among the elite families of the city; and the role of women in these networks and structures, which Jaher called a "signal contribution to Brahmin studies and an important addition to the field of family history and women's history."

Family: The Making of an Idea, an Institution, and a Controversy in American Culture is a "well-informed, smoothly written synthesis of recent work about the history and sociology of American families, one that acknowledges the behavioral as well as symbolic dimensions of families," commented reviewer John R. Gillis in the *Journal of Interdisciplinary History.* Farrell "reviews research by sociologists and historians to address current tensions in popular and academic debates on the changing American family," noted *Social Forces* reviewer R. Kelly Raley. In the book's opening chapter, Farrell outlines the academic study of families and describes a number of significant public concerns about the changing nature of the family, including issues such as single-parent families, the stresses of work on families, divorce and its impact on families, the continued erosion of the traditional nuclear family, and child safety and standards of living. Farrell looks at four dimensions of family—childhood, adolescent sexuality, marriage, and aging—and how they developed and shifted from Colonial American times to the present day. She notes that the idealized vision of family often varies from the reality, with profound ambivalence and contradiction present in all four family dimensions. The symbolic importance of family is at an all-time high, Farrell notes, but she also reports that families and family members often do not, and cannot, live up to the ideal, causing conflict and stress. She considers carefully whether government involvement is necessary to preserve the concept, if not the reality, of families. "At it's base," Farrell's book "is an argument about whether families are necessary and whether state involvement does more harm than good," Raley observed. Gillis concluded that Farrell's work is a "concise, balanced, and readable treatment of a subject that, because of its cultural significance, can never be free of controversy."

BIOGRAPHICAL AND CRITICAL SOURCES:

PERIODICALS

Journal of Interdisciplinary History, summer, 1995, Frederic Cople Jaher, review of *Elite Families: Class and Power in Nineteenth-Century Boston,* p. 141; summer, 2000, John R. Gillis, review of *Family: The Making of an Idea, an Institution, and a Controversy in American Culture,* p. 123.
Social Forces, September 2000, R. Kelly Raley, review of *Family,* p. 353.

ONLINE

Perseus Books Group Web site, http://www.perseus booksgroup.com/ (November 25, 2006), biography of Betty G. Farrell.*

FAVOR, J. Martin

PERSONAL: Education: University of Michigan, Ph.D., 1993.

ADDRESSES: Home—NH. *Office*—Department of English, Dartmouth College, 6032 Sanborn House, Hanover, NH 03755. *E-mail*—J.Martin.Favor@ dartmouth.edu.

CAREER: Dartmouth College, Hanover, NH, associate professor of English, chair of African and African American studies department.

WRITINGS:

Authentic Blackness: The Folk in the New Negro Renaissance, Duke University Press (Durham, NC), 1999.

Contributor to periodicals, including *Callaloo* and *Soul: A Journal of Black Politics, Culture, and Society.*

SIDELIGHTS: African American studies scholar J. Martin Favor explores the concept of racial identity in *Authentic Blackness: The Folk in the New Negro Renaissance.* In doing so, he relies on four texts of the Harlem Renaissance era that include James Weldon Johnson's *Autobiography of an Ex-Colored Man,* Jean Toomer's *Cane,* Nella Larsen's *Quicksand,* and George Schuyler's *Black No More.* Michele Gates-Moresi noted in *American Studies International* that Favor "questions a privileging of the folk, especially in the theories of Houston Baker and Henry Louis Gates Jr., and its meaning for literary constructions of racial identity. Baker posits authentic blackness in the lower classes (blues performance) and Gates privileges the vernacular as a basis for literary theory by asserting a particular African American cultural experience." Favor feels that their approaches avoid the issue of race itself. "*Authentic Blackness* is an important contribution to African American literary study because it prompts consideration of how various discourses privilege, shroud, and (re)produce African American identity," wrote Adam Hotek in *American Literature.* "Favor attempts to rehabilitate, to recenter, the agency of a black 'speaking subject' who seeks to 'transform' race as an 'older category' into a 'significant, controllable literary trope that resists deterministic, essentializing categorization.'"

BIOGRAPHICAL AND CRITICAL SOURCES:

PERIODICALS

American Literature, June, 2002, Adam Hotek, review of *Authentic Blackness: The Folk in the New Negro Renaissance,* p. 419.

American Studies International, October, 2001, Michele Gates-Moresi, review of *Authentic Blackness,* p. 84.*

*   *   *

FEIN, Melvyn L. 1941-
(Melvyn Leonard Fein)

PERSONAL: Born August 22, 1941, in Brooklyn, NY; son of Samuel J. and Florence D. Fein. *Education:* Brooklyn College of the City University of New York, B.A., 1963; City University of New York, Ph.D., 1983. *Hobbies and other interests:* Walking, reading.

ADDRESSES: Home—Canto, GA. *Office*—Department of Sociology, Kennesaw State University, Kennesaw, GA 20144-5591.

CAREER: Office of Vocational Rehabilitation, Rochester, NY, rehabilitation counselor, 1978-90; Kennesaw State University, Kennesaw, GA, associate professor, 1991-96, professor of sociology, 1996—. University Center of Georgia, chair of interdepartmental group for sociology, 1996.

MEMBER: Sociological Practice Association (member of board of directors, 1992; editor, 1994-96), American Sociological Association, Southern Sociological Society, Georgia Sociological Association (member of board of directors, 1991-95; president, 2000).

WRITINGS:

Role Change: A Resocialization Perspective, Praeger (New York, NY), 1990.

Analyzing Psychotherapy: A Social Role Interpretation, Praeger (New York, NY), 1992.

I.A.M.: A Common Sense Guide to Coping with Anger, Praeger (Westport, CT), 1993.

Hardball without an Umpire: The Sociology of Morality, Praeger (Westport, CT), 1997.

The Limits of Idealism: When Good Intentions Go Bad, Kluwer Academic (New York, NY), 1999.

Race and Morality: How Good Intentions Undermine Social Justice and Perpetuate Inequality, Kluwer Academic (New York, NY), 2001.

The Great Middle-Class Revolution: Our Long March toward a Professionalized Society, Kennesaw State University Press (Kennesaw, GA), 2005.

SIDELIGHTS: Melvyn L. Fein told *CA:* "I write because I want to share hard-won ideas. My social views have changed considerably over the years, but I have always believed in pursuing the truth. That is what I attempt to do in my books. What has surprised me most is how unreceptive many intellectuals are to fresh ideas. When I was young I assumed that insightful views, clearly expressed, would command assent. Now I know better. Too often intelligent people are committed to reading—and understanding—only that with which they already agree."

BIOGRAPHICAL AND CRITICAL SOURCES:

PERIODICALS

Choice, October, 1992, M.W. York, review of *Analyzing Psychotherapy: A Social Role Interpretation,* p. 385; March, 1998, review of *Hardball without an Umpire: The Sociology of Morality,* p. 1280; April, 2000, L. Braude, review of *The Limits of Idealism: When Good Intentions Go Bad,* p. 1551; April, 2002, K.M. McKinley, review of *Race and Morality: How Good Intentions Undermine Social Justice and Perpetuate Inequality,* p. 1504.

Reference & Research Book News, February, 1998, review of *Hardball without an Umpire,* p. 78; February, 2000, review of *The Limits of Idealism,* p. 91; August, 2001, review of *Race and Morality,* p. 54; November, 2006, review of *The Great Middle-Class Revolution: Our Long March toward a Professionalized Society.*

*   *   *

FEIN, Melvyn Leonard
See FEIN, Melvyn L.

FIFFER, Sharon 1951-
(Sharon Sloan Fiffer)

PERSONAL: Born 1951; married Steve Fiffer (a writer and editor); children: three.

ADDRESSES: Home—Evanston, IL. *E-mail*—janewheel@gmail.com.

CAREER: Writer, editor, educator, and novelist. Instructor in writing programs and English departments at the University of Illinois, Barat College, and Northwestern University.

AWARDS, HONORS: Literary Award, Illinois Arts Council, for short story "The Power of Speech"; Artist's Fellowship in Fiction.

WRITINGS:

NONFICTION

Imagining America: Paul Thai's Journey from the Killing Fields of Cambodia to Freedom in the U.S.A., Paragon House (New York, NY), 1991.
(With Steve Fiffer) *Fifty Ways to Help Your Community: A Handbook for Change,* Doubleday (New York, NY), 1994.
(Editor, with Steve Fiffer) *Home: American Writers Remember Rooms of Their Own,* Pantheon (New York, NY), 1995.
(Editor, with Steve Fiffer) *Family: American Writers Remember Their Own,* afterword by Jane Smiley, Pantheon (New York, NY), 1996.
(Editor, with Steve Fiffer) *Body,* Bard (New York, NY), 1999.

"JANE WHEEL" MYSTERY SERIES; NOVELS

Killer Stuff, St. Martin's Minotaur (New York, NY), 2001.
Dead Guy's Stuff, St. Martin's Minotaur (New York, NY), 2002.
The Wrong Stuff, St. Martin's Minotaur (New York, NY), 2003.
Buried Stuff, St. Martin's Minotaur (New York, NY), 2004.

Hollywood Stuff, St. Martin's Minotaur (New York, NY), 2006.

Other Voices, coeditor, c. 1985-91.

SIDELIGHTS: Novelist, editor, and educator Sharon Fiffer is the author of a series of mystery novels centering on collector, antiques picker, collectibles consultant, and flea-market maven Jane Wheel. Separated from her husband, a professor, and laid off from her job at a Chicago advertising agency, Jane decides to become a "picker" for an antiques dealer, scouring sales, shops, and markets looking for unnoticed or undervalued items that can be acquired cheaply and resold for a profit. In the first book of the series, *Killer Stuff,* Jane's amateur sleuthing skills are required when a neighbor is murdered. Her efforts, however, are hampered by a rumor that she is having an affair with the dead woman's husband, having been caught giving him a surreptitious kiss at a dinner party. Despite the rumor, homicide detective Bruce Oh is willing to work with Jane to solve the crime, especially after she uncovers a second body and the unique object used in the murder. With assistance from her best friend, Tim, a gay antiques dealer, Jane sorts the treasures from the clutter in her search for a murderer. *Booklist* reviewer Stuart Miller called the novel "an auspicious debut featuring a popular pastime."

In *Dead Guy's Stuff,* Jane uncovers a trove of antique bar memorabilia that she intends to use to decorate her parents' bar in Kankakee, Illinois. Among the items, however, Jane finds a disturbing relic: a human finger floating in a jar. When she contacts detective Bruce Oh to help reunite the digit with its original owner, the investigation reveals an unexpected connection between the finger and her parents. "Humor and a great many details" about collectors of "stuff" and the collector's mentality "make this a fascinating, fun story," observed *Booklist* reviewer Sue O'Brien. A *Kirkus Reviews* contributor called the book "hilarious stuff" and "worth reading cover to cover."

The Wrong Stuff finds Jane determined to reduce the unwieldy masses of objects in her own home after she loses her son's field trip permission slip. While fielding an invitation from Bruce Oh to join his new private detective agency, Jane helps Bruce and his wife, Claire, herself an antiques dealer, with a deal gone bad.

Another infuriated antiques buyer has accused Claire of substituting a fake item for an extremely rare and valuable chest. When the buyer is discovered murdered, suspicion falls on the beleaguered Claire. Jane agrees to investigate, and accompanied by her best pal, Tim, she heads off to determine what happened to the original chest when it was sent away for restoration. A second murder convinces Jane that whoever is interested in the chest is willing to go to any lengths to retain it. Detailed information on the often unseen world of antiques "picking, dealing, and restoring, as well as clutter removal, offer added dimensions to an enjoyable series," commented O'Brien in another *Booklist* review.

BIOGRAPHICAL AND CRITICAL SOURCES:

PERIODICALS

Booklist, November 1, 1995, Mary Carroll, review of *Home: American Writers Remember Rooms of Their Own,* p. 449; November 1, 1996, Jim O'Laughlin, review of *Family: American Writers Remember Their Own,* p. 474; June 1, 1999, Donna Seaman, review of *Body,* p. 1770; August, 2001, Stuart Miller, review of *Killer Stuff,* p. 2095; October 1, 2002, Sue O'Brien, review of *Dead Guy's Stuff,* p. 303; September 15, 2003, Sue O'Brien, review of *The Wrong Stuff,* p. 214; November 15, 2004, Sue O'Brien, review of *Buried Stuff,* p. 565; May 1, 2006, Sue O'Brien, review of *Hollywood Stuff,* p. 22.

Kirkus Reviews, August 1, 1991, review of *Imagining America: Paul Thai's Journey from the Killing Fields of Cambodia to Freedom in the U.S.A.,* p. 981; October 1, 1996, review of *Family,* p. 1440; May 15, 1999, review of *Body,* p. 771; July 15, 2001, review of *Killer Stuff,* p. 982; August 15, 2002, review of *Dead Guy's Stuff,* p. 1177; September 1, 2003, review of *The Wrong Stuff,* p. 1101; September 15, 2004, review of *Buried Stuff,* p. 893; April 15, 2006, review of *Hollywood Stuff,* p. 381.

Library Journal, August, 1991, Glenn Masuchika, review of *Imagining America,* p. 128; November 1, 2002, Rex E. Klett, review of *Dead Guy's Stuff,* p. 132; November 1, 2003, Rex E. Klett, review of *The Wrong Stuff,* p. 128.

Los Angeles Times Book Review, December 24, 1995, Bernard Cooper, "Home for the Holidays," p. 1.

Publishers Weekly, July 5, 1991, review of *Imagining America,* p. 52; August 28, 1995, review of *Home,* p. 93; September 2, 1996, review of *Family,* p. 101; May 3, 1999, review of *Body,* p. 58; August 6, 2001, review of *Killer Stuff,* p. 65; September 23, 2002, review of *Dead Guy's Stuff,* p. 53; October 13, 2003, "November Publications," review of *The Wrong Stuff,* p. 61; April 10, 2006, review of *Hollywood Stuff,* p. 49.

Tribune Books (Chicago, IL), September 9, 2001, review of *Killer Stuff,* p. 3.

ONLINE

Sharon Fiffer Home Page, http://www.sharonfiffer.com (December 3, 2006).

*   *   *

**FIFFER, Sharon Sloan
    See FIFFER, Sharon**

*   *   *

FINLAY, Victoria

PERSONAL: Education: Attended the University of St. Andrews, Scotland, and the College of William and Mary, VA.

ADDRESSES: Home—Somerset, England.

CAREER: Journalist and writer. Has worked for the Alliance of Religion and Conversation (ARC), Bath, England. Previously worked as a journalist in Hong Kong, China, including five years as editor of the *South China Morning Post* and as a weekly radio commentator, then for Reuters in London, England, and Scandinavia.

WRITINGS:

Colour: Travels through a Paintbox, Sceptre (London, England), 2002, published as *Color: A Natural History of the Palette,* Ballantine Books (New York, NY), 2003.

Jewels: A Secret History, Ballantine Books (New York, NY), 2006, published in England as *Buried Treasure: Travels through the Jewel Box,* Sceptre (London, England), 2006.

Contributor to periodicals, including the *London Times.*

SIDELIGHTS: A longtime journalist, Victoria Finlay left her position at the *South China Morning Post* to write *Color: A Natural History of the Palette,* published in England as *Colour: Travels through a Paintbox.* In addition to presenting what amounts to the story of each color, including what specific colors mean to various people in different societies, the author also presents a book that is part travelogue as she recounts her various journeys, such as her search for the ochre Australian Aborigines once mined, and her visit to Chilean plantations to learn of the red chochineal beetles.

Writing in *Kirkus Reviews,* a contributor referred to *Color* as "a well-rounded exploration of the properties and associations of colors from an engagingly personal vantage." The reviewer went on to note: "The writing is tight, yet her warm, anecdotal approach keeps the reader engaged." In his review in *Biotechnic & Histochemistry,* Jim Elsam wrote that "this book is a large collection of small stories and, if one thinks of a story as something that carries us toward understanding, Finlay hits the spot both in the carrying and the destinations." A *Publishers Weekly* contributor wrote: "Thanks to Finlay's impeccable reportorial skills and a remarkable degree of engagement, this is an utterly unique and fascinating read."

Finlay was inspired by an engagement ring from her fiancé to write *Jewels: A Secret History,* published in England as *Buried Treasure: Travels through the Jewel Box.* In her book, the author presents some of the world's most valuable gems, from the malleable amber to the hardest gem in the world—the diamond. As in her previous book, *Color,* Finlay provides a travelogue to accompany her explanation of the myths and popularity surrounding the gems she focuses on. For example, she describes how her search for the origins of gems led her to the Egyptian desert, a Baltic beach, and many other locales, where she interviews miners, gem cutters, sellers and others associated with the gem trade. The author also presents numerous anecdotes about gems, such as the story of a cat skeleton that turned into opal.

In a review of *Jewels* in *Booklist,* Kristine Huntley noted that "this rich, comprehensive book will no doubt appeal to jewelry lovers." Jo Sargent, writing in the *Geographical,* called the book "a captivating rummage through the various gems our planet produces" and "a fascinating volume." A *Kirkus Reviews* contributor wrote that the book contains "many sparkling anecdotes about jewels." John De Falbe, writing in the *Spectator,* noted: "This book plainly involved a huge amount of travelling, but it is only significant as it illuminates the scarcity and mystique of the gems. The point is always what Finlay finds when she gets there, both the stories and the stone itself."

BIOGRAPHICAL AND CRITICAL SOURCES:

PERIODICALS

Biotechnic & Histochemistry, February, 2004, Jim Elsam, review of *Colour: Travels through a Paintbox,* p. 53.
Booklist, December 1, 2002, Donna Seaman, review of *Color: A Natural History of the Palette,* p. 636; August 1, 2006, Kristine Huntley, review of *Jewels: A Secret History,* p. 22.
Geographical, July, 2006, Jo Sargent, review of *Buried Treasure: Travels through the Jewel Box,* p. 83.
Guardian (London, England), April 29, 2006, Veronica Horwell, review of *Buried Treasure.*
Kirkus Reviews, November 1, 2002, review of *Color,* p. 1587; June 1, 2006, review of *Jewels,* p. 555.
Library Journal, February 1, 2003, Jack Perry Brown, review of *Color,* p. 82; August 1, 2006, Regina M. Beard, review of *Jewels,* p. 101.
Publishers Weekly, December 16, 2002, review of *Color,* p. 58; May 29, 2006, review of *Jewels,* p. 47.
Spectator, June 30, 2006, John De Falbe, review of *Buried Treasure.*
Time International, December 16, 2002, Tim Mcgirk, "The Color of Passion: British Adventurer Victoria Finlay Embarks on a Journey to Discover the Cradles of Our Colors," p. 50.

ONLINE

Curled Up with a Good Book, http://www.curledup.com/ (January 18, 2007), Poornima Apte, review of *Color.*

Random House Web site, http://www.randomhouse. com/ (January 18, 2007), Mo Wu, "A Conversation with Victoria Finlay."*

*   *   *

FLANAGAN, Caitlin

PERSONAL: Born in Berkeley, CA; married; children: two (twin boys). *Education:* University of Virginia, B.A., M.A.

CAREER: Writer, critic, and magazine journalist. Has worked as a teacher at Harvard-Westlake School in Los Angeles, CA.

AWARDS, HONORS: National Magazine Award finalist (four times), for reviews in the *Atlantic.*

WRITINGS:

To Hell with All That: Loving and Loathing Our Inner Housewife, Little, Brown (New York, NY), 2006.

Contributor to books, including *Best American Magazine Writing,* 2002, 2003, and 2004, *Best American Essays,* 2003, *Best American Travel Writing,* 2006, and *50 Best Book Reviews from the Atlantic Monthly.*

Contributor to periodicals, including the *Atlantic* and the *New Yorker.*

SIDELIGHTS: Writer, critic, and journalist Caitlin Flanagan is the author of *To Hell with All That: Loving and Loathing Our Inner Housewife,* which *Booklist* reviewer Barbara Jacobs called "an insightful, incisive look at the multiple demands on American women in the new millennium." In a series of recast articles from the *Atlantic* and the *New Yorker,* Flanagan examines the sometimes paradoxical demands placed on women in modern society and ponders the ancient conflict between the rights and privileges of being a woman and the power and control of masculinity. "Flanagan is a sparkling stylist, and she is definitely on to something with her idea of an 'inner

housewife,' that secret part of emancipated womanhood that clings to old-fashioned feminine roles even as the outer lawyer, or whatever, rejects them," commented Meghan Cox Gurdon in the *Weekly Standard.* Flanagan observes that, paradoxically, women might well resent the constant struggle against entropy represented by the unceasing need for cleaning and tidying, but she also notes that in some way, a clean house or clean laundry evokes a feeling of accomplishment. For Flanagan, child-rearing duties are best left to the woman of the house, even as stay-at-home dads and hired nannies proliferate as sources of caring for children. Working mothers are trapped in a situation in which they will inevitably lose a portion of their lives with their children, no matter if working motherhood is socially approved or disapproved. The contrast between women's stated positions on domestic issues, and the actual social reality of the home sphere, forms the core of Flanagan's book. "What makes Flanagan's book original and vital is that she is a realist, willing to acknowledge the essential gray areas in too often polarized positions," commented Pamela Paul in the *New York Times.* In the often emotionally charged arena of domestic life, bracketed by old-fashioned housewife values on one side and modern feminism on the other, with numerous gradations of opinion and reaction in between, Flanagan's viewpoints often provoke deep ire from readers and detractors. However, Paul observed: "Here's what I think really bothers Flanagan's critics: No matter how vociferously they disagree with her on some things, they find themselves agreeing with much of what she writes."

"Flanagan writes with intelligence, wit and brio. She's likable," Paul remarked. Gurdon called Flanagan's book a "witty, elegantly written, and charming mix of self-deprecation and social commentary" and observed that Flanagan herself is a "wonderfully readable observer of the peculiarities of modern domestic life."

BIOGRAPHICAL AND CRITICAL SOURCES:

PERIODICALS

Booklist, April 15, 2006, Barbara Jacobs, review of *To Hell with All That: Loving and Loathing Our Inner Housewife,* p. 9.
New York Times, April 16, 2006, Pamela Paul, "Mother Superior," review of *To Hell with All That.*

Reason, October, 2006, Shannon Chamberlain, "The Real Mommy Wars: Both Left and Right Attack Mothers for the Choices They Make," review of *To Hell with All That,* p. 56.

Weekly Standard, August 14, 2006, Meghan Cox Gurdon, "Kitchen Confidential: Inside Every Feminist, a Woman Yearns to Break Free," review of *To Hell with All That.*

ONLINE

Atlantic Online, http://www.theatlantic.com/ (December 9, 2006), biography of Caitlin Flanagan.

*   *   *

FLEMING, Anne 1964-

PERSONAL: Born 1964.

ADDRESSES: Home—Vancouver, British Columbia, Canada. *Office*—Faculty of Creative and Critical Studies, University of British Columbia, Okanagan, 3333 University Way, Kelowna, British Columbia V1V 1V7, Canada.

CAREER: Writer, novelist, short-story writer, poet, screenwriter, playwright, and educator. University of British Columbia, Okanagan, British Columbia, Canada, assistant professor of creative writing. Instructor in creative writing at University of British Columbia, Emily Carr Institute of Art and Design, Kwantlen University College, and Douglas College. Former member of faculty, Banff Centre for the Arts Wired Writing Studio.

AWARDS, HONORS: Canadian National Award for fiction; Journey Prize shortlist; Danuta Gleed Award shortlist; Ethel Wilson Prize shortlist; Canadian Governor-General's Award nomination for *Pool-Hopping and Other Stories.*

WRITINGS:

Pool-Hopping and Other Stories, Polestar Book Publishers (Victoria, British Columbia, Canada), 1998.

Anomaly, Raincoast Books (Vancouver, British Columbia, Canada), 2005.

Contributor to anthologies, including *Meltwater: Fiction and Poetry from the Banff Centre,* edited by Edna Alford, Don McKay, Rhea Tregebove, and Rachel Wyatt, Banff Centre Press (Banff, Alberta, Canada), 2003; and *Second Chapter: The Canadian Writers Photography Project,* photography by Don Denton, Banff Centre Press (Banff, Alberta, Canada), 2004. Contributor to periodicals, including *Toronto Life, New Quarterly,* and the *Georgia Straight.*

SIDELIGHTS: Anne Fleming is an award-winning Canadian author and educator who has taught in universities throughout Canada. She currently serves as an assistant professor of creative writing at the University of British Columbia, Okanagan. As a lesbian, Fleming balances the expectations the literary world has for "queer writers" with her desire to write evocative fiction that does not serve as a showcase for lesbian theory or homosexual stereotype. "I'm not interested in manifesting lesbian theory in my fiction," Fleming remarked to interviewer Zoe Whittall in *This Magazine.* "Theory and specific people: it's not always an exact fit." Whittall observed that "regardless of politics, Fleming's work really comes down to a love of language and story."

Fleming's *Pool-Hopping and Other Stories* contains thirteen short stories. A reviewer in *Herizons* remarked that "most of Fleming's characters are either living through, or attempting to understand the 'defining moments' in their lives." George, the sixty-eight-year-old protagonist of "You Would Know What to Do," has lost his wife and is estranged from his gay son. He is no longer the head of the "happy family" that he perceives himself to be and, in his clouded thinking, a desperate move is required to restore the balance. In an attempt to reconnect with his family, he considers robbing a bank. The reader follows George as he makes his fateful decision. Craig, the narrator of "Solar Plexus," a seventeen-year-old who looks many years older than he is, moves carefully but deliberately to convince a girl whose father is dying of cancer to sleep with him. Abruptly, he goes too far, with unexpected results. A group of lesbian friends gathers for Christmas in "Atmospherics," where Susan resents the presence of punk-rock chick Marla, her ex's new lover. Susan is pregnant by artificial insemination, and when she discovers that lesbian Marla got pregnant the old-fashioned way, her attitude toward her softens. In the title story, Julie endures a heat wave and reflects on her past after the death of her twin, and recalls a time when she and her friends bested another heat wave by trespassing in their wealthier neighbors' swimming pools. "Most of Fleming's stories leave you wanting so much you ache," observed the reviewer in *Herizons.* "At once ruthlessly precise with her descriptions . . . and generous to her characters, she makes a bracing, truthful debut with these thirteen stories," commented a *Publishers Weekly* reviewer.

By all outward appearances, the Riggs family, featured in Fleming's novel *Anomaly,* are a normal, happy family. The family consists of two parents, a mischievous brother, and two sisters. However, the anomaly of the title is represented by Carol, an albino, and how her condition influences her and the people around her. The story centers around mother Rowena, her daughters Carol and Glynnis, and the aged girl-guide troop leader Miss Beryl Balls, a tough but wise "old spinster" who has never really been able to come out of the closet. "Fleming faultlessly captures the range and register of these four voices, and each is equally strong and distinctive," commented Claire Robson in *Herizons.* Fleming's story follows Carol and Glynnis from childhood into the tumult of adolescence, when Carol takes up a punk rock lifestyle and Glynnis struggles to deal with her nascent lesbian feelings. The girls must also deal with their issues as siblings, including the perpetual specter of a disabling injury Carol once inflicted on Glynnis. There is "nothing precious about these growing pains, and the two central characters are exquisitely drawn," commented a *Publishers Weekly* contributor. As the girls navigate the difficult terrain of adolescence and their own conflicted relationship with each other, Rowena becomes drawn more and more to the religious life of the ministry, while Miss Balls nurtures precious memories of an unconsummated relationship she had with another nurse during the war. "Fleming's ability to fully inhabit the consciousness of her characters is flawless, as are her portraits of the ordinary and extraordinary life of adolescent girls," remarked a *Kirkus Reviews* critic. *Booklist* reviewer Maureen O'Connor remarked: "This first novel is a triumph of language and story."

BIOGRAPHICAL AND CRITICAL SOURCES:

PERIODICALS

Booklist, August 1, 2006, Maureen O'Connor, review of *Anomaly,* p. 40.

Herizons, summer, 2000, review of *Pool-Hopping and Other Stories,* p. 31; spring, 2006, Clare Robson, review of *Anomaly,* p. 34.

Kirkus Reviews, May 15, 2006, review of *Anomaly,* p. 482.

Publishers Weekly, February 22, 1999, review of *Pool-Hopping and Other Stories,* p. 67; May 22, 2006, review of *Anomaly,* p. 26.

ONLINE

Anne Fleming Home Page, http://annefleming.ca (December 20, 2006).

Banff Centre Web site, http://www.banfcentre.ca/ (December 20, 2006), biography of Anne Fleming.

Eighteenth Vancouver International Writers and Readers Festival Web site, http://www.writersfest.bc.ca/ (December 20, 2006), biography of Anne Fleming.

This Magazine, http://www.thismagazine.com/ (September, 2005), Zoe Whittall, "Dyke Type," profile of Anne Fleming.

University of British Columbia, Okanagan, Department of Creative Studies Web site, http://web.ubc.ca/okanagan/ (December 1, 2006), biography of Anne Fleming.*

*   *   *

FLYNN, Gillian 1971-

PERSONAL: Born 1971, in Kansas City, MO. *Education:* Northwestern University, M.A.

ADDRESSES: Home—Chicago, IL. *Office*—Entertainment Weekly, P.O. Box 60001, Tampa, FL 33660-0001 *Agent*—Stephanie Kip Rostan, Levine Greenberg Literary Agency, 307 7th Ave., Ste. 2407, New York, NY 10001.

CAREER: Entertainment Weekly, Tampa, FL, film and television critic.

WRITINGS:

Sharp Objects (novel), Shaye Areheart Books (New York, NY), 2006.

Contributor to *Entertainment Weekly.*

SIDELIGHTS: Gillian Flynn serves as film and television critic for *Entertainment Weekly* and writes fiction in her free time. Flynn's first novel, *Sharp Objects,* was delayed for a time when Flynn earned the prime assignment to cover the making of Peter Jackson's *The Lord of the Rings* trilogy during its filming in New Zealand. However, Flynn returned to her novel after the film project was completed, and the result was a well-received thriller about a reporter named Camille, who returns to the small Midwestern town where she was raised in order to investigate the murders of a number of children. During the investigation, Camille also finds herself forced to deal with her own dysfunctional family and her scarred psyche. Flynn credits her own prolific reading and reviewing of mystery novels with her ability to maintain suspense throughout her own work, as well as her efforts to set a specific atmosphere for the book. In an interview for the *Redbook Bookclub Online,* Flynn stated: "I wanted *Sharp Objects* to have the feel of a fairy-tale gone really wrong: The evil, jealous queen (Camille's mother), the town surrounded by haunted woods, the attacks on children. Camille, then, is the beautiful young girl in serious danger that every good fairy tale has. In this story, she's as much in danger from herself as she is from outside forces." Joanne Wilkinson, in a review for *Booklist,* found that Flynn's effort was "fueled by stylish writing and compelling portraits of desperate housewives, southern style," calling the book an "impressive debut novel." A contributor for *Kirkus Reviews* called the book "a savage debut thriller that renders the Electra complex electric, the mother/daughter bond a psychopathic stranglehold."

BIOGRAPHICAL AND CRITICAL SOURCES:

PERIODICALS

Booklist, August 1, 2006, Joanne Wilkinson, review of *Sharp Objects,* p. 49.
Bookmarks, January-February, 2007, review of *Sharp Objects,* p. 43.
Chicago Tribune Books, October 29, 2006, Alan Cheuse, "A Sharply Written, Compelling Debut Novel," review of *Sharp Objects,* p. 6.
Entertainment Weekly, September 29, 2006, Gilbert Cruz, review of *Sharp Objects,* p. 89.
Kirkus Reviews, July 15, 2006, review of *Sharp Objects,* p. 690.

Library Journal, August 1, 2006, Nancy McNicol, review of *Sharp Objects,* p. 68.
People, October 30, 2006, Natalie Danford, review of *Sharp Objects,* p. 45.
Publishers Weekly, August 14, 2006, Suzanne Mantell, review of *Sharp Objects,* p. 88; August 21, 2006, review of *Sharp Objects,* p. 50.

ONLINE

Random House Web site, http://www.randomhouse. com/ (January 13, 2007), author spotlight.
Redbook Bookclub Online, http://youarehere.redbook. ivillage.com/ (January 13, 2007), Rebecca Davis, author interview.*

*   *   *

FORBES, Flores A.

PERSONAL: *Education:* New York University, Robert F. Wagner School of Public Service, M.S.

ADDRESSES: *Home*—NY. *Office*—Abyssinian Development Corporation, 4 W. 125th St., New York, NY 10027.

CAREER: Abyssinian Development Corporation, New York, NY, chief strategic officer.

WRITINGS:

Will You Die with Me? My Life and the Black Panther Party (memoir), Atria Books (New York, NY), 2006.

SIDELIGHTS: Flores A. Forbes is an expert in urban planning policy and economic and community development, and serves as the chief strategic officer for the Abyssinian Development Corporation. Forbes spent his early years as a pivotal member of the radical separatist Black Panther Party, joining in the late 1960s and working as a bodyguard, enforcer, and an inner circle gunman. He eventually killed a friend, went on the run, then finally turned himself in for sentencing. In his book, *Will You Die with Me? My*

Life and the Black Panther Party, Forbes writes about his experiences during that period of his life and how he broke free of the Black Panthers. He also offers readers an inside look at the development of the organization. Stanley Crouch, in a review for the *New York Times,* remarked of Forbes's effort: "Part of the power of the book is seeing this man slowly shocked free of the iceberg of ideology to which he had submitted and for which he was willing to achieve goals 'by any means necessary.' Much of its value is that it helps to make up for a decided shortcoming of our national literature, which has never sufficiently examined the radical politics of the 60's." A contributor for *Kirkus Reviews* called the book "a dark and disturbing read," while Francisca Goldsmith, writing for the *School Library Journal,* found it to be "a compelling nonfiction read."

BIOGRAPHICAL AND CRITICAL SOURCES:

BOOKS

Forbes, Flores A., *Will You Die with Me? My Life and the Black Panther Party,* Atria Books (New York, NY), 2006.

PERIODICALS

Kirkus Reviews, June 1, 2006, review of *Will You Die with Me?,* p. 555.
New York Times, September 10, 2006, Stanley Crouch, "By Any Means Necessary," review of *Will You Die with Me?*
San Francisco Chronicle, July 9, 2006, Austin Considine, review of *Will You Die with Me?,* p. M1.
School Library Journal, November, 2006, Francisca Goldsmith, review of *Will You Die with Me?,* p. 172.

ONLINE

New York Public Radio Web site, http://www.wnyc.org/ (July 26, 2006), author biography.
Turnstile Web site, http://turnstile.cssny.org/ (January 21, 2007), author biography.*

*   *   *

FORD, Christine 1953-

PERSONAL: Born 1953, in Pittsfield, MA.

ADDRESSES: Home and office—Arlington, TX. *E-mail*—crsford@comcast.net.

CAREER: Author and poet. Teaches picture-book-writing workshops for adults.

MEMBER: Society of Children's Book Writers and Illustrators.

WRITINGS:

Snow!, illustrated by Candace Whitman, HarperFestival (New York, NY), 1999.
Scout (novel), Delacorte (New York, NY), 2006.
(With Trish Holland) *The Soldiers' Night before Christmas,* illustrated by John Manders, Golden Books (New York, NY), 2006.

SIDELIGHTS: Poet Christine Ford is the author of the picture books *Snow!* and *The Soldiers' Night before Christmas,* as well as the middle-grade novel *Scout.* Ford made her publishing debut in 1999 with *Snow!,* a work in verse illustrated by Candace Whitman. In the book, a father spends a wintry day playing outdoors with his son and daughter and their pet dog. The family goes sledding, throws snowballs, and builds a snowman before heading indoors. Kathy Broderick, writing in *Booklist,* noted that Ford's "couplets work well with Whitman's watercolor collage illustrations" and called *Snow!* a "fine picture book." *School Library Journal* contributor Tana Elias stated that Ford's "rhymes are pleasant."

Based on Clement Moore's famous holiday poem, Ford's *The Soldiers' Night before Christmas,* written with Trish Holland, appeared in 2006. Set on a U.S. Army base, the work begins: "'Twas the night before Christmas, and all through the base / Only sentries were stirring—they guarded the place." The poem's narrator, a young soldier, is awakened in the middle of the night by the arrival of cigar-smoking Sergeant McClaus in a Blackhawk helicopter, followed by eight brightly decorated Humvees laden with gifts from home. *School Library Journal* reviewer Virginia Walter deemed *The Soldiers' Night before Christmas* "a lighthearted, even humorous, retelling," and a *Kirkus Reviews* contributor wrote that the authors "offer a witty parody that serves up a unique vision of a Santa who is very different from the traditional St. Nick."

In 2006 Ford also published *Scout,* a novel written in free verse. According to a critic in *Kirkus Reviews,* "Ford shows considerable skill in distilling the messy complexity of grief and emotional renewal in poetry that often sings." The book concerns Cecelia, nicknamed Scout, a motherless eleven-year-old who escapes her loneliness by playing in the nature area near her home. Cecelia makes friends with Redbud, a new student at her school who lives with his stern father, a former Marine. "At first Cecelia admits that she finds the father's power fascinating," observed *Booklist* reviewer Hazel Rochman, but as the pair grows closer, she learns that Redbud is being abused. When Redbud is injured in a hit-and-run accident, Cecelia blames herself and is consumed with grief, prompting her emotionally distant father to rekindle his bond with his daughter. *Scout* "explores love for family and friends, courage, grief, guilt, and loss," in the words of *School Library Journal* critic Nancy P. Reeder. "In the end, it is a story of hope."

BIOGRAPHICAL AND CRITICAL SOURCES:

BOOKS

Ford, Christine, and Trish Holland, *The Soldiers' Night before Christmas,* Golden Books (New York, NY), 2006.

PERIODICALS

Booklist, January 1, 2000, Kathy Broderick, review of *Snow!,* p. 936; January 1, 2006, Hazel Rochman, review of *Scout,* p. 101.

Kirkus Reviews, March 1, 2006, review of *Scout,* p. 229; November 1, 2006, review of *The Soldiers' Night before Christmas,* p. 1130.

School Library Journal, December, 1999, Tana Elias, review of *Snow!,* p. 96; May, 2006, Nancy P. Reeder, review of *Scout,* p. 123; October, 2006, Virginia Walter, review of *The Soldiers' Night before Christmas,* p. 97.

ONLINE

Christine Ford Home Page, http://www.christineford. com (January 10, 2007).

FORD, Gerald R. 1913-2006
(Gerald Rudolph Ford, Jr.)

OBITUARY NOTICE— See index for *CA* sketch: Born July 14, 1913, in Omaha, NE; died December 26, 2006, in Rancho Mirage, CA. Politician and author. Ford was the thirty-eighth president of the United States who is often remembered for his efforts in healing the nation's wounds after President Nixon's resignation. Born Leslie Lynch King, Jr., Ford was two years old when his birth parents divorced. His mother remarried, and her son was named after his stepfather. It was not until he was seventeen that Ford would meet his biological father, and it was not a pleasant experience for him; he learned that his father had not paid the court-ordered alimony and child support all those years he was growing up. On the other hand, Ford had huge respect and admiration for his stepfather, who was a paint salesman but, more importantly, a kind and honorable man. His mother and stepfather instilled a strong work ethic in Ford, who came to believe that hard work would bring its due rewards. Attending the University of Michigan, he was a football and boxing coach and played for the Wolverines as the star center of the football team. He was named most valuable player in his senior year. The Detroit Lions and Green Bay Packers both offered to put Ford on their teams, but Ford decided he was more interested in pursuing the law. He graduated from the Yale Law School in 1941 and was admitted to the Michigan Bar that year. Establishing a law practice in his home town of Grand Rapids, he joined the navy the next year after the attack on Pearl Harbor. Because of his education and athletic background, the navy at first tried to keep him stateside as a physical trainer. Ford, however, had other ideas. He applied for front-line duty for over a year before finally being transferred to the aircraft carrier *Monterey.* The future president saw action in the Pacific theater, including at the battles at Wake Island and in the Philippines, and was awarded ten battle stars. Returning home in 1946, he joined the law firm Butterfield, Kenney & Amberg, but his war experiences had changed him. He began to have an interest in world and national politics. Ford ran for the U.S. House of Representatives and was a surprise winner in the 1948 elections. It would be the first of a string of political victories that saw Ford maintain his seat for two dozen years. A Republican, he rose to the post of minority leader in the Democrat-controlled Congress. Ford long aspired to win the post of speaker of the House, but because the Republicans remained a minority party during his career the job eluded him. Instead, he satisfied himself with work on the Appropriations Committee and in leading his party in the House. He developed a reputation as a loyal conservative and supporter of presidents Eisenhower and Nixon, and his friendly personality won him many political allies. Some critics would later argue that Ford was not a very effective legislator, having never written a major bill on his own; Ford, however, responded that he was far too busy on the Appropriations Committee to author legislation. It was because he was not a controversial figure in the Republican Party that many speculated Ford became President Richard Nixon's choice for replacing the indicted Spiro Agnew, who had been found guilty of tax evasion. Ford, realizing he would not win the speaker of the House seat, thought the vice presidency would be a good way to end his political career, and so he accepted the offer. Taking the office in 1973, Ford was the first vice president to fill the post on the U.S. Constitution's Twenty-fifth Amendment, which allowed the president to select a vice president should the office become unexpectedly open. Ford found himself in the middle of the Watergate era in which Nixon was accused of orchestrating the break-in at Democratic headquarters at the Watergate complex. Told that the president was in no way involved, Ford at first took the word of Nixon and his associates and defended the president. As evidence mounted against Nixon, however, Ford finally publicly declared on August 6, 1974, that he could no longer defend the president. Two days later, Nixon resigned rather than face impeachment. It was an alarming twist of fate for Ford, who had never aspired to sit in the White House, but he found himself taking the oath of office on August 9. He was the first man to ever serve as U.S. president without being elected. Realizing this, Ford took his responsibility with utmost seriousness. Seeking to heal the nation's wounds from the Watergate scandal, perhaps the most memorable action he took was to pardon the disgraced Richard Nixon. Ford would be criticized for this for years, but in the long run he was validated by historians who saw it as the correct course of action. As Ford realized before almost anyone else, a long trial against President Nixon would only rub salt into the wounds the nation had suffered. Better to put the past behind and get back to national issues than to become distracted by court actions that could last for years, Ford reasoned. Though he only served in the office for a little over two years, the president presided over some significant developments in the country. During his administration, America finally saw the end of the Vietnam War;

he began talks with Panama that would eventually turn control of the canal to the Panamanians during President Jimmy Carter's term; and he supported the Helsinki Accords, which many experts now feel helped to bring about the demise of the Soviet Union by encouraging political resistance in Eastern Europe. Inflation began to come under control and unemployment rates fell, too, under Ford's watch. Ford's conservative policies often irked liberal legislators, however. The president did not believe in government handouts, which some political pundits thought counterintuitive from a man who many knew was generous to a fault on a personal level. Some were resentful of his policies, and two assassination attempts were made in 1975 on his life: one by Lynette Fromme, a follower of convicted murderer Charles Manson, and a second by another woman whose name was Sara Jane Moore. Most criticisms of how Ford ran the country proved minor, however, compared to continuing resentment over the Nixon pardon. It was this act, still fresh in the public's mind, that was blamed for Ford's loss of the 1976 election to Jimmy Carter. After leaving office, Ford became a successful public speaker, and he worked for the Ronald Reagan and George H.W. Bush presidential campaigns. Finally retiring to California after suffering a stroke in 2000, the president enjoyed golf and living a quiet life. The next year, Ford was given a Profile in Courage Award; he was also the recipient of the 1999 Presidential Medal of Freedom and the Congressional Gold Medal, as well as the 1972 National Football Foundation and Hall of Fame Award. Interestingly, the president never wrote an autobiography, though he did publish several nonfiction works and speech selections, as well as *Humor and the Presidency* (1987).

OBITUARIES AND OTHER SOURCES:

PERIODICALS

Chicago Tribune, December 28, 2006, Section 1, pp. 6-7.
New York Times, December 28, 2006, pp. A29, A31; December 29, 2006, p. A2; January 3, 2007, p. A2.
Times (London, England), December 28, 2006, p. 58.

*   *   *

FORD, Gerald Rudolph, Jr.
    See FORD, Gerald R.

FORD, Marcia

PERSONAL: Married; husband's name John (a distribution center supervisor); children: Elizabeth, Sarah. *Education:* Monmouth College (now Monmouth University, West Long Branch, NJ), B.A., 1972; Jersey Shore Bible Institute, Asbury Park, NJ, 1975-77. Graduate, education for ministry program, University of the South, Sewanee, TN.

ADDRESSES: Home—Orange City, FL. *E-mail*—misfit@marciaford.com.

CAREER: Writer, editor, journalist, and manager. *Asbury Park Press,* Asbury Park, NJ, reporter, 1973-77, religion editor, 1974-83, education editor, 1977-78, copy editor, 1978-83; *Monmouth Business Talk,* managing editor, 1987; *Charisma,* news editor, 1994-96, associate editor, 1996; *Ministries Today,* news editor, 1994-96, associate editor, 1996; *Christian Retailing,* managing editor, 1997-98, news editor, 1998-99; freelance writer and editor, 1999—.

MEMBER: Emergent Village, Advanced Writers and Speakers Association, Florida Writers Association, National Association of Women Writers, National Writers Union, Toastmasters (served as officer).

AWARDS, HONORS: Royal Palm Literary Award, Florida Writers Association, first place, autobiography, 2004, for *Memoir of a Misfit;* first place, inspirational, 2004, for *101 Most Powerful Promises in the Bible.*

WRITINGS:

Charisma Reports: The Brownsville Revival, Creation House (Lake Mary, FL), 1997.

(With Scott Marshall) *Restless Pilgrim: The Spiritual Journey of Bob Dylan,* Relevant (Lake Mary, FL), 2002.

101 Most Powerful Promises in the Bible, edited by Steve and Lois Rabey, Warner Faith (New York, NY), 2003.

Meditations for Misfits: Finding Your Place in the Family of God, Jossey-Bass (San Francisco, CA), 2003.

Memoir of a Misfit: Finding My Place in the Family of God, foreword by Phyllis Tickle, Jossey-Bass (San Francisco, CA), 2003.

God between the Covers: Finding Faith through Reading, Crossroad Publishing (New York, NY), 2005.

Finding Hope: Cultivating God's Gift of a Hopeful Spirit, SkyLight Paths (Woodstock, VT), 2006.

The Sacred Art of Forgiveness: Forgiving Ourselves and Others through God's Grace, SkyLight Paths (Woodstock, VT), 2006.

Traditions of the Ancients: Vintage Faith Practices for the 21st Century, Broadman & Holman (Nashville, TN), 2006.

SIDELIGHTS: Writer, editor, and inspirational author Marcia Ford is a thirty-year veteran of the writing and editing business. A former newspaper reporter and magazine editor, Ford has been a freelance book editor and a managing editor. Much of her magazine work has been for Christian-based publications, and her books often reflect associated religious and inspirational themes. In *101 Most Powerful Promises in the Bible,* Ford highlights biblical promises and advice from both the Old and New Testaments. She stresses passages that provide readers with instruction, hope, and inspiration and explains how the lessons from the passages can be applied to particular situations and to daily life. She includes historical information and commentary on the biblical verse she highlights. Ford successfully elucidates "key biblical principles, providing her readers with substantial truths to reflect upon long after the book has been closed," noted a *Publishers Weekly* reviewer.

With *Finding Hope: Cultivating God's Gift of a Hopeful Spirit,* Ford "manages to communicate the essence of hope with intelligence, humor, and grace," commented a contributor to *Publishers Weekly.* At the time of the book's writing, Ford was suffering from a severe illness and reeling from the effects of a fire that had damaged her home, yet she still found encouragement in her Christian faith and advice for readers searching for a source of hope when their own lives turn bleak. She endorses placing one's ultimate hope in God and illustrates this notion with stories from history, popular culture, the Bible, and her own life. She also provides idea-triggering questions for readers to consider and suggests practices such as meditation and journaling as methods for restoring clarity and hope.

The Sacred Art of Forgiveness: Forgiving Ourselves and Others through God's Grace contains Ford's meditation and consideration of the often difficult act of forgiveness. Using a structure similar to that of her previous books, Ford illustrates the liberating power of forgiveness with stories from history and from her own personal experience. She offers questions for readers to ponder and lists practical exercises to be undertaken by those seeking a better understanding of forgiveness and what it can mean in their lives. Ford finds the greatest source of forgiveness in the divine and in the great forgiveness demonstrated by God. As a practical matter, Ford also considers the difficulty in forgiving someone who is dangerous or abusive, noting that forgiving someone does not necessarily require reuniting with them. A *Publishers Weekly* writer concluded: "This primer belongs in the hands of anyone who needs to give or receive forgiveness."

Ford's interest in religion extends beyond the traditional branches of Christianity, as demonstrated in *Traditions of the Ancients: Vintage Faith Practices for the 21st Century.* In this book Ford describes twenty-eight spiritual practices, some forgotten or little used, from the biblical tradition and early Christian worship. Ford describes such practices as praying for the gift of tears and bereavement; using solitude and silence as an enhancement to religious observance; participating in prayer at fixed hours; consuming memorial meals; and more. Ford "offers some interesting ideas to readers wishing to climb out of ruts in their prayer and worship habits," observed a *Publishers Weekly* critic.

BIOGRAPHICAL AND CRITICAL SOURCES:

PERIODICALS

Publishers Weekly, August 11, 2003, review of *101 Most Powerful Promises in the Bible,* p. 274; January 30, 2006, review of *Traditions of the Ancients: Vintage Faith Practices for the 21st Century,* p. 63; February 13, 2006, review of *The Sacred Art of Forgiveness: Forgiving Ourselves and Others through God's Grace,* p. 84; September 11, 2006, review of *Finding Hope: Cultivating God's Gift of a Hopeful Spirit,* p. 51.

ONLINE

Marcia Ford Home Page, http://www.marciaford.com (December 9, 2006).

FOSTER, Thomas A.

PERSONAL: Education: Cornell University, B.A.; North Carolina State University, M.A.; Johns Hopkins University, Ph.D.

ADDRESSES: Home—Chicago, IL. *Office*—Department of History, DePaul University, 1 E. Jackson Blvd., Chicago, IL 60604. *E-mail*—tfoster4@ depaul.edu.

CAREER: DePaul University, Chicago, IL, assistant professor of history.

WRITINGS:

Sex and the Eighteenth-Century Man: Massachusetts and the History of Sexuality in America, Beacon Press (Boston, MA), 2006.
(Editor) *Long before Stonewall: Histories of Same-Sex Sexuality in Early America,* New York University Press (New York, NY), 2007.

Contributor of scholarly articles to various journals, including the *William and Mary Quarterly.*

SIDELIGHTS: Thomas A. Foster serves as an assistant professor of history at DePaul University in Chicago, Illinois, where his primary areas of research interest include early America, U.S. women's and gender history, the American Revolution, the history of sexuality, and U.S. social and cultural history. In his *Sex and the Eighteenth-Century Man: Massachusetts and the History of Sexuality in America,* Foster presents an alternative to the traditional views of American sexual behavior in the eighteenth century, claiming it was not the chaste, puritanical society most commonly reported. Instead, Foster argues that the nation's founding fathers considered sex to be a part of daily life, and treated the subject in a frank and open manner, and that sexuality, along with religion and economics, was a vital part of how men defined themselves during the period. Maurice Gold, writing for the *Gay & Lesbian Review Worldwide,* noted that the book originated as a doctoral thesis, but added: "Foster's prose is more readable than many similar books, and for the most part he avoids turgid postmodernese." Matthew Price, in a review for the

New York Times, called Foster's effort a "plodding if occasionally saucy book." A contributor for *Publishers Weekly* remarked that Foster "uncovers intriguing and historically important examples that provoke rethinking of the history of gender in America."

BIOGRAPHICAL AND CRITICAL SOURCES:

PERIODICALS

Gay & Lesbian Review Worldwide, November-December, 2006, Maurice Gold, review of *Sex and the Eighteenth-Century Man: Massachusetts and the History of Sexuality in America,* p. 44.

New York Times, January 7, 2007, Matthew Price, review of *Sex and the Eighteenth-Century Man.*

Publishers Weekly, July 24, 2006, review of *Sex and the Eighteenth-Century Man,* p. 51.

ONLINE

Booksense, http://semcoop.booksense.com/ (January 14, 2007), author biography.

DePaul University Web site, http://condor.depaul.edu/ (January 14, 2007), faculty biography.*

*   *   *

FOURNIER, Ron

PERSONAL: Born in Detroit, MI; married; wife's name Lori; children: three. *Education:* University of Detroit, graduated.

ADDRESSES: Home—Arlington, VA. *E-mail*—authors@applebeesamerica.com.

CAREER: Sentinel-Record, Hot Springs, AR, reporter, 1985-87; *Arkansas Democrat-Gazette,* Little Rock, reporter, 1987-89; Associated Press, 1989—, Washington correspondent, 1992—, chief political writer.

AWARDS, HONORS: Sigma Delta Chi Award, Society of Professional Journalists, for coverage of the 2000 presidential election; three-time winner of the Merriman Smith Award, White House Correspondents Association.

WRITINGS:

(With Douglas B. Sosnik and Matthew J. Dowd) *Applebee's America: How Successful Political, Business, and Religious Leaders Connect with the New American Community,* Simon & Schuster (New York, NY), 2006.

SIDELIGHTS: For Sidelights, see *CA* entry on Matthew J. Dowd.

BIOGRAPHICAL AND CRITICAL SOURCES:

PERIODICALS

American Prospect, October, 2006, E.J. Dionne, Jr., review of *Applebee's America: How Successful Political, Business, and Religious Leaders Connect with the New American Community,* p. 52.

Booklist, September 15, 2006, Vanessa Bush, review of *Applebee's America,* p. 13.

Library Journal, September 1, 2006, Carol J. Elsen, review of *Applebee's America,* p. 158.

Publishers Weekly, July 24, 2006, review of *Applebee's America,* p. 52.

San Francisco Chronicle, September 18, 2006, Austin Considine, review of *Applebee's America.*

Washington Post, September 12, 2006, Amy Goldstein, review of *Applebee's America,* p. A21.

ONLINE

Applebee's America Web site, http://www.applebeesamerica.com (January 11, 2007).

Think and Ask, http://www.thinkandask.com/ (September 3, 2006), review of *Applebee's America.**

*   *   *

FRANKEL, Alison

PERSONAL: Married Dan Fagin; children: Anna and Lily. *Education:* Graduated from Dartmouth College.

ADDRESSES: Home—Sea Cliff, NY. *E-mail*—afrankel@alm.com

CAREER: Writer. *American Lawyer,* senior writer.

WRITINGS:

Double Eagle: The Epic Story of the World's Most Valuable Coin, W.W. Norton (New York, NY), 2006.

SIDELIGHTS: As a senior writer for *American Lawyer,* Alison Frankel has written on topics ranging from controversial judicial rulings to the top-grossing U.S. law firms. Her research skills as a journalist served her well on another newsworthy story, this one the focus of her first book: *Double Eagle: The Epic Story of the World's Most Valuable Coin.* In the field of numanistics (the collection and preservation of coins), the Double Eagle was long considered the "Holy Grail" among collectors, since the 1933 gold coin was the last of its kind made in the United States and was never placed into official circulation. In *Double Eagle,* Frankel shares background information on its design and production and recounts with dramatic flair a story spanning seven decades as the only known surviving Double Eagle is chased across continents, ultimately surfacing at a 2002 Sotheby's auction.

A *Publishers Weekly* reviewer commented that "Frankel demonstrates her journalistic skill with sparkling accounts," further adding that the book is a "great read for the obsessed collector and general public alike." A contributor to *Kirkus Reviews* described *Double Eagle* as "a gripping read" and a "readable and authoritative history of a phenomenon for the numismatic ages."

BIOGRAPHICAL AND CRITICAL SOURCES:

PERIODICALS

Kirkus Reviews, April 1, 2006, review of *Double Eagle: The Epic Story of the World's Most Valuable Coin,* p. 333.

Publishers Weekly, February 13, 2006, review of *Double Eagle,* p. 71.

ONLINE

American Lawyer, http://www.americanlawyer.com/ (November 26, 2006).

*   *   *

FREEMAN, Brian 1963-

PERSONAL: Born 1963, in Chicago, IL; married; wife's name Marcia. *Education:* Carleton College, B.A., 1984.

ADDRESSES: Home—MN. *E-mail*—brian@bfreeman books.com.

CAREER: Writer, novelist, marketing director, and communications professional. Faegre & Benson (an international law firm), former director of marketing and public relations.

MEMBER: Phi Beta Kappa.

AWARDS, HONORS: Macavity Award for best first novel, Edgar Award finalist, Dagger Award finalist, Anthony Award finalist, and Barry Award finalist, all for *Immoral.*

WRITINGS:

Immoral, St. Martin's Minotaur (New York, NY), 2005.
Stripped, St. Martin's Minotaur (New York, NY), 2006.

Freeman's books have been translated into sixteen languages.

SIDELIGHTS: Mystery novelist Brian Freeman is a former marketing and communications professional. In his first novel, *Immoral,* Freeman "delivers a near pitch-perfect first novel that soars with believable characters, crisp dialogue and, for the most part, logical twists and turns," commented reviewer Oline H. Cogdill in the *South Florida Sun-Sentinel*. Protagonist Jonathan Stride is a police detective in Duluth, Minnesota. Stride's partner, Maggie Bei, is a colleague who has long been in love with Detective Stride from afar. Stride is called in to investigate the disappearance of teenage Rachel Deese, who vanished after returning home from school. He contrasts the current case with another disappearance from the same school fourteen months earlier, when sixteen-year-old Kerry McGrath also went missing. The local media suspect a serial killer at large in Duluth, but the thoughtful, meticulous Stride does not. He notes considerable differences in the personalities and characters of the two missing girls. Kerry was a pleasant, sweet, and largely innocent young woman. Rachel, in contrast, was sexually promiscuous, supremely manipulative, and a difficult personality. In many ways, she is not a likable character. Cogdill observed that it is "risky to provide a flawed victim, but the author manages to make her both imperfect and sympathetic." As Stride's investigation unfolds, he uncovers evidence that Rachel might have been the victim of unwanted sexual advances from her stepfather, Graeme Stoner, a wealthy local banker. Stoner is indicted for murder and the trial goes forward, even though Rachel's body has not been found. A devastating revelation stops the trial, and three years later, a mysterious tip reignites the case. With *Immoral*, Freeman "turns in a psychologically gripping, virtuoso performance," creating a detective with the potential to carry a series, stated Roland Person in the *Library Journal*.

In *Stripped*, Freeman's second novel to feature Jonathan Stride, a forty-year-old murder continues to have deadly repercussions. Stride, now based in Las Vegas, works with transsexual investigative partner Amanda Gillen and courts police officer Serena Dial. In the course of investigating a rash of recent murders, Stride discovers connections between the killings and the death, forty years earlier, of gorgeous dancer Amira Luz. Hugely popular and desired by everyone from businessmen to mobsters, Amira was the star of the hottest show in Vegas. Her charmed career came to an abrupt end when she was murdered in her hotel pool, ostensibly by a deranged fan. Now, however, Stride finds that a series of recent murder victims were in some way associated with Amira Luz. While pursuing the case, Stride riles several members of the local power elite, who have secrets they wish to keep buried

with the long-dead Amira. "Murder, money, suspense and sex are accounted for as Freeman consistently hits his thriller marks, keeping the action coming and the tension high," commented a contributor to *Kirkus Reviews*. *Stripped* "fully illustrates Freeman's strength as an author," showcasing his "well-shaped characters" and "strong storytelling skills," Cogdill remarked in another *South Florida Sun-Sentinel* review.

BIOGRAPHICAL AND CRITICAL SOURCES:

PERIODICALS

Booklist, August 1, 2006, Allison Block, review of *Stripped*, p. 49.
Kirkus Reviews, July 15, 2005, review of *Immoral*, p. 753; August 1, 2006, review of *Stripped*, p. 742.
Library Journal, August 1, 2005, Roland Person, review of *Immoral*, p. 67; March 15, 2006, Barbara Hoffert and Ann Burns, "All New, All Distinct," review of *Immoral*, p. 48.
M2 Best Books, April 13, 2006, "Nominees for Edgar Awards Announced."
PR Newswire, June 27, 2006, "Brian Freeman's *Immoral:* The Suspense Novel Sold around the World . . . Now in Paperback," review of *Immoral;* October 3, 2006, "Prepare to Get *Stripped:* Award-Winning Author Brian Freeman Releases His New Thriller Today."
Publishers Weekly, July 25, 2005, review of *Immoral*, p. 40; October 31, 2005, audiobook review of *Immoral*, p. 52; August 7, 2006, review of *Stripped*, p. 31.
South Florida Sun-Sentinel (Ft. Lauderdale, FL), August 31, 2005, Oline H. Cogdill, review of *Immoral;* September 27, 2006, Oline H. Cogdill, review of *Stripped*.
St. Paul Pioneer Press (St. Paul, MN), February 1, 2006, Mary Ann Grossman, "Debut Whodunit Gets Nod: *Immoral* Is Nominee for Coveted Edgar," review of *Immoral*.
Swiss News, May, 2006, review of *Immoral*, p. 60.

ONLINE

Brian Freeman Home Page, http://www.bfreeman books.com (December 20, 2006).
Brian Freeman Web log, http://holtzbrinckinternet. typepad.com/bfreeman (December 20, 2006).

FREUDENBERGER, Nell 1975-

PERSONAL: Born April 21, 1975, in New York, NY. *Education:* Harvard University, B.A., 1997; New York University, M.F.A., 2000.

ADDRESSES: Home—New York, NY.

CAREER: Writer. Worked as an editorial assistant at the *New Yorker.*

AWARDS, HONORS: PEN/Malamud Award for excellence in short fiction; Sue Kaufman prize for first fiction, 2004, for *Lucky Girls;* O. Henry Prize Stories, Best American Short Stories, 2004, for "The Tutor."

WRITINGS:

Lucky Girls: Stories, Ecco (New York, NY), 2003.
The Dissident (novel), Ecco (New York, NY), 2006.

Stories have appeared in periodicals, including the *New Yorker, Granta,* and the *Paris Review.*

SIDELIGHTS: Nell Freudenberger is a short-story writer and novelist whose first collection of short stories, *Lucky Girls: Stories,* features young women who come from privileged lives and who often are traveling abroad. "Freudenberger seems particularly interested in the way Westerners interact with Asian cultures, and travel through Asia is a common thread pulled through these five stories," wrote Elisa Ludwig in the *San Francisco Chronicle.* For example, in the story "Outside the Western Gate," Freudenberger tells the tale of an American writer who goes to an apartment long owned by her family in New Delhi. While there, she ponders her Indian mother, thinking about how her mother thirty years earlier once loaded up the family car with chocolates and art supplies and took her sister but not her on a trip through the Khyber pass. She also remembers her mother's love of America and tries to reconcile it with the fact that she eventually committed suicide in Hollywood.

In "The Tutor," which garnered Freudenberger an O. Henry Prize, the author writes of Zubin, an aspiring poet in Bombay who takes a job tutoring an American businessman's daughter, Julia, so she can get a high S.A.T. score for entrance to a good college in America. Zubin himself attended Harvard and finds himself emotionally stranded between America and India. "Their relationship is fraught with cross-cultural longing and the erotic unlawfulness of teacher-student fantasies," wrote Ludwig, adding that Freudenberger "juggles the power dynamics of social status and gender, both of which are, of course, further complicated by geography." Writing in *Booklist,* Ellen Loughran called *Lucky Girls* "an excellent addition to all short story collections."

Freudenberger's first novel, *The Dissident,* focuses on Yuan Zhao, a visitor from China, and the host family he ends up staying with in Beverly Hills. A performance artist, Zhao is also part of a subversive Chinese community of artists. When he arrives at the Traverses house, he finds himself enmeshed in an American family's life that reveals an uncaring husband, a wife whose only recourse to a sexless marriage is to cheat on her husband with his brother, and children (one with a potential eating disorder and the other suicidal) who are so focused on themselves that they care little for their parents or anyone else. Interspersed with his experience in America is Zhao's narration of his own story as a dissident in China.

"Freudenberger fulfills the promise of her 2003 collection of short stories, *Lucky Girls,* in her expansive first novel," wrote a *Publishers Weekly* contributor. Starr E. Smith, writing in the *Library Journal,* noted: "Energetic, witty writing sparkles throughout." In a review in *Booklist,* Michele Leber noted the author's "facile, insightful prose and strong characterizations." In his review in the *New York Times,* A.O. Scott commented: "Every character in the book . . . is endowed with a sharp individuality. This is no small feat, given how crowded the novel feels, the bustle of a single house in Beverly Hills no less—indeed, more—than the largest city in the most populous country in the world."

BIOGRAPHICAL AND CRITICAL SOURCES:

PERIODICALS

Booklist, September 1, 2003, Ellen Loughran, review of *Lucky Girls: Stories,* p. 54; August 1, 2006, Michele Leber, review of *The Dissident,* p. 41.

Carolina Quarterly, winter, 2004, Hilary Elkins, review of *Lucky Girls,* p. 55.

Entertainment Weekly, August 22, 2003, Karen Valby, "Do You Feel 'Lucky'? Well, Do You, Nell?," brief profile of author, p. 135; August 18, 2006, Karen Valby, review of *The Dissident,* p. 141.

Kirkus Reviews, July 1, 2003, review of *Lucky Girls,* p. 874; June 1, 2006, review of *The Dissident,* p. 535.

Library Journal, August. 2003, Rebecca Stuhr, review of *Lucky Girls,* p. 138; August 1, 2006, Starr E. Smith, review of *The Dissident,* p. 68.

New York Times, September 14, 2003, Jennifer Schuessler, review of *Lucky Girls;* September 10, 2006, A.O. Scott, review of *The Dissident.*

People, September 22, 2003, Jeremy Jackson, review of *Lucky Girls,* p. 57.

Publishers Weekly, June 30, 2003, review of *Lucky Girls,* p. 51; July 10, 2006, review of *The Dissident,* p. 49; July 10, 2006, Marshall Heyman, "PW talks with Nell Freudenberger," p. 51.

San Francisco Chronicle, August 31, 2003, Elisa Ludwig, review of *Lucky Girls,* p. M1.

Time International, November 24, 2003, Bryan Walsh, review of *Lucky Girls,* p. 116.

Village Voice, August 11, 2006, Hua Hsu, review of *The Dissident.*

ONLINE

Barnes and Noble Web site, http://www.barnesandnoble.com/ (January 18, 2007), "Meet the Writers: Nell Freudenberger," interview with author.*

*   *   *

FRIEND, David 1955-

PERSONAL: Born January 31, 1955, in Chicago, IL; married Nancy Paulsen; children: Sam and Molly (twins). *Education:* Amherst College, B.A., 1977.

ADDRESSES: E-mail—dfriend@davidfriend.net.

CAREER: Publishing executive, writer, editor, and poet. *Life* magazine, New York, NY, correspondent, 1978-86, senior editor, 1987-92, director of photography and new media, 1992-98, director of photography and assistant managing editor, 1998; *Vanity Fair,* New York, NY, editor of creative development, beginning 1998. Also member of numerous national and international photography award juries; cocurator of numerous photography exhibitions, including *Somalia's Cry;* video contributions include *LIFE at Woodstock;* producer of CD-ROM *The Face of Life, 1936-72;* helped place first independent photography exhibition on genocide in Bosnia at the U.S. Holocaust Memorial Museum in Washington, DC. Also created the Alfred Eisenstaedt Awards for Magazine Photography under the auspices of Columbia University's Graduate School of Journalism.

MEMBER: International Center of Photography (president's council), Overseas Press Club.

AWARDS, HONORS: Photojournalism editing award, National Press Photographers Association; Emmy and Peabody Awards, as an executive producer of the documentary *9/11,* Columbia Broadcasting System (CBS).

WRITINGS:

Baseball, Football, Daddy, and Me (juvenile), pictures by Rick Brown, Viking (New York, NY), 1990.

(With the editors of *Life*) *The Meaning of Life: Reflections in Words and Pictures on Why We Are Here,* Little, Brown (Boston, MA), 1991.

(Editor, with the editors of *Life*) *More Reflections on the Meaning of Life,* Little, Brown (Boston, MA), 1992.

(Editor, with Gigi Benson) Harry Benson, *First Families: An Intimate Portrait from the Kennedys to the Clintons,* forewords by Rosalynn Carter, Nancy Reagan, and Barbara Bush, Bulfinch Press (Boston, MA), 1997.

(Editor, with Graydon Carter) *Vanity Fair's Hollywood,* text by Christopher Hitchens, Viking Studio (New York, NY), 2000.

(With Graydon Carter) *Oscar Night from the Editors of Vanity Fair: 75 Years of Hollywood Parties,* afterword by Dominick Dunne, Knopf (New York, NY), 2004.

Watching the World Change: The Stories behind the Images of 9/11, Farrar, Straus & Giroux (New York, NY), 2006.

Contributor of articles, essays, and cartoons to periodicals, including the *London Sunday Times, Playboy, National Lampoon, Contemporary Literary Criticism, Life, Washington Post, Discover, Common Review,* and the *New York Times.* Served as editorial director of *Life* magazine Web site. Also contributor of poetry to periodicals, including the *New Yorker.*

SIDELIGHTS: David Friend is a writer and publishing executive whose wide-ranging works include everything from a children's book to a book featuring photographs of the 9/11 terrorist attacks in New York City. In his children's book, *Baseball, Football, Daddy, and Me,* with pictures by Rick Brown, Friend tells the story of a father and his young son who go to various sporting events, forming a strong bond and many memories. Jeff Unger, writing in *Entertainment Weekly,* noted that "there will be few fathers who finish this book without planning a trip to a game." A *People* contributor referred to the book as a "sweet little story."

Friend collaborates with the editors of *Life* for *The Meaning of Life: Reflections in Words and Pictures on Why We Are Here.* The book features the replies of various people—from the famous to unknowns such as taxi drivers—to the question of what they think the meaning of life may be, as posed by the editors of *Life* magazine. The book features 173 responses and 132 photographs by various photographers. In a review in *People,* Ralph Novak noted that many of the answers are "provocative, funny and/or enlightening." Novak added: "Most of these answers probably tell us more about the people giving them than the nature of the universe, but that's OK."

Friend and Graydon Carter take a look at the biggest night in Hollywood in their book *Oscar Night from the Editors of Vanity Fair: 75 Years of Hollywood Parties.* The book chronicles through text and photographs the famous awards night beginning with the 1929 affair. The photographs feature movie stars of the past such as Janet Gaynor and Tyrone Power, as well as modern fan favorites such as Brad Pitt. "The people love celebrity, and VF serves it to them with style and brains," wrote Heather McCormack in the *Library Journal.*

Friend takes on a more serious subject matter in his book *Watching the World Change: The Stories behind the Images of 9/11.* The book features both the photographs and recollections of a wide range of photographers, from professionals to amateurs, who witnessed the terrorist attacks of 9/11 and who took photographs of the event in progress, as well as its aftermath. As they discuss this day, many ponder issues such as the ethics of photographing the terrible event that killed so many people. The author also writes about the overall effect of photography on the modern society's perception of the world. "A brief review can't do justice to *Watching the World Change,* a lucid, thoughtful and wide-ranging book," wrote Garrison Keillor in the *New York Times.* "In truth, Friend's excellent writing conveys more of the truth of the day than photographs can." In a review in *Booklist,* Vanessa Bush noted that "this compelling book demonstrates the power and pathos of an unforgettable event." A *Kirkus Reviews* contributor referred to *Watching the World Change* as "an informed and intimate account—accompanied by some disturbing photos—of one of the worst days in American history."

BIOGRAPHICAL AND CRITICAL SOURCES:

PERIODICALS

Booklist, September 15, 2006, Vanessa Bush, review of *Watching the World Change: The Stories behind the Images of 9/11,* p. 18.

Entertainment Weekly, May 15, 1992, Jeff Unger, review of *Baseball, Football, Daddy, and Me,* p. 74.

Kirkus Reviews, July 1, 2006, review of *Watching the World Change,* p. 661.

Library Journal, October 15, 2004, Heather McCormack, review of *Oscar Night from the Editors of Vanity Fair: 75 Years of Hollywood Parties,* p. 64; October 1, 2006, Melissa M. Johnson, review of *Watching the World Change,* p. 92.

New York Times, September 3, 2006, Garrison Keillor, "Bearing Witness," review of *Watching the World Change.*

People, May 14, 1990, review of *Baseball, Football, Daddy, and Me,* p. 36; April 15, 1991, Ralph Novak, review of *The Meaning of Life: Reflections in Words and Pictures on Why We Are Here,* p. 22.

Publishers Weekly, February 9, 1990, Diane Roback, review of *Baseball, Football, Daddy, and Me,* p. 59; June 26, 2006, review of *Watching the World Change,* p. 44.

FRISCH, Morton J. 1923-2006

OBITUARY NOTICE— See index for *CA* sketch: Born January 26, 1923, in Chicago, IL; died of pulmonary fibrosis, December 24, 2006, in DeKalb, IL. Philosopher, educator, and author. A retired professor at Northern Illinois University, DeKalb was widely noted as a scholar of the history of political philosophy. After completing high school, he enlisted in the U.S. Army and was stationed in England, where he assisted in antiaircraft defense during World War II. He then saw action in Belgium and the Battle of the Bulge, for which service he was awarded that country's Croix de Guerre. Returning home, he attended Roosevelt University on the G.I. Bill. He completed his B.A. in 1949, then attended the University of Chicago, where he was influenced by Leo Strauss, a political philosopher who was on the faculty there. Earning an M.A., he then went to Pennsylvania State University for his Ph.D., graduating in 1953. His first faculty position was at the College of William and Mary, where he was an assistant professor until 1961, and an associate professor of

government for the next three years. Frisch joined the Northern Illinois University faculty in 1964, where he established a graduate program in political theory and became respected for his work in the history of political philosophy. Becoming a full professor of political science in 1966, Frisch continued to build his department, helping to draw in noted scholars in the field to its faculty. He retired in 1992, but continued to teach graduate seminars for several more years. Frisch wrote and edited nine books, including *Franklin D. Roosevelt: The Contribution of the New Deal to American Political Thought and Practice* (1975) and *Alexander Hamilton and the Political Order: An Interpretation of His Political Thought and Practice* (1990). His last book was scheduled to be published posthumously.

OBITUARIES AND OTHER SOURCES:

PERIODICALS

Chicago Tribune, January 13, 2007, Section 3, p. 7.

G

GALLAGHER, Susan E.

PERSONAL: Education: Ramapo College of New Jersey, B.A., 1983; New School for Social Research, M.A., 1989, Ph.D., 1996.

ADDRESSES: Office—Department of Political Science, University of Massachusetts, Lowell, 850 Broadway St., Ste. 4, Lowell, MA 01854. *E-mail*—susan_gallagher@uml.edu.

CAREER: University of Massachusetts, Lowell, assistant professor, 1996-2002, associate professor of political science, 2002—. Also adjunct instructor at various universities, including New York University, Rutgers University, and Ramapo College of New Jersey

WRITINGS:

Daniel Defoe's "Moll Flanders," illustrated by Kenneth Lopez, Research & Education Association (Piscataway, NJ), 1996.
The Rule of the Rich? Adam Smith's Argument against Political Power, Pennsylvania State University Press (University Park, PA), 1998.

SIDELIGHTS: Susan E. Gallagher is an associate professor of political science at the University of Massachusetts, Lowell. Her academic background focuses primarily on political and feminist theories. Her 1998 publication, *The Rule of the Rich? Adam Smith's Argument against Political Power,* stems from extensive research into British political theory and economist Adam Smith.

In the book, Gallagher addresses the views of Adam Smith in the context of his time and place and also offers a survey of his predecessors, including Mandeville, Bolingbroke, and Hume. In providing this alternative view of Smith, Gallagher contends that he was not an advocate of limited government for the sake of individual freedom, but rather, as a means to curb the influence of the commercial aristocracy. Mark E. Yellin, writing in the *American Political Science Review,* called the book "a provocative, interesting, and clearly written work that . . . challenges recent revisionist accounts of Adam Smith's political and economic thought." In an *Ethics* review, Patricia H. Werhane found that the book was an "important contribution." In a *Perspectives on Political Science* review, Richard F. Flannery called *The Rule of the Rich* "an arresting monograph, but to appreciate it readers will need to know something about social thought or eighteenth-century history." Yellin concluded, however, that "because of its readability and concise length, it is accessible to those with little background who would like to know more about Mandeville, Bolingbroke, [Hume], and Smith."

BIOGRAPHICAL AND CRITICAL SOURCES:

PERIODICALS

American Political Science Review, March, 2000, Mark E. Yellin, review of *The Rule of the Rich? Adam Smith's Argument against Political Power,* p. 172.

English Historical Review, June, 2000, J.C.D. Clark, review of *The Rule of the Rich?,* p. 743.

Ethics, October, 2002, Patricia H. Werhane, review of *The Rule of the Rich?,* p. 193.

Library Journal, October 15, 1998, Brent A. Nelson, review of *The Rule of the Rich?,* p. 84.

Perspectives on Political Science, fall, 1999, Richard F. Flannery, review of *The Rule of the Rich?,* p. 239.

Review of Politics, spring, 2000, James E. Alvey, review of *The Rule of the Rich?,* p. 398.

ONLINE

University of Massachusetts Lowell Web site, http://www.uml.edu/ (January 18, 2007), author profile.*

*   *   *

GAMBACCINI, Piero 1923-

PERSONAL: Born October 26, 1923, in Rome, Italy; son of Riccardo (a physician) and Ernesta (a homemaker) Gambaccini; married Bettie Gage Lippitt (a homemaker and translator), July 16, 1956; children: Riccardo, Alessandra (Sciascia) Gambaccini. *Ethnicity:* "Italian." *Education:* Attended University of Pisa between 1940 and 1946; earned medical degree in Florence, 1946, specialization in radiology, 1949, and university teaching qualification in Rome, 1957. *Religion:* Roman Catholic.

ADDRESSES: Home—Italy. *E-mail*—pierog@infol.it.

CAREER: University of Florence, Florence, Italy, professor of radiology, 1952-55; University of Rome, Rome, Italy, professor of radiology, 1955-59; San Giovanni di Dio (hospital), Florence, chief radiologist, 1959-81; Torrepalli Hospital, Florence, chief radiologist and medical director, 1981-84; retired, 1985. Founder of the first school in Italy for radiological technicians; founder of first treatment center for drug addicts in Florence, 1973; Lenitherapy Foundation of the Terminally Ill, founding member; Cassa di Rismarmio Bank, member of board of charitable distributions. Worked as volunteer missionary in Thailand.

WRITINGS:

I Mercanti della Salute, 2002, published as *Mountebanks and Medicasters: A History of Italian Charlatans from the Middle Ages to the Present,* McFarland (Jefferson, NC), 2004.

Contributor to medical journals. Co-author of two volumes of *Tattato di Radiologia Medica.* Also a lecturer at many national and international radiological conferences.

SIDELIGHTS: Piero Gambaccini told *CA:* "Following in my father's footsteps, I became a medical doctor and then a professor of radiology. I practiced and taught radiology, both diagnostic and therapeutic, at the universities of Florence and Rome until, in 1958, I received an appointment as chief radiologist at the Florentine hospital San Giovanni di Dio, founded in the fifteenth century by Amerigo Vespucci's uncle, Simone. I remained in this position until the hospital was moved to a new building, where I remained as chief radiologist and medical director until 1985, when I retired.

"During my professional years, my interest in traditional and alternative medicine took me to India, Afghanistan, and Niger. After retiring, I worked as a volunteer with the Catholic missionary order of Saint Camillus in Thailand, procuring and installing medical equipment for hospitals, leper colonies, and the Cambodian refugee camps. My work there was officially recognized by the Thai royal family and the government of Thailand. In 1986, still during the Cold War, I collaborated with the then Apostolic Nuncius, Archbishop Renato Martino (who was made a cardinal in 2003), providing radiological equipment to the Mahosot Hospital in Vientiane, Laos.

"Although I have published many medical papers and a treatise on radiology, I have always been fascinated by the psychological aspects of medicine and the relationship between doctor and patient. I especially admire the way American and English authors are able to explain complicated scientific or historical issues so that they can be read and understood by lay readers. I hope I have been able to accomplish this in my book *Mountebanks and Medicasters: A History of Italian Charlatans from the Middle Ages to the Present.* Seemingly a history of Italian medical quacks, the book explores the placebo effect, the relationship between doctor and patient, and offers a critique of modern medical practice."

BIOGRAPHICAL AND CRITICAL SOURCES:

PERIODICALS

Choice, May, 2004, M. Kroger, review of *Mountebanks and Medicasters: A History of Italian Charlatans from the Middle Ages to the Present,* p. 1697.
SciTech Book News, March, 2004, review of *Mountebanks and Medicasters,* p. 79.

*   *   *

GANSWORTH, Eric L.

PERSONAL: Born at Tuscarora Indian Nation, New York State.

ADDRESSES: Office—Department of English, Canisius College, 2001 Main St., Buffalo, NY 14222. *E-mail*—eric.gansworth@canisius.edu.

CAREER: Canisius College, Buffalo, NY, associate professor of English and Lowery writer in residence; Associated Colleges of the Twin Cities, visiting writer in residence, 2004. Began career as a visual artist, including work with Herd about Buffalo Project; Hallwalls Contemporary Art Center, member of board of directors; New York Foundation for the Arts, past member of artists advisory committee. Enrolled member of Onondaga Nation. *Exhibitions:* Work exhibited in the solo show "Nickel Eclipse: Iroquois Moon," Olean Public Library, 1999, then Castellani Museum, 2000; also represented in group shows throughout the state of New York.

MEMBER: Wordcraft Circle of Native Writers and Storytellers, Native Writers Circle of the Americas.

WRITINGS:

Indian Summers (novel), Michigan State University Press (East Lansing, MI), 1998.

Nickel Eclipse: Iroquois Moon (poetry and paintings), Michigan State University Press (East Lansing, MI), 2000.
Smoke Dancing (novel), Michigan State University Press (East Lansing, MI), 2004.
Mending Skins (novel), University of Nebraska Press (Lincoln, NE), 2005.
Breathing the Monster Alive, Bright Hills Press (Treadwell, NY), 2006.

Work represented in anthologies, including *Growing Up Native,* Morrow (New York, NY); *Red Earth,* Doubleday (New York, NY); *Iroquois Voices,* Bright Hill Press (Treadwell, NY); *Nothing but the Truth: An Anthology of Native American Literature,* Prentice-Hall; and *Stories for Winter Nights,* White Pine; work also included on the audio tape *Roadkillbasa.* Contributor of poetry, nonfiction, and fiction to periodicals, including *Shenandoah, Cream City Review, Slipstream, American Indian Culture and Research Journal,* and *Blueline.*

BIOGRAPHICAL AND CRITICAL SOURCES:

PERIODICALS

Publishers Weekly, February 21, 2005, review of *Mending Skins,* p. 158.*

*   *   *

GARDNER, James N.

PERSONAL: Married Lynda Nelson (in business). *Education:* Yale University, B.A.; Yale Law School, J.D.

CAREER: Writer, complexity theorist, attorney, senator, and science writer. United States Supreme Court, Washington, DC, law clerk for Associate Justice Potter Stewart, 1975; Oregon State Senate, Portland, state senator, 1978-84; cofounder, with Lynda Nelson Gardner, of law and government affairs firm, 1992.

WRITINGS:

Effective Lobbying in the European Community, Kluwer Law and Taxation Publishers (Boston, MA), 1991.

Biocosm: The New Scientific Theory of Evolution: Intelligent Life Is the Architect of the Universe, Inner Ocean Publishing (Makawao, HI), 2003.

Intelligent Universe: AI, ET, and the Emerging Mind of the Cosmos, New Page Books (Franklin Lakes, NJ), 2007.

Contributor of technical articles and scientific papers to periodicals, including *Complexity, Acta Astronautica,* and *Journal of the British Interplanetary Society.* Contributor of popular science articles to *Wired, Nature Biotechnology, Wall Street Journal,* and *World Link.* Former feature editor, *Yale Scientific Magazine;* former drama critic, *Yale Daily News;* former article editor, *Yale Law Journal.*

SIDELIGHTS: Trained in philosophy and theoretical biology, James N. Gardner is an attorney, science writer, and complexity theorist who has written widely on issues related to cosmology, law, philosophy, evolution, and other topics. In *Biocosm: The New Scientific Theory of Evolution: Intelligent Life Is the Architect of the Universe,* Gardner proposes a new mechanism for the complexity of the cosmos that he calls the "Selfish Biocosm"—the "struggle of the creative force of life against the disintegrative acid of entropy, of emergent order against encroaching chaos, and ultimate power of mind against the brute intransigence of lifeless matter," as he puts it on his home page.

Though life as it is known occupies only an infinitesimally small fraction of the universe, Gardner notes that if some major characteristics of the greater physical world were only slightly different, life would have had no chance to develop or continue. A universe expanding at a greater rate, for example, would not be favorable to life. Minor differences in the gravitational constant, the charge of an electron, or the speed of light would create a universe inimical to life. Gardner's theory posits that it is not random chance that the physical laws of the universe favor the emergence of carbon-based life. Instead, he believes that a superintelligent race living in a "mother universe" created and designed the universe humans live in, carefully adjusting all the fundamental physical laws to make them favorable to life. Once established, the force of life itself becomes dedicated to its propagation. Much as humans have a biological imperative to pass on their DNA to new generations, life itself seeks to propagate, expand, and perpetuate itself in all areas of the universe. Evolution, to Gardner, is not a random Darwinian event in which prominent characteristics are favored; instead, evolution has a purpose, and that purpose is to continue the expansion and development of life in the universe. Eventually, this universe will grow to develop its own form of superintelligence, giving it the ability to create "baby universes" of its own, and continuing the ongoing cosmic cycle.

Gardner does not suggest the influence of a deity as understood in religious terms, though his theory does have some characteristics in common with notions of intelligent design. Instead, the "selfish biocosm" deliberately expands and propagates intelligent life within itself, and will continue to do so on a grand, almost unimaginable scale. For those who do not "favor an explanation for the creation of life that involves a deity of some sort, then Gardner's theory seems a plausible alternative" to theories of both divine creation and intelligent design, noted a *Publishers Weekly* reviewer. In a *Harper's* review of *Biocosm,* John Leonard wrote: "This is the best popular account I've seen of the argument for 'intelligent design'. . . . [Gardner] speculates himself into a radiant evolutionary future." In stating his argument, noted a reviewer on the *Deep Change* Web site, Gardner offers an "eloquent and lucid synthesis of the most recent advances in physics, cosmology, biology, biochemistry, astronomy, and complexity theory."

BIOGRAPHICAL AND CRITICAL SOURCES:

PERIODICALS

Harper's, October, 2003, John Leonard, review of *Biocosm: The New Scientific Theory of Evolution: Intelligent Life Is the Architect of the Universe,* pp. 75-76.

Publishers Weekly, July 21, 2003, review of *Biocosm,* p. 184.

ONLINE

Biocosm Online, http://www.biocosm.org (December 20, 2006).

Deep Change Web site, http://www.deep-change.com/ (December 20, 2006), biography of James N. Gardner and review of *Biocosm.*

International Society for Complexity, Information, and Design, http://www.iscid.org/ (December 20, 2006), biography of James N. Gardner.

KurzweilAI.net, http://www.kurzweilai.net/ (December 20, 2006), biography of James N. Gardner.

Scientist Errant Web site, http://errant.scienceboard. net/ (April 15, 2006), Michael J. Corey, review of *Biocosm;* (April 29, 2006), Michael J. Corey, review of *Biocosm;* (May 30, 2006), Michael J. Corey, review of *Biocosm.*

Seti League Web site, http://www.setileague.org/ (December 20, 2006), David Ocame, review of *Biocosm.**

*   *   *

GAVALDA, Anna 1970-

PERSONAL: Born December 9, 1970 in Boulogne-Billancourt, Hauts-de-Seine, France; divorced; children: two.

CAREER: Writer and journalist.

AWARDS, HONORS: Grand Prix RTL-Lirem, 2000, for *I Wish Someone Were Waiting for Me Somewhere.*

WRITINGS:

Je voudrais que quelqu'un m'attende quelque part (short stories), [France] 1999, translation by Karen L. Marker published as *I Wish Someone Were Waiting for Me Somewhere,* Riverhead Books (New York, NY), 2003.

Il était une fois—l'automobile, Roger-Viollet (Paris, France), 2000.

Je l'aimais (novel), Dilettante (Paris France), 2002, translation by Catherine Evans published as *Someone I Loved,* Riverhead Books (New York, NY), 2005.

95 Pounds of Hope (juvenile novel), translated by Gill Rosner, Viking (New York, NY), 2003.

Ensemble, c'est tout (novel), Dilettante (Paris, France), 2004, translated by Alison Anderson as *Hunting and Gathering,* Chatto & Windus (London, England), 2006, Riverhead Books (New York, NY), 2007.

Contributor to periodicals, including *Elle* magazine. Books have also been translated into several languages, including Spanish.

ADAPTATIONS: Ensemble, c'est tout, was adapted for film, c. 2007.

SIDELIGHTS: Anna Gavalda is a French short-story writer and novelist. Her collection of short stories, *I Wish Someone Were Waiting for Me Somewhere,* was first published to wide critical acclaim in France in 1999 as *Je voudrais que quelqu'un m'attende quelque part.* The stories are told by first-person narrators who are often seeking love and even more often finding heartbreak instead. In other stories, disastrous events follow everyday circumstances. For example, in one story, two teenage friends borrow a Jaguar from one of their fathers, crash into a wild boar, load it into the car, and then have the boar totally destroy the car after the boar comes back to its senses. Vin Patel, writing on the *Bookreporter.com,* noted that "at times, these stories may lead you to think more deeply about your own past, your secrets and fears." A *Publishers Weekly* contributor wrote that "this uneven but entertaining collection displays a deliciously Gallic insouciance." Patricia M. Gathercole, writing in *World Literature Today,* referred to *I Wish Someone Were Waiting for Me Somewhere* as "entertaining and thought-provoking."

In Gavalda's novel *95 Pounds of Hope,* the thirteen-year-old narrator, Gregory Dubosc, has attention deficit disorder, hates school, and suffers the scorn and teasing of his classmates. In the meantime, Gregory ponders the things he does like in life, including his grandfather and his love of woodworking. As Gregory tells his story, his grandfather is comatose but still coaches Gregory through life until one day Gregory is able to return the kindness by willing his grandfather back to health. Ed Sullivan, writing in *Booklist,* called Gregory "an interesting character with an engaging voice." A *Kirkus Reviews* contributor called *95 Pounds of Hope* "a hopeful, genuine story that will be an asset to any collection."

In her debut adult novel, *Someone I Loved,* Gavalda tells the story of Chloe, who serves as the tale's narrator. Through Chloe's words, the reader learns of her husband's infidelity and eventual abandonment, the attachment she forms with her father-in-law, and the subsequent revelation during a long conversation with her father-in-law that he was also unfaithful to his wife. Whitney Scott, writing in *Booklist,* noted the author's technique of "using the conversation to explore the motivations and nuances involved in marriage." A *Publishers Weekly* reviewer commented: "At the book's best moments, mundane details mingle with Chloe's despair to create an even deeper sadness." Referring to the novel as "compelling," a *Kirkus Reviews* contributor added: "Intense and immediate as a late-night conversation between lovers, this should draw readers to the best-selling Gavalda." In a review of the French version of the novel, titled *Je l'aimais,* *World Literature Today* reviewer Lucille F. Becker wrote: "Gavalda's talent for writing and her gift for dialogue make reading her work a delight."

Gavalda is also the author of *Hunting and Gathering,* published in France as *Ensemble, c'est tout.* The novel tells the story of a group of oddballs and nonconformists who come together in Paris. A contributor to the *French Book News* Web site referred to the novel as "original, full of wry humour and razor-sharp observation."

BIOGRAPHICAL AND CRITICAL SOURCES:

PERIODICALS

Booklist, September 15, 2003, Ed Sullivan, review of *95 Pounds of Hope,* p. 1174; March 1, 2005, Whitney Scott, review of *Someone I Loved,* p. 1142.

Kirkus Reviews, September 15, 2003, review of *95 Pounds of Hope,* p. 1174; February 1, 2005, review of *Someone I Loved,* p. 136.

Library Journal, April 1, 2005, Prudence Peiffer, review of *Someone I Loved,* p. 85.

Publishers Weekly, August 25, 2003, review of *95 Pounds of Hope,* p. 65; January 26, 2004, review of *I Wish Someone Were Waiting for Me Somewhere,* p. 232; March 14, 2005, review of *Someone I Loved,* p. 45.

School Library Journal, November, 2003, Barbara Auerbach, review of *95 Pounds of Hope,* p. 139.

World Literature Today, July-September, 2003, Lucille F. Becker, review of *Je l'aimais,* p. 115; September-December, 2004, Patricia M. Gathercole, review of *I Wish Someone Were Waiting for Me Somewhere,* p. 115.

ONLINE

Bookreporter.com, http://www.bookreporter.com/ (January 19, 2007), Vin Patel, review of *I Wish Someone Were Waiting for Me Somewhere.*

French Book News, http://www.FrenchBookNews. com/ (January 19, 2007), review of *Hunting and Gathering.*

International Movie Database, http://www.imdb.com/ (January 17, 2007), information on author's film work.*

*   *   *

GELLER, Jonny 1968(?)-

PERSONAL: Born c. 1968; married; children: two sons.

ADDRESSES: Home—London, England. *Office*—Curtis Brown Group, Ltd., Haymarket House, 28-29 Haymarket, London SW1Y 4SP, England.

CAREER: Curtis Brown Group, Ltd., London, England, literary agent, 1993—.

WRITINGS:

Yes, but Is It Good for the Jews?, Bloomsbury (London, England), 2006.

SIDELIGHTS: Jonny Geller trained as an actor but moved into the publishing industry in 1993. Since then, he has become one of the senior members of Curtis Brown Group, Ltd., England's largest independent literary agency. Among the top authors he represents are Hari Kunzru, Sean Hughes, Phil Whitaker, Tracy Chevalier, and James Flint. Geller has a reputation for scoring his authors six-figure advances. Geller's critics say that the high advance only raises the expectations for the works of first-time novelists. In a *Financial Times* article, Geller responded to this criticism by noting: "All my big six-figure sums have worked—all of them have sold over 100,000 copies, strengthening my argument that the higher advance, the better."

In 2006 Geller published his first book, *Yes, but Is It Good for the Jews?* outlining his comic perception of various items, events, and people in contemporary society. He uses a mathematical equation to rate each topic on a scale of one to seven. Some score favorably: Monica Lewinsky and *The Godfather* films. Others do not: Easter and the Toyota Prius. A *Publishers Weekly* reviewer noted that, "in some cases, the effort to find a Jewish connection feels strained, and most of the discussions are lightweight." Zoe Strimpel disliked the Jewish-centric approach that the book takes. In a *Financial Times* review, Strimpel commented: "One might equally ask how good books like this are for the Jews."

BIOGRAPHICAL AND CRITICAL SOURCES:

PERIODICALS

Booklist, September 15, 2006, Ilene Cooper, review of *Yes, but Is It Good for the Jews?*, p. 16.
Financial Times, March 18, 2002, Sathnam Sanghera, "Making Advances"; December 16, 2006, Zoe Strimpel, review of *Yes, but Is It Good for the Jews?*, p. 41.
Jewish News Weekly, November 10, 2006, Dan Pine, review of *Yes, but Is It Good for the Jews?*
Publishers Weekly, July 10, 2006, review of *Yes, but Is It Good for the Jews?*, p. 61.

ONLINE

Curtis Brown Group, Ltd. Web site, http://www.curtisbrown.co.uk/ (January 19, 2007), author profile.
IdeasFactory.com Web site, http://www.ideasfactory.com/ (January 19, 2007), Michele Kirsch, "Agent Provocateur."
IsItGoodForTheJews.com Web site, http://www.isitgoodforthejews.com (January 19, 2007), author profile.*

* * *

GILFOYLE, Timothy J. 1956-
(Timothy Joseph Gilfoyle)

PERSONAL: Born March 24, 1956, in Harrisburg, PA; son of Joseph Daniel Gilfoyle and Mary Dorothy Norton; married Mary Rose Alexander, August 19, 1990; children: Maria Adele, Danielle Louise. *Education:* Columbia University, B.A., 1979, M.A., 1980, Ph.D., 1987. *Hobbies and other interests:* Basketball.

ADDRESSES: *Office*—Department of History, Loyola University, 6525 N. Sheridan Rd., Chicago, IL, 60626-5385. *E-mail*—tgilfoy@luc.edu.

CAREER: Historian, educator, and writer. Sarah Lawrence College, Bronxville, New York, NY, visiting professor, 1987-88; Barnard College, New York, NY, visiting professor, 1988-89; Loyola University, Chicago, IL, assistant professor, 1989-95, associate professor, 1995-2003, professor of American history, 2003—. Member of the board of directors for the Chicago Metro History Education Center and the Museum of Sex, New York, NY; trustee of the Chicago History Museum.

MEMBER: American Historical Association, American Studies Association, Organization of American History, Urban History Association.

AWARDS, HONORS: Allan Nevins Prize, Society of American Historians, and Dixon Ryan Fox Prize, New York State Historical Association, both for *City of Eros;* National Endowment for the Humanities/Lloyd Lewis Fellow at the Newberry Library in Chicago, 1993-94; Senior fellow at the Museum of American History, Smithsonian Institution, 1997; John Simon Guggenheim Memorial Foundation fellow, 1988-99; Minow Family Foundation fellow, 2001-02; Best Article, Society for the History of Children and Youth, 2005, for "Street-Rats and Gutter-Snipes: Child Pickpockets and Street Culture in New York City, 1850-1900"; Dixon Ryan Fox Prize, New York State Historical Association; best book of the year citation, *Chicago Tribune* and *London Times,* 2006, for *A Pickpocket's Tale: The Underworld of Nineteenth-Century New York*; best book of the year citation, *Chicago Tribune,* 2006, for *Millennium Park: Creating a Chicago Landmark;* New York State Archives Award, 2006.

WRITINGS:

City of Eros: New York City, Prostitution, and the Commercialization of Sex, 1790-1920, W.W. Norton (New York, NY), 1992.

Millennium Park: Creating a Chicago Landmark, University of Chicago Press (Chicago, IL), 2006.

A Pickpocket's Tale: The Underworld of Nineteenth-Century New York, W.W. Norton (New York, NY), 2006.

Contributor to periodicals, including the *American Quarterly, Prospects, New York History, Missouri Review,* and the *Atlantic Monthly.* Author of regular "Making History" feature in *Chicago History.* Associate editor of the *Journal of Urban History,* and coeditor of the"Historical Studies in Urban America" series, University of Chicago Press. Has served on numerous editorial boards, including the boards for *New York History, The Encyclopedia of New York City, The Encyclopedia of Chicago History,* and the *New-York Journal of American History.*

SIDELIGHTS: Timothy J. Gilfoyle is a history professor who specializes in American urban and social history. In his first book, *City of Eros: New York City, Prostitution, and the Commercialization of Sex, 1790-1920,* Gilfoyle focuses on a social history of prostitution in New York City. The author recounts how a growing population combined with various social factors—such as a high rate of transience, low wages for women, and a male subculture that threw aside age-old beliefs about proper sexual behavior—led to a growing trade in prostitution. Referring to the book as "scholarly yet ribald," a *Publishers Weekly* contributor wrote: "The details—erotic or shocking, depending on one's point of view—are here." David Nasaw, writing in the *New York Times Book Review,* called *City of Eros* "a fascinating study." Nasaw wrote: "Mr. Gilfoyle . . . does not simply catalogue the omnipresence of the prostitutes. He situates their trade in the economic life of the city." The reviewer continued: "*City of Eros* is social history at its best, beautifully written, with a mosaic of rich detail that informs but does not overwhelm the narrative line."

In his monograph *Millennium Park: Creating a Chicago Landmark,* the author provides a history of how the city of Chicago between the years of 1998 and 2004 took twenty-four acres of neglected land and turned it into a widely admired urban park. In the process, Gilfoyle details the history of the site as a railroad depot that the owners refused to sell for decades, long after the depot was gone, and while the tracks crisscrossing it remained. The author also delves into the creation of the park's landmarks, which include sculptures, a theater for music and dance, and a music pavilion. "Gilfoyle has written a thorough account of the creation of these works," commented Michael J. Lewis in the *New York Times Book Review.*

Gilfoyle returns to the environs of New York City with *A Pickpocket's Tale: The Underworld of Nineteenth-Century New York.* Focusing on the late nineteenth-century pickpocket and con man George Appo, the author explores the criminal underworld of post-Civil War New York. The author follows Appo on his criminal meanderings through the city, his spending habits (which included visiting opium dens), and his eventually notoriety when he testifies in court about police corruption. Appo even appears as himself on Broadway. In a review in *Booklist,* Gilbert Taylor commented that "Appo and his story acquire meaningful context in Gilfoyle's professional historical reconstruction." A *Publishers Weekly* contributor called *A Pickpocket's Tale* "a colorful, evocative social history." Referring to the author's research as "prodigious," a *Kirkus Reviews* contributor called the book "eye-opening and grand, good fun to read." Glenn C. Altschuler, writing in the *Philadelphia Inquirer,* noted that the author "provides . . . a fascinating examination of late-19th-century America's urban underworld, with its opium dens, houses of prostitution, neighborhood gangs, 'fences' of stolen goods, cops, courts, and correctional institutions."

BIOGRAPHICAL AND CRITICAL SOURCES:

PERIODICALS

Booklist, August 1, 2006, Gilbert Taylor, review of *A Pickpocket's Tale: The Underworld of Nineteenth-Century New York,* p. 15.

Entertainment Weekly, August 11, 2006, Whitney Pastorek, review of *A Pickpocket's Tale,* p. 73.

Financial Times, September 23, 2006, Ludovic Hunter-Tilney, review of *A Pickpocket's Tale,* p. 49.

Kirkus Reviews, May 15, 2006, review of *A Pickpocket's Tale,* p. 505.

New York Times Book Review, August 30, 1992, David Nasaw, review of *City of Eros: New York City, Prostitution, and the Commercialization of Sex, 1790-1920,* p. 9; August 6, 2006, Michael J.

Lewis, review of *Millenium Park: Creating a Chicago Landmark,* p. 1; August 9, 2006, William Grimes, review of *A Pickpocket's Tale.*

Philadelphia Inquirer, September 27, 2006, Glenn C. Altschuler, review of *A Pickpocket's Tale.*

Publishers Weekly, July 27, 1992, review of *City of Eros,* p. 55; May 1, 2006, review of *A Pickpocket's Tale,* p. 46.

ONLINE

University of Loyola Chicago Web site, http://www.luc.edu/ (January 20, 2007), faculty profile of author.

*   *   *

GILFOYLE, Timothy Joseph
    See GILFOYLE, Timothy J.

*   *   *

GISBERT, Francesc Capdevila
    See MAX

*   *   *

GLICK, Daniel 1956-

PERSONAL: Born 1956, in CA; divorced; children: Kolya (son), Zoe. *Education:* University of California at Berkeley, M.J.

ADDRESSES: Home—CO.

CAREER: Newsweek magazine, investigative reporter, c. 1988-2001, including national correspondent in Washington, DC, and special correspondent covering Rocky Mountain region, c. 1994-2001; freelance writer, 2001—. Has also worked as an English teacher and yak herder in Tibet. Associate producer of documentary on JonBenet Ramsey, *JonBenet's America.*

AWARDS, HONORS: Ted Scripps fellowship, 1999-2000; Knight International Journalism Fellowship; Colorado Book Award, for *Monkey Dancing.*

WRITINGS:

Powder Burn: Arson, Money, and Mystery on Vail Mountain, PublicAffairs Books (New York, NY), 2001, revised edition, 2003.
Monkey Dancing: A Father, Two Kids, and a Journey to the Ends of the Earth, PublicAffairs Books (New York, NY), 2003.

Contributor to periodicals, including *New York Times Magazine, Washington Post Sunday Magazine, Outside, Esquire, Men's Journal, Sports Afield, National Wildlife, National Geographic, Rolling Stone, Smithsonian, Harper's,* and *Wilderness.* Author's works have been translated into Italian, Korean, and Japanese.

SIDELIGHTS: Daniel Glick spent more than a decade as a staff reporter for *Newsweek* magazine, undertaking assignments as varied as reporting on the demise of the Siberian tiger in the Russian Far East and the murder-suicides at Columbine High School. He was deeply involved in reporting on the death of child beauty queen JonBenet Ramsey and the subsequent investigation into the high-profile murder, and appeared many times on television as a commentator on the case. Elsewhere, Glick's reportage has covered politics, science—especially environmental issues—and news items of international interest arising in the Rocky Mountain region, where he was based from 1994 through 2001. Since 2001 Glick has been a freelance writer, placing work in national magazines and publishing two nonfiction books on ecological issues.

Powder Burn: Arson, Money, and Mystery on Vail Mountain examines the mysterious fire in October, 1998, that destroyed an exclusive ski resort in Vail, Colorado. What Glick uncovers in the course of his investigation defies the easy black-and-white picture of eco-terrorism first painted in the press to explain the twelve-million-dollar arson. As a reviewer noted in a *Trail & Timberline* piece, what emerges in *Powder Burn* "is nothing less than the riveting story of the complete corporatization . . . not only of our public lands, but also the social, economic, political, cultural, and environmental sphere within a thirty-mile radius of the town of Vail." Glick shows that the ownership of the resort, Vail Resorts, Inc., had incurred the wrath of many local interests beyond merely the environmentalists seeking to protect a lynx habitat. Those in op-position to Vail Resorts, Inc., included migrant labor-ers, local businesses edged out by the resort's opening its own restaurants, stores, and tours, and even middle-class skiers who resented the corporation's decisions to cater to an ever more exclusive elite.

Washington Monthly correspondent Bill McKibben called *Powder Burn* "a detective story where the crime turns out to be nowhere near the most evil act," and Sam Weller in the Chicago *Tribune Books* deemed the work "a savvy, engrossing whodunit." In a review for the *St. Petersburg Times,* Jack Reed noted: "While he gives us a look into the secretive world of radical environmentalism, Glick's greatest accomplishment is his insightful critique of the ski resort business." *GearReview* contributor Steve Mann observed that the book "exposes the raw nerves of political, economic, recreational, and environmental forces playing out over the entire West. The blazes on Vail Mountain symbol-ize the smoldering conflict between industrial tourism and land preservation." Brian Howard, writing in *E Magazine: The Environmental Magazine,* called Glick's book a "valuable template for understanding the roots of eco-terrorism" in the United States and throughout the world.

Monkey Dancing: A Father, Two Kids, and a Journey to the Ends of the Earth provides new challenges for Glick. For the first time he writes in the first person, and the story of his decision—in the wake of his dif-ficult divorce and his brother's death—to take his two young children on an extended trip around the world is intensely personal. At the same time, *Monkey Danc-ing* addresses many of the issues that Glick sees as globally important. These include habitat destruction and the extinction of species, the challenge of living an engaged life, and the political implications of travel-ing as an American in foreign countries as the terrorist attack events of September 11, 2001, were unfolding in New York. Throughout the narrative, he reflects on his brother's life and his death from a rare form of male breast cancer. He also works to reconcile his feel-ings about his divorce and the fact that his wife left him for another woman. Glick uses the trip as a means of reaching peace with himself and his life, and also as a means of building a closer bond between himself and his children. In doing so, he works to instill in them a love and appreciation of the natural world and the living things within it.

A *Kirkus Reviews* critic called the book a "fine and mordant account of experiencing things before they melt into air, stitching the remnants of a family's old lives into a whole new cloth." A *Publishers Weekly* critic commented, "This unusual, superbly written and deeply human story of their travels is a consistently rewarding odyssey." In her *Los Angeles Times Book Review* critique, Bernadette Murphy wrote that Glick's "rich narrative traces [the family's] five-month sojourn, a trip filled with wonder and awe." Murphy added: "Although readers may disagree with some of Glick's parenting choices along the way, we see clearly how huge an endeavor it is to travel around the world as a single father with two children."

BIOGRAPHICAL AND CRITICAL SOURCES:

PERIODICALS

Amicus Journal, summer, 2001, Marc Peruzzi, review of *Powder Burn: Arson, Money, and Mystery on Vail Mountain,* p. 35.
E Magazine: The Environmental Magazine, May-June, 2001, Brian Howard, "Arson on the Mountain," review of *Powder Burn,* p. 60.
Kirkus Reviews, April 15, 2003, review of *Monkey Dancing: A Father, Two Kids, and a Journey to the Ends of the Earth,* p. 584.
Library Journal, May 1, 2003, Rebecca Bollen, review of *Monkey Dancing,* p. 144.
Los Angeles Times Book Review, July 8, 2003, Berna-dette Murphy, "A Global Journey of Discovery for Self and Family."
Publishers Weekly, May 5, 2005, review of *Monkey Dancing,* p. 213.
St. Petersburg Times (St. Petersburg, FL), March 4, 2001, Jack Reed, "Investigating Ecotage on Vail Mountain."
Trail & Timberline, May-June, 2001, "Glick's *Powder Burn* a Literary Powder Keg."
Tribune Books (Chicago, IL), June 17, 2001, Sam Weller, review of *Powder Burn,* p. 3.
Washington Monthly, May, 2001, Bill McKibben, "Ski Moguls," review of *Powder Burn,* p. 52.

ONLINE

Daniel Glick Home Page, http://www.danielglick.net (October 1, 2003).

GearReview, http://www.gearreview.com/ (October 1, 2003), Steve Mann, review of *Powder Burn.*

Grist, http://www.grist.org/ (February 19, 2001), Florangela Davila, "Dance of the Burning Vails," review of *Powder Burn.*

* * *

GOLD, Robin

PERSONAL: Female.

ADDRESSES: Home—New York, NY.

CAREER: Development executive, independent film producer, and actor.

WRITINGS:

The Perfectly True Tales of a Perfect Size 12, Plume (New York, NY), 2007.

SIDELIGHTS: Robin Gold works in independent film production in New York City. Her experience ranges from acting in the movie *My Ex-Girlfriend's Wedding Reception* to her role as associate producer in the film *Romance & Cigarettes.* This film put her in the company of director John Turturro and a celebrated cast, including Susan Sarandon, James Gandolfini, Kate Winslet, and Christopher Walken.

Gold made her publishing debut in the chick-lit genre with *The Perfectly True Tales of a Perfect Size 12.* The creative Delilah White finds herself in competition with Margo, a rival coworker, for a promotion on their lifestyle television show. Because Delilah is confident she will get the job based on merit, she takes a vacation in the Catskills to relax. Margo follows and complicates matters by trying to steal Delilah's new love interest. A reviewer in *Publishers Weekly* called the book an "affable debut." A critic writing in *Kirkus Reviews* found the book to contain "a memorable character stuck in a forgettable story." Patty Engelmann, writing in *Booklist,* described the story as "fun and uplifting" and noted that the party at the conclusion of the book is "one of fiction's most hilarious and outrageous."

BIOGRAPHICAL AND CRITICAL SOURCES:

PERIODICALS

Booklist, October 15, 2006, Patty Engelmann, review of *The Perfectly True Tales of a Perfect Size 12,* p. 28.

Kirkus Reviews, September 1, 2006, review of *The Perfectly True Tales of a Perfect Size 12,* p. 865.

Publishers Weekly, October 16, 2006, review of *The Perfectly True Tales of a Perfect Size 12,* p. 29.

ONLINE

Internet Movie Database, http://www.imdb.com/ (January 22, 2007), author profile.*

* * *

GOLDEN, Daniel 1957-

PERSONAL: Born 1957. *Education:* Harvard University, B.A.

ADDRESSES: Office—Wall Street Journal, 200 Burnett Road, Chicopee, MA, 01020.

CAREER: Journalist. *Springfield Daily News,* Springfield, MA, staff reporter, 1978-81; *Boston Globe,* Boston, MA, regional correspondent, 1981, Sunday "Focus" section writer, 1986-93, medical investigative reporter, 1993-94, projects reporter, 1994-98; *Wall Street Journal,* Boston, MA, reporter, 1999-2000, senior special writer, 2000, became deputy bureau chief.

AWARDS, HONORS: Pulitzer Prize, 2004, for beat reporting; George Polk Award, 1985, for business reporting, 2004, for education reporting; National Headliner Award, 1989, feature writing category, 1999, for beat reporting category; First Place Award, Sigma Delta Chi, 1989, for magazine reporting; First Place Award, Sunday Magazine Editors, 1990, for investigative reporting; First Place Award, AP Sports

Editors, 1993, for investigative reporting; National Award, Education Writers Association, 2002, 2004, for education reporting.

WRITINGS:

The Price of Admission: How America's Ruling Class Buys Its Way into Elite Colleges—and Who Gets Left Outside the Gates, Crown (New York, NY), 2006.

SIDELIGHTS: Daniel Golden is a journalist whose professional career saw him based in Massachusetts for most of his life. Starting as a staff reporter for the *Springfield Daily News,* Golden moved up the journalistic ranks with his work at the *Boston Globe* before becoming deputy bureau chief at the Boston office of the *Wall Street Journal.* During his time at the *Wall Street Journal,* Golden published his first book, *The Price of Admission: How America's Ruling Class Buys Its Way into Elite Colleges—and Who Gets Left Outside the Gates.*

Centered around the American secondary education system, *The Price of Admission* exposes the admission policies of the top-tier universities in the United States and how money and parental alumni status mean more than one's SAT scores and grades. Golden offers statistics, interviews from Ivy-League admissions officers, and stories about the children of America's rich and famous. Matt Fleischer-Black, reviewing the book in *Corporate Counsel,* found that "it makes for an eye-opening report about how the affluent maintain their hold on the top rungs of the class ladder." In the *New York Times Book Review,* Michael Wolff found Golden to be bitter about top college admissions practices, commenting: "Golden is something of an avenger, exacting retribution for too much wealth and status by dishing about every rich and famous father's kid's lackluster SAT scores." It is the very stories, however, that a critic writing in *Kirkus Reviews* most enjoyed about the book, stating: "While the fact that the rich and famous are treated differently is hardly news, this report's abundance of juicy stories of outrageous favoritism makes for an absorbing read."

BIOGRAPHICAL AND CRITICAL SOURCES:

PERIODICALS

Atlantic Monthly, October, 2006, review of *The Price of Admission: How America's Ruling Class Buys*

Its Way into Elite Colleges—and Who Gets Left Outside the Gates, p. 126.
Corporate Counsel, October, 2006, Matt Fleischer-Black, review of *The Price of Admission,* p. 147.
Kirkus Reviews, June 15, 2006, review of *The Price of Admission,* p. 615.
New York Times Book Review, September 17, 2006, Michael Wolff, review of *Price of Admission,* p. 20.
Publishers Weekly, June 12, 2006, review of *The Price of Admission,* p. 41.
University Business, November, 2006, review of *The Price of Admission,* p. 20.*

*　　*　　*

**GOLDSWORTHY, Adrian
(Adrian Keith Goldsworthy)**

PERSONAL: Born 1969. *Education:* St. John's College, Oxford, Ph.D., 1994.

CAREER: Historian.

WRITINGS:

The Roman Army at War: 100 B.C.-A.D. 200, Clarendon Press (New York, NY), 1996.
(Editor, with Ian Haynes) *The Roman Army as a Community: Including Papers of a Conference Held at Birkbeck College, University of London, on 11-12 January 1997,* Journal of Roman Archaeology (Portsmouth, RI), 1999.
Roman Warfare, Cassell (London, England), 2000.
The Punic Wars, Cassell (London, England), 2000.
Cannae, Cassell Military (London, England), 2001.
In the Name of Rome: The Men Who Won the Roman Empire, Weidenfeld & Nicolson (London, England), 2003.
The Fall of Carthage: The Punic Wars, 265-146 B.C., Cassell (London, England), 2003.
The Complete Roman Army, Thames & Hudson (New York, NY), 2003.
Caesar's Civil War, 49-44 B.C., Routledge (New York, NY), 2003.
Caesar: Life of a Colossus, Yale University Press (New Haven, CT), 2006.

General editor, *Roman Warfare,* Collins/Smithsonian (New York, NY), 2005.

SIDELIGHTS: Adrian Goldsworthy is a recognized authority on Roman military history. He has written exclusively on his favorite subject, ranging from the days of the military in the early Roman Republic to the final years as the empire began to crumble. Tom Holland, writing in the *Spectator,* called Goldsworthy "indisputably our leading authority on the Roman way of war." The critic did note, though, that the historian is fairly conservative in his writing and does not often speculate or theorize about the Roman military.

Though he has only been publishing histories at a regular pace since about 2000, Goldsworthy has been very active since the release of such titles as *Roman Warfare* and *The Punic Wars.* The historian is often praised for his accurate research, offering both academic and general readers a plethora of facts in a readable manner. Of course, much of this history has been covered by other scholars before, but in a review of *The Punic Wars* by Jay Freeman in *Booklist,* for example, the critic held that the stories have been told "rarely as well."

In some cases, such as *In the Name of Rome: The Men Who Won the Roman Empire* and *The Complete Roman Army,* Goldsworthy offers expansive histories covering many centuries of change in the Roman military. In the former title, for instance, Goldsworthy discusses fifteen of the most important military commanders in the empire, comparing their accomplishments and effects on history, and sometimes noting how the Roman legions differed or were similar to modern military machines. Reviewing this book in the *Spectator,* Allan Massie asserted that "Goldsworthy's study of these commanders is thoroughly researched, and authoritative. He is lucid in exposition and narrative. The result is a book which academics will value and which nevertheless must appeal to anyone interested in the art of war and the making and defence of the Roman Empire." In what *Historian* contributor John Dayton called "an outstanding general study of the Roman military system," *The Complete Roman Army* shows how the Roman army evolved from troops formed of civilian farmers to a highly trained force of professional soldiers, then declined as internal strife tore the army and Rome apart. While Dayton noted some small errors in the book, such as an occasional

misspelling of a Latin word and the lack of reference citations, the reviewer considered it a "most beneficial" resource for those interested in the subject. "For anyone interested in the nuts and bolts of the soldier's life in the Roman army, this is an invaluable reference book," Susanna Shadrake similarly stated in *History Today.*

After writing a book about the Roman Civil War, featuring Caesar as the central figure, Goldsworthy focused on this most famous of Roman leaders in his 2006 title, *Caesar: Life of a Colossus.* It is a largely sympathetic portrait of the man who led Rome to domination of a continent and became its first emperor, only to be assassinated by those who yearned for the return of the Republic. Goldsworthy's biography discusses Caesar's military and political ambitions, as well as his personal life. According to one *Publishers Weekly* reviewer, "Goldsworthy's exhaustive, lucid, elegantly written life makes its subject the embodiment of his age." "The analysis of Caesar's generalship is predictably excellent, and the account of the Gallic wars, in particular, has rarely been bettered," reported Holland in the *Spectator,* who praised the historian for extracting quality facts from a wide array of resources. The critic, though, regretted that Goldsworthy does not seem to capture "the sheer excitement of political life in the late Republic," and added that the detailed military aspects offered make for some "foot-slogging" reading. He also commented that "the result is an impressively detailed book, but one that rarely, outside the account of the Gallic campaigns, comes alive." Sean Fleming, writing in *Library Journal,* admitted that Goldsworthy offers no new information here, but asserted that *Caesar* is "an engaging and well-drawn resource."

BIOGRAPHICAL AND CRITICAL SOURCES:

PERIODICALS

Atlantic Monthly, October, 2006, review of *Caesar: Life of a Colossus,* p. 126.

Booklist, April 1, 2001, Jay Freeman, review of *The Punic Wars,* p. 1445; September 15, 2006, Gilbert Taylor, review of *Caesar,* p. 18.

Contemporary Review, February, 2004, review of *The Complete Roman Army,* p. 128.

Historian, spring, 2005, John Dayton, review of *The Complete Roman Army,* p. 155.

History Today, November, 2003, Susanna Shadrake, review of *The Complete Roman Army,* p. 67.

Library Journal, September 15, 2006, Sean Fleming, review of *Caesar,* p. 67.

Publishers Weekly, July 24, 2006, review of *Caesar,* p. 45.

Spectator, November 22, 2003, Allan Massie, "Arms and the Men," review of *In the Name of Rome: The Men Who Won the Roman Empire,* p. 60; April 29, 2006, Tom Holland, "Never Simply a Soldier," review of *Caesar.**

* * *

GOLDSWORTHY, Adrian Keith
See GOLDSWORTHY, Adrian

* * *

GORDON, Michael R. 1951-

PERSONAL: Born 1951, in New York, NY. *Education:* Columbia Journalism School, B.A.; Columbia University, M.A.

ADDRESSES: Home—Washington, DC. *Office*—New York Times, 229 W. 43rd St., New York, NY 10036.

CAREER: During early career, worked for the United Nations and as a Washington, DC, reporter for the *National Journal; New York Times,* New York, NY, staff member, 1985—, currently chief military correspondent.

WRITINGS:

(With Bernard E. Trainor) *The Generals' War: The Inside Story of the Conflict in the Gulf,* Little, Brown (Boston, MA), 1995.

(With Bernard E. Trainor) *Cobra II: The Inside Story of the Invasion and Occupation of Iraq,* Pantheon Books (New York, NY), 2006.

SIDELIGHTS: Michael R. Gordon is a war correspondent who has covered conflicts in many of the world's hot spots, including Kosovo, Afghanistan, Chechnya, and the Middle East. After graduating from the Columbia School of Journalism, he worked for the United Nations, mostly covering issues in Namibia for three years. He then became a reporter for the *National Journal* in Washington, DC. During the early 1980s, he covered the Pentagon, before being hired by the *New York Times* in 1985. Military issues and foreign policy became his specialty. Teaming up with retired army general Bernard E. Trainor, Gordon has written two books about American wars in the Middle East: *The Generals' War: The Inside Story of the Conflict in the Gulf,* and *Cobra II: The Inside Story of the Invasion and Occupation of Iraq.*

The Generals' War is about the first Gulf War—also known by the operation names of Desert Shield and Desert Storm—and the decisions made by Generals Colin Powell and Norman Schwarzkopf during the George H.W. Bush presidency. The American invasion of Kuwait to oust invading Iraqi forces was like a German blitzkrieg. Yet despite the quick success of liberating the small, oil-rich country, the ultimate end of the conflict is seen by many as a failure because of President Bush's decision not to relentlessly pursue and destroy Iraqi President Saddam Hussein's Republican Guard. Hence, Saddam remained comfortably in power in Iraq, and eventually became the target of a second, disastrous war for the Americans. Gordon and Trainor attempt to answer the big question as to why the Americans did not destroy the Republican Guard in what Eugene Sullivan called a "fascinating and sustained analysis" in his *Booklist* review. *Washington Monthly* contributor David Evans praised the "thoroughly researched" book, which makes use of declassified government documents and numerous interviews with military personnel and political bureaucrats. While the authors conclude that the military's performance in the war was exemplary, they largely lay the blame on General Schwarzkopf for not being forcefully insistent on finishing the job. For this reason and other reasons, the American forces stalled at the end of the conflict, and allowed the Iraqis to safely flee. Gordon and Trainor also point out that the air attacks, though heavy, still left the Iraqis with the ability to respond with Scud missiles; also, there was a notable lack of communication and coordination between the various branches of the service and the commanders in charge of the operation. While Evans regretted that the authors do not "satisfactorily" explain why the air attacks did not completely succeed, the critic appreciated the many other "juicy details" of what went awry.

A *Publishers Weekly* contributor concluded that *The Generals' War* is a "meticulous reconstruction of American leadership in Desert Shield/Desert Storm."

Cobra II depicts a much different military under much different leadership. Under President George W. Bush, son of the previous Bush, and his Secretary of State, Donald Rumsfeld, there was a fundamental shift in the concept of what the U.S. military should be. Rumsfeld felt that the military under previous administrations was cumbersome, outdated, and geared more toward the problems of the Cold War era than toward the twenty-first-century dilemmas of conflicts in the Middle East and terrorism. Rumsfeld and President Bush believed that smaller forces, using high-tech weaponry and support, could succeed much more quickly and efficiently in military operations. This idea was put to the test when President Bush unilaterally decided to invade Iraq and overthrow Saddam Hussein. In *Cobra II* Gordon and Trainor explore what led to this fateful decision and the numerous mistakes in policy and decision-making that caused the Americans to become bogged down for years in a quagmire of endless violence and civil unrest. The authors discuss how Bush, and especially Rumsfeld, developed such tunnel vision that they refused to adapt their strategy when they met with unexpected resistance after successfully toppling the Iraqi regime. They grossly underestimated the number of American forces that would be required, and they did not expect to create a civilian insurgency against which the American military had little experience in overcoming. "Gordon and Trainor lucidly lay out the story of how perception and personality played decisive roles in planning for the war and the subsequent occupation from the moment the administration cast a baleful eye on Iraq," reported Gregory Fontenot in the *Military Review*. While Fontenot complained that the authors sometimes do not provide supporting documentation for their arguments, the critic concluded that they "argue effectively that the planning effort was flawed by poor communication and a top-down approach that brooked almost no contrary points of view." An *Economist* contributor was disappointed that the authors barely touch on the extended occupation of Iraq, focusing instead on what led up to it, but asserted that the book "will be hard to improve upon." Also commenting on the "riveting . . . descriptions of the war" and "stupendous research," Jacob Heilbrunn concluded in his *New York Times Book Review* assessment that "*Cobra II* is everything that the Bush administration's

plan for the war was not. It is meticulously organized, shuns bluff and bombast for lapidary statements, and is largely impervious to attack."

BIOGRAPHICAL AND CRITICAL SOURCES:

PERIODICALS

Booklist, January 15, 1995, Eugene Sullivan, review of *The Generals' War: The Inside Story of the Conflict in the Gulf,* p. 893.
Economist, April 8, 2006, "Led by Donkeys; War in Iraq," review of *Cobra II: The Inside Story of the Invasion and Occupation of Iraq,* p. 83.
Military Review, July-August, 2006, Gregory Fontenot, review of *Cobra II,* p. 114.
New Yorker, April 3, 2006, Steve Coll, "Deluded," review of *Cobra II,* p. 27.
New York Times Book Review, April 30, 2006, Jacob Heilbrunn, "The Rumsfeld Doctrine," review of *Cobra II,* p. 9.
Publishers Weekly, November 7, 1994, review of *The Generals' War,* p. 53.
Spectator, May 13, 2006, Allan Mallinson, "No End of a Lesson," review of *Cobra II.*
Washington Monthly, January-February, 1995, David Evans, review of *The Generals' War,* p. 41.

ONLINE

Institute of International Studies Web site, http://globetrotter.berkeley.edu/ (March 21, 2006), Harry Kreisler, interview with Michael R. Gordon.*

*   *   *

GRANDBOIS, Peter

PERSONAL: Married; children: three. *Education:* Bennington College, M.F.A.; University of Denver, Ph.D., 2006. *Hobbies and other interests:* Flamenco guitar.

ADDRESSES: Home—Davis, CA. *Office*—California State University, Sacramento, 6000 J St., Sacramento, CA 95819. *E-mail*—pgrandbo@csus.edu.

CAREER: California State University, Sacramento, professor of creative writing and contemporary literature, 2006—. Former member of the United States National Fencing Team.

AWARDS, HONORS: Silver medalist, 1993, U.S. National Fencing Championships; Pushcart Prize honorable mention, for short story "All or Nothing at the Fabergé"; "Discover Great New Writers" series citation, Barnes & Noble, and "Original Voices" series citation, Borders Books, both for *The Gravedigger.*

WRITINGS:

The Gravedigger: A Novel, Chronicle Books (San Francisco, CA), 2006.
(Translator) Edgardo Rodríguez Juliá, *San Juan: Ciudad Soñada,* University of Wisconsin Press (Madison, WI), 2007.

Also author of *A Single, Straight Line* (short stories; includes "All or Nothing at the Fabergé").

SIDELIGHTS: Peter Grandbois's book *The Gravedigger: A Novel* evokes the spirit of the school of magic realism made famous in the works of Latin American writers Alejo Carpentier, Mario Vargas Llosa, and Gabriel García Márquez. His story features a protagonist named Juan Rodrigo, who lives and works at his trade in a small Spanish village. Juan has the ability—inherited from his father and grandfather before him—to hear and understand the stories the ghosts of the dead tell him. "The real story," however, related a reviewer for *Book Fetish,* "is Juan's life, told partially through his communications with his late wife, Carlota, who died in childbirth, and partially through the most distressing aspect of this novel." Juan's own story is told to the ghost of his only child, his daughter Esperanza, while he is digging her grave in the mountains of Andalusia. Despite the stories of the various ghosts, stated Peter Warzel in the *Rocky Mountain News,* "the magic and sorrow of the novel is in how Juan Rodrigo tells the story of his adored daughter's life and how she probes and pushes him to reveal his own life in the process." The novel, concluded Kel Munger in the *Sacramento News and Review,* "has more the tenor of a fable than of the wandering, language-driven narratives that make up

the work of García Márquez. That's not a bad thing. We have a García Márquez. What's really wonderful is to make the welcome discovery of a Grandbois."

BIOGRAPHICAL AND CRITICAL SOURCES:

PERIODICALS

Booklist, April 15, 2006, Allison Block, review of *The Gravedigger: A Novel,* p. 27.
Kirkus Reviews, April 15, 2006, review of *The Gravedigger,* p. 370.
Publishers Weekly, March 20, 2006, review of *The Gravedigger,* p. 34.
Rocky Mountain News, August 29, 2006, Peter Warzel, "'Gravedigger' Uncovers Charm, Beauty."
Sacramento News and Review, August 24, 2006, Kel Munger, "Ghost Stories."

ONLINE

Book Fetish, http://www.bookfetish.org/ (July 10, 2006), review of *The Gravedigger.*
Brothers Grandbois Web site, http://www.brothers grandbois.com/ (November 29, 2006), author biography and author interview with Alex Stein.
DU Today, http://www.du.edu/ (November 29, 2006), Jordan Ames, "Grandbois Takes Circuitous Route to Literary Success."

*   *   *

GRESCOE, Taras 1966-

PERSONAL: Born 1966, in Toronto, Ontario, Canada.

ADDRESSES: Home—Montreal, Quebec, Canada. *Agent*—Michelle Tessler, Tessler Literary Agency, 27 W. 20th St., Ste. 1003, New York, NY 10011. *E-mail*—tgrescoe@hotmail.com.

CAREER: Teacher of English in Paris, France, c. 1990-94; travel journalist based in Montreal, Quebec, Canada, beginning 1996. Has also worked variously as a newspaper boy, concession stand worker in a movie theater, video store clerk, delivery driver, and researcher.

AWARDS, HONORS: Mavis Gallant Prize for nonfiction, 2000, Quebec Writers' Federation First Book Award, 2000, and Edna Staebler Award for creative nonfiction, 2001, all for *Sacré Blues: An Unsentimental Journey through Quebec.*

WRITINGS:

Sacré Blues: An Unsentimental Journey through Quebec, Macfarlane, Walter & Ross (Toronto, Ontario, Canada), 2000.

The End of Elsewhere: Travels among the Tourists, Macfarlane, Walter & Ross (Toronto, Ontario, Canada), 2003.

The Devil's Picnic: Around the World in Pursuit of Forbidden Fruit, Bloomsbury Publishers (New York, NY), 2005.

Author's books have been translated into Japanese, German, French, and Chinese. Contributor to periodicals, including the London *Times, Chicago Tribune Magazine, Wired, New York Times, National Geographic Traveler, Saturday Night, Canadian Geographic, Gourmet, The Independent, The Guardian, New York Times Magazine,* and *Condé Nast Traveler.*

SIDELIGHTS: Taras Grescoe is a Canadian journalist and author who uses travel pieces to engage in commentary upon human nature, politics, history, and exotic and mundane locations not immediately accessible to average readers. Grescoe's first full-length book, *Sacré Blues: An Unsentimental Journey through Quebec,* grew from his decision to settle in Quebec after growing up in western Canada and also living in Paris for four years. His status as an outside observer of the Quebecois allowed him to explore the distinctiveness of the culture without preconceived political or social prejudices, and he wrote *Sacré Blues* as a meditation on one of North America's unique societies.

Grescoe traveled through the province, interviewing prominent intellectuals and citizens on the street, eating the favorite local foods, and watching the popular television shows. He covers the region's holidays, politics, and generational differences, its evolving language patterns, and its citizens' perception of their place in North America and the world. In a *Canadian Geographic* review of *Sacré Blues,* Joel Yanofsky commended Grescoe as a "thorough, unflagging and quirky researcher." Yanofsky also observed that Grescoe's enthusiasm "will probably help the rest of the country understand a little better Quebec's neverending ambivalence about its place in Canada." Describing the book as "lively" and "information-packed," Padma Viswanathan concluded in *Quill & Quire* that "Grescoe is opinionated and has great affection for Quebec, but remains skilful and professional throughout."

The End of Elsewhere: Travels among the Tourists finds Grescoe in Europe and Asia, taking pre-packaged tours to popular destinations and musing on the history of the tourist trade and its impact on native cultures and the ecology. Toronto *Globe and Mail* writer Kisha Ferguson called the work "one of the most original travel books to come out in years." In a review for the *Montreal Review of Books,* Ian McGillis commented: "Grescoe comes up with a twist that ought to set his book apart in a crowded and competitive genre. What raises the book a further notch, though, is that for all the author's stated determination to set self-consciousness aside, he ends up revealing a lot about his own need to wander." In a review for *LauraHird.com,* Marc Goldin wrote: "This book is an unbelievably honest look at the state of travel and tourism in general and at one man's life spent in the pursuit of this, specifically. . . . More than that, it was well written and poetic at moments and philosophical always, in its examination of the state of our world in these times."

Grescoe's third book took him on another epic journey around the world, this time searching out substances that are illegal or taboo in many cultures and reflecting on the sociological impact of prohibition. *The Devil's Picnic: Around the World in Pursuit of Forbidden Fruit* was described by *Straight.com* reviewer Alexander Varty as "an insightful, witty, and ultimately sobering analysis of pleasure." *New Statesman* contributor Ned Denny called the book a "perceptive, cogent and witty analysis of the enduring folly that is prohibition." In a *Washington Post* review, Josh Friedland said of Grescoe: "Behind this culinary risk-taker hides a true policy wonk, deeply interested in the regulations that make so many forbidden foods, drinks and drugs . . . forbidden." Writing for the *National Post,* Robert Wiersema called *The Devil's Picnic* "a feast of delights for the armchair gourmet," adding that "it is difficult not to gorge oneself on Grescoe's writing."

BIOGRAPHICAL AND CRITICAL SOURCES:

PERIODICALS

Canadian Geographic, September, 2000, Joel Yanofsky, "Newcomer Takes a Brazen Romp through La Belle Province," p. 81.

Globe and Mail (Toronto, Ontario, Canada), May 3, 2003, Kisha Ferguson, review of *The End of Elsewhere: Travels among the Tourists.*

Maclean's, November 13, 2000, "A Tour of Quebec Quirkiness," p. 50.

Montreal Review of Books, October 1, 2003, Andy Brown, "Explaining Poutine"; spring-summer, 2003, Ian McGillis, review of *The End of Elsewhere.*

National Post, March 4, 2006, Robert Wiersema, "Traverse the World's Offbeat and Verboten," p. WP16.

New Statesman, March 6, 2006, Ned Denny, "Illegal Highs," p. 55.

Quill & Quire, September, 2000, Padma Viswanathan, review of *Sacré Blues: An Unsentimental Journey through Quebec,* p. 50.

Washington Post, October 23, 2005, Josh Friedland, review of *The Devil's Picnic: Around the World in Pursuit of Forbidden Fruit,* p. T08.

ONLINE

LauraHird.com, http://www.laurahird.com/ (December 25, 2006), Marc Goldin, review of *The End of Elsewhere.*

Straight.com, http://www.straight.com/ (March 2, 2006), Alexander Varty, review of *The Devil's Picnic.*

Wilfrid Laurier University Web site, http://www.wlu.ca/ (September 18, 2001), Kathryn Wardropper, "*Sacré Blues* Wins Edna Staebler Award for Creative Nonfiction."

H

HAINE, W. Scott

PERSONAL: Education: University of California, Berkeley, B.A.; University of Wisconsin-Madison, M.A., Ph.D.

ADDRESSES: Home—Half Moon Bay, CA. *Office*— Holy Names University, 3500 Mountain Blvd., Oakland, CA 94619. *E-mail*—shaine@aol.com.

CAREER: Historian, educator, and writer. Teaching positions at University of Maryland University College, Adelphi, College of San Mateo, San Mateo, CA, and Cañada College, Redwoord City, CA; Holy Names University, Oakland, CA, lecturer in European history.

WRITINGS:

The World of the Paris Café: Sociability among the French Working Class, 1789-1914, Johns Hopkins University Press (Baltimore, MD), 1996.
The History of France, Greenwood Press (Westport, CT), 2000.
Culture and the Customs of France, Greenwood Press (Westport, CT), 2006.

SIDELIGHTS: In his book *The World of the Paris Café: Sociability among the French Working Class, 1789-1914,* French cultural historian W. Scott Haine explores the café culture of Paris, which included almost all of the social classes as well as a strong contingent of artists, writers, and academics. According to Haine, this culture played an important role in how the various classes both formed and expressed their identity. In this comprehensive history, the author explores how cafés were perceived and the various elements of café etiquette. He delineates the role of gender in café society and how this society contributed to relations among family members, various politicians, and a wide range of professionals who conducted business within their confines. In the end, according to Haine, the café society fostered debate among the classes that ultimately led to a blue-collar, or common, public forum.

David Garrioch, writing in the *English Historical Review,* commented: "The central theme of W. Scott Haine's *The World of the Paris Café . . .* is the role of the cafe as one of the pillars of working-class identity." Garrioch went on to write that "there is valuable material here for all those interested in the social history of nineteenth-century Paris." *Historian* contributor Judith A. DeGroat wrote: "Drawing on newspapers; medical, social reform, and political tracts; and upon court records for crime and bankruptcy, Haine constructs a microhistory of the cafe milieu of Paris from the French Revolution to the Great War." The reviewer added: "All told, this book makes a useful contribution to the study of working-class culture." In a review of *The World of the Paris Café* in the *Economist,* a contributor commented that the author's "academic study of their place in French social history is worthwhile and in places even interesting." Jill Harsin wrote in the *Journal of Modern History* that the author "has found a subject that intersects many of the most vital areas of nineteenth-century urban life: the development of neighborhoods and sociability, the evolution of gender and class identities, the transformation of leisure and play." Harsin added: "His treatment, both entertaining and analytical, sheds new light and provides important new perspectives for all of these issues."

In *The History of France,* the author provides a history for beginning students and the general public. Beginning with the prehistory of France, Haine traces the country's development through ancient and medieval times. He writes of the establishment of the French monarchy and delves into the genesis of the French Revolution and the downfall of Napoleon. As he moves into the twentieth century, the author recounts the fascist elements of Vichy France during World War II and how Charles de Gaulle played a primary role in reestablishing a stable political climate following the war. The history ends with the beginning of the twenty-first century. The book includes a timeline of historical events and various biographical sketches. Jack B. Ridley, writing in *History: Review of New Books,* commented that the book "is highly recommended as an introduction to the rich, varied, and influential history of France."

BIOGRAPHICAL AND CRITICAL SOURCES:

PERIODICALS

Economist, July 20, 1996, review of *The World of the Paris Café: Sociability among the French Working Class, 1789-1914,* p. S6.
English Historical Review, April, 1998, David Garrioch, review of *The World of the Paris Café,* p. 507.
Historian, fall, 1997, Judith A. DeGroat review of *The World of the Paris Café,* p. 165.
History: Review of New Books, winter, 2001, Jack B. Ridley, review of *The History of France,* p. 79.
Journal of Modern History, December, 1997, Jill Harsin, review of *The World of the Paris Café,* p. 854.
Journal of Social History, winter, 1997, Steven M. Beaudoin, review of *The World of the Paris Café,* p. 200.

*   *   *

HALEY, David B. 1936-

PERSONAL: Born 1936. *Education:* Harvard University, A.B., Ph.D.

ADDRESSES: Home—MN. *Office*—Department of English, University of Minnesota, 310C Lind Hall, 207 Church St. S.E., Minneapolis, MN 55455. *E-mail*—dbhaley@umn.edu.

CAREER: University of Minnesota, Minneapolis, from assistant professor to professor of English, currently professor emeritus.

WRITINGS:

Shakespeare's Courtly Mirror: Reflexivity and Prudence in "All's Well That Ends Well," University of Delaware Press (Newark, DE), 1993.
Dryden and the Problem of Freedom: The Republican Aftermath, 1649-1680, Yale University Press (New Haven, CT), 1997.
(Editor, with others) *"A Certain Text": Close Readings and Textual Studies in Shakespeare and Others in Honor of Tom Clayton,* University of Delaware Press (Newark, DE), 2002.

SIDELIGHTS: David B. Haley is a professor of English and author of a number of volumes, including *Shakespeare's Courtly Mirror: Reflexivity and Prudence in "All's Well That Ends Well."* It is a study of a complex play that is similar to Shakespeare's earlier history plays in that it mirrors the heroism of princes and courtiers. "Haley considers the play a dialectic between courtly prudence and Divine Providence," remarked C.B. Hardman in the *Review of English Studies.* In the play, Count Bertram is forced by the king to marry a low-born beauty named Helena after she cures the king of a fistula. "Throughout the play from the recovery of the sick king, Haley suggests that a continued analogy with the alchemical process is maintained," observed Hardman, who concluded: "When Haley discusses the roles of Bertram and Helena, the persona of the courtier, courtly society, and courtly praxis, he is sometimes interesting, even when one does not accept his conclusions."

Haley is also the author of *Dryden and the Problem of Freedom: The Republican Aftermath, 1649-1680,* in which he "assembles symptomatic and contextualized readings of Dryden's poems chronologically," remarked Donna Landry and Gerald MacLean in *Studies* in English Literature, 1500-1900. "Haley's book will be read with great interest by those devoted to Dryden's poetic accomplishments."

BIOGRAPHICAL AND CRITICAL SOURCES:

PERIODICALS

Review of English Studies, November, 1995, C.B. Hardman, review of *Shakespeare's Courtly Mirror: Reflexivity and Prudence in "All's Well That Ends Well,"* p. 567.
Studies in English Literature, 1500-1900, summer, 1998, Donna Landry and Gerald MacLean, review of *Dryden and the Problem of Freedom: The Republican Aftermath, 1649-1680,* p. 553.*

*   *   *

HANNA, Martha

PERSONAL: Education: University of Winnipeg, B.A. (with honors), 1977; University of Toronto, M.A., 1978; Georgetown University, Ph.D., 1989.

ADDRESSES: Office—Department of History, University of Colorado, Campus Box 234, Boulder, CO 80309-0234. *E-mail*—martha.hanna@colorado.edu.

CAREER: University of Colorado, Boulder, instructor, 1988, assistant professor, 1989-96, associate professor of history, 1996—. Cambridge University, visiting fellow of Clare Hall, 2003-04.

MEMBER: American Historical Association, Society for French Historical Studies, Western Society for French History (member of council, 1994-97; vice president, 2005-06).

AWARDS, HONORS: Grant from American Council of Learned Societies, 1996; fellow of National Endowment for the Humanities, 2004.

WRITINGS:

The Mobilization of Intellect: French Scholars and Writers during the Great War, Harvard University Press (Cambridge, MA), 1996.

Your Death Would Be Mine: Paul and Marie Pireaud in the Great War, Harvard University Press (Cambridge, MA), 2006.

Member of editorial board, *French Historical Studies,* 2004-07.

BIOGRAPHICAL AND CRITICAL SOURCES:

PERIODICALS

Journal of Modern History, March, 1999, Daniel J. Sherman, review of *The Mobilization of Intellect: French Scholars and Writers during the Great War,* p. 218.

ONLINE

Martha Hanna's Home Page, http://spot.colorado.edu/~hanna (January 5, 2007).*

*   *   *

HARDYMENT, Christina 1946-

PERSONAL: Born 1946; daughter of Eiliv Odd Hauge (a writer) and Diana Hardyment; married Tom Griffith, 1969 (divorced, 1991); children; four daughters. *Education:* Attended Newnham College, Cambridge, 1964-67.

ADDRESSES: Home—Oxford, England. *Agent*—Gill Coleridge, Rogers, Coleridge & White Ltd., 20 Powis Mews, London W11 1JN, England.

CAREER: Writer, journalist, and historian. Taught at Blackheath High School, England, for two years.

WRITINGS:

Dream Babies: Three Centuries of Good Advice on Child Care, Harper & Row (New York, NY), 1983, Frances Lincoln Publishing, 2007.

The Canary-Coloured Cart: One Family's Search for Storybook Europe, Heinemann (London, England), 1987, published as *Heidi's Alp: One Family's Search for Storybook Europe,* Atlantic Monthly Press (New York, NY), 1988.

Arthur Ransome and Captain Flint's Trunk, Jonathan Cape (London, England), 1988, Frances Lincoln Publishers (London, England), 2007.

From Mangle to Microwave: The Mechanization of Household Work, Basil Blackwell (New York, NY), 1988.

Home Comfort: A History of Domestic Arrangements in Association with the National Trust, Academy Chicago in Association with the National Trust (Chicago, IL), 1992.

Slice of Life: The British Way of Eating since 1945, BBC Books (London, England), 1995.

Perfect Parents: Baby-Care Advice Past and Present, Oxford University Press (New York, NY), 1995.

Behind the Scenes: Domestic Arrangements in Historic Houses, National Trust (London, England), 1997.

Literary Trails, National Trust (London, England), 2000.

Malory: The Knight Who Became King Arthur's Chronicler, HarperCollins Publishers (New York, NY), 2005.

SIDELIGHTS: Christina Hardyment began her writing career writing about family life in a social context within the home. For example, in *Home Comfort: A History of Domestic Arrangements in Association with the National Trust,* Hardyment chronicles the great houses of England with a focus on how the houses were run and the people who ran them, from the kitchen help to the houses' various owners. Writing about houses now owned by England's National Trust, the author chronicles how domestic requirements and duties changed over the years due to modern contrivances, such as indoor plumbing, and also details how the domestic help handled common household chores and problems, such as removing stains from clothes. She also provides some common recipes of the times. A contributor to the *Economist* noted that "though the days of levigated hartshorn, grist, spree, limbecks and cucurbits have a period charm, [the author] is fairly unsentimental about their passing."

In *Slice of Life: The British Way of Eating since 1945,* Hardyment details the development of British cuisine, writing about contributions from such notables as Elizabeth David. Writing in the *New Statesman & Society,* Chris Savage King noted that the author "details the sometimes ridiculous trials it took for British food and cooking to reach its current excellence."

Hardyment turns her view to a literary topic with her book *Malory: The Knight Who Became King Arthur's Chronicler.* In her biography of one of the founding father's of English literature, the author bases much of her writing on conjecture since little is known about the details of Malory's life. "Hardyment overcomes this by sketching out a 'likely career' for her subject, chronicling his training in the chivalric arts and his experience of war in France," wrote Kathy Watson in the *New Statesman.* Watson went on to note, "Her description of Malory's christening is a memorable performance, with flaming torches, flickering candles, the superstitious placing of a crust of bread under the baby's mattress to keep witches away, and feasting and dancing." A *Kirkus Reviews* contributor commented that the author "has shaped an admittedly speculative life with creative, highly intelligent and persuasive guesswork." A *Publishers Weekly* reviewer noted: "Camelot echoes marvelously through Hardyment's biography, making palpable Malory's desire for valor and honor." In a review in the *Guardian,* Richard Barber wrote that "there are huge gaps in the Malory story, and Hardyment plugs these gaps by presenting speculations as to what might have been happening to him set against a picture of the society and political history of the age." Barber also noted that "this is a book which any reader interested in the middle ages should try for themselves."

BIOGRAPHICAL AND CRITICAL SOURCES:

PERIODICALS

Economist, April 4, 1992, review of *Home Comfort: A History of Domestic Arrangements in Association with the National Trust,* p. 108.

Guardian (London, England), September 3, 2005, Richard Barber, review of *Malory: The Knight Who Became King Arthur's Chronicler.*

Kirkus Reviews, June 1, 2006, review of *Malory,* p. 556.

New Statesman & Society, October 27, 1995, Chris Savage King, review of *Slice of Life: The British Way of Eating since 1945,* p. 46.

New Statesman, September 12, 2005, Kathy Watson, review of *Malory,* p. 55.
Publishers Weekly, May 22, 2006, review of *Malory,* p. 44.

ONLINE

Christina Hardyment Home Page, http://www. christinahardyment.co.uk (January 21, 2007).

*   *   *

HARMON, Byron 1969-

PERSONAL: Born July 20, 1969, in Lake Charles, LA. *Education:* Attended Southern University.

ADDRESSES: Home—New York, NY. *Office*—CBS 2 News, 524 W. 57 St., New York, NY 10019. *Agent*—Lane Zachary, Zachary Shuster Harmsworth, 1776 Broadway, Ste. 1405, New York, NY 10019.

CAREER: WCBS-TV, New York, NY, executive producer of *Early Morning News;* has also worked at television stations in Baton Rouge, LA, Tulsa, OK, and Baltimore, MD. *Military service:* Served in U.S. Army.

AWARDS, HONORS: Eight Emmy Awards for television work.

WRITINGS:

NOVELS

All the Women I've Loved, Pocket Books (New York, NY), 2004.
Mistakes Men Make, Pocket Books (New York, NY), 2005.
Crabs in a Barrel, Agate (Chicago, IL), 2006.

SIDELIGHTS: Byron Harmon, an Emmy Award-winning television producer, is the author of such novels as *Mistakes Men Make* and *Crabs in a Barrel.* *Mistakes Men Make* follows the trials and triumphs of Eric Swift, a former football superstar who lands his dream job as a New York City sports anchor. The charismatic bachelor quickly gets swept up in the glitz and glamour of the Big Apple, however, and becomes addicted to cocaine. With the help of his coworker, Eden Alexander, Swift attempts to regain control of his life. *Mistakes Men Make* is "a candid, unflattering look into the world of sports journalism," according to Glenn Townes, writing in the *Black Issues Book Review.*

A luxury yacht is shipwrecked and its passengers stranded on a remote island in *Crabs in a Barrel.* The diverse group of African American passengers, including a waitress, a corporate lawyer, a comedian, and a drug dealer, must depend on each other for survival, but their varied social and economic backgrounds threaten to tear them apart. As the days pass, the storm that forced the crew onto the island develops into a Category Three hurricane. When the Coast Guard calls off its search because of the approaching storm, the father of one of the passengers enlists a friend's help to find the castaways. A critic in *Kirkus Reviews* praised "the clever interweaving of [the] subplot."

BIOGRAPHICAL AND CRITICAL SOURCES:

PERIODICALS

Black Issues Book Review, January-February, 2006, Glenn Townes, review of *Mistakes Men Make,* p. 61.
Kirkus Reviews, June 15, 2006, review of *Crabs in a Barrel,* p. 592.

ONLINE

Byron Harmon's Home Page, http://www.byron harmon.com (January 15, 2007).*

*   *   *

HASSINGER, Amy 1972-

PERSONAL: Born 1972, in Newton, MA; married; children: one daughter, one son. *Education:* Barnard College, B.A., 1994; studied at the Iowa Writers' Workshop. *Hobbies and other interests:* Yoga, reading, cooking, chatting with friends, singing.

ADDRESSES: Home—Urbana, IL. *Agent*—Stephanie Abou, The Joy Harris Literary Agency, 156 5th Ave., Ste. 617, New York, NY 10010. *E-mail*—amy@amyhassinger.com.

CAREER: Writer and teacher. University of Nebraska at Omaha, teacher in low-residency M.F.A. writing program. Has taught creative writing at Iowa Writers' Workshop and Iowa State University.

AWARDS, HONORS: Peter S. Prescott Prize, 1994, for short story "The Kiss"; Joseph E. and Ursi I. Callen Scholarship, Iowa Writers' Workshop,1999–2001; Teaching-writing fellow, Iowa Writers' Workshop, 2000–01; Listen Up! Award, *Publishers Weekly,* 2003, and Audiobook of the Year Award, *ForeWord* magazine, 2003, both for audio edition of *Nina: Adolescence;* Finalist Award in Prose, Illinois Arts Council, 2006.

WRITINGS:

Finding Katahdin: An Exploration of Maine's Past (history), University of Maine Press (Orono, ME), 2001
Nina: Adolescence(novel), Putnam (New York, NY), 2003.
The Priest's Madonna (novel), Putnam (New York, NY), 2006

Contributor to periodicals, including *Arts and Letters* and *Hunger Mountain.*

SIDELIGHTS: Amy Hassinger's debut novel, *Nina: Adolescence,* uses the story of one shaken family to explore themes of adolescent sexuality, artistic license, and coping strategies in the face of tragedy. Eager to help her parents deal with their grief over the accidental drowning of her younger brother, fifteen-year-old Nina encourages her artist-mother to begin painting again. When her mother chooses to paint a series of nudes of Nina—in effect documenting Nina's burgeoning femininity—the whole family must deal with the issues surrounding the mother's decision to display the portraits in a show. "Hassinger perfectly captures the guilt and thirst for affection," recorded a *Publishers Weekly* writer, "that compels Nina to pose nude," stemming from her role in her brother's death and from her need to reconnect with her parents.

One of the issues she encounters in her career as her mother's model centers on Nina's mother's ex-boyfriend, photographer Leo Beck, who abuses Nina's trust by photographing her naked and beginning a serious relationship with her. "The story is beautifully told," wrote *Kliatt* critic Susan Allison, "arousing sympathy for each member of the family caught in this web, but especially for Nina and her father Henry." *Booklist* contributor Gillian Engberg called *Nina* "an unsettling and acutely sensitive debut" and a "powerful, disturbing story," and a *Kirkus Reviews* correspondent noted that Hassinger "builds her touching drama with a refreshingly undramatic simplicity."

Hassinger's second novel, *The Priest's Madonna,* traces the story of the nineteenth-century affair between a small-town French girl, Marie Dernanaud, and the priest who serves her village. During renovations to the village church Marie uncovers evidence about the purported relationship between Mary Magdalene and Jesus. Hassinger parallels Marie's story with Mary's, showing how each woman has to struggle to "serve the man she loves," declared Anna M. Nelson in *Library Journal,* "without destroying him and his faith." "What is riveting about this novel is NOT . . . the sexual relationship," noted Viviane Crystal on the *Best Reviews* Web site. "What grips the reader is how people find and lose faith because of their immersion in either material things or belief in worldly ideas." "Hassinger brings historical characters to life," *Booklist* critic Michele Leber stated, "in this vivid and affecting account of love and faith."

Hassinger told *CA:* "I have always loved to read, and after a while, it occurred to me that I might like to write something of my own. I am a very disciplined writer, or was until I had small children anyway. In the days before little ones, I wrote every day for four hours, shooting for 1,000 words a day. I'll get back there someday, when I can afford more babysitting hours. I find that consistency with the work is one of the most important things in my process.

"I hope [that my] stories will enthrall people, and that the sentences will jazz them, maybe make them want to write something of their own. On a deeper level, I hope they'll encourage people to step into my characters' shoes for a while, and see the world through their eyes."

When asked to state the most surprising thing she has discovered as a writer, Hassinger responded: "That I can actually write a novel. Who knew?"

BIOGRAPHICAL AND CRITICAL SOURCES:

PERIODICALS

Booklist, May 1, 2003, Gillian Engberg, review of *Nina: Adolescence,* p. 1579; November 15, 2003, Nancy Spillman, review of *Nina,* p. 616; February 15, 2006, Michele Leber, review of *The Priest's Madonna,* p. 41; October 1, 2006, Mary Frances Wilkens, review of *The Priest's Madonna,* p. 70.

Kirkus Reviews, April 15, 2003, review of *Nina,* p. 558.

Kliatt, September, 2004, Susan Allison, review of *Nina,* p. 20.

Library Journal, February 1, 2004, Nancy R. Ives, review of *Nina,* p. 142; March 1, 2006, Anna M. Nelson, review of *The Priest's Madonna,* p. 77.

Publishers Weekly, September 1, 2003, review of *Nina* p. 32; January 30, 2006, review of *The Priest's Madonna,* p. 36.

ONLINE

Amy Hassinger Home Page, http://www.amyhassinger.com (December 20, 2006), author biography.

Best Reviews, http://www.thebestreviews.com/ (December 20, 2006), Viviane Crystal, review of *The Priest's Madonna.*

LitLine: A Web site for the Independent Literary Community, http://www.litline.org/ (December 20, 2006), author biography.

*   *   *

HATCHER, Teri 1964-
(Teri Lynn Hatcher)

PERSONAL: Born December 8, 1964, in Sunnyvale, CA; daughter of Owen (a nuclear physicist) and Esther (a computer programmer) Hatcher; married Marcus Leithold, June 4, 1988 (divorced, 1989); married Jon Tenney (an actor), May 27, 1994 (divorced, March, 2003); children: (second marriage) Emerson Rose. *Education:* Attended De Anza College; trained for the stage at American Conservatory Theater, San Francisco, CA. *Hobbies and other interests:* Playing golf.

CAREER: Actress. Made television debut in an episode of *The Love Boat,* 1977; appeared as Penny Parker in the series *MacGyver,* 1985, as Lois Lane in *Lois and Clark: The New Adventures of Superman,* and as Susan Mayer in the series *Desperate Housewives,* beginning 2004; appeared in episodes of other television series. Appeared on stage as Sally Bowles in the touring production of the musical *Cabaret,* 1999. Gold Rush (cheerleaders for the San Francisco 49ers football team), cheerleader, 1984.

AWARDS, HONORS: Golden Globe Award, lead actress in a comedy series, Hollywood Foreign Press Association, and Screen Actors Guild Award, outstanding female actor in a comedy series, both c. 2005, for *Desperate Housewives;* two awards, women of the year awards, U.S. television actress of the year and special award, *Glamour,* 2005; World Actress Award, Women's World Awards, 2005.

WRITINGS:

Burnt Toast and Other Philosophies of Life (autobiography), Hyperion (New York, NY), 2006.

ADAPTATIONS: Hatcher's autobiography *Burnt Toast and Other Philosophies of Life* was released as an audiobook with the author as reader, 2006.*

*   *   *

HATCHER, Teri Lynn
See HATCHER, Teri

*   *   *

HAZELWOOD, Robin 1971(?)-

PERSONAL: Born c. 1971, in Milwaukee, WI. *Education:* Yale University, B.A., 1992; New York University, M.B.A., 1999.

ADDRESSES: Agent—Suzanne Gluck, William Morris Agency, 1325 Avenue of the Americas, New York, NY 10019.

CAREER: Model and writer. LinkShare, senior director of marketing, c. 1999-2002.

WRITINGS:

Model Student: A Tale of Co-Eds and Cover Girls, Crown (New York, NY), 2006.

SIDELIGHTS: Robin Hazelwood has had a varied professional life. As a child, she qualified for the Olympic Trials for the 100 m breaststroke in both 1984 and 1988 and started a modeling career shortly afterward. She graduated from Yale University in 1992 and continued with her international modeling career until taking up full-time studies at New York University in 1998. After graduating with an M.B.A, Hazelwood worked for an online marketing company for several years before focusing all her attention on writing.

Her first book, *Model Student: A Tale of Co-Eds and Cover Girls,* introduces Emily, a character who is based in part on Hazelwood herself. Born in Milwaukee and working her way up the modeling ladder, Emily attempts to balance her career with her studies at a top-tier university. Rebecca Vnuk, reviewing the book in the *Library Journal,* said fans of *America's Next Top Model* television show would find this book "just right." A reviewer in *Publishers Weekly* called the dialogue "bright and authentic" and noted that Emily "will have readers rooting for her all the way."

BIOGRAPHICAL AND CRITICAL SOURCES:

PERIODICALS

Kirkus Reviews, June 1, 2006, review of *Model Student: A Tale of Co-Eds and Cover Girls,* p. 537.
Library Journal, June 1, 2006, Rebecca Vnuk, review of *Model Student,* p. 110.
Publishers Weekly, May 29, 2006, review of *Model Student,* p. 38.

ONLINE

Conversations with Famous Writers Web log, http:// conversationsfamouswriters.blogspot.com/ (January 23, 2007), author interview.

Jungle Magazine, http://www.mbajungle.com/ (January 23, 2007), author profile.
Robin Hazelwood's Home Page, http://robin hazelwoodbooks.com (January 23, 2007), author biography.*

*   *   *

HEADLEY, Justina Chen 1968-

PERSONAL: Born 1968, in PA; married; children. *Education:* Stanford University, graduate; studied writing at University of Washington. *Hobbies and other interests:* Running, walking, reading, yoga.

ADDRESSES: Home—Seattle, WA. *Agent*—Steven Malk, Writers House, 21 W. 26th St., New York, NY 10010. *E-mail*—justina@justinachenheadley.com.

CAREER: Writer. Microsoft Corp., Seattle, WA, formerly worked in marketing; editor and publisher of periodicals in Sydney, New South Wales, Australia; StrataGem (consultant to nonprofit organizations), Seattle, founder; founder of scholarship contest for young writers.

MEMBER: Society of Children's Book Writers and Illustrators.

WRITINGS:

The Patch (picture book), illustrated by Mitch Vane, Charlesbridge (Watertown, MA), 2006.
Nothing but the Truth (and a Few White Lies) (young-adult novel), Little, Brown (New York, NY), 2006.
Girl Overboard (young-adult novel), Little, Brown (New York, NY), 2008.

SIDELIGHTS: Called an "impressive debut" by a *Publishers Weekly* contributor, Justina Chen Headley's young-adult novel *Nothing but the Truth (and a Few White Lies)* introduces readers to fifteen-year-old Patty Ho, a Taiwanese American whose efforts to fit in with her Caucasian schoolmates while also placating her old-world relatives are made easier to bear because of the teen's healthy sense of humor. When Patty is sent to a summer math camp at Stanford University, she finds herself on her own and free from others' expectations for the first time in her life. With the help of a caring aunt and some family photos that help her make sense of her single mom's frustration and her absent father, Patty also finds a new best friend in the self-reliant Jasmine, experiences her first kiss with the good-looking Stu, and gains a stronger sense of self. Praising Headley's use of "creative wordplay," the *Publishers Weekly* critic also cited Headley's ability to let her heroine's "lively, first-person narrative" track the girl's "emotional maturation during the course of an eventful summer," and in *Kirkus Reviews* a contributor wrote that Headley's likeable narrator "never loses her nervy bounce or her need to tell it all as it's happening." Noting Headley's focus on "those who live between two distinct cultures," *School Library Journal* reviewer Amy S. Pattee added that, with its "funny and thoughtful moments," *Nothing but the Truth (and a Few White Lies)* shows Headley's voice to be "a new and much-needed one that shows great promise."

Geared for younger readers, Headley's picture book *The Patch* was inspired by her own daughter's amblyompia. In Headley's story, five-year-old Becca is confronted by a disease of the eyes that required her to wear not only eyeglasses (yuck!), but a patch over one eye in order to see. Facing the other students in her kindergarten class is made easier when Becca, wearing purple eyeglasses and a pink eye patch, uses her vivid imagination to create a team of alter-egos. With the help of Becca the Ballerina Pirate and Becca the Private Eye, she inspires her classmates to wish for eye patches of their own. Calling *The Patch* "a lovely and surprising story" in which "Becca's exuberance shines through," *School Library Journal* reviewer Genevieve Gallagher predicted that the book would be popular with story-hour fans, while in *Booklist* Gillian Engberg described it as a "well-paced, reassuring offering on an unusual topic."

Headley, who is involved with nonprofit groups through her own company, StrataGem, donated the proceeds of her first two children's books to charitable causes; in 2006 she sponsored the Nothing but the Truth essay contest, the winner of which received a five-thousand-dollar college scholarship, and a portion of the proceeds from *The Patch* were donated to In-

fantSEE, which provides parents of infants with no-cost eye assessments.

BIOGRAPHICAL AND CRITICAL SOURCES:

PERIODICALS

Booklist, February 1, 2006, Gillian Engberg, review of *The Patch,* p. 55.
Bulletin of the Center for Children's Books, June, 2006, Loretta Gaffney, review of *Nothing but the Truth (and a Few White Lies),* p. 454.
Kirkus Reviews, January 1, 2006, review of *The Patch,* p. 42; March 15, 2006, review of *Nothing but the Truth (and a Few White Lies),* p. 291.
Publishers Weekly, January 30, 2006, review of *The Patch,* p. 69; April 10, 2006, review of *Nothing but the Truth (and a Few White Lies),* p. 72.
School Library Journal, February, 2006, Genevieve Gallagher, review of *The Patch,* p. 103; July, 2006, Amy S. Pattee, review of *Nothing but the Truth (and a Few White Lies),* p. 104.
Voice of Youth Advocates, April, 2006, Rebecca C. Moore, review of *Nothing but the Truth (and a Few White Lies),* p. 46.

ONLINE

BookLoons, http://www.bookloons.com/ (February 7, 2007), Hillary Williamson, review of *Nothing but the Truth (and a Few White Lies).*
Cynsations, http://www.cynthialeitichsmith.blogspot.com/ (January 4, 2006), Cynthia Leitich Smith, interview with Headley.
Justina Chen Headley Home Page, http://www.justinachenheadley.com (February 7, 2007).

*   *   *

HEATH-STUBBS, John 1918-2006
(John Francis Alexander Heath-Stubbs)

OBITUARY NOTICE— See index for *CA* sketch: Born July 9, 1918, in London, England; died December 26, 2006, in London, England. Author. Heath-Stubbs was a noted poet inspired by traditional forms and mythology. Born with poor eyesight, he would become completely blind by the time he was sixty. Despite this handicap, he was a prolific poet, as well as a translator, critic, and editor. As a youth, he transferred to several schools before being taught by private tutors and also attending the Worcester College for the Blind. He enrolled at Queen's College, Oxford, in 1939, where he was influenced by fellow classmate C.S. Lewis and the playwright Charles Williams. By the early 1940s, he was publishing poems in anthologies and his own collections, the first of the latter being *Wounded Thammuz* (1942). Never a slave to modern trends in verse, Heath-Stubbs followed his own muse. He enjoyed references to ancient myths and emulating epic stanzas, though he also wrote light verse and other forms. Sometimes considered unfashionable by literary critics, he was labeled a neo-Romantic whose Christian faith was evident in his writing. Though his primary focus in life was his writing, Heath-Stubbs held several jobs over the years. After work as an English master at Hall School in Hampstead from 1944 to 1945, he was an editorial assistant for *Hutchinson's Illustrated Encyclopedia* for a year. He taught at Leeds University during the early 1950s, and from 1955 to 1958 was a visiting professor at the University of Alexandria in Egypt. His academic career stabilized later in life. He was a part-time lecturer at the College of St. Mark and St. John in England from 1963 to 1972, and a tutor at Merton College, Oxford, from 1975 to 1991. Over the years, he penned almost forty poetry collections, nine translated works, seven works of criticism, and ten edited works. His memoirs were released in 1993 as *Hindsights*. Heath-Stubbs won the prestigious Queen's Gold Medal for Poetry in 1973, the Cholmondeley Award in 1989, and the Cross of St. Augustine in 1999, among other honors, and was appointed to the Order of the British Empire in 1988. Despite his lifelong struggle with failing sight, Heath-Stubbs was remembered for producing quality literary works and always maintaining a good sense of humor—as can be seen in the title of his autobiography, as well as his self-mocking poem "Epitaph." Among his notable books are the light verse collection *A Charm and a Toothache* (1954), *Selected Poems* (1966), and the epic *Artorius* (1970).

OBITUARIES AND OTHER SOURCES:

BOOKS

Heath-Stubbs, John, *Hindsights,* Hodder & Stoughton (London, England), 1993.

PERIODICALS

Times (London, England), December 30, 2006, p. 48.
Washington Post, December 27, 2006, p. B5.

*　　*　　*

HEATH-STUBBS, John Francis Alexander See HEATH-STUBBS, John

*　　*　　*

HELM, Sarah

PERSONAL: Female.

ADDRESSES: Home—London, England.

CAREER: Sunday Times, London, England, former reporter and feature writer; *Independent,* London, founding member, 1986—, became diplomatic editor, Middle East correspondent, and European correspondent.

AWARDS, HONORS: British Press Award; Laurence Stern fellowship, *Washington Post.*

WRITINGS:

A Life in Secrets: Vera Atkins and the Missing Agents of WWII, Nan A. Talese (New York, NY), 2005.

SIDELIGHTS: British journalist Sarah Helm is the author of *A Life in Secrets: Vera Atkins and the Missing Agents of WWII,* a history of a British spy who left behind documentation of her role in the Special Operations Executive (SOE) when she died in 2000. Helm met Atkins in 1998, when the latter was nearly ninety years old. Atkins was a Jew who generally passed as upper-class British, although she did experience prejudice by some who knew the truth and who tried to prevent her from advancing in her career. She had been born to a German father named Rosenberg and a South African mother, who then moved to

Romania, where she was born. Her secret was that she dealt with the Nazis herself in order to secure freedom for members of her family. After the war she was reported to have been a fierce interrogator when she became attached to the war crimes unit.

The highest-ranking female officer in the French section, Atkins, who was based in London, sent four hundred agents to France, including thirty-nine women she had recruited and supervised. Most were turned over by a double agent to the Gestapo. Atkins's incompetent superior, Maurice Buckmaster, refused to believe that the operation had failed until Hitler sent a message thanking him for the guns and cash. In 1945, after the war had ended, Atkins attempted to track down her missing "girls" by traveling to Germany and interviewing survivors and officials from the concentration camps. She did learn the fates of several, including children's book author Noor Inayat Khan, who was shot at Dachau.

Vanessa Juarez concluded in an *Entertainment Weekly* review that Atkins "was mysterious, with a lot to be mysterious about. Ms. Helm, to her great credit, digs to the very bottom of it and lays it out for the world to see." A *Publishers Weekly* contributor called *A Life in Secrets* "a searing history of female courage and suffering during WWII."

BIOGRAPHICAL AND CRITICAL SOURCES:

PERIODICALS

Booklist, August 1, 2006, Gilbert Taylor, review of *A Life in Secrets: Vera Atkins and the Missing Agents of WWII,* p. 31.

Contemporary Review, summer, 2006, Edward Bradbury, review of *A Life in Secrets,* p. 251.

Economist, August 6, 2005, review of *A Life in Secrets,* p. 69.

Entertainment Weekly, August 25, 2006, Vanessa Juarez, review of *A Life in Secrets,* p. 89.

Kirkus Reviews, June 1, 2006, review of *A Life in Secrets,* p. 557.

Library Journal, June 15, 2006, Ed Goedeken, review of *A Life in Secrets,* p. 82.

New Statesman, June 6, 2005, Paul Laity, review of *A Life in Secrets,* p. 52.

New York Times, August 30, 2006, William Grimes, review of *A Life in Secrets.*

Pittsburgh Post-Gazette, October 29, 2006, Peter B. King, review of *A Life in Secrets.*

Publishers Weekly, April 17, 2006, review of *A Life in Secrets,* p. 173.*

*   *   *

HERINGA MASON, Marcia J. 1945-

PERSONAL: Born January 24, 1945, in Chicago, IL; daughter of John (in sales) and Johanna (a homemaker) Heringa; married William C. De Vries (divorced June, 1992); married Philip P. Mason (a historian and professor), March 12, 1993; children: (first marriage) Heather Leigh De Vries Briody, Cori Jo De Vries Vanderley, Rachel Suzanne De Vries Sterner. *Education:* Trinity Christian College, A.A., 1966; Spring Arbor College, B.A., 1990; Wayne State University, M.A., 1995. *Politics:* Democrat. *Religion:* Protestant. *Hobbies and other interests:* Birding, gardening, geology, natural history, Navajo culture, textile history.

ADDRESSES: Home—Prescott, AZ; Dearborn, MI. *E-mail*—mhmhistory@aol.com.

CAREER: Teacher at a day school in El Paso, TX, 1982-87; Edsel and Eleanor Ford House, Grosse Pointe Shores, MI, public relations and marketing director, 1988-93; Henry Ford Museum, Dearborn, MI, interpreter and archivist, 1993-97; Ford Motor Co., Dearborn, archivist, 1997-2000; Desert Caballeros Western Museum, Wickenburg, AZ, marketing and exhibit manager, 2001-03; writer and oral historian, 2003—. Sharlot Hall Museum Archives, volunteer; member of Henry Ford Museum, Sharlot Hall Museum, Smoki Museum, and Northern Arizona Museum.

MEMBER: National Wildlife Federation, Nature Conservancy, National Trust for Historic Preservation, Audubon Society, Grand Canyon Association.

WRITINGS:

(Editor) *Remember the Distance That Divides Us: The Family Letters of Philadelphia Quaker Abolition-*

ist and Michigan Pioneer, Elizabeth Margaret Chandler, 1830-1842, Michigan State University Press (East Lansing, MI), 2005.

SIDELIGHTS: Marcia J. Heringa Mason told *CA:* "My motivation for editing *Remember the Distance That Divides Us: The Family Letters of Philadelphia Quaker Abolitionist and Michigan Pioneer, Elizabeth Margaret Chandler, 1830-1842* was to make available to a wide audience the remarkable story of Elizabeth Margaret Chandler. The book is a significant contribution to the history of women and to life in Philadelphia and frontier Michigan in the 1830s.

"My writing process involves extensive research in the relevant subjects surrounding the story, oral history interviews, then writing a narrative that both teaches and draws the reader into the subject's life. I am particularly motivated to offer history from the bottom up, especially from a woman's perspective."

*   *   *

HEWARD, Edmund 1912-2006
(Edmund Rawlings Heward)

OBITUARY NOTICE— See index for *CA* sketch: Born August 19, 1912, in London, England; died December 11, 2006. Attorney and author. A former chief master of the British Supreme Court, Heward was also noted for writing biographies and books on the law. After suffering measles as a teenager, his hearing was severely impaired. Nevertheless, he graduated from Trinity College, Cambridge, with a master's in 1933. He enlisted in the Royal Artillery during World War II, serving as an antiaircraft gunner in England and then in India, where he rose to the rank of major. After the war, he was a partner in the law firm of Rose, Johnson & Hicks. In 1959 he earned his Supreme Court post as master of the Chancery Division. He was chief master from 1980 until 1985, when he retired. Heward was the admired author of the law book *Guide to Chancery Practice* (1962; 5th edition, 1979), but also wrote several respected biographies on English justices. Among these are *The Great and the Good: A Life of Lord Radcliffe* (1994) and *A Victorian Law Reformer: A Life of Lord Selborne* (1998).

OBITUARIES AND OTHER SOURCES:

PERIODICALS

Times (London, England), February 14, 2007, p. 67.

HEWARD, Edmund Rawlings
See HEWARD, Edmund

*   *   *

HOLDEN, Kate 1972-

PERSONAL: Born 1972, in Melbourne, Victoria, Australia; daughter of Geoffrey and Margot Holden. *Education:* University of Melbourne, honours degree in classics and literature, graduate diploma in professional writing and editing.

CAREER: Author, 2005—. Formerly a sex worker in St. Kilda, Australia.

WRITINGS:

In My Skin: A Memoir, Arcade (New York, NY), 2005.

SIDELIGHTS: Kate Holden's *In My Skin: A Memoir* is, in the words of Allison Block writing in *Booklist,* a "breathtakingly candid memoir" recounting her years as a heroin addict and sex worker in suburban St. Kilda, Victoria, Australia. Two things, however, make Holden's story stand out from those of thousands of women in similar circumstances around the world: first, she was the daughter of middle-class parents, a college graduate with a solid job when she became addicted, and second, she took on the job of prostitute as a career, built a sense of self-esteem on it, and eventually was able to break her addiction. "Her depictions of the dark realities she lived through are at times graphic," declared a *Publishers Weekly* reviewer, ". . . but always clear-eyed."

Later Holden went back to college, earned a graduate degree in writing, and began work on her memoir—in part, she said in an Australian Broadcasting Corporation interview with Joanna Murray-Smith, because she "had a really strong impulse to communicate my story to people." "I felt really strongly that there weren't very many stories that were told by people who had actually overcome heroin addiction or drug addiction," she continued. "And it was partly out of a desire to show people what it was really like being a prostitute." "I don't believe prostitution itself is inherently exploitative, but it can be," Holden concluded in her *Readings* interview. "I found my own experience, ultimately, empowering."

BIOGRAPHICAL AND CRITICAL SOURCES:

BOOKS

Holden, Kate, *In My Skin: A Memoir,* Arcade (New York, NY), 2005.

PERIODICALS

Age (Melbourne, Australia), September 17, 2005, Juliette Hughes, "East of Time."

Asia Africa Intelligence Wire, October 9, 2005, "Descent into Heroin Hell: A Writer's Tale"; October 15, 2005, Ceridwen Spark, "A Close Look at the Oldest Trick in the Book."

Booklist, October 1, 2006, Allison Block, review of *In My Skin: A Memoir,* p.12.

Europe Intelligence Wire, May 6, 2006, "A College Girl in the Skin Trade."

Kirkus Reviews, August 15, 2006, review of *In My Skin,* p. 822.

Library Journal, October 1, 2006, Elizabeth Brinkley, review of *In My Skin,* p. 94.

New Statesman, June 19, 2006, Mary Fitzgerald, "Like a True Professional," p. 67.

Observer (London, England), May 14, 2006, Stephanie Merritt, "A Beautiful Loser Makes Good."

Publishers Weekly, October 2, 2006, review of *In My Skin,* p. 52.

ONLINE

Australian Broadcasting Corporation, http://www.abc.net.au/ (December 27, 2006), Joanna Murray-Smith, "Leaving Lucy."

Canberra Review Online, http://www.canberrareview.com.au/ (December 27, 2006), Rebekah Beare, review of *In My Skin.*

Readings, http://www.readings.com.au/ (December 27, 2006), author interview.*

*   *   *

HOLLOWAY, Kris

PERSONAL: Born in Granville, OH; married John Bidwell; children: two sons. *Education:* Alleghany College, B.A.; University of Michigan, M.P.H.

ADDRESSES: *Home*—Northampton, MA. *E-mail*—kris@moniquemangorains.com.

CAREER: Served in the Peace Corps in Mali, 1989-91; consultant to nonprofit organizations, educational institutions, and businesses; fundraiser for the National Priorities Project.

WRITINGS:

Monique and the Mango Rains: Two Years with a Midwife in Mali (memoir), Waveland Press (Long Grove, IL), 2007.

SIDELIGHTS: Kris Holloway spent two years in the Peace Corps stationed in Mali, beginning in 1989, where she first intended to apply her skills as a forestry and natural resources expert. Instead of planting trees, however, she soon found herself assisting twenty-four-year-old midwife Monique Dembele. Holloway, who was twenty-two, lived with Monique, and the women forged a strong friendship in spite of their differences. Monique was in charge of all births and cared for the often malnourished expectant mothers in her makeshift clinic in the village of Nampossela, as well as for the population in general. The women had no form of birth control and often suffered malnourishment and physical exhaustion in a village without electricity, running water, or the most basic of medical equipment. Many were abused and exploited. Monique was in an arranged marriage, and the men of her family often took her pay. She died during the birth of her fifth child. Her story of poverty and struggle is representative of other women in many parts of Africa, and one which Holloway began to write about after returning to Mali in 1999. *Monique and the Mango Rains: Two Years with a Midwife in Mali* is a memoir honoring her friend. "Holloway does not disguise the realities of life in a poor rural African village, and yet she is never condescending," reported a *Kirkus Reviews* contributor. "While Holloway's story is a personal one . . . the rhythm of life and death in Mali itself shines through all the pages," concluded Mary Grace Flaherty in *Library Journal.*

BIOGRAPHICAL AND CRITICAL SOURCES:

BOOKS

Holloway, Kris, *Monique and the Mango Rains: Two Years with a Midwife in Mali,* Waveland Press (Long Grove, IL), 2007.

PERIODICALS

Entertainment Weekly, Abby West, review of *Monique and the Mango Rains,* p. 82.

Kirkus Reviews, June 15, 2006, review of *Monique and the Mango Rains,* p. 616.

Library Journal, September 15, 2006, Mary Grace Flaherty, review of *Monique and the Mango Rains,* p. 77.

Publishers Weekly, May 15, 2006, review of *Monique and the Mango Rains,* p. 56.

ONLINE

Kris Holloway Home Page, http://www.monique mangorains.com (January 11, 2006).

Peace Corps Online, http://peacecorpsonline.org/ (August 28, 2006), Sonja Brodie, review of *Monique and the Mango Rains.*

Peace Corps Writers, http://peacecorpswriters.org/ (June 9, 2006), interview with Kris Holloway.

*   *   *

HUNT, Laird

PERSONAL: Married Eleni Sikelianos (a poet); children: Eva Grace. *Education:* Naropa University, M.F.A.; has also studied at the Sorbonne.

ADDRESSES: Home—Boulder, CO. *E-mail*—lairdhunt@earthlink.net.

CAREER: Denver University, Denver, CO, faculty member in creative writing program. Former United Nations press officer. Has been a resident at the MacDowell Colony and the Camargo Foundation, Cassis, France.

WRITINGS:

FICTION

The Paris Stories (short stories), Smokeproof Press (Boulder, CO), 2000.

The Impossibly (novel), Coffee House Press (Minneapolis, MN), 2001.

(Editor) Gojmir Polajnar, *Don't Kill Anyone, I Love You,* translated by Aaron Gillies, Spuyten Duyvil (New York, NY), 2001.

Indiana, Indiana: (The Dark and Lovely Portions of the Night) (novel), Coffee House Press (Minneapolis, MN), 2003.

The Exquisite (novel), Coffee House Press (Minneapolis, MN), 2006.

Contributor to periodicals, including *Ploughshares, McSweeney's, Fence, Mentor, Unculte, Zoum Zoum, Brick, Conjunctions,* and *Bomb.*

SIDELIGHTS: A creative writing instructor who is the author of short stories and novels, Laird Hunt is known for composing fiction that is experimental and challenging to audiences. Admitting to Andrew Ervin in an interview on the *Bookslut* Web site that "the reader does need to pull out a mental dance step or two to avoid tripping up" in such works as *The Exquisite.* The author made no apologies and felt that many readers could negotiate his subtle and recondite narratives. "I do think there are far more readers up for the unexpected than we tend to imagine," Laird asserted, "and that some few of them might be willing to follow along with a narrator who can't quite get the who, what, where, when and how to function as much more than a jumble and who, on top of it, has more than one version of events to propose."

In his debut novel, *The Impossibly,* Laird is never direct about just what is happening in the plot and why. Apparently, the unnamed narrator and all the other characters he meets are, in one way or another, associated with some sort of powerful and often nefarious organization that rules their lives. Referred to only as "the organization," the book never says what the organization does or why it often tortures or kills people. The narrator begins his tale as a pawn of the organization, but, through his love for a woman that he eventually loses, resolves later in his life to break off his ties to the organization. Even conversations and events in the novel are obscure, and Laird leaves the mysteries up to his readers to resolve. Within the basic progression of the story, the narrator jumps around chronologically, and his thoughts are desultory as well. "This interruptive narrative seems to be an accurate map of the human mind trying to make sense of the world," theorized Kelly Everding in a *Rain Taxi* Web site review. The critic concluded that Laird's debut "is a challenging and inventive work, alternately chilling and humorous, that breaks new ground in the world of speculative fiction."

Laird's novel *The Exquisite* is no less difficult to figure out. Set shortly after the 9/11 terrorist attacks of 2001, the story features two alternating plotlines that seem to feature the same characters in different forms. In one story, a thief named Henry is enamored of the sexy Tulip, who asks him to steal something from the apartment of a man named Kindt. It is Kindt's business to arrange the fake demises of his clients, but now he seems to ask Henry to "kill" him. In the other story, Tulip is a doctor at a hospital, with Henry and Kindt as her patients. Whether the two tales are related is unclear; neither is it clear whether or not these are the same people. It could be that Henry has gone insane, perhaps because of something that happened during the attacks, or maybe not. In a way, the confusion of the story reflects the confusion in America that followed the September 11 terrorist acts. "*The Exquisite* is an excellent exploration of a shattered life," attested Carrie Jones on the *KGBBar* Web site. "Hunt's two compellingly imagined shards suggest so many others in such a way as to almost command the reader to question his or her own sense of just what has happened in the last five years." Matthew Tiffany, writing for the *Pop Matters* Web site, concluded: "This is an exceptionally well-written and well-constructed story. . . . Hunt has an easy mastery of noir, and the sheer joy with which he tells this story is addictive. His sentences stretch out with wonderful, funny word choices that come across as perfectly fitting coming from the mouth of a man who finds great delight in holding forth (at length) on the luminescence of herring."

BIOGRAPHICAL AND CRITICAL SOURCES:

ONLINE

Bookslut, http://www.bookslut.com/ (December 1, 2006), Andrew Ervin, "An Interview with Laird Hunt."
KGBBar, http://www.kgbbar.com/ (January 17, 2007), Carrie Jones, review of *The Exquisite.*

Laird Hunt Home Page, http://lairdhunt.net (January 17, 2007).
Pop Matters, http://www.popmatters.com/ (January 17, 2007), Matthew Tiffany, review of *The Exquisite.*
Rain Taxi, http://www.raintaxi.com/ (January 17, 2007), Kelly Everding, review of *The Impossibly.*

*   *   *

HUSSEY, Andrew 1963-

PERSONAL: Born in 1963, in Liverpool, England.

ADDRESSES: Office—Department of French and Comparative Studies, University of London Institute in Paris, 9-11 Rue de Constantine, Cedex 97, Paris 75340, France. *E-mail*—a.hussey@ulip.lon.ac.uk.

CAREER: Historian and author. University of Wales, Aberystwyth, lecturer in politics and French literature; University of London Institute, Paris, France, head of French and comparative studies. British Council, Morocco, began as writer-in-residence, 2002, became director of Trans-Mahgreb Creative Writing Project; Abdemaalik University, Tetouan, Morocco, visitng professor of intercultural studies.

AWARDS, HONORS: British Council writer-in-residence for Morocco, 2004-05.

WRITINGS:

The Inner Scar: The Mysticism of Georges Bataille (religious studies), Rodopi (Atlanta, GA), 2000.
The Game of War: The Life and Death of Guy Debord (biography), J. Cape (London, England), 2001.
(Editor) *The Beast at Heaven's Gate: Georges Bataille and the Art of Transgression,* Rodopi (New York, NY), 2006.
Paris: The Secret History, Bloomsbury (New York, NY), 2007.

Author of weekly column for *New Statesman.* Contributor to periodicals, including the *Observer.*

SIDELIGHTS: Andrew Hussey's *Paris: The Secret History* examines the hidden life of the City of Light throughout the two thousand years of its existence.

Instead of concentrating on major figures of the city's history, however, he looks at "Paris from the perspective of the city's marginal and subversive elements—insurrectionists, criminals, immigrants and sexual outsiders," explained a *Publishers Weekly* contributor. "He guides us through important French poetry, novels, films, music—but also along the rivers of blood running in the streets in just about every century," said a *Kirkus Reviews* contributor. "On every page," critic Tim Martin wrote in the *Independent,* "fragments of sinister trivia and captivating alternative histories bob up with the regularity of the corpses that have thronged the Seine since the time of the Parisii." "Paris may be the world's favorite city," Donald Morrison reported in *Time International,* "but few of the 25 million annual visitors realize that its handsome streets are paved with blood and *merde.*"

Many critics—and Hussey himself—have compared *Paris* to Peter Ackroyd's *London: The Biography,* another history that examines a major world city through the lives of colorful characters and criminal elements. Through much of the city's history, Hussey reports, Paris was ruled directly by the kings of France. Personalities—like Charles VI, who labored under the impression that he was made of glass and wore clothes interwoven with iron bars to prevent breakage, and Henri III, who threw his jester into prison for telling him that poor people lived in Paris—play a prominent role in Hussey's story. Like Ackroyd's volume, Martin wrote, *Paris* "brims with rubbernecker's trouvailles. Breaking off from an erudite passage on the Templars, for example, he moves seamlessly to a description of the present-day Bar-Tabac des Templiers, where members of the Milice du Christ rub shoulders with Dan Brown dilettantes to debate the mysteries of the Order."

"Hussey's sympathies lie far more with the working class, the drunkards, bohemians, decadents and *flâneurs* of Paris than with the clichéd and commodified picture-postcard city," Ian Pindar wrote in the *Guardian.* "He is more interested in Belleville or Les Halles than in the 'sterile grandeur' of Versailles. He is also a sympathetic guide to *les événements* of May 1968 and reminds us that the first major student unrest in Paris took place in 1229, so it's a venerable tradition." "Paris teems with characters straight out of a novel by Honore de Balzac, Victor Hugo or Emile Zola," Morrison stated, "who are themselves among the book's colorful players." Hussey comes to the conclusion, Marie Marmo Mullaney explained in the *Library Journal,* that in the final analysis the "'typical' Parisian" was a myth, "and that for its first 1000 years Paris was not a great or beautiful city." "This book," concluded *New York Times* contributor Alan Riding, "is a lengthy reminder that urban history is about artisans, criminals, conspirators, prostitutes, priests, immigrants, students and intellectuals no less than emperors, kings and presidents."

Hussey told *CA:* "I've always been keen on French writers—the novels that had an impact on me as a teenager were by Albert Camus and then Louis-Ferdinand Céline. It's hard to say why this was so. I grew up in the suburbs of Liverpool and in cultural and political terms couldn't have been further from Paris or North Africa, where my career has taken me. I suppose it was intellectual curiosity and a desire to go beyond my immediate surroundings that drove me on—a familiar scenario for any writer I think. I am also an admirer of Georges Bataille who, apart from being known as a dedicated erotomane, was obsessed by the idea of transcendence in writing—to some extent that is what drives me on, pretentious as it may sound. These days I am a big fan of the Spanish writer Juan Goytisolo, whose work crosses boundaries all the time, and the Scottish singer and writer Momus, who always manages to be perverse, tender, and clever all at once. I think the best poet currently at work in English is Mark E Smith."

When asked to state the most surprising thing he has learned as a writer, Hussey said: "The sheer hard work is no surprise. The big business of publishing is really no surprise either. The fickle pace of change in journalism is also well known. But the pettiness and jealousy of other writers can come as a shock. I was also surprised by how nerve-wracking and exhausting the whole business of publication and promotion can be. Like most writers, I want to be read and known but find self-promotion vaguely unsettling."

When asked what effect he hopes his books will have, Hussey said: "Pleasure. People seem to think that any entertaining book is either cheap or rubbish or intellectually insignificant; I'd like to prove that the opposite is the case."

BIOGRAPHICAL AND CRITICAL SOURCES:

PERIODICALS

Guardian, July 8, 2006, Ian Pindar, "The Hidden City: Ian Pindar Enjoys Andrew Hussey's Tour of the Erogenous Zones of Paris."

Independent, July 16, 2006, Tim Martin, review of *Paris: The Secret History.*

Kirkus Reviews, October 15, 2006, review of *Paris,* p. 1057.

Library Journal, November 15, 2006, Marie Marmo Mullaney, review of *Paris,* p. 78.

New York Times, December 21, 2006, Alan Riding, "Paris from the Beginning: More Than a City of Light."

Publishers Weekly, October 16, 2006, review of *Paris,* p. 44.

Time International, July 17, 2006, Donald Morrison, "City of Light's Dark Side," p. 45.

I-J

ISIN, Engin F. 1959-
(Engin Fahri Isin)

PERSONAL: Born 1959. *Education:* University of Toronto, Ph.D.

ADDRESSES: Office—Urban Studies Program, York University, 305 Calumet College, Downsview, Ontario M3J 1P3, Canada.

CAREER: York University, Downsview, Ontario, Canada, professor of urban studies and Canada Research Chair for the arts, 2001-06; Open University, Milton Keynes, England, professor of politics, chair in citizenship, and director of the Centre for Citizenship, Identities, and Governance, 2007—

WRITINGS:

Cities without Citizens: Modernity of the City as a Corporation, Black Rose Books (Montreal, Quebec, Canada), 1992.

(Editor) *Toronto Region in the World Economy* (symposium proceedings), Urban Studies Program, York University (Downsview, Ontario, Canada), 1994.

(With Thomas Osborne and Nikolas Rose) *Governing Cities: Liberalism, Neoliberalism, Advanced Liberalism,* Urban Studies Program, York University (Downsview, Ontario, Canada), 1998.

(With Patricia K. Wood) *Citizenship and Identity,* Sage Publications (London, England), 1999.

(Editor) *Democracy, Citizenship, and the Global City,* Routledge (London, England), 2000.

(Editor, with Bryan S. Turner) *Handbook of Citizenship Studies,* Sage Publications (London, England), 2002.

Being Political: Genealogies of Citizenship, University of Minnesota Press (Minneapolis, MN), 2002.

(Editor, with Gerard Delanty) *Handbook of Historical Sociology,* Sage Publications (London, England), 2003.

Chief editor, *Citizenship Studies.* Contributor to periodicals and books.

BIOGRAPHICAL AND CRITICAL SOURCES:

PERIODICALS

Canadian Journal of Urban Research, winter, 2002, Patti Tamara Lenard, review of *Being Political: Genealogies of Citizenship,* p. 363.

ONLINE

Engin F. Isin Home Page, http://www.enginfisin.eu (May 10, 2007).

Open University Web site, http://www.open.ac.uk/ (May 10, 2007), faculty profile of author.

*   *   *

ISIN, Engin Fahri
See ISIN, Engin F.

JACKSON, Rob 1961-
(Robert Bradley Jackson)

PERSONAL: Born 1961; married; children: Robert, David, Will. *Education:* Rice University, B.S., 1983; Utah State University, M.S. (ecology), 1990, M.S. (statistics), 1992, Ph.D., 1992.

ADDRESSES: Home and office—Durham, NC. *Office*—Department of Biology and Nicholas School of the Environment, Duke University, Box 91000, B226, LSRC, Durham, NC 27708-1000. *E-mail*—jackson@duke.edu.

CAREER: Writer. Dow Chemical Company, chemical engineer for four years; Stanford University, Distinguished Postdoctoral Fellow for Global Change; University of Texas, assistant professor; Duke University, Durham, NC, professor and director of Center on Global Change.

AWARDS, HONORS: Murray F. Buell Award, Ecological Society of America, 1990; Presidential Early Career Award in Science and Engineering, National Science Foundation, 1999.

WRITINGS:

(Coeditor) *Methods in Ecosystem Science,* Springer Publishing (New York, NY), 2000.
The Earth Remains Forever: Generations at a Crossroads, foreword by John Graves, University of Texas Press (Austin, TX), 2002.
Animal Mischief: Poems (for children), illustrations by Laura Jacobsen, Boyds Mills Press (Honesdale, PA), 2006.

SIDELIGHTS: Rob Jackson has a rather unusual resume for a children's author: in fact, he had already established himself as a biological and environmental researcher when he wrote his first children's book, *Animal Mischief: Poems.* A professor of biology at Duke University with numerous peer-reviewed scientific publications and several awards to his credit, Jackson became a children's writer only by chance. While on sabbatical in Argentina with his family, Jackson wrote poems to entertain his two oldest sons, then aged seven and nine. "It was a way of passing time while we traveled," the author noted in an online interview for Duke University's *News and Communications.* When his verses met with his sons' enthusiasm, Jackson was inspired to consider them for publication. Grounded in science, each of the collection's eighteen poems profiles a single creature, providing fascinating information for imaginative future scientists.

"I wanted the poems to be fun for the reader," Jackson explained to the *News and Communications* interviewer, "but I also wanted the kids to learn something." To add to the informational value of *Animal Mischief* he includes an afterword in which he presents in-depth details about each species featured. In *Kirkus Reviews,* a critic praised *Animal Mischief* as a collection of "sly, humorous animal poems," the reviewer predicting that Jackson's poetry "will tickle the funny bone of young readers." Dubbing Jackson's short poems "witty," Carolyn Phelan wrote in *Booklist* that while poetry collections focusing on animals are not exactly a rare species within children's literature, "few so successfully integrate zoology with amusing verse" as Jackson does in *Animal Mischief.*

BIOGRAPHICAL AND CRITICAL SOURCES:

PERIODICALS

Booklist, April 1, 2006, Carolyn Phelan, review of *Animal Mischief: Poems,* p. 45.
Kirkus Reviews, March 1, 2006, review of *Animal Mischief,* p. 232.
Quarterly Review of Biology, December, 2003, Marty Condon, review of *The Earth Remains Forever: Generations at a Crossroads,* p. 495.
School Library Journal, May, 2006, Carol L. Mackay, review of *Animal Mischief,* p. 112.
Virginia Quarterly Review, spring, 2003, review of *The Earth Remains Forever,* p. 63.

ONLINE

Duke University News and Communications Online, http://dukenews.duke.edu/ (January 4, 2007), "Duke Biologist/Poet Is Up to 'Animal Mischief.'"

Rob Jackson Home Page, http://fds.duke.edu/ (January 4, 2007).*

*   *   *

JACKSON, Robert Bradley
See JACKSON, Rob

*   *   *

JACOBSEN, John Kurt 1949-

PERSONAL: Born 1949.

ADDRESSES: Office—Department of Political Science, University of Chicago, Chicago, IL 60637.

CAREER: University of Chicago, Chicago, IL, research associate in political science.

WRITINGS:

Chasing Progress in the Irish Republic: Ideology, Democracy, and Dependent Development, Cambridge University Press (New York, NY), 1994.
Dead Reckonings: Ideas, Interests, and Politics in the "Information Age" (collected essays), Humanities Press (Atlantic Highlands, NJ), 1997.
Technical Fouls: Democratic Dilemmas and Technological Change, Westview Press (Boulder, CO), 2000.
(Editor, with Lloyd I. Rudolph) *Experiencing the State,* Oxford University Press (New Delhi, India), 2006.

BIOGRAPHICAL AND CRITICAL SOURCES:

PERIODICALS

Bulletin of the Atomic Scientists, March, 2001, Michael S. Reidy, review of *Technical Fouls: Democratic Dilemmas and Technological Change,* p. 75.

Perspectives on Political Science, spring, 2001, Carl Grafton, review of *Technical Fouls.*

ONLINE

H-Net: Humanities and Social Sciences Online, http://h-net.org/ (February, 1998), review of *Dead Reckonings: Ideas, Interests, and Politics in the "Information Age."**

*   *   *

JACOBY, Sanford M. 1953-
(Sanford Mark Jacoby)

PERSONAL: Born May 13, 1953, in New York, NY; married, 1984; children: two. *Education:* University of Pennsylvania, A.B., 1974; University of California, Berkeley, Ph.D., 1981.

ADDRESSES: Office—University of California, Los Angeles, Los Angeles, CA, 90095-1481; fax: 310-825-0218. *E-mail*—sanford.jacoby@anderson.ucla.edu.

CAREER: Economics historian, educator, writer, and editor. University of California, Los Angeles, professor, 1980—, Sanford M. Jacoby Howard Noble professor of management and vice chairman, associate director of the Institute of Industrial Relations. Former economic and business historian for the U.S. Department of Labor. Visiting scholar, Cornell University, Meiji University, and the University of Tokyo.

MEMBER: National Academy of Social Insurance.

AWARDS, HONORS: George R. Terry Book Award, Academy of Management, 1986; National Endowment for the Humanities fellowship, 1990; Philip Taft Prize in Labor History, 1998; Piper Memorial Lecturer, Chicago-Kent Law School, 1999; Abe fellow, Japan Foundation and Social Science Research Council, 2000.

WRITINGS:

Employing Bureaucracy: Managers, Unions, and the Transformation of Work in American Industry, 1900-1945, Columbia University Press (New

York, NY), 1985, revised edition published as *Employing Bureaucracy: Managers, Unions, and the Transformation of Work in the 20th Century,* Lawrence Erlbaum (Mahwah, NJ), 2004.

(Editor) *Masters to Managers: Historical and Comparative Perspectives on American Employers,* Columbia University Press (New York, NY), 1991.

(Editor) *The Workers of Nations: Industrial Relations in a Global Economy,* Oxford University Press (New York, NY), 1995.

Modern Manors: Welfare Capitalism Since the New Deal, Princeton University Press (Princeton, NJ), 1997.

The Embedded Corporation: Corporate Governance and Employment Relations in Japan and the United States, Princeton University Press (Princeton, NJ), 2005.

Coeditor of *Comparative Labor Law and Policy Journal;* serves on numerous editorial boards, including *California Management Review, Enterprise & Society, Industrial Relations, Labor History,* and *Work & Occupations.*

SIDELIGHTS: Sanford M. Jacoby is an economics historian whose primary research and writing interests are twentieth-century U.S. business, economic, and labor history. In his book *Modern Manors: Welfare Capitalism since the New Deal,* the author presents a business history that focuses on labor relations in non-union companies with the goal of exploring welfare capitalism, primarily from the 1920s through the 1950s. Focusing on Kodak, Sears, and Thompson Products, the author chronicles how the idea of welfare capitalism virtually disappeared in the 1930s—due to the economic turmoil caused by the Great Depression—only to reemerge in the 1940s. Writing in the *Business History Review,* Sven Beckert noted that "all three companies created viable labor relations that helped forge a workforce strongly attached to their employers, and that succeeded in keeping away organized labor." Similarly, *Business History* contributor Joseph Melling noted: "Jacoby shows how each firm adapted to the conditions of the Depression and sought to develop practices which would enable the corporate structure to encompass the legal requirements of the New Deal years whilst also providing workers with a strategic reason to remain loyal to the enterprise." In his book, the author also details how welfare capitalism changed from the 1920s to its reemergence in the 1940s and also discusses subsequent changes to the philosophy in the later part of the century.

In his review of *Modern Manors,* Beckert called the book "a tour de force, taking readers on a journey through the largely unexplored universe of labor relations." Beckert went on to note: "It is business history, at its best, firmly rooting the analysis of company policies in discussions of the macroeconomic environment, the history of labor and its institutions, and employers' collective action and politics." In a review in the *Administrative Science Quarterly,* Larry W. Hunter wrote: "In *Modern Manors,* Jacoby sets out to amend our understanding of welfare capitalism and succeeds admirably." Hunter added: "The significance of his work, however, goes beyond the history itself. In *Modern Manors,* the roles of managers and their ideologies get their due: the subtle ways they differ across companies, change over time, and influence outcomes and practices of critical importance to their workforces." *American Journal of Sociology* contributor Christopher Howard wrote: "Leaving readers wanting to know more is often the sign of good scholarship, and *Modern Manors* is a very good book. Each case study weaves together developments internal to the company, in the relevant industry, in unionized firms, and in Washington—no mean feat."

In his 2005 book *The Embedded Corporation: Corporate Governance and Employment Relations in Japan and the United States,* Jacoby delves into the question of whether different types of capitalism are becoming more similar due to globalization. His research and analysis focus on senior human relations executives in large U.S. and Japanese corporations. Gary Herrigel, writing in *Enterprise & Society,* commented: "This is a very interesting examination of the fate of human relations (HR) departments."

BIOGRAPHICAL AND CRITICAL SOURCES:

PERIODICALS

Administrative Science Quarterly, December, 1999, Larry W. Hunter, review of *Modern Manors: Welfare Capitalism since the New Deal,* p. 826; March, 2005, Emilio J. Castilla, review of *The Embedded Corporation: Corporate Governance and Employment Relations in Japan and the United States,* pp. 143-148.

American Journal of Sociology, November, 1998, Christopher Howard, review of *Modern Manors,* p. 946.

American Political Science Review, December, 1998, Charles Noble, review of *Modern Manors,* p. 946.

British Journal of Industrial Relations, December, 2005, Frank Dobbin, review of *The Embedded Corporation,* pp. 569-576.

Business History Review, summer, 1999, Sven Beckert, review of *Modern Manors,* p. 300.

Business History, April, 1999, Joseph Melling, review of *Modern Manors,* p. 151.

Enterprise & Society, March, 2006, Gary Herrigel, review of *The Embedded Corporation,* pp. 181-183.

Journal of Economic Issues, December, 1998, Dell Champlin, review of *Modern Manors,* p. 1200.

Journal of Industrial Relations, December, 2005, Peter Waring, review of *The Embedded Corporation,* pp. 484-486.

Journal of Socio-Economics, Volume 36, 2007, John W. Budd, review of *The Embedded Corporation,* pp. 161-165.

Labor History, August, 1998, Jeffrey Haydu, review of *Modern Manors,* p. 347.

ONLINE

Department of History UCLA Web site, http://www.history.ucla.edu/ (January 21, 2007), faculty profile of author.

* * *

JACOBY, Sanford Mark
   See JACOBY, Sanford M.

* * *

JENNINGS, Ken 1974-

PERSONAL: Born 1974, near Seattle, WA; married Mindy Boam (a preschool teacher); children: Dylan. *Education:* Attended University of Washington for a year; Brigham Young University, B.A., B.S., 2000. *Religion:* Mormon

ADDRESSES: Home—WA. *Agent*—Jud Laghi, LJK Literary Management, 708 3rd Ave., 16th Fl., New York, NY 10017.

CAREER: Worked for CompHealth, Salt Lake City, UT, software engineer; National Academic Quiz Tournaments, freelance question writer.

WRITINGS:

Brainiac: Adventures in the Curious, Competitive, Compulsive World of Trivia Buffs, Villard (New York, NY), 2006.

SIDELIGHTS: Ken Jennings is best known for being the contestant to maintain his *Jeopardy!* champion status for seventy-five consecutive weeks before finally relinquishing his podium. A software engineer from Utah, Jennings was born in Washington state, but grew up abroad, living primarily in Korea and Singapore with his family. After attending the University of Washington for a year, Jennings took time off to spend two years in Madrid, Spain, on a Mormon mission. He then returned to the United States and completed his education at Brigham Young University. Jennings was fascinated with pop culture even as a child and, after graduating, began writing questions for the National Academic Quiz Tournaments on a freelance basis. He also went to work as a software engineer, and was employed by CompHealth in Salt Lake City, Utah, when he became a *Jeopardy!* contestant in 2004. Jennings has written about his own adventures and the world of trivia on the whole in his book, *Brainiac: Adventures in the Curious, Competitive, Compulsive World of Trivia Buffs.* He analyzes the reasons why people are so fascinated with trivia, including his own personal experiences and interviews with other trivia experts, as well as the history of this area of pop culture, while including trivia challenges for readers. A contributor for *Kirkus Reviews* called the book "a report from the contestant's podium of particular interest to anyone who endeavors to become a human equivalent of Google." Lev Grossman, in a review for *Time,* remarked: "Jennings is actually a very charming, insightful writer. Instead of obsessing about the Streak, he explores the wider subculture of trivia."

BIOGRAPHICAL AND CRITICAL SOURCES:

BOOKS

Jennings, Ken, *Brainiac: Adventures in the Curious, Competitive, Compulsive World of Trivia Buffs,* Villard (New York, NY), 2006.

PERIODICALS

Entertainment Weekly, September 15, 2006, Ken Tucker, "Trivial Pursuits," review of *Brainiac,* p. 78.

Kirkus Reviews, May 15, 2006, review of *Brainiac,* p. S16; June 1, 2006, review of *Brainiac,* p. 557.

Library Journal, September 15, 2006, Jennifer Zarr, review of *Brainiac,* p. 77.

Publishers Weekly, May 29, 2006, review of *Brainiac,* p. 45.

Time, September 25, 2006, Lev Grossman, "Obsessive Nerds for $1,000, Alex" review of *Brainiac,* p. 83.

ONLINE

Ken Jennings Home Page, http://www.ken-jennings.com (January 29, 2007).*

*   *   *

JOHNSON, Cynthia
   See RICHARDSON, Evelyn

*   *   *

JOHNSON, Lisa 1967-

PERSONAL: Born 1967.

ADDRESSES: E-mail—lisa@reachgroupconsulting.com.

CAREER: Reach Group Consulting, CEO.

WRITINGS:

(With Andrea Learned) *Don't Think Pink: What Really Makes Women Buy—and How to Increase Your Share in This Crucial Market,* AMACOM (New York, NY), 2004.

(With Cheri Hanson) *Mind Your X's and Y's: Satisfying the 10 Cravings of a New Generation of Consumers,* Free Press (New York, NY), 2006.

Contributor to periodicals, including *New York Times* magazine and *Chicago Tribune;* contributor to National Public Radio's *Marketplace.*

SIDELIGHTS: Lisa Johnson is a marketing consultant and the author of books that include *Don't Think Pink: What Really Makes Women Buy—and How to Increase Your Share in This Crucial Market,* written with Andrea Learned and published by AMACOM, the publishing arm of the American Management Association. The book points out that women head forty percent of both American households and American companies. They also make the majority of consumer decisions. The authors contend that in spite of the buying power of women, most companies fail to appeal to them and to their specific needs and interests, which vary by age and lifestyle. They provide examples of companies that have given more consideration to women consumers by appealing to minority groups and hotels, for example, that offer safety measures such as security cameras and better lighting. A *Publishers Weekly* contributor remarked: "This is a solid guide for marketers at any corporation who want to reach the women's market."

With Cheri Hanson, Johnson wrote *Mind Your X's and Y's: Satisfying the 10 Cravings of a New Generation of Consumers.* This volume is a guide to marketing to Generation X, who are those Americans born between 1965 and 1979, and Generation Y, which includes those born from 1980 to 1997. These groups are notable for their strong commitment to technology; the authors call them "The Connected Generation." Brands that have been successful with this age group are noted and the challenges in reaching them discussed. "The result is effective as both a marketing workbook and a study of social trends," concluded David Siegfried in *Booklist.*

Johnson told *CA:* "My first book, *Don't Think Pink,* was born out of preparation for a three-day seminar on marketing to women (twenty-four hours of curriculum). Once I had worked through my ideas on the topic, writing a book didn't seem so intimidating.

"I write books about what I want to learn, instead of what I already understand. The act of writing a book is a structured, deadline-driven way to dive into a topic and come out enriched and transformed. I am officially addicted to the process.

"I am most influenced by my desire to crack a code or provide clarity on a topic that has people baffled. That is why I am so fascinated right now with the modern marketplace and the role technology is playing in how we work and play.

"Most days my mouth is far ahead of my typing fingers, and I end up speaking into a recorder or to my writing partner, Cheri Hanson. Once I empty my brain and we capture the main thoughts, the development and editing process can begin. This is a system that has worked well for me for years.

"My latest book, *Mind Your X's and Y's,* was built on a treasure hunt and code-cracking mission to discover the ten cravings of the connected generation. I still get a little chill thinking about the process. It was a rocket ride!

"I was surprised by the power in the act of discovery. I now make it my goal to orchestrate an experience where the reader discovers truth and has their own 'A-HA' moment. The act of discovery makes information both magical and memorable.

"I hope my readers will see people and the marketplace with fresh eyes and feel equipped to transform insight into action."

BIOGRAPHICAL AND CRITICAL SOURCES:

PERIODICALS

Booklist, September 15, 2006, David Siegfried, review of *Don't Think Pink: What Really Makes Women Buy—and How to Increase Your Share in This Crucial Market,* p. 12.
Harvard Business Review, September, 2006, Julia Kirby, review of *Mind Your X's and Y's: Satisfying the 10 Cravings of a New Generation of Consumers,* p. 32.
Publishers Weekly, May 3, 2004, review of *Don't Think Pink,* p. 183; July 10, 2006, review of *Mind Your X's and Y's,* p. 66.

*   *   *

JOHNSON, Walter 1967-

PERSONAL: Born 1967. *Education:* Princeton University, Ph.D., 1995.

ADDRESSES: Home—NY. *Office*—Department of History, Harvard University, Center for Government and International Studies—South, 1730 Cambridge St., Cambridge, MA 02138. *E-mail*—johnson2@fas.harvard.edu.

CAREER: New York University, New York, NY, professor of social and cultural analysis, history; Harvard University, Cambridge, MA, professor of history and African American studies.

AWARDS, HONORS: Avery O. Craven Prize, Organization of American Historians, 2000; Frederick Jackson Turner Award (cowinner), Organization of American Historians, for *Soul by Soul: Life inside the Antebellum Slave Market,* 2000; SHEAR Book Prize, Society of Historians of the Early American Republic, 2000; John Hope Franklin Prize, American Studies Association, 2000; Francis B. Simkins Award (cowinner), Southern Historical Association, 2001.

WRITINGS:

Soul by Soul: Life inside the Antebellum Slave Market, Harvard University Press (Cambridge, MA), 1999.
(Editor) *The Chattel Principle: Internal Slave Trades in the Americas,* Yale University Press (New Haven, CT), 2005.

Contributor of articles to periodicals and anthologies, including *Lincoln Center Theater Review, Journal of the Early Republic, Journal of Social History, Law and Social Inquiry,* and *New Perspectives on American Slavery.*

SIDELIGHTS: Walter Johnson provides a penetrating look at the horrors of slavery in his book *Soul by Soul: Life inside the Antebellum Slave Market.* The author begins his study in the 1820s, when the institution of slavery was strengthened by a cotton boom in the South. Between the 1820s and the 1850s, approximately one million slaves were marched from the Atlantic coast, where farmland was becoming exhausted from tobacco cultivation, to the fertile new cotton fields of the Mississippi Valley. The hub of the slave trade was the market in New Orleans, and this is the central focus of Johnson's book. Using letters, court records, slave narratives, and other documentation, the author portrays dealers, traders, auctioneers, and slaves in very personal terms. *Soul by Soul* is "a superior examination of the speculation in slaves as individuals conducted it," stated Gilbert Taylor in *Booklist*. A *Publishers Weekly* writer remarked: "The evil business of slavery has seldom been exposed with so much humanity and insight as in this eloquent study." Randall M. Miller, assessing the book in *Library Journal*, called it "the fullest, most penetrating examination of the antebellum slave market to date." *The Chattel Principle: Internal Slave Trades in the Americas*, which Johnson edited, collects a series of essays addressing the institution of slavery in North and South America. John David Smith, in a contribution for the *North Carolina Historical Review*, called the work "a useful collection that historians of slavery will welcome."

BIOGRAPHICAL AND CRITICAL SOURCES:

PERIODICALS

American Historical Review, October, 2001, Bertram Wyatt-Brown, review of *Soul by Soul: Life inside the Antebellum Slave Market*, p. 1359; June, 2005, review of *The Chattel Principle: Internal Slave Trades in the Americas*, p. 916.
American Literature, September, 2002, David Barry Gaspar, review of *Soul by Soul*, p. 637.
Black Issues Book Review, November, 2000, review of *Soul by Soul*, p. 66.
Book World, February 27, 2000, review of *Soul by Soul*, p. 2; December 3, 2000, review of *Soul by Soul*, p. 2.
Booklist, February 15, 2000, Gilbert Taylor, review of *Soul by Soul*, p. 1077.
Books & Culture, November-December, 2001, Randal M. Jelks, "Slavery and Broken Souls," p. 34.
Business History Review, winter, 2005, David Eltis, review of *The Chattel Principle*, p. 863.
Choice: Current Reviews for Academic Libraries, June, 2000, review of *Soul by Soul*, p. 1876.
Ebony, April, 2000, "Ebony Bookshelf," review of *Soul by Soul*, p. 20.
H-Net: Humanities and Social Sciences Online, June, 2000, review of *Soul by Soul*.
Historian, summer, 2001, review of *Soul by Soul*, p. 808; summer, 2001, John Zaborney, review of *Soul by Soul*, p. 836; spring-summer, 2002, Robert Hunt, review of *Soul by Soul*, p. 758.
History: Review of New Books, spring, 2000, Theodore Kornweibel, Jr., review of *Soul by Soul*, p. 106.
Journal of American History, September, 2001, Dylan Pennigroth, review of *Soul by Soul*, p. 644.
Journal of American Studies, December, 2001, review of *Soul by Soul*, p. 535; December, 2002, Emily West, review of *Soul by Soul*, p. 527.
Journal of Interdisciplinary History, winter, 2001, Gavin Wright, review of *Soul by Soul*, p. 469.
Journal of Southern History, August, 2001, review of *Soul by Soul*, p. 649.
Journal of the Early Republic, spring, 2001, Steven Deyle, review of *Soul by Soul*, p. 184.
Kirkus Reviews, November 1, 1999, review of *Soul by Soul*, p. 1716.
Labour/Le Travail, spring, 2003, Alvin Finkel, review of *Soul by Soul*, p. 344.
Library Journal, November 15, 1999, Randall M. Miller, review of *Soul by Soul*, p. 80.
New York Review of Books, November 2, 2000, George M. Frederickson, review of *Soul by Soul*, p. 61.
New Yorker, March 13, 2000, Nicholas Lemann, review of *Soul by Soul*, p. 93.
North Carolina Historical Review, January, 2006, John David Smith, review of *The Chattel Principle*, pp. 110-111.
Publishers Weekly, December 20, 1999, review of *Soul by Soul*, p. 64.
Reviews in American History, December, 2000, Jan Ellen Lewis, review of *Soul by Soul*, p. 538.
TLS: Times Literary Supplement, May 12, 2000, review of *Soul by Soul*, p. 32.

*   *   *

JUNGSTEDT, Mari 1962-

PERSONAL: Born 1962, in Stockholm, Sweden; married; mother of two.

ADDRESSES: Home—Stockholm, Sweden. *Agent*—Kontakt: Niclas Salomonsson eller Emma Tibblin, Skeppsbron 32, 103 18 Stockholm, Sweden.

CAREER: Writer. Works as radio and television journalist in Stockholm, Sweden.

WRITINGS:

Den du inte ser (mystery novel), [Sweden], 2003, translation by Tiina Nunnally published as *Unseen,* St. Martin's Minotaur (New York, NY), 2006.

SIDELIGHTS: Mari Jungstedt has worked as a radio and television journalist in Stockholm, Sweden, for well over a decade. During summers, she spends time with her husband and children on the island of Gotland, which is just off the Swedish coast, and which has served as the inspiration for the setting of her mystery series. *Unseen,* the first title in the series and also the first to be translated into English, first appeared in Sweden in 2003. The novel is a police procedural that follows the investigation into the murder of Helena Hillerstrom. Helena goes out for a run with her dog one morning and is later found dead, having been killed with an axe. On the previous night, her boyfriend took his aggressions out on Helena, making him a prime suspect. But then other women are found murdered, and Detective Superintendent Anders Knutas is called in to investigate. A contribu-

tor for *Kirkus Reviews* remarks that the book includes "foreboding atmosphere, plausible police work, a pat ending, several loose ends and a particularly handsome use of those endless days in a Swedish June." A *Library Journal* critic concluded that *Unseen* was "a solid, compellingly readable police procedural with a nicely rounded protagonist."

BIOGRAPHICAL AND CRITICAL SOURCES:

PERIODICALS

Kirkus Reviews, June 15, 2006, review of *Unseen,* p. 603.
Library Journal, July 1, 2006, review of *Unseen.*
Publishers Weekly, May 29, 2006, review of *Unseen,* p. 38.

ONLINE

Minotaur Books Web site, http://www.minotaurbooks. com/ (January 29, 2007), author biography.*

K

KALDER, Daniel 1974-

PERSONAL: Born 1974, in Fife, Scotland. *Education:* Graduated from Edinburgh University.

ADDRESSES: *Agent*—Emma Parry, Fletcher & Parry LLC., 78 5th Ave., 3rd Fl., New York, NY 10011.

CAREER: Writer. Worked variously in the BSE crisis unit and as a private tutor and magazine writer in Moscow.

WRITINGS:

Lost Cosmonaut: Observations of an Anti-Tourist (travel memoir), Scribner (New York, NY), 2006.

SIDELIGHTS: Born in Fife, Scotland, writer Daniel Kalder has spent a decade in the former Soviet Union, uncovering the most unlikely of tourist destinations. Rather than visiting locations known for beautiful scenery, fine food, excellent shopping opportunities, or historical significance, Kalder has invested his time in more obscure, contemporary settings in order to see what they have to offer. The reality of the places he visited, which were often broken down, littered with trash, economically unsound, and architecturally stark, fits in to Kalder's premise of traveling as an "anti-tourist." Kalder himself stated, in an interview for the London *Times:* "I'm really fascinated by things that nobody cares about, precisely because nobody cares about them. It's a type of pity, I suppose. The travel writer usually tries to fake authenticity and pretend they're constantly stumbling on beautiful places off the beaten track. I thought it'd be amusing for the writer to go off the track and wish he'd never left it." His book, *Lost Cosmonaut: Observations of an Anti-Tourist,* chronicles his experiences and describes many of his discoveries over the course of his travels, including his interest in the various people who made up the territories that were swallowed up by the Soviet Union, such as Tatarstan, Kalmykia, Mari El, and Udmurtia. Viv Groskop, in a review for the *New Statesman,* remarked that "the places Daniel Kalder visits are real enough, but he refuses to find anything interesting about them. He may think this is hilarious, but in fact it merely emphasises how misguided his book is." Dusko Doder, writing for the *Guardian,* opined: "Kalder has written a readable book that for the first time assembles essential historical and factual information about the four republics. This is a considerable achievement, as the process of Russification was so successful that there are very few people who still remember old traditions and practices."

Richard B. Woodward, in a review for the *New York Times,* remarked of Kalder that his "distaste for package tourism (and travel writing) is at times compromised by a preening self-regard and a nostalgie de la boue." Woodward went on to add: "What redeems the book from smugness is that he pours as much scorn on himself as on others," while a contributor for *Kirkus Reviews* commented: "His cavalier narration works best when taken in small doses, as do the jarring moments when the author openly admits to the fabrication of several dramatically detailed interactions." However, Askold Krushelnycky, in a contribution for the *Independent,* noted: "Much of this fine first book is hilarious and often abrasive. But Kalder's observations are always underpinned by a fondness for these hidden Europeans, and the cultures edging towards extinction." Mark Eleveld, reviewing the title for *Booklist,* called Kalder's account of his adventures "cool, wry, lively, and fun." Writing for the *Times Literary Supplement,* Zinovy Zinik called the book a "revelatory study . . . full of sharp absurdist insights into uncharted territories of boredom, distant lands of bizarre institutions and strange bureaucratic habits."

BIOGRAPHICAL AND CRITICAL SOURCES:

BOOKS

Kalder, Daniel, *Lost Cosmonaut: Observations of an Anti-Tourist,* Scribner (New York, NY), 2006.

PERIODICALS

Booklist, August 1, 2006, Mark Eleveld, review of *Lost Cosmonaut,* p. 30.
Bookseller, December 16, 2005, Caroline Sanderson, "Travelling with an Anti-Tourist," review of *Lost Cosmonaut,* p. 37; June 2, 2006, Andrew Steed, review of *Lost Cosmonaut,* p. 13.
Kirkus Reviews, June 1, 2006, review of *Lost Cosmonaut,* p. 558.
New Scientist, January 28, 2006, David Cohen, "Off the Beaten Track," review of *Lost Cosmonaut,* p. 50.
New Statesman, February 27, 2006, Viv Groskop, "Lonely Planet," review of *Lost Cosmonaut,* p. 55.
Publishers Weekly, May 22, 2006, review of *Lost Cosmonaut,* p. 41.
Times Literary Supplement, April 7, 2006, Zinovy Zinik, "Going Nowhere," review of *Lost Cosmonaut,* p. 36.

ONLINE

Daniel Kalder Home Page, http://www.danielkalder. com (January 29, 2007).
Guardian Online, http://books.guardian.co.uk/ (March 25, 2006), Dusko Doder, "Lost Lands the Size of Scotland," review of *Lost Cosmonaut.*

Independent Online, http://enjoyment.independent.co. uk/ (March 7, 2006), Askold Krushelnycky, review of *Lost Cosmonaut.*
New York Times Online, http://www.nytimes.com/ (December 24, 2006), Richard B. Woodward, "Armchair Traveler," review of *Lost Cosmonaut.*
Times Online (London, England), http://www. timesonline.co.uk/ (January 29, 2007), Allan Brown, "Having a Terrible Time, Wish You Were Here," review of *Lost Cosmonaut.*

*   *   *

KAMP, David

PERSONAL: Male.

ADDRESSES: E-mail—david@davidkamp.com.

CAREER: Writer.

WRITINGS:

(With Steven Daly) *The Rock Snob's Dictionary: An Essential Lexicon of Rockological Knowledge,* illustrated by Ross MacDonald, Broadway Books (New York, NY), 2005.
(With Lawrence Levi) *The Film Snob's Dictionary: An Essential Lexicon of Filmological Knowledge,* illustrated by Ross MacDonald, Broadway Books (New York, NY), 2006.
The United States of Arugula: How We Became a Gourmet Nation, Broadway Books (New York, NY), 2006.

Contributor to periodicals, including *Vanity Fair* and *GQ.*

SIDELIGHTS: In *The United States of Arugula: How We Became a Gourmet Nation,* writer David Kamp explores both the chefs and the social factors that have impacted American cooking over the past five decades. "Food is my passion in my private life. I love to cook, to eat and go out to restaurants," Kamp told Scott Hume in an interview on the *Restaurants & Institutions* Web site. "In my lifetime, I've been continually awed and pleased by the accelerated pace at which food has gotten better, in terms of ingredients and shopping and in sophistication and restaurants; the breadth of what's available and the talents of the chefs themselves. And I thought, what a wonderful thing to write about because it appeals very strongly to me as a food person and it's that rarest of things, an upbeat cultural development."

In his book, Kamp writes about longtime venerated chefs and food authorities such as James Beard, Julia Child, and Craig Claiborne. He also details the influence of the modern television chefs who have their own programs on the Food Network and also appear on other television shows and commercials and who often write hugely popular books. These include Emeril Lagasse, Mario Batali, and Rachael Ray. The author delves into various food trends that have taken hold in the United States, from French and nouvelle cuisines to a growing emphasis on organic foods and cooking. He also provides an historical look at how American cuisine changed from the time of the American Revolution to modern times, with an emphasis on the twentieth century, which saw the country's reputation for cuisine rise from being very low to being compared to the best of European foods.

"Kamp has accomplished a marvelous feat in collecting the telling details and anecdotes of those who have helped shaped American tastes," observed Cheryl L. Reed in a review of *The United States of Arugula* in the *Chicago Sun-Times*. "Reading him is like gathering around the prep table gossiping with the line cooks." Reed went on to note: "*Arugula* is sure to entertain anyone who shops at Williams-Sonoma or Crate and Barrel, watches the Food Network and regularly forks out a few Franklins for an epicurean experience." In a review in the *Seattle Post-Intelligencer*, John Marshall noted that the author "covers the vast culinary territory in a deliciously entertaining fashion, with marvelous profiles of celeb chefs and other luminaries that capture their outsized egos, competitive natures and bitchy relationships with others in the kitchen trade." Writing on *AmericanHeritage.com*, Jon Grinspan commented: "*The United States of Arugula* vividly portrays several eras of American culture while leaving the reader genuinely pleased with the changes in our national diet." *New York Times* contributor A.O. Scott noted: "Without quite saying so—and with admirable lightness of touch for just that reason— Kamp uses food to suggest a broader history, a tale of tastes and trends embedded in the grand epic of American consumer capitalism."

BIOGRAPHICAL AND CRITICAL SOURCES:

PERIODICALS

Chicago Sun-Times, December 17, 2006, Cheryl L. Reed, review of *The United States of Arugula: How We Became a Gourmet Nation*.
New York Times, October 1, 2006, A.O. Scott, review of *The United States of Arugula*.
Seattle Post-Intelligencer, September 29, 2006, John Marshall, review of *The United States of Arugula*.

ONLINE

AmericanHeritage.com, http://www.americanheritage.com/ (September 13, 2006), Jon Grinspan, "Fast-Food Nation or Gourmet Nation?," review of *The United States of Arugula*.
David Kamp Home Page, http://www.davidkamp.com (January 21, 2007).
Restaurants & Institutions, http://www.rimag.com/ (January 21, 2007), Scott Hume, "Interface: David Kamp," interview with author.*

* * *

KARPF, Anne

PERSONAL: Married; children: two daughters.

ADDRESSES: Home—London, England. *Agent*—Natasha Fairweather, A.P. Watt Ltd., 20 John St., London WC1N 2DR, England.

CAREER: Writer, journalist, sociologist, broadcaster. *Cosmopolitan*, former contributing editor; *New Statesman*, columnist; *Jewish Chronicle*, columnist; *Guardian* (London, England), columnist; British Broadcasting Corporation (BBC) Radio 3 and 4, broadcaster. London Metropolitan University, senior lecturer.

WRITINGS:

NONFICTION

Doctoring the Media: The Reporting of Health and Illness, Routledge (London, England), 1988.

The War After: Living with the Holocaust, Minerva (London, England), 1996.

The Human Voice: The Story of a Talent, Bloomsbury (London, England), 2006, published as *The Human Voice: How This Extraordinary Instrument Reveals Essential Clues about Who We Are,* Bloomsbury (New York, NY), 2006.

The Human Voice, has been translated into German, French, and Japanese. *The War After* was translated into German.

Contributor to books, including *Nothing Makes You Free,* edited by Melvyn Bucket, W.W. Norton, 2003. Contributor of articles to periodicals, including *Cosmopolitan, Times* (London, England), *Guardian* (London, England), the *Mail on Sunday,* and the *New Statesman.*

ADAPTATIONS: *The War After: Living with the Holocaust* was serialized in the London *Times* and the *Mail on Sunday.*

SIDELIGHTS: British author Anne Karpf is known for her nonfiction work on the reporting of health care, *Doctoring the Media: The Reporting of Health and Illness,* and for her family memoir of the holocaust, *The War After: Living with the Holocaust.* A BBC radio broadcaster and instructor at the University of London, she has also been a columnist for several major British periodicals. Her 2006 work, *The Human Voice: How This Extraordinary Instrument Reveals Essential Clues about Who We Are* (published in England as *The Human Voice: The Story of a Talent,*) introduced her writing to readers in the United States as well.

The Human Voice is, according to a *Kirkus Reviews* critic, a "wide-ranging examination of the human voice, drawing on the fields of anatomy, child development, linguistics, psychology, anthropology and cultural studies." Karpf examines the power of the voice and talking from many angles. She looks at the anatomical means by which speech is produced in humans, noting that the human vocal chords vibrate more than a million times per day. She further inspects the timbre and sound of voices of broadcasters as well as mothers. For example, she examined the voice of former British prime minister, Margaret Thatcher, and the manner in which she would change her voice from

a higher register when she was railing against something or someone, to lower tones when she wanted to comfort the audience. A *Publishers Weekly* reviewer felt this "lively and intelligent guide reveals how powerfully and pervasively the human voice shapes our everyday world." This is true not only in the oratorical skills of politicians and broadcasters but also in the soothing tones of a mother to her child. Following this line of study, Karpf observes the impact of the mother's voice on the baby and on the baby's developing linguistic skill. In this context, she also points out that linguists have shown that "baby talk" is an international language. She further looks at the variety of ways an individual's voice can change, depending on the circumstances, and investigates gender and voice, observing, for example, that women's voices have lowered in the past half-century as women increasingly compete in the marketplace and society with men. Karpf ends with a discussion of new voice technologies, including voiceprints and voice machines.

Karpf's *The Human Voice* won critical praise on both sides of the Atlantic. Writing in *Library Journal,* Michael C. Cramer found it a "unique and fascinating book" that "skillfully articulates the science and anthropology behind the voice." The *Publishers Weekly* contributor went on to call the book a "fluent study," while *Entertainment Weekly* contributor Chris Willman called it a "delightful distillation." Similarly, the *Kirkus Reviews* critic felt it was an "entertaining account." Reviewing the British publication in the *Times,* Fiona Shaw termed it "thrilling" and a work that "explores with enthusiastic brio this fundamental capacity."

BIOGRAPHICAL AND CRITICAL SOURCES:

BOOKS

Karpf, Anne, *The War After: Living with the Holocaust,* Minerva (London, England), 1996.

PERIODICALS

Booklist, July 1, 2006, Bryce Christensen, review of *The Human Voice: How This Extraordinary Instrument Reveals Essential Clues about Who We Are,* p. 16.

Entertainment Weekly, August 25, 2006, Chris Willman, review of *The Human Voice,* p. 90.

Herizons, winter, 2007, review of *The Human Voice,* p. 9.

Kirkus Reviews, May 15, 2006, review of *The Human Voice,* p. 506.

Library Journal, Michael D. Cramer, review of *The Human Voice,* p. 100.

Publishers Weekly, April 24, 2006, review of *The Human Voice,* p. 46.

Sunday Times (London, England), June 11, 2006, Russell Davies, review of *The Human Voice: The Story of a Remarkable Talent.*

Times (London, England), August 5, 2006, Fiona Shaw, review of *The Human Voice.*

Times Literary Supplement, August 30, 1996, Caroline Moorehead, review of *The War After,* p. 36; September 29, 2006, Jennifer Coates, review of *The Human Voice,* p. 34.

ONLINE

A.P. Watt Ltd. Web site, http://www.apwatt.co.uk/ (January 27, 2007), "Anne Karpf."

Bloomsbury Publishers Web site, http://www. bloomsburyusa.com/ (January 27, 2007), "Anne Karpf."

*   *   *

KARPYSHYN, Drew

PERSONAL: Married; wife's name Jennifer. *Education:* Earned B.A.

ADDRESSES: Home—Sherwood Park, Alberta, Canada.

CAREER: BioWare, Edmonton, Alberta, Canada, software developer and writer, 2000—. Also worked as a loans officer.

WRITINGS:

Baldur's Gate II: Throne of Bhaal, Wizards of the Coast (Renton, WA), 2001.

Temple Hill, Wizards of the Coast (Renton, WA), 2001.

Darth Bane: Path of Destruction, Del Rey Ballantine Books (New York, NY), 2006.

SIDELIGHTS: Drew Karpyshyn worked as a loans officer and investment advisor before a car accident left him without a vehicle to get to and from work each day. Karpyshyn used this as an excuse to move in a new direction with his life. After some additional secondary studies and a day on the television quiz show *Jeopardy,* Karpyshyn began work for BioWare, a software game publisher. Here he began writing scripts and story lines for various games. This resulted in novelizations of several of the games and led to his first published book in 2001, *Baldur's Gate II: Throne of Bhaal.*

Karpyshyn also began writing for the "Old Republic" *Star Wars* series and published *Darth Bane: Path of Destruction* in 2006. This book is set a thousand years before the onset of George Lucas's six-part movie story line in a time when Jedi and Sith numbers were equal. Darth Bane reorganizes the Brotherhood of the Sith and clarifies the Rule of Two as he rises to the top of the hierarchy of the Dark Side of the Force. A reviewer in *Publishers Weekly* concluded that the book is "sure to satisfy the *Star Wars* faithful." Dana Cobern-Kullman, reviewing the book for the *School Library Journal,* agreed that "fans won't be disappointed," and called the novel "an entertaining read, well written, and consistent in its history."

BIOGRAPHICAL AND CRITICAL SOURCES:

PERIODICALS

Booklist, September 1, 2006, Roland Green, review of *Darth Bane: Path of Destruction,* p. 67.

Hollywood Reporter, March 26, 2004, Chris Marlowe, "'Knights' Crowned Vid Games King," p. 6.

Library Journal, August 1, 2006, Jackie Cassada, review of *Darth Bane,* p. 77.

Publishers Weekly, July 24, 2006, review of *Darth Bane,* p. 41.

School Library Journal, November, 2006, Dana Cobern-Kullman, review of *Darth Bane,* p. 171.*

*   *   *

KELLEY, Mary L.

PERSONAL: Born in San Antonio, TX.

ADDRESSES: Home—Beaumont, TX. *Office*—Department of History, Lamar University, P.O. Box 10009, Beaumont, TX 77710.

CAREER: Lamar University, Beaumont, TX, assistant professor of history.

AWARDS, HONORS: Fulbright scholarship.

WRITINGS:

The Foundations of Texan Philanthropy, Texas A&M University Press (College Station, TX), 2004.

*   *   *

KERNEY, Kelly 1979-
(Kelly A. Kerney)

PERSONAL: Born 1979. *Education:* Bowdoin College, B.A., 2002; University of Notre Dame, M.F.A., 2004.

ADDRESSES: Home—Richmond, VA.

CAREER: Writer.

AWARDS, HONORS: University of Notre Dame, Nicholas Sparks Postgraduate Fellowship, 2004.

WRITINGS:

Born Again (novel), Harcourt (Orlando, FL), 2006.

SIDELIGHTS: Kelly Kerney loved to read from a young age, but it was only thanks to the encouragement of one of her professors during her time at Bowdoin College that she began to seriously consider becoming a writer herself. Anthony Walton was Writer-in-Residence at Bowdoin when Kerney enrolled in the English department, and it was Walton who encouraged Kerney to take her own writing to the next level. In an interview for the Bowdoin College Web site, Kerney explained: "I never thought I could write (professionally) until I worked with Professor Walton. He opened my eyes to contemporary literature, and the more I read, the more I believed that I could do it." Walton not only helped Kerney develop as a writer, but pointed her in the direction of books and authors whose works he felt would assist in her development. The result of Kerney's hard work was graduate school at the University of Notre Dame, followed by a Sparks Fellowship from author Nicholas Sparks that enabled her to spend an entire year writing. Kerney began work on her first novel, *Born Again,* partway through graduate school. The novel builds on themes from her own childhood, and tells the story of Mel, a Pentecostal and Bible Quiz champ, who decides to take on Darwin's theory of evolution. A contributor for *Kirkus Reviews* called the book "a seamless blend of snark and sincerity." Amy Johnson, in a review for the *San Francisco Chronicle,* found Kerney's book to be "a humorous portrait of an adolescent awakening from the blind faith of childhood and learning to see, think and believe with adult awareness."

BIOGRAPHICAL AND CRITICAL SOURCES:

PERIODICALS

Booklist, August 1, 2006, Jennifer Mattson, review of *Born Again,* p. 41.
Kirkus Reviews, June 1, 2006, review of *Born Again,* p. 537.
Library Journal, September 15, 2006, Heather McCormack, review of *Born Again,* p. 49.
Publishers Weekly, May 29, 2006, review of *Born Again,* p. 34.

ONLINE

BookLoons, http://www.bookloons.com/ (December 26, 2006), Lyn Seippel, review of *Born Again.*
Bowdoin College Web site, http://www.bowdoin.edu/ (September 16, 2006), "Kelly Kerney '02 Garners Big Attention for Debut Novel."
Kelly Kerney's My Space Page, http://profile.myspace.com/ (December 26, 2006), author biography.
San Francisco Chronicle Online, http://www.sfgate.com/ (August 31, 2006), Amy Johnson, review of *Born Again.*

KERNEY, Kelly A.
See KERNEY, Kelly

*   *   *

KING, Rosemary A. 1966-

PERSONAL: Born December 2, 1966, in Erie, PA; daughter of Thomas L. (an accountant) and Dolores A. (a homemaker) King. Ethnicity: "Caucasian." Education: U.S. Air Force Academy, B.S., 1988; Harvard University, M.A., 1991; Arizona State University, Ph. D., 2000.

ADDRESSES: Home—Washington, DC. Office—The Pentagon, Room 2E667, Washington, DC 20318-5134. E-mail—rosemary.king@js.pentagon.mil.

CAREER: U.S. Air Force, career officer, 1988—; present rank, lieutenant colonel.

WRITINGS:

Border Confluences: Borderland Narratives from the Mexican War to the Present, University of Arizona Press (Tucson, AZ), 2004.

SIDELIGHTS: Rosemary A. King told CA: "My first book, Border Confluences: Borderland Narratives from the Mexican War to the Present, explores narratives set along the U.S.-Mexico border. I have been interested in the borderlands since I was a child growing up in Mexico City in the early 1980s. Favorite authors include Cormac McCarthy, Miguel Méndez, and Leslie Marmon Silko."

*   *   *

KIRKPATRICK, Jeane D.J. 1926-2006
(Jeane Duane Jordan Kirkpatrick)

OBITUARY NOTICE— See index for CA sketch: Born November 19, 1926, in Duncan, OK; died of congestive heart failure, December 7, 2006, in Bethesda, MD. Political scientist, educator, diplomat, and author.

Kirkpatrick is best remembered for her role as the U.S. ambassador to the United Nations during President Ronald Reagan's first term in office. Her education included an A.A. from Stephens College, a B.A. from Barnard College in 1948, an M.A. from Columbia University in 1950, and a Ph.D. from that institution in 1967; she also attended graduate courses at the Institut de Science Politique at the University of Paris from 1952 to 1953. After completing her master's degree, she worked as a research analyst for the U.S. State Department, and was a research associate at George Washington University and at the Fund for the Republic during the mid-1950s. Kirkpatrick began her academic career in earnest at Trinity College, where she was an assistant professor of political science from 1962 to 1967. She then joined the Georgetown University faculty, where she rose to become Leavey Professor in Foundations of Freedom in 1978. For much of her life, Kirkpatrick was a Democrat with strong liberal leanings. However, she was a staunch anticommunist as early as the 1950s, when she first became aware of the many social injustices perpetrated in the Stalinist Soviet Union. In the early 1970s, she joined the Coalition for a Democratic Majority, an organization that tried to wrest control of the party from the followers of George McGovern, and in 1978 she joined the American Enterprise Institute. Kirkpatrick remained loyal to Democratic ideals concerning workers' rights and other social issues, but she became increasingly frustrated with her party's positions on foreign relations. She came to believe in a strong U.S. military and favored American support of right-wing governments that she felt might eventually turn toward democracy. After publishing an article critical of President Jimmy Carter's foreign policies, she attracted the attention of Republican presidential hopeful Ronald Reagan. After Reagan won the election, he appointed her U.S. ambassador to the United Nations. Here, her willingness to express her opinions, even when they did not fully reflect the administration's, sometimes rankled her superiors. However, Kirkpatrick supported Reagan on such issues as opposition to the Sandinistas in Nicaragua and support of the 1982 Israeli invasion of Lebanon. A particular moment in the spotlight came in 1983, when she presented a film to the U.N. showing the Soviets shooting down a South Korean passenger airplane. A woman who was also officially a Democrat in a government dominated by Republican men, Kirkpatrick often felt frustrated in her government post. She was, nevertheless, disappointed and surprised when Reagan did not ask her to return to his team when he won reelection. Kirkpatrick switched to the

Republican Party in 1985. She returned to Georgetown University, where she continued to teach until her 2002 retirement. She also was a member of the President's Foreign Intelligence Advisory Board from 1985 to 1993 and of the Defense Policy Review Board from 1985 to 1993, and she chaired the Commission on Fail Safe and Risk Reduction from 1990 to 1992. In 2003, as well, she headed the U.S. Delegation to the Human Rights Commission. Kirkpatrick was the author of many books on politics, including *Political Women* (1974), *The Reagan Doctrine and U.S. Foreign Policy* (1985), and *Good Intentions: Lost on the Road to the New World Order* (1996). She earned many honors for her contributions over the years, including the 1982 B'nai B'rith Humanitarian award, the 1984 French Prix Politique, the 1985 Presidential Medal of Freedom, the 1996 Jerusalem 2000 award, the 1999 Hungarian Presidential Gold medal, and the 2000 Living Legends medal from the Library of Congress.

OBITUARIES AND OTHER SOURCES:

PERIODICALS

Chicago Tribune, December 9, 2006, Section 1, pp. 1, 11.
New York Times, December 9, 2006, pp. A1, A15.
Times (London, England), December 9, 2006, p. 76.
Washington Post, December 9, 2006, pp. A1, A9.

*   *   *

KIRKPATRICK, Jeane Duane Jordan
   See KIRKPATRICK, Jeane D.J.

*   *   *

KÖENINGS, N.S. 1970-
   (Nathalie Arnold)

PERSONAL: Born 1970. *Education:* Bryn Mawr College, B.A., 1991; Indiana University, M.F.A., Ph.D.

ADDRESSES: Office—Creative Writing Program, Hampshire College, 893 West St., Amherst, MA 01002. *E-mail*—naia@hampshire.edu.

CAREER: Writer, artist. Previously worked for Human Rights Watch; Hampshire College, Amherst, MA, visiting assistant professor of creative writing and anthropology.

WRITINGS:

The Blue Taxi (novel), Little, Brown (New York, NY), 2006.

Contributor of short fiction to periodicals, including *Story Quarterly* and *Glimmer Train;* published her novella *Setting Up Shop,* as a chapbook, White Eagle Coffee Store Press, 2004.

SIDELIGHTS: N.S. Köenings has a colorful, varied background that shines through in her writing. Raised primarily in Europe and East Africa, Köenings earned her B.A. in African studies from Bryn Mawr College and a Ph.D. in sociocultural anthropology from the University of Indiana, where she also earned an M.F.A. in fiction. Extremely aware of culture and social climates, she has worked for Human Rights Watch and written about the political culture and occult in Zanzibar. Her novel, *The Blue Taxi,* takes place in a fictionalized African city such as the ones she lived in during her childhood and then later as an adult. In an interview for the Warner Books Web site, she explained: "East Africa is not, for me, a symbolic repository of 'memories'; it's definitely not a mythical or charmed, mysterious region of my imagination. The capital cities, the more provincial and coastal towns, and the rural areas I've been in, they're just places, like wherever a person has grown up or worked or lived is just an ordinary place." The novel is seeped in the locale, but also addresses the ways in which ordinary people's lives connect after a small boy is hit by a bus and nearly killed. Emily Cook, in a review for *Booklist,* remarked that the book "is lush and charismatic yet lacks verve as it slowly plods along." A critic for the *New Yorker* noted that "the characters display a frustrating inertia" or "sleep-walking quality." Todd Pruzan, writing for *New York Times Book Review,* had a more positive reaction to the pace: "Köenings examines the minutiae of her endearingly flawed characters in slow motion and at high, exacting resolution." A contributor for *Publishers Weekly* wrote: "The world Köenings has created in her accomplished debut is tragic and exhilarating."

BIOGRAPHICAL AND CRITICAL SOURCES:

PERIODICALS

Booklist, September 15, 2006, Emily Cook, review of *The Blue Taxi,* p. 28.

Kirkus Reviews, July 15, 2006, review of *The Blue Taxi,* p. 692.

Library Journal, August 1, 2006, Leigh Anne Vrabel, review of *The Blue Taxi,* p. 71.

New York Times Book Review, December 31, 2006, Todd Pruzan, review of *The Blue Taxi.*

New Yorker, November 27, 2006, review of *The Blue Taxi.*

Publishers Weekly, August 7, 2006, review of *The Blue Taxi,* p. 29.

ONLINE

Compulsive Reader, http://www.compulsivereader. com/ (December 26, 2006), Brenda A. Snodgrass, review of *The Blue Taxi.*

* * *

KOOPMANS, Loek 1943-

PERSONAL: Born May 16, 1943, in Haarlem, Netherlands; son of Oege (a social worker) and Toos (a homemaker) Koopmans; married Marijke Berghauser Pont (a therapist), July 8, 1973; children: Frank, Rozemarijn. *Education:* Attended School of Modern Design, Arnhem, Netherlands. *Hobbies and other interests:* Sports, philosophy.

ADDRESSES: Home—Zwolle, Netherlands. *E-mail*—loekkoopmans@hetnet.nl.

CAREER: Writer and illustrator of children's books. Freelance oil painter.

AWARDS, HONORS: Awards from Society of Dutch Illustrators, 1993, 1996.

WRITINGS:

CHILDREN'S BOOKS; AUTHOR AND ILLUSTRATOR

Kiep kantel, kiep kantel, Stichting voor de Collectieve Propaganda van het Nederlandse Boek (Amsterdam, Netherlands), 1984.

Het sprookje van de bron, Werkgroep Kinderboekenweek Zolle (Zolle, Netherlands), 1989.

Kan ik er ook nog bij? Een prentenboek, Christofoor (Zeist, Netherlands), 1990.

Ein Märchen im Schnee: Eine alte Geschichte, Mangold (Graz, Austria), 1991, published as *Any Room for Me?,* Floris (Edinburgh, Scotland), 1992, published as *The Woodcutter's Mitten: An Old Tale,* Crocodile Books (New York, NY), 1995.

Ein Märchen im Sommerwald: Eine alte Geschichte, Mangold (Graz, Austria), 1992, published as *The Pancake That Ran Away,* Floris (Edinburgh, Scotland), 1993.

Een dikke vette pannekoek: Een oude geschiedenis, Christofoor (Zeist, Netherlands), 1993, 3rd edition, 2005.

Die Wurst an der Nase: die unglückselige und doch so vergnügliche Geschichte vom unzufriedenen Holzfäller und seinen drei Wünschen, Mangold (Graz, Austria), 1995.

Kan ik er ook nog bij? Een prentenboek, Christofoor (Zeist, Netherlands), 1998.

Waar komt de sneeuw vandaan?, Christofoor (Zeist, Netherlands), 2006.

ILLUSTRATOR:

L.G.J. Bloemink-Rehwinkel, *Appels,* Nienhuis (Amsterdam, Netherlands), 1974.

L.G.J. Bloemink-Rehwinkel, *Apen,* Nienhuis (Amsterdam, Netherlands), 1974.

L.G.J. Bloemink-Rehwinkel, *De agent,* Nienhuis (Amsterdam, Netherlands), 1974.

L.G.J. Bloemink-Rehwinkel, *Bloemen,* Nienhuis (Amsterdam, Netherlands), 1974.

L.G.J. Bloemink-Rehwinkel, *Bijen,* Nienhuis (Amsterdam, Netherlands), 1974.

L.G.J. Bloemink-Rehwinkel, *De hond,* Nienhuis (Amsterdam, Netherlands), 1974.

L.G.J. Bloemink-Rehwinkel, *Kikkers,* Nienhuis (Amsterdam, Netherlands), 1974.

L.G.J. Bloemink-Rehwinkel, *Van alles wat,* Nienhuis (Amsterdam, Netherlands), 1974.

Jeanette Kleinveld, *Samenwerking tegen vervuiling,* Versluys (Amsterdam, Netherlands), 1974, 2nd edition, 1977.

Miep Klomp, *Zuinig zijn met energie,* Versluys (Amsterdam, Netherlands), 1975, 2nd edition, 1979.

Jeanette Kleinveld, *Op reis in Suriname,* Versluys (Amsterdam, Netherlands), 1977.

Jeanette Kleinveld, *Ons drinkwater,* Versluys (Amsterdam, Netherlands), 1977, 2nd edition, 1982.

Toos Olden, *Van huisvuil tot mest,* Versluys (Amsterdam, Netherlands), 1978.

Toos Olden, *Vuilverbranding,* Versluys (Amsterdam, Netherlands), 1979.

Huub Reijnders, *Stap voor stap lezen,* Volumes 10-11, Zwijsen (Tilburg, Netherlands), 1981.

Jetty Krever, *Wij lopen samen weg,* Zwijsen (Tilburg, Netherlands), 1981.

Jan Naaijkens, *De blauwe vis,* M. Stenvert (Meppel, Netherlands), 1981.

Hanke Kleinstra, *Ook water voor Abdi,* M. Stenvert (Meppel, Netherlands), 1982.

Gerrit de Boer, *De wenspillen van professor Kreupelhout,* M. Stenvert (Meppel, Netherlands), 1982.

J. Kokmeijer, *Mirjam en de ekster,* M. Stenvert (Meppel, Netherlands), 1982.

Geertje Gort, *Letter-greep: niveau lezen voor het voortgezet onderwijs,* Nijgh & van Ditmar Educatief (Amsterdam, Netherlands), Volume 2A: *Toen de dooi inviel; Zijn vader; Uit het dagboek van Suna,* 1983, Volume 2B: *Triestheid speciaal; Ups en downs; Padjelanta,* 1983, Volume 2C: *Is dat het nou? Ik heb geen naam; Lange maanden,* 1983, Volume 3A: *Liefdewerk, oud papier; De heks van Amersfoort; Weg uit het verleden,* 1984, Volume 3B: *Het onzichtbare licht; Filiz; De jongen met het litteken,* 1984, Volume 3C: *Ben is dood; Koude kermis; Bart (Lumberjack in Canada),* 1984.

J. Kokmeijer, *Red de molen,* M. Stenvert (Meppel, Netherlands), 1984.

A.J. Pleysier, *De konijntjes,* Kok Educatief (Kampen, Netherlands), 1984, 2nd edition, 1994.

A.J. Pleysier, *Loebas, de hond,* Kok Educatief (Kampen, Netherlands), 1984, 2nd edition, 1994.

A.J. Pleysier, *Rebbel, de parkiet,* Kok Educatief (Kampen, Netherlands), 1984, 2nd edition, 1992.

A.J. Pleysier, *De muis,* Kok Educatief (Kampen, Netherlands), 1984, 2nd edition, 1993.

Miek Koopmans, *Aardje Klaar en Grote Vaar,* Stichting voor de Collectieve Propaganda van het Nederlandse Boek (Amsterdam, Netherlands), 1985.

Gerrit de Boer, *Avontuur in Frankrijk,* M. Stenvert (Meppel, Netherlands), 1986.

Anny Matti, *Eem handvol mieren,* Meulenhoff Educatief (Utrecht, Netherlands), 1987.

Anny Matti, *Sneeuw onder de evenaar,* Meulenhoff Educatief (Utrecht, Netherlands), 1988.

Anny Matti, *De ondergang van De Marskramer,* Meulenhoff Educatief (Utrecht, Netherlands), 1989.

Frank Herzen, *De put van Avalach,* Zwijsen (Tilburg, Netherlands), 1989.

Peter Vervloed, *Een mislukt eiland,* La Rivière & Voorhoeve (Kampen, Netherlands), 1990.

Jennine Staring, *De bliesblazers, de groggel en het mannetje van de regenboog,* Christofoor (Zeist, Netherlands), 1991.

Jennine Staring, *Der alte Garten und Tanjas geheimnisvolle Freunde,* Urachhaus (Stuttgart, Germany), 1992.

Frank Herzen, *Duivel van de zee,* Elzenga (Amsterdam, Netherlands), 1992, 3rd edition, 1998.

Miek Dorrestein, *Met de stroom mee,* Van Holkema & Warendorf (Houten, Netherlands), 1994.

Jacob Grimm, *Gelukkige Hans: Een sprookje van de gebroeders Grimm,* Christofoor (Zeist, Netherlands), 1994.

Anneliese Lussert, *The Christmas Visitor,* translated by Rosemary Lanning, North-South Books (New York, NY), 1995.

Mariette Vanhalewijn, *Nog niet zo lang geleden: Bekende verhalen van Mariette Vanhalewijn,* Lannoo (Tielt, Belgium), 1996.

Anneli Vermeer, *Het land achter de bergen,* Christofoor (Zeist, Netherlands), 1997.

Wolfram Hänel, *The Gold at the End of the Rainbow,* translated by Anthea Bell, North-South Books (New York, NY), 1997.

Marijke Bouwhuis, *Een rare dag met oma,* Malmberg ('s Hertogenbosch, Netherlands), 1998.

Charles Perrault, *Assepoester,* De Vier Windstreken (Rijswijk, Netherlands), 1999.

Charles Perrault, *Cinderella: A Fairy Tale,* translated by Anthea Bell, North-South Books (New York, NY), 1999.

Mariëlle Koster, *Haal het doek maar op: Kinderboek; Josje in het theater,* Schouwburg Odeon (Zwolle, Netherlands), 2000.

René Berends, *Het web van Anansi,* Malmberg ('s Hertogenbosch, Netherlands), 2000.

Elly Zuiderveld, *De sleutel van Andermansland,* Callenbach (Nijkerk, Netherlands), 2001.

Günter Spang, *The Ox and the Donkey: A Christmas Story,* translated by Marianne Martens, North-South Books (New York, NY), 2001.

Willem van den Akker, *Vergif,* Wolters-Noordhoff (Groningen, Netherlands), 2001.

Marijke Bouwhuis, *Hou op, Tes!,* Clavis (Amsterdam, Netherlands), 2001.

Hella de Groot, *De pest,* Wolters-Noordhoff (Groningen, Netherlands), 2002.

Frans Weeber, Heksen, Wolters-Noordhoff (Groningen, Netherlands), 2004.

Jane B. Mason, *Stella and the Berry Thief,* Marshall Cavendish (New York, NY), 2004.

Frog, Bee, and Snail Look for Snow, Floris (Edinburgh, Scotland), 2006.

Illustrator of additional books published in German, Japanese, and Korean; contributor of illustrations to other books.

SIDELIGHTS: Loek Koopmans told *CA:* "Writing and illustrating picture books is important. These books help very young children to develop as adults. They also provide the author or illustrator with a very special responsibility. A picture book illustrator has to be conscious of the power and influence he has on children. He has to study the nature of children and search for or subscribe to opinions on the development of children into adults. This is the way a picture book illustrator can develop his own style.

"My writing and illustrating process started at the most important point of life: the universe and the sun—the source of all life! In my work the sunlight is never absent, but there is no sun without clouds because clouds are the creation of the sun itself. Light and dark are inseparable, and so are good and evil. So are fairy tales: they contain eternal truth."

BIOGRAPHICAL AND CRITICAL SOURCES:

ONLINE

Loek Koopmans Home Page, http://www.loek koopmans.tk (December 27, 2006).

*   *   *

KOSNER, Edward 1937-

PERSONAL: Born 1937, in New York, NY; married second wife, Julie Baumgold (a writer). *Education:* City College of the City University of New York, B.A., 1958. *Religion:* Jewish

ADDRESSES: Agent—Amanda Urban, ICM, 825 8th Ave., New York, NY 10019.

CAREER: Journalist, editor, publisher. *New York Post,* New York, NY, 1958-63, began as rewrite man, became assistant city editor; *Newsweek,* New York, NY, 1963-79, began as national affairs writer, became editor; *New York,* New York, NY, 1980-93, began as editor, became editor and president; *Esquire,* New York, NY, editor-in-chief, 1993-97; *Daily News,* New York, NY, began as Sunday editor, became editor-in-chief, 1998-2003.

AWARDS, HONORS: Townsend Harris Medal, from City College of New York, 1979: Robert F. Kennedy Journalism Award and the American Bar Association's Silver Gavel, both for "Justice on Trial."

WRITINGS:

It's News to Me: The Making and Unmaking of an Editor (memoir), introduction by Pete Hamill, Thunder's Mouth Press (New York, NY), 2006.

Contributor to numerous periodicals, including the *New York Times, New York, Wall Street Journal, Newsweek, New York Post,* and the *Daily News.*

SIDELIGHTS: Edward Kosner graduated from City College of the City University of New York in 1958, and immediately embarked on a career in journalism that would last more that four decades. While still in school, he worked as the City College correspondent to the *New York Times.* In subsequent years, he has served as editor of *Newsweek, New York, Esquire,* and the *Daily News,* and written for numerous other periodicals. In 1979, City College awarded Kosner the Townsend Harris Medal, and his writing has also won various prizes, including the Robert F. Kennedy Journalism Award and the American Bar Association's Silver Gavel, both for "Justice on Trial," an article he wrote for *Newsweek.* In *It's News to Me: The Making and Unmaking of an Editor,* Kosner chronicles his life as a journalist, including the ups and downs of the job, and explains both the joys and the hardships of his career. Jack Shafer, writing for the *New York Times,* cited Kosner's string of successes and opined: "As any editor can tell you, a book that's mostly about having it all isn't much of a book. This memoir marks one of the rare instances in which Kosner failed to get the story." However, a contributor for *Kirkus Reviews* called the book "a meaty memoir" and "a compelling chronicle that follows a journalist—and journalism—from the age of typewriters to the era of BlackBerries."

BIOGRAPHICAL AND CRITICAL SOURCES:

BOOKS

Kosner, Edward *It's News to Me: The Making and Unmaking of an Editor,* Thunder's Mouth Press (New York, NY), 2006.

PERIODICALS

Booklist, September 1, 2006, Vanessa Bush, review of *It's News to Me,* p. 23.
Kirkus Reviews, June 15, 2006, review of *It's News to Me,* p. 618.

ONLINE

Los Angeles Times Online, http://calendarlive.com/books/ (September 26, 2006), Josh Getlin, "A Media Memoir: Longtime Newspaper and Magazine Editor Edward Kosner Offers a Cautionary Tale about Survival in That Professional Arena."
New York Times Online, http://www.nytimes.com/ (October 1, 2006), Jack Shafer, "New York Confidential," review of *It's News to Me.*
Nonstop NY Web site, http://members.aol.com/nonstopny/eventbio.htm (January 29, 2007), City University of New York honors announcements.

*   *   *

KOZLOFF, Nikolas

PERSONAL: *Education:* Attended University of Miami; Oxford University, Ph.D.

ADDRESSES: *Home*—Carroll Gardens, NY.

CAREER: Council on Hemispheric Affairs, Washington, DC, senior research fellow.

WRITINGS:

Hugo Chávez: Oil, Politics, and the Challenge to the United States, Palgrave Macmillan (New York, NY), 2006.

Contributor to periodicals, including *Counterpunch, Political Affairs,* and the *Brooklyn Rail.*

SIDELIGHTS: Nikolas Kozloff is a Latin American scholar and researcher who was trained at Oxford University. Kozloff publishes articles about Latin American politics, particularly that of Venezuela and the Hugo Chávez government, in various periodicals, including *Counterpunch, Political Affairs,* and the *Brooklyn Rail.*

Hugo Chávez: Oil, Politics, and the Challenge to the United States, Kozloff's first published book, deals with the relations between Venezuela and its larger-than-life president and the United States. Chávez reformed Venezuela, the fifth-largest oil producer in the world, in a way that differed greatly from that of U.S. President George W. Bush and allied himself with international enemies of the Bush administration, causing a significant political and ideological challenge to U.S. hegemony in the region.

A *Publishers Weekly* reviewer noticed "a leftist bias toward Chávez" and found that the ample historical information mixed with personal stories of the Venezuelan leader created an "uneven read." However, the reviewer called the book a "thoughtful, well-researched alternative to the majority of information available on Chávez in the English-speaking world." Tony Pecinovsky, reviewing the book in *People's Weekly World,* wrote that the book suffers from "little original research, . . . wastes time on miniature biographies," and contains too much of the author's own life experiences mixed in. *Library Journal* reviewer Deborah Lee, however, found *Hugo Chávez* "useful both for its biographical background material on Chávez" and "its pertinent insights into his ways."

BIOGRAPHICAL AND CRITICAL SOURCES:

PERIODICALS

Library Journal, September 15, 2006, Deborah Lee, review of *Hugo Chávez: Oil, Politics, and the Challenge to the United States,* p. 76.

People's Weekly World, September 28, 2006, Tony Pecinovsky, review of *Hugo Chávez.*

Publishers Weekly, July 24, 2006, review of *Hugo Chávez,* p. 53.

ONLINE

Council on Hemispheric Affairs Web site, http://www.coha.org/ (September 15, 2006), author's employer Web site.*

* * *

KUCZYNSKI, Alex 1968(?)-
  (Alexandra Louise Kuczynski)

PERSONAL: Born c. 1968, in Lima, Peru; daughter of Pedro-Pablo Kuczynski (former Peruvian government minister); married Charles Porter Stevenson, Jr. (an investor), November 30, 2002. *Education:* Graduated from Barnard College.

ADDRESSES: Home—New York, NY, and Ketchum, ID. *Office*—New York Times, 229 W. 43rd St., New York, NY 10036. *E-mail*—alex@alexkuczynski.com; alexk@nytimes.com; alexk@zebra.net.

CAREER: Journalist. *New York Times,* New York, NY, reporter and Styles columnist. Previously worked at the *New York Observer.*

WRITINGS:

Beauty Junkies: Inside Our $15 Billion Obsession with Cosmetic Surgery, Doubleday (New York, NY), 2006.

"Thursday Styles Critical Shopper" columnist for the *New York Times.* Also contributor to periodicals and magazines, including *Vanity Fair, Harper's Bazaar, Allure, New York Times Magazine, Elle,* and the *New York Times Book Review.*

SIDELIGHTS: Alex Kuczynski began reporting for the *New York Times* in the late 1990s and spent most of that time as the author of the "Thursday Styles Critical Shopper" column. Aside from writing her column, Kuczynski also contributes to numerous other periodicals.

Kuczynski's first book, *Beauty Junkies: Inside Our $15 Billion Obsession with Cosmetic Surgery,* was published in 2006. In it she describes how America's Hollywood-driven average citizens strive to achieve and then maintain the appearance of a model or actor through plastic surgery. Kuczynski, who has also undergone numerous surgeries to improve her appearance, calls it a national addiction. In an *Entertainment Weekly* review, Jennifer Reese likened the book to a "women's magazine piece stretched to 278 pages." Both Kathryn Masterson, in a *Chicago Tribune* review, and Toni Bentley, in a *New York Times Book Review* article, found different strong points in the book. Masterson noted that Kuczynski "has a keen eye and a talent for description, and she is at her best exposing the hucksters and snake-oil sellers in the business." Bentley stated: "Kuczynski's book is most interesting when she switches from the confessional to the informative, as in her brief but fascinating chapter on the history of plastic surgery."

BIOGRAPHICAL AND CRITICAL SOURCES:

PERIODICALS

America's Intelligence Wire, October 2, 2006, John Gibson, author interview.

Booklist, September 1, 2006, Barbara Jacobs, review of *Beauty Junkies: Inside Our $15 Billion Obsession with Cosmetic Surgery,* p. 32.

Chicago Tribune, November 1, 2006, Kathryn Masterson, review of *Beauty Junkies.*

Entertainment Weekly, October 20, 2006, Jennifer Reese, review of *Beauty Junkies,* p. 85.

Houston Chronicle, October 6, 2006, Barbara Liss, review of *Beauty Junkies.*

New York Post, October 16, 2006, Liz Smith, review of *Beauty Junkies.*

New York Times Book Review, October 22, 2006, Toni Bentley, review of *Beauty Junkies.*

Newsweek, October 30, 2006, Barbara Kantrowitz, review of *Beauty Junkies,* p. 54.

Publishers Weekly, January 26, 2006, review of *Beauty Junkies,* p. 40; July 24, 2006, Penny Kaganoff, "Chasing Beauty," p. 46.

* * *

KUCZYNSKI, Alexandra Louise
  See KUCZYNSKI, Alex

KUIPERS, Dean 1964(?)-

PERSONAL: Born c. 1964, in MI; partner of Meg Cranston; children: Spenser. *Education:* Graduated from Kalamazoo College.

ADDRESSES: Home—Los Angeles, CA. *Office*—Los Angeles CityBeat, 5900 Wilshire Blvd., Ste. 2211, Los Angeles, CA 90036.

CAREER: Journalist. *Los Angeles CityBeat,* Los Angeles, CA, deputy editor. Former editor at *Spin* and *Raygun* magazines. Has worked on numerous short films.

WRITINGS:

(Author of essays, coeditor, with Chris Ashworth) *Ray Gun: Out of Control,* introduction by Marvin Scott Jarrett, Simon & Schuster (New York, NY), 1997.
I Am a Bullet: Living in Accelerated Culture, photographs by Doug Aitken, Crown (New York, NY), 2000.
Burning Rainbow Farm: How a Stoner Utopia Went Up in Smoke, Bloomsbury (New York, NY), 2006.

Contributor of text to both the book and the film *Diamond Sea,* by Doug Aitken. Contributor to periodicals, including *Playboy, Rolling Stone, Los Angeles Times, Interview, Travel & Leisure, Outside, LA Weekly,* and *Spin.*

SIDELIGHTS: Dean Kuipers is a native of Michigan who left for Los Angeles after finishing college in Kalamazoo. Since graduating he has edited a number of alternative periodicals, including *Spin, Raygun,* and *Los Angeles CityBeat.* His journalistic experience is rounded off by also contributing to mainstream periodicals, including *Playboy, Rolling Stone, Travel & Leisure,* and the *Los Angeles Times.*

Burning Rainbow Farm: How a Stoner Utopia Went Up in Smoke is set just down the road from where Kuipers grew up. A blue-collar, libertarian couple, Tom Crosslin and Rollie Rohm, lived on a farm which frequently held concerts and get-togethers for decriminalizing marijuana use. Neighbors were mostly indifferent to the proceedings or lifestyle of the two men.

In 2001, shortly before the September 11 terrorist attacks, District Attorney Scott Teter arranged to have Rohm's son taken into protective custody and to seize the land and property. The two men refused this heavy-handed government invasion and armed themselves to protect their land. The end of the five-day standoff resulted in the burning of the farm and both men shot dead, despite never firing at a law enforcement officer.

Reviews of *Burning Rainbow Farm* were mostly positive. A contributor to *Kirkus Reviews* called the book "an excellent look at the marijuana subculture, deluded or not, aspiring to the Middle-American mainstream." Whitney Pastorek, reviewing the book in *Entertainment Weekly,* noted that it was "exhaustively researched" but "criminally underedited." In a *Seattle Post-Intelligencer* review, John Marshall stated: "Kuipers has a gift for trenchant incident and information, but he has filled the book with way too many minor characters and other plot diversions." Marshall conceded that the book "remains a riveting, and often shocking, account of government law enforcement gone wild."

BIOGRAPHICAL AND CRITICAL SOURCES:

PERIODICALS

Booklist, July 1, 2006, Mike Tribby, review of *Burning Rainbow Farm: How a Stoner Utopia Went Up in Smoke,* p. 13.
Entertainment Weekly, June 16, 2006, Whitney Pastorek, review of *Burning Rainbow Farm,* p. 80.
Kirkus Reviews, May 15, 2006, review of *Burning Rainbow Farm,* p. 506.
New York Times Book Review, July 20, 1997, Steven Heller, review of *Ray Gun: Out of Control.*
Publishers Weekly, May 8, 2006, review of *Burning Rainbow Farm,* p. 54.
Reference & Research Book News, November, 2006, review of *Burning Rainbow Farm.*
Seattle Post-Intelligencer, August 18, 2006, John Marshall, review of *Burning Rainbow Farm.*

ONLINE

Dean Kuipers Home Page, http://www.deankuipers online.com (January 26, 2007), author biography.*

KUNZMANN, Richard 1976-

PERSONAL: Born 1976, in Namibia. *Education:* Earned master's degree (with honors), 2002.

ADDRESSES: Home—South Africa. *Agent*—Gillon Aitken Associates, 18-21 Cavaye Pl., London SW10 9PT, England.

CAREER: Writer. Previously worked as a bookseller in London, England.

WRITINGS:

CRIME NOVELS

Bloody Harvests, Macmillan (London, England), 2004, Thomas Dunne Books (New York, NY), 2006.
Salamander Cotton, Macmillan (London, England), 2006.

SIDELIGHTS: Richard Kunzmann was born in Namibia, educated in South Africa, and worked in London while publishing his first novel, *Bloody Harvests.* The book incorporates his interest in Africa's myths and legends. With a background in criminology and psychology, Kunzmann introduced the South African equivalent of Sherlock Holmes, Detective Inspector Jacob Tshabalala. Working in the poorest area of Johannesburg, Tshabalala and his partner, Harry Mason, try to uncover the murder of a child whose organs were harvested out of her living body. Many suspect this was the work of a witch doctor, causing tribal beliefs and personal connections to tear at the relationship of the detectives.

Gloria Feit, reviewing the book on the *Spine Tingler Magazine* Web site, called it "a dense and dark novel, filled with intensity, complex characterizations, and rich in sense of place of this fascinating culture and country." Jo Ann Vicarel, writing in *Library Journal,* noted that "this outstanding novel is sure to win readers everywhere." In *Publishers Weekly,* a critic wrote that "the complex narrative perhaps switches directions too often," but concluded that Kunzmann "does a fine job." A *Kirkus Reviews* contributor commented that the book contains "lots of characters to like" and "lots of vivid evocations of an interesting time and place."

BIOGRAPHICAL AND CRITICAL SOURCES:

PERIODICALS

Booklist, December 1, 2006, David Pitt, review of *Bloody Harvests,* p. 26.
Kirkus Reviews, October 1, 2006, review of *Bloody Harvests,* p. 991.
Library Journal, November 1, 2006, Jo Ann Vicarel, review of *Bloody Harvests,* p. 54.
Publishers Weekly, October 1, 2006, review of *Bloody Harvests,* p. 38.

ONLINE

Gillon Aitken Associates Web site, http://www.gillon aitkenassociates.co.uk/ (January 26, 2007), author biography.
Spine Tingler Magazine, http://www.spinetinglermag. com/ (October 22, 2006), Gloria Feit, review of *Bloody Harvests.**

L

LABARRE, Polly G.

PERSONAL: Education: Yale University, B.A. (summa cum laude).

ADDRESSES: Home—New York, NY. *Agent*—Lavin Agency, 77 Peter St., 4th Fl., Toronto, Ontario M5V 2G4, Canada. *E-mail*—polly@mavericksatwork.com.

CAREER: Writer, editor, and speaker. *Industry Week,* Cleveland, OH, served as bureau editor, book-review editor, reporter, and coproducer of interactive service and executive conferences; *Fast Company,* New York, NY, cofounder, founding editor, and senior editor for eight years. Also worked in book publishing, including literary scout for foreign book publishers and for Amblin Entertainment with Maria Campbell Associates. Has appeared on television, including *Good Morning America, Today,* and *Nightly Business Report.* Serves on the board of advisors of TakingITGlobal.

WRITINGS:

(With William C. Taylor) *Mavericks at Work: Why the Most Original Minds in Business Win,* William Morrow (New York, NY), 2006.

Contributor to the book *The Big Moo: Stop Trying to Be Perfect and Start Being Remarkable,* Portfolio Hardcover, 2005; contributor to periodicals, including the *New York Times.*

SIDELIGHTS: Polly G. LaBarre is a business writer and editor and author, with William C. Taylor, of *Mavericks at Work: Why the Most Original Minds in Business Win.* In their book, LaBarre and Taylor present the strategies, tactics, and advice of business leaders who took unique ideas and approaches and created successful companies. Some of the companies profiled include Netflix, Google, and Pixar. Much of the book focuses on how companies and their leaders are establishing a new agenda for business in the twenty-first century through a combination of innovative strategy, service, and organization. In an interview on the *How to Change the World* Web Blog, LaBarre commented on the mavericks profiled in the book, noting: "I was struck by how unfailingly generous these mavericks were—and by how creative they were in their generosity. One of the big lessons of the book is that generosity begets prosperity."

"*Mavericks* is wide-ranging: Taylor and LaBarre muse on everything from open-source innovation to the value of open-book management," wrote a *Business Week* contributor. The reviewer added: "To their credit, Taylor and LaBarre have some caveats about their 'mavericks' and describe cases where a few have gone astray." David Siegfried, writing in *Booklist,* commented that LaBarre and Taylor "have identified positive developments in a business environment that is struggling to emerge from slow growth." A contributor to the *Economist* referred to *Mavericks at Work* as "a pivotal work in the tradition of *In Search of Excellence.*"

BIOGRAPHICAL AND CRITICAL SOURCES:

PERIODICALS

Booklist, September 15, 2006, David Siegfried, review of *Mavericks at Work: Why the Most Original Minds in Business Win,* p. 12.

Business Week, October 2, 2006, review of *Mavericks at Work,* p. 104.

Economist, November 18, 2006, review of *Mavericks at Work,* p. 86.

Newsweek, October 2, 2006, John Sparks, review of *Mavericks at Work.*

ONLINE

Fast Company.com, http://www.fastcompany.com/ (January 22, 2007), brief profile of author.

How to Change the World Blog, http://blog.guykawasaki.com/ (October 9, 2006), "Ten Questions with Polly LaBarre."

Journal of Business Strategy, http://www.journalofbusinessstrategy.com/ (January 22, 2007), Timothy Leffel, "Why Maverick Companies Succeed in a Competitive Environment: An Interview with Polly LaBarre."

Lavin Agency Web site, http://www.thelavinagency.com/ (January 22, 2007), profile of author.

MavericksatWork.com, http://www.mavericksatwork.com (January 22, 2007), brief profile of author.*

* * *

LAMOUREUX, Florence 1932-

PERSONAL: Born November 24, 1932, in Coventry, RI; daughter of Howard K. (a small-business operator) and Myrtle (an elementary schoolteacher) Kettelle; married Charles H. Lamoureux (a university professor), August 28, 1954 (deceased); children: Mark H., Anne M. *Ethnicity:* "Caucasian." *Education:* University of Rhode Island, B.A., 1954; University of Hawaii at Manoa, M.A., 1980.

ADDRESSES: Home—Honolulu, HI. *E-mail*—flolam@hawaii.rr.com.

CAREER: National Biological Institute, Bogor, Indonesia, English language teacher to Indonesian scientists, 1972-73, 1979-80; University of Hawaii at Manoa, Honolulu, administrative assistant and program coordinator for Centers for Southeast Asian and Philippine Studies, 1982-91, and National Resource Center for Southeast Asian Studies, 1991-97, associate director of Center for Southeast Asian Studies, 1997-2004; retired, 2004. Language Learning Unlimited, Honolulu, English language teacher, 1981; leader of study tours.

WRITINGS:

(Translator) Mochtar Lubis, *The Indonesian Dilemma,* Graham Brash (Singapore), 1982.

(Editor, with Soenjono Dardowidjojo, and contributor of translations) Mochtar Lubis, *In the Surau: Seven Islamic Short Stories from Indonesia,* Southeast Asian Studies, University of Hawaii at Manoa (Honolulu, HI), 1983.

(Translator) Mochtar Lubis, *Tiger!* (novel), Select Books (Singapore), 1991.

Indonesia: A Global Studies Handbook, American Bibliographical Center-Clio Press (Santa Barbara, CA), 2003.

Also translator of shorter works. Contributor to periodicals, including *Social Science Record. Education about Asia,* past member of editorial board.

SIDELIGHTS: Florence Lamoureux told *CA:* "I was fortunate to live in Indonesia in 1972 and 1973 during my husband's sabbatical leave. I returned home with the intent of learning more about this unique Asian country, and as a result I began to study its language, history, and culture. My career as a writer began as a translator of short stories from Indonesian into English. I went on to translate a detailed essay on environmental issues and later a novel. The Indonesian journalist and activist Mochtar Lubis wrote both. I also translated a book of short stories by Lubis that were written in 1955: an interesting period in Indonesia's history of seeking independence from the Dutch. Lubis was my primary inspiration as an author. I not only admire the style in which he wrote, but I also agree with his philosophy.

"During my years at the University of Hawaii I wrote a variety of K-12 educational materials on Southeast Asian countries and issues. A high school level book on East Timor was my last publication for that center. I later wrote *Indonesia: A Global Studies Handbook.* It was especially enjoyable for me to write this book, as I got to research and explore Indonesian culture in great detail. I had lived in Indonesia for more than three years. I have also traveled extensively throughout the archipelago."

LANKFORD, Andrea
(Andrea R. Lankford)

PERSONAL: Married. *Education:* University of Tennessee, Knoxville, graduated 1986.

ADDRESSES: Agent—Jeff Kellogg, Pavilion Literary Management, 660 Massachusetts Ave., Ste. 4, Boston, MA 02118. *E-mail*—arlankford@hotmail.com.

CAREER: National Park Service, park ranger for twelve years.

WRITINGS:

(And photographer) *Biking the Arizona Trail: The Complete Guide to Day-Riding and Thru-Biking,* Westcliffe Publishers (Englewood, CO), 2002.

(And photographer) *Biking the Grand Canyon Area,* Westcliffe Publishers (Englewood, CO), 2003.

Haunted Hikes: Spine Tingling Tales and Trails from North America's National Parks, Santa Monica Press (Santa Monica, CA), 2006.

SIDELIGHTS: Andrea Lankford spent twelve years as a ranger for the National Park Service enforcing laws, fighting fires, and practicing wilderness medicine in locations such as Cape Hatteras, Zion, Yosemite, and the Grand Canyon. After leaving the Park Service, Lankford embarked on personal adventures that included hiking, kayaking, and mountain biking the Grand Canyon and the Arizona Trail, both of which touring adventures she recounts in her first two books.

In *Haunted Hikes: Spine Tingling Tales and Trails from North America's National Parks,* Lankford highlights fifty hikes, each of which is associated with a true or spooky story, many of which involve murdered or missing persons. The true stories include bleeding trees, a lake that burps, and brain-eating amoebas. *Library Journal* contributor Susan Belsky described the volume as being a "guide for the morbidly curious."

Lankford rates the fright factor of each story with from one to five skulls. Her curses, tales, and histories of people such as Charles Manson, who retreated to Death Valley, are contained in eight geographically themed chapters. Familiar legends such as Bigfoot and Sasquatch appear in various stories, but other lesser-known creatures like Florida's Skunk Ape are also included. In a review for the *RoadTrip America* Web site, Megan Edwards wrote, "The book would be valuable for the maps and descriptions of routes alone, but the well-told tales add a fascinating dimension. . . . Enhanced with photographs and loaded with plenty of suggestions for further research and reading, *Haunted Hikes* is no mere guidebook. It's a highly entertaining tapestry of stories that add a human (or inhuman) element to natural landscapes."

Lankford told *CA:* "My time as a park ranger continues to be a major influence in my work. I loved having a job that allowed me to enjoy nature every day, but I quickly learned that life as a park ranger was not all waterfalls and sunsets. Yet, despite many search and rescue missions with tragic endings, I also see an odd, undeniable beauty in frightening things that occur in gorgeous landscapes, such as the Grand Canyon, Yosemite, and Yellowstone. *Haunted Hikes* was my first attempt to share my passion for the stories behind the scenery in our national parks."

BIOGRAPHICAL AND CRITICAL SOURCES:

PERIODICALS

Library Journal, August 1, 2006, Susan Belsky, review of *Haunted Hikes: Spine Tingling Tales and Trails from North America's National Parks,* p. 110.

ONLINE

Andrea Lankford Home Page, http://www.haunted hiker.com (December 12, 2006).

eTorch (University of Tennessee), http://pr.tennessee. edu/etorch/ (December 12, 2006), review of *Haunted Hikes.*

RoadTrip America, http://www.roadtripamerica.com/ (October 8, 2006), Megan Edwards, review of *Haunted Hikes.*

*   *   *

LANKFORD, Andrea R.
See LANKFORD, Andrea

LANPHER, Katherine 1959-

PERSONAL: Born May 27, 1959; divorced. *Education:* Northwestern University, B.A.; University of Chicago, M.A.

ADDRESSES: Home—New York, NY. *E-mail*—leapdays@gmail.com.

CAREER: Radio personality and columnist. *St. Paul Pioneer-Press,* St. Paul, MN, reporter, 1972-82, columnist, 1982-88; "Midmorning," Minnesota Public Radio, radio host, 1988-2004; "Weeknights with Katherine Lanpher," KSTP-AM 1500, Maplewood, MN, radio host, 1995-96; "Al Franken Show," Air America Radio, New York, NY, cohost, 2004-05. Guest host on National Public Radio and commentator for CNN, MSNBC, and CNBC.

WRITINGS:

Leap Days: Chronicles of a Midlife Move (memoir), Springboard Press (New York, NY), 2006.

Contributor to the *New York Times* and *More* magazine.

SIDELIGHTS: Katherine Lanpher spent many years in the Twin Cities of Minnesota. Her sixteen-year tenure with the *St. Paul Pioneer-Press* followed by nearly sixteen years hosting Minnesota Public Radio's "Midmorning" show made her a regional celebrity. Lanpher's career turned to the national stage when she was asked to cohost the "Al Franken Show" on Air America Radio in New York. The move from three decades in Minnesota to New York was a significant moment in her life. Lanpher only remained with Air America for two years, leaving the show to fully devote her time to writing her first book, *Leap Days: Chronicles of a Midlife Move.*

The book, primarily a memoir, talks about the personal difficulty she faced involving changing careers in a new city during her midlife years. A critic writing in *Kirkus Reviews* called the book "tempting fare for anyone who's ever wondered: 'Who am I and how did I get here?'" *People* contributor Bethanne Patrick gave the book a four-star rating and labeled it "high flying." Writing in the *New York Times Book Review,* Eve Co-

nant noted that "some of Lanpher's writing is hokey" but conceded that "it's hard not to warm to her transparency." A reviewer in *Publishers Weekly* concluded that the writing is filled with "poignant candor and unconcealed wonder."

BIOGRAPHICAL AND CRITICAL SOURCES:

BOOKS

Lanpher, Katherine, *Leap Days: Chronicles of a Midlife Move,* Springboard Press (New York, NY), 2006.

PERIODICALS

Kirkus Reviews, June 15, 2006, review of *Leap Days,* p. 619.
New York Times, February 19, 2006, Stephen P. Williams, "Celebrity from the Midwest Finds a New Life in New York."
New York Times Book Review, December 10, 2006, Eve Conant, review of *Leap Days,* p. 34L.
People, October 16, 2006, Bethanne Patrick, review of *Leap Days,* p. 55.
Publishers Weekly, June 12, 2006, review of *Leap Days,* p. 38.
Villager (New York, NY), October 11-17, 2006, Steven Snyder, "Katherine Lanpher's Midlife Move."

ONLINE

Katherine Lanpher Home Page, http://www.katherinelanpher.com (January 26, 2007), author biography.*

*   *   *

LARSEN, Judy Merrill 1960-

PERSONAL: Born April, 1960, in Whittier, CA; married; children: five. *Education:* Graduated from the University of Wisconsin, Madison, 1982; earned master's degree from Washington University.

ADDRESSES: Home—St. Louis, MO. *Agent*—Marly Rusoff & Associates, Inc., P.O. Box 542, Bronxville, NY 10708.

CAREER: Writer and educator. Worked variously as a waitress, grocery checker, copy center clerk, deli clerk, sales clerk, substitute teacher, and English teacher.

WRITINGS:

All the Numbers (novel), Ballantine Books (New York, NY), 2006.

SIDELIGHTS: Judy Merrill Larsen moved around a lot as a child before studying in Wisconsin and settling in St. Louis, Missouri, with her husband and five children. Along with holding a number of different addresses, Larsen held numerous jobs. She stopped teaching to write her first novel, *All the Numbers.* Larsen explained her motivation in deciding to become a full-time writer in an interview on the Harford County Public Library Web site. She stated: "I had set a goal for myself that I would get to Europe and write a novel before I turned 40. So, in the summer of 1999, I took my sons to Europe for 17 days and then came home and wrote the first draft of this book. I turned 40 the following April."

All the Numbers tells the story of a woman, who after losing her youngest son in an accident, copes with her loss, her other son, and her attitude towards the teen responsible for his death. A contributor to *Kirkus Reviews* liked the way Larsen "builds a tender portrait" of the family but noted that "the story is too predictable." A *Publishers Weekly* reviewer concluded that "there are bright moments, but the book feels like a novella stretched too thin." Deborah Donovan, writing in *Booklist,* commented that "Larsen depicts a mother's year of grief and recovery with a sure and honest voice."

BIOGRAPHICAL AND CRITICAL SOURCES:

PERIODICALS

Booklist, June 1, 2006, Deborah Donovan, review of *All the Numbers,* p. 37.

Kirkus Reviews, June 1, 2006, review of *All the Numbers,* p. 537.
Publishers Weekly, May 1, 2006, review of *All the Numbers,* p. 31.

ONLINE

BookLoons, http://www.bookloons.com/ (January 27, 2007), Hilary Williamson, review of *All the Numbers.*
Harford County Public Library Web site, http://www. harf.lib.md.us/ (January 27, 2007), author interview.
Judy Merrill Larsen Home Page, http://www.judy merrilllarsen.com (January 27, 2007), author biography.
Random House Web site, http://www.randomhouse. com/ (January 27, 2007), author interview.

*			*			*

LEDUFF, Charlie 1967-

PERSONAL: Born 1967; married. *Education:* University of Michigan, B.A.; University of California, Berkeley, M.A.

ADDRESSES: Office—New York Times, 229 W. 43rd St., New York, NY 10036.

CAREER: New York Times, New York, NY, 1995—, began as reporter for metropolitan desk, became national correspondent in Los Angeles bureau. Worked previously as a reporter for *Alaska Fisherman's Journal,* as a middle-school teacher, baker, bartender, cannery worker, and gang counselor. Star of ten-part television series *Only in America;* star and narrator of documentary *United Gates of America.*

AWARDS, HONORS: Pulitzer Prize for National Reporting, 2001, for series "How Race Is Lived in America"; Meyer Berger Award, Columbia University Graduate School of Journalism, for writing style and stories reflecting the lives of everyday New Yorkers.

WRITINGS:

NONFICTION

Work and Other Sins: Life in New York City and Thereabouts, Penguin Press (New York, NY), 2004.

US Guys: The True and Twisted Mind of the American Man, Penguin Press (New York, NY), 2006.

SIDELIGHTS: Charlie LeDuff is a correspondent for the *New York Times* who contributed to a Pulitzer Prize-winning series of articles about race in America. LeDuff held a variety of jobs before taking up journalism, and as a reporter has frequently researched his articles by immersing himself in new professions. After working a variety of jobs, LeDuff began his writing career as an intern for the *Alaska Fisherman's Journal.* An outstanding obituary LeDuff wrote for a friend, a Russian youth who had died after the fall of the Soviet Union, caught the attention of some key people at the *New York Times,* and LeDuff was offered a ten-week chance to work with the prestigious newspaper. After the ten weeks were up, his term was extended into a six-month trial, then a three-year apprenticeship. LeDuff was hired as a full-fledged staff member shortly before starting work on the series that won the Pulitzer in 2001.

For his contribution to the prize-winning series, LeDuff went to North Carolina and got a job at the country's largest pork-processing plant. He found that while Caucasians, African-Americans, Hispanics, and Native Americans could all get jobs at the plant, the areas in which they worked were strictly, if unofficially, segregated. LeDuff described the brutality of slaughterhouse work and the unofficial politics of the workplace. LeDuff has written more than four hundred articles for the *Times,* his assignments ranging from roaming New York City in the guise of a blind person, to reporting on the war in Iraq while embedded in a unit of Marines.

LeDuff's first book was *Work and Other Sins: Life in New York City and Thereabouts.* In it, he offers profiles of various working people in New York, including a doorman, a gravedigger, slaughterhouse workers, a florist, a prostitute, and even an animal trapper. His portraits are "compelling and entertaining," stated Donna Seaman in *Booklist,* adding that they are "spiked with social commentary and graced with frank wonder" at the character of the people he writes about. A *Publishers Weekly* writer remarked on the author's respect for his subjects, and noted: "His carefully dry, clipped style honors their experiences and habits." Nevertheless, that writer did feel that LeDuff's tone was perhaps too detached, and stated that the author

"does little to advance the interests of his subjects." Another reviewer, Karen Valby in *Entertainment Weekly,* praised LeDuff's collection of character sketches as "extraordinary."

LeDuff again sought to illuminate the lives of ordinary Americans in his second book, *US Guys: The True and Twisted Mind of the American Man.* His "gonzo exploits in this book are nothing short of inspired," according to a *Publishers Weekly* writer. LeDuff tells of getting into a fight at a biker club, going out on assignment with homicide police in Detroit, spending time with gay rodeo riders, and discussing racial issues with football players in Texas. In the process he searches for insights into both the male psyche and the American way of life. The *Publishers Weekly* reviewer found LeDuff's work at times "self-consciously stylized," but praised it overall as "angry, touching, entertaining, and flawed."

BIOGRAPHICAL AND CRITICAL SOURCES:

PERIODICALS

Booklist, January 1, 2004, Donna Seaman, review of *Work and Other Sins: Life in New York City and Thereabouts,* p. 815.
Commentary, April, 2004, Luc Sante, review of *Work and Other Sins,* p. 75.
Entertainment Weekly, January 23, 2004, Karen Valby, review of *Work and Other Sins,* p. 105.
Kirkus Reviews, November 1, 2003, review of *Work and Other Sins,* p. 1301.
Library Journal, December, 2003, Suzanne W. Wood, review of *Work and Other Sins,* p. 147; November 1, 2006, Joseph L. Carlson, review of *US Guys: The True and Twisted Mind of the American Man,* p. 98.
PR Newswire, August 22, 2005, "Pulitzer Prize-Winning New York Times Reporter Charlie LeDuff Explores the Unique Subcultures That Exist Only in America."
Publishers Weekly, October 16, 2006, review of *US Guys,* p. 43; November 17, 2003, review of *Work and Other Sins,* p. 57.

ONLINE

Journalism Jobs, http://www.journalismjobs.com/ (January 18, 2007), interview with Charlie LeDuff.

Neiman Foundation for Journalism at Harvard University Web site, http://www.nieman.harvard.edu/ (January 18, 2007), biographical information about Charlie LeDuff.

San Francisco, http://www.sanfran.com/ (January 18, 2007), Bruce Kelley, "Charlie LeDuff's Bay Area Secrets."*

*   *   *

LEE, Rebecca 1967-

PERSONAL: Born 1967. *Education:* St. Olaf College, B.A., 1989; Iowa Writers' Workshop, M.F.A., 1992.

ADDRESSES: Office—Department of Creative Writing, University of North Carolina at Wilmington, 601 S. College Rd., Wilmington, NC 28403-5938. *E-mail*—leer@uncw.edu.

CAREER: University of North Carolina at Wilmington, professor of creative writing.

AWARDS, HONORS: Rona Jaffe Award for fiction, and National Magazine Award for fiction, both 2001; Radcliffe Institute fellow, 2001-02.

WRITINGS:

The City Is a Rising Tide (novel), Simon & Schuster (New York, NY), 2006.

Contributor to periodicals, including *Atlantic Monthly, Outside,* and *Zoetrope;* author of the screenplay *Emerson and Thoreau: The Winter of 1842.*

SIDELIGHTS: Rebecca Lee is the author of short stories, a play, and a novel titled *The City Is a Rising Tide,* set in the early 1990s. The narrator, Justine Laxness, spent much of her early life in Mao's China with her wealthy missionary parents and now lives in New York where she works for the Aquinas Foundation, a nonprofit intent on establishing a New Age healing center on the Yangtze River in China. The project is threatened by the government's plan to build a dam extension that will flood the land they wish to use.

Justine is in love with her boss, Peter, who is unattainable. She has known him since they first met in 1970s Beijing, when she was a child and he was working for Richard Nixon. At that time Peter was in love with Justine's nanny, Su Chen, who was at one time a companion to Mao and whose life ended tragically. It is in her memory that Peter wants to build the healing center.

A *Kirkus Reviews* contributor wrote: "Lee conjures affecting images of city vistas and (especially) the embracing presence of the Hudson River, observing such scenes with a deft balance of clinical precision and romantic hyperbole." Donna Seaman commented in *Booklist* that the novel "is significant and extraordinarily astute as rising tides literal and figurative threaten to drown dreams, love, and peace."

BIOGRAPHICAL AND CRITICAL SOURCES:

PERIODICALS

Booklist, June 1, 2006, Donna Seaman, review of *The City Is a Rising Tide,* p. 38.
Kirkus Reviews, May 15, 2006, review of *The City Is a Rising Tide,* p. 487.
Library Journal, June 1, 2006, David A. Berona, review of *The City Is a Rising Tide,* p. 108.
Publishers Weekly, May 8, 2006, review of *The City Is a Rising Tide,* p. 48.

*   *   *

LEFLORE, Lyah Beth 1970-

PERSONAL: Born 1970, in St. Louis, MO. *Education:* Stephens College, B.A.

ADDRESSES: Home—Los Angeles, CA.

CAREER: Nickelodeon, assistant to the vice president of programming, 1991-93; Uptown Entertainment, 1993-96, began as director of development, became associate producer of series *New York Undercover;* Haymon Development, vice president of television production and development, 1996-2004; writer, 2004—.

MEMBER: Alpha Kappa Alpha.

AWARDS, HONORS: Named as one of the "25 to watch under 25" by *Essence* magazine, 1995.

WRITINGS:

(With Charlotte Burley) *Cosmopolitan Girls* (novel), Harlem Moon/Broadway Books (New York, NY), 2004.

Last Night a DJ Saved My Life: A Novel, Harlem Moon/Broadway Books, 2006.

SIDELIGHTS: Lyah Beth LeFlore began a successful television career in her early twenties and has been involved in the development of many popular shows and series. She left television after the publication of her first novel, *Cosmopolitan Girls,* to concentrate on her writing.

LeFlore's debut, written with Charlotte Burley, was one of the early black chick-lit successes, about young women who may not have it all, but do have most of it, similar to their white counterparts in the hit Home Box Office series *Sex and the City.* Also set in New York, the story begins with the new friendship of copywriter Charlie Thornton and television producer Lindsey Bradley, forged over cosmopolitans in the Shark Bar. Both women are in unsatisfactory relationships from which they must free themselves. They provide support to each other as they face the business and relationship hurdles of modern life. *Booklist* contributor Lillian Lewis wrote that the authors "have many touching things to say about the nature of true friendship."

LeFlore's second book, *Last Night a DJ Saved My Life: A Novel,* features protagonist Destiny Day, a party planner who leads a chaotic life. Denise M. Doig reviewed the book in the *Black Issues Book Review,* noting that LeFlore reveals the dark side of wealth in addition to the glamour, and felt that the novel ranged "from downright funny to sad."

BIOGRAPHICAL AND CRITICAL SOURCES:

PERIODICALS

Black Issues Book Review, September-October, 2006, Denise M. Doig, review of *Last Night a DJ Saved My Life: A Novel,* p. 45.

Booklist, January 1, 2004, Lillian Lewis, review of *Cosmopolitan Girls,* p. 818.

Essence, July, 2006, Imani Powell, "Leaving the Glamorous Life: In Her Follow-up to the Popular *Cosmopolitan Girls,* Lyah Beth LeFlore Finds Pleasure in the Simple Things," p. 80.

New York Times, May 31, 2004, Lola Ogunnaike, review of *Cosmopolitan Girls.*

ONLINE

Bookreporter.com, http://www.bookreporter.com/ (February 3, 2006), Terry Miller, review of *Cosmopolitan Girls.*

Lyah Beth LeFlore Home Page, http://www.lyahbethleflore.com (February 3, 2007).

Philadelphia Inquirer Online, http://www.philly.com/ (July 12, 2006), Dwayne Campbell, review of *Last Night a DJ Saved My Life.*

Stephens College Web site, http://www.stephens.edu/ (February 3, 2007), author biography.*

* * *

LEGENDRE, Thomas

PERSONAL: Born in ME; married Allyson Stack (a creative writing instructor); children: two. *Education:* Attended the University of New Hampshire and University of Delaware; Arizona State University, M.F.A.

ADDRESSES: Home—Edinburgh, Scotland.

CAREER: Prescott College, Prescott, AZ, English instructor; writer.

WRITINGS:

The Burning: A Novel, Little, Brown (New York, NY), 2006.

SIDELIGHTS: Maine native Thomas Legendre was living in Edinburgh, Scotland, where his wife, writer Allyson Stack, was teaching and studying, when he completed his first book, *The Burning: A Novel.* Legendre was a student of economics who switched to the study of literature and creative writing, but economics is a major theme in the story, the opening of which was inspired by a successful evening playing blackjack in a Las Vegas casino.

The protagonist, Logan Smith, is in Las Vegas celebrating the completion of his doctoral dissertation. There he meets beautiful blackjack dealer Dallas Cole, who becomes his wife two years later. Like his creator, Logan accepts a teaching position in Arizona, where he revisits the neoclassical free market view of economics while Dallas, who does not adapt well to the new city nor to the idea of her husband spending all of his time working on his theories, develops a serious gambling problem and spends Logan's trust fund. Logan falls in love with Keris Aguilar, an astrophysicist who introduces him to Nicholas Georgescu, an economist who adds the missing pieces to Logan's work. Keris is also pursued by Deck, Logan's supply-sider department rival.

"The love affair between Logan and Keris is rendered with remarkable feeling and credibility," wrote Stephen Amidon in the *New Statesman.* "But the novel's greatest accomplishment is Dallas, a woman of great passions and considerable guile who is nevertheless being burned alive by an economic system that sees human beings as little more than fuel for its mindless and ultimately self-destructive growth."

In reviewing the novel in the *Independent,* contributor Matt Thorne wrote that "as well as being one of the few novels of ideas which actually gives the reader something to think about beyond the standard nihilism usually found in such books, Legendre is brilliant at three-dimensional descriptions, bringing to life everything from soda cans to distant constellations. His narrative grip never slackens, even in moments of dense economic theory, and *The Burning* provides enormous emotional and intellectual satisfaction."

BIOGRAPHICAL AND CRITICAL SOURCES:

PERIODICALS

Booklist, May 15, 2006, Joanne Wilkinson, review of *The Burning: A Novel,* p. 23.

Entertainment Weekly, July 21, 2006, Tina Jordan, review of *The Burning,* p. 75.
Kirkus Reviews, June 15, 2006, review of *The Burning,* p. 595.
New Statesman, March 20, 2006, Stephen Amidon, review of *The Burning,* p. 56.
Publishers Weekly, May 1, 2006, review of *The Burning,* p. 35.
Sunday Times (London, England), February 26, 2006, Anna Burnside, review of *The Burning.*

ONLINE

Guardian Unlimited, http://www.guardian.co.uk/ (April 15, 2006), Carrie O'Grady, review of *The Burning.*
Independent Online Edition, http://enjoyment. independent.co.uk/ (March 12, 2006), Matt Thorne, review of *The Burning.**

*   *   *

LESLAU, Wolf 1906-2006

OBITUARY NOTICE— See index for *CA* sketch: Born November 14, 1906, in Krzepice, Poland; died November 18, 2006, in Fullerton, CA. Linguist, educator, and author. A specialist in Semitic languages, Leslau was renowned for his work in recording disappearing tongues and dialects in Ethiopia. Eventually becoming fluent in seventeen languages, he attended the Sorbonne as a college student. Here he earned a degree in 1934; that year he also received a diploma from the Ecole des Hautes Etudes. His Ph.D. from the Sorbonne would be earned later, in 1953. Remaining at the latter institution, he lectured in southern Arabic until 1939. Germany would soon invade France, and Leslau, a Polish Jew, was sent to a concentration camp. Good fortune came in 1942, however, when an international organization secured his release. Along with his wife, Leslau fled to New York City, where he taught Semitic studies at the Ecole des Hautes Etudes' local campus. After World War II, he made what would be the first of numerous trips to Ethiopia while working for the Asia Institute. The African country had a number of Semitic communities, and Leslau set out to record their dying languages, such as the Gafat tongue. His dictionaries and grammar guides are the first written studies of many of these languages that belonged to tribes with oral traditions. He would win the Haile Selassie Award for Ethiopian Studies in 1965 for his work there. Leslau taught at Brandeis University in the early 1950s before moving to the University of California at Los Angeles in 1955. Here he was professor of Hebrew and Semitic languages and was founding chair of the university's department of Near Eastern and African languages. He retired in 1976. Also the recipient of the Lidzbarski Gold Medal Award in 1996 from the International Oriental Societies, Leslau was the author of numerous scholarly texts. Among these are *A Dictionary of Moca: Southwestern Ethiopia* (1958), *Harari* (1965), *Soddo* (1968), *Gurage Folkore: Ethiopian Folk Tales, Proverbs, Beliefs, and Riddles* (1982), and *Reference Grammar of Amharic* (1995).

OBITUARIES AND OTHER SOURCES:

PERIODICALS

Los Angeles Times, November 23, 2006, p. B9.

*   *   *

LESSING, Stephanie

PERSONAL: Married; children: one son, one daughter. *Education:* Boston University, graduated 1983.

ADDRESSES: Home—Demarest, NJ.

CAREER: Writer. *Mademoiselle* magazine, began as copywriter, became copy chief.

WRITINGS:

NOVELS

She's Got Issues, Avon Books (New York, NY), 2005.
Miss Understanding, Avon Books (New York, NY), 2006.

Also author of an unpublished book of essays, *A Girl's Guide to Girls.* Contributor to a tribute anthology honoring author Judy Blume. Contributor to periodi-

cals, including *Vogue, Vanity Fair, Glamour,* and *Mademoiselle.* Contributing editor to *Vogue, Glamour, Vanity Fair,* and *Mademoiselle.* Author of an advice column.

SIDELIGHTS: Stephanie Lessing began her writing career as a copywriter for *Mademoiselle* magazine, and her popular first novel, *She's Got Issues,* drew on her experiences in the world of fashion journalism. The novel grew out of an unpublished collection of essays, *A Girl's Guide to Girls.* When that book failed to find a publisher, Lessing reworked some of her essay material into fiction. "I chose one essay, 'Girl Boss,' and decided to see what it would be like to interview with the type of woman I describe in that essay," Lessing said in an interview for *Gothamist.* "Once I sent Chloe, the heroine of *She's Got Issues,* on her first interview, the book was as good as written. She became a human being as soon as she sat down in the reception area and I became fascinated by the way she reacted to the other girls around her. I just kept following her around and mimicking her. She wrote the book. I had nothing to do with it. I was nothing more than an observer with a pen throughout the entire process." Chloe Rose, who works at a fashion magazine called *Issues,* is a naive character who means well, but constantly finds herself getting into problematic situations and then telling little lies to get out of them. Sue Waldeck, a reviewer on the *Road to Romance* Web site, wrote: "Chloe is a sweet, naive, honest girly-girl who is charming and ditzy yet brilliant in her own way. I fell for her instantly."

Chloe's sister Zoe is the focus of Lessing's next book, *Miss Understanding.* Unlike Chloe, Zoe is quite intelligent, yet she remains "strangely clueless," according to Lisa Davis-Craig in *Library Journal.* She is hypochondriacal, obsessive-compulsive, and lacking in fashion sense. A former columnist for a publication called *The Radical Mind,* Zoe seems an unlikely choice to take over the editorship of *Issues,* yet so she does. Before long, however, Zoe begins the process of changing the magazine—renamed *Miss Understanding*—into a serious, feminist publication. One of her goals is to illuminate the reasons that women are sometimes so mean to each other. Yet Zoe is soon caught up in the sort of female power struggle she abhors, as members of her staff resist her plans to change the magazine in various ways. To complicate matters further, Zoe becomes pregnant, and so must endure her staff's mutiny while dealing with the many side effects of her condition. Reviewing Lessing's novel for *Booklist*, Aleksandra Kostovski found that it was overcrowded with strange characters and plot twists, but appreciated the author's "weird and unique take" on life in the modern workplace.

BIOGRAPHICAL AND CRITICAL SOURCES:

PERIODICALS

Booklist, September 15, 2006, Aleksandra Kostovski, review of *Miss Understanding*, p. 28.
Kirkus Reviews, September 1, 2006, review of *Miss Understanding*, p. 868.
Library Journal, September 15, 2006, Lisa Davis-Craig, review of *Miss Understanding*, p. 49.
PR Newswire, December 1, 2005, "Hudson Booksellers Announced National Distribution of Author Stephanie Lessing's 'She's Got Issues.'"
Publishers Weekly, August 21, 2006, review of *Miss Understanding*, p. 47.

ONLINE

BookLoons, http://www.bookloons.com/ (January 15, 2006), Marie Hashima Lofton, review of *She's Got Issues*.
Conversations with Famous Writers, http://conversationsfamouswriters.blogspot.com/ (October 7, 2005), interview with Stephanie Lessing.
Gothamist, http://www.gothamist.com/ (August 16, 2005), review of *She's Got Issues*.
Road to Romance, http://www.roadtoromance.ca/ (January 16, 2006), Sue Waldeck, review of *She's Got Issues*.
Stephanie Lessing Home Page, http://www.stephanie lessing.com (January 15, 2006).*

*   *   *

LI, Laura Tyson 1963(?)-

PERSONAL: Born c. 1963, in San Francisco, CA; married; two children. *Education:* Dartmouth College, B.A., 1985.

ADDRESSES: Home—New York, NY. *Agent*—Elizabeth Sheinkman, Elaine Markson Literary Agency, 44 Greenwich Ave., New York, NY 10011. *E-mail*—lauratysonli@hotmail.com.

CAREER: Journalist. *South China Morning Post*, former business reporter; *Financial Times*, Taiwan correspondent, 1994-98.

WRITINGS:

Madame Chiang Kai-Shek: China's Eternal First Lady, Atlantic Monthly (New York, NY), 2006.

Contributor to publications, including the *Economist*.

SIDELIGHTS: Laura Tyson Li was raised in Cornwall, Connecticut, and went on to major in East Asian Studies at Dartmouth College in New Hampshire. From there, she moved to Asia, where she spent a decade studying and working in China, Hong Kong, and Taiwan. She served as a business reporter for the *South China Morning Post* and the Taiwan correspondent for the *Financial Times*. Eventually, Li returned to the United States, where she settled in New York City with her husband and daughter, and began concentrating on her first book. *Madame Chiang Kai-Shek: China's Eternal First Lady*, a biography, is the result of Li's longtime interest in the woman. She first wrote about her for the weekend section of the *Financial Times* when Madame was celebrating her one hundredth birthday in 1997. Li was captivated by the varying opinions people held regarding the woman, even after she had been living abroad for decades. Donna Seaman, writing for *Booklist*, remarked: "Li brilliantly analyzes a fearless and profoundly conflicted woman of extraordinary force." A contributor for *Kirkus Reviews* called the book "a well-balanced biography of one of the most powerful women in Chinese history" and "an interesting and detailed account." A reviewer for *Publishers Weekly* found the book to be "a well-researched, fluently written assessment."

BIOGRAPHICAL AND CRITICAL SOURCES:

PERIODICALS

Booklist, June 1, 2006, Donna Seaman, review of *Madame Chiang Kai-Shek: China's Eternal First Lady*, p. 28.

Kirkus Reviews, June 15, 2006, review of *Madame Chiang Kai-Shek,* p. 619.
Los Angeles Times, November 10, 2006, review of *Madame Chiang Kai-Shek.*
Publishers Weekly, May 22, 2006, review of *Madame Chiang Kai-Shek,* p. 41.

ONLINE

Daily Record Online, http://www.dailyrecord.com/ (January 19, 2006), Meredith Napolitano, "A Dragon Lady's Life."
Laura Tyson Li Home Page, http://www.lauratysonli.com (March 14, 2007).

* * *

LINS, Paulo 1958-

PERSONAL: Born 1958, in Rio de Janeiro, Brazil; son of a house painter and a domestic helper.

ADDRESSES: Home—Rio de Janeiro, Brazil.

CAREER: Universidade Federal do Rio de Janeiro, Rio de Janeiro, Brazil, professor. University of California, Berkeley, Center for Latin American Studies, Mario de Andrade Chair in Brazilian Culture, 2004; cofounder of Cooperativa de Poetas; member of jury of Premio Casa de las Américas.

WRITINGS:

Cidade de Deus (novel), Companhia das Letras (São Paulo, Brazil), 1997, translation by Alison Entrekin published as *City of God,* Black Cat (New York, NY), 2006.

Author of *Sob o Sol,* a poetry collection. Also author of two screenplays.

ADAPTATIONS: City of God was adapted as a motion picture, 2002.

SIDELIGHTS: Paulo Lins is the author of *City of God,* "a sprawling epic of gang life in the shantytowns of Rio de Janeiro," remarked *Library Journal* critic Jack Shreve. Lins, a native of Rio, grew up in a wretched, crime-plagued housing project known as Cidade de Deus ("City of God"), originally created in the 1960s for displaced flood victims. "Everything that happened in that book is drawn from reality," the author stated on the *Latin America News* Web site. His novel, first published in 1997, gave many Brazilians their first look at life in a favela, or slum. "These are two different worlds that have no contact with each other," Lins added. "The elite is ignorant of the favela because it doesn't want to see, and the favela doesn't know the rest of Brazil because it is deprived of the means and the opportunity."

Covering three decades, *City of God* chronicles the lives of the myriad gangsters who inhabit the projects, including Hellraiser, Sparrow, and Tiny, who vie for control of the city's drug dens. "A multiethnic horde of minor characters flit in and out of the gangsters' truncated lives as they plot and execute holdups, whack friends, relatives and rivals, obsessively pursue women, drugs, samba prowess, revenge and loot," noted a contributor in *Kirkus Reviews.* According to a *Publishers Weekly* reviewer, Lins "serves up a Scarface-like urban epic, bursting with encyclopedic, graphic descriptions of violence, punctuated with lyricism and longing."

Despite the success of his novel, Lins remains humble. "Just in the City of God alone there are hundreds of people exactly like me, with the same aspirations and even the same abilities," he remarked on the *Latin America News* Web site. "The favela has left its mark on me as much as them, but the difference is that I managed to find a way to circumvent the social structure and conditions that hold back the resident of the favela, and was able to get out."

BIOGRAPHICAL AND CRITICAL SOURCES:

PERIODICALS

Booklist, September 1, 2006, Keir Graff, review of *City of God,* p. 55.
Kirkus Reviews, July 15, 2006, review of *City of God,* p. 693.
Library Journal, November 1, 2006, Jack Shreve, review of *City of God,* p. 69.

Publishers Weekly, August 7, 2006, review of *City of God,* p. 29.

ONLINE

Latin America News Web site, http://lamnews.com (April 27, 2004), "Out of the Slums of Rio, an Author Finds Fame."*

*   *   *

LION, Melissa 1976-

PERSONAL: Born 1976, in CA. *Education:* Saint Mary's College, M.F.A.

ADDRESSES: *Home and office*—San Francisco, CA. *E-mail*—melissalion@hotmail.com.

CAREER: Bookseller and writer. Instructor at Saint Mary's College.

WRITINGS:

Swollen, Wendy Lamb (New York, NY), 2004.
Upstream, Wendy Lamb (New York, NY), 2005.

Contributor of fiction to periodicals, including *Santa Monica Review* and *Other Voices.* Contributor to anthologies, including *The Crucifix Is Down,* Red Hen Press.

SIDELIGHTS: Melissa Lion's novel *Swollen* focuses on a young woman's struggle to come to terms with her unwillingness to trust others. Samantha's parents are divorced; her mother is absent, and her womanizing father cheats on his live-in and pregnant girlfriend, Ruth, whom Samantha admires. Two events ultimately cause Samantha's life to change: for one, a popular boy in her high school—and the star of the school's track team to which she also belongs—mysteriously dies, and for the other, she begins a romantic relationship with Farouk, an immigrant student. Torn between her love of running and her romance with Farouk, Samantha leaves the track team, but when the relationship ends it confirms Samantha's

suspicion that all men cheat. Fortunately, Ruth's decision to finally exhibit some self-respect impacts Samantha more positively, and the teen ultimately finds sanctuary with Ruth and her new baby brother.

While a *Publishers Weekly* contributor faulted *Swollen* for building to a conclusion that the reviewer characterized as somewhat "ambiguous," other critics found Lion's conclusion more satisfying. Susan Riley, reviewing the book for *School Library Journal,* praised Lion's fiction debut as "an achingly beautiful story that shows one young woman's growing strength as she realizes that she deserves better."

Lion found her inspiration for writing *Swollen* while watching a group of teen girls running track near her home in La Jolla, California. "I wondered what it was like to be the most middle girl in the pack," she explained to an online interviewer for *Bookselling This Week.* "I wasn't on any sports team and I hated to run, but I remember longing to be in the lead, in anything." Commenting on the author's focus on the girl in the middle, Reyhan Harmanci commented in the *San Francisco Chronicle* that "rarely . . . has a high school protagonist perched between social groups been rendered as skillfully and soulfully as Samantha." Debbie Carton, reviewing *Swollen* for *Booklist,* concluded that, with its "clear, distinctive language," *Swollen* "will keep teens reading and savoring."

Lion's second novel, *Upstream,* features a more confident protagonist. Grieving over the death of her boyfriend, high school senior Martha struggles to deal with the pity she receives from her Alaskan community. Lion uses the Alaskan landscape to mirror Martha's inner journey, depicting the teen's grief and guilt at the part she played in the accident that led to her boyfriend's death. "It is this very concrete evocation of place and people that makes this offering stand out," concluded Vicky Smith in a *Horn Book* review of *Upstream.* "Lion writes with sensitivity and depth," *Booklist* critic Gillian Engberg noted of the book, while Johanna Lewis commented in *School Library Journal* that Lion's "descriptions, especially of emotion or moment, are resonant and truthful." Reviewing the novel for *Kliatt,* Claire Rosser maintained that Lion "continues to demonstrate her skill and her commitment to her YA readers" in her sophomore effort, while in *Kirkus Reviews* a contributor deemed the novelist "a YA author to watch."

Lion's vivid memory of her teen years serves her well in her career as an author. As she told Carolyn Juris in an interview for *Teen Reads* online, "I remember so clearly what they [teen girls] are going through. And I watch them and my own emotions are right there."

BIOGRAPHICAL AND CRITICAL SOURCES:

PERIODICALS

Booklist, October 15, 2004, Debbie Carton, review of *Swollen,* p. 398; June 1, 2005, Gillian Engberg, review of *Upstream,* p. 1786.
Bulletin of the Center for Children's Books, October, 2004, Karen Coats, review of *Swollen,* p. 87.
Horn Book, March-April, 2005, Vicky Smith, review of *Upstream,* p. 205.
Journal of Adolescent and Adult Literacy, March, 2005, Nicole Denourie, review of *Swollen,* p. 525.
Kirkus Reviews, July 15, 2004, review of *Swollen,* p. 690; April 15, 2005, review of *Upstream,* p. 477.
Kliatt, July, 2004, Claire Rosser, review of *Swollen,* p. 10; May, 2006, Claire Rosser, review of *Swollen,* p. 20; March, 2005, Melissa Lion, "Why I Write," pp. 4-5; May, 2005, Claire Rosser, review of *Upstream,* p. 15.
Publishers Weekly, September 13, 2004, review of *Swollen,* p. 80.
San Francisco Chronicle, September 26, 2004, Reyhan Harmanci, "Running through High School, Tripped Up by Death," p. M6.
School Library Journal, August, 2004, Susan Riley, review of *Swollen,* p. 126; July, 2005, Johanna Lewis, review of *Upstream,* p. 105.
Voice of Youth Advocates, August, 2004, review of *Swollen,* p. 221; June, 2005, Leslie Carter, review of *Upstream,* p. 132.

ONLINE

Bookselling This Week Online (American Booksellers Association), http://news.bookweb.org/ (September 23, 2004), Nomi Schwartz, "Looking at Life from Both Sides Now: Melissa Lion, Bookseller/ Author."
Melissa Lion Home Page, http://www.melissalion.com (January 11, 2007).
Random House Web site, http://www.randomhouse. com/ (January 11, 2007), "Melissa Lion."
Teen Reads Web site, http://www.teenreads.com/ (June 15, 2005), Carolyn Juris, interview with Lion.*

LIPARULO, Robert

PERSONAL: Born in NY; married; wife's name Jodi; children: Melanie, Matthew, Anthony, Isabella. *Education:* Graduate of Weber State University. *Hobbies and other interests:* Swimming, scuba diving, travel, movies, reading, family.

ADDRESSES: Home—CO. *Agent*—Joel Gotler, Intellectual Property Group, 9200 Sunset Blvd., Ste. 820, Los Angeles, CA 90069-3607. *E-mail*—joel@ipglm. com.

CAREER: Writer.

WRITINGS:

Comes a Horseman (novel), WestBow Press (Nashville, TN), 2005.
Germ (novel), WestBow Press (Nashville, TN), 2006.
Deadfall (novel), WestBow Press (Nashville, TN), 2007.

Contributor to books, including *Thriller,* Mira Books (Ontario, Canada), 2006. Contributor to periodicals, including *Travel & Leisure, Consumer's Digest, Reader's Digest, Modern Bride, Chief Executive,* and the *Arizona Daily Star;* celebrity interviewer and author of screenplays. *New Man* magazine, contributing editor.

ADAPTATIONS: Movie rights to *Comes a Horseman* were purchased by Mace Neufeld. Movie and video game rights to *Germ* were purchased by Red Eagle Entertainment.

SIDELIGHTS: Early in his career, Robert Liparulo wrote screenplays and reviewed celebrities, including rock-and-roll stars like Bruce Springsteen. He then began writing action-adventure thrillers. Responding to a question regarding his faith and how it affects his writing posed by an interviewer for *Christian Fandom* online, he responded: "Jesus Christ is my Lord and Savior. Without Him, we'd all be on a hell-bound train. My gifts and skills as a writer come from Him. They are not for me or my own benefit, but given to me to bless others. I want to honor Him by doing the best job I can do. I trust that He is in everything I do, even if I'm not conscious about 'putting' Him there." Liparulo doesn't shy away from the darker side of mankind, however. In an interview with Robin Parrish of *Infuze* online, he said: "I don't mind depicting sin in fiction, because as long as it's depicted as a problem, as long as that sin does what sin does. As long as it brings you down or attracts more sin. Paint it for what it is; don't glorify it. But I don't mind seeing real sin depicted in fiction."

Liparulo's *Comes a Horseman,* was described by *Christianity Today* reviewer Cindy Crosby, as being a "chilling debut," part *The DaVinci Code,* part "Left Behind," and part Tom Clancy thriller. Luco Scaramuzzi supposes himself to be the long-promised antichrist and will be supported by the Watchers, who have been awaiting his arrival, if he can prove that he is. Federal agent Brady Moore is recovering from the death of his wife, and agent Alicia Wagner, who has feelings for him, wisely lets him heal. They are investigating a series of beheadings of people who seem to have no connection with each other. In reviewing the novel for *Bookreporter.com,* Joe Hartlaub wrote: "Liparulo puts the reader right in the room during the investigation of one of these murders, and it's not a pretty sight. . . . . His characters, particularly Moore, are unforgettable, and his villains are everything that bad guys should, and shouldn't, be."

Germ is a thriller in which an Ebola virus has been programmed to seek out and destroy specific targets by identifying their DNA. The story opens with Despesorio Vero, lab assistant to scientist Karl Litt, watching a patient die as his organs liquefy. Time passes and Despesorio and agent Goodwin Donnelly are killed by assassin Atropos, who is eliminating everyone connected to the investigation. Before thousands are killed, special agent Julia Matheson must find the source of the virus, with the help of a memory chip and clue left behind by Goodwin, who was her partner. The creator of the virus is revealed, as well as the origins of the research begun in Germany during World War II.

A *Publishers Weekly* contributor wrote: "Plenty of technical details . . . help differentiate this story from the run-of-the-mill thriller." W. Terry Whalin reviewed *Germ* for *FaithfulReader.com,* concluding that "Liparulo has crafted a multi-strand page turner and a highly recommended thriller."

Liparulo told *CA:* "I started writing poems when I was about eight. I went door to door selling the poems for pennies. My neighbors were very kind. I started a novel when I was thirteen and published my first article in a newspaper when I was fourteen. I started writing short stories for magazines, and when that market dried up, switched to nonfiction articles—celebrity profiles, movie and book reviews, investigative pieces. Right after college, I edited an entertainment magazine in Colorado, so I got a chance to hang out backstage and interview a lot of rock'n'roll greats: Bruce Springsteen, The Who, Chicago, etc. I wrote several screenplays, about half of which sold, but never got off the ground.

"I lean toward horror, psychological suspense, and action, so I think the authors who really shaped the way I approach writing and my writing style are: Richard Matheson—his *I Am Legend* shocked me, in a good way, when I read it at age eleven. It showed me how powerful stories can be. Stephen King's *The Stand* and Tolkien's *Lord of the Rings* showed me that there are no limits to the size and scope and majesty of novels, and Peter Straub's *Ghost Story* proved that 'little' stories can be 'big.' Thomas Perry's *The Butcher's Boy* helped me fine-tune what I liked about thrillers and taught me about irony. David Morrell's *Testament* introduced me to the horror that can spin off of real life. James Dickey's *Deliverance* is about as perfect a novel as can be written. I loved the literary classics, as well: *The Turn of the Screw, The House of the Seven Gables, Moby Dick,* and *The Last of the Mohicans.* As diverse as this list seems, really they primarily fall into two genres: action or suspense, and that's what I write.

"My advice to writers: 1. To paraphrase Winston Churchill: 'Never, never, never give up.' 2. Develop your own style. Don't try to mimic someone else's and don't let an editor mess with it. At the end of the day, style is really all you bring to the table. Stories and plots are a dime a dozen. Style is what makes you different from all the other writers out there. 3. Understand that the craft of writing is only half of what it takes to be a published author. The other half is working with editors, meeting deadlines, marketing your books and yourself, and all that other stuff that feels like garbage because it's not writing."

BIOGRAPHICAL AND CRITICAL SOURCES:

PERIODICALS

Christianity Today, November, 2005, Cindy Crosby, review of *Comes a Horseman,* p. 100.

Gazette Telegraph, December 9, 2006, Paul Asay, "Label Breaker."

Publishers Weekly, September 5, 2005, review of *Comes a Horseman,* p. 35; September 25, 2006, review of *Germ,* p. 47.

ONLINE

Bookreporter.com, http://www.bookreporter.com/ (December 16, 2006), Joe Hartlaub, review of *Comes a Horseman.*

Christian Fandom, http://www.swcp.com/christian-fandom/oli-rl.html/ (December 17, 2006), "Interview: Robert Liparulo."

Comes a Horseman Web site, http://www.comesa horsemanbook.com (December 17, 2006).

FaithfulReader.com, http://www.faithfulreader.com/ (December 17, 2006), W. Terry Whalin, review of *Germ.*

Infuze, http://www.infuzemagazine.com/ (December 17, 2006), Robin Parrish, author interview.

Robert Liparulo Home Page, http://www.robert liparulo.com (December 17, 2006).

Who Dunnit, http://www.who-dunnit.com/ (December 17, 2006), Alan Paul Curtis, review of *Comes a Horseman.*

*   *   *

LIPSET, Seymour Martin 1922-2006

OBITUARY NOTICE— See index for *CA* sketch: Born March 18, 1922, in New York, NY; died of a stroke, December 31, 2006, in Arlington, VA. Sociologist, political scientist, educator, and author. An eminent political sociologist, Lipset was renowned for his groundbreaking work in studying American society and how the unique history and character of the nation influenced the course of its politics. The son of Jewish immigrants from Russia, he was born in Harlem and grew up in the Bronx. His parents wanted him to study dentistry, so that he could eventually take over his uncle's practice. After one year in college, however, Lipset became more interested in history and politics. While at the City College of New York, he was drawn to the active student socialist community there and became a member of the Young People's Socialist League. Among this group were such future luminaries as critic Alfred Kazin, political journalist Nathan Glazer, and sociologist Daniel Bell. Lipset graduated in 1943, and by this time had become fascinated with a sociopolitical problem: why had the United States so stringently resisted becoming a communist country when Karl Marx had predicted it would be the first nation to convert to this political model? To better understand this problem, he traveled to neighboring Canada to study how its government and society differed from that in the United States. He analyzed the Co-operative Commonwealth Federation in Saskatchewan, Canada's most prominent leftist party at the time, and compared it with America in his classic work *Agrarian Socialism* (1950). The issue was further explored in such volumes as *The First New Nation* (1963) and *North American Cultures: Values and Institutions in Canada and the United States* (1990). Meanwhile, Lipset completed his Ph.D. at Columbia University in 1949 and taught at the University of Toronto in the early 1950s. He then joined the Columbia University faculty, where he was assistant director of the Bureau of Applied Social Research. Moving on to the University of California at Berkeley in 1956, he directed its Institute of International Studies from 1962 to 1966. Over the years, Lipset became more conservative. Though still a Democrat, he was one of the first prominent scholars associated with the neoconservative movement. He came to understand that it was the American belief in the importance of individualism that made the United States resistant to communism; indeed, the politics of the country even prevented a major socialist party from successfully forming. Lipset discussed in clear, jargon-free prose his many conclusions and theories in his important most work, *Political Man* (1960), which was later expanded as *Political Man: The Social Basis of Politics* (1981). Here he covered topics ranging from industrialization and social hierarchies to public opinion and democratic ideals. A nominee for the National Book Award, it was published all over the world and sold over four hundred thousand copies. He would be nominated for a second National Book Award for *The First New Nation: The U.S. in Historical and Comparative Perspective* (1963; 2nd edition, 1981). Lipset would later teach at Harvard, where he was George D. Markham Professor of Government; from 1975 to 1992 he was a professor at Stanford University, retiring as Caroline S.G. Munro Professor. A former president of both the American Political Science Association and the American Sociological Association, he would become active in the B'nai B'rith Hillel Foundation as he reconnected with his Jewish roots. Deeply concerned about the conflicts in the Middle East, he was a former president of American Professors for Peace in the Middle East and the Progressive Foundation, chaired the U.S. Institute for Peace and the Aurora Foundation, and was cochair of the executive committee for the International Center for Peace in the Middle East. Among his other important publications are *Revolution and Counterrevolution* (1968; revised edition, 1988), *Opportunity and Welfare in the First New Nation* (1974), *The Confidence Gap: Business, Labor, and Government in the Public Mind* (1983), *American Exceptionalism: A Double-edged Sword* (1996), and *It Didn't Happen Here: Why Socialism Failed in the United States* (2000).

OBITUARIES AND OTHER SOURCES:

PERIODICALS

Times (London, England), January 11, 2007, p. 60.
New York Times, January 4, 2007, p. A21.

*   *   *

LIPSTEIN, Kurt 1909-2006

OBITUARY NOTICE— See index for *CA* sketch: Born March 19, 1909, in Frankfurt am Main, Germany; died December 2, 2006. Educator and author. Lipstein was a former Cambridge University professor of comparative law and a noted expert on private international law. A 1931 graduate of the University of Berlin, he was a member of the Prussian Judicial Service for two years before enrolling at Cambridge University. Here he completed a Ph.D. in 1936 and was later a faculty secretary there. He was hired as a lecturer at Cambridge in 1946 and was a director of research for the International Association for Legal Science from 1954 to 1959. Lipstein was made a fellow of Clare College in 1956 and a reader in conflict of laws at Cambridge in 1962. From 1973 to 1976 he served as professor of comparative law. Earning the Humboldt Prize in 1980, he also held honorary degrees from Cambridge and the University of Würzburg. Lipstein was the author of such works as *The Law of the European Economic Community* (1974) and *Principles of the Conflict of Laws: National and International* (1981).

OBITUARIES AND OTHER SOURCES:

PERIODICALS

Times (London, England), January 18, 2007, p. 57.

*   *   *

LISTER, Michael

PERSONAL: Married; wife's name Pam; children: two. *Hobbies and other interests:* Rock, blues, and alternative music, basketball, reading, movies, art, religion, Mustangs.

ADDRESSES: Home—Wewahitchka, FL. *Office*— Sunshine and Crime, P.O. Box 35038, Panama City, FL 32412. *E-mail*—michaellister@mchsi.com.

CAREER: Florida Department of Corrections, chaplain, 1993-2000; Triple Horse Entertainment, Atlanta, GA, senior staff writer; freelance writer, 2000—. Owner, with Jamie Lester, and writer and editor, of the *Gulf Country Breeze* (newspaper), Wewahitchka, FL, 2003—; Gulf Coast Community College, adjunct professor. Founder of the Direct Effect Project, Michael Lister Ministries, Pottersville Press, and Pottersville Productions.

WRITINGS:

(Editor) *North Florida Noir,* Pottersville Press (Panama City, FL), 2006.

"JOHN JORDAN" MYSTERY SERIES

Power in the Blood, Pineapple Press (Sarasota, FL), 1997.
Blood of the Lamb, Bleak House Books (Madison, WI), 2004.
Flesh and Blood and Other John Jordan Stories, Pottersville Press (Panama City, FL), 2006.

Reviewer at *Sunshine and Crime* online.

SIDELIGHTS: Before becoming a writer in 2000, Michael Lister was the youngest chaplain to work in the Florida Department of Corrections. He has continued his work on behalf of those who need it through his ministry and nonprofit, the Direct Effect Project, all the proceeds from which go to support the incarcerated, hungry, and sick, and provide educational support for children. Lister also teaches and speaks about writing, art, life, and religion and founded his own publishing and production companies, Pottersville Press and Pottersville Productions, the names of which were obviously inspired by one of his favorite films, *It's a Wonderful Life.* He continues to volunteer in the prison system.

Lister began a series of books featuring the character John Jordan with *Power in the Blood,* called "a promising first novel" by *Library Journal* reviewer Rex E. Klett. John is a former police detective, now a prison chaplain, a flawed man of faith who does not believe in organized religion and who suffers from depression and alcoholism. In this story he witnesses what seems to be the death of a prisoner who was trying to escape, and investigates to learn the truth. His progress is hindered by Tom Daniels, his former father-in-law and a state prison inspector, and helped by nurse Strickland, classification officer Anna Rodden, and Merrill Monroe, the black guard who is his best friend. John fears that he may have contracted AIDS from the blood of an HIV-positive inmate, and struggles to control his lust for Laura, a Federal Express driver. The plot becomes more complex with the death of a local banker. Mary Frances Wilkens wrote in *Booklist* that "this competent, authentic tale carves a nice niche for itself."

The second book in the series is *Blood of the Lamb,* and Lister followed with *Flesh and Blood and Other John Jordan Stories,* a collection of seven tales about seven different cases, which a *Publishers Weekly* reviewer felt "will appeal more to a Christian audience than general mystery readers." In one story a young virgin nun who flees Hurricane Katrina becomes pregnant, and in another John's ailing mother asks him to investigate the healing properties of the Shroud of Turin. In a review for the Panama City, Florida, *News Herald,* David Vest noted that each of the stories "provides a separate character study of Jordan. That character includes a strong current of spirituality—whether he likes it or not. The current runs outside the prison walls as well as within, often bumping up against Jordan's skepticism and strong sense of reason."

BIOGRAPHICAL AND CRITICAL SOURCES:

PERIODICALS

Booklist, September 15, 1997, Mary Frances Wilkens, review of *Power in the Blood,* p. 214.
Library Journal, August, 1997, Rex E. Klett, review of *Power in the Blood,* p. 139.
News Herald (Panama City, FL), November 12, 2006, David Vest, review of *Flesh and Blood and Other John Jordan Stories.*
Publishers Weekly, July 21, 1997, review of *Power in the Blood,* p. 188; October 2, 2006, review of *Flesh and Blood,* p. 42.

ONLINE

Direct Effect Project Web site, http://www.directeffect.com/ (December 16, 2006).
Michael Lister Home Page, http://www.michaellister.com (December 16, 2006).
Sunshine and Crime, http://www.sunshineandcrime.com/ (December 16, 2006).

*   *   *

LLERENA, Mario 1913-2006
(Rafael Mario Ramón Llerena, Ara Niemoller)

OBITUARY NOTICE— See index for *CA* sketch: Born March 5, 1913, in Placetas, Las Villas, Cuba; died December 10, 2006, in Miami, FL. Activist, journalist, and author. A supporter of Cuba's Fidel Castro before Castro took power, Llerena later became a critic of the revolutionary leader when Castro revealed himself to be a communist. A 1940 graduate of the University of Havana, where he was a philosophy major, he taught elementary and high school classes in Cuba until 1942. Contemplating a career in the ministry, he attended Princeton Theological Seminary, but then decided to become a writer. A Spanish instructor at Duke University from 1948 to 1952, Llerena then traveled to Mexico. It was there that he first met Castro, who was living in exile and planning to overthrow the government of General Fulgencio Batista in Cuba. Llerena became a Castro supporter and wrote a pamphlet, *Nuestra Razón,* that was published in Mexico and stated the justification for a Cuban revolution. His writing skills and connections in the United States made him an ideal public relations person for Castro; he had his articles published in the *New York Times* and other newspapers in support of the cause. In 1957, when rumors were flying that Castro had died, Llerena made it known that he was alive and raising an army in the mountains of Cuba. He served as chair of the July 26 Movement in New York, the organization that supported Castro, and he also worked for freedom of speech in Cuba as head of the Committee for Cultural Freedom there. Castro and Llerena fell into a disagreement, however, when the latter participated in peace talks with the Batista government. Castro felt that Llerena had overstepped his bounds and the two parted ways. When Castro came to power two years later, the new Cuban leader made his true colors known. Llerena had thought that Castro would bring democracy to Cuba; instead, he showed himself to be a communist dictator. Llerena remained in his homeland for several years, working as a freelance writer and publishing articles against Castro's policies. He left Cuba in 1960, however, moving to New York City and then Miami. He was an assistant editor at the University of Miami Press from 1967 to 1972, later becoming chief editor of LOGOI, Inc. Llerena penned books about the Cuban Revolution, including *The Unsuspected Revolution: The Birth and Rise of Castroism* (1978) and *The Myth and the Mirage: Six Essays on Revolution* (1995).

OBITUARIES AND OTHER SOURCES:

PERIODICALS

New York Times, December 12, 2006, p. A29.

     *   *   *

LLERENA, Rafael Mario Ramón
   See LLERENA, Mario

LOKKO, Lesley 1964-
   (Lesley Naa Norle Lokko)

PERSONAL: Born 1964, in Dundee, Scotland; daughter of a surgeon father. *Education:* Attended Oxford University; Bartlett School of Architecture, B.Sc., 1992, Diploma in Architecture, 1995; University of London, Ph.D., 2007.

ADDRESSES: Home—Accra, Ghana, and London, England. *Agent*—Christine Green, 6 Whitehorse Mews, Westminster Bridge Rd., London SE1 7QD, England.

CAREER: Architect, educator, and writer. Taught at Bartlett School of Architecture, London Metropolitan University, Kingston University, Iowa State University, University of Illinois at Chicago, and University of Capetown; currently visiting professor at Westminster University.

WRITINGS:

NOVELS

Sundowners, Orion (London, England), 2003.
Saffron Skies, Orion (London, England), 2005, St. Martin's Press (New York, NY), 2006.
Bitter Chocolate, Orion (London, England), 2007.

NONFICTION

(Editor and contributor) *White Papers, Black Marks: Architecture, Race, Culture,* University of Minnesota Press (Minneapolis, MN), 2000.

Contributor to periodicals, including the *Guardian.*

SIDELIGHTS: Lesley Lokko, a writer, educator, and architect, is the author of several of popular romance novels, including *Sundowners* and *Saffron Skies.* Lokko, who was born in Scotland and grew up in Ghana, made her publishing debut in 2000, serving as the editor for *White Papers, Black Marks: Architecture, Race, Culture,* a work that examines how racial ideology affects architectural design. "I've tried to argue that architecture is not just a technical discipline, it's also a cultural discipline, and issues of history, identity and migration are very much part of the culture," she told Susan Mansfield in the *Scotsman*. "Different cultures look at space, surface, line, beauty, and have different ways of understanding them. I'm interested in trying to make a space where students can explore these things."

Between 1992 and 1994, Lokko worked as an architect in South Africa, where she was inspired to try her hand at fiction. More than a decade later, she published *Sundowners*, "a big, glamorous doorstop of a book full of designer labels and luxury houses in the mould of the 1980s blockbusters by Jackie Collins or Judith Krantz," Mansfield observed. Set against the backdrop of the apartheid era in South Africa, the work follows the lives of four women over a span of twenty years. According to Pamela Buxton in *Building Design,* the novel "is bursting with inflamed passions but it's certainly more than mere chick-lit—as well as following the romantic fortunes of the protagonists, the novel's backbone is South African politics and human rights." In Lokko's family saga *Saffron Skies,* a young woman tries to win the love and approval of her wealthy, globe-trotting father. A *Kirkus Reviews* reviewer called *Saffron Skies* "a family saga spanning three continents and 30 years," that is "ultimately satisfying."

BIOGRAPHICAL AND CRITICAL SOURCES:

PERIODICALS

Architectural Review, April, 2003, Edward Robbins, review of *White Papers, Black Marks: Architecture, Race, Culture,* p. 94.
Building Design, January 30, 2004, Pamela Buxton, "Sections and Shopping," interview with Lesley Lokko, p. 18.
Kirkus Reviews, September 1, 2006, review of *Saffron Skies,* p. 868.
Publishers Weekly, September 11, 2006, review of *Saffron Skies,* p. 36.
Scotsman, November 11, 2004, Susan Mansfield, "Meet the Scottish Jackie Collins."

ONLINE

Orion Books Web site, http://www.orionbooks.co.uk/ (December 12, 2006), "Lesley Lokko Talks to Danuta Kean about How to Write a Blockbuster."

Trashionista Web site, http://www.trashionista.com/ (January 12, 2007), review of *Sundowners.*

*   *   *

LOKKO, Lesley Naa Norle
   See LOKKO, Lesley

*   *   *

LOPEZ DZUR, Carlos 1955-
   (Zorro Viejo)

PERSONAL: Born September 1, 1955, in the United States; widower; children: Gabriela. *Ethnicity:* "Latino." *Education:* University of Puerto Rico, B.A.; San Diego State University, M.A.; additional graduate study at Montana State University. *Religion:* "Jewish/Tantrist."

ADDRESSES: Home—Orange County, CA. *E-mail*—baudelaire1998@yahoo.com.

CAREER: Writer, educator, researcher, and Web master.

MEMBER: Ateneo de San Sebastián.

AWARDS, HONORS: Winner of Chicano literary contest, University of California, Irvine, 1982, for the poetry collection *El hombre extendido.*

WRITINGS:

El hombre extendido, 1987.
Simposio de Tlacuilos (novel), Ediciones Nuevo Espacio, 2000.
Las máscaras del Tabú (novel), BookSurge Publishing, 2001.
Comevacas y tiznaos: Partidas sediciosas en El Pepino de 1898, Outskirts Press (Parker, CO), 2005.
El corazón del monstruo: Estampas y anecdotario existencial (short stories), Outskirts Press (Parker, CO), 2006.

Numerous other writings include the novel *Berkeley y yo.* Some writings appeared under pseudonym Zorro Viejo.

BIOGRAPHICAL AND CRITICAL SOURCES:

ONLINE

Carlos Lopez Dzur y la Generation del '70, http://www.geocities.com/baudelaire1998/Indexlopez.htm (May 16, 2007), author's home page.

* * *

LUEDERS, Bill 1959-

PERSONAL: Surname is pronounced "leaders"; born 1959, in Milwaukee, WI; married; wife's name Linda.

ADDRESSES: Home—Madison, WI. *Office*—Isthmus Publishing Company, 101 King St., Madison, WI 53703. *E-mail*—Blueders101@yahoo.com; blueders@isthmus.com.

CAREER: Cofounder of *The Crazy Shepherd* newspaper (now called *Shepherd Express*), Milwaukee, WI, 1982; *Isthmus,* Madison, WI, news editor, 1986—. Wisconsin Freedom of Information Council, president, 2004—.

WRITINGS:

An Enemy of the State: The Life of Erwin Knoll, Common Courage Press (Monroe, ME), 1996.
Cry Rape: The True Story of One Woman's Harrowing Quest for Justice, University of Wisconsin Press (Madison, WI), 2006.

SIDELIGHTS: Bill Lueders, an editor for the *Isthmus,* a weekly newspaper in Madison, Wisconsin, is the author of the 1996 biography *An Enemy of the State: The Life of Erwin Knoll* and the 2006 nonfiction work *Cry Rape: The True Story of One Woman's Harrowing Quest for Justice.* In *An Enemy of the State,* Lueders recounts the life of the Austrian immigrant who fled

Nazi persecution and became one of America's most controversial and defiant journalists. Beginning in 1973, Knoll served as editor of the *Progressive,* a monthly political magazine that champions social and economic justice. "For 21 years until his death in 1994 his fiery defense of free speech, his attacks on the military-industrial complex, and his scornful contempt for electoral politics made him a lion on the American Left, while his ideas were made known to millions by occasional appearances on public television," noted Samuel H. Day, Jr., in the *Bulletin of the Atomic Scientists.* "But he remained best known for his role in challenging nuclear secrecy, which prompted an historic First Amendment battle over prior restraint—government suppression of an article before its publication." That battle, which revolved around the *Progressive*'s intent to publish "The H-Bomb Secret: How We Got It, Why We're Telling It," an article by Howard Morland, caused a furor in political and journalistic circles; the case was eventually dropped, however, when it was determined that the information was already in the public domain. As Day wrote, Lueders "has provided the definitive account of a landmark conflict between freedom of the press and nuclear secrecy—a momentous contest still at issue, despite the victory of the intrepid little magazine and its doughty editor." According to Eyal Press, writing in the *Nation,* "One of the many virtues of . . . *An Enemy of the State,* is that it reminds us of the dignity that can come with being uncompromising."

In *Cry Rape,* Lueders details the true story of a rape victim who was pressured to recant her story by members of her city's police force. On September 4, 1997, an intruder entered the home of Patty, a legally blind single mother living in Madison, and raped her at knifepoint. The lead detective on the case, Tom Woodmansee, suspected Patty was lying about the sexual assault; at one point in the investigation, he kept Patty in a windowless interrogation room until she admitted that she had fabricated the incident. Patty was eventually charged with obstruction, though the charges were dropped, and DNA evidence later confirmed her story. "Lueders walks readers through Patty's years-long struggle for justice—which exacted a devastating financial and emotional toll—and his own fight for access to police records and crime scene analysis, turning thousands of pages of police reports, court transcripts, medical records, and interviews into a gripping mystery," commented Linda Lutton in the

Chicago Reader. According to Doug Moe, writing in the *Capital Times,* Lueder's "achievement is large—the book is not a polemic, the tone is not angry, but the systemic fallibility *Cry Rape* reveals is frightening." As Connie Fletcher noted in *Booklist,* "This is a powerful example of how an investigative reporter can right injustices and expose the need for further reform."

BIOGRAPHICAL AND CRITICAL SOURCES:

PERIODICALS

American Journalism Review, December, 1996, Carl Sessions Stepp, review of *An Enemy of the State: The Life of Erwin Knoll,* p. 45.
Booklist, September 1, 2006, Connie Fletcher, review of *Cry Rape: The True Story of One Woman's Harrowing Quest for Justice,* p. 28.

Bulletin of the Atomic Scientists, May-June, 1997, Samuel H. Day, Jr., review of *An Enemy of the State,* p. 57.
Capital Times, September 9, 2006, Doug Moe, "Injustice in 'Patty' Case Haunts Writer," p. A2.
Chicago Reader, November 10, 2006, Linda Lutton, "A True Crime."
Kirkus Reviews, July 15, 2006, review of *Cry Rape,* p. 713.
Nation, April 21, 1997, Eyal Press, review of *An Enemy of the State,* p. 30.
Publishers Weekly, September 18, 2006, review of *Cry Rape,* p. 47.

ONLINE

Bill Lueders Home Page, http://www.geocities.com/blueders101/bill.html (December 15, 2006).
Cry Rape Web Site, http://www.cryrapebook.com (December 15, 2006).

M

MACAVINTA, Courtney

PERSONAL: Married. *Education:* San Francisco State University, B.A. (cum laude), 1996.

ADDRESSES: Home and office—San Jose, CA. *E-mail*—courtney@respectgirls.com.

CAREER: Sacramento Bee, Sacramento, CA, online editor, 1996; CNET News.com, San Francisco, CA, senior writer, 1996-2000; ChickClick, editorial director, 2000-01; freelance journalist; RespectRx.com, Web publisher and writer.

AWARDS, HONORS: First-place award for Best News Story, Computer Press Awards, 1997; Internet Investigation of the Year award, Internet Freedom Awards, 1999; James Madison Freedom-of-Information Award, Society of Professional Journalists, 2000.

WRITINGS:

(With Andrea Vander Pluym) *Respect: A Girl's Guide to Getting Respect and Dealing When Your Line Is Crossed,* Free Spirit Publishing (Minneapolis, MN), 2005.

Contributor to periodicals and Web sites, including *Washington Post, American Leadership Forum, Red Herring,* and *Wired News.*

SIDELIGHTS: Raised in San Jose, California, Courtney Macavinta grew up in a working-class family that had its fair share of troubles, including poverty, substance abuse, and issues of racism. Beyond her family's struggles, Macavinta also battled the typical issues of many American girls: feelings of self-doubt, concerns with her physical image, and confusion about her multiracial heritage. Learning to overcome her personal insecurities, Macavinta pursued a career as an investigative reporter and has earned several awards within the journalistic field. Her desire to help young girls struggling with the same issues of self-identity and low self-esteem that she had once battled inspired Macavinta to write *Respect: A Girl's Guide to Getting Respect and Dealing When Your Line Is Crossed.* As the journalist maintains on her home page, "respect is always within reach because true respect starts on the inside."

Written in collaboration with Andrea Vander Pluym, *Respect* channels Macavinta's message of self-love and provides young women with the tools needed to gain the self-confidence required in order to inspire others to treat one with respect. In addition to suggestions regarding ways of appropriately responding to the words and actions of others, the book deals with such things as sexual harassment, date rape, peer pressure, drug and alcohol use, and peer relationships. As a reviewer for *NEA Today* noted, Macavinta and Pluym "keep the advice real" in their straightforward prose. Sara Catherine Howard, writing an assessment of *Respect* for *Research Library,* noted that the coauthors offer "definitive measures . . . without being didactic," while in *Kliatt* Sherri Ginsberg pointed out that *Respect* "gives the reader verbal weapons to manage these stressful years."

BIOGRAPHICAL AND CRITICAL SOURCES:

PERIODICALS

Kliatt, January, 2006, Sherri Ginsberg, review of *Respect: A Girl's Guide to Getting Respect and Dealing When Your Line Is Crossed,* p. 30.
NEA Today, November, 2006, review of *Respect,* p. 56.
Research Library (annual), 2006, Sara Catherine Howard, review of *Respect,* p. 66.

ONLINE

Courtney Macavinta Home Page, http://www.courtneymacavinta.com (January 7, 2007).
Free Spirit Publishing Web site, http://www.freespirit.com/ (January 7, 2007), "Courtney Macavinta."*

* * *

MacKINNON, Colin

PERSONAL: Married; wife's name Diane. *Education:* Columbia University, M.S.; University of California, Los Angeles, Ph.D.

ADDRESSES: *Home*—Chevy Chase, MD. *Agent*—Philip G. Spitzer Literary Agency, 50 Talmage Farm Ln., East Hampton, NY 11937.

CAREER: American Institute of Iranian Studies, Tehran, Iran, director, mid-1970s; Amnesty International USA, New York, NY, Iran country coordinator, 1995-97. Served as chief editor for *Middle East Executive Reports,* Washington, DC; has taught at Tehran University, University of Jondi Shapur, Columbia University, and Georgetown University.

WRITINGS:

NOVELS

Finding Hoseyn, Arbor House (New York, NY), 1986.

Morning Spy, Evening Spy, St. Martin's Press (New York, NY), 2006.

SIDELIGHTS: Colin MacKinnon, a Middle East expert who has worked and taught in Iran, is the author of the political thrillers *Finding Hoseyn* and *Morning Spy, Evening Spy.* Set in Tehran in 1977, during the final days of the Shah's regime, *Finding Hoseyn* follows an American journalist's efforts to find the killer of an Israeli spy. His search takes him throughout Europe and the Middle East, as he chases a shadowy figure known as Hoseyn. In MacKinnon's debut novel, wrote *New York Times Book Review* critic Newgate Callendar, "we get a good idea of what life in Iran was like in pre-Khomeini days, of how the country was ripe for revolution, of the fanaticism of the religious element, of the determination of the terrorists and of the gossipy approach of the foreign press contingent. Mr. MacKinnon does not preach but merely stands outside his political world, reporting. And a splendid reporter he is."

Two decades after his first book appeared, MacKinnon published *Morning Spy, Evening Spy,* "a haunting, disturbingly realistic portrait of the failings, organizational and personal, that opened up the skies for 9/11," wrote *Booklist* critic Frank Sennett. In the book, CIA agent Paul Patterson investigates the murder of an operative in Pakistan who had been providing intelligence on Osama Bin Laden. As he gathers information, Patterson realizes that he has stumbled upon a huge al-Qaeda operation, but his findings are lost amidst a sea of governmental red tape. A *Publishers Weekly* reviewer praised the novel, stating that MacKinnon "shows great insight into the inner workings of U.S. intelligence," and a contributor in *Kirkus Reviews* noted that the author "has a quiet, spare style and a knack for nailing down just the right details. It's an approach that lends the story an air of authenticity."

BIOGRAPHICAL AND CRITICAL SOURCES:

PERIODICALS

Booklist, September 1, 2006, Frank Sennett, review of *Morning Spy, Evening Spy,* p. 62.
Kirkus Reviews, July 15, 2006, review of *Morning Spy, Evening Spy,* p. 693.

New York Times Book Review, March 16, 1986, Newgate Callendar, "Crime," review of *Finding Hoseyn.*

Publishers Weekly, August 7, 2006, review of *Morning Spy, Evening Spy,* p. 30.

*   *   *

MADISON, Amber 1984-

PERSONAL: Born 1984, daughter of Roger Madison (a neurobiologist) and Jane Leserman (a professor of sociology). *Education:* Graduate of Tufts University, 2005.

ADDRESSES: Home—Somerville, MA. *E-mail*—media@ambermadisononline.com.

CAREER: Writer. Worked in Boston-area bars.

WRITINGS:

Hooking Up: A Girl's All-Out Guide to Sex and Sexuality, Prometheus Books (Amherst, NY), 2006.

Wrote column "Between the Sheets" for the Tufts University newspaper.

SIDELIGHTS: Amber Madison, who grew up in a communal environment with very open-minded parents, wrote a sex column for the Tufts University newspaper while studying community health, for which she took a human sexuality class. What she discovered while penning "Between the Sheets" was that there were huge gaps in her peer group's knowledge of the subject and that they seldom had someone in their life to whom they could go for information. She then wrote *Hooking Up: A Girl's All-Out Guide to Sex and Sexuality,* a guide for teen girls and older, but which is also a good resource for boys and even parents. She begins with basic anatomy and then covers subjects that most similar books will not, such as why girls should take control of their own sexuality, what constitutes rape, the right time to lose one's virginity, and same-sex attractions.

In a *Boston Globe* interview and article, Mark Shanahan wrote that the book "is equal parts how-to and how-*not*-to, a mix of straightforward information and personal anecdote." Madison told Shanahan: "We are so ridiculous about how we approach sex and sexuality in our culture. We have tons of media that is all about sex all the time—if it's a car ad, it's about sex; if it's a perfume ad, it's about sex—but when it comes to actually talking about sex, people just won't do it."

A *News & Observer* contributor noted: "Using examples from her own life, as well as interviews with other young women, Amber writes about everything from contraception to sexually transmitted diseases to virginity to pregnancy and sexual assault. Depending on the situation, she sometimes uses slang terms for body parts and sexual practices. She wants the book to reflect 'how people really talk. Not how doctors talk.'" "Sensitive issues are approached with humor and realism," commented a *Publishers Weekly* reviewer. "This is the book you wish you'd had as a teenage girl."

BIOGRAPHICAL AND CRITICAL SOURCES:

PERIODICALS

America's Intelligence Wire, September 20, 2006, Kristen Casazza, review of *Hooking Up: A Girl's All-Out Guide to Sex and Sexuality.*

Boston Globe, September 12, 2006, Mark Shanahan, "Hooking Up with Amber: At 22, She Graduates from College Columnist to Author with Some Frank Talk about Sex" (interview).

Cosmopolitan, March, 2003, Alexandra Robbins, "Meet the 'New Sexperts,'" p. 206.

News & Observer (Raleigh, NC), October 3, 2006, Matt Ehlers, "Sex Is Her Subject: And She Wants Other Young Women to Know All about It, Too."

Publishers Weekly, July 24, 2006, review of *Hooking Up,* p. 55.

ONLINE

Amber Madison Home Page, http://www.ambermadisononline.com (February 3, 2007).

Play, http://www.playnewhaven.com/ (September 20, 2006), Jon Cooper, "Hooking Up with Amber Madison" (interview).*

MADOC, Gwen 1931-
  (Doreen Edwards)

PERSONAL: Born June 1, 1931, in Swansea, Wales; married; husband's name Harry. *Education:* Attended Open University.

ADDRESSES: Home—Swansea, Wales.

CAREER: Writer. Formerly worked as a medical secretary.

WRITINGS:

FICTION

Daughter of Shame, Hodder & Stoughton (London, England), 2000.
By Lies Betrayed, Hodder & Stoughton (London, England), 2001.
Bad to the Bone, Hodder & Stoughton (London, England), 2003.
No Child of Mine, Hodder & Stoughton (London, England), 2004.
Her Mother's Sins, Hodder & Stoughton (London, England), 2005.
The Stolen Baby, Hodder & Stoughton (London, England), 2005.
Take My Child, Severn House (Sutton, England), 2006.

FICTION UNDER PSEUDONYM DOREEN EDWARDS

Follow Every Rainbow, Piatkus (London, England), 1997.
Dreaming of Tomorrow, Piatkus (London, England), 1997.
A Better Love Next Time, Piatkus (London, England), 1999.

BIOGRAPHICAL AND CRITICAL SOURCES:

PERIODICALS

Booklist, September 15, 2006, Patty Engelmann, review of *Take My Child,* p. 28.*

MADSEN, Deborah L. 1960-
  (Deborah Lea Madsen)

PERSONAL: Born December 13, 1960, in Melbourne, Victoria, Australia; daughter of Michael and Vivienne Margaret Jones; married Mark Sandberg, February 23, 1989; children: Selene Deborah, Dana Marcia, Aurora Leigh, James Mark Sandberg. *Education:* University of Adelaide, B.A. (with honors), 1981, M.A., 1984; University of Sussex, D.Phil., 1988.

ADDRESSES: Office—Department of English, University of Geneva, CH-1211, Geneva-4, Switzerland. *E-mail*—deborah.madsen@lettres.unige.ch.

CAREER: University of Leicester, Leicester, England, lecturer, 1989-95, reader in English, 1995-97, and director of American Studies program; London South Bank University, London, England, professor of English, 1997-2002; University of Geneva, Geneva, Switzerland, professor of American literature and culture, 2002—. Visiting lecturer at the University of Adelaide, 2004, University of Bern, 2005, and the University of Fribourg, 2006. Guest lecturer at conferences and universities.

MEMBER: Modern Language Association, International Association of University Professors of English, European Association for American Studies, Swiss Association for North American Studies, Swiss Association of University Teachers of English, Society for Multi-Ethnic Studies in Europe and America, Swiss Association for North American Studies, American Antiquarian Society,.

WRITINGS:

NONFICTION

The Postmodernist Allegories of Thomas Pynchon, St. Martin's Press (New York, NY), 1991.
Rereading Allegory: A Narrative Approach to Genre, St. Martin's Press (New York, NY), 1994.
(Editor) *Visions of America since 1492,* St. Martin's Press (New York, NY), 1994.
Postmodernism: A Bibliography, 1926-1994, Rodopi (Amsterdam, Netherlands), 1995.

Allegory in America: From Puritanism to Postmodernism, St. Martin's Press (New York, NY), 1996.

American Exceptionalism, University Press of Mississippi (Jackson, MS), 1998.

(Editor) *Post-Colonial Literatures: Expanding the Canon,* Pluto Press (Sterling, VA), 1999.

Feminist Theory and Literary Practice, Pluto Press (Sterling, VA), 2000.

Maxine Hong Kingston, Thomson Gale (Detroit, MI), 2000.

Understanding Contemporary Chicana Literature, University of South Carolina Press (Columbia, SC), 2000.

Chinese American Writers, Thomson Gale (Detroit, MI), 2001.

The Woman Warrior and China Men, Thomson Gale (Detroit, MI), 2001.

(Editor) *Beyond the Borders: American Literature and Post-Colonial Theory,* Pluto Press (Sterling, VA), 2003.

(Editor) *Asian American Writers,* Thomson Gale (Detroit, MI), 2005.

(Editor, with Michael Hanrahan) *Teaching, Technology, Textuality: Approaches to New Media,* Macmillan (New York, NY), 2006.

Contributor to books, including *Approaches to Teaching Thomas Pynchon's "The Crying of Lot 49 and Other Works,"* edited by Thomas Schaub, MLA (New York, NY); and *Companion to Australian Literature,* Boydell & Brewer (Elizabethtown, NY). Contributor to periodicals, including *Concentric: Literary and Cultural Studies, Journal of Intercultural Studies, History of European Ideas, Journal of American Studies,* and *Canadian Review of American Studies.* Member of editorial board, *European Journal of American Culture,* and *Journal of Contemporary Women Writers.*

SIDELIGHTS: Educated in Australia and England, Deborah L. Madsen is a scholar specializing in American literature. Her interests also include feminism, the study of transnational ethnic literatures, and American Exceptionalism, or the idea that the United States is set apart from other modern nations because of its unique history and political and religious organizations.

One of Madsen's first books, *Allegory in America: From Puritanism to Postmodernism,* examines the use of allegory in American literature. Beginning with a

brief history of allegory in Hellenistic, Judaistic, and Christian literature, she moves to colonial New England in the second chapter, and from these on through the twentieth century. Included are discussions of narratives written by authors who had been taken captive by Native Americans; these are compared to a slave narrative written in the nineteenth century. "The congruence of postmodernist terminology and the language of traditional allegory is strikingly demonstrated here, and in the successful (though regrettably short) chapter on John Barth," reported Brian Harding in the *Modern Language Review.*

In *American Exceptionalism,* Madsen takes a concise but thorough look at the belief that the United States is a unique nation, set apart from others. This widespread notion has led to significant decisions in national policy. Madsen's book traces the roots of Exceptionalism in six chapters, starting with the Puritans in the seventeenth century and leading up to modern times. According to a reviewer for *H-Net Online,* those reading the book will appreciate "the author's clear, fast-paced, and mercifully jargon-lite prose" as she discusses American movies, poetry, prose, and theology. Ideologies that oppose the notion of Exceptionalism are also presented; these are drawn from works by African American, Native American, and Chicano writers.

The book begins with the early years in the Massachusetts Bay Colony, when the Puritans truly embraced the idea of their colony as a unique place, selected by God for a special purpose. While praising Madsen's coverage of the Puritans as the first to believe in America's fateful position among nations, the *H-Net Online* reviewer did state that "there are disagreements over such matters and Madsen ought to have explored them." The *H-Net Online* writer concluded by stating that, in fact, many countries besides the United States have considered themselves special and somehow critically important, raising the point that perhaps American Exceptionalism is really nothing unique. "She could have done more to answer that question," noted the reviewer. "Still, it is only bold works such as Madsen's that raise such important issues."

Madsen told *CA:* "My favorite book is always my next book. Writing is inseparable from thinking for me; I do a lot of my thinking in the process of writing . . . and editing.

"It sounds trite to say that I hope readers of my books will come to know anew that things have histories, but I think it is very important to be aware that the ways in which we use language, in figures of speech and the like, are historically determined. My interest is in taking aspects of who we are now, in the Western anglophone world, and tracing the history of the rhetoric that informs our cultural habits."

BIOGRAPHICAL AND CRITICAL SOURCES:

PERIODICALS

Journal of Southern History, August, 2000, Michael O'Brien, review of *American Exceptionalism,* p. 605.
Library Journal, February 1, 2001, Nedra C. Evers, review of *Understanding Contemporary Chicana Literature,* p. 89.
Modern Language Review, July, 1998, Brian Harding, review of *Allegory in America: From Puritanism to Postmodernism,* p. 805.
Reference & Research Book News, November, 2005, review of *Asian American Writers.*
Research in African Literatures, winter, 2001, Anuradha Dingwaney Needham, review of *Post-Colonial Literatures: Expanding the Canon,* p. 221.

ONLINE

H-Net Online, http://www.h-net.org/ (January 22, 2007), "The Complexities of American Exceptionalism."

*   *   *

MADSEN, Deborah Lea
    See MADSEN, Deborah L.

*   *   *

MAGNUS, Shulamit S. 1950-

PERSONAL: Born 1950. *Education:* Barnard College, B.A., 1972; Columbia University, M.Phil., 1977; Columbia University, Ph.D., 1988.

ADDRESSES: Office—Department of History, Oberlin College, Rice Hall 316, 10 N. Professor St., Oberlin, OH 44074-1095. *E-mail*—shulamit.magnus@oberlin.edu.

CAREER: Historian, educator, and writer. Columbia University, New York, NY, reader in history, 1974-75, lecturer on the Holocaust, 1979-1980; Reconstructionist Rabbinical College, director of modern Jewish civilization program, 1982-1991; Stanford University, Palo Alto, CA, acting assistant professor of history, 1991-94, affiliated scholar at the Institute for Research on Women and Gender, 1994-98; Oberlin College, Oberlin, OH, associate professor of history and Jewish studies, 1998—, chair and director of Jewish studies program, 2001-2006.

AWARDS, HONORS: Fellowships from Columbia University, 1972-76, 1978-81, Memorial Foundation for Jewish Culture, 1976, National Foundation for Jewish Culture, 1978-79, 1980-81, Yad Hanadiv and Barecha Foundation, 1988-89, and Community Foundation of Santa Clara, 1994-95; Legacy Grant for historical research on Jewish women, 1994-95; National Endowment for the Humanities translation grant, 1995-97.

WRITINGS:

Jewish Emancipation in a German City: Cologne, 1798-1871, Stanford University Press (Stanford, CA), 1997.

Contributor to books, including *Encyclopaedia Judaica,* 2006. Contributor of articles and reviews to periodicals, including *Polin: Studies in Polish Jewry, Association for Jewish Studies Review, Modern Judaism, Lifecycles, Slavic Review, German History,* and *Response.*

SIDELIGHTS: A historian specializing in Jewish studies, Shulamit S. Magnus is the author of *Jewish Emancipation in a German City: Cologne, 1798-1871.* In her book, the author focuses on the repeal of ancient laws discriminating against Jews in the city of Cologne. The laws, which were common throughout Europe, forbade Jews from becoming citizens. Magnus chronicles the political events and social changes that led the laws' repeal in Cologne. For example, she examines the dynamics of the relationship among the political leaders of the city, various territorial governments, and the city of Berlin, as well as the role that the strong Jewish banking industry played in the shift toward allowing Jews to become citizens. The author segments her study into four major periods: Cologne under French rule, the city under Prussian rule, the 1840s time period of new advocacy for Jewish rights, and the subsequent new influence of Jews in the political and social environments.

"Magnus makes no claim for Cologne as representative of the emancipation process elsewhere in Germany," wrote *Canadian Journal of History* contributor Lionel B. Steiman in a review of *Jewish Emancipation in a German City.* Steiman went on to refer to the book as "a thoroughly researched, beautifully written analysis, and an important contribution to its field." Noting that the author's "book is not the first major study of the Jews of Cologne," Michael A. Meyer, writing in the *Historian,* added that nevertheless "Magnus has gone far beyond . . . [a previous] account for the early nineteenth century, not only utilizing new archival sources and employing quantitative analysis, but presenting a much more integrated image of the Jewish community within its non-Jewish environment." In a review in the *Journal of Social History,* James M. Brophy wrote: "The great strength in this study is Magnus's close attention to the differing forms of anti-Jewish behavior and her sharp analysis of why antisemitic attitudes changed over time. Her nuanced arguments point up the need for exacting research to understand the contingencies that both hindered and aided the goal of Jewish civic equality."

BIOGRAPHICAL AND CRITICAL SOURCES:

PERIODICALS

Canadian Journal of History, December, 1997, Lionel B. Steiman, review of *Jewish Emancipation in a German City: Cologne, 1798-1871,* p. 464.
Historian, spring, 1999, Michael A. Meyer, review of *Jewish Emancipation in a German City,* p. 715.
Journal of Social History, spring, 1999, James M. Brophy, review of *Jewish Emancipation in a German City,* p. 747.

ONLINE

Oberlin Department of History Web site, http://www.oberlin.edu/history/ (January 22, 2007), faculty profile of author.

MAHLER, Sarah J. 1959-

PERSONAL: Born 1959. *Education:* Ph.D.

ADDRESSES: Office—Florida International University, 11200 S.W. 8th St., Miami, FL 33199. *E-mail*—Sarah.Mahler@fiu.edu.

CAREER: University of Vermont, Burlington, VT, former member of anthropology faculty; Florida International University, Miami, FL, professor of sociology/anthropology and director of the Transnational & Comparative Studies Center.

WRITINGS:

American Dreaming: Immigrant Life on the Margins, Princeton University Press (Princeton, NJ), 1995.
Salvadorans in Suburbia: Symbiosis and Conflict, Allyn & Bacon (Boston, MA), 1995.

SIDELIGHTS: Anthropologist Sarah J. Mahler began her initial research for a her first book by setting out to understand competing behaviors among immigrants on Long Island. When she was done, however, she ended up with a much more thorough discussion of South American and Salvadoran immigrants to the United States titled *American Dreaming: Immigrant Life on the Margins.* Through extensive interviews with immigrants and analysis of government data, she comes up with a "vivid, analytically keen account of the sociopolitical shadowland inhabited by undocumented immigrants from the Americas," according to Matthew Jacobson in the *Journal of American Ethnic History.* Mahler seeks to discover not only why immigrants from her chosen countries come to America, but also what happens when they arrive here, and why some who leave again often come back to the United States. Here she finds many disillusioned people who become frustrated by the high expense of living in America—even though their pay is higher than in their native lands—and immigration policies that make their lives more difficult because they are considered "illegal." "Deepest of the immigrants' disappointments, however," related Jacobson, "is the perceived erosion of solidarity within the ethnic community."

In her interviews, Mahler repeatedly found that immigrants were saddened by how their fellow countrymen's attitudes changed for the worse, and the feeling of community they once had is lost. Alan Wolfe, writing for the *New York Times Book Review,* was impressed by how "Mahler's narrative skills bring these people to life," but put off by "her didactic intrusions and overweening political opinions." Wolfe felt that the author's goal is to make "Americans . . . feel guilty for the way they treat the immigrants in their midst. But one can also feel proud to belong to a country that offers immigrants a chance." Many other reviewers, however, had high praise for *American Dreaming.* It "advances our understanding of intraethnic relations in the communities studied," asserted Elizabeth J. Mueller in the *International Migration Review,* adding: "Most importantly, *American Dreaming* challenges us to rethink the prevalence of 'ethnic solidarity.'" Richard M. Krieg concluded in the *Social Service Review:* "*American Dreaming* contains multiple insights that will be valuable to practitioners who are interested in or who work with low-income immigrants."

BIOGRAPHICAL AND CRITICAL SOURCES:

PERIODICALS

International Migration Review, spring, 1997, Elizabeth J. Mueller, review of *American Dreaming: Immigrant Life on the Margins,* p. 191.
Journal of American Ethnic History, fall, 1997, Matthew Jacobson, review of *American Dreaming,* p. 89; spring, 1998, Elliott Robert Barkan, "From the Field: Four Studies of New Americans," review of *Salvadorans in Suburbia: Symbiosis and Conflict,*" p. 94.
New York Times Book Review, December 17, 1995, Alan Wolfe, "Displaced Persons," review of *American Dreaming.*
Social Service Review, March, 1998, Richard M. Krieg, review of *American Dreaming,* p. 150.

*   *   *

MAHONEY, Daniel J. 1960-

PERSONAL: Born 1960. *Education:* College of Holy Cross, B.A., 1982; Catholic University of America, M.A., 1984, Ph.D., 1988.

ADDRESSES: Office—Assumption College, 500 Salisbury St., Worcester, MA 01609.

CAREER: Assumption College, Worcester, MA, professor of political science.

AWARDS, HONORS: Prix Raymond Aron, 1999.

WRITINGS:

The Liberal Political Science of Raymond Aron: A Critical Introduction, Rowman & Littlefield (Lanham, MD), 1992.
De Gaulle: Statesmanship, Grandeur, and Modern Democracy, foreword by Pierre Manent, Praeger (Westport, CT), 1996, published with new introduction by Mahoney, Transaction Publishers (New Brunswick, NJ), 2000.
Aleksandr Solzhenitsyn: The Ascent from Ideology, Rowman & Littlefield (Lanham, MD), 2001.
(Translator, with Paul Seaton) Pierre Manent, *The Wars of the Twentieth Century,* c. 2002.
Bertrand de Jouvenel: The Conservative Liberal and the Illusions of Modernity, ISI Books (Wilmington, DE), 2005.

EDITOR

Raymond Aron, *In Defense of Political Reason: Essays,* Rowman & Littlefield (Lanham, MD), 1994.
(With Paul Seaton, and translator with Seaton, and author of introduction) Pierre Manent, *Modern Liberty and Its Discontents: Selected Writings of Pierre Manent,* Rowman & Littlefield (Lanham, MD), 1998.
(And author of introduction) Aurel Kolnai, *"Privilege and Liberty" and Other Essays in Political Philosophy,* foreword by Pierre Manent, Lexington Books (Lanham, MD), 1999.
(With Robert Faulkner) Alexander Shtromas, *Totalitarianism and the Prospects for World Order: Closing the Door on the Twentieth Century,* Lexington Books (Lanham, MD), 2003.
(With Edward E. Ericson, Jr.) Aleksandr Solzhenitsyn, *The Solzhenitsyn Reader: New and Essential Writings, 1947-2005,* ISI Books (Wilmington, DE), 2006.

Contributor to periodicals, including *National Interest, Perspectives on Political Science, First Things,* and the *Wall Street Journal.* Associate editor, *Perspectives on Political Science.* Book review editor, *Society.*

SIDELIGHTS: Daniel J. Mahoney is a scholar of political science who is well known for his written and edited books on French philosophers and political thinkers, his acclaimed work on Russian writer Aleksandr Solzhenitsyn, and his interest in the politics of totalitarian regimes. After publishing a work on the twentieth-century French sociologist, political scientist and philosopher Raymon Aron, *The Liberal Political Science of Raymond Aron: A Critical Introduction,* Mahoney edited a collection of his essays and then completed *De Gaulle: Statesmanship, Grandeur, and Modern Democracy.* Here, the author examines the former French president's influential political philosophy by analyzing the statesman's speeches and writings. In what *Foreign Affairs* contributor Stanley Hoffmann called a "perceptive and eloquent" work, Mahoney notes the similarities between Charles de Gaulle's thought and the ideas of Alexis de Tocqueville and Max Weber and "provides new insight into some of the more problematic aspects of the general's career," according to Iain Ogilvie in *Perspectives on Political Science.* Appreciating how Mahoney employs "textual analysis" to arrive at his conclusions, Ogilvie asserted that "one of the chief merits of the book is that it rescues discourse on the subject from the stereotypical straitjackets of 'personality cult,' 'strong leadership,' and 'tyranny.'" The critic found that the book lacked a strong summary paragraph, but concluded that *De Gaulle* "is a seminal contribution to providing a more balanced account" of de Gaulle.

Even more appreciated is Mahoney's *Aleksandr Solzhenitsyn: The Ascent from Ideology.* Published in 2001, this study was released at a time when Western academics had begun to dismiss the Russian author and philosopher as increasingly irrelevant in the post-Soviet world. Mahoney, on the other hand, defends Solzhenitsyn, representing him as a writer and thinker who has become misunderstood and unjustly denigrated as anti-Semitic and pro-Tsarist. "He reminds us that everything that we have learned since the fall of the Berlin Wall vindicates Solzhenitsyn," commented Robert P. Kraynak in a *First Things* review. Kraynak pointed out that many liberal intellectuals have a hard time reconciling Solzhenitsyn's conservative ideas of Christianity and the state with his equally important belief in individual freedoms. The author supports his thesis by quoting from and analyzing often ignored writings and speeches by the Russian author, in particular his 1993 Liechtenstein Address in which, although Solzhenitsyn remains critical of Western-style materialism, he also makes apparent his love of democracy and faith in this important political experiment. Mahoney also comments on Solzhenitsyn's championing of the work of former Russian Prime Minister Peter Stolypin, who favored a gradual evolution of politics in Russia from Tsarism to more liberal practices, rather than the abrupt and extreme revolution that came in 1917. "In Mahoney's view," Kraynak continued, "Solzhenitsyn is best understood as a Tocquevillean deeply committed to local self-government. To defend this somewhat surprising claim, Mahoney looks to Solzhenitsyn's personal observations of Switzerland's Appenzell region, whose citizens impressed him with their old-fashioned character and devotion to local liberty." Although Kraynak was disappointed that Mahoney does not point out the influence of St. Augustine on Solzhenitsyn's philosophy, the reviewer concluded that "Mahoney provides the most fair-minded and attractive account of Solzhenitsyn's political thought to date. The great Russian writer comes alive as an original thinker who combines ancient spiritual wisdom with modern political freedom."

Other critics of *Aleksandr Solzhenitsyn* were equally enthusiastic about the importance of Mahoney's work. Echoing Kraynak, Edward E. Ericson, Jr., asserted in the *American Enterprise* that "Mahoney's book restores the Russian writer to the relevance he had before Western critics turned away from him. Beyond that, it advances the field of Solzhenitsyn criticism by a quantum leap . . . and Mahoney's mastery of Solzhenitsyn's texts is encyclopedic." Ericson noted that the author reveals the Russian as a distinctly moderate political thinker, further praising Mahoney for practicing "the lost art of close reading" in his analysis of texts. Mahoney "dispels widespread misunderstandings through attention to both the breadth and the depth of Solzhenitsyn's corpus," Flagg Taylor wrote in *Perspectives on Political Science,* reinforcing what other reviewers have said, and "demonstrates Solzhenitsyn's continuing relevance today."

Mahoney also published *Bertrand de Jouvenel: The Conservative Liberal and the Illusions of Modernity,* which is about another French philosopher and political scientist. Continuing "his ever-widening exploration of the religiopolitical question in modernity" with this work, according to Will Morrisey in *Perspectives on Political Science,* Mahoney describes de Jouvenel as a "conservative liberal." Reminiscent of Solzhenitsyn, de Jouvenel also treasured tradition and those values of the old aristocracy that were important, as well as Christian spirituality. He also, however, championed political and individual freedoms. "Mahoney shows himself unmatched among his generation of political scientists in his ability to introduce a thinker to new readers while illuminating him for old readers," reported Morrisey. A contributor to *First Things* concluded that the author has "done a brilliant job of bringing [his subject] to life."

BIOGRAPHICAL AND CRITICAL SOURCES:

PERIODICALS

American Enterprise, April-May, 2002, Edward E. Ericson, Jr., review of *Aleksandr Solzhenitsyn: The Ascent from Ideology,* p. 52.
First Things, December, 1998, Russell Hittinger, review of *Modern Liberty and Its Discontents: Selected Writings of Pierre Manent,* p. 42; December, 2001, Robert P. Kraynak, review of *Aleksandr Solzhenitsyn,* p. 46.
Foreign Affairs, September-October, 1996, Stanley Hoffmann, review of *De Gaulle: Statesmanship, Grandeur, and Modern Democracy,* p. 146; June-July, 2006, review of *Bertrand de Jouvenel: The Conservative Liberal and the Illusions of Modernity,* p. 54.
Modern Age, winter-spring, 2004, David J. Bobb, "Resisting the Ideological Lie," review of *Aleksandr Solzhenitsyn,* p. 113.
National Review, December 31, 2006, Paul Hollander, "Writer and Prophet," review of *The Solzhenitsyn Reader: New and Essential Writings, 1947-2005,* p. 46.
Perspectives on Political Science, winter, 1997, Iain Ogilvie, review of *De Gaulle,* p. 60; spring, 1999, Marc D. Guerra, review of *Modern Liberty and Its Discontents,* p. 117; summer, 2000, "Philosophy," review of *"Privilege and Liberty" and Other Essays in Political Philosophy,* p. 191; summer, 2002, review of *The Wars of the Twentieth Century,* p. 139; Flagg Taylor, review of *Aleksandr Solzhenitsyn,* p. 173; spring, 2006, Will Morrisey, review of *Bertrand de Jouvenel,* p. 116.
Review of Metaphysics, December, 2000, Paul Seaton, review of *"Privilege and Liberty" and Other Essays in Political Philosophy,* p. 447.

MALARKEY, Tucker

PERSONAL: Education: Georgetown University, B.A; attended Iowa Writers' Workshop.

ADDRESSES: Home—CA. *E-mail*—tuckermalarkey@yahoo.com.

CAREER: Writer, journalist. *Washington Post,* reporter on foreign desk. Assistant to Haynes Johnson, *Sleepwalking through History. Tin House* magazine, former editor-at-large. ESL instructor, Kenya and South Africa.

AWARDS, HONORS: Michener Grant, 1995.

WRITINGS:

NOVELS

An Obvious Enchantment, Random House (New York, NY), 2000.
Resurrection, Riverhead Books (New York, NY), 2006.

ADAPTATIONS: Resurrection was adapted for audio, Penguin Audio, 2006.

SIDELIGHTS: Raised in San Francisco, California, novelist Tucker Malarkey was a journalist for the *Washington Post* before she decided to travel to Africa. There, she lived for a time on an island near Kenya and in South Africa, deciding to focus on fiction rather than journalism. She has put her African experiences to use in her subsequent work. *An Obvious Enchantment,* her debut novel of 2000, is set on a remote island off the coast of Africa. American anthropologist Ingrid Holz travels there to search for her missing professor, but along the way she encounters a group of expatriates living on the island. First, there is Finn, an American who has been raised by Swahilis and to whom Ingrid is attracted. Then there is Stanley Wicks, who has left England to try to recreate some of the splendor of his lost family home, building a hotel on the island. And there is also the professor himself, Templeton, who has gone missing while tracing the origins of Islam on Africa's east coast. Templeton is a cipher: Ingrid and the reader never really know if he is a savior for the people or a malevolent force similar to Kurtz in Joseph Conrad's *Heart of Darkness.*

Reviewing the novel in *Booklist,* Bill Ott called it a "gripping story" as well as an "impressive debut." Similar praise came from a *Publishers Weekly* reviewer who found it a "multifaceted, ambitious debut." *Library Journal* contributor Barbara Hoffert had a less favorable impression of the same work, commenting that despite the presence of "some evocative passages," the book struggled with pace and ultimately left the reader unsatisfied. While Richard Bernstein, writing in the *New York Times Book Review,* found that the novel was "far from entirely convincing," he observed that "its virtues are distinguished enough for us to keep reading with pleasure and a sense of edification about a faraway world." Bernstein also called this first novel "entertainingly piquant."

Malarkey also uses an African setting for her 2006 novel, *Resurrection.* World War II has just concluded, and British nurse Gemma Bastian travels to Cairo to investigate the sudden death of her archaeologist father, Charles. There she finds that he has unearthed the Nag Hammadi, a papyrus that tells a very different story of Jesus Christ from the one found in the New Testament. This discovery made Charles a target for murder, and now Gemma sets out to find the perpetrator. *Library Journal* contributor Andrea Y. Griffith felt that *Resurrection,* despite its genre elements, was "more novel than thriller," with a greater focus on character than one would usually find in works of suspense. A *Kirkus Reviews* critic who found the book "passable entertainment," commented that Malarkey's "mix of shattering scriptural revelations and skullduggery should be combustible, but the fire never catches." Bryce Christensen, writing in *Booklist,* found more to like, noting that while "some readers may enjoy Malarkey's novel simply as a literary thriller, many will find themselves wrestling with theological conundrums." Likewise, *USAToday.com* reviewer Carol Memmott remarked that the author "writes deftly about spiritual discovery, and the religious history she weaves into her story gives the novel some heft."

BIOGRAPHICAL AND CRITICAL SOURCES:

PERIODICALS

Booklist, Bill Ott, August, 2000, review of *An Obvious Enchantment,* p. 2114; July 1, 2006, Bryce Christensen, review of *Resurrection,* p. 38.

Kirkus Reviews, May 15, 2006, review of *Resurrection,* p. S6; June 1, 2006, review of *Resurrection,* p. 538.
Library Journal, May 15, 2000, Barbara Hoffert, review of *An Obvious Enchantment,* p. 125; July 1, 2006, Andrea Y. Griffith, review of *Resurrection,* p. 68.
New York Times Book Review, September 1, 2000, Richard Bernstein, "Mystery upon Mystery in the Shadows," review of *An Obvious Enchantment.*
Publishers Weekly, June 19, 2000, review of *An Obvious Enchantment,* p. 58; June 5, 2006, review of *Resurrection,* p. 36.

ONLINE

Bookreporter.com, http://www.bookreporter.com/ (January 27, 2007), Marcia Ford, review of *Resurrection.*
Powells.com, http://www.powells.com/ (September 19, 2000), Dave Weich, "Tucker Malarkey."
Random House Web site, http://www.randomhouse.com/ (January 27, 2007), "Tucker Malarkey."
Resurrection Web site, http://www.resurrection thebook.com (January 27, 2007).
USAToday.com, http://www.usatoday.com/ (July 24, 2006), Carol Memmott, review of *Resurrection.*

*   *   *

MANNING, Harvey 1925-2006
(Harvey Hawthorne Manning)

OBITUARY NOTICE— See index for *CA* sketch: Born July 16, 1925, in Ballard, WA; died of complications from colon cancer, November 12, 2006, in Seattle, WA. Conservationist, editor, publisher, and author. As founding editor of Mountaineer Books, Manning was best known as the author of hiking and nature guides and for his efforts to preserve endangered habitats. A 1946 graduate of the University of Washington, he worked in a variety of jobs through the 1950s. Among these were clerk, tool salesman, newspaper salesman, and radio station manager and salesman. By the late 1950s he was becoming more involved in the publishing business, working for such companies as Macmillan Company and Rinehart Company in New York City. His first book, *High Worlds of the Mountainclimber* (1959), would mark the beginning of many other collaborations with photographers Bob and Ira Spring. Manning was a writer and editor for the University of Washington from 1961 to 1971 before he founded Mountaineer Books. The publishing house focused on books about the outdoors, and Manning produced dozens of titles in the "100 Hikes" and "Footsore" series. An active conservationist, he also was instrumental in getting the 1984 Washington Wilderness Act passed, thus preserving over one million acres of wild lands in the state. Also the editor of *Mountaineering: The Freedom of the Hills* (1960; revised edition, 1967), later taken over by other editors and now in its seventh edition, Manning penned such additional works as *Backpacking: One Step at a Time* (1971; revised edition, 1986), *Oregon Wildlife Areas* (1978), *Fifty Years of Climbing Together* (1988), *Hiking the Great Northwest* (1998), and *Gallery of Mountain Flowers* (2002).

OBITUARIES AND OTHER SOURCES:

PERIODICALS

Los Angeles Times, November 15, 2006, p. B9.

*   *   *

MANNING, Harvey Hawthorne
    See MANNING, Harvey

*   *   *

MARGULIES, Joseph

PERSONAL: Married. *Education:* Cornell University, B.A. (with distinction), 1982; Northwestern University, J.D. (cum laude), 1988.

ADDRESSES: Home—Chicago, IL. *Office*—Northwestern University School of Law, 357 E. Chicago Ave., Chicago, IL 60611. *E-mail*—j-margulies@law.northwestern.edu.

CAREER: Office of the Honorable William Hart, Northern District of Illinois, clerkship; Texas Capital Resource Center, attorney for men and women on Death Row in Texas; attorney in private practice in Minneapolis, MN, beginning 1994; Cornell University Law School, Ithaca, NY, Distinguished Practitioner in Residence, 2002; University of Chicago Law School, 2004-06; Northwestern University Law School, clinical associate professor of law, assistant director of MacArthur Justice Center. Witness at Senate Judiciary Committee hearing on detainee issues, 2005. Lecturer on civil liberties.

WRITINGS:

Guantanamo and the Abuse of Presidential Power (nonfiction), Simon & Schuster (New York, NY), 2006.

SIDELIGHTS: Joseph Margulies is an attorney and civil rights activist whose book *Guantanamo and the Abuse of Presidential Power* analyzes the treatment of the prisoners held at the American prison at Guantanamo Bay, Cuba. Prisoners at Guantanamo were captured during American military actions in the Middle East. They were incarcerated indefinitely and many were held only on suspicion, never charged with any crime. Allegations of torture were made by some of the prisoners. Margulies served as the lead counsel in the Supreme Court case *Rasul v. Bush,* a case brought on behalf of Guantanamo inmates from Australia and Great Britain, and consolidated with another similar case involving prisoners from Kuwait. The prisoners in both cases alleged they were held without reason. The case resulted in the decision that courts in the United States may hear suits from foreign citizens contesting the legality of their imprisonment.

Despite his personal involvement in the case, Margulies's book on Guantanamo has drawn praise as being fairly balanced. "Surprisingly, the book is not a polemic but presents both sides," remarked Brian J. Foley in the *National Law Journal.* "It's masterfully written, reasoned and sourced—an enlightening explanation of how our government reached this failed policy."

Margulies states his view that human-rights violations have occurred at Guantanamo, and that they have seriously marred the reputation of the United States among other countries of the world. He speculates that the deeply flawed policies at Guantanamo came about because the members of the Bush administration believed that everyone held at Guantanamo was a trained guerilla fighter, conditioned to resist interrogation. Because of this, Defense Secretary Donald Rumsfeld and others felt that extreme tactics of disorientation and humiliation were required to instill feelings of helplessness and fear, in order to extract information from the inmates. Margulies believes that the civil-rights violations at Guantanamo have been allowed—even approved—because of the administration's absolute conviction that it's perceptions are correct.

In addition to giving an overarching view of the entire situation Margulies recalls the key court case, *Rasul v. Bush,* "in fascinating detail," according to Karl Helicher in *Library Journal.* "In addition, he includes gruesome examples of beatings and techniques of emotional abuse approved by Defense Secretary Donald Rumsfeld." The importance of this book was emphasized in the *New York Times* by Adam Liptak, who wrote: "Mr. Margulies is a resourceful advocate, a serious and sober legal analyst and a fine, sometimes luminous writer. In his new book Mr. Margulies weaves together a history of wartime interrogation, a consideration of the legal standards that apply to it and an assessment of the toll that Guantanamo has taken on the men and boys held there, and on the nation's reputation and values."

BIOGRAPHICAL AND CRITICAL SOURCES:

PERIODICALS

Booklist, August 1, 2006, Brendan Driscoll, review of *Guantanamo and the Abuse of Presidential Power,* p. 18.

Economist, July 1, 2006, review of *Guantanamo and the Abuse of Presidential Power,* p. 75.

Kirkus Reviews, May 15, 2006, review of *Guantanamo and the Abuse of Presidential Power,* p. 508.

Legal Times, June 26, 2006, Vanessa Blum, review of *Guantanamo and the Abuse of Presidential Power.*

Library Journal, June 1, 2006, Karl Helicher, review of *Guantanamo and the Abuse of Presidential Power,* p. 138.

National Law Journal, June 25, 2006, Brian J. Foley, review of *Guantanamo and the Abuse of Presidential Power.*

New York Times, July 13, 2006, Adam Liptak, review of *Guantanamo and the Abuse of Presidential Power,* p. E1.

New York Times Book Review, July 30, 2006, Jonathan Mahler, review of *Guantanamo and the Abuse of Presidential Power,* p. 6.

Publishers Weekly, May 15, 2006, review of *Guantanamo and the Abuse of Presidential Power,* p. 62.

Recorder, September 22, 2006, Vanessa Blum, review of *Guantanamo and the Abuse of Presidential Power.*

*   *   *

MARKS, Diana F. 1950-

PERSONAL: Born May 1, 1950, in Boulder, CO; daughter of Earl (a teacher) and Shirley (a homemaker) Heuchemer; married Peter Marks (a teacher), June 7, 1973; children: Kevin, Colin. *Education:* University of Southern Colorado, B.S., 1972; College of New Jersey, M.Ed., 1977.

ADDRESSES: Office—P.O. Box 451, Washington Crossing, PA 18977. *E-mail*—deemarks@comcast.net.

CAREER: Kit Carson School District, Kit Carson, CO, teacher, 1972-73; Neshaminy School District, Bucks County, PA, teacher, 1973-79; Council Rock School District, Bucks County, PA, teacher of gifted children, 1979—, currently at Wrightstown Elementary School.

MEMBER: Delta Kappa Gamma.

WRITINGS:

Glues, Brews, and Goos: Recipes and Formulas for Almost Any Project, Teacher Ideas Press, 1996.

Let's Celebrate Today, Libraries Unlimited (Westport, CT), 1998, 2nd edition, 2003.

Glues, Brews, and Goos: Recipes and Formulas for Almost Any Project, Volume 2, Libraries Unlimited (Westport, CT), 2003.

Children's Book Award Handbook, Libraries Unlimited (Westport, CT), 2006.

Contributor to periodicals, including *Learning, Gifted Child Today, Challenge, Good Apple,* and *Spark.*

SIDELIGHTS: Diana F. Marks told *CA:* "I was a writer before I was a reader. When I was about three years old, I would ask my mother for a piece of lined paper. I would 'write' my story, filling the page with small circles. Then I would 'read' my story to my mother and ask for another piece of paper. When I was about ten years old, my teacher raved about a story that I had written about the marriage of some vegetables. The bride was a tomato. The bride's mother was a potato, crying her eyes out. I wrote throughout high school and college. When my sons were young, I had little time for writing. However, when I found myself driving them to soccer practices, et cetera, I learned to write anywhere and anytime. Now that my sons are older, I can write more.

"I like to research little-known subjects, and I love to interview people. Many people have led interesting lives, and those stories should be shared with others.

"I hope that my books will prove to be valuable to children and all who care about children."

*   *   *

MAWER, Granville Allen 1943-

PERSONAL: Born July 20, 1943, in Gate Burton, Lincolnshire, England; married; children: one daughter. *Education:* University of Sydney, B.A. (with honors), 1966.

ADDRESSES: E-mail—gamawer@bigpond.net.au.

CAREER: Australian federal public servant and public policy consultant, 1966-95; maritime historian and writer, 1994—.

WRITINGS:

Fast Company: The Lively Times and Untimely End of the Clipper Ship "Walter Hood," 1852-1870, Plainwords Press (Hughes, Australian Capital Territory, Australia), 1994.

Most Perfectly Safe: The Convict Shipwreck Disasters of 1833-42, Allen & Unwin (St. Leonard's, New South Wales, Australia), 1997.

Ahab's Trade: The Saga of South Sea Whaling, St. Martin's Press (New York, NY), 1999.

The Devil's Gambit, released online, 2003.

The Wild Colonial Boy: The Life & Legend of Jack Doolan, Mulini Press (Canberra, Australian Capital Territory, Australia), 2004.

South by Northwest: The Magnetic Crusade and the Contest for Antarctica, Wakefield Press (Kent Town, South Australia, Australia), 2006.

SIDELIGHTS: Granville Allen Mawer is an Australian maritime historian who specializes in the eighteenth and nineteenth centuries. His best-known book, *Ahab's Trade: The Saga of South Sea Whaling,* explores all facets of the international whaling industry as it developed between 1650 and 1924. Not only does Mawer provide details about the evolution of whaling in America and Europe, but he also describes whaling efforts in the Pacific undertaken by British and Australian interests. Mawer's study examines life aboard whaling ships, the many uses to which whale oil and other whale products were put, and how whaling techniques changed over time— without ever becoming foolproof or entirely safe. To quote W. Jeffrey Bolster in the *New York Times Book Review: Ahab's Trade* "steeps readers in whaling lore."

Ahab's Trade was welcomed by reviewers for its comprehensive look at a livelihood that was so important in the eighteenth and nineteenth centuries that it influenced politics and drove some species of whales to the brink of extinction. "Among the many strengths of Mawer's work are the ways he makes clear whaling's role in terms of international relations and warfare," wrote Andrew G. Wilson in the *Historian.* Bolster noted, "One of Mawer's accomplishments is interleaving British and Australian whaling histories with that of the Yankees. Led by Nantucket Quakers, New Englanders dominated the industry from the late 18th to the late 19th centuries, and their story has generally been told by Americans without reference to competitors. Yet whaling was central to Australia's founding, too, and might have remained big business there but for the nemesis of British tariff policy." In *Quadrant,* Warren Reed wrote: "An outstanding strength of *Ahab's Trade* is its clever blending of the rise and fall of the industry with the methodology used to catch the whales themselves. Few other books have come close to striking a balance, and it is this achievement which makes the work so readable, for readers with either a general or specialised interest."

According to *Time International* contributor Elizabeth Feizkhah, "Mawer chronicles the rise of this first global industry with novelistic verve; as he remarks, the truth of whaling life was often as strange as fiction." Reed similarly observed, "If you have ever wondered how much truth there is in Herman Melville's *Moby Dick,* this book will answer your questions. Actually, *Moby Dick* wasn't far from reality. There were, indeed, massive bull whales which could take their revenge on a vessel. The Nantucket whale ship Essex was sunk by just such a giant in 1820 in mid-Pacific, and what happened to the captain and crew of that ship thereafter is a story which surpasses that of *Moby Dick. Ahab's Trade* tells that story well, as it does man's longstanding quest to profit from the largest creature of the sea." Gilbert Taylor in *Booklist* felt that the work "bespeaks its author's enthusiasm, widely shared, for the history of South Pacific whaling fishery." According to Bolster, Mawer "has written a rousing, largely anecdotal and . . . elegant 'saga'. . . . Inspired passages . . . live up to Mawer's stated desire 'to evoke the past as much as to explain it.'"

Among Mawer's other books is *Most Perfectly Safe: The Convict Shipwreck Disasters of 1833-42,* an account of several convict ships that were destroyed by shipwreck en route from England to Australia. In her *Australian Book Review* appraisal of the title, Margaret Steinberger concluded that Mawer "exploits the potential for history to read as exciting adventure and intrigue."

BIOGRAPHICAL AND CRITICAL SOURCES:

PERIODICALS

American Studies International, February, 2001, Kenneth Speirs, review of *Ahab's Trade: The Saga of South Sea Whaling,* p. 65.
Australian Book Review, July, 1997, Margaret Steinberger, review of *Most Perfectly Safe: The Convict Shipwreck Disasters of 1833-42,* p. 65.
Booklist, December 15, 1999, Gilbert Taylor, review of *Ahab's Trade,* p. 745.
Bulletin with Newsweek, June 27, 2006, Ashley Hay, "Freeze Company," review of *South by Northwest: The Magnetic Crusade and the Contest for Antarctica,* p. 132.
Historian, summer, 2001, Andrew G. Wilson, review of *Ahab's Trade,* p. 891.
Library Journal, January, 2000, Stanley Itkin, review of *Ahab's Trade,* p. 132.
New England Quarterly, September, 2000, Robert Lloyd Webb, review of *Ahab's Trade,* p. 526.
New York Times Book Review, January 30, 2000, W. Jeffrey Bolster, "Catch Willy," review of *Ahab's Trade,* p. 26.
Publishers Weekly, December 6, 1999, review of *Ahab's Trade,* p. 67.
Quadrant, July, 2001, Warren Reed, review of *Ahab's Trade,* p. 112.
SciTech Book News, June, 2000, review of *Ahab's Trade,* p. 111.
Sea History, summer, 2000, review of *Ahab's Trade,* p. 44.
Time International, January 29, 2001, Elizabeth Feizkhah, "Princes of Whales," p. 48.
Time Literary Supplement, July 7, 2000, review of *Ahab's Trade,* p. 32.

* * *

MAX 1956-

(Francesc Capdevila Gisbert)

PERSONAL: Born 1956, in Barcelona, Spain.

ADDRESSES: Home—Mallorca, Spain.

CAREER: Illustrator and writer. Associated with El Rrollo, an artist's group, beginning 1973; cofounder of *El Víbora,* a comics magazine, 1979; cofounder of *Nosotros somos los muertos,* a comics magazine, 1995.

AWARDS, HONORS: Prize for best work, Sixth International Comic Fair, 1988; prize for best work, 1996, for *Como perros*; prize for best story, for "El prolongado sueño del Sr. T," 1998.

WRITINGS:

COLLECTIONS

Gustavo Contra la Actividad del Radio, Ediciones La Cúpula (Barcelona, Spain), 1981.

Peter Pank, Ediciones La Cúpula (Barcelona, Spain), 1985, Catalan Communications (New York, NY), 1991.

Peter Pank el Licantropunk, Ediciones La Cúpula (Barcelona, Spain), 1987.

El Beso Secreto, Ediciones La Cúpula (Barcelona, Spain), 1987.

Peter Pank Pankdinista!, Ediciones La Cúpula (Barcelona, Spain), 1990.

Gustavo en Comecocometrón, Ediciones La Cúpula (Barcelona, Spain), 1994.

Como Perros!, Ediciones La Cúpula (Barcelona, Spain), 1995.

El Canto del Gallo, Ediciones La Cúpula (Barcelona, Spain), 1996.

El prolongado sueño del señor T, Ediciones La Cúpula (Barcelona, Spain), 1998, published as *The Extended Dream of Mr. D,* Drawn & Quarterly (Montreal, Canada), 2000.

Bardin the Superrealist, Fantagraphics (Seattle, WA), 2006.

ILLUSTRATOR:

Mique Beltrán, *Mujeres Fatales,* Ediciones la Cúpula (Barcelona, Spain), 1989.

El león y el ratón y La liebre y la tortuga, La Galera (Barcelona, Spain), 1993.

Yoshi y la lluvia, La Galera (Barcelona, Spain), 1999.

Jorge Zentner, *La Muerte Húmeda + El Carnaval de los Ciervos,* Ediciones La Cúpula (Barcelona, Spain), 1999.

Oriol Izquierdo, adapter, *La Sirenita,* La Galera (Barcelona, Spain), 1999, translation published as *The Little Mermaid/La Sirenita,* Chronicle Books (San Francisco, CA), 2003.

Juan sin miedo, La Galera (Barcelona, Spain), 2000.

Caterina Valrui, adapter, *Thumbelina/Pulgarcita,* Chronicle Books (San Francisco, CA), 2004.

Hans Christian Andersen, *El Muneco De Nieve,* Grupo Anaya Comercial, 2005.

Hans Christian Andersen, *El ruiseñor* (title means "The Nightingale"), Combel Editorial (Barcelona, Spain), 2006.

Sandra Comino, *Morning Glory,* Groundwood Books (Toronto, Ontario, Canada), 2006.

Maria Eulalia Valeri, adapter, *The Hare and the Tortoise/La liebre y la tortuga,* Chronicle Books (San Francisco, CA), 2006.

Also illustrator of *Órficas,* 1994, and *Monlogo y alucinacin del gigante blanco,* 1996.

SIDELIGHTS: Artist and illustrator Francesc Capdevila Gisbert, who publishes under the name of Max, is a pioneering figure in Spain's underground comics scene. He first came to prominence in the 1970s as a member of El Rrollo, an artists' collective, and later cofounded *El Víbora,* an independent comics journal. "*El Víbora* advertised itself as a magazine for the sick-minded, and featured the most demented comic strips on the market, vigorously marking out for itself a separate territory from the typical sci-fi, Moebius-esque magazines," noted Marcos Castrillón on the *Ninth Art* Web site. Max published his first collection, *Gustavo Contra la Actividad del Radio,* in 1981, and four years later he published *Peter Pank,* the first of three volumes featuring the anarchic title character. *Peter Pank* "is in equal parts an homage to J.M. Barrie's original play, and a ruthless parody of 80s trash culture," Castrillón stated.

In *Bardin the Superrealist,* Max collects a number of single-page strips and short stories, as well as one long work, featuring the title character. "Bardin, a big-headed balding man in a suit, is blessed with mystical powers that put him in touch with his own unconscious as well as the global (universal) unconscious mind," observed Bart Beaty on the *Comics Reporter* Web site. "Guided by Dali and Bunuel's *Chien Andalou,* Bardin moves through multiple worlds, debating the holy trinity in its many forms, and ruminating on his own philosophical beliefs." "In *Bardin,* over ten years' worth of work has been reproduced in beautiful stochastic printing, which uses 'frequency-modulated dot patterns' to create rich colors and intricate detail," noted Jason Baxter on *IGN.com.* "The method suits Max's clean, consummate style, which features the effortless line work, understanding of pacing, and comic staging that only a master can possess." In *Bardin the Superrealist* and other works, "Max has managed to completely overshadow his comix heritage, and sails a sea of surrealist storytelling and futuristic conceptual design," Castrillón wrote.

BIOGRAPHICAL AND CRITICAL SOURCES:

PERIODICALS

Booklist, September 1, 2006, Ray Olson, review of *Bardin the Superrealist,* p. 70.
Publishers Weekly, October 2, 2006, review of *Bardin the Superrealist,* p. 46.

ONLINE

Comics Reporter Web site, http://www.comicsreporter.com/ (July 13, 2006), Bart Beaty, review of *Bardin the Superrealist;* (October 27, 2006), review of *Bardin the Superrealist.*
IGN.com, http://comics.ign.com/ (October 18, 2006), Jason Baxter, "Trippin' in the Superreal World," review of *Bardin the Superrealist.*
Ninth Art Web site, http://www.ninthart.com/ (April 23, 2004), Marcos Castrillón, "Beyond Borders."*

*   *   *

McCAFFER, Ron
    See McCAFFER, Ronald

*   *   *

McCAFFER, Ronald 1943-
    (Ron McCaffer)

PERSONAL: Born December 8, 1943, in Glasgow, Scotland; son of John Gregg and Catherine Turner McCaffer; married Margaret Elizabeth Warner (a schoolteacher), August 13, 1966; children: Malcolm Andrew. *Ethnicity:* "Caucasian." *Education:* University of Strathclyde, B.Sc., 1965, D.Sc., 1998; Loughborough University of Technology, Ph.D., 1977.

ADDRESSES: Office—Department of Civil Engineering, Loughborough University of Technology, Loughborough, Leicestershire LE11 3TU, England. *E-mail*—r.mccaffer@lboro.ac.uk.

CAREER: Loughborough University of Technology, Loughborough, Leicestershire, England, member of engineering faculty.

MEMBER: Royal Academy of Engineering (fellow), Institution of Civil Engineers (fellow), Chartered Institute of Building (fellow), American Society of Civil Engineers.

WRITINGS:

Management of Off-Highway Plant and Equipment, Taylor & Francis (Philadelphia, PA), 2003.
(With Frank Harris) *Modern Construction Management,* Blackwell Scientific Publishing (London, England), 2006.

BIOGRAPHICAL AND CRITICAL SOURCES:

ONLINE

Ronald McCaffer Home Page, http://www.mccaffer.com (October 21, 2006).

*   *   *

McCANDLESS, Sarah Grace 1974(?)-

PERSONAL: Born c. 1974, in Chicago, IL. *Education:* Michigan State University, B.A., 1996.

ADDRESSES: Agent—Jenny Bent, Trident Media Group, 41 Madison Ave., 36th Fl., New York, NY 10010.

CAREER: Dark Horse Comics, Portland, OR, marketing director, 1999-2004; freelance writer, 2004—.

WRITINGS:

Grosse Pointe Girl: Tales from a Suburban Adolescence (novel), illustrated by Christine Norrie, Simon & Schuster (New York, NY), 2004.
The Girl I Wanted to Be (novel), Simon & Schuster Paperbacks (New York, NY), 2006.

Contributor to *Sexy Chix: An Anthology of Women Writers and Artists,* illustrated by Joelle Jones, Dark Horse Comics, 2006. Contributor to periodicals, including *Mudsugar, Daily Candy,* and *Venus.*

SIDELIGHTS: Sarah Grace McCandless left her job as a marketing director for Dark Horse Comics to become a freelance writer. Her first two books since setting off on her own are *Grosse Pointe Girl: Tales from a Suburban Adolescence* and *The Girl I Wanted to Be,* both of which, while featuring teenaged protagonists, have been marketed toward both adult and young adult audiences. *Grosse Pointe Girl* draws on many autobiographical elements from the author, who grew up in Michigan. Set in the 1980s, the novel features Emma Harris, a sixth grader who has just moved to a suburb of Detroit. Here, she meets some wealthy kids and becomes friends with Katrina, before her parents divorce and she, just like McCandless herself, has to move to an apartment. McCandless writes with humor about the various typical episodes the young Emma lives through, but "these tales are darker and more elegiac than the bouncy prose suggests," according to a *Kirkus Reviews* writer, who noted episodes about drinking, sex, and even suicide. Other reviewers focused more on the author's ability to capture her characters well. Gillian Engberg, writing for *Booklist,* lauded McCandless's "wickedly funny descriptions and her unerring ear for teen dialogue," while *People* critic Lori Gottlieb felt she "hilariously captures teen politics."

In the follow-up novel, *The Girl I Wanted to Be,* the story features a slightly older girl, fourteen year old Presley Moran. Presley greatly admires her Aunt Betsi, whom she regards as a mentor as the girl gets ready to enter high school, and is attracted to her handsome cousin Barry. She is thus mortified when she learns that these two important people in her life are having a love affair. Presley looks for emotional support from her friends at school, but only finds it from Jack, a friend of Barry's. According to a *Kirkus Reviews* critic, this second novel "capture[s] some of the nuances of adolescence, but while the story hangs together well, it isn't deep enough to transcend the alienating tone of youth." On the other hand, a writer for *Publishers Weekly* felt that, although the plot itself does not "come as a surprise . . . the delicate manner in which sophomore novelist McCandless . . . relays the affair does."

BIOGRAPHICAL AND CRITICAL SOURCES:

PERIODICALS

Booklist, May 1, 2004, Gillian Engberg, review of *Grosse Pointe Girl: Tales from a Suburban*

Adolescence, p. 1546; April 15, 2006, Gillian Engberg, review of *The Girl I Wanted to Be,* p. 29.

Kansas City Star, June 24, 2006, John Mark Eberhart, "I've Got a Secret? It's Tough to Make the Right Choices at 14."

Kirkus Reviews, April 15, 2004, review of *Grosse Pointe Girl,* p. 353; April 15, 2006, review of *The Girl I Wanted to Be,* p. 373.

Library Journal, June 15, 2004, Jan Blodgett, review of *Grosse Pointe Girl,* p. 59; May 1, 2006, Jan Blodgett, review of *The Girl I Wanted to Be,* p. 80.

People, June 28, 2004, Lori Gottlieb, review of *Grosse Pointe Girl,* p. 47.

Publishers Weekly, April 3, 2006, review of *The Girl I Wanted to Be,* p. 37.

ONLINE

Book Slut, http://www.bookslut.com/ (January 1, 2004), review of *Grosse Pointe Girl.*

Dcist, http://www.dcist.com/ (June 7, 2006), profile of Sarah Grace McCandless.

Future Tense Books, http://www.futuretensebooks. com/ (December 1, 2006), "Sarah Grace McCandless Interview."

Sarah Disgrace: The Official Web Site of Author Sarah Grace McCandless, http://www.sarah disgrace.com (December 1, 2006).*

*   *   *

McCLOUD, Catriona
   See McPHERSON, Catriona

*   *   *

McDONALD, Iverach 1908-2006

OBITUARY NOTICE— See index for *CA* sketch: Born October 23, 1908; died December 14, 2006. Journalist and author. A longtime correspondent and editor for the London *Times,* McDonald was particularly known as an expert on Russia. Coming from a prominent Scottish family whose members included university professors, ministers, farmers, and journalists, the young McDonald was influenced most by his uncle, who was the owner of the *Northern Times* and *Highland News* newspapers. He therefore resolved to become a journalist himself, getting his start as an assistant editor at the *Yorkshire Post* in the early 1930s. He then joined the Times Publishing Company, working in London as a subeditor and then in Berlin as a correspondent just before World War II. He quickly rose from assistant to diplomatic correspondent, also reporting from places such as Munich and Prague. When England entered World War II, McDonald enlisted. By then, his long interest in Russia had given him a solid command of the language. This was a highly valued skill in the army, but McDonald was disappointed when the result was that he had to serve out his time in military intelligence, rather than in action. He continued to send in reports to the *Times,* as well, notably making the accurate prediction that Adolf Hitler would invade Russia, creating a second front. When the war ended, McDonald returned to his assistant editor post, but was promoted to foreign editor in 1952. The Cold War was now heating up, and McDonald's knowledge of Russia and its Soviet satellites was becoming increasingly important. Because the journalist had a well-rounded appreciation of Russians and their history and culture, he understood the people better because he did not view them just as Soviet communists, as many others did. McDonald fostered respectful relationships with many Soviet leaders, and had many contacts in that country that came in handy for his newspaper work. At the *Times* he rose to managing editor in 1965, associate editor in 1967, and director from 1968 to 1973, when he retired. After his retirement, McDonald published two books: *A Man of the Times: Talks and Travels in a Disrupted World* (1976) and *Struggles in War and Peace, 1939-1966* (1984), which was part of the "History of the Times" series released by Times Books.

OBITUARIES AND OTHER SOURCES:

PERIODICALS

Times (London, England), December 18, 2006, p. 42.

*   *   *

McFADYEN, Cody 1968-

PERSONAL: Born 1968, in TX; married; children: one daughter.

ADDRESSES: Home—Moorpark, CA. *E-mail*—cody@codymcfadyen.com.

CAREER: Author. Has worked in numerous fields, including in drug counseling, construction, fund raising, landscaping, Web site design, and in management; raised venture capital and ran Digital Snow, Inc. (a video game development company).

WRITINGS:

Shadow Man (thriller novel), Bantam Books (New York, NY), 2006.
Face of Death (thriller novel), Bantam Books (New York, NY), 2007.

ADAPTATIONS: Shadow Man was adapted as an audio recording by Random House Audio, 2006.

SIDELIGHTS: "I have written, on and off, since I was 9 years old. I always had the idea of wanting to be a writer, but I was distracted by life, it's ups and downs and whirligigs," commented Cody McFadyen on his home page. After many years trying various occupations, ranging from drug counseling and fund raising to Web site design, McFadyen finally pursued his old dream by publishing the thriller novel *Shadow Man*. Having been a fan of the genre for many years, "first-time novelist McFadyen writes like an old pro," reported David Pitt in a *Booklist* review of the author's debut. A number of other critics were impressed as well by the novel. McFadyen begins with a premise about an Internet stalker who believes he is related to Jack the Ripper; his purpose is to seek out women who are performing sexual acts on pornography Web sites and kill them. One of the victims was a friend of FBI agent Smoky Barrett. Barrett did not know her friend was involved in the dark world of virtual porn, but the case brings her back into action after suffering tragic personal losses. In an earlier case, Barrett's husband and daughter were murdered by a man she eventually killed herself, but the aftermath resulted in depression and thoughts of suicide. McFadyen mixes his protagonist's personal life and a heady plot of violence successfully, according to a number of reviewers. A *Publishers Weekly* contributor, for instance, called Barrett a "memorable protagonist" and praised the author's writing as "crisp and smart." "Brisk and fascinating" was how a *Kirkus Reviews* writer characterized the debut novel.

BIOGRAPHICAL AND CRITICAL SOURCES:

PERIODICALS

Booklist, May 1, 2006, David Pitt, review of *Shadow Man*, p. 22.

Hollywood Reporter, June 12, 2006, Jerry Bartell, "Women, Take Your Mark: 'Shadow,' 'Fear,' 'Dead,'" p. 14.

Kirkus Reviews, April 1, 2006, review of *Shadow Man*, p. 318.

Library Journal, May 1, 2006, Susan O. Moritz, review of *Shadow Man*, p. 80.

Publishers Weekly, April 17, 2006, review of *Shadow Man*, p. 163.

South Florida Sun-Sentinel, review of *Shadow Man*.

ONLINE

Cody McFadyen Home Page, http://www.codymcfadyen.com (November 30, 2006).

Shots, http://www.shotsmag.co.uk/ (November 30, 2006), "Cody McFadyen Talks to Shots Ezine about Writing His Debut Thriller, *Shadow Man*."

* * *

McINTOSH, Pat

PERSONAL: Born in Lanarkshire, Scotland. *Education:* Graduate of Glasgow University.

CAREER: Writer.

WRITINGS:

"GIL CUNNINGHAM" MYSTERY SERIES

The Harper's Quine, Carroll & Graf (New York, NY), 2004.

The Nicholas Feast, Constable (London, England), 2005.

The Merchant's Mark, Carroll & Graf (New York, NY), 2006.

St. Mungo's Robin, Carroll & Graf (New York, NY), 2007.

SIDELIGHTS: Pat McIntosh is the author of a series of mystery books featuring protagonist Gil Cunningham and set in Medieval Scotland. In the first novel in the series, *The Harper's Quine*, Cunningham is undergoing legal training but ultimately wants to become a priest and notary, following in the footsteps of his uncle, Canon David Cunningham. When a local landowner's wife leaves him because of abuse and takes up with a musician, she later turns up dead on a construction site. Gil begins investigating the case, with the primary focus on the woman's husband, John Semphill, and his new love, the also brutal Lady Euphemia Campbell. In the meantime, Gil meets a mason's daughter, Alys, who is starting to turn his eye away from the priesthood. "Lovers of quality historicals will welcome McIntosh's debut," wrote a reviewer in *Publishers Weekly*. A *Kirkus Reviews* contributor commented: "In spite of all the violence, the affectionate family relationships and warm characterizations shine most brightly here: a charming plaid debut."

Gil returns in *The Nicholas Feast* and has left his goal of entering the priesthood behind as he is now engaged to Alys. Attending the Nicholas Feast at Glasgow University, Gil is asked to help solve a crime when the unlikable William Irvine, a bastard member of the Montgomery clan, is found strangled. Gil soon finds that Irvine was a blackmailer with plenty of enemies and begins to unravel the case by decoding Irvine's shorthand notebook with the help of Alys. A subplot involves Gil's mother trying to convince him not to marry. "A satisfying story, studded with tidbits of medieval custom, hearty as a raisin scone," wrote a *Kirkus Reviews* contributor. Rex E. Klett, writing in the *Library Journal*, referred to *The Nicholas Feast* as "a nicely involving historical, well-written and tidily plotted." In a review on the *Shots Magazine* Web site, Ayo Onatade wrote that the mystery is "just as good" as the author's debut, adding: "The characters are well drawn and a lot more fleshed out in this second book."

The Merchant's Mark features Gil involved in a book import business. However, when he and his partner, the merchant Augie Morison, receive their shipment of books, they also find a man's head in a barrel of brine along with a treasure in a leather pouch. When Augie is accused of murder, Gil sets out to solve the case. Margaret Flanagan, writing in *Booklist*, commented that the author "provides an intelligent, authentic, and suspenseful historical whodunit." A *Kirkus Reviews* contributor called the mystery "a convincing tale of loving families and brutal killers that delves deep into medieval Scottish life." A *Publishers Weekly* reviewer noted that the author's "characterizations and period detail are first-rate."

BIOGRAPHICAL AND CRITICAL SOURCES:

PERIODICALS

Booklist, June 1, 2006, Margaret Flanagan, review of *The Merchant's Mark,* p. 44.

Kirkus Reviews, July 1, 2004, review of *The Harper's Quine,* p. 607; May 15, 2005, review of *The Nicholas Feast,* p. 565; May 15, 2006, review of *The Merchant's Mark,* p. 499.

Library Journal, July, 2004, Rex E. Klett, review of *The Harper's Quine,* p. 63; July 1, 2005, Rex E. Klett, review of *The Nicholas Feast,* p. 57.

Publishers Weekly, July 12, 2004, review of *The Harper's Quine,* p. 47; May 15, 2006, review of *The Merchant's Mark,* p. 51.

ONLINE

MyShelf.com, http://www.myshelf.com/ (December 31, 2006), review of *The Nicholas Feast* and *The Merchant's Mark.*

Shots Magazine, http://www.shotsmag.co.uk/ (December 31, 2006), Ayo Onatade, review of *The Nicholas Feast.*

* * *

McKEITHEN, Madge 1955-

PERSONAL: Born 1955, in Fayetteville, NC; divorced; children: Isaac and Nicholas Levy. *Education:* Graduate of the College of William and Mary and Johns Hopkins School of Advanced International Studies; Queens University of Charlotte, M.F.A. 2006.

ADDRESSES: Home—New York, NY. *E-mail*—Madge.mckeithen@gmail.com.

CAREER: Writer. Has worked as a teacher and as a researcher and editor for a U.S. congressman and the World Bank. New School, New York, NY, teacher of creative writing, 2006—.

WRITINGS:

Blue Peninsula: Essential Words for a Life of Loss and Change (memoir; essays), Farrar, Straus & Giroux (New York, NY), 2006.

SIDELIGHTS: In her memoir, *Blue Peninsula: Essential Words for a Life of Loss and Change,* Madge McKeithen tells of the transformation she underwent due to a mysterious illness afflicting her son Ike and how she turned to poetry for consolation. Ike's symptoms begin with leg stiffness that soon causes him to lose the use of his legs. As times passes, Ike's illness worsens until he beings suffering from blood irregularities and dementia. The book follows the first eight years of Ike's illness and McKeithen's attempts to deal with her child's problem. Eventually, she begins to compulsively read poetry as a way to escape and maintain her emotional equilibrium. The author also opens each chapter with a poem that has affected her deeply. Karen Campbell, writing in the *Boston Globe,* commented: "For [McKeithen], poetry has offered both flights of fancy and moments of profound truth." Campbell also noted: "McKeithen's is a sobering yet compelling story," adding that "the writing is vivid, sometimes eloquently metaphorical, other times blazingly direct." A reviewer writing on the *BookPage* Web site, called *Blue Peninsula* "an unusual hybrid of health memoir and 'favorite poems.'" A *Publishers Weekly* contributor noted: "Readers will come away reminded of poetry's powerful ability to enlighten personal struggles."

BIOGRAPHICAL AND CRITICAL SOURCES:

BOOKS

McKeithen, Madge, *Blue Peninsula: Essential Words for a Life of Loss and Change,* Farrar, Straus & Giroux (New York, NY), 2006.

PERIODICALS

Boston Globe, July 3, 2006, Karen Campbell, review of *Blue Peninsula.*

Publishers Weekly, February 27, 2006, review of *Blue Peninsula,* p. 43.

New York Times May 23, 2006, Dinitia Smith, review of *Blue Peninsula*.

ONLINE

BookPage, http://www.bookpage.com/ (December 31, 2006), review of *Blue Peninsula.*
Literature, Arts, and Medicine Database, http://litmed. med.nyu.edu/ (February 16, 2007), review of *Blue Peninsula.*
Madge McKeithen Home Page, http://www.madge mckeithen.com (December 31, 2006).
Poems.com, http://www.poems.com/ (December 31, 2006), brief biography of author.
Queens University of Charlotte Web site, http://www. queens.edu/ (December 31, 2006), brief biography of author.

*   *   *

McKENDRICK, Scot 1958-

PERSONAL: Born March 26, 1958, in Dundee, Scotland; son of James Irvine (an industrial engineer) and June Jean McKendrick; married Alison Mary Adger, 1985; children: Iona Jean Euphemia, Imogen Mary Jessie, Alexander James Michael. *Ethnicity:* "Scottish." *Education:* Oxford University, M.A. (hons.), 1982; Courtauld Institute of Art, London, Ph. D., 1988. *Religion:* Church of Scotland.

ADDRESSES: Home—Cockham, Berkshire, England. *Office*—Department of Manuscripts, British Library, 96 Euston Rd., London NW1 2DB, England. *E-mail*— scot.mckendrick@bl.uk.

CAREER: British Library, London, England, curator responsible for Latin and Greek manuscripts, 1986-97, curator of classical, Byzantine, and biblical manuscripts, 1997-2003, head of medieval and earlier manuscripts, 2003-05, head of western manuscripts, 2006—. Royal Commission on Historical Manuscripts, curator, 1989; London Research Center for Illuminated Manuscripts, member; J. Paul Getty Museum, Los Angeles, CA, guest scholar, 1999; Stanley Spencer Gallery, trustee, 2004—; Sir Winston Churchill Archive trust, trustee, 2006; consultant. University of London, faculty member at School of Advanced Studies, 1995—, fellow of Courtauld Institute of Art, 1997—; speaker at other institutions, including Metropolitan Museum of Art, New York, NY, and universities of Cambridge, Bristol, Leeds, and Oxford, England, Berlin, Germany, Lille and Paris, France, and Leiden, Netherlands.

MEMBER: Society of Antiquaries (fellow), Association for Manuscripts and Archives in Research Collections.

AWARDS, HONORS: Eugène Baie Prize, best publication on the history of Flemish civilization, culture, or art, 1998-2002, and Eric Mitchell Prize, best exhibition catalog, 2002-03, both for *Illuminating the Renaissance: The Triumph of Flemish Manuscript Painting in Europe.*

WRITINGS:

(Coeditor) *The British Library Catalogue of Additions to the Manuscripts (New Series), 1976-1980,* British Library (London, England), 1995.
The History of Alexander the Great: An Illuminated Manuscript of Vasco da Lucena's French Translation of the Ancient Text by Quintus Curtius Rufus, J. Paul Getty Museum (Los Angeles, CA), 1996.
(Coeditor) *Illuminating the Book: Makers and Interpreters; Essays in Honour of Janet Backhouse,* British Library (London, England), 1998.
(Editor) *The Summary Catalogue of Greek Manuscripts in the British Library,* Volume 1, British Library (London, England), 1999.
(Coeditor and contributor) *The Bible as Book: The Transmission of the Greek Text,* British Library (London, England), 2003.
(Coauthor) *Illuminating the Renaissance: The Triumph of Flemish Manuscript Painting in Europe* (exhibition catalog), J. Paul Getty Museum (Los Angeles, CA), 2003.
Flemish Illuminated Manuscripts, 1400-1550, British Library (London, England), 2003.
In a Monastery Library: Preserving Codex Sinaiticus and the Greek Written Heritage, British Library (London, England), 2006.
(Coauthor) *Bible Manuscripts,* British Library (London, England), 2007.

Contributor to books, including *Fake? The Art of Deception,* edited by M. Jones, British Museum (London, England), 1990; *England and the Low*

Countries in the Late Middle Ages, edited by C.M. Barron and N. Saul, 1995; *Medieval Boom Production: The Latin Classics,* edited by C. Chavannes-Mazel and M. Smith, 1996; *The Mythical Quest,* British Library, 1996; and *Under the Influence: The Concept of Influence and the Study of Illuminated Manuscripts,* edited by A. Bovey and J. Lowden, Brepols (Turnhout, Belgium), 2006; and to exhibition catalogs. Contributor to periodicals, including *British Library Journal, English Manuscript Studies, 1100-1700,* and *Burlington.*

*   *   *

McMANNERS, John 1916-2006

OBITUARY NOTICE— See index for *CA* sketch: Born December 25, 1916, in Durham, England; died November 4, 2006. Historian, priest, educator, and author. A former Oxford University ecclesiastical history professor, McManners was a noted authority on the history of the Church in France. The son of an Anglican minister, he became enamored of history as a student at St. Edmund Hall, Oxford, where he was influenced by medieval historian A.B. Emden. He graduated in 1939, just as World War II broke out. McManners enlisted in the British Army's Royal Northumberland Fusiliers. He saw action in North Africa, commanding a unit at the battles of Alamein and Tunis, for which service he was awarded the Order of King George II of the Hellenes by the King of Greece. Returning home, he completed his master's degree at Oxford, then studied theology at the University of Durham. He earned a diploma in theology in 1947 and was ordained a priest in the Church of England the next year. McManners found employment as a fellow and chaplain at St. Edmund Hall, but a long-standing interest in Australia led him to accept a post at the University of Tasmania in 1956. Here, he was chair of the history department. Internal politics, however, made his stay at the university uncomfortable, and McManners moved to the University of Sydney two years later. McManners enjoyed his years in Australia, but in 1967 he returned to England to be closer to his aging parents. The University of Leicester hired him as professor of history in 1968, and five years later he went back to Oxford as Regius Professor of Ecclesiastical History; he was also given a canonry at Christ Church. By this time, McManners already had a solid reputation as a scholar of French religious history. Beginning with *French Ecclesiastical*

Society under the Ancien Regime: A Study of Angers in the Eighteenth Century (1960), the professor had earned the esteem of colleagues and critics alike for his knowledge of the subject. His reputation continued to grow with books such as *The French Revolution and the Church* (1969), *Church and State in France, 1870-1914* (1972), and *Death and Enlightenment* (1981), which won the Wolfson Literary Award. McManners retired from Christ Church in 1984 to accept a fellowship and chaplaincy at All Souls. He remained college chaplain until 2001 and was an honorary fellow thereafter. Among his later literary achievements are the comprehensive *The Oxford Illustrated History of Christianity* (1990), which he edited, and the works *Church and Society in Eighteenth-Century France* (1998) and *All Souls and the Shipley Case, 1808-1810* (2002). He recalled his days in the army in the autobiography *Fusilier: Recollections and Reflections, 1939-1945* (2002).

OBITUARIES AND OTHER SOURCES:

PERIODICALS

McManners, John, *Fusilier: Recollections and Reflections, 1939-1945,* Michael Russell (Wilby, England), 2002.

PERIODICALS

Times (London, England), November 14, 2006, p. 54.

*   *   *

McPHERSON, Catriona 1965-
(Catriona McCloud)

PERSONAL: Born 1965, in South Queensferry, Scotland; married. *Education:* University of Edinburgh, M.A., Ph.D.

ADDRESSES: Home—Galloway, Scotland. *Agent*—Coombs Moylett, 3 Askew Rd., London NW1 3BH, England. *E-mail*—cmcpherson@dial.pipex.com.

CAREER: Writer. Previously worked in a bank, then at the Edinburgh City Libraries, Edinburgh, Scotland; University of Leeds, Yorkshire, England, lecturer of English, 1999-2000; Open University, Scotland, tutor.

WRITINGS:

(As Catriona McCloud) *Growing Up Again,* Orion (London, England), 2007.

"DANDY GILVER" SERIES

After the Armistice Ball, Constable (London, England), 2005.

The Burry Man's Day, Constable (London, England), 2006.

SIDELIGHTS: Catriona McPherson is author of the "Dandy Gilver" series of historical mystery novels set in the 1920s. In the first novel in the series, *After the Armistice Ball,* McPherson introduces the reader to Dandy Gilver, a woman who grew up in the Victorian era but is now living in a changing world of more freedom for women. When the local yearly celebration of the end of World War I, called an armistice ball, is held at the Duffy's house, the family diamonds go missing. With her children—whom she has ambivalent feelings about—away at school and her unlikable husband working, Dandy accepts an offer from her friend Daisy Duffy to help find the missing diamonds, leading her to uncover dark secrets in the Duffy family and to encounter a murderer.

"Memorable supporting characters . . . plus vivid descriptions of the Scottish landscape enhance a compelling mystery," wrote a *Publishers Weekly* contributor of *After the Armistice Ball.* Sue O'Brien, writing in *Booklist,* noted that "details of Daisy's well-to-do lifestyle . . . evoke the time period and a certain class of people." Rex E. Klett commented in a review in the *Library Journal* on the novel's "perfect settings, class peculiarities, wry humor, and seamless prose."

McPherson's next "Dandy Gilver" mystery is titled *The Burry Man's Day,* named after an annual, ancient Scottish festival in which a local man is dressed in burrs and thorny seeds and then walks through town to deter evil spirits while being given free drinks of whiskey in the process. On a visit to her old friend, Buttercup, in South Queensferry, Scotland, Dandy becomes suspicious when the Burry Man falls over dead during his walk and she finds out that some of the townsfolk

think he has been poisoned even though the police have ruled that the death is due to a heart attack. "The Burry Man is the best ready-made character a writer could hope for," McPherson told Brian Ferguson for an article in the *Scotsman.* The author continued: "It's the combination of his disguise, the fact that he's never alone all day and the number of different people who pour him nips of whisky. He's made to be the star of a murder mystery."

"Dandy makes a wonderfully real narrator and protagonist," wrote a reviewer on *MyShelf.com.* The reviewer added that *The Burry Man's Day* is a "well-researched historical novel that brings the past to life." Writing in *Booklist,* Barbara Bibel noted that the mystery features a "lively cast of characters and a strong Scottish atmosphere." A *Kirkus Reviews* contributor wrote of the book: "Dandy and her friends are charming period pieces who are given an interesting and heartbreaking mystery to solve." A *Publishers Weekly* reviewer referred to the book as an "altogether satisfying cozy."

McPherson told *CA:* "My three older sisters taught me to read and write long before I went to school—they were always the teachers when we played, and I was always the pupil—so I can't remember a time before I could write and before I wanted to write stories. I started with pastiches of Enid Blyton fairy tales and went on from there.

"With six full-length stories completed so far, I'm beginning to see that what I come back to again and again is family, love, and secrets. Also, I don't think I could ever write a wholly solemn book.

"My writing process has been a great disappointment to my scientist husband, who thought that when I gave up academia I would start to wear wispy garments and work in a romantic lair of scribbled notes and inspirational objects, and that he would wake at three in the morning to find me typing by candlelight. In fact, when I'm writing a first draft, I start at nine in the morning, Monday through Friday, write until twelve, take two hours off for lunch and a walk, and then write, edit, or do admin until six. My study is tidier than his.

"My most surprising discovery is how much more like exploration and less like creation writing is than I would have expected. Every time so far, I've made a decision to change something big at the end of the writing process (e.g., the identity of the murderer) and found that the book is already set up as though that were going to happen.

"My favorite book is my first—unpublished— manuscript. It's the one that proved I could sit down at a blank screen and end up with a hundred thousand words of connected prose. Until I had done it the first time it seemed a ludicrous thing to suppose I could achieve, and I'm glad I don't have that particular worry any more."

BIOGRAPHICAL AND CRITICAL SOURCES:

PERIODICALS

Booklist, September 1, 2005, Sue O'Brien, review of *After the Armistice Ball,* p. 70; September 15, 2006, Barbara Bibel, review of *The Burry Man's Day,* p. 32.

Kirkus Reviews, August 1, 2006, review of *The Burry Man's Day,* p. 757.

Library Journal, September 1, 2005, Rex E. Klett, review of *After the Armistice Ball,* p. 117.

Publishers Weekly, July 18, 2005, review of *After the Armistice Ball,* p. 187; August 7, 2006, review of *The Burry Man's Day,* p. 36.

Scotsman (Edinburgh, Scotland), July 20, 2006, Biran Ferguson, "Novel Idea Brings Old Custom to Life," profile of author; July 23, 2006, "Catriona McPherson," interview with author.

ONLINE

Dandy Gilver Series Web site, http://www.dandygilver.co.uk (December 31, 2006).

Euro Crime, http://www.eurocrime.co.uk/ (December 31, 2006), Karen Meek, review of *After the Armistice Ball.*

MurderExpress.net, http://www.murderexpress.net/ (December 31, 2006), brief biography of author.

MyShelf.com, http://www.myshelf.com/ (December 31, 2006), review of *After the Armistice Ball* and the *The Burry Man's Day.*

Mystery Scene Magazine, http://www.mysteryscenemag.com/ (December 31, 2006), Molly Adams, review of *After the Armistice Ball.*

MEEHAN, Eileen R. 1951-

PERSONAL: Born August 3, 1951, in San Francisco, CA; daughter of James (a cemetery worker) and K. (a telephone operator) Meehan; married Alfred J. Babbitt, Jr. (self-employed), August 15, 1978. *Ethnicity:* "Irish-American." *Education:* San Francisco State University, B.A. (summa cum laude), 1973; University of Pennsylvania, M.A., 1975; University of Illinois at Urbana-Champaign, Ph.D., 1983.

ADDRESSES: Home—Baton Rouge, LA. *Office*—Manship School of Mass Communication, Louisiana State University, Baton Rouge, LA 70803. *E-mail*—emeeha1@lsu.edu.

CAREER: University of Iowa, Iowa City, lecturer, 1982, assistant professor of communication studies, 1982-89; University of Arizona, Tucson, assistant professor, 1989-93, associate professor of media arts, 1993-2003, affiliate of Graduate Interdisciplinary Program in Comparative Cultural and Literary Studies, 1992-2003; University of New Mexico, Albuquerque, holder of Garry Carruthers Endowed Visiting Chair, 2002-03; Louisiana State University, Baton Rouge, associate professor and holder of Lemuel Heidel Brown Endowed Chair in Media and Political Economy, 2003—. University of Wisconsin—Madison, visiting assistant professor, 1992.

AWARDS, HONORS: Dallas Smythe Award, Union for Democratic Communications, 1999.

WRITINGS:

(Editor, with Janet Wasko and Mark Phillips, and contributor) *Dazzled by Disney? The Global Disney Audiences Project,* Continuum Publishing Group (New York, NY), 2001.

(Editor, with Ellen Riordan, and contributor) *Sex and Money: Feminism and Political Economy in Media Studies,* University of Minnesota Press (Minneapolis, MN), 2002.

Why TV Is Not Our Fault: Television Programming, Viewers, and Who's Really in Control, Rowman & Littlefield (Lanham, MD), 2006.

Contributor to books, including *The Many Lives of Batman: Critical Approaches to a Superhero and His Media,* edited by W. Uricchio and R.E. Pearson, Routledge, 1991; *Ruthless Criticism: New Perspectives in U.S. Communication History,* edited by W. Solomon and R. McChesney, University of Minnesota Press, 1993; *The Postmodern Presence,* edited by A.A. Berger, Alta Mira Press, 1998; *Consuming Audiences? Production and Reception in Media Research,* edited by Janet Wasko and I. Hagen, Hampton Press, 2000; and *A Companion to Television,* edited by Janet Wasco, Blackwell Publishers, 2005. Contributor of articles and reviews to periodicals, including *Journal of Communication Inquiry, Media, Culture, and Society, Journal of Broadcasting and Electronic Media, Camera Obscura, Television and New Media, Critical Studies in Media and Communication, Feminist Media Studies, International Journal of Media and Cultural Politics, Journal of Media Economics,* and *Critical Studies in Mass Communication.*

*   *   *

MEISTER, Ellen

PERSONAL: Born in Bronx, NY; married; husband's name Mike; children: two sons and a daughter. *Education:* Graduated from University of Buffalo (magna cum laude).

ADDRESSES: Home—Long Island, NY. *Agent*—Annelise Robey, Jane Rotrosen Agency, 318 E. 51st St., New York, NY 10022. *E-mail*—ellen@ellenmeister.com.

CAREER: Writer. Previously worked at various jobs, including as a promotion assistant for a medical publisher, a literary agency, a trade association doing publicity and promotion, various magazines as a copywriter, and then as founder of a sales promotion agency.

WRITINGS:

Secret Confessions of the Applewood PTA (novel), W. Morrow (New York, NY), 2006.

Author of blog *Side Dish.*

ADAPTATIONS: Secret Confessions of the Applewood PTA, has been adapted for audio, Brilliance Audio, 2006.

SIDELIGHTS: In her first novel, *Secret Confessions of the Applewood PTA* Ellen Meister tells the story of three women—Maddie, Ruth, and Lisa—who are on the Applewood PTA committee and receive the job of sprucing up the town's reputation when Hollywood starts scouting Applewood to shoot a movie starring George Clooney. In addition to their public relations duties, however, the three women must also deal with problems in their own lives, including a bad marriage, a secret affair due to a husband's impotency, and an alcoholic mother who has ruined her singing career. Commenting on where the idea for the book came from, the author told a contributor to the *Ink Pot* Web site: "I had walked into a PTA meeting . . . feeling like I had this big secret. No one there knew I wanted to write. No one even knew I had an inner life." The author continued: "Then I got to wondering if all the women in the room were thinking more or less the same thing. That's when I knew I needed to write about these women, and to explore the depth of their lives."

Carol Haggas, writing in *Booklist,* noted that *Secret Confessions of the Applewood PTA* is filled "with sexy characters, sharp dialogue, and snappy pacing." A *Kirkus Reviews* contributor wrote that the novel's premise "leads to madcap escapades and silly sniping amongst the women," adding that it's a "comical yet poignant read without too much melodrama." Amy Brozio-Andrews commented in the *Library Journal* that the author's "debut novel is heartbreakingly funny."

Meister told *CA:* "I suspect that for most writers, the infection begins in the tender, heartsick teen years, when we're so open to falling in love. It was certainly that way for me. Like most kids my age, I pored over J.D. Salinger's paragraphs as if they were a treasure map to enlightenment. Oddly enough, though, it wasn't *Catcher in the Rye* that gave me that first woosh of love for the craft. It was 'A Perfect Day for Bananafish' from [Salinger's] *Nine Stories.* It's a brilliant piece filled with exquisite sentences, but there was one simple line of dialogue that hit me in such a sweet spot my heart caved in. And that was it."

BIOGRAPHICAL AND CRITICAL SOURCES:

PERIODICALS

Booklist, June 1, 2006, Carol Haggas, review of *Secret Confessions of the Applewood PTA,* p. 39.

Kirkus Reviews, May 15, 2006, review of *Secret Confessions of the Applewood PTA,* p. 489.
Library Journal, June 15, 2006, Amy Brozio-Andrews, review of *Secret Confessions of the Applewood PTA,* p. 60.
Publishers Weekly, May 8, 2006, review of *Secret Confessions of the Applewood PTA,* p. 45.

ONLINE

Ellen Meister Home Page, http://ellenmeister.com (January 1, 2007).
Ink Pot, http://www.inkpots.net/ (January 1, 2007), "Ellen Meister," interview with author.
insolent rudder, http://www.insolentrudder.net/ (January 1, 2007), "A Quarterly Conversation with . . . Ellen Meister."
Syosset-Jericho Tribune Web site, http://www.antonnews.com/syossetjerichotribune/ (April 8, 2005), "Jericho Author Ellen Meister Writes Debut Novel."

*   *   *

MERCER, Bill 1926-
   (William A. Mercer)

PERSONAL: Born February 13, 1926, in Muskogee, OK; son of Frank (a clinical assistant) and Maynie (a homemaker) Mercer; married Ilene Love Hargis (a teacher); children: F. David A., Daniel Evan, Martin Andrew, Laura Ilene Mercer Tiedemann. *Ethnicity:* "Caucasian." *Education:* Attended Northeastern State College (now State University), 1946-48; University of Denver, B.A., 1949; North Texas State University (now University of North Texas), M.A., 1966. *Politics:* Democrat. *Religion:* Episcopalian. *Hobbies and other interests:* Tennis, reading.

ADDRESSES: *Home*—Richardson, TX. *E-mail*—w-mercer@sbcglobal.net.

CAREER: KMUS-Radio, Muskogee, OK, sports reporter and staff announce, 1951-53; KRLD-Television and Radio, Dallas, TX, sports and news reporter, 1953-64; Dallas Cowboys, Dallas, announcer, 1965-72; Texas Rangers, Arlington, announcer, 1972-73; Chicago White Sox, Chicago, IL, announcer,

1974-75; KVIL-Radio, Dallas, affiliate, 1976-83. Dallas Texans, announcer, 1960-62. University of North Texas, affiliate, 1957-94. *Military service:* U.S. Navy, signal operator, 1943-46; received four battle stars.

MEMBER: American Federation of Television and Radio Artists (retired member).

AWARDS, HONORS: Inducted into Texas Baseball Ex-Pros Hall of Fame, 1983, Hall of Fame, Athletic Department, University of North Texas, 1992, and Texas Radio Hall of Fame, 2002; Bill Teegins Award, Oklahoma Sports Museum 2006; cowinner, Katie Award, Dallas Press Club, 2006, for best play-by-play.

WRITINGS:

(With Bob Huffaker, Wes Wise, and George Phenix) *When the News Went Live: Dallas 1963,* Taylor Trade Publishing (Lanham, MD), 2004.
Play-by-Play: Tales from a Sportscasting Insider, Taylor Trade Publishing (Lanham, MD), 2007.

Sports columnist, *Denton Record Chronicle.* Contributor to periodicals.

SIDELIGHTS: Bill Mercer told *CA:* "As a radio-television journalist and sports announcer my writing had been limited to current stories, narrations, and public relations material. My thesis for my master's degree was on the how-to of sports play-by-play broadcasting—never published. In 2002 Bub Huffaker, a former fellow journalist at KRLD-Television and Radio, was approached about writing a book on the coverage of the Kennedy assassination in Dallas. Bob called on me, Wes Wise, and George Phenix (all former journalists at KRLD) to contribute chapters about our experiences covering the assassination for KRLD. The book is *When the News Went Live.*

"After that publication I was asked to write a book on the history of radio and television broadcasting as they relate to the evolution of sports broadcasting. *Play-by-Play: Tales from a Sportscasting Insider* includes chapters on baseball, football, and professional wrestling. I had broadcast all of these from high school, college, and minor leagues to the highest level in each sport. I trace the beginning of sports broadcasting from its inception to the current time.

"In the early 1990s I had been asked to write a summary history of landing craft infantry, large (LCI-L) for the national LCI association annual publication. It is this brief history that I intend to enlarge for my next book. The LCI was originally designed to transport troops from an embarkation point to island or area being invaded. It was considered expendable. However, as World War II progressed, the LCI was probably the most versatile ship created for that war. I promised my shipmates during one of our reunions that I would write a book about our 439. There are fewer of those mates left. It is that story that I wish to tell.

"I never expected to become a college teacher or writer. These evolved out of my early efforts to become a respected professional play-by-play sports broadcaster. At the age of eighty, I imagine the LCI book will be my final chapter as an author."

*   *   *

MERCER, William A.
See MERCER, Bill

*   *   *

MERINO, José María 1941-

PERSONAL: Born 1941 in La Coruna, Spain.

CAREER: Writer.

AWARDS, HONORS: Premio Novelas y Cuentos, 1976, for *La novela de Andres Choz;* Critica Prize, 1985, for *La orilla oscura;* Nacional de Literatura Juvenil, 1993, for *Los trenes de verano.*

WRITINGS:

Cien años de cuentos (1899-1998) (short stories), 1999.
Dias imaginarios, 2003.
El heredero, Alfaguara (Madrid, Spain), 2003.
Ficción continua, Seix Barral (Barcelona, Spain), 2004.

Cuentos de los días raros, Alfaguara (Madrid, Spain), 2004.
Intramuros, illustrated by Enrique Flores, Anaya (Madrid, Spain), 2004.
Cuentos del libro de la noche, Alfguara (Madrid, Spain), 2005.
El anillo judío y otros cuentos, Castilla Ediciones (Valladolid, Spain), 2005.
Cumpleaños lejos de casa: poesía reunida, Seix Barral (Barcelona, Spain), 2006.
Tres semanas de mal dormis: diario nocturno, limited edition, Seix Barral (Barcelona, Spain), 2006.

Other writings, include *La novela de Andres Choz; La orilla oscura;* and *Los trenes de verano.*

BIOGRAPHICAL AND CRITICAL SOURCES:

PERIODICALS

World Literature Today, July-September, 2002, Luis Larios Vandrell, review of *Dias imaginarios,* p. 145.*

*   *   *

MEYER, Allan 1932-

PERSONAL: Born August 18, 1932, in NE; son of Arthur and Alma Meyer; married; wife's name Sharon (in real estate sales). *Education:* University of Nebraska, B.A.; Catholic University of America, M.A.; Nova University, Ed.D., 1987. *Hobbies and other interests:* Music.

ADDRESSES: Home—Tucson, AZ *E-mail*—ameyer32@aol.com.

CAREER: Cochise College, Douglas, AZ, instructor in philosophy, 1970-92. Worked for WJAG-Radio, Norfolk, NE, KJAY-Radio, Topeka, KS, and KLIN-Radio, Lincoln, NE.

WRITINGS:

Right and Wrong: A Useful Fiction (nonfiction), Second Thoughts Press (Eugene, OR), 2006.

SIDELIGHTS: Allan Meyer told *CA:* "As a college philosophy teacher, I was not able to defend traditional views of morality and religion. I took notes on writings by Will Durant, B.F. Skinner, E.O. Wilson, Antonio Damasio, Richard Dawkins, and others. My background in literature, history, and arts helped make my writing style effective. Hard work and lots of library time did the rest."

* * *

MEYER, Maisie J. 1939-
(Maisie Joy Meyer)

PERSONAL: Born October 20, 1939, in Calcutta, India; British subject; daughter of Saul (in import-export business) and Seemah Gloria (a homemaker) Sadka; married Benjamin Meyer (a structural engineer), August 20, 1961; children: Deborah Meyer Kelman, David, Saul. *Education:* Loreto College, B.A. (English), 1961; earned B.A. (humanities), 1986; London School of Economics and Political Science, London, M.A., 1988, Ph.D., 1994. *Religion:* Jewish.

ADDRESSES: Home—London, England. *E-mail*—mjmeyer@email.com.

CAREER: Historian.

WRITINGS:

From the Rivers of Babylon to the Whangpoo: A Century of Sephardi Jewish Life in Shanghai, University Press of America (Lanham, MD), 2003.

Contributor to periodicals, including *Immigrants and Minorities, Jewish Culture and History,* and *Jewish Quarterly.*

SIDELIGHTS: Maisie J. Meyer told *CA:* "In the course of worldwide research for my doctoral thesis on the Baghdadi Jewish community of Shanghai, I collected a wealth of fascinating material that I wanted to share with a wide readership. Being of Baghdadi Jewish origin, and born and brought up in India, I was particularly interested in Baghdadi Jewish immigration to the East.

"I found a striking similarity between writing this book and childbirth. Researching was comparable to the exciting courtship period. My husband, Benny, was as essential to the conception of our children as he was to the book's formation. Coordinating the mountain of research and editing the umpteen drafts was like a pregnancy. The increasingly heavy load made me feel broody and isolated. The pains of editing the final draft and not least preparing the index were as excruciating as those of labor and childbirth. I expected the analogy would end here because whereas everyone finds something to admire in a baby, I expected readers to be critical. Happily, I had extremely good reviews and above all, the community whose history I recorded was most appreciative. All my efforts seemed worthwhile when one member who has sadly become blind told me that he has so much enjoyment listening to tapes of my book which his daughter recorded. This 'baby' seems to have brought me as much joy as my other children. I am delighted that there is a now going to be a reprint of my book."

BIOGRAPHICAL AND CRITICAL SOURCES:

PERIODICALS

China Review International, spring, 2004, Jonathan Goldstein, review of *From the Rivers of Babylon to the Whangpoo: A Century of Sephardi Jewish Life in Shanghai,* p. 146.
Choice, January, 2004, K.E. Stapleton, review of *From the Rivers of Babylon to the Whangpoo,* p. 968.
Reference & Research Book News, August, 2003, review of *From the Rivers of Babylon to the Whangpoo,* p. 47.

* * *

MEYER, Maisie Joy
See MEYER, Maisie J.

* * *

MEYERS, Robin
See MEYERS, Robin R.

MEYERS, Robin R. 1952-
(Robin Meyers, Robin Rex Meyers)

PERSONAL: Born 1952, in Oklahoma City, OK; married; wife's name Shawn (an artist); children: Blue, Chelsea, and Cass. *Education:* Phillips University Graduate Seminary, M.Div.; Drew University, D.Min.; University of Oklahoma, Ph.D. *Religion:* Christian.

ADDRESSES: Office—Mayflower Congregational Church, 3901 N.W. 63rd St., Oklahoma City, OK 73116. *E-mail*—rmeyers@okcu.edu.

CAREER: Minister, educator, and writer. Mayflower Congregational UCC Church, Oklahoma City, OK, senior minister, 1985—; Oklahoma City University Philosophy Department, professor of rhetoric, 1991—. Earl Preacher for the Earl Lectures at Berkeley, CA, 2000; *Oklahoma Gazette,* columnist. Also served in churches in Summit, NJ, and Detroit, MI. Has appeared on television, including *Dateline NBC,* and as a commentator on National Public Radio; sermons broadcast in Oklahoma on KOKC-AM 1520, c. 1994—; appeared in the documentary *The Execution of Wanda Jean,* 2002.

WRITINGS:

With Ears to Hear: Preaching as Self-Persuasion, Pilgrim Press (Cleveland, OH), 1993.
Morning Sun on a White Piano: Simple Pleasures and the Sacramental Life, Doubleday (New York, NY), 1998.
The Virtue in the Vice: Finding Seven Lively Virtues in the Seven Deadly Sins, Health Communications (Deerfield Beach, FL), 2004.
(As Robin Meyers) *Why the Christian Right Is Wrong: A Minister's Manifesto for Taking Back Your Faith, Your Flag, Your Future,* Jossey-Bass (San Francisco, CA), 2006.

SIDELIGHTS: Robin R. Meyers is a minister and author who writes about preaching, communication, and Christianity. In his book *Morning Sun on a White Piano: Simple Pleasures and the Sacramental Life,* Meyers focuses on what he perceives to be the "simple pleasures" of everyday life, from writing a letter to parenting to interaction with pets. He also

makes specific recommendations for living a more simple and sacramental life, such as turning off the television set. A *Publishers Weekly* contributor wrote that the "short meditations are charming and eloquent explorations into the holiness of ordinary life." Writing in the *Library Journal,* Robert Nixon commented that *Morning Sun on a White Piano* contains "a number of excellent insights into what makes life worth living." William C. Graham, writing in the *National Catholic Reporter,* recommended the book to "those who wish to better appreciate the joys of simple living."

Meyers presents an alternative view to the political Christian Right movement in his book *Why the Christian Right Is Wrong: A Minister's Manifesto for Taking Back Your Faith, Your Flag, Your Future.* Meyers presents his case that many Christians, especially those on the religious right, fail to understand the true meaning of Christianity and Christ's words, or they simply ignore them. Based on the primary points in a speech Meyers gave in 2004 at the Oklahoma University Peace Rally, which was widely disseminated through the Internet, *Why the Christian Right Is Wrong* presents the author's opposition to much of the right-wing political agenda and his belief that Christians should in fact lean towards liberalism. Focusing primarily on Jesus' teachings, Meyers points out, for example, that Christians should be against the death penalty based on Christ's own words and that Christians should also be good stewards of the Earth as commanded by God and, thus, support protection of the environment. In an interview with Mary Lane Gallagher in the *Bellingham Herald,* Meyers explained his position this way: "I'm not opposed to anybody holding traditional values. I'm opposed to taking the person who was the first nonviolent revolutionary, who was so radical in his subversive ministry, that he got executed, and use that person as the great guardian of sort of a nostalgic, traditional view of life." The author went on to note: "The book is intentionally provocative. I'm certain once or twice, at least, it crosses over a line."

Writing in the *Library Journal,* Leroy Hommerding commented: "Certainly, his points deserve a reading." Hommerding also wrote that the author provides "a spirited approach to economic survival and what constitutes humble and compassionate citizens." A *Publishers Weekly* contributor noted that the author "delivers an unambiguous, palpable blueprint" for those Christians dissatisfied with where the country is headed.

BIOGRAPHICAL AND CRITICAL SOURCES:

PERIODICALS

Bellingham Herald (Bellingham, WA), July 13, 2006, Mary Lane Gallagher, "Minister Gains Notoriety for Treatise against the Religious Right."

Library Journal, February 15, 1998, Robert Nixon, review of *Morning Sun on a White Piano: Simple Pleasures and the Sacramental Life,* p. 148; June 1, 2006, Leroy Hommerding, review of *Why the Christian Right Is Wrong: A Minister's Manifesto for Taking Back Your Faith, Your Flag, Your Future,* p. 126

National Catholic Reporter, April 3, 1998, William C. Graham, review of *Morning Sun on a White Piano,* p. 18.

Publishers Weekly, February 9, 1998, review of *Morning Sun on a White Piano,* p. 91; February 27, 2006, review of *Why the Christian Right Is Wrong,* p. 56.

ONLINE

Live Journal, http://community.livejournal.com/christianleft/105456.html (November 14, 2004), Robin Meyers, "Real Moral Values," speech by author.

Mayflower Congregational Church Web site, http://www.mayflowerucc.org/ (November 24, 2006), profile of author.

*   *   *

MEYERS, Robin Rex
    See MEYERS, Robin R.

*   *   *

MILLER, Mark Edwin 1966-

PERSONAL: Born November 22, 1966, in San Antonio, TX; son of Charles Edwin (in sales) and Prentice Miller; married Gia De Giovanni (a doctor), May 29, 1998; children: Delaney, Regan. *Ethnicity:* "White." *Education:* Texas A&M University, B.A.,

1989; University of Arizona, M.A., 1994, Ph.D., 2001. *Religion:* Protestant. *Hobbies and other interests:* Hiking, travel, camping, fishing.

ADDRESSES: Home—Cedar City, UT. *Office*—Department of History, Southern Utah University, 225 Centrum, Cedar City, UT 84720. *E-mail*—miller@suu.edu.

CAREER: Locke Purnell Rain & Harrel, Dallas, TX, legal assistant, 1989-91; Ouachita Baptist University, Arkadelphia, AR, assistant professor of history, 2001-06; Southern Utah University, Cedar City, assistant professor of history, 2006—.

MEMBER: American Society for Ethnohistory, Association of Borderlands Studies, Western History Association, Southwestern Social Sciences Association, Phi Alpha Theta.

AWARDS, HONORS: Littleton-Griswold Prize, American Historical Association.

WRITINGS:

Forgotten Tribes: Unrecognized Indians and the Federal Acknowledgement Process, University of Nebraska Press (Lincoln, NE), 2004.

*   *   *

MILLER, Mary Beth 1964-

PERSONAL: Born 1964; married; children: four. *Education:* Attended Fairfield University, Fairfield, CT. *Hobbies and other interests:* Quilting and horse riding.

CAREER: Writer. Previously worked for a medical and nursing publishing house.

WRITINGS:

Aimee: A Novel, Dutton Books (New York, NY), 2002.

On the Head of a Pin (novel), Dutton Books (New York, NY), 2006.

SIDELIGHTS: In her first young adult novel, *Aimee: A Novel,* author Mary Beth Miller tackles the subject of a teen suicide. The novel's narrator is a young girl named Zoe whose best friend, Aimee, is dead. As Zoe tells the story in a journal she is keeping as part of her therapy treatment, she drifts back and forth from the past to present, revealing that she has been accused of murdering Aimee. Living in a new town with her parents, Zoe must deal with anorexia and her parents' eventual breakup, which comes not only as a result of the ordeal over Aimee but also due to their own faults as people and parents. As the novel progresses, the reader begins to learn what drove Aimee to kill herself. "A fascinating character study that will intrigue readers wanting to go beyond sensationalistic headlines," wrote a Kirkus Reviews contributor of the novel. Claire Rosser, writing in *Kliatt* commented: "This is a tale of woe almost on every page." In an article in the *Pittsburgh Post-Gazette,* Karen MacPherson noted that the author "masterfully controls the book's narrative so that the reader isn't quite certain until the very end of the book exactly what happened the night Aimee died." A *Publishers Weekly* reviewer wrote that "readers will readily recognize the feelings and conflicts that fuel this engrossing novel." Debbie Carton, writing in *Booklist,* called the novel "edgy" and noted: "The portrayal of therapy is especially good."

Miller's next novel, *On the Head of a Pin,* tells a story death and lies. High school student Andy accidentally shoots and kills a young girl named Helen, the high school's homecoming queen, while fooling around with a gun at his father's cabin. Panicking, Andy and his friends Josh and Victor drug Helen's boyfriend, an artist named Michael, and then go out and bury Helen. Josh is a devout Catholic who wants to tell the truth but is threatened by Andy and Victor. As a result, of the boys' deception, Michael, who comes from a poor family and was seeing Helen despite her parents' objections, becomes the prime suspect in Helen's murder, leading to a catastrophic chain of events that changes the boys and their parents' lives forever. "Alternating between Josh's and Michael's perspectives, the author delves deep into the psyches of these two sensitive and vulnerable boys," wrote a *Publishers Weekly* contributor. "This is a book that asks big questions," wrote Myrna Marler in *Kliatt,* noting that the novel "also brings up religious themes." Frances Bradburn, writing in *Booklist,* commented that the author "skillfully weaves together numerous strands to create a horrifying yet thought-provoking and disturbingly real scenario." In a review in the *School Library Journal,* Johanna Lewis wrote that the author's "beautifully rendered narrators [Michael and Josh] manage to compel readers on to the last page."

BIOGRAPHICAL AND CRITICAL SOURCES:

PERIODICALS

Booklist, May 1, 2002, Debbie Carton, review of *Aimee: A Novel,* p. 1518; February 15, 2006, Frances Bradburn, review of *On the Head of a Pin,* p. 95.
Kirkus Reviews, May 1, 2002, review of *Aimee,* p. 661; January 15, 2006, review of *On the Head of a Pin,* p. 87.
Kliatt, May, 2002, Claire Rosser, review of *Aimee,* p. 11; March, 2006, Myrna Marler, review of *On the Head of a Pin,* p. 15.
Pittsburgh Post-Gazette, October 1, 2002, Karen MacPherson "Deft Whodunit Gracefully Handles Teen Suicide Topic," interview with author.
Publishers Weekly, May 20, 2002, review of *Aimee,* p. 68; February 27, 2006, review of *On the Head of a Pin,* p. 63.
School Library Journal, April, 2006, Johanna Lewis, review of *On the Head of a Pin,* p. 144.

ONLINE

Mary Beth Miller Home Page, http://www.marybeth miller.net (January 1, 2007).*

*　　　*　　　*

MILLMAN, Chad

PERSONAL: Son of Barry J. and Temmy Millman; married Stacy Ellen Kronland (an architect), June 20, 1998; children: Zachary. *Education:* Graduate of Indiana University.

ADDRESSES: Home—Montclair, NJ. *E-mail*—chad@ chadmillman.com.

CAREER: Journalist and writer. Former reporter, *Sports Illustrated,* New York, NY, then CNNSI correspondent, c. 1993-98; *ESPN The Magazine,* contributor then senior editor, beginning 1998.

WRITINGS:

(With Lars Anderson) *Pickup Artists: Street Basketball in America,* Verso (New York, NY), 1998.

The Odds: One Season, Three Gamblers, and the Death of Their Las Vegas, PublicAffairs (New York, NY), 2001.

The Detonators: The Secret Plot to Destroy America and an Epic Hunt for Justice, Little, Brown (New York, NY), 2006.

(With Vince Papale) *Invincible: My Journey from NFL Fan to NFL Captain,* Hyperion (New York, NY), 2006.

SIDELIGHTS: Chad Millman is a former sports reporter and the author of several nonfiction books, including *Pickup Artists: Street Basketball in America,* written with Lars Anderson. In *Pickup Artists,* Millman briefly outlines the history of basketball and then focuses in on rule changes that led to the ensuing growth of the sport's popularity on the streets of major cities, such as New York, Los Angeles, and Chicago. The author discusses how the new young players from both the ghettos and America's working-class families eventually created major changes in how the game was played. He also profiles some of the most famous "street players," as well as notable women players who played long before women's basketball became popular. A *Publishers Weekly* contributor called *Pickup Artists* a "significant contribution to the history of the game."

In his book *The Odds: One Season, Three Gamblers, and the Death of Their Las Vegas,* Millman provides a portrait of Las Vegas and the gambling mania that surrounds sports betting, such as college basketball's playoffs (known as "March Madness"). As he follows a bookmaker, an experienced professional gambler, and a gambler just starting out as a pro, Millman describes a gambling city that is slowly being turned into a kind of DisneyLand for tourists as its former stranglehold on legal gambling is threatened by developers, off-shore betting sites, and increasing legalized gambling in other states. "This is not a

Reefer Madness-style expose designed to scare gamblers straight," wrote Jim Burns in the *Library Journal.* Charles Hirshberg, writing in *Sports Illustrated,* referred to *The Odds* as "an intimate, hilarious and, at times, terribly sad portrait."

The Detonators: The Secret Plot to Destroy America and an Epic Hunt for Justice recounts the story of a 1916 terror bombing of New Jersey's Black Tom munitions plant by three German agents. The explosion, which occurred before the United States entered World War I, was so strong that it could be heard in parts of Maryland and killed a baby by blasting it out of its crib. The bombing was considered the single worst terrorist act in America up to that time. The author follows the German operatives in the United States and those who worked with them for financial motives, as well as the legal battles that followed the end of the war as lawyers tried to sue Germany for twenty million dollars in damages. Gilbert Taylor, writing in *Booklist,* commented: "From a storytelling perspective, Millman commendably rises above a dry recitation of briefs and rulings." A *Kirkus Reviews* contributor called *The Detonators* "an intriguing, bracing tale, and not just for history buffs." Another reviewer writing in *Publishers Weekly* commented that the "emphasis on the personal stories of the main characters involved in hatching the Black Tom plot and those who solved it makes for gripping reading."

BIOGRAPHICAL AND CRITICAL SOURCES:

PERIODICALS

Booklist, July 1, 2006, Gilbert Taylor, review of *The Detonators: The Secret Plot to Destroy America and an Epic Hunt for Justice,* p. 25.

Entertainment Weekly, June 30, 2006, Jennifer Reese, review of *The Detonators,* p. 166.

Kirkus Reviews, May 1, 2006, review of *The Detonators,* p. 448.

Library Journal, May 1, 2001, Jim Burns, review of *The Odds: One Season, Three Gamblers, and the Death of Their Las Vegas,* p. 96; June 15, 2006, Edwin B. Burgess, review of *The Detonators,* p. 84.

Publishers Weekly, May 4, 1998, review of *Pickup Artists: Street Basketball in America,* p. 193; May 8, 2006, review of *The Detonators,* p. 58.

Sports Illustrated, April 2, 2001, Charles Hirshberg, review of *The Odds,* p. R4.

ONLINE

Chad Millman Home Page, http://www.chadmillman. com (January 1, 2006).
Gotham Gazette, http://www.gothamgazette.com/ (October 18, 2006), "The Forgotten Attack on NYC," interview with author.
New York Observer Online, http://observer.com/ (January 1, 2007), Glenn C. Altschuler, review of *The Detonators.**

* * *

MIN, Katherine 1959(?)-

PERSONAL: Born c. 1959, in Champaign, IL (one source says Urbana, IL); married; children. *Education:* Amherst College, B.A.; Columbia University, M.A.

ADDRESSES: Home—NH.

CAREER: Writer and educator. Plymouth State University, Graduate Studies Division, Plymouth, NH, adjunct faculty, writer-in-residence, and diversity scholar. Also teaches at the Iowa Writing Festival.

AWARDS, HONORS: Pushcart Prize, for short story "Courting a Monk"; National Endowment for the Arts grant, 1992; MacDowell Colony fellowship, 1995, 1996, 1999, 2001; New Hampshire State Council on the Arts fellowship, 1995; Wallace-Reader's Digest fellow; Tennessee Williams scholar.

WRITINGS:

Secondhand World: A Novel, Knopf (New York, NY), 2006.

Short stories have been anthologized in the *The Pushcart Book of Stories: The Best Short Stories from a Quarter-Century of the Pushcart Prize,* and featured on National Public Radio; stories have also appeared in periodicals, including *TriQuarterly, Ploughshares, Threepenny Review,* and *Prairie Schooner.*

SIDELIGHTS: In her first book, *Secondhand World: A Novel,* Katherine Min draws on her own family's background as immigrants from Korea to tell the story of Isadora Myung Hee Sohn, or Isa, a young Korean-American caught between the traditional world of her Korean parents and an American world that seems little interested in traditions of any kind. Living in New York near Schenectady, Isa is thrown into turmoil when her brother is killed in an accident, leading her parents to honor the dead in a traditional Korean way that makes Isa suspect that they care more for him in death than her in life. When she becomes enamored of an albino boy named Hero and travels with him to California, she leaves behind family and Korean ways. Nevertheless, when Isa suspects that her mother is having an affair, she is drawn back into the world of Korean tradition.

"Min poignantly captures the dilemma of second-generation Americans . . . but she also tells of a quest for self-discovery, which is universal," wrote Pat Bangs of *Secondhand World* in a review in the *School Library Journal.* Referring to Min's debut novel as "lovely," a *Kirkus Reviews* contributor noted that the author "evokes period and place as well as characters with stringent attention and honesty." Shirley N. Quan, writing in the *Library Journal,* commented: "Touching and bittersweet, this novel is filled with universal themes."

BIOGRAPHICAL AND CRITICAL SOURCES:

PERIODICALS

America's Intelligence Wire, Nov 15, 2006, Shirley Chen, review of *Secondhand World: A Novel.*
Entertainment Weekly, October 6, 2006, Allyssa Lee, review of *Secondhand World,* p. 74.
Kirkus Reviews, June 15, 2006, review of *Secondhand World,* p. 596.
Library Journal, June 1, 2006, Shirley N. Quan, review of *Secondhand World,* p. 109.
Los Angeles Times, November 26, 2006, Deborah Vankin, review of *Secondhand World.*

School Library Journal, October, 2006, Pat Bangs, review of *Secondhand World,* p. 188.

ONLINE

Katherine Min Home Page, http://www.katherinemin. com (January 22, 2007).

New Hampshire State Council on the Arts Web site, http://www.nh.gov/nharts/ (January 22, 2007), profile of author.

You Are Here/Redbook Web site, http://youarehere. redbook.ivillage.com/time/ (January 22, 2007), "Book Club: Katherine Min," interview with author.*

*   *   *

MISAKIAN, Jo Ellen Priest

PERSONAL: Born in Allen, OK; daughter of Frederick (a farmer) and Velma (a homemaker) Priest; married Johnny Lee Misakian, Sr. (a manager); children: Johnny Lee, Jr., Jeffrey Dale, James Kevin. *Education:* New York Institute of Technology, B.S., 1992; San Jose State University, M.L.S., 1993. *Politics:* Republican. *Religion:* Protestant. *Hobbies and other interests:* Reading, computer activities.

ADDRESSES: Home—Fresno, CA. *Office*—Fresno Pacific University, 1717 S. Chestnut Ave., Fresno, CA 93702.

CAREER: Library technician for public school system in Sanger, CA, 1971-94; Fresno County Office of Education, Fresno, CA, library services specialist, 1994-99; Fresno Pacific University, Fresno, program director and interim dean, 1999—. Heartland Regional Library Network, executive director; Teacher Librarian Advisory Board, member, 2003—.

MEMBER: American Library Association, American Association of School Librarians (regional director, 2003-05), California School Library Association (president, 2000-01).

AWARDS, HONORS: Professional Services Award, Northern Section, California School Library Association, 2005.

WRITINGS:

The Essential School Library Glossary, Linworth Publishing (Worthington, OH), 2005.

SIDELIGHTS: Jo Ellen Priest Misakian told *CA:* "*The Essential School Library Glossary* was created in response to a need for school library personnel to have a handy reference to check the meanings of words particular to libraries. It was deliberately kept small—but containing the essential words—to provide a quick resource to library personnel new to the profession.

"I am in awe of authors who create books, especially those who write for young people. They are the true celebrities in my estimation and deserve to be treated as such.

"When I was working in the library at Lone Star School, my students signed a petition requesting the book *The Outsiders* be made into a movie. Francis Coppola agreed to produce the movie, which is dedicated to the students of Lone Star and to me. This is an example of how the love of a special book changed the lives of some seventh- and eighth-grade students."

*   *   *

MITCHELL, Bob 1944-
(Robert L. Mitchell)

PERSONAL: Born 1944; married; wife's name Susan (an artist); children: three. *Education:* Williams College, B.A. (magna cum laude); Columbia University, M.A.; Harvard University, Ph.D. *Hobbies and other interests:* Sports, travel, animals, music, art, food and wine, acoustic guitar.

ADDRESSES: Home—Santa Barbara, CA. *Agent*—Joelle Delbourgo, Joelle Delbourgo Associates, Inc., 516 Bloomfield Ave., Ste. 5, Montclair, NJ 07042. *E-mail*—bmitch44@verizon.net.

CAREER: Writer and educator. Taught French for eleven years at Harvard University, Cambridge, MA; Purdue University, West Lafayette, IN; and Ohio State

University, Columbus OH; taught for a year in France. Worked in advertising in New York, NY, as a copywriter and then creative director, beginning 1981; special consultant for commercial film writing and production, Tel Aviv, Israel, 1994.

MEMBER: Phi Beta Kappa.

AWARDS, HONORS: Woodrow Wilson fellow; Fulbright fellow.

WRITINGS:

The Heart Has Its Reasons: Reflections on Sports and Life, Diamond Communications (South Bend, IN), 1995.
The Tao of Sports, Frog (Berkeley, CA), 1997.
How My Mother Accidentally Tossed Out My Entire Baseball-Card Collection: And Other Sports Stories, Frog (Berkeley, CA), 1999.
Match Made in Heaven (novel), Kensington Books (New York, NY), 2006.

Also author of four books about nineteenth- and twentieth-century French poetry. *Match Made in Heaven* has been printed in several foreign languages, including Spanish, Hungarian, Indonesian, Korean, and Turkish.

ADAPTATIONS: Match Made in Heaven has been made into an audiobook, Brilliance Audio, 2006.

SIDELIGHTS: After writing three nonfiction books about his passion for sports, Bob Mitchell turned to the novel with *Match Made in Heaven.* The story revolves around Harvard Professor Elliott Goodman, who suffers a massive heart attack and pleads for his life while being worked on in a hospital operating room. To Goodman's surprise, God appears on the ceiling and wants to know why Goodman should be saved. The professor cannot give a good reason, but God decides to give him a chance anyway. He challenges Goodman to a game of golf, and promises to spare Goodman if he wins. However, Goodman will not play God but will have to compete against a different historical character on each hole, from Leonardo da Vinci and W.C. Fields to John Lennon and Socrates. As the game progresses, Goodman has

discussions about life with each of his opponents. "The novel is all about the life lessons Elliott learns from these amazing characters and from the amazing game of golf," wrote Gina Holmes on the *Novel Journey* Blog site. "At a deeper level, it's really about why a human life is worth saving and what is so precious about human existence here on earth." A *Kirkus Reviews* contributor commented that the conversations between Goodman and his opponents are "chockful of notable quotables," adding that "this is a kind of greatest-hits of the world's wisdom traditions—each aphorism served up entertainingly." John Mort, writing in *Booklist,* noted that the author "strikes an agreeable tone and is often amusing."

Mitchell once told *CA:* "Ever since I was a little kid, I've always loved to write. I can't explain it, and I do think it's in the genetic helical matter. Not that my upbringing and education didn't have a huge impact one me. Certainly reading and loving the classics was very inspiring to me, writers like Flaubert, Proust, Dostoevsky, Tolstoy, Dickens, Joyce, and so on. Plus a number of poets, including Rimbaud, Mallarmé, Valéry, Whitman, Yeats, Eliot, Auden, Thomas, and Stevens. But the bottom line, as Rilke so brilliantly posits in 'Letters to a Young Poet,' was that deep inside I always asked, 'Must I write?' And the answer was always a resounding 'Yes!'

"Aside from admiring these classical writers, I try not to be influenced too much by other writers. The reason is that I am not overly fond of 'genre' novels, which comprise a huge percentage of popular fiction these days. I guess it's part of my personality to not be a follower, and to do things that are far from the madding crowd, so to speak. When I write, I like to choose a topic that is utterly distinctive and that has never been written about before in the history of the world. And to write about it in an utterly distinctive style and voice. Such, for example, is the subject matter and writing manner of the two novels I've written so far, *Match Made in Heaven* and *The Secrets of Solomon Stein* [not yet published].

"For me, I don't write at all 'to have an effect.' That is, to affect potential readers in one way or another. I write for me primarily: I express what I need to in the way I need to, and I let the chips fall. Of course, my books inherently contain elements (in the writing) of humor, drama, and introspection, so naturally, if readers end up laughing, being moved, and thinking, that is always nice. But I would say that, as pleasant as it is to hear from readers that these 'effects' were realized, they are more a byproduct of the writing than its actual motivating force."

BIOGRAPHICAL AND CRITICAL SOURCES:

PERIODICALS

Booklist, April 15, 2006, John Mort, review of *Match Made in Heaven,* p. 28.
Kirkus Reviews, April 1, 2006, review of *Match Made in Heaven,* p. 318.
Santa Barbara Independent, May 18, 2006, Matt Kettmann, "Discussing Life and Golf with the Author of *Match Made in Heaven.*"

ONLINE

Bob Mitchell Home Page, http://www.bobmitchell books.com (November 25, 2006).
Novel Journey Blog site, http://noveljourney.blogspot. com/ (June 12, 2006), Gina Holmes, "Author Interview—Bob Mitchell."
Refreshment in Refuge Blog site, http://refreshment refuge.blogspot.com/ (November 25, 2006), Gina Burgess, interview with author.

*   *   *

MITCHELL, Robert L.
   See MITCHELL, Bob

*   *   *

MODINE, Matthew 1959-
   (Matthew Avery Modine)

PERSONAL: Born March 22, 1959, in Loma Linda, CA; son of Mark (a manager of drive-in theaters) and Dolores (a bookkeeper) Modine; married Caridad Rivera, October 31, 1980; children: Bowman, Ruby.

ADDRESSES: Agent—Untitled Entertainment NY, 451 Greenwich St., 7th Fl., New York, NY 10013.

CAREER: Actor director, editor, producer, cinematographer, and writer. Appeared in numerous films, including *Baby It's You,* Paramount, 1983; *Private School,* Universal, 1983; *Streamers,* United Artists, 1983; *The Hotel New Hampshire,* Orion, 1984; *Mrs. Soffel,* Metro-Goldwyn-Mayer/United Artists, 1984; *Birdy,* TriStar, 1984; *Vision Quest* (also known as *Crazy for You*), Warner Bros., 1987; *Full Metal Jacket* (also known as *Stanley Kubrick's Full Metal Jacket*), Warner Bros., 1987; *Orphans,* Lorimar, 1987; *Married to the Mob,* Orion, 1987; *Gross Anatomy* (also known as *A Cut Above*), Buena Vista, 1989; *La partita* (also known as *The Gamble*), CG Reteitalia/ Warner Bros., 1988; *Memphis Belle,* Warner Bros., 1990; *Pacific Heights,* Twentieth Century-Fox, 1990; *The Lemon Sisters,* Miramax, 1991; *Wind,* TriStar, 1992; *Equinox* (also known as *Isimeria*), IRS Releasing, 1993; *Short Cuts,* Fine Line, 1993; *The Browning Version,* Paramount, 1994; *Bye Bye, Love,* Twentieth Century-Fox, 1995; *Cutthroat Island* (also known as *Corsari, Die Piratenbraut* and *L'ile aux pirates*), Metro-Goldwyn-Mayer/United Artists, 1995; (voice) *Fluke,* Metro-Goldwyn-Mayer, 1995; *The Real Blonde,* Paramount, 1997; *The Blackout,* Trimark, 1997; *Notting Hill,* MCA/Universal, 1999; *Any Given Sunday* (also known as *Any Given Sunday, Gridiron, Monday Night, On Any Given Sunday, The League,* and *Playing Hurt*), Warner Bros., 1999; *Very Mean Men,* Miracle Entertainment, 2000; *Bamboozled,* New Line Cinema, 2000; *Nobody's Baby,* 2001; *In the Shadows,* Lions Gate Films, 2001; *The Shipment,* Promark Entertainment Group, 2001; *Hollywood North,* 2003; *Funky Monkey,* 2004; *Transporter 2,* 2005; *Mary,* 2005; and *Opa!,* 2005. Director, producer, editor, and cinematographer for *Smoking,* Pyramide International, 1993; director of the play *Twelve Angry Men,* New Mercury Theatre. Also acted in numerous television movies (including *And the Band Played On,* HBO), specials, series, and miniseries; appeared in the stage production *Breaking Up,* 1990, and *Resurrection Blues,* c. 2005.

AWARDS, HONORS: Best Actor Golden Lion Award (shared), 1984, for performance in *Streamers;* Volpi Cup for Best Ensemble Cast and Golden Globe for Best Ensemble cast (shared), for performance in *Shortcuts;* Golden Globe and Emmy Award nominations, for performance in *And the Band Played On.*

WRITINGS:

When I Was a Boy (screenplay), Mercury Film, 1993.

(And director and actor) *If . . . Dog . . . Rabbit . . . ,* (screenplay), Franchise Pictures, 1998.
Full Metal Jacket Diary (memoir), Rugged Land (New York, NY), 2005.

Also author of the screenplay for the film *Ecce Pirate,* 1997.

SIDELIGHTS: With his limited-edition book *Full Metal Jacket Diary,* which has a metal cover, actor Matthew Modine records his experiences making the Stanley Kubrick Vietnam war film *Full Metal Jacket.* Aided by numerous photographs taken by Modine during filming, the author recounts his nearly two years working on the film via a diary he kept at the time. In his book, Modine, who has also written several screenplays, discusses the famous director Kubrick and his process for making films. The author also writes of his own experiences, including eating leftover army food rations from the Vietnam war. "It's the portrait of an actor as a young man, someone going through a heart of darkness," Modine told Kevin Filipski in an article on the *Go Brooklyn* Web site. "I was like Gilligan, but I was lost on an island called England. First it was three months, then six months, and then it became two whole years out of my life. It was a real interesting journey." In an article on the *Filmmaker* Web site, a contributor wrote that the book "alternates between screenplay format and military-style dispatches, with the images presented in both standard and collage form." A *Publishers Weekly* contributor commented that "the work succeeds in expressing Modine's attitude—'I'm going to make you feel the horror of death.'"

BIOGRAPHICAL AND CRITICAL SOURCES:

BOOKS

Contemporary Theatre, Film and Television, Volume 45, Thomson Gale (Detroit, MI), 2002.
Modine, Matthew, *Full Metal Jacket Diary,* Rugged Land (New York, NY), 2005.

PERIODICALS

Chicago Sun-Times, November 25, 2005, Bill Zwecker, "Face Time: Q&A with Matthew Modine."

Daily News (New York, NY), October 25, 2005, "'Full Metal' Casting Call."
Publishers Weekly, August 8, 2005, review of *Full Metal Jacket Diary,* p. 224.

ONLINE

Filmmaker, http://www.filmmakermagazine.com/ (November 25, 2006), review of *Full Metal Jacket Diary.*
Go Brooklyn, http://www.go-brooklyn.com/ (November 25, 2006), Kevin Filipski, "'Jacket Required,'" review of *Full Metal Jacket Diary.*
Internet Movie Database, http://www.imdb.com/ (November 25, 2006), information on author's film work.
Mathew Modine Home Page, http://www.matthew modine.com (November 25, 2006).*

*   *   *

MODINE, Matthew Avery
    See MODINE, Matthew

*   *   *

MOGEN, Pamela
    See AIDAN, Pamela

*   *   *

MONK, Bathsheba 1966-

PERSONAL: Born 1966.

ADDRESSES: Home—Allentown, PA. *Agent*—David Kuhn, Kuhn Projects, LLC, 126 5th Ave., Ste. 3A, New York, NY 10011. *E-mail*—bathshebamonk@hotmail.com.

CAREER: Writer. *Military service:* U.S. Army.

WRITINGS:

Now You See It . . . : Stories from Cokesville, PA (short stories), Farrar, Straus & Giroux (New York, NY), 2006.

Has contributed to periodicals, including *Los Angeles Times* and *New York Times Sunday Magazine.*

SIDELIGHTS: In her first book, *Now You See It . . . : Stories from Cokesville, PA,* Bathsheba Monk presents seventeen linked short stories that take place between 1948 and 1994. The stories reflect life in the fictional eastern Pennsylvania industrial town and present a range of fictional characters over several generations who struggle with a difficult life or leave town in search of a new one, such as Tess who goes off to Hollywood and becomes a soap-opera star. Nevertheless, even those who leave remain connected to the town and its hard living and slightly off-kilter inhabitants. In one story, a steelworker, Bruno Gojuk, falls into a vat of molten metal and his widow is given a 175-pound ingot, representing the weight of the man when he signed on to work at the plant, even though he weighed 200 pounds when he died. The ingot takes Bruno's place at his wake. A *Kirkus Reviews* contributor called the story collection "a pleasurable . . . examination of hardscrabble lives and hapless dreams." Carlo Rotella, writing in the *Chicago Tribune,* commented: "The decline and fall of American heavy industry forms the narrative backdrop against which the individual stories unfold, a great transformation that alternately pounds down [Monk's] characters and sets them bewilderingly adrift." In a review on the *Rain Taxi* Web site, William Bush referred to the author's "quietly confident prose." Reba Leiding noted in the *Library Journal* that the author "makes us see that we are all exiles in a changing world."

BIOGRAPHICAL AND CRITICAL SOURCES:

PERIODICALS

Boston Globe, July 7, 2006, Amanda Heller, review of *Now You See It . . . : Stories from Cokesville, PA.*

Chicago Sun-Times, July 9, 2006, Teresa Budsai, review of *Now You See It . . . .*

Chicago Tribune, May 28, 2006, Carlo Rotella, review of *Now You See It . . . .*

Kirkus Reviews, April 15, 2006, review of *Now You See It . . . ,* p. 374.

Library Journal, March 1, 2006, Reba Leiding, review of *Now You See It . . . ,* p. 80.

New Yorker, June 19, 2006, review of *Now You See It . . . .*

Philadelphia Inquirer, July 26, 2006, Karen Heller, review of *Now You See It . . . .*

Plain Dealer (Cleveland, OH), July 30, 2006, review of *Now You See It . . . .*

Times-Picayune, June 25, 2006, Susan Larson, review of *Now You See It . . . .*

Wall Street Journal, June 30, 2006, Kate Flately, review of *Now You See It . . . .*

ONLINE

Bathsheba Monk Home Page, http://www.bathshebamonk.com (November 26, 2006).

Esquire.com, http://www.esquire.com/ (June 21, 2006), Anna Godbersen, review of *Now You See It . . . .*

Rain Taxi, http://www.raintaxi.com/ (November 26, 2006), William Bush, review of *Now You See It . . . .*

*   *   *

MONTGOMERY, Charles 1968-

PERSONAL: Born 1968.

ADDRESSES: *Home*—Vancouver, British Columbia, Canada. *Agent*—Anne McDermid & Associates, 83 Willcocks St., Toronto, Ontario M5S 1C9, Canada. *E-mail*—chuckum@telus.net.

CAREER: Journalist and writer.

AWARDS, HONORS: Western Magazine Awards Best Travel/Leisure Feature, 2001, for "Coast Rage," *Vancouver* magazine; Western Magazine Awards Gold Award for Best Article: B.C./Yukon, 2002, for "Psychedelic Renaissance," *Georgia Straight* magazine; Western Canada Magazine Awards Best Arts and Culture Feature, 2003, for "Lowry's Ghosts," *Vancouver* magazine; American Society of Travel Writers Foundation Lowell Thomas Silver Award for Best U.S./Canada Magazine Travel Article, 2003, for "Storm Coast," *Canadian Geographic;* Western Magazine Awards best travel feature, Canadian

National Magazine Awards Silver for best travel story, both 2004, both for "Heaven Can Wait," *Western Living* magazine; Charles Taylor Prize for Literary Nonfiction, Hubert Evans Nonfiction Prize, BC Book Prizes, both 2005, both for *The Last Heathen*; Canadian National Magazine Awards Gold, 2005, for "Into the Megalopolis," *Explore* magazine.

WRITINGS:

The Last Heathen: Encounters with Ghosts and Ancestors in Melanesia, Douglas & McIntyre (Vancouver, British Columbia, Canada), 2004, also published as *The Shark God: Encounters with Ghosts and Ancestors in the South Pacific,* HarperCollins (New York, NY), 2005.

Contributor to the anthology *Way Out There;* contributor to periodicals, including *Canadian Geographic* and *Western Living.*

SIDELIGHTS: Charles Montgomery is a freelance journalist and author of *The Last Heathen: Encounters with Ghosts and Ancestors in Melanesia,* published worldwide as *The Shark God: Encounters with Ghosts and Ancestors in the South Pacific.* Montgomery recounts his experiences retracing a journey in Melanesia made by his great-grandfather, the Right Reverend Henry Hutchinson Montgomery, more than a century earlier. The author's journey was sparked by his discovery of a book left by his great-grandfather containing old photographs and an account of his missionary journey. Once in the South Seas, Montgomery finds that the Melanesians no longer practice cannibalism, but they continue to blend their ancient rituals and myths with Christianity, sometimes creating new religions in the process. The author also details his journey to discover the culture's ancient rituals and practice of shamanism. George Cohen, writing in *Booklist,* noted: "The . . . documentation and analyses of these people and their world is a haunting reading experience." A *Kirkus Reviews* contributor wrote: "Montgomery is a talented writer, and this tour is delivered in vivid, precise prose." In a review in *Geographical,* Michael Moran referred to *The Shark God* as a "uniquely disturbing travel book [that] should be required reading for anyone with a sense of unease at the development of the modern world."

BIOGRAPHICAL AND CRITICAL SOURCES:

PERIODICALS

Booklist, March 15, 2006, George Cohen, review of *The Shark God: Encounters with Ghosts and Ancestors in the South Pacific,* p. 19.
Geographical, July, 2006, Michael Moran, review of *The Shark God,* p. 84.
Globe and Mail, (Toronto, Ontario, Canada), September 25, 2004, Simon Winchester, review of *The Last Heathen: Encounters with Ghosts and Ancestors in Melanesia,* p. D3; November 27, 2004, Martin Levin and H.J. Kirchhoff, "The Globe 100: Of All the Year's Writings, Few Meet the Test," p. D3; March 1, 2005, Rebecca Caldwell, "B.C. Writer Wins $25,000," p. R1.
Guardian (London, England), August 5, 2006, Kevin Rushby, review of *The Shark God.*
Kirkus Reviews, April 15, 2006, review of *The Shark God,* p. 394.
Library Journal, April 15, 2006, Joel Jones, review of *The Shark God,* p. 97.
New York Times Book Review, August 6, 2006, Holly Morris, review of *The Shark God.*
Publishers Weekly, May 1, 2006, review of *The Shark God,* p. 51.

ONLINE

Charles Montgomery Home Page, http://www.charlesmontgomery.ca (November 26, 2006).

* * *

MONTGOMERY, Lee

PERSONAL: Married.

ADDRESSES: Home—Portland, OR. *Office*—Tin House Books, 2601 N.W. Thurman St., Portland, OR 97210.

CAREER: Tin House Books, Portland, OR, editorial director; *Santa Monica Review,* CA, editor; *Iowa Review,* fiction editor. Tufts University, Medford, MA, worked in department of psychology; worked at Oregon Health and Science University, Portland.

AWARDS, HONORS: Iowa Short Fiction Prize, 2007, for *Whose World is This? Stories.*

WRITINGS:

NONFICTION

(Editor, with Mary Hussmann and David Hamilton) *Transgressions: The Iowa Anthology of Innovative Fiction,* University of Iowa Press (Iowa City, IA), 1994.

(Editor) *Absolute Disaster: Fiction from Los Angeles,* Dove Books (Los Angeles, CA), 1996.

(With David L. Lander) *Fall Down, Laughing: How Squiggy Caught Multiple Sclerosis and Didn't Tell Nobody,* Jeremy P. Tarcher/Putnam (New York, NY), 2000.

The Things between Us: A Memoir, Free Press (New York, NY), 2006.

Whose World is This? Stories, University of Iowa Press (Iowa City, IA), 2007.

Executive editor, *Tin House.* Contributor to *Story, Black Clock, Denver Quarterly,* and *Iowa Review.*

SIDELIGHTS: Lee Montgomery is an editor and writer who won widespread acclaim for her book *The Things between Us: A Memoir.* Montgomery grew up in a quirky New England family. Her mother was a heavy drinker who started the day with gin; her beloved father apparently ignored his wife's serious case of alcoholism. Montgomery's book recounts her youth, and her conflicts with her flamboyant, troubled mother. As a young person, Montgomery seeks escape through drinking and drugs; later, she moves to the Pacific Coast. In her new life on the other side of the continent, she keeps in close touch with both her parents, but she and her siblings—a sister nine years her senior, and a brother six years older than she—stay away from their childhood home as much as possible.

Then the family is drawn back together when their father faces impending death, due to stomach cancer. The author shifts between her own feelings about her past and her dread of the future, to recounting the daily progress of her father's disease, to an account of her mother's drinking, which continues to spiral out of control. A *Publishers Weekly* writer credited Montgom-

ery with writing in a "lyric and nuanced" style, one that avoided "both sentimentality and New England stoicism" to make "a tender portrait of modern death and real American families." *Library Journal* contributor Nancy R. Ives praised the author for writing "with precision and grace, showing how a parent's decline and ultimate death can unite a family and lead to self-discovery, forgiveness, and healing." Elaina Richardson reviewed the memoir for *O, The Oprah Magazine,* and remarked that Montgomery's family members "undeniably qualify as dysfunctional, but they are also quick-witted, charming, voracious storytellers, and as fearful as the rest of us in the face of death."

"The title refers to the obstacles that keep family members alone and apart but also the idiosyncratic ways in which family members pull together when confronted with the unthinkable," remarked Amy Finch in the Boston *Phoenix.* "*The Things between Us* is a beautiful tribute to a funny old guy who laughed loud and often, and whose daughter did the best she could to make him less lonely as he left the planet."

In an interview with Dave Weich on *Powells.com,* Montgomery mused: "Death is a great advisor, and I'm not the first person to say that. When you look at life through death, that lens, it's much more precious. Trespasses are much more forgivable. You're able to appreciate the things that did go right, in my case the lovely things about our family and my parents. It provided perspective."

BIOGRAPHICAL AND CRITICAL SOURCES:

BOOKS

Montgomery, Lee, *The Things between Us: A Memoir,* Free Press (New York, NY), 2006.

PERIODICALS

Booklist, July 1, 2006, Margaret Flanagan, review of *The Things between Us,* p. 14.

Kirkus Review, June 15, 2006, review of *The Things between Us,* p. 621.

Library Journal, August 1, 2006, Nancy R. Ives, review of *The Things between Us,* p. 98.

O, The Oprah Magazine, August, 2006, Elaina Richardson, review of *The Things between Us,* p. 148.

Phoenix (Boston, MA), September 27, 2006, Amy Finch, review of *The Things between Us.*

Publishers Weekly, September 19, 1994, review of *Transgressions: The Iowa Anthology of Innovative Fiction,* p. 52; December 16, 1996, review of *Absolute Disaster: Fiction From Los Angeles,* p. 45; June 26, 2006, review of *The Things between Us,* p. 46.

Review of Contemporary Fiction, spring, 1995, Brooke Horvath, review of *Transgressions,* p. 181.

Studies in Short Fiction, spring, 1996, Kevin J.H. Dettmar, review of *Transgressions,* p. 302.

ONLINE

Powells.com, http://www.powells.com/ (January 21, 2007), Dave Weich, interview with Lee Montgomery.

* * *

MOORE, James 1951-
(James C. Moore)

PERSONAL: Born 1951.

CAREER: Writer, journalist. Former television news correspondent. Has appeared on television and radio programs, including the *Today Show,* National Broadcasting Company (NBC), *American Morning,* Cable News Network (CNN), *Real Time with Bill Maher, Hardball with Chris Matthews,* Microsoft-National Broadcasting Company (MSNBC), *CBS Evening News,* Columbia Broadcasting System (CBS), *Morning Edition,* National Public Radio (NPR), and Air America Radio.

AWARDS, HONORS: Emmy Award; Edward R. Murrow Award, Radio Television News Director's Association; Individual Broadcast Achievement Award, Texas Headliner's Foundation.

WRITINGS:

NONFICTION

(With Wayne Slater) *Bush's Brain: How Karl Rove Made George W. Bush Presidential,* John Wiley (New York, NY), 2003.

Bush's War for Reelection: Iraq, the White House, and the People, John Wiley (New York, NY), 2004.

(With Wayne Slater) *The Architect: Karl Rove and the Master Plan for Absolute Power,* Crown (New York, NY), 2006.

(With Wayne Slater) *Rove Exposed: How Bush's Brain Fooled America,* John Wiley (New York, NY), 2006.

Also author of Web log, *James Moore,* found on *The Huffington Post* Web site.

ADAPTATIONS: Bush's Brain: How Karl Rove Made George W. Bush Presidential was adapted for a documentary film, 2004, by BB Productions, directed by Michael Paradies Shoob and Joseph Mealey.

SIDELIGHTS: James Moore is a former television journalist and the author of several hard-hitting nonfiction books on the presidency of George W. Bush and his chief political strategist, Karl Rove. Working with journalist Wayne Slater, Moore published the 2003 *Bush's Brain: How Karl Rove Made George W. Bush Presidential,* an examination of how Rove took a reluctant and unprepared candidate, in the opinion of the authors, and turned him into the president of the United States. According to Moore and Slater, Rove's use of wedge issues was a major part of his election strategy. For example, Rove focused attention on West Virginia, a usual Democratic stronghold, but a state where hunters and mine workers were at odds with the environmental and gun-control policies of the previous Democratic administration. Bush campaigned hard in the state opposing those policies and as a result was able to capture its five electoral votes, which were desperately needed in the close election of 2000. Writing in the libertarian magazine *Reason,* John F. Pitney, Jr., felt that Moore's analysis of the West Virginia case was "the only good thing" about *Bush's Brain,* which otherwise Pitney found to be a "mess," a book that "relies overmuch on uneducated speculation." Other reviewers had a far more positive assessment of *Bush's Brain,* however, and its analysis of Rove's influence. Rove, as Moore and Slater portray him, has only one idea: winning. To that end he will sacrifice conviction and the truth. Mick Hume, writing in the *New Statesman* noted, "This book provides a detailed insider account of how Rove guided Bush through the Republican primaries and the presidential campaign." *USA Today Magazine* reviewer Gerald F. Kreyche felt it "is not unfair to characterize the work as muckraking," in the positive sense of such investigative journalism. Kreyche continued: "One almost has the impression that the authors strongly dislike Rove, but admire his successes, reluctantly giving the devil his due." Writing in the *New York Times Book Review*, Nicholas Confessore called the same book a "trenchant chronicle."

Working on his own, Moore wrote the 2004 *Bush's War for Reelection: Iraq, the White House, and the People*, which lays bare what Moore finds to be deceptions and manipulations that got the United States into the war in Iraq. Numerous other writers addressed themselves to this theme at the time, but, as Maria D. Jones noted in a review for *Curled Up with a Good Book*, "what makes this book stand out from many other Bush-bashings is the focus on the military men and women in Iraq and the suffering they endure because of the ideologies of a small group of neoconservative men who have never seen battle themselves." Teaming up again with Slater, Moore further explored the mind and life of Rove in the 2006 title *The Architect: Karl Rove and the Master Plan for Absolute Power*, "an indictment of the man himself as a cynical and manipulative hypocrite who will do anything to win," according to Confessore. Moore and Slater attempt to document what they see as the lies and deceptions employed by Rove to cement absolute Republican hegemony despite a very slim majority in the polls. For Confessore, this book is a "blistering sequel" yet one which "rapidly descends into self-parody." Confessore believed that the authors gave Rove too much credit as the architect of all Republican machinations. Pointing to the use of such divisive wedge issues as gay marriage and tort reform, Moore and Slater credit Rove with designing a divide-and-conquer plan for the Republicans to hold power for a generation or more. Writing in *Library Journal*, Jill Ortner called *The Architect* "well-documented." Further praise came from a *Publishers Weekly* reviewer who found the work "a compulsive page-turner," and from *Booklist* contributor Vanessa Bush, who termed it "riveting investigative journalism."

BIOGRAPHICAL AND CRITICAL SOURCES:

PERIODICALS

Booklist, July 1, 2006, Vanessa Bush, review of *The Architect: Karl Rove and the Master Plan for Absolute Power*, p. 5.

Campaigns & Elections, June, 2003, review of *Bush's Brain: How Karl Rove Made George W. Bush Presidential*, p. 14.
Kirkus Reviews, July 1, 2006, review of *The Architect*, p. 667.
Library Journal, August 1, 2006, Jill Ortner, review of *The Architect*, p. 107.
New Statesman, May 12, 2003, Mick Hume, review of *Bush's Brain*, p. 52.
New York Times Book Review, October 15, 2006, Nicholas Confessore, "Strategist in Chief," review of *The Architect*.
Publishers Weekly, July 24, 2006, review of *The Architect*, p. 52.
Reason, October, 2003, John F. Pitney, Jr., "Accidental Genius," review of *Bush's Brain*, p. 58.
Spectator, May 24, 2003, George Osborne, review of *Bush's Brain*, p. 39.
Variety, March 29, 2004, Joe Leydon, review of *Bush's Brain* (film), p. 85.
Video Business, August 30, 2004, Ed Hulse, review of *Bush's Brain* (film), p. 18.
USA Today Magazine, July, 2003, Gerald F. Kreyche, review of *Bush's Brain*, p. 81.

ONLINE

BuzzFlash.com, http://www.buzzflash.com/ (June 2, 2003), "Who Is Bush's Brain?"
Curled Up with a Good Book, http://www.curledup.com/ (January 27, 2007), Marie D. Jones, review of *Bush's War for Reelection: Iraq, the White House, and the People*.
KarlRove.com, http://www.karlrove.com (January 27, 2007).*

*   *   *

MOORE, James C.
See MOORE, James

*   *   *

MOORES, Ted 1943-

PERSONAL: Born June 25, 1943, in Oshawa, Ontario, Canada; son of Fred (a printer) and Dorothy (a homemaker) Moores; married Joan Barrett (a business partner), 1974; children: Daisy, Jennifer.

ADDRESSES: Home and office—Peterborough, Ontario, Canada. *E-mail*—info@bearmountainboats.com.

CAREER: Boatbuilder. Also works as graphic artist and teacher. Member of Canadian Canoe Museum.

MEMBER: Antique and Classic Boat Society.

WRITINGS:

Canoecraft, Firefly Books (Richmond Hill, Ontario, Canada), 1983.
Kayaks You Can Build, Firefly Books (Richmond Hill, Ontario, Canada), 2004.

*   *   *

MOORHOUSE, Roger 1968-

PERSONAL: Born October 14, 1968, in Stockport, Cheshire, England; married; children: two. *Education:* University of London, M.A., 1994; postgraduate research at the Heinrich Heine Universtät, Düsseldorf, Germany and University of Strathclyde, Glasgow, Scotland.

ADDRESSES: Home—Leighton Buzzard, Bedfordshire LU7 9EY, England; fax: +44(0)1296 660988. *E-mail*—roger@rogermoorhouse.com.

CAREER: Historian, writer, editor, and translator. Senior researcher and editorial assistant to Professor Norman Davies, 1995—.

WRITINGS:

(With Norman Davies) *Microcosm: Portrait of a Central European City,* Jonathan Cape (London, England), 2002.
Killing Hitler: The Plots, the Assassins, and the Dictator Who Cheated Death, Bantam Books (New York, NY), 2006.

Contributor to periodicals, including *BBC History* magazine.

SIDELIGHTS: Roger Moorhouse is an historian and author who wrote his first book, *Microcosm: Portrait of a Central European City,* with Norman Davies. In their book, the authors tell the story of Wroclaw, a city in modern-day Poland, close to the borders with the Czech Republic and Germany. The city has had many names over its long existence, most notably the German name Breslau, which it carried until the end of World War Two. It has also undergone numerous changes in government and national and ethnic influence over the years. Moorhouse and Davies explore such issues as national identity and examine the city's many instances of social turmoil. "Davies and Moorhouse set out to present the history of the city, a microcosm of Central Europe, as evenhandedly as possible, freeing it from the straitjackets of German and Polish nationalisms, and giving due weight to its Jewish and Czech components," wrote Richard Butterwick in the *English Historical Review.* Butterwick added that "*Microcosm* must be acclaimed as exemplary." Writing in the *Spectator,* Antony Beevor noted the book's "scholarship and objectivity," adding that it "also makes a fascinating story."

As the author of *Killing Hitler: The Plots, the Assassins, and the Dictator Who Cheated Death,* Moorhouse presents case studies of eight attempts to assassinate Adolf Hitler. The author examines the people and reasons behind the attempts and also explores how each of the failures, along with the other many failed attempts to assassinate the dictator, helped to lead Hitler and his coterie to the belief that they were unstoppable. "Moorhouse's documentation and analysis of this comprehensive history will keep readers interested to the end," wrote George Cohen in *Booklist.* A *Publishers Weekly* contributor wrote: "Accessible prose, suspenseful narration and ample historical context make this a page-turner."

BIOGRAPHICAL AND CRITICAL SOURCES:

PERIODICALS

Booklist, March 1, 2006, George Cohen, review of *Killing Hitler: The Plots, the Assassins, and the Dictator Who Cheated Death,* p. 57.
Economist, April 27, 2002, review of *Microcosm: Portrait of a Central European City.*
English Historical Review, June, 2004, Richard Butterwick, review of *Microcosm,* p. 743.

Library Journal, March 1, 2006, Frederic Krome, review of *Killing Hitler,* p. 103.

Publishers Weekly, February 27, 2006, review of *Killing Hitler,* p. 52.

Spectator, March 30, 2002, Antony Beevor, review of *Microcosm,* p. 42.

ONLINE

Random House Web site, http://www.randomhouse. com/ (November 28, 2006), brief profile of author.

Roger Moorhouse Home Page, http://www. rogermoorhouse.com (November 27, 2006).

*　　*　　*

MORAN, Martin 1959-

PERSONAL: Born December 29, 1959, in Denver, CO; son of Martin, Sr. (a newspaper journalist) and Carol (a court reporter) Moran; companion of Henry Stram (an actor). *Ethnicity:* "Caucasian." *Education:* Attended Stanford University, 1978-80, and American Conservatory Theater, 1980; State University of New York Empire State College, B.F.A., 1990. *Politics:* Democrat. *Religion:* "Raised Roman Catholic; now practicing Buddhist."

ADDRESSES: Home—New York, NY. *Agent*—Malaga Baldi, 233 W. 99th St., Ste. 19C, New York, NY 10025.

CAREER: Professional actor, 1982—. Appeared in the solo show *The Tricky Part,* McGinn-Cazale Theater, New York, NY, 2004, and Signature Theater, Washington, DC, 2007, and as Sir Robin, *Spamalot* (musical), Shubert Theater, New York, NY, 2006-07; numerous other stage appearances include roles of the Ghost of Christmas Past, *A Christmas Carol,* a Londoner, *Oliver!,* Huckleberry Finn, *Big River,* Mr. Tackaberry and J.P. Finch, *How to Succeed in Business without Really Trying,* Harold Bride, *Titanic,* Ernst Ludwig, *Cabaret,* and Dr. Kitchell, *Bells Are Ringing,* all Broadway productions; as Zonker, *Doonesbury,* tour of U.S. cities; off-Broadway appearances include Clinton, *Legacy,* and Alfred Hersland, *The Making of Americans,* both Music Theater Group; the Mad Hatter, *Once on a Summer's Day,* Ensemble

Studio Theater; Avi's son, *One, Two, Three, Four, Five,* Manhattan Theater Club; Skeets Miler, *Floyd Collins,* Playwrights Horizons Theater; Grant Winkle and Wilbur Walsh, *Cider House Rules,* Atlantic Theater Company; and Ernie Lally, *A Man of No Importance,* Lincoln Center Theater; also appeared in regional and repertory productions. Film appearances include roles of George Swain, *The West;* chairman's assistant, *Private Parts;* and member of museum board, *The Next Big Thing.* Television appearances include role of Mary's coworker in the movie *Mary and Rhoda,* American Broadcasting Companies; and appearances in episodes of the series *Law & Order: Criminal Intent,* National Broadcasting Co., and *Dellaventura.*

MEMBER: Actors' Equity Association, Screen Actors Guild, American Federation of Television and Radio Artists, American Civil Liberties Union.

AWARDS, HONORS: Special Obie Award, *Village Voice,* 2004, Outer Critics Circle Award nomination, and two Drama Desk Award nominations, all for *The Tricky Part;* Lambda Literary Award and Publishing Triangle Award, both 2005, for *The Tricky Part: One Boy's Fall from Trespass into Grace.*

WRITINGS:

The Tricky Part (stage script; solo show; performed in New York, NY, at McGinn-Cazale Theater, 2004, and in Washington, DC, at Signature Theater, 2007), Dramatists Play Service (New York, NY), 2004.

The Tricky Part: One Boy's Fall from Trespass into Grace (memoir), Beacon Press (Boston, MA), 2005, paperback published as *The Tricky Part: A Boy's Story of Sexual Trespass, a Man's Journey to Forgiveness,* Anchor Books (New York, NY), 2006.

The Cellist (one-act play), 2006.

SIDELIGHTS: Martin Moran told *CA:* "I write to find out what I think, to seek meaning in events. Poetry influences my work tremendously. Though I don't write poetry, I find that I turn to the work of Mary Oliver, Stanley Kunitz, Shakespeare, Marie Howe, Mark Doty, and many others.

"I write very, very slowly. Writing for me is primarily a process of constant rewriting, first with pen and paper, then several typewritten drafts: endless, happy editing.

"*The Tricky Part* was a story I had to tell. I felt I had no choice. There was an ache, an imperative to use language to make sense, to find meaning in the past, and therefore the present."

BIOGRAPHICAL AND CRITICAL SOURCES:

ONLINE

Martin Moran Home Page, http://www.thetricky partbook.com (December 28, 2006).

*　　*　　*

MORGAN, Jody 1957-

PERSONAL: Born September 26, 1957, in Brantford, Ontario, Canada; daughter of Jack (a commissioner) and Norma (a homemaker) Kay; married Clive Morgan (a laboratory technologist), June, 2004; children: Blair, Adrienne. *Education:* University of Guelph, B.Sc. (with honors), 1982; Queen's University, Kingston, Ontario, Canada, B.Ed., 1983. *Hobbies and other interests:* Music (flute and piano), Triathlons.

ADDRESSES: Home—Yarker, Ontario, Canada. *E-mail*—clive.morgan@sympatico.ca.

CAREER: University of Guelph, Guelph, Ontario, Canada, researcher in biology, 1981-83; Queen's University, Kingston, Ontario, researcher in biology, 1984-86; *Equinox,* Camden East, Ontario, associate editor and photograph researcher, 1986-93. *Harrowsmith,* worked as assistant editor.

AWARDS, HONORS: Henry Bergh Children's Book Honor, American Society for the Prevention of Cruelty to Animals, 2004, for *Elephant Rescue: Changing the Future for Endangered Wildlife.*

WRITINGS:

Elephant Rescue: Changing the Future for Endangered Wildlife, Firefly Books (Buffalo, NY), 2004.

*　　*　　*

MORRIS, Emily S. 1976(?)-
(Libby Street, a joint pseudonym)

PERSONAL: Born c. 1976; daughter of Randy and Shawn Morris. *Education:* Ohio University, M.A.

ADDRESSES: Home—New York, NY. *E-mail*—libby@libbystreet.com.

CAREER: Writer, novelist, and advertising executive at a pharmaceutical marketing firm.

WRITINGS:

WITH SARAH BUSHWELLER UNDER JOINT PSEUDONYM LIBBY STREET

Happiness Sold Separately, Downtown Press (New York, NY), 2005.
Accidental It Girl, Downtown Press (New York, NY), 2006.

Author's works have been translated into German and Dutch.

SIDELIGHTS: For Sidelights, see BUSHWELLER, Sarah.

BIOGRAPHICAL AND CRITICAL SOURCES:

PERIODICALS

Booklist, June 1, 2005, review of *Happiness Sold Separately,* p. 1757; September 15, 2006, Aleksandra Kostovski, review of *Accidental It Girl,* p. 29.

Delaware State News, June 14, 2004, Jenna Kania, "Dover Natives a Novel Pair," profile of Sarah Bushweller and Emily S. Morris.

News Journal (Wilmington, DE), December 7, 2004, Christopher Yasiejko, "Dover Friends Always Finish Each Other's Thoughts, Decide to Write a Book," profile of Sarah Bushweller and Emily S. Morris.

ONLINE

Book Fetish, http://www.bookfetish.org/ (January 22, 2007), Vivian Whipp, review of *Accidental It Girl.*

BookLoons, http://www.bookloons.com/ (January 22, 2007), Tarah Schaeffer, review of *Happiness Sold Separately;* Kim Atchue-Cusella, review of *Accidental It Girl.*

ChickLitGurrl Web log, http://chicklitgurrl.blogspot.com/ (November, 2006), profile of Sarah Bushweller and Emily S. Morris.

Fallen Angel Reviews, http://www.fallenangelreviews.com/ (January 22, 2007), review of *Accidental It Girl.*

Libby Street's Home Page, http://www.libbystreet.com (January 22, 2007).*

*   *   *

MULLEN, Thomas 1974(?)-

PERSONAL: Born c. 1974, in Providence, RI; married; children: a son. *Education:* Graduate of Oberlin College. *Hobbies and other interests:* Music, film, travel, and hiking.

ADDRESSES: Home—Washington, DC. *Agent*—Susan Golomb, Susan Golomb Literary Agency, 875 Avenue of the Americas, Ste. 2302, New York, NY 10001.

CAREER: Writer. Has worked for a fast food company, consulting firm, a senior-citizen-run thrift store, a research center on alcohol and drug addictions, and a small publisher of newsletters.

WRITINGS:

The Last Town on Earth: A Novel, Random House (New York, NY), 2006.

ADAPTATIONS: The Last Town on Earth has been optioned for film by DreamWorks.

SIDELIGHTS: In his first book, *The Last Town on Earth: A Novel,* author Thomas Mullen writes of a murder in the woods near Commonwealth, Washington, a utopian timber town that seeks to keep out the horrific 1918 influenza epidemic by quarantining itself. As the story begins, the novel's protagonist, sixteen-year-old Philip Worthy, son of the timber mill owner Charles Worthy, is on guard duty with Graham Stone. Their orders are to keep people out. When a tired and hungry soldier comes by and fails to heed their warning to stay away, he is shot dead by Graham. Nevertheless, the epidemic finally hits Commonwealth with tragic results. In the meantime, a second soldier held prisoner has also been killed by Graham, leading Philip, who comes down with the virulent flu, to confront the man he once admired.

Noting that the author makes his tale analogous to modern-day concerns about "contagious viruses, obsession with foreign operatives, and repression of political dissent," Joanne Wilkinson also noted in *Booklist* the novel's "foreboding atmosphere." A *Kirkus Reviews* contributor commented that the author's "debut gets mileage out of the gruesome epidemic and contains some interesting historical nuggets." Max Byrd, writing in the *New York Times Book Review,* referred to *The Last Town on Earth* as "remarkable," adding that "time and again, Mullen's suspenseful storytelling pulls us forward." Byrd continued: "Time and again, his imagery—from the 'logs bobbing on the water's surface like corpses' to the whole town, seen 'in full eclipse'—is devastatingly right."

BIOGRAPHICAL AND CRITICAL SOURCES:

PERIODICALS

Booklist, July 1, 2006, Joanne Wilkinson, review of *The Last Town on Earth: A Novel,* p. 31.

Entertainment Weekly, August 25, 2006, Karen Karbo, review of *The Last Town on Earth,* p. 91.

Kirkus Reviews, May 15, 2006, review of *The Last Town on Earth,* p. S10; June 15, 2006, review of *The Last Town on Earth,* p. 59.

Library Journal, July 1, 2006, Jim Coan, review of *The Last Town on Earth,* p. 68.

New York Times Book Review, September 3, 2006, Max Byrd, review of *The Last Town on Earth,* p. 15.

Publishers Weekly, June 6, 2005, Jason Anthony, "Update: First-Time Author Thomas Mullen Got a Double-Dose of Immediate Gratification Last Week Courtesy of the Publishing and Film Worlds," p. 10.

USA Today, September 6, 2006, Jocelyn McClurg, review of *The Last Town on Earth.*

ONLINE

Thomas Mullen Home Page, http://www.thomas mullen.net (January 22, 2007).*

*   *   *

MURRELL, Kathleen Berton 1936-
(Kathleen Berton)

PERSONAL: Born September 10, 1936, in Ottawa, Ontario, Canada; married Geoffrey Murrell (a diplomat), November 26, 1962; children: Sarah, Timothy, Kate, Alice Murrell Castle. *Ethnicity:* "White." *Education:* University of Manitoba, B.A., 1956; Queen's University, Kingston, Ontario, Canada, B.A. (hons.), 1957; London School of Economics and Political Science, M.Sc., 1960.

ADDRESSES: Home—London, England.

CAREER: Diplomat with the Canadian Foreign Service, 1960-64; writer.

WRITINGS:

(Under name Kathleen Berton) *Moscow: An Architectural History,* Macmillan (New York, NY), 1977.

(Under name Kathleen Berton; with John Freeman) *Moscow Revealed,* Abbeville Press (New York, NY), 1991.

(Under name Kathleen Berton) *The British Embassy Residence, Moscow,* British Foreign Office (London, England), 1991.

Moscow: History, Art, and Architecture, Troika, 1993.

St. Petersburg: History, Art, and Architecture, Troika, 1993.

Moscow Art Nouveau, Philip Wilson (London, England), 1997.

Russia (juvenile), Alfred Knopf (New York, NY), 1998.

Moscow: An Illustrated History, Hippocrene Books (New York, NY), 2003.

Discovering the Moscow Countryside: A Travel Guide to the Heart of Russia, I.B. Tauris (London, England), 2003.

BIOGRAPHICAL AND CRITICAL SOURCES:

PERIODICALS

Booklist, July, 1998, Kay Weisman, review of *Russia,* p. 1876.

Interior Design, July, 1998, Stanley Abercrombie, review of *Moscow Art Nouveau,* p. 100.

Library Journal, June 1, 2001, Melinda Stivers Leach, review of *Discovering the Moscow Countryside: A Travel Guide to the Heart of Russia,* p. 2000.

*   *   *

MURTAGH, Niall

PERSONAL: Born in Dublin, Ireland; married; wife's name Miyuki; children: two. *Education:* University College Dublin, master's degree, 1979; Tokyo Institute of Technology, Ph.D.; also diplomas from Osaka Gaidai (University of Foreign Studies) and Alliance Francaise de Paris.

ADDRESSES: Home—Japan. *E-mail*—nm1@ niallmurtagh.info.

CAREER: Writer, consultant, and educator. OM-Consulting, founder and director, 2005—; Kokugakuin University, Tokyo, Japan, lecturer. Worked as a volunteer in Bangladesh, an engineer on a construction site in New South Wales, a teacher in a pacifist school in the mountains of Fukushima, and for Mitsubishi Electric Corporation.

WRITINGS:

The Blue-Eyed Salaryman: From World Traveller to Lifer at Mitsubishi (memoir), Profile (London, England), 2005.

Contributor to periodicals and academic journals.

SIDELIGHTS: Niall Murtagh has had a wide-ranging career working mainly in the Far East, and is a long-time resident of Japan. In his first book, *The Blue-Eyed Salaryman: From World Traveller to Lifer at Mitsubishi,* the author chronicles his younger days as a world traveler and then his decision to join Mitsubishi, one of Japan's most traditional and conservative corporations. The author then details life as a Westerner, that is, an outsider, in the Japanese corporate world, where he is referred to by the Japanese alias of Muruta-san and works as a computer programmer. He details his efforts to fit into a corporate culture, where he even receives a reprimand for parking his bicycle in the wrong place. In fact, according to Murtagh, the company's rules are so exhaustive that they touch upon almost every aspect of the employee's life, both within and outside the company.

"The book is full of wonderful vignettes and details," wrote Harriet Sergeant in the *Spectator.* Sergeant also commented: "In simple, straightforward language Murtagh tells how it is. This is not a romanticised version of Japan, but a Japan instantly recognisable to the majority of Japanese—the life of the traditional salaryman." A *Kirkus Reviews* contributor noted that author's "sometimes cynical, always waggish, text." A reviewer writing in *Management Today* commented: "There are several years' worth of anecdotes in the book, providing a comical picture of life on the corporate frontline. Murtagh makes us laugh at the oddities of Japanese working life without being condescending." In his review in the *New Statesman,* William Leith referred to *The Blue-Eyed Salaryman* as "a fascinating book," adding that "it will make you look at the logos of Japanese products and feel full of wonder."

BIOGRAPHICAL AND CRITICAL SOURCES:

BOOKS

Murtagh, Niall, *The Blue-Eyed Salaryman: From World Traveller to Lifer at Mitsubishi,* Profile (London, England), 2005.

PERIODICALS

Kirkus Reviews, June 1, 2006, review of *The Blue-Eyed Salaryman,* p. 561.
Management Today, May 31, 2005, review of *The Blue-Eyed Salaryman,* p. 35.
New Statesman, March 21, 2005, William Leith, review of *The Blue-Eyed Salaryman,* p. 53.
Spectator, April 2, 2005, Harriet Sergeant, review of *The Blue-Eyed Salaryman,* p. 45.
Yomiuri Shimbun/Daily Yomiuri (Japan), February 12, 2006, review of *The Blue-Eyed Salaryman.*

ONLINE

Niall Murtagh Home Page, http://www.niallmurtagh.info (January 23, 2007).
OM-Consulting, http://www.om-c.biz/ (January 23, 2007), brief profile of author.
Profile Books Web site, http://www.profilebooks.co.uk/ (January 23, 2007), brief profile of author.

*   *   *

MYERS, Jack 1913-2006
  (Jack Edgar Myers)

OBITUARY NOTICE— See index for *CA* sketch: Born July 10, 1913, in Boyds Mills, PA; died of cancer, December 28, 2006, in Austin, TX. Biologist, educator, and author. Myers was noted for his work in researching the uses of algae as a food source, but he was also a prolific children's author who explained concepts to young audiences as the science editor of *Highlights for Children.* His educational background included a B.S. from Juniata College in 1934, an M.S. from Montana State University in 1935, and a Ph.D. from the University of Minnesota in 1939. He joined the University of Texas faculty in 1941, becoming a professor of botany and zoology. Myers would teach there until 1980, but he remained at the university as a researcher until he finally retired in 1999. An expert on the processes of photosynthesis and phototropism, he had a special fascination for the potential of algae as a food source. His research demonstrated that algae could be used as a protein source that could be grown at rates sixty times more efficient than soy beans. He also worked with NASA to see how algae could be used both for food and for converting carbon dioxide to oxygen in space vehicles. This work result in a Founders Award from the American Society for Gravitational and Space Biology in 1998. Myers was the son of Gary and Caroline Myers, who were the founders of the educational magazine *Highlights for Children*. Beginning in 1960, he assisted with the periodical, writing articles, editing the science section, and answering thousands of letters from children over the years. He strongly believed in making science understandable and fascinating for young people. Toward this end, he authored many science books for children. Among these titles are *Can Birds Get Lost? And Other Questions about Animals* (1991), *Do Cats Really Have Nine Lives? And Other Questions about Your World* (1993), and *How Dogs Came from Wolves: And Other Explorations of Science in Action* (2001).

OBITUARIES AND OTHER SOURCES:

PERIODICALS

New York Times, January 6, 2007, p. A13.

* * *

MYERS, Jack Edgar
    See MYERS, Jack

N-O

NASHT, Simon

PERSONAL: Male.

ADDRESSES: Office—Real Pictures Pty Ltd., P.O. Box 507, Avalon, New South Wales 2107, Australia. *E-mail*—simon@nasht.com.

CAREER: Writer, journalist, screenwriter, movie producer, movie director, and television producer. Films produced include *Rite of Pasage* (television), 2001; *Wildest Show on Earth,* 2001; *New York Justice* (television series), 2001; *Voyage of the Nautilus* (television; and director), 2002; and *Tasmanian Devil,* 2005. Also appeared in the Australian television series *Beyond 2000.*

WRITINGS:

The Last Explorer: Hubert Wilkins: Australia's Unknown Hero, Hodder Australia (Sydney, New South Wales, Australia), 2005, published as *The Last Explorer: Hubert Wilkins, Hero of the Great Age of Polar Exploration,* Arcade (New York, NY), 2006.

Also author and director of the documentary films *Frank Hurley: The Man Who Made History,* (television), 2004, and *The Bridge* (also producer), 2007.

SIDELIGHTS: Simon Nasht is a documentary film writer, producer, and director, who has written a book and made a film about a noted Arctic explorer. In *The Last Explorer: Hubert Wilkins: Australia's Unknown Hero* the author details Wilkins's early life growing up on a sheep farm in Australia followed by a chronicle of his exploits and contributions to early twentieth-century exploration. For example, Nasht writes about Wilkins's foresight in being the first to use modern technological developments such as the airplane and submarine for exploration and his accomplishment of completing a world map in eight months based on his numerous flights. Nasht also explores how Wilkins combined his explorations with his scientific background to produce scientific firsts, such as revealing the relationship between the world's weather and the Arctic poles, an achievement that garnered Wilkins knighthood.

"It was most gratifying . . . to find . . . a well-written biography of Wilkins, with much new factual information about his activities," wrote Stuart E. Jenness in *Arctic.* Jenness also wrote: "Nasht has done a fine job of retelling Wilkins's remarkable life," adding: "His brisk, detailed, and down-to-earth style of writing holds one's interest from beginning to end, and his many informative endnotes reflect the depth of his research." George Cohen, writing in *Booklist,* commented: "Anyone interested in the history of polar exploration will want to read this book." In a review of Nasht's documentary film about filmmaker Frank Hurley, *Frank Hurley: The Man Who Made History, Quadrant* contributor Neil McDonald noted that the film "is thoroughly researched, handsomely shot with extensive extracts from Hurley's films and selections of his stills interwoven with just the right balance between interviews with the participants and commentators."

BIOGRAPHICAL AND CRITICAL SOURCES:

PERIODICALS

Arctic, September, 2006, Stuart E. Jenness, review of The Last Explorer: Hubert Wilkins: Australia's Unknown Hero, p. 328.
Booklist, September 15, 2006, George Cohen, review of The Last Explorer, p. 22.
Quadrant, September, 2005, Neil McDonald, review of film Frank Hurley: The Man Who Made History, p. 72.

ONLINE

Internet Movie Database, http://www.imdb.com/ (January 23, 2007), information on author's film work.*

* * *

NEAMAN, Elliot Yale 1957-

PERSONAL: Born 1957. Education: University of British Columbia, B.A., 1979; Freie Universitat Berlin, M.A., 1985; University of California, Berkeley, Ph.D., 1992.

ADDRESSES: Home—San Francisco, CA. Office—Department of History, University of San Francisco, 2130 Fulton St., San Francisco, CA 94117-1080. E-mail—neamane@usfca.edu; elliotyale2@mac.com.

CAREER: Historian, educator, and writer. Two Cities School, Zurich, Switzerland, English teacher, beginning 1980; Academy for Foreign Languages, Berlin, Germany, English teacher, beginning 1982; University of San Francisco, San Francisco, CA, graduate student instructor, 1990-92; assistant professor of history, 1993-98, associate professor of history, 1999—. Also editorial assistant for Tikkun magazine, 1992.

AWARDS, HONORS: Outstanding Student Instructor, University of California, Berkeley, 1992; Distinguished Research Award, University of San Francisco, 1999.

WRITINGS:

A Dubious Past: Ernst Jünger and the Politics of Literature after Nazism, University of California Press (Berkeley, CA), 1999.

Contributor to books, including Rechtextremismus—Ideologie und Gewal, edited by Hajo Funke, Edition Hentrich (Berlin, Germany), 1995; Antisemitism and Xenophobia in Germany after Unification, edited by Rainer Erb and Werner Bergmann, Oxford University Press (New York, NY), 1997; Fascism's Return: Scandal, Revision and Ideology, edited by Richard Golsan, University of Nebraska Press (Lincoln, NE), 1998; The Encyclopedia of Historiography, edited by Daniel Woolf, Garland (New York, NY), 1998; Amerika, dich hasst sich's besser, Die USA in Wahn und Wirklichkeit, edited by Thomas Uwer and Thomas von der Osten-Sacken, Konkret Verlag, 2003; Rhinecrossings; Berlin-Paris, edited by Aminia Brueggeman and Peter Schulman, State University of New York Press (Albany, NY), 2005; New History of German Literature, edited by Judith Ryan et al., Harvard University Press (Cambridge, MA), 2005; Anti-Semitism, edited by Mark McKain, Greenhaven Press (Westport, CT), 2005; Scribner's Encyclopedia of Europe 1789-1914, Scribner (New York, NY), 2006. Contributor of articles and reviews to periodicals, including the New York Times, Dissent, Constellations, Tikkun, New German Critique, Critical Review, Central European History, Frankfurter Allgemeine Zeitung, Lingua Franca, Telos, and German Politics and Society.

SIDELIGHTS: Elliot Yale Neaman is a historian whose primary interests are European intellectual history, German conservatism and right-wing politics, and the Holocaust. In his book A Dubious Past: Ernst Jünger and the Politics of Literature after Nazism, the author explores the legacy of German intellectual Jünger, who wrote about a wide range of topics and often created controversy, especially during his early writings of intellectual fascism. Neaman examines Jünger's published writings as well as his unpublished works, such as letters. The author also delves into interviews with Jünger and explores how Jünger's own public career mirrored German political history. "Elliot Neaman's book on the life and work of this controversial figure is a timely reminder of the confusion over Jünger's place among German authors of the twentieth century, illustrated by the numerous debates over Jünger's complicity with fascism that persisted until his death," wrote Daniel P. Reynolds in the *Rocky Mountain Review of Language and Literature.* Referring to the book as "carefully documented and meticulously argued," Reynolds added that the author explains why Jünger is "one of German literature's most ambiguous figures." In a review in *German History,* Geoff Eley commented that the author's "new study provides a first-rate basis in the English language for judging the fullness of Jünger's career." Eley also wrote: "*A Dubious Past* provides a model of ambitiously conceived and carefully contextualized intellectual history, which leaves twentieth-century historians in its debt."

BIOGRAPHICAL AND CRITICAL SOURCES:

PERIODICALS

German History, Volume 19, 2001, Geoff Eley, review of *A Dubious Past: Ernst Jünger and the Politics of Literature after Nazism,* p. 643.
Rocky Mountain Review of Language and Literature, Volume 55, number 2, 2001, Daniel P. Reynolds, review of *A Dubious Past,* pp. 115-116.

ONLINE

Academic Keys for the Humanities Web site, http://humanities.academickeys.com/ (January 24, 2007), profile of author.
University of San Francisco College of Arts & Sciences Web page, http://artsci.usfca.edu/ (January 24, 2007), faculty profile of author.*

*   *   *

NEEDHAM, Rodney 1923-2006
(Rodney Phillip Needham)

OBITUARY NOTICE— See index for *CA* sketch: Born May 15, 1923, in Kent, England; died December 4, 2006. Anthropologist, educator, and author. A former Oxford professor, Needham favored the structural anthropology approach first formulated by Claude Levi-Strauss. Before he enrolled in college, World War II broke out and Needham enlisted in the British Army. He fought with the First Gurkha Rifles in Burma and in 1944 was seriously wounded in the leg. Despite his war experiences, he would be fascinated by the cultures of Southeast Asia, where he would later return to conduct field research. Needham was educated at Oxford University, receiving his Ph.D. from Merton College. He also studied Chinese for two years at the School of Oriental and African Studies. During the early 1950s, he did field work in Sarawak, Borneo, and in Indonesia. He returned to England in 1956 and became a lecturer in anthropology at Oxford. Needham was promoted to Professor of Social Anthropology and Fellow of All Souls College in 1976 and retired in 1990. As a scholar, he specialized in social anthropology and was enamored of Levi-Strauss's idea of structural anthropology, the theory that all people organize their concepts of the world in terms of binary opposites. Needham related his thoughts on structuralism in his first book, *Structure and Sentiment: A Test Case in Social Anthropology* (1962), as well as in other books, such as his acclaimed *Belief, Language and Experience* (1972). Also an editor and translator of anthropology books, Needham was the author of such other works as *Primordial Characters* (1978), *Against the Tranquility of Axioms* (1983), and *Mamboru: History and Structure in a Domain of Northwestern Sumba* (1987).

OBITUARIES AND OTHER SOURCES:

PERIODICALS

Times (London, England), February 19, 2007, p. 53.

*   *   *

NEEDHAM, Rodney Phillip
See NEEDHAM, Rodney

*   *   *

NELSON, Craig

PERSONAL: Education: Graduate of the University of Texas at Austin.

ADDRESSES: Home—New York, NY. *E-mail*—craig@craignelson.us.

CAREER: Writer, editor. Former executive editor and vice president at Harper & Row, Hyperion, Random House, and Villard. Has also worked at a zoo and as a literary agent.

MEMBER: Boy Scouts of America (Eagle Scout).

AWARDS, HONORS: Henry Adams Prize, 2006, for *Thomas Paine: Enlightenment, Revolution, and the Birth of Modern Nations.*

WRITINGS:

Bad TV: The Very Best of the Very Worst, Delta (New York, NY), 1995.
Finding True Love in a Man-Eat-Man World: The Intelligent Guide to Gay Dating, Sex, Romance, and Eternal Love, Dell (New York, NY), 1996.
Let's Get Lost: Adventures in the Great Wide Open, Warner Books (New York, NY), 1999.
The First Heroes: The Extraordinary Story of the Doolittle Raid—America's First World War II Victory, Viking (New York, NY), 2002.
Thomas Paine: Enlightenment, Revolution, and the Birth of Modern Nations, Viking (New York, NY), 2006.

Contributor of articles to periodicals, including *New York Observer, New England Review, New York Rocker, California Quarterly, Salon.com, Blender, Show International,* and *Genre,* among others.

ADAPTATIONS: Thomas Paine: Enlightenment, Revolution, and the Birth of Modern Nations was adapted for audio, Recorded Books, 2006.

SIDELIGHTS: Craig Nelson is a former publishing editor and the author of numerous nonfiction works. His first book title, *Bad TV: The Very Best of the Very Worst,* was a tongue-in-cheek ode to woefully bad television programming. Nelson covers forty years of television, including situation comedies, made-for-television movies, and children's shows, to find the worst television ever produced. Reviewing *Bad TV* in *Entertainment Weekly,* Vanessa V. Friedman felt the author deals with the topic in "an appropriately awestruck tone."

In his 2002 title, *The First Heroes: The Extraordinary Story of the Doolittle Raid—America's First World War II Victory,* Nelson takes on a more sober topic, focusing on the April, 1942, raid on Tokyo and other Japanese cities by American bombers. The sixteen bombers under the command of Lieutenant Colonel Jimmy Doolittle provided an enormous morale boost for Americans and also created a sense of fear and dread in the Japanese, who had hitherto felt safe and well protected in their islands. This psychological factor was greater than any physical destruction that the raid accomplished. After the raid the pilots and crew had to bail out of their planes, which were out of fuel. Their planned escape route was through Japanese-occupied China, and many did not survive the mission. Nelson, who is both a son and nephew of World War II veterans, approaches the story from the viewpoint of twenty crew members in a "a thrilling real-life saga that both informs and inspires," according to *Booklist* contributor Jay Freeman. Other critics added to the praise. A writer for *Kirkus Reviews* lauded Nelson's "passionately fresh perspective to this amazing story," and further called the book "riveting" as well as a "gripping drama . . . nearly impossible to put down."

Nelson turns to an earlier era of American history in his 2006 work, *Thomas Paine: Enlightenment, Revolution, and the Birth of Modern Nations.* Here he tackles the enigma of Paine, who at age forty, with little formal education, penned one of the most important tracts in Western history. His seventy-seven-page pamphlet, *Common Sense,* was, according to *New Yorker* contributor Jill Lepore, "an anonymous, fanatical, and brutally brilliant . . . pamphlet that would convince the American people of what more than a decade of taxes and nearly a year of war had not: that it was nothing less than their destiny to declare independence from Britain." Historians have long wondered at Paine's ability to synthesize Enlightenment thought in this hard-hitting work, and, as Lepore noted, Nelson "argues that Paine soaked up the ideas of the Enlightenment, especially Newtonian rationalism, during the years he spent in London, and that may be the best explanation anyone ever gets." For Lepore, Nelson's book was a "rewarding new biography." Further praise came from *Library Journal* contributor Thomas J. Schaeper, who commended Nelson's "storyteller's gift for the dramatic." Similarly, a reviewer for *Publishers Weekly* called Nelson's *Thomas Paine* a "brisk, intellectually sophisticated study."

BIOGRAPHICAL AND CRITICAL SOURCES:

PERIODICALS

Booklist, September 1, 2002, Jay Freeman, review of *The First Heroes: The Extraordinary Story of the Doolittle Raid—America's First World War II Victory,* p. 50; October 15, 2006, Jay Freeman, review of *Thomas Paine: Enlightenment, Revolution, and the Birth of Modern Nations,* p. 9.

Entertainment Weekly, January 13, 1995, Vanessa V. Friedman, review of *Bad TV: The Very Best of the Very Worst,* p. 56.

History Today, May, 2003, review of *The First Heroes,* p. 84.

Kirkus Reviews, August 1, 2002, review of *The First Heroes,* p. 1103.

Library Journal, July, 1999, Janet Ross, review of *Let's Get Lost: Adventures in the Great Wide Open,* p. 119; August, 2002, Edwin B. Burgess, review of *The First Heroes,* p. 118; September 15, 2006, Thomas J. Schaeper, review of *Thomas Paine,* p. 69.

New Criterion, October, 2006, Joseph Rago, "Doubting Thomas," review of *Thomas Paine,* p. 25.

New Yorker, October 16, 2006, Jill Lepore, "The Sharpened Quill," review of *Thomas Paine.*

Publishers Weekly, July 24, 2006, review of *Thomas Paine,* p. 47.

ONLINE

Craig Nelson Home Page, http://www.craignelson.us (January 28, 2007).

*   *   *

NEWHART, Bob 1929-
(George Robert Newhart)

PERSONAL: Born September 5, 1929 (some sources say September 29, 1929), in Oak Park, IL; son of George David and Julia Pauline Newhart; married Virginia Quinn, January 12, 1964; children: Robert William, Timothy, Jennifer, Courtney. *Education:* Loyola University, Chicago, B.S., 1952.

ADDRESSES: Agent—William Morris Agency, 151 S. El Camino Dr., Beverly Hills, CA 90212.

CAREER: Comedian, actor, and writer. Actor in films and on television, including the television shows *The Bob Newhart Show,* 1961; *The Bob Newhart Show,* 1972-78; *Newhart,* 1982-90; *Bob,* 1992-94; and *George and Leo,* 1997-98; also appeared on numerous television specials and other series. Previously worked as accountant for the U.S. Gypsum Co. and copywriter for the Fred Niles Film Co., 1958. Theatrical films include *Hell Is For Heroes,* 1962; *Hot Millions,* 1968; *On a Clear Day You Can See Forever,* 1970; *Catch 22,* 1970; *Cold Turkey,* 1971; *First Family,* 1980; *Little Miss Marker,* 1980; *In & Out,* 1997; *Elf,* 2003; *Legally Blonde 2: Red, White & Blonde,* 2003. Also supplied voices for the animated films *The Rescuers,* 1977; *The Rescuers Down Under,* 1990, and *Rudolph the Red-Nosed Reindeer: The Movie,* 1998. Television movies include *Thursday's Game,* 1974; *Marathon,* 1980; *Packy,* 1987; *The Entertainers,* 1991; *The Librarian: Quest for the Spear,* 2004; and *The Librarian: Return to King Solomon's Mines,* 2006. *Military service:* U.S. Army, 1952-54.

AWARDS, HONORS: Grammy awards (three): Best New Artist, Best Comedy Performance (Spoken Word), and Album of the Year, 1961, for *The Button Down Mind of Bob Newhart;* Emmy award, 1961; Peabody award, 1961; Sword of Loyola award, 1976; Legend to Legend award, 1993; Kennedy Center Mark Twain award, 2002; Icon award, TVLand, 2005; named to Television Academy of Arts & Sciences Hall of Fame, 1993; honored as an American Master (*Bob Newhart: Unbuttoned*), Public Broadcasting Service (PBS), 2005.

WRITINGS:

I Shouldn't Even Be Doing This! And Other Things That Strike Me as Funny (memoir), Hyperion (New York, NY), 2006.

Writer and performer on numerous comedy albums, including *The Button-Down Mind of Bob Newhart,* 1961; *The Button-Down Mind Strikes Back,* 1962; *Bob Newhart's Button-Down Concert,* Nick at Nite Records, 1997; *Something Like This . . . The Bob Newhart Anthology,* Warner Archives/Rhino, 2001. Other albums include *Behind the Button-Down Mind, The Button-Down Mind on TV, Bob Newhart Faces Bob Newhart, Windmills Are Weakening, This Is It, Bob Newhart Deluxe Edition, Best of Bob Newhart,* and *Very Funny Bob Newhart.*

SIDELIGHTS: Bob Newhart is a comedian best known for his deadpan stand-up comedy routines and for his highly successful television series *The Bob Newhart Show* and *Newhart.* In his memoir, *I Shouldn't Even Be Doing This! And Other Things That Strike Me as Funny,* Newhart writes about his life and nearly fifty-year career. Nevertheless, during an interview that appeared in *America's Intelligence Wire,* Newhart noted that he did not consider his book to be a memoir, noting that "memoirs are for Marquis de Sade and Geishas. They write memoirs." The author writes about both his successes and failures, his fear of flying, his love of golf, and about many of his celebrity friends, such as comedians Don Rickles and the late Buddy Hackett. In addition to writing about his life, the author includes numerous asides that feature his comical take on life. Newhart also writes about various comedians and comedy styles and how he created his own famous comedy routines. A *Publishers Weekly* contributor commented on Newhart's writing style of "treating the reader almost as a personal friend." Writing in *Kirkus Reviews,* a contributor noted: "There are no revelations, dark or otherwise." Nevertheless, the reviewer added that *I Shouldn't Even Be Doing This!* is "full of the wry, understated self-deprecation that Newhart has perfected."

BIOGRAPHICAL AND CRITICAL SOURCES:

BOOKS

Contemporary Theatre, Film and Television, Volume 44, Thomson Gale (Detroit, MI), 2002.
Newhart, Bob, *I Shouldn't Even Be Doing This! And Other Things That Strike Me as Funny,* Hyperion (New York, NY), 2006.

St. James Encyclopedia of Popular Culture, St. James Press (Detroit, MI), 2000.

PERIODICALS

America's Intelligence Wire, October 2, 2006, interview with author; October 20, 2006, Frazier Moore, review of *I Shouldn't Even Be Doing This!*
Buffalo News, December 3, 2006, Greg Connors "Newhart, Borowitz Shed a Humorous Light on Hecklers, Politicians."
Dailey Variety, February 7, 2005, "Dr. Sitcom," p. SS23; July 14, 2005, Army Archerd, "Just for Variety," interview with author, p. 2.
Entertainment Weekly, September 26, 1997, Bruce Fretts, "Love That Bob," p. 36; November 1, 1999, Bruce Fretts, "78 Bob Newhart: Comedy Was Never So Pefectly Straight," p. 131.
Hollywood Reporter, July 20, 2005, Barry Garron, "Newhart Still on TV's Mind: Comic Saluted on PBS' 'Masters,'" p. 5.
Kirkus Reviews, May 15, 2006, "Previewing the New Season of 'Writing with Celebrities,'" p. S4; June 1, 2006, review of *I Shouldn't Even Be Doing This!,* p. 562.
Life, October 1997, Alison Adato, "He's Back. All Together Now: 'Hi, Bob!,'" interview with author, p. 27.
New York Times Book Review, October 8, 2006, Dwight Garner, review of *I Shouldn't Even Be Doing This!*
People, May 9, 1983, Ralph Novak, "Same to You, Fella! Bob Newhart, TV's Most Durable Sitcomic, Takes on His Deadpan Image Head to Head," p. 60.
Publishers Weekly, July 10, 2006, review of *I Shouldn't Even Be Doing This!,* p. 68.
U.S. News & World Report, April 11, 2005, Marc Silver, "Doctor Hartley Is 'In,'" interview with author, p. 19.

ONLINE

Comedy Couch, http://comedycouch.com/ (April 14, 2006), "The Interview."
Internet Movie Database, http://www.imdb.com/ (January 24, 2007), information on author's film and television career.*

NEWHART, George Robert
    See NEWHART, Bob

*   *   *

NIEMOLLER, Ara
    See LLERENA, Mario

*   *   *

OBER, Karl Patrick
    See OBER, K. Patrick

*   *   *

OBER, K. Patrick 1949-
    (Karl Patrick Ober)

PERSONAL: Born April 7, 1949, in Ames, IA; son of Jestin (a veterinarian) and Maridale (a homemaker) Ober; married Cathy Irene Collison (a homemaker), March 24, 1971; children: Christopher Patrick, Rebecca Irene. *Ethnicity:* "Caucasian (Western European)." *Education:* Michigan State University, B.S., 1970; University of Florida, M.D., 1974.

ADDRESSES: Home—Clemmons, NC. *Office*—School of Medicine, Wake Forest University, Medical Center Blvd., Winston-Salem, NC 27157. *E-mail*—kober@triad.rr.com.

CAREER: Wake Forest University, Winston-Salem, NC, member of medical faculty, 1979—, associate dean for education.

MEMBER: American College of Physicians, Endocrine Society, American Diabetes Association.

WRITINGS:

(Editor) *Endocrinology of Critical Diseases,* Humana Press (Totowa, NJ), 1997.

Mark Twain and Medicine: "Any Mummery Will Cure," University of Missouri Press (Columbia, MO), 2003.

Contributor to medical journals. Past guest editor of periodicals published by Endocrinology and Metabolism Clinics of North America and Medical Clinics of North America.

SIDELIGHTS: K. Patrick Ober told *CA:* "I am particularly interested in the relationship between the humanities and the practice of medicine. One of my medical journal articles uses the lessons from the Uncle Remus stories by Joel Chandler Harris to illustrate the dilemmas faced by modern-day doctors in solving difficult clinical problems. My area of greatest interest, however, stems from my lifelong passion with the writings of Mark Twain as the quintessential spokesman for all of humanity. My specific focus is on Twain's medical experiences and writings, which continue to be as insightful and humorous as they were in the nineteenth century."

BIOGRAPHICAL AND CRITICAL SOURCES:

PERIODICALS

Choice, April, 2004, R. Nadelhaft, review of *Mark Twain and Medicine: "Any Mummery Will Cure,"* p. 1473.
New England Journal of Medicine, June 10, 2004, Stephanie Brown Clark, review of *Mark Twain and Medicine,* p. 2529.
Library Journal, February 1, 2004, A.J. Wright, review of *Mark Twain and Medicine,* p. 117.
Reference & Research Book News, February, 2004, review of *Mark Twain and Medicine,* p. 244.
SciTech Book News, September, 1997, review of *Endocrinology of Critical Diseases,* p. 80.

*   *   *

OLSEN, Christopher J. 1966-
    (Christopher John Olsen)

PERSONAL: Born March 19, 1966, in Fargo, ND; son of Richard Donald and Verna Jean Catherine Olsen; married Jennifer Ann Ross, March 18, 1995; children: Emma Catherine, Charlotte Ann, Ross Christopher.

Education: North Dakota State University, B.A., 1988; University of Nebraska, M.A., 1990; University of Florida, Ph.D., 1996. *Hobbies and other interests:* Golf.

ADDRESSES: Home—Terre Haute, IN. *E-mail*—c-olsen@indstate.edu; colsen@isugw.indstate.edu.

CAREER: Historian, educator, and writer. University of Florida, Gainesville, adjunct professor, 1995-96; Virginia Wesleyan College, Norfolk, assistant professor, 1996-99; Indiana State University, Terre Haute, assistant professor of history, 1999-2002, associate professor of history, 2002—.

MEMBER: Organization of American Historians, Southern Historical Association, Society for Historians of the Early American Republic, Indiana Historical Society, South Dakota Historical Society, Phi Alpha Theta, Phi Beta Kappa.

AWARDS, HONORS: Graduate Council doctoral fellowship, University of Florida, 1990-91; Samuel Proctor Graduate Teaching Award, History Department, University of Florida, 1992-93; recipient of numerous grants.

WRITINGS:

Political Culture and Secession in Mississippi: Masculinity, Honor, and the Antiparty Tradition, 1830-1860, Oxford University Press (New York, NY), 2000.
The American Civil War: A Hands-On History, Hill & Wang (New York, NY), 2006.

Contributor to books, including *Reader's Guide to American History,* edited by Peter J. Parish, Fitzroy Dearborn Publishers (Chicago, IL), 1998; *Americans at War: Society, Culture, and the Homefront,* edited by John P. Resch, Macmillan (New York, NY), 2004; *The United States at War,* ABC-Clio (New York, NY), 2005; *The Mississippi Encyclopedia,* edited by Charles Reagan Wilson, University Press of Mississippi (Jackson, MS), 2006; *Georgia Women,* Volume I, edited by Sarah E. Gardner and Ann Short Chirhart,

University of Georgia Press (Athens, GA), 2007; *Southern Families,* University of Georgia Press (Athens, GA), c. 2007. Contributor of articles and book reviews to periodicals, including *Alabama Review, Georgia Historical Quarterly, American Historical Review, Journal of Illinois History, Journal of American History, Journal of Women's History, Journal of Military History, Filson History Quarterly, Journal of the Early Republic, Journal of the Early Republic Australasian Journal of American Studies, Southern Historian, Florida Historical Quarterly,* and the *Journal of Mississippi History.*

SIDELIGHTS: Christopher J. Olsen is a historian whose primary interests include Southern and Civil War history. In his first book, *Political Culture and Secession in Mississippi: Masculinity, Honor, and the Antiparty Tradition, 1830-1860,* the author explores Mississippi politics during the antebellum period and presents his theory that, at that time, Mississippians were largely unconcerned about specific parties but were primarily influenced by face-to-face encounters with politicians. "They emphasized masculine honor as the bulwark of their political values," wrote *Journal of Southern History* contributor Nicole Etcheson in her review of *Political Culture and Secession in Mississippi.* Noting that the author supports his case by close examination of voting records, Etcheson went on to write: "The statistical material is nicely balanced with literary and anecdotal evidence, ensuring that the stories of real people are never obscured." The reviewer added: "This is not a dreary read." Carlton Jackson, writing in the *Mississippi Quarterly,* commented: "At least with Mississippi . . . Professor Christopher J. Olsen sees secession as the ultimate act of masculinity."

The American Civil War: A Hands-On History provides an overview of the Civil War by presenting the basic issues that led to the Civil War, those that arose during the course of the war, and the numerous concerns that followed in its aftermath. The author writes about the politics and social issues of the times and details numerous battles. "Effective interplay between context and contingency is Olsen's authorial forte," wrote Gilbert Taylor in *Booklist.* A *Kirkus Reviews* contributor commented that the author "gets the basic points across clearly and effectively." Another reviewer writing in *Publishers Weekly* commented that the author "has produced a tightly written book ideal for anyone looking for a quick introduction to" the Civil War.

BIOGRAPHICAL AND CRITICAL SOURCES:

PERIODICALS

Booklist, June 1, 2006, Gilbert Taylor, review of *The American Civil War: A Hands-On History,* p. 22.

Journal of Southern History, May, 2002, Nicole Etcheson, review of *Political Culture and Secession in Mississippi: Masculinity, Honor, and the Antiparty Tradition, 1830-1860,* p. 448.

Kirkus Reviews, June 1, 2006, review of *The American Civil War,* p. 562.

Library Journal, August 1, 2006, Randall M. Miller, review of *The American Civil War,* p. 101.

Mississippi Quarterly, spring, 2002, Carlton Jackson, review of *Political Culture and Secession in Mississippi,* p. 288.

Publishers Weekly, May 15, 2006, review of *The American Civil War,* p. 58.

ONLINE

Indiana University Department of History Web site, http://www.indstate.edu/history/ (January 24, 2007), faculty profile of author and author's curriculum vitae.*

* * *

OLSEN, Christopher John
    See OLSEN, Christopher J.

* * *

OTTERNESS, Philip 1955-

PERSONAL: Born February 14, 1955, in Kadoka, SD. *Education:* University of Pennsylvania, B.A., M.S., 1977; Cambridge University, M.A., 1979; Johns Hopkins University, M.A., 1982; University of Iowa, Ph.D., 1996.

ADDRESSES: Office—No. 6042, Warren Wilson College, P.O. Box 9000, Asheville, NC 28815. *E-mail*—pottern@warren-wilson.edu.

CAREER: Warren Wilson College, Asheville, NC, professor of history and political science, 1996—.

WRITINGS:

Becoming German: The 1709 Palatine Migration to New York, Cornell University Press (Ithaca, NY), 2004.

* * *

OZ, Daphne 1986(?)-

PERSONAL: Born c. 1986; daughter of Mehmet (a cardiologist and author) and Lisa (an author) Oz. *Education:* Attended Princeton University.

ADDRESSES: E-mail—daphne@newmarketpress.com.

CAREER: Writer, 2006—.

WRITINGS:

The Dorm Room Diet: The 8-Step Program for Creating a Healthy Lifestyle Plan That Really Works, Newmarket Press (New York, NY), 2006.

Contributor to *ELLEgirl* magazine.

SIDELIGHTS: In *The Dorm Room Diet: The 8-Step Program for Creating a Healthy Lifestyle Plan That Really Works,* college student Daphne Oz offers her fellow students a way to escape poor eating habits that dormitory living can make worse—which can in turn lead to weight gain, often as much as fifteen pounds during the freshman year alone. The daughter of a diet expert and a heart surgeon, Oz struggled with weight issues of her own through high school. "When I was accepted to college, I realized that this represented an entirely new stage in my life," she wrote in an author interview published on her home page. "If I didn't seize the opportunity to change now, when would I? So I began the process of changing my lifestyle, and I haven't looked back since." She continued: "I realized that I was not the only one interested in this stuff. I decided to put together a book so that anyone who wanted the information could get it easily."

"This is a great book to pack between the extra-long twin sheets and study lamp," concluded a *Publishers Weekly* reviewer. "Readers of all ages," *Booklist* contributor Gillian Engberg declared, "may glean plenty of new facts and, perhaps most of all, encouragement" from *The Dorm Room Diet.*

BIOGRAPHICAL AND CRITICAL SOURCES:

PERIODICALS

Booklist, September 1, 2006, Gillian Engberg, review of *The Dorm Room Diet: The 8-Step Program for Creating a Healthy Lifestyle Plan That Really Works,* p. 32.

Library Journal, September 1, 2006, Beth Hill, review of *The Dorm Room Diet,* p. 169.

New York Times Upfront, November 13, 2006, "How to Stave Off the 'Freshman 15,'" p. 6.

Publishers Weekly, July 24, 2006, review of *The Dorm Room Diet,* p. 55.

ONLINE

Daphne Oz Home page, http://www.dormroomdiet. com (January 24, 2007), author biography and interview.

Washington Post Online, http://www.washingtonpost. com/ (September 12, 2006), "The Dorm Room Diet," author interview.*

P

PADOWICZ, Julian

PERSONAL: Married. *Education:* Graduated from Colgate University.

ADDRESSES: *Home*—Stamford, CT.

CAREER: Writer, documentary filmmaker, and producer of audio tapes.

AWARDS, HONORS: Golden Eagle Award, Committee on International Non-Theatrical Events, for educational film *The People Shop.*

WRITINGS:

Mother and Me: Escape from Warsaw 1939 (memoir), Academy Chicago Publishers (Chicago, IL), 2006.

Author of numerous audiobooks, including *Runaway Horses, Chickens, and Other Upset People* (young adult novel); *Jesse* (young adult novel); *Gordon* (novel); *Seeing the Franklin Roosevelt Home with Julian Padowicz; 100 Minutes to Better Photography; 60 Minutes towards Computer Literacy; Cat Lovers Only; Soliciting the Major Gift; Stalking the Corporate Dollar;* and *Public Relations in Support of Development.*

SIDELIGHTS: *Mother and Me: Escape from Warsaw 1939* is Julian Padowicz's story of how he and his mother—and some of their relatives—escaped from Nazi persecution after the fall of Poland in 1939. The small party of refugees fled to Soviet-controlled Ukraine, and then Padowicz and his mother trekked over the Carpathian Mountains to reach Hungary. "Julian Padowicz's perilous escape from Warsaw is an exciting adventure, made all the more engrossing because he conveys so much about his feelings and impressions of this time in his life," wrote Patricia F. D'Ascoli in the *Jewish Ledger.* "The young Julian, who seems at times wise beyond his years, has a wonderfully wry outlook on the varied circumstances in which he finds himself during the course of his journey."

The moving force behind Julian's flight is his mother, a wealthy woman who lost her second husband during the war. "Beautiful and manipulative," explained a *Publishers Weekly* contributor, Basia Padowicz Weisbrem's "self-absorption and lack of concern for consequences alienate[d] her in-laws." She and Julian were finally abandoned by their guide in the Carpathians and were forced to find their own way through the wilderness into free Hungary. She "did whatever she had to—from telling lies to flirting with Soviet officers," concluded a *Kirkus Reviews* contributor, "to get provisions for her family." In the final analysis it is Basia Weisbrem, declared the *Kirkus Reviews* writer, who "emerges as the real hero of this tale."

BIOGRAPHICAL AND CRITICAL SOURCES:

BOOKS

Padowicz, Julian, *Mother and Me: Escape from Warsaw 1939,* Academy Chicago Publishers (Chicago, IL), 2006.

PERIODICALS

Booklist, April 15, 2006, George Cohen, review of *Mother and Me,* p. 24.

Jewish Ledger, August 30, 2006, Patricia F. D'Ascoli, "An Engaging Memoir from a Stamford Author."

Kirkus Reviews, June 15, 2006, review of *Mother and Me,* p. 622.

Publishers Weekly, May 15, 2006, review of *Mother and Me,* p. 60.

* * *

PAGNAMENTA, Peter 1941-

PERSONAL: Born April 12, 1941, in Oxford, England; son of Charles Francis and Daphne Isabel Pagnamenta; married Sybil Healy, April 13, 1966; children: Zoe and Robin. *Education:* Cambridge University, M.A., 1963.

ADDRESSES: Home—London, England.

CAREER: Television producer and writer. British Broadcasting Corporation (BBC), script writer, 1964-65, assistant producer of *Tonight,* 1965, producer of *24 Hours,* 1966, producer in New York office, 1968, editor of *24 Hours,* 1971, editor of *Midweek,* 1972, editor of *Panorama,* 1975, producer of *All Our Working Lives* (ten-part series), editor of *Real Lives* series, 1984; head of Current Affairs Group Television, 1985, producer of *Nippon,* 1990, producer of *People's Century* (twenty-six-part series), 1995-99; Pagnamenta Associates, founder, 1997.

AWARDS, HONORS: Shell Award; Industrial Journalism Award; British Film Institute Archive Award; National Viewers and Listeners Award; International Emmy, 1996, and Peabody Award, 1997, both for *People's Century.*

WRITINGS:

(With Richard Overy) *All Our Working Lives,* British Broadcasting Corporation (London, England), 1984.

(Editor) *The Hidden Hall: Portrait of a Cambridge College,* Third Millennium (London, England), 2004.

(With Momoko Williams) *Sword and Blossom: A British Officer's Enduring Love for a Japanese Woman,* Penguin Press (New York, NY), 2006, also published as *Falling Blossom: A British Officer's Enduring Love for a Japanese Woman,* Century (London, England), 2006.

SIDELIGHTS: Peter Pagnamenta is a television producer and author who collaborated with Momoko Williams to write *Sword and Blossom: A British Officer's Enduring Love for a Japanese Woman,* which was published in England as *Falling Blossom: A British Officer's Enduring Love for a Japanese Woman.* The book tells of the romance between a British career officer, Arthur Hart-Synnot, and Masa Suzuki, the daughter of a Tokyo barber. Based largely on love letters from Arthur to Masa that were discovered in 1982, *Sword and Blossom* recounts how the two met in Tokyo in 1904 when Arthur was sent on an assignment to Japan, and continues the story to their ultimate separation. Although the two eventually have two sons together, Masa refuses to marry Arthur and the two of them are often separated as Arthur receives various assignments throughout the world. A *Kirkus Reviews* contributor referred to *Sword and Blossom* as "a polished account that segues elegantly from a personal saga to a larger cultural history." A *Publishers Weekly* contributor noted that the authors "offer a deeply sympathetic portrayal of this doomed long-distance romance." In a review in the *Library Journal,* Charles W. Hayford wrote: "This is grand history on a human scale, vivid and sweeping."

BIOGRAPHICAL AND CRITICAL SOURCES:

BOOKS

Pagnamenta, Peter, and Momoko Williams, *Sword and Blossom: A British Officer's Enduring Love for a Japanese Woman,* Penguin Press (New York, NY), 2006.

PERIODICALS

Entertainment Weekly, June 16, 2006, Tim Purtell, review of *Sword and Blossom,* p. 79.

Europe Intelligence Wire, June 17, 2006, review of *Falling Blossom: A British Officer's Enduring Love for a Japanese Woman.*

Guardian (London, England), May 13, 2006, Anthony Thwaite, review of *Falling Blossom.*

Independent (London, England), July 23, 2006, Charlie Lee-Potter, review of *Falling Blossom.*

Kirkus Reviews, April 1, 2006, review of *Sword and Blossom,* p. 338.

Library Journal, June 1, 2006, Charles W. Hayford, review of *Sword and Blossom,* p. 136.

Publishers Weekly, April 17, 2006, review of *Sword and Blossom,* p. 182.

ONLINE

PBS Web site, http://www.pbs.org/ (November 28, 2006), brief profile of author.

*   *   *

PALAHNIUK, Volodymir Ivanovich
See PALANCE, Jack

*   *   *

PALANCE, Jack 1919-2006
(Volodymir Ivanovich Palahniuk, Walter Jack Palance)

OBITUARY NOTICE— See index for *CA* sketch: Born February 18, 1919, in Lattimer Mines, PA; died November 10, 2006, in Montecito, CA. Actor, artist, and author. Palance was an Oscar- and Emmy-winning actor known for his performances in such films as *Shane, Sudden Fear,* and *City Slickers.* Growing up in Pennsylvania coal mining country, Palance was born Volodymir Ivanovich Palahniuk. He had no desire to sweat out his life as a miner, and managed to win a football scholarship to the University of North Carolina. He dropped out of college before earning a degree, however, and instead pursued a professional boxing career. Palance did well with a 12-2 record to his credit before deciding that getting beaten up was no way to make a living. By this time, America had entered World War II, and Palance enlisted in the U.S. Army Air Forces. He became a bomber pilot and suf-

fered serious facial injuries after his plane crashed following an engine failure. Honorably discharged, he next attended Stanford University, where he studied to be a journalist and graduated in 1947. It was after the war, too, that he changed his surname to Palance. The *San Francisco Chronicle* hired him as a sports writer, but even with earning extra money as a radio broadcaster Palance wanted a better income. He took a friend's suggestion and traveled to Broadway to see if he could become an actor. This idea met with surprising success, and within a month he was appearing on stage. He was an understudy for Marlon Brando in the famous *A Streetcar Named Desire* production, and in 1950 Palance was praised for his performance in *Darkness at Noon.* That same year, he made his film debut with *Panic in the Street,* where he was credited under the name Walter Palance. Now known as Jack Palance, the actor received Academy Award nominations for his roles in *Sudden Fear* (1952) and *Shane* (1953), and he won an Emmy for playing a boxer in 1956's *Requiem for a Heavyweight.* By this time, Palance had a reputation for playing tough, often unsympathetic roles. His rough exterior concealed a much softer side, however. While shooting spaghetti Westerns in Italy, he became fascinated by the art world that surrounded him, and consequently took up painting. Favoring abstract and impressionistic styles, he became fairly accomplished as a painter and held several exhibits of his work. He also later showed his sensitive side by penning the poetry book *The Forest of Love* (1996). Acting, however, was his main vocation. Focusing mostly on film and television work, Palance would continue to work into his eighties. His television credits include starring roles in the series *The Greatest Show on Earth* (1963-64), *Bronk* (1975-76), and *Ripley's Believe It or Not* (1982-86), and films such as *Hell's Brigade* (1969), *Portrait of a Hitman* (1977), *Young Guns* (1988), *City Slickers* (1991), and *City Slickers II: The Legend of Curly's Gold* (1994). It was for the comedy *City Slickers* that he actually won his first and only Oscar, playing the part of a scary cowboy who whips some soft, urban professionals into shape. Palance wowed audiences during the Oscar ceremony when he did one-handed push-ups on stage to prove he was in top physical condition.

OBITUARIES AND OTHER SOURCES:

PERIODICALS

Chicago Tribune, November 11, 2006, Section 1, p. 10.

Los Angeles Times, November 11, 2006, p. B12.
New York Times, November 11, 2006, p. B10; November 15, 2006, p. A2.
Times (London, England), November 13, 2006, p. 62.

* * *

PALANCE, Walter Jack
      See PALANCE, Jack

* * *

PARADIZ, Valerie 1963-

PERSONAL: Born 1963, in CO; children: Elijah Wapner. Education: City University of New York, Ph.D.

ADDRESSES: Home and office—Woodstock, NY. Office—The Asperger Institute, P.O. Box 55, Woodstock, NY 12498. E-mail—val@valerieparadiz.com.

CAREER: Educator, author, and activist. Instructor in German and writing at Bard College, Brooklyn College, and State University of New York, New Paltz. School for Autistic Strength, Purpose, and Independence in Education (ASPIE), founder and director; speaker on autism and Asperger syndrome; Global Regional Asperger Syndrome Partnership, member of board of directors.

WRITINGS:

Teenage Refugees from Haiti Speak Out, Rosen Publishing Group (New York, NY), 1995.
Elijah's Cup: A Family's Journey into the Community and Culture of High-Functioning Autism and Asperger's Syndrome, Free Press (New York, NY), 2002.
Clever Maids: The Secret History of the Grimm Fairy Tales, Basic Books (New York, NY), 2005.

SIDELIGHTS: Many believe that the stories known as the Grimms' fairy tales are based on peasant fables collected by two German brothers: Jacob and Wilhelm Grimm. Educator and writer Valerie Paradiz casts aside this long-held theory with her book Clever Maids: The Secret History of the Grimm Fairy Tales. In Clever Maids, Paradiz contends that the stories collected by the Brothers Grimm were actually gathered from educated female friends of the German-born brothers. As Paradiz theorizes, Wilhelm Grimm's wife, Dorchen Wild, was the actual creator of the familiar story "Rumplestiltskin," and family friends the Hassenflug twins were the originators of "Puss in Boots" and "Little Red Riding Hood." In her assessment of Clever Maids, Nancy R. Ives wrote in Library Journal that Paradiz's work "will appeal to readers of women's history and literature and to anyone interested in the Grimm tales."

In addition to her expertise in German literature, Paradiz is also an authority on Asperger syndrome, an autism spectrum disorder. As the cofounder and director of education at New York's Open Center for Autism, she works with young adults dealing with their autism by providing educational and leisure programs. Paradiz's knowledge of autism was acquired through her personal experiences as a mother of a high-functioning autistic son, and she chronicles these experiences in Elijah's Cup: A Family's Journey into the Community and Culture of High-Functioning Autism and Asperger's Syndrome. Discussing what it means to be a parent to a high-functioning autistic child, Paradiz also includes current medical findings with regard to the disorder. Kathryn Atwood, in a review for BookPleasures.com, noted that Elijah's Cup "is a must-read for anyone interested in exploring the fascinating world of high-functioning autism."

BIOGRAPHICAL AND CRITICAL SOURCES:

PERIODICALS

Library Journal, February 1, 2005, Nancy R. Ives, review of Clever Maids: The Secret History of the Grimm Fairy Tales, p. 80.

ONLINE

Autism Society of America Web site, http://asa.confex.com/ (January 4, 2007).
BookPleasures.com, http://www.bookpleasures.com/ (January 4, 2007), Kathryn Atwood, review of Elijah's Cup: A Family's Journey into the Community and Culture of High-Functioning Autism.

Omega Institute Web site, http://www.eomega.org/ (January 4, 2007), "Valerie Paradiz."

Open Center for Autism Web site, http://www. aspieschool.org/ (January 4, 2007).

Valerie Paradiz Home Page, http://www.valerie paradiz.com (January 4, 2007).

*   *   *

PARKER, Alison M.
(Alison Marie Parker)

PERSONAL: Education: University of California, Berkeley, B.A., 1988; Johns Hopkins University, M.A., 1990, Ph.D., 1993.

ADDRESSES: Office—History Department, State University of New York College at Brockport, 350 New Campus Dr., Brockport, NY 14420-2914. *E-mail*—aparker@brockport.edu.

CAREER: Writer, educator. State University of New York College at Brockport, NY, associate professor.

AWARDS, HONORS: Ford Foundation Travel Grants for Women's Studies Projects, Johns Hopkins University, 1990, 1991, 1993; dissertation research grant, the Arthur and Elizabeth Schlesinger Library on the History of Women in America, Radcliffe College, 1991; National Endowment for the Humanities Summer Seminar, Stanford University, 2002.

WRITINGS:

Purifying America: Women, Cultural Reform, and Pro-censorship Activism, 1873-1933, University of Illinois Press (Urbana, IL), 1997.

(Editor, with Stephanie Cole) *Women and the Unstable State in Nineteenth-Century America,* introduction by Sarah Barringer Gordon, Texas A&M University Press (College Station, TX), 2000.

(Editor, with Stephanie Cole) *Beyond Black & White: Race, Ethnicity and Gender in the U.S. South and Southwest,* Texas A&M University Press (College Station, TX), 2004.

Contributor of articles to professional journals, including *Journal of Women's History* and *Reviews in American History,* and to books, including *Movie*

Censorship and American Culture, edited by Francis Couvares, Smithsonian Institution Press, 1996; *Votes for Women: A Concise History of the Suffrage Movement,* Oxford University Press, 2002; and *The American Congress: Building of Democracy,* edited by Julian Zelizer, Houghton Mifflin, 2004.

SIDELIGHTS: Alison M. Parker is an American academic and historian whose area of study focuses on issues of gender and race. Her 1997 work, *Purifying America: Women, Cultural Reform, and Pro-censorship Activism, 1873-1933,* examines the effect that women had on censorship. Parker pays particular attention to the role of the Woman's Christian Temperance Union (WCTU) and its Department for the Suppression of Impure Literature, as well as the work of the American Library Association (ALA) in its pro-censorship activities. Both of these organs attempted to control culture at the "point of consumption" and the "point of production," as Kate Wittenstein explained in a *Michigan Historical Review* article. Thus, in addition to mounting campaigns against certain forms of literature, art, ballet, and entertainments such as burlesque, the WCTU also tried to shape young minds with its publications, such as *Young Crusader* and *Oak and Ivy Leaf.* According to Wayne A. Wiegand, writing in *Library Quarterly,* these publications "carried fiction in which adolescent characters manifested what the union thought were appropriate social and moral behaviors." The WCTU also campaigned vigorously to get censorship legislation passed, and their movement was supported by a large section of middle-class and upper-class Americans. The ALA, however, was against such legislation, feeling that laws would deprive them of their professional responsibility of guiding cultural norms through a proper selection of literature. Both the WCTU and the ALA managed to avoid criticism of suppression of free speech by restricting their activities to cultural rather than political arenas. By 1925 the WCTU had also taken on the new movie industry; its Department of Literature was transformed into the Department of Motion Pictures. Wittenstein found Parker's book a "multilayered revisionist account." Wiegand also had qualified praise for Parker's study, noting, "Despite . . . admirable contributions, however, [Parker's] perspectives on librarians are too narrow." Wiegand went on to point out that by 1933 librarians were not of one mind regarding the role of censorship.

Working as editor with Stephanie Cole, Parker produced the 2000 title, *Women and the Unstable State* in *Nineteenth-Century America,* a collection of essays which examine "American women's relationship to electoral politics from 1800 through the end of Reconstruction," as Rebecca Edwards described the book in *Journal of Southern History.* The six essays attempt to demonstrate, Edwards further commented, that "women who tried to exert political power had to surmount the twin obstacles of subordination in marriage and lack of voting rights. Surprisingly, many succeeded." Edwards concluded, "These essays illuminate not only the history of such women, but the broader systems of law, partisanship, and kinship in which they labored." Lee Chambers-Schiller, writing in the *North Carolina Historical Review,* also had praise for the collection, calling it a "volume to savor, an introduction to women's political history for the uninitiated with challenging contributions for those steeped in the literature."

Again working with Cole, Parker edited the 2004 volume *Beyond Black & White: Race, Ethnicity and Gender in the U.S. South and Southwest.* According to Linda W. Reese, writing in the *American Historical Review,* this collection of essays "probes the boundaries and contradictions of the traditional understanding of race in nineteenth and early twentieth-century America as a bifurcation of 'black' and 'white.'" Fay A. Yarbrough, writing in the *Journal of Southern History,* had praise for both Parker and Cole, noting that they "have put together a selection of essays that forces a reconsideration of how historians conceptualize both the American South and the operation of race."

BIOGRAPHICAL AND CRITICAL SOURCES:

PERIODICALS

American Historical Review, April, 2005, Linda W. Reese, review of *Beyond Black & White: Race, Ethnicity and Gender in the U.S. South and Southwest,* p. 462.
Journal of Southern History, February, 2002, Rebecca Edwards, review of *Women and the Unstable State in Nineteenth-Century America,* p. 162; May, 2005, Fay A. Yarbrough, review of *Beyond Black & White,* p. 510.
Library Quarterly, October, 1998, Wayne A. Wiegand, review of *Purifying America: Women, Cultural Reform, and Pro-censorship Activism, 1873-1933,* p. 511.
Michigan Historical Review, spring, 2000, Kate Wittenstein, review of *Purifying America,* p. 165.
North Carolina Historical Review, October, 2001, Lee Chambers-Schiller, review of *Women and the Unstable State in Nineteenth-Century America,* p. 502.

ONLINE

SUNY Brockport Web site, http://www.brockport.edu/ (January 30, 2007), "Faculty Page: Dr. Alison M. Parker."*

*   *   *

PARKER, Alison Marie
    See PARKER, Alison M.

*   *   *

PARKER, Derrick

PERSONAL: Male.

CAREER: Author, 2006—. Former head of New York Police Department special forces unit. Rap-related crime expert, appearing in *Rolling Stone, New York* magazine, *Blender, Vibe, New York Times, Newsday,* and other magazines and newspapers; also appeared on television, including MTV, Fox, VH1, *Unsolved Mysteries,* and CourtTV.

WRITINGS:

(With Matt Diehl) *Notorious C.O.P.: The Inside Story of the Tupac, Biggie, and Jam Master Jay Investigations from the NYPD's First "Hip-Hop Cop,"* St. Martin's Press (New York, NY), 2006.

SIDELIGHTS: "Derrick Parker," wrote Mark Lelinwalla on the Web site *Vibe.com,* "was the Hip Hop Cop, who was put on assignment to monitor and keep tab on all of moves that MCs in the city were making." In *Notorious C.O.P.: The Inside Story of the Tupac, Biggie, and Jam Master Jay Investigations from the NYPD's First "Hip-Hop Cop,"* Parker relates stories drawn from his years keeping track of the violence associated with major rap artists. "I had to earn the respect of the rappers," Parker told Abran Maldonado in an interview on *AllHipHop.com,* "not to go out there and treat them all like criminals; you can't do that in the rap community. I earned their respect and that's why they could come to me and I can go to the people that other cops couldn't approach." Although Parker created a rapport with major rap figures, he failed to win the backing of his colleagues, a writer for *Kirkus Reviews* stated, "giving the impression [in *Notorious C.O.P.*] that he was often fighting a lone battle against hip-hop-related crime." "Full of engaging detail," declared Mike Tribby in his *Booklist* review of the volume, "this is a gritty trip to the nexus of big-money rap and ongoing gang rivalries." "Parker," concluded a *Publishers Weekly* contributor, "proves his assertion that there is a 'seemingly insurmountable divide between the NYPD and the hip-hop world.'"

BIOGRAPHICAL AND CRITICAL SOURCES:

PERIODICALS

Booklist, May 15, 2006, Mike Tribby, review of *Notorious C.O.P.: The Inside Story of the Tupac, Biggie, and Jam Master Jay Investigations from the NYPD's First "Hip-Hop Cop,"* p. 10.

Entertainment Weekly, July 21, 2006, Michael Endelman, Chris Willman, Gilbert Cruz, and Clark Collis, "Chapter and Verse," p. 69.

Kirkus Reviews, May 15, 2006, review of *Notorious C.O.P.,* p. 509.

Library Journal, June 15, 2006, Craig Shufelt, review of *Notorious C.O.P.,* p. 72.

New York Times Book Review, October 1, 2006, Dave Itzkoff, "Music Chronicle."

Publishers Weekly, May 1, 2006, review of *Notorious C.O.P.,* p. 50.

ONLINE

AllHipHop.com, http://www.allhiphop.com/ (January 24, 2007), Abran Maldonado, "Derrick Parker: The Sound of the Police," author interview.

Vibe.com, http://www.vibe.com/ (January 24, 2007), Mark Lelinwalla, "Derrick Parker: Notorious C.O. P.," author interview.*

PARSHALL, Sandra

PERSONAL: Born in SC; married to a journalist.

ADDRESSES: Home—McLean, VA. *Agent*—Jacky Sach, BookEnds LLC, 136 Long Hill Rd., Gilette, NJ 07933. *E-mail*—sparshall@verizon.net.

CAREER: Writer, novelist, and journalist. Worked as a reporter for newspapers, including the *Spartanburg Herald,* Spartanburg, SC, and the *Baltimore Evening Sun,* Baltimore, MD.

WRITINGS:

NOVELS

The Heat of the Moon, Poisoned Pen Press (Scottsdale, AZ), 2006.

Disturbing the Dead, Poisoned Pen Press (Scottsdale, AZ), 2007.

SIDELIGHTS: Mystery writer Sandra Parshall is a reporter and journalist who made her fiction debut with the novel *The Heat of the Moon.* Protagonist Rachel Goddard, a twenty-seven-year-old veterinarian, is content with her career at a clinic in McLean, VA, though her personal life is a bit more rocky. Her relationship with her mother and sister is not as strong as she would like, even though they all still share the same home. When a client rushes in with the family dog, struck by a car, Rachel finds herself comforting the owner's distraught younger daughter. The event brings back a vivid, traumatic memory from her own childhood that she believes has to do with the death of her father, who died when she was very young. These haunting memories and flashbacks become more and more prominent, until Rachel has no choice but to look for answers. Her mother, however, is unwilling to talk about the matter, becoming hostile when pressed. She is encouraged to continue looking for answers by her boss, veterinarian Luke Campbell, with whom she shares a budding romantic relationship. As she struggles against her cold, domineering mother and weak, submissive sister, answers slowly emerge that reveal a troubled past unlike anything Rachel had ever imagined. "For a first novel, this book is surprisingly polished and accomplished—Parshall knows her stuff, and it shows," remarked Hank Wagner on the *Mystery Scene* Web site. *Booklist* critic Jenny McLarin named it a "standout debut that effectively crosses sub-genres," while a reviewer on the *Spinetingler Magazine* Web site found it to be "stunning," "tightly written," and "breathtaking." A *Publishers Weekly* reviewer remarked, "The fresh, mesmerizing plot will keep readers turning the pages to the very end."

Parshall told *CA:* "I have been making up stories and writing them down since I was a child printing words in pencil on a lined tablet. The ability to create an imaginary world has always seemed an irresistible form of magic to me. The starting point is usually in the real world, though— a person, a place, an event captures my attention and I build my own created world around that point of inspiration. I enjoy books that raise psychological or social questions, stories that stay with me long after I've turned the last page, and if I can produce a book that has that effect on readers, while also entertaining them, I will have succeeded as a writer."

BIOGRAPHICAL AND CRITICAL SOURCES:

PERIODICALS

Booklist, March 15, 2006, Jenny McLarin, review of *The Heat of the Moon,* p. 32.
Publishers Weekly, April 10, 2006, review of *The Heat of the Moon,* p. 49.

ONLINE

Mysterious Musings, http://juliabuckley.blogspot.com/ (August 17, 2006), Julia Buckley, interview with Sandra Parshall.
Mystery Scene, http://www.mysteryscenemag.com/ (December 19, 2006), Hank Wagner, review of *The Heat of the Moon.*
Sandra Parshall Home Page, http://www.sandraparshall.com (November 30, 2006).
Spinetingler Magazine, http://www.spinetinglermag.com/ (December 19, 2006), Andrea Maloney, review of *The Heat of the Moon.*

*   *   *

PATON, Bruce C.

PERSONAL: Born in India. *Education:* University of Edinburgh, M.D.

ADDRESSES: Home—Denver, CO. *Office*—5380 E. Mansfield Ave., Denver, CO 80237; fax: 303-692-8225. *E-mail*—cardsurg@comcast.net.

CAREER: Writer, historian, physician, artist, and surgeon. University of Colorado Health Sciences center, clinical professor of surgery; physician in private practice in Denver, CO, now retired. Wilderness Medical Society, former president; Colorado Outward Bound School, former chairman; Given Institute, director, 1999—. *Military service:* Served in the Royal Marine Command (Great Britain); became lieutenant.

MEMBER: American Association for Thoracic Surgery, American Surgical Association, Society for Cardiothoracic Surgeons in Great Britain and Ireland. Fellow of the Royal College of Surgeons of Edinburgh and the Royal College of Physicians of Edinburgh.

WRITINGS:

Lewis & Clark: Doctors in the Wilderness, Fulcrum Publishing (Golden, CO), 2001.
Adventuring with Boldness: The Triumph of the Explorers, Fulcrum Publishing (Golden, CO), 2006.

Contributor of art to books, including *Eric Shipton: Everest and Beyond,* Mountaineers Books, 1998. Has also published 200 medical papers on cardiac surgery, frostbite, hypothermia, and medical history.

SIDELIGHTS: Bruce C. Paton is an author and physician. Born in India, he was educated in Scotland and served as a doctor in Scotland and Kenya before moving to the United States, where he worked as a research fellow in surgery, according to a biographer on the Fulcrum Publishing Web site. Paton is an avid outdoors adventurer who has twice climbed Africa's Mount Kilimanjaro. An expert in wilderness medicine, he cofounded the Wilderness Medical Society and writes on issues related to adventuring and outdoors medicine.

In *Lewis & Clark: Doctors in the Wilderness,* Paton delves into the medical history of the storied Lewis and Clark expedition, examining the state of medical science in the eighteenth century and uncovering facts about the medical care afforded to the members of the expedition as they opened up sections of the American West. Paton recounts the expedition's more prominent medical events and emergencies, and describes how medical care was administered to those who needed it. Notably, Paton concludes that Lewis and Clark, "although minimally trained in the medical arts of the day, were arguably able to assess, diagnose, and treat wilderness illness and injury with as much (if not more) competence as most physicians of the period," observed George W. Rodway in *Wilderness and Environmental Medicine*. Paton "is clearly at his best when employing his expertise as a backcountry medicine expert. Ailments related to altitude and climate—frostbite and heat exhaustion, diet and water deficiencies—these are the areas where Paton competently suggests new ways of looking at old material," remarked Dawn Nickel, writing in *Montana*. "By drawing upon his background as a surgeon and wilderness medicine expert, Dr. Paton has produced a very readable, nontechnical, and often entertaining book," Rodway commented.

Adventuring with Boldness: The Triumph of the Explorers contains Paton's examination of the lives and motivations of nine famous explorers, adventurers, and other bold seekers of the unknown. Some adventurers succeeded wildly while others failed or, at worst, perished, and Paton investigates the characteristics and motivations that separate the two. He focuses on a number of individuals and expeditions from the eighteenth and nineteenth centuries, some more famous than others, including Lewis and Clark, Zebulon Pike, and even the notorious Captain Bligh. He covers the explorers' missions, expedition personnel, accomplishments, and, when necessary, failures. Paton uncovers how success often hinged not on grand schemes and expansive goals, but on attention to small but crucial details. A *Publishers Weekly* reviewer commented that the book has "elements of an accessible textbook and an informative field manual."

BIOGRAPHICAL AND CRITICAL SOURCES:

PERIODICALS

Montana, summer, 2002, Dawn Nickel, review of *Lewis & Clark: Doctors in the Wilderness*.

Publishers Weekly, February 27, 2006, review of *Adventuring with Boldness: The Triumph of the Explorers*, p. 42.
Wilderness and Environmental Medicine, Volume 14, number 1, George W. Rodway, review of *Lewis & Clark*.

ONLINE

Fulcrum Publishing Web site, http://www.fulcrumbooks.com/ (November 30, 2006), biography of Bruce C. Paton.
University of Colorado Health Sciences Center Web site, http://www.uchsc.edu/ (November 30, 2006), biography of Bruce C. Paton.

*   *   *

PATTEN, Fred 1940-

PERSONAL: Born December 11, 1940, in Los Angeles, CA; son of Beverly Walter and Shirley Marie Patten. *Education:* University of California, Los Angeles, B.A., 1962, M.L.S., 1963. *Politics:* Democrat. *Religion:* Roman Catholic.

ADDRESSES: Home—Golden State Colonial Convalescent Hospital, 10830 Oxnard St., North Hollywood, CA 91606. *E-mail*—fredpatten@earthlink.net.

CAREER: Freelance writer and librarian, 1965-69; Hughes Aircraft Co., El Segundo, CA, librarian, 1969-90; Streamline Pictures, Los Angeles, CA, manager, 1991-2002; freelance writer, 2002—.

MEMBER: International Animated Film Society (AS-IFA-Hollywood), Comic Art Professional Society, Los Angeles Science Fantasy Society.

WRITINGS:

(Editor) Trish Ledoux and Doug Ranney, *The Complete Anime Guide: Japanese Animation Video Directory and Resource Guide*, Tiger Mountain Press (Issaquah, WA), 1995.

An Anthropomorphic Bibliography, Yarf! (Cupertino, CA), 1995, 3rd edition, 2000.

(Editor) *Best in Show: Fifteen Years of Outstanding Furry Fiction,* Sofawolf Press (St. Paul, MN), 2003, published as *Furry! The World's Best Anthropomorphic Fiction,* iBooks (New York, NY), 2006.

Watching Anime, Reading Manga: 25 Years of Essays and Reviews, Stone Bridge Press (Berkeley, CA), 2004.

Has also contributed to books, including *Animation Art: From Pencil to Pixel, the History of Cartoon, Anime & CGI,* HarperCollins (New York), 2004; and *The Animated Movie Guide: The Ultimate Illustrated Reference to Cartoon, Stop-Motion, and Computer-Generated Feature Films,* Chicago Review Press (Chicago, IL), 2005. Book reviewer for *Anthro.*

SIDELIGHTS: Fred Patten told *CA:* "I began reading science-fiction magazines in my early teens. I read everything in them; the stories, the editorials, the science fiction book and movie reviews, and the letters from readers. When I became active in science fiction fandom during college, many of the fans were publishing their own fanzines in the format of the professional magazines; with amateur stories, editorials and reviews. I was invited to become a science fiction reviewer for several fanzines, and was soon publishing my own. Within ten years I was writing reviews and articles for newsstand popular-culture magazines, mostly on science fiction. From 1975 to 1977 I was the publisher and coeditor, with Richard Delap of, *Delap's F&SF Review,* a monthly science fiction book review magazine for librarians. My fondness for science fiction led me to discover Japanese science fiction animation in the mid-1970s, and I began specializing in articles about anime and manga for the general public, eventually writing enough to fill a book with them."

*   *   *

PAYTON, B.A.
   See PAYTON, Brian

*   *   *

PAYTON, Brian 1966-
   (B.A. Payton)

PERSONAL: Born April 23, 1966, in Torrance, CA.

ADDRESSES: Home—Vancouver, British Columbia, Canada.

CAREER: Writer, c. 1996—.

AWARDS, HONORS: Lowell Thomas Silver Award for best North American travel essay, Society of American Travel Writers, 2001 and 2003. MacDowell Fellow; three-time winner of Northern Lights Awards for excellence in travel journalism.

WRITINGS:

Hail Mary Corner (novel), Beach Home Publishing (Vancouver, British Columbia, Canada), 2001.
Shadow of the Bear: Travels in Vanishing Wilderness, Bloomsbury/Holtzbrinck Publishers (New York, NY), 2006, published as *In Bear Country,* Old Street Publishing (London, England), 2007.

Contributor to periodicals, including the *New York Times, Los Angeles Times, Chicago Tribune, Boston Globe, Globe and Mail,* and *Canadian Geographic.* Contributor to *Literary Trips 2: Following in the Footsteps of Fame.*

SIDELIGHTS: Brian Payton's *Shadow of the Bear: Travels in Vanishing Wilderness* relates the story of the travel writer's journeys in search of the different species of bear that still survive in the modern world. According to Payton, only eight different ursine species are left: the sloth bear, sun bear, spectacled bear, polar bear, giant panda, brown/grizzly bear, Asiatic black bear, and American black bear. Bear species, Payton finds, "now are disappearing 100 times faster than normal," explained George Cohen in *Booklist,* "because of human activities." At the same time, however, Payton recognizes that loss of habitat (the major threat to the bears' survival) is inevitable in a world where the poorest people have to encroach on bear territory in order to survive themselves. For example, Cambodia presents Payton with a vexing conservation question: 'Just how far are we willing to go?'" declared a *Kirkus Reviews* contributor. "He sees desperately poor people trying to survive; the only land available is sun-bear turf."

For Payton, bears are not merely one of the largest land predators—they are metaphors used universally to evoke the idea of the wilderness. "Bears have inhabited our memories and even our dreams," stated Robert E. Bieder on *globeandmail.com.* "*Shadow of the Bear* is also an exploration of how bears have shaped the psyche of humankind," declared Shelagh Plunkett on the *Bear Matters BC* Web site. "Why do we fear them? Why do we worship them? What makes a sensible person want to pat a carnivorous half-ton polar bear?" "Indeed, it was a dream about a bear that propelled Brian Payton on his journeys, resulting in *Shadow of the Bear,*" Bieder continued. That dream, as interpreted by a Navajo medicine man, concluded a *Publishers Weekly* contributor, told the author that he "has a responsibility to tell his stories in respectful acknowledgment of 'the spirit of the bear.'"

BIOGRAPHICAL AND CRITICAL SOURCES:

PERIODICALS

Booklist, May 15, 2006, George Cohen, review of *Shadow of the Bear: Travels in Vanishing Wilderness,* p. 12.
Canadian Geographic, March, 2001, Rick Boychuk, "Treading Softly in a Grizzly Sanctuary," p. 11.
Kirkus Reviews, May 15, 2006, review of *Shadow of the Bear,* p. 509.
Publishers Weekly, April 24, 2006, review of *Shadow of the Bear,* p. 46.
Vancouver Sun, July 22, 2006, Shelagh Plunkett, "Brian Payton Is Curious, Humble, and Self-Effacing Enough to Make a Good Guide on a Round-the-World Bear-Watching Trip."

ONLINE

Brian Payton Home Page, http://www.brianpayton.com (January 26, 2007), author biography.
globeandmail.com, http://www.globeandmail.com/ (July 15, 2006), Robert E. Bieder, review of *Shadow of the Bear.*

*   *   *

PEARCE, Philippa 1920-2006
  (Ann Philippa Christie)

OBITUARY NOTICE— See index for *CA* sketch: Born January 23, 1920, in Great Shelford, Cambridgeshire, England; died December 21, 2006. Editor and author. Pearce was an award-winning children's book author

famous for her classic 1958 tale, *Tom's Midnight Garden.* Educated at Girton College, Cambridge, where she studied English and history and earned a master's degree in 1942, she then joined the British Civil Service. After World War II, however, she pursued a more pleasurable career as a writer and producer for the school broadcasting department at the British Broadcasting Corporation. While still working for the BBC, she released her first children's title, *Minnow on the Say* (1954), which was published in the United States four years later as *The Minnow Leads to Treasure.* Though it earned a Lewis Carroll Shelf Award, the success of this book was nothing compared to *Tom's Midnight Garden,* a fantasy tale that touched the hearts of millions. It was translated in versions all over the world and adapted several times to television. As with its predecessor, it won another Lewis Carroll Shelf Award, but, in addition, a Carnegie Medal. The popularity of the book was such that Pearce quit her job at the BBC, returning only to part-time work in 1960. She had also worked as an editor in the education department at Clarendon Press for a year, and from 1960 to 1967 she was the editor of children's books for Andre Deutsch. Pearce would publish many more children's tales over the next four decades, including the Whitbread Award-winning *The Battle of Bubble and Squeek* (1978). Among her other works are *What the Neighbours Did, and Other Stories* (1972), *A Picnic for Bunnykins* (1984), *Children of Charlecote* (1989), *The Little White Hen* (1986), and the more recent *The Ghost in Annie's Room* (2000), *The Peddler of Swaffham* (2001), *Familiar and Haunting Collected Stories* (2002), and *Little Gentleman* (2004). Named to the Order of the British Empire for her literary contributions, she reflected on her childhood in the privately printed autobiography *Logbook* (2000).

OBITUARIES AND OTHER SOURCES:

BOOKS

Pearce, Philippa, *Logbook,* privately printed, 2000.

PERIODICALS

Times (London, England), December 21, 2006.

*   *   *

PELTIER, Melissa Jo

PERSONAL: Female.

ADDRESSES: Home—Los Angeles, CA, and Nyack, NY. *Office*—MPH Entertainment, Inc., 1033 N. Hollywood Way, Ste. F, Burbank, CA 91505.

CAREER: Writer, movie producer, television director, and television producer. Producer of films, including (as executive producer), *Men Seeking Women* (also known as *The Bet*), IFM Film Associates, 1997; and (as coexecutive producer), *My Big Fat Greek Wedding,* IFC Films, 2002. Also director, producer, coproducer, executive producer, or coexecutive producer of numerous television shows, including *Dog Whisperer with Cesar Millan,* and films for the History Channel.

WRITINGS:

(With Cesar Millan) *Cesar's Way: The Natural, Everyday Guide to Understanding and Correcting Common Dog Problems,* Harmony Books (New York, NY), 2006.

TELEVISION SHOWS

Abortion Denied: Shattering Young Women's Lives, TBS, 1990.
Scared Silent: Exposing and Ending Child Abuse, ABC, CBS, NBC, and PBS, 1992.
Break the Silence: Kids against Child Abuse, CBS, 1994.
Titanic (contains the segments *"Death of a Dream"* and *"The Legend Lives On"*), Arts and Entertainment, 1994.
Arnold Schwarzenegger: Flex Appeal, Arts and Entertainment, 1996.
(With Susan Berman, Paul Kaufman, and Jim Milio) *Las Vegas* (contains the segments *"Gamble in the Desert"* and *"House of Cards"*), Arts and Entertainment, 1996.
(And coexecutive producer) *Pirates of the Barbary Coast,* History Channel, 1998.
Discovery Channel Eco-Challenge (also known as *Discovery Eco-Challenge Australia*), Discovery Channel, 1998.
Martian Mania: The True Story of "War of the Worlds," Sci-Fi Channel, 1998.
The First Detective, History Channel, 1999.
The History of Sex, History Channel, 1999.
(With Steve Muscarella) *The Inquisition,* History Channel, 1999.

(With Max M. Fletcher) *Founding Fathers,* History Channel, 2000.
Palm Beach: Money, Power, and Privilege, Arts and Entertainment, 2000.
Ghost Ship of the Confederacy, History Channel, 2001.
Gossip: Tabloid Tales, Arts and Entertainment, 2002.
The Roswell Crash: Startling New Evidence, Sci-Fi Channel, 2002.

Also author of the television shows *Sea Tales: The Doomed Voyage of the St. Louis,* (with Christopher Meindl), c. 1999; *Sea Tales: Lusitania, Murder on the Atlantic,* (with Kelly McPherson), c. 1999; *The New Roswell: Kecksburg Exposed,* 2003; *Nightwaves,* 2003; and *The True Story of Hannibal,* 2005. Contributing writer of segments for *Dog Whisperer with Cesar Millan.* 2006.

SIDELIGHTS: Melissa Jo Peltier has written for and produced numerous television shows, including the popular *Dog Whisperer with Cesar Millan.* Peltier also teamed with Millan to write *Cesar's Way: The Natural, Everyday Guide to Understanding and Correcting Common Dog Problems.* The book sets forth Millan's unique approach to dog training, with an emphasis on problem dogs and on the foibles of the humans who can't control them. The book also recounts Millan's humble beginnings in Mexico, where he worked on a farm and learned about pack behavior among dogs. The authors write about Millan's successes in rehabilitating dogs and some of his failures. The book includes numerous photographs depicting dogs in their various states, such as dogs in submissive or aggressive states. Writing in the *New York Times Book Review,* Liesl Schillinger noted that the book includes tales about "the pets of [Millan's] famous clientele to illustrate his precepts." Rachel Quagliariello, writing on *HollywoodJesus.com,* commented: "Every word in this book is evidence of Cesar's love for nature and animals." Quagliariello added: "If you have a dog, or you're considering adoption, *Cesar's Way* will challenge you to count the cost." In a review on the *Fun with Dead Trees* Web site, a contributor called the book "compelling" and noted: "If you have a dog or are thinking about getting one, *Cesar's Way* . . . is definitely worth checking out."

BIOGRAPHICAL AND CRITICAL SOURCES:

BOOKS

Contemporary Theatre, Film and Television, Volume 49, Thomson Gale (Detroit, MI), 2003.

PERIODICALS

Bookseller, August 4, 2006, "Hodder Wins Dog Whisperer," p. 11.

New York Times Book Review, February 26, 2006, Liesl Schillinger, review of *Cesar's Way: The Natural, Everyday Guide to Understanding and Correcting Common Dog Problems.*

ONLINE

Fun with Dead Trees, http://kapgar.typepad.com/fwdt/ (January 24, 2007), review of *Cesar's Way.*

HollywoodJesus.com, http://www.hollywoodjesus.com/ (January 24, 2007), Rachel Quagliariello, review of *Cesar's Way.*

Internet Movie Database, http://www.imdb.com/ (January 24, 2007), information on author's film and television work.*

*   *   *

PEYTON, John 1919-2006

(John Wynne William Peyton, John Peyton, Baron of Yeovil)

OBITUARY NOTICE— See index for *CA* sketch: Born February 13, 1919, in England; died November 22, 2006. Politician and author. Peyton was a conservative minister during the government of Britain's Prime Minister Edward Heath. A law student at Trinity College, Oxford, his education was interrupted by World War II. Peyton enlisted in the 15th/19th Hussars, but was captured in Belgium in 1940. He spent the rest of the duration as a prisoner of war. After the Americans liberated his prison camp in 1945, Peyton returned home and completed a master's degree at Trinity. Called to the Bar of the Inner Temple, he spent a year in India assisting with the transfer of power of this former part of the British Empire. Back in England again, he worked as a broker and then sought office on the Conservative ticket. He subsequently won the 1950 election for the Yeovil seat in Parliament. During his political career, Peyton held a variety of seats, including service in the Ministry of Defense, as secretary of the Ministry of Power in the early 1960s, and as minister of Transport Industries in the early 1970s. When the Conservatives lost power in 1974, Peyton was a candidate for prime minister, though no one, not even he, thought he had a serious chance at the office. He continued in Parliament as opposition spokesman for agriculture, a position of little prominence, and quit government work for good in 1979. Peyton then focused on the business world. He was United Kingdom chair of Texas Instruments from 1974 to 1990, and was also director for Alcan Aluminum from 1985 to 1991. A big supporter of the London Zoo, he served as the treasurer of the Zoological Society of London from 1984 to 1991 and was chair of Zoo Operations Ltd. from 1988 to 1991. Peyton reflected on his life in the autobiography *Without Benefit of Laundry* (1997) and was also the author of *Solly Zuckerman: A Scientist Out of the Ordinary* (2001).

OBITUARIES AND OTHER SOURCES:

BOOKS

Peyton, John, *Without Benefit of Laundry,* Bloomsbury (London, England), 1997.

PERIODICALS

Times (London, England), November 24, 2006, p. 79.

*   *   *

PEYTON, John, Baron of Yeovil
See PEYTON, John

*   *   *

PEYTON, John Wynne William
See PEYTON, John

*   *   *

PHILLIPS, Julie

PERSONAL: Born in Seattle, WA; married (husband a translator); children: two.

ADDRESSES: Home—Amsterdam, Netherlands. *E-mail*—jp@julie-phillips.com.

CAREER: Writer. *Seattle Weekly,* Seattle, WA, reporter; *Village Voice,* New York, NY, reporter.

AWARDS, HONORS: National Book Critics Circle Award, National Book Critics Circle, *Salon.com* best nonfiction books citation, *New York Times* notable book, best book of the year citations, *Publishers Weekly, Kansas City Star, Seattle Times, Washington Post,* and *Times Literary Supplement,* all 2006, all for *James Tiptree, Jr.: The Double Life of Alice B. Sheldon.*

WRITINGS:

James Tiptree, Jr.: The Double Life of Alice B. Sheldon (biography), St. Martin's Press (New York, NY), 2006.

Contributor of articles to periodicals, including *Newsday, Interview, Ms., Voice Literary Supplement,* and *Mademoiselle.*

SIDELIGHTS: Julie Phillips's biography *James Tiptree, Jr.: The Double Life of Alice B. Sheldon* recounts the story of one of the great science fiction writers of the twentieth century. The book, according to Matthew Cheney on the *Strange Horizons* Web site, "is an extraordinarily well-crafted study of an extraordinary life—the life of a woman who traveled to Africa as a child with her high-society parents, worked for the U.S. government during World War II, published a story in the *New Yorker,* analyzed intelligence for the CIA in its early days, earned a Ph.D. in experimental psychology, and then wrote science fiction stories under the name 'James Tiptree, Jr.,' an identity she would keep secret from the world at large for years, even as she gained more and more notice as a significant writer." "Artist, CIA operative, gender-bending literary seductress with a Hemingwayesque alter-ego," Elizabeth Hand wrote in a *Magazine of Fantasy and Science Fiction* review, "Sheldon insured there'd be no Hollywood ending when, in a suicide pact, she murdered her elderly husband, then shot herself in their suburban home."

From 1967 to 1977, Alice Bradley Sheldon, writing as Tiptree, produced some of the most innovative speculative fiction in the history of the genre, before her identity was revealed. Nonetheless, her opus helped redefine her chosen genre in the 1970s—and it did so in a way that surprised everyone. "When Tiptree was unmasked, Sheldon was 61," Susanna J. Sturgis revealed in the *Women's Review of Books.* "Science fiction was widely thought to be a young man's game, then one of its giants turned out to be a woman who produced her entire oeuvre in her fifties and sixties. And everyone who assumed Tiptree was a man—based not only on the author's name but on the style and subjects of the stories and what was known of the author's life—had some rethinking to do about gender."

Phillips's biography also reveals that Sheldon herself was deeply conflicted about her own gender and sexual identity. Working from personal letters (Sheldon maintained an extensive correspondence, under her own name as well as under both the Tiptree pseudonym and as Raccoona Sheldon, with other science fiction writers), Phillips reconstructs the ways in which the author dealt with her sexuality and her understanding of the role of women in twentieth-century society. "She was an enthusiastic supporter of second-wave feminism," explained Laura Miller in a review for *Salon.com,* "who joined NOW and subscribed to *Ms.* Magazine from the outset. She started and abandoned several sympathetic treatises on the dilemma of women, especially those women with 'atypical' ambitions and desires." Fellow female science fiction writer Joanna Russ, Miller wrote, "who came out of the closet as a lesbian during her epistolary friendship with Tiptree, received Sheldon's confession of similar yearnings: 'I *like* some men a lot, but from the start, before I knew anything, it was always girls and women who lit me up.'"

Reviewers celebrated Phillips's accomplishment in documenting and revealing Sheldon's life. "With painstaking research, frequent quotes from Sheldon's letters (as Tiptree and not), and respectful but thorough attention to motives and emotions," declared Russ Allbery on *Eyrie.org,* "she has recorded the story of a person in all of her flaws, triumphs, and bright-edged tragedy." "In assembling such a cohesive account of Sheldon's life," Dave Itzkoff wrote in the *New York Times Book Review,* "Phillips has produced a kind of photo-negative of an archetypal Tiptree story: instead of scrupulously withholding details from the reader until the last possible moment, she doles them out generously, without excessive editorializing or undue reverence for her subject. Yet her writing achieves its own kind of narrative tension," Itzkoff concluded, "a spell that obliges even the readers already clued in to Tiptree's secret to turn the book's pages with increasing suspense as they wait for its real-life inhabitants to catch up with them."

BIOGRAPHICAL AND CRITICAL SOURCES:

PERIODICALS

Booklist, June 1, 2006, Carl Hays, review of *James Tiptree, Jr.: The Double Life of Alice B. Sheldon,* p. 29.

Entertainment Weekly, August 18, 2006, Jennifer Reese, "Male Delivery," p. 142.

Kirkus Reviews, May 15, 2006, review of *James Tiptree, Jr.,* p. 510.

Los Angeles Times Book Review, December 3, 2006, Gavin Grant, "Julie Phillips on James Tiptree, Jr."

Magazine of Fantasy and Science Fiction, October-November, 2006, Elizabeth Hand, review of *James Tiptree, Jr.,* p. 40.

New York Times Book Review, August 20, 2006, Dave Itzkoff, "Alice's Alias," p. 1.

Publishers Weekly, March 20, 2006, review of *James Tiptree, Jr.,* p. 44.

Seattle Times Book Review, August 4, 2006, Nisi Shawl, review of *James Tiptree, Jr.*

Women's Review of Books, November-December, 2006, Susanna J. Sturgis, "The Man Who Didn't Exist," p. 3.

ONLINE

Bookforum, http://www.bookforum.com/ (March 14, 2007), Carter Scholz, "Invisible Man: A New Biography Explores the Woman Who was James Tiptree, Jr."

Julie Phillips Home Page, http://www.julie-phillips.com (January 26, 2007), author biography.

Eyrie.org, http://www.eyrie.org/ (January 26, 2007), Russ Allbery, review of *James Tiptree, Jr.*

Salon.com, http://www.salon.com/ (January 26, 2007), Laura Miller, "Stranger Than Science Fiction."

SciFi.com, http://www.scifi.com/ (January 26, 2007), John Joseph Adams, "Biography Unveils Tiptree/Sheldon."

Strange Horizons, http://www.strangehorizons.com/ (January 26, 2007), Matthew Cheney, "Interview: Julie Phillips."

*   *   *

PHILLIPS, Lisa A.

PERSONAL: Married Bill Mead; children: Clara.

ADDRESSES: Home—Woodstock, NY. *Agent*—Jennie Dunham, Dunham Literacy, Inc., 156 5th Ave., Ste. 625, New York, NY 10010-7002. *E-mail*—mail@lisaaphillips.com.

CAREER: Writer, journalist, educator, and broadcaster. State University of New York at New Paltz, professor of journalism. Has worked as reporter and announcer for numerous public radio stations throughout the United States.

AWARDS, HONORS: New York Foundation for the Arts fiction award, 2002; National Society for Arts and Letters Pittsburgh chapter award; Scott Turow award; Edward R. Murrow Award (four-time recipient); New York Festival Award; Associated Press honors; honors from *Communicator.*

WRITINGS:

Public Radio: Behind the Voices, CDS Books (New York, NY), 2006.

Contributor to periodicals, including the *New York Times.*

SIDELIGHTS: Writer, broadcaster, and journalist Lisa A. Phillips is a professor of journalism and an avid supporter of public radio, having worked at six different public radio stations in five states. In her book, *Public Radio: Behind the Voices,* Phillips explores the diverse people and personalities behind the eclectic programming found on America's public radio stations. She "provides an excellent, incredibly thorough look at most of the NPR personalities," commented Scott Butki in an interview with Phillips on

Blogcritics. "She describes what it is like to meet some of these people, what their insecurities are about their voices and abilities, and relays anecdote after anecdote that are hilarious and revealing."

"There's something to the relationship listeners have with public radio hosts that goes beyond simply the voice that delivers the news, etc., and I wanted to take that relationship further," Phillips told Butki. In forty-three profiles underscored by in-depth interviews, Phillips looks at the career path, broadcast experience, and distinctive features of public radio hosts who specialize in music, news, analysis, entertainment, and commentary. She covers individuals such as public radio pioneer Susan Stamberg; talk show host Tavis Smiley; the Magliozzi brothers, who host the popular automotive help program "Car Talk"; Ira Glass, known for his commentary and on-air essays from "This American Life"; "Prairie Home Companion" humorist and raconteur Garrison Keillor; musician and "Piano Jazz" host Marian McPartland; journalist and news commentator Nina Totenberg; and many others. A *Publishers Weekly* contributor observed: "Phillips is a gifted journalist, able to draw out her subjects' vibrant presence on the printed page." *Booklist* reviewer Vanessa Bush concluded, "Public radio fans will enjoy this personal look at their favorite personalities."

Phillips told *CA:* "I started out as a fiction writer. Though I couldn't seem to publish much fiction, understanding story form has been key to my approach to *Public Radio* and my reporting career. I look for the best stories from my sources, knowing that they are what makes the reader keep reading.

"I know from my years in public radio that listeners have a connection to public radio hosts that goes beyond simply listening to the news. Listeners are intensely curious about public radio people and want to know about their lives. My book reveals that the lives of public radio hosts have many of the qualities of the radio they bring to us. Their personal stories are fascinating and significant—stories that enlarge our sense of history and humanity."

BIOGRAPHICAL AND CRITICAL SOURCES:

PERIODICALS

Booklist, May 15, 2006, Vanessa Bush, review of *Public Radio: Behind the Voices,* p. 12.

Publishers Weekly, February 13, 2006, *Public Radio,* p. 78.

ONLINE

Blogcritics, http://www.blogcritics.org/ (September 6, 2006), Scott Butki, interview with Lisa A. Phillips.
Public Radio: Behind the Voices Web site, http://www.publicradiobehindthevoices.com (November 30, 2006), biography of Lisa A. Phillips.

*   *   *

PIPER, Karen Lynnea 1965-

PERSONAL: Born 1965. *Education:* Earned an M.A.; University of Oregon, Ph.D., 1996.

ADDRESSES: Home—Columbia, MO. *Office*—Department of English, University of Missouri-Columbia, 107 Tate Hall, Columbia, MO 65211-1500. *E-mail*—piperk@missouri.edu.

CAREER: University of Missouri-Columbia, associate professor of English.

AWARDS, HONORS: Sierra Nature Writing Award, 1996; National Endowment of the Humanities grant, 2000; Huntington fellowship, 2000-01.

WRITINGS:

Cartographic Fictions: Maps, Race, and Identity, Rutgers University Press (New Brunswick, NJ), 2002.
Left in the Dust: How Race and Politics Created a Human and Environmental Tragedy in L.A., Palgrave Macmillan (New York, NY), 2006.

Contributor to journals, including *Cultural Critique, American Indian Quarterly, MELUS,* and *Postcolonial Literatures: Expanding the Canon.*

SIDELIGHTS: Karen Lynnea Piper is a member of the English department faculty at the University of Missouri at Columbia. *Cartographic Fictions: Maps,*

Race, and Identity, Piper's first book, looks at the ways in which mapping and cartographic techniques can be affected by gender and race. Eric H. Ash, in a review for *Isis,* noted that the book "provides a valuable analysis of the role played by modern cartographic technologies," adding that "Piper's writing is generally lucid, engaging, and free of jargon." Geoffrey Stacks, writing for *Modern Fiction Studies,* stated that Piper's effort "makes a strong case for the map as an essential tool of power both for the colonizer and the colonized."

In *Left in the Dust: How Race and Politics Created a Human and Environmental Tragedy in L.A.,* Piper looks at a toxic dust problem in Los Angeles and the environmental discrimination it revealed. When Owens Lake was drained in the diversion of a river, the result was a dust bowl that produced toxic wind and polluted air—air that Piper herself grew up breathing. Donna Seaman, writing for *Booklist,* remarked: "Global concerns about the increase in windblown dust make Piper's hard-hitting report especially significant."

BIOGRAPHICAL AND CRITICAL SOURCES:

PERIODICALS

Booklist, July 1, 2006, Donna Seaman, review of *Left in the Dust: How Race and Politics Created a Human and Environmental Tragedy in L.A.,* p. 14.
Choice, December, 2002, G.J. Martin, review of *Cartographic Fictions: Maps, Race, and Identity,* p. 683.
International History Review, December, 2003, Norman Etherington, review of *Cartographic Fictions,* p. 994.
Isis, March, 2004, Eric H. Ash, review of *Cartographic Fictions,* p. 134.
Kirkus Reviews, June 1, 2006, review of *Left in the Dust,* p. 562.
Modern Fiction Studies, summer, 2004, Geoffrey Stacks, review of *Cartographic Fictions,* pp. 526-528.
Publishers Weekly, May 15, 2006, review of *Left in the Dust,* p. 59.

ONLINE

College of DuPage Web site, http://www.cod.edu/ (January 30, 2007), Heart of Darkness lecture series speaker biography.
University of Missouri-Columbia English Department Web site, http://english.missouri.edu/ (January 30, 2007), faculty biography.

*   *   *

PITT, William
See PITT, William Rivers

*   *   *

PITT, William Rivers 1971-
(William Pitt)

PERSONAL: Born 1971, in Washington, DC; son of Charles Redding Pitt (a politician). *Education:* Graduated from Holy Cross College.

ADDRESSES: Home—Cambridge, MA.

CAREER: Writer, editor, journalist, educator, political activist, and political commentator. Progressive Democrats of America, editorial director. Worked as a high school teacher for several years. Political analyst, Institute for Public Accuracy; former managing editor and senior writer, currently contributor, *Truthout.org.* Press secretary for the presidential campaign of Dennis Kucinich, 2004.

WRITINGS:

(With Scott Ritter) *War on Iraq: What Team Bush Doesn't Want You to Know,* Context Books (New York, NY), 2002.
The Greatest Sedition Is Silence: Four Years in America, Pluto Press (Sterling, VA), 2003.
Our Flag, Too: The Paradox of Patriotism, Context Books (New York, NY), 2003.
House of Ill Repute: Reflections on War, Lies, and America's Ravaged Reputation, PoliPointPress (Sausalito, CA), 2006.

Author of blog *Pitt Stop.*

SIDELIGHTS: William Rivers Pitt is a left-wing political analyst and writer who has been outspoken in his criticism of U.S. president George W. Bush and the 2003 military invasion of Iraq. He is the editorial director of Progressive Democrats of America, and is a contributor to the liberal Web site *Truthout.org*.

In 2002, Pitt collaborated with Scott Ritter on the book *War on Iraq: What Team Bush Doesn't Want You to Know*. Ritter, a former weapons inspector for the United Nations, claimed that Iraq had no nuclear weapons capabilities, and that a U.S.-led invasion was unnecessary and unjustified. His remarks took on extra significance because he had supported Bush in the presidential election of 2000. Ritter and Pitt clearly outline the positive and negative aspects of War in Iraq, and make it clear that there is no justification for the war based on Iraq's alleged possession of weapons of mass destruction—Iraq has no such weapons, the authors state. In an interview on *BuzzFlash.com*, Pitt related his assertion that the War in Iraq and continued American presence in the Middle East has little to do with defusing weapons or installing democracy, but is instead centered around U.S. oil interests and the desire to increase American influence and control of Middle Eastern oil.

Pitt continues his criticism of the Bush administration and its policies in *The Greatest Sedition Is Silence: Four Years in America*, published in 2003. A reviewer for *Publishers Weekly* described Pitt as "an angry leftist" who airs his complaints about Bush and his administration, the media, and the influence of corporate oil interests on policymaking. The reviewer noted that many of Pitt's remarks are "too far off-center and inflammatory for the majority of even those who oppose the president," and stated that his extreme views undercut his "more salient complaints." However, *Ecologist* reviewer David Mitchell observed that Pitt "does not shy away from confronting the issues" of American politics, media acquiescence to White House pressure, corporate scandals, disastrous public policies, continued erosion of privacy and personal liberty, and poorly justified military actions.

BIOGRAPHICAL AND CRITICAL SOURCES:

PERIODICALS

Ecologist, September, 2003, David Mitchell, review of *The Greatest Sedition Is Silence: Four Years in America*, p. 61.

Los Angeles Times Book Review, November 3, 2002, Andrew Cockburn, review of *War on Iraq: What Team Bush Doesn't Want You to Know*, p. R3.

New Statesman, October 7, 2002, review of *War on Iraq*, p. 22.

Publishers Weekly, October 7, 2002, review of *War on Iraq*, p. 22; April 28, 2003, review of *The Greatest Sedition Is Silence*, p. 58.

ONLINE

BuzzFlash.com, http://www.buzzflash.com/ (September 25, 2002), "William Rivers Pitt, Essayist and Author of *War on Iraq*," interview with William Rivers Pitt.

Truthout, http://www.truthout.org (January 2, 2007).*

* * *

POMFRET, John 1961(?)-

PERSONAL: Born c. 1961, in Milwaukee, WI; married (wife is an interpreter); children: two. *Education:* Stanford University, B.A., M.A.; attended Nanjing University, China, c. 1981-82.

ADDRESSES: Office—Washington Post, P.O. Box 17370, Arlington, VA 22216.

CAREER: Journalist and writer. *Washington Post*, Washington, DC, beginning 1991—, bureau chief in Beijing, China, 1998-2003, Los Angeles bureau chief, c. 2003—. Previously reported for the Associated Press; worked as a bartender in Paris, France.

AWARDS, HONORS: Fulbright scholar at Singapore's Institute of Southeast Asian Studies, 1983-84; Osborne Elliott Award for Excellence in Asian Journalism, Asia Society, 2003; Alicia Patterson Journalism fellowship, 2004.

WRITINGS:

Chinese Lessons: Five Classmates and the Story of the New China, H. Holt (New York, NY), 2006.

SIDELIGHTS: Journalist John Pomfret, who worked for many years as a foreign correspondent in China and other Asian countries, was one of the first Westerners to attend Nanjing University in early 1981. In his book, *Chinese Lessons: Five Classmates and the Story of the New China,* the author examines three decades of Chinese history through the lives of five former classmates at Nanjing University, as well as through his own personal observations and diaries. In his story, the author tells how some of his five classmates—who were children of parents caught up in the political purges directed by the Chinese leader Mao as part of the Great Leap Forward and also the Cultural Revolution—witnessed the deaths of their own parents and were sometimes forced to act as accomplices with the Chinese government in their arrests and convictions. "It's his detailed reporting about their lives before and after graduation . . . that sets this book apart," noted a *Kirkus Reviews* contributor, who went on to refer to *Chinese Lessons* as "a moving account of individual experiences." Orville Schell, writing in the *New York Times Book Review,* called the book "a highly personal, honest, funny and well-informed account of China's hyperactive effort to forget its past and reinvent its future." Orville added: "What makes this book particularly rewarding is that Pomfret not only describes China today, he also reminds us what came before." A *Publishers Weekly* contributor noted that the author's "palpable and pithy first-hand depiction . . . offers a swift, elucidating introduction to [China's] awesome energies and troubling contradictions."

BIOGRAPHICAL AND CRITICAL SOURCES:

BOOKS

Pomfret, John, *Chinese Lessons: Five Classmates and the Story of the New China,* H. Holt (New York, NY), 2006.

PERIODICALS

Booklist, August 1, 2006, Steven Schroeder, review of *Chinese Lessons,* p. 34.
Entertainment Weekly, August 11, 2006, Brian Palmer, review of *Chinese Lessons,* p. 72.
Kirkus Reviews, June 15, 2006, review of *Chinese Lessons,* p. 623.

Library Journal, August 1, 2006, Charles Hayford, review of *Chinese Lessons,* p. 104.
New York Times Book Review, August 6, 2006, Orville Schell, review of *Chinese Lessons.*
New York Times, August 4, 2006, William Grimes, review of *Chinese Lessons.*
Publishers Weekly, June 19, 2006, review of *Chinese Lessons,* p. 57.
Washington Monthly, November, 2006, T.A. Frank, review of *Chinese Lessons,* p. 43.

ONLINE

Asia Pacific Business Outlook 2006, http://www.apbo2006.com/ (January 25, 2007), brief profile of author.
Asia Society Web site, http://www.asiasociety.org/ (February 25, 2004), "Asia Society Announces Winner of the Osborn Elliott Prize for Excellence in Asian Journalism."
China Digital Times, http://chinadigitaltimes.net/ (July 24, 2006), Sophie Beach, "CDT Bookshelf: Interview with John Pomfret."
Frontline Web site, http://www.pbs.org/ (January 25, 2007), "Interview with John Pomfret."
John Pomfret Home Page, http://www.johnpomfret.net (January 25, 2007).
Leigh Bureau Web site, http://www.leighbureau.com/ (January 25, 2007), profile of author.
Prince Roy's Realm, http://www.princeroy.org/ (September 12, 2006), review of *Chinese Lessons.**

* * *

PONCE de LEON, Charles L.

PERSONAL: Education: University of California at Santa Barbara, B.A., 1981, Rutgers University, Ph.D., 1992.

ADDRESSES: Office—Purchase College, 735 Anderson Hill Rd., 2008 HUM Building, Purchase, NY 10577. *E-mail*—charles.poncedeleon@purchase.edu.

CAREER: Princeton University, Princeton, NJ, lecturer, 1992-94; State University of New York, Purchase College, Purchase, NY, assistant professor, 1994-2001, associate professor of history, 2001—.

AWARDS, HONORS: Smithsonian Institution fellow-ship, 1988-89; junior faculty development award, 1998-99.

WRITINGS:

NONFICTION

Self-Exposure: Human-Interest Journalism and the Emergence of Celebrity in America, 1890-1940, University of North Carolina Press (Chapel Hill, NC), 2002.
Fortunate Son: The Life of Elvis Presley, Hill & Wang (New York, NY), 2006.

Contributor to *The Airplane and American Culture,* edited by Domenic J. Pisano, Smithsonian Institution Press (Washington, DC), 1996.

SIDELIGHTS: Charles L. Ponce de Leon explored the nature of celebrity in his first book, *Self-Exposure: Human-Interest Journalism and the Emergence of Celebrity in America, 1890-1940.* In his next book, *Fortunate Son: The Life of Elvis Presley,* he brought his insight to the life of one of America's most famous celebrities.

Discussing the emergence of celebrity in an interview with Scott McLemee for the *Chronicle of Higher Education,* Ponce de Leon stated that in the period between 1890 and 1940, journalism changed significantly in its treatment of human-interest stories. During the 1890s, stories that took a human-interest perspective were often omitted altogether from major newspapers, or were very limited. By 1940, however, the human-interest angle of news reporting had crept into almost every area of magazine and newspaper journalism. This created many new opportunities for people who had not really done anything newsworthy, but who hoped to promote themselves in some way. The era of celebrity was emerging, but along with the advantages for those who sought media attention, there was the drawback of having their personal lives violated in ways they would not have asked for. Ponce de Leon commented to McLemee: "Today you find a coexistence of forms that seemingly shouldn't coexist in one culture. . . . publications that claim, . . . to present the real selves of celebrities. . . . And

alongside them, there will be accounts that are all about . . . the idea that everyone is manipulating everyone else."

Reviewing *Self-Exposure* for *Hedgehog Review,* Andrew Witmer stated that Ponce de Leon "masterfully illuminates" the emergence of celebrity. He went on to say that the author makes two important points: "First, he shows that American fascination with celebrities is best understood in light of the social and economic developments associated with modernity. Second, he demonstrates that even seemingly superficial reporting about celebrities carried powerful ideas about matters as fundamental as human identity, the good life, politics, race relations, class status, and gender roles."

Ponce de Leon's biography of Elvis Presley begins with the singer's childhood and upbringing in the South. The first half of the book recounts his rise to fame, while the second goes over his years on the top and his descent into depression, multiple addictions, and death. He shows how Elvis's celebrity made it impossible for him to live a normal life, and how it also thwarted his artistic ambitions. Though the material reveals nothing new, *Fortunate Son* is "well written, fast-paced, and accurate," commented Dave Szatmary in *Library Journal.* Another favorable review came from a *Kirkus Reviews* writer, who acknowledged that while Elvis's story has been frequently told, Ponce de Leon "retells it well, with respect for his subject and the working-class Southern culture."

BIOGRAPHICAL AND CRITICAL SOURCES:

PERIODICALS

Booklist, July 1, 2006, Benjamin Segedin, review of *Fortunate Son: The Life of Elvis Presley,* p. 19.
Chronicle of Higher Education, September 13, 2002, Scott McLemee, interview with Charles L. Ponce de Leon.
Hedgehog Review, spring, 2005, Andrew Witmer, review of *Self-Exposure: Human-Interest Journalism and the Emergence of Celebrity in America,* p. 88.
Journalism History, winter, 2003, Joseph Bernt, review of *Self-Exposure,* p. 198.

eriodicals

Kirkus Reviews, June 1, 2006, review of *Fortunate Son,* p. 563.

Library Journal, June 15, 2006, Dave Szatmary, review of *Fortunate Son,* p. 72.

Washington Post Book World, August 20, 2006, Joe Heim, review of *Fortunate Son,* p. 9.

ONLINE

Elvis Information Network, http://www.elvisinfonet. com (February 8, 2007), Susan MacDougall, review of *Fortunate Son.*

*　　*　　*

PONZEK, Debra

PERSONAL: Married Gregory Addonizio; children: Remy (daughter), Cole, Gray (sons).

CAREER: Writer and chef. Aux Délices (a restaurant and catering business), Riverside, CT, owner and operator. Montrachet Restaurant, New York, NY, former executive chef.

AWARDS, HONORS: Rising Star Chef of the Year award, James Beard Foundation; Chef of the Year award, Chefs of America; Ten Best New Chefs distinction, *Food & Wine* magazine.

WRITINGS:

(With Joan Schwartz) *French Food, American Accent: Debra Ponzek's Spirited Cuisine,* Clarkson Potter (New York, NY), 1996.

(With Geralyn Delaney Graham) *The Summer House Cookbook: Easy Recipes for When You Have Better Things to Do with Your Time,* Clarkson Potter (New York, NY), 2003.

The Family Kitchen: Easy and Delicious Recipes for Parents and Kids to Make and Enjoy Together, Clarkson Potter (New York, NY), 2006.

SIDELIGHTS: Chef, food writer, and cookbook author Debra Ponzek is an entrepreneur and owner of Aux Délices, a restaurant and catering business in Riverside, Connecticut, and other locations throughout the state. In addition to her food service business, Ponzek and her staff also offer cooking classes and instruction for both adults and children. Ponzek further stresses the connection between adults and kids in her cookbook, *The Family Kitchen: Easy and Delicious Recipes for Parents and Kids to Make and Enjoy Together.* In the book, Ponzek offers 125 recipes that can involve even the youngest children, and which also provide ways in which parents and kids can interact and bond while creating tasty dishes for all to enjoy. The recipes are "simple," but "they are not dumbed down," remarked Judith Sutton, writing in *Library Journal.* Ponzek includes meals for breakfast, lunch, and dinner, and structures the instructions in such a way that children will learn valuable lessons about kitchen safety, food preparation, and cooking techniques. Dishes include golden gazpacho, grilled shrimp satay with ginger and lime, grilled spicy red snapper tacos, double hot chocolate with homemade marshmallows, and patchwork apple pie. "Ponzek's experience as a chef and mother assures that each dish is homey yet sophisticated," observed a *Publishers Weekly* reviewer.

The Summer House Cookbook: Easy Recipes for When You Have Better Things to Do with Your Time, by Ponzek and coauthor Geralyn Delaney Graham, includes quick, easy recipes intended for vacations, relaxation times, and other times when warmer weather discourages kitchen work and more attractive summertime activities vie for attention. The authors offer readers "simple but generally sophisticated recipes for those lazy summer days," commented Sutton in another *Library Journal* review.

BIOGRAPHICAL AND CRITICAL SOURCES:

PERIODICALS

House Beautiful, August, 2006, Devon S. Fredericks, "Cookbook: Does American Home-Style Cooking Really Mean Opening a Can? Our Reviewer Weighs a Top-Selling Cookbook against Debra Ponzek's Much Healthier *The Family Kitchen,*" review of *The Family Kitchen: Easy and Delicious Recipes for Parents and Kids to Make and Enjoy Together,* p. 48.

Library Journal, April 15, 2003, Judith Sutton, review of *The Summer House Cookbook: Easy Recipes for When You Have Better Things to Do with Your Time,* p. 117; February 15, 2006, Judith Sutton, review of *The Family Kitchen,* p. 143.

Parenting, May 1, 2002, Rosemary Black, "Four-Star Family Meals: Three Noted Chefs Share Their Favorite Recipes for Cooking with Their Kids," profile of Debra Ponzek, p. 170.

Publishers Weekly, February 27, 2006, review of *The Family Kitchen,* p. 54.

Redbook, March, 1999, Tamara Holt, "School-Night Gourmet (Save Time with Packaged Foods)," p. 152.

ONLINE

Aux Délices Foods Web site, http://www.auxdelices foods.com/ (November 30, 2006), biography of Debra Ponzek.*

*　　　*　　　*

PORTMAN, Frank 1964-
　(Dr. Frank)

PERSONAL: Born 1964; married. *Education:* Obtained degree.

ADDRESSES: Home—CA. *E-mail*—mail@frank portman.com.

CAREER: Musician and writer. Mr. T Experience, Berkeley, CA, founding member, singer, songwriter, guitarist, 1985—. Recordings include *Everybody's Entitled to Their Own Opinion,* 1986, *Night Shift at the Thrill Factory,* 1987, *Big Black Bugs Bleed Blue Blood,* 1989, *Making Things with Light,* 1990, *Milk, Milk, Lemonade,* 1992, *Gun Crazy,* 1993, *Our Bodies, Our Selves,* 1994, *The Mr. T Experience!. . . And the Women Who Love Them,* 1995, *Alternative Is Here to Stay,* 1995, *Love Is Dead,* 1996, *Revenge Is Sweet, and So Are You,* 1997, *Alcatraz,* 1999, *Show Business Is My Life,* 1999.

WRITINGS:

King Dork (young adult novel), Delacorte Press (New York, NY), 2006.

Author of blog *Dr. Frank Web Log.*

SIDELIGHTS: Frank Portman is a founding member of the punk rock band, Mr. T Experience. The band, formed in the San Francisco Bay Area in 1985, has rotated through many new members, but Portman remains its anchor, having been featured in nearly one dozen albums. Aside from writing lyrics for the band's songs, Portman ventured into writing novels for the young adult genre. His debut book, *King Dork,* has already received wide attention and its movie rights have already been optioned by Will Ferrell. On making the switch from songwriter to book writer, Portman said in an *Entertainment Weekly* interview that "writing a novel takes up your whole day for, like, two years. With music you roll out of bed and you play something, but [with a book] it's like being back in school: You've got this homework project, and anytime you do anything else you think, 'Man, I really should be working on that novel, otherwise I'm going to have to give the advance back!'"

King Dork is a story about high school as narrated by the lead character, Tom Henderson. Tom, an intelligent kid who loves rock music, has only one friend but many enemies at school. A subplot involving Tom finding his dead father's copy of *Catcher in the Rye* full of secret codes in the margins gives the protagonist a chance to learn more about his father and the mystery surrounding his death.

Critics were pleased with Portman's literary debut. Dave Housley, writing in a review on *PopMatters.com,* called the book "one of the funniest books of the year, maybe of any year." Miranda Doyle's review in *School Library Journal* found the book "original, heartfelt, and sparkling with wit and intelligence." She called Tom's character "engaging." A reviewer in *Publishers Weekly* concluded that "the author's biting humor and skillful connection of events will keep pages turning."

BIOGRAPHICAL AND CRITICAL SOURCES:

BOOKS

Contemporary Musicians, Volume 29, Thomson Gale (Detroit, MI), 2000.

PERIODICALS

Booklist, May 15, 2006, Cindy Dobrez, review of *King Dork,* p. 41.

Bulletin of the Center for Children's Books, May, 2006, Deborah Stevenson, review of *King Dork,* p. 419.

Children's Bookwatch, August, 2006, review of *King Dork.*

Entertainment Weekly, April 28, 2006, Jennifer Reese, review of *King Dork,* p. 138; May 15, 2006, Bob Cannon, "'King' of Rock."

Kirkus Reviews, March 15, 2006, review of *King Dork,* p. 298.

Library Media Connection, March, 2006, Cynthia Schulz, review of *King Dork,* p. 69.

Publishers Weekly, March 13, 2006, review of *King Dork,* p. 68.

San Francisco Chronicle, April 27, 2006, Tony Du-Shane, "Out Loud He Pities the Fool," p. H25.

School Library Journal, April, 2006, Miranda Doyle, review of *King Dork,* p. 146.

Teacher Librarian, December, 2006, review of *King Dork,* p. 24.

Voice of Youth Advocates, April, 2006, Kathie Fitch, review of *King Dork,* p. 50.

Washington Times, April 30, 2006, Clive Davis, review of *King Dork.*

ONLINE

Bookslut, http://www.bookslut.com/ (December 29, 2006), Michael Schaub, author interview.

Brink, http://www.brink.com/ (December 29, 2006), Chuck Prophet, author interview.

BuzzFeed, http://www.buzzfeed.com/ (December 29, 2006), author profile.

Frank Portman Home Page, http://www.frankportman.com (December 29, 2006), author biography.

Frank Portman MySpace Profile, http://www.myspace.com/doctorfrank (December 29, 2006), author profile.

Metroactive, http://www.metroactive.com/ (May 27, 1999), Gina Arnold, author profile.

Pop Goes The Library, http://www.popgoesthelibrary.com/ (March 6, 2006), Sophie Brookover, author interview.

Pop Matters, http://www.popmatters.com/ (May 1, 2006), Dave Housley, review of *King Dork.*

teenreads.com, http://www.teenreads.com/ (December 29, 2006), Brian Farrey, review of *King Dork.*

*   *   *

POUNDSTONE, Paula 1959-

PERSONAL: Born December 29, 1959, in Huntsville, AL; children: Toshia, Allison, and Thomas E.

ADDRESSES: Home—Santa Monica, CA. *Agent*—Debbie Keller, Personal Publicity, 12831 S. 71st St., Tempe, AZ 85284.

CAREER: Comedian. National Public Radio, *Wait Wait . . . Don't Tell Me!,* panelist. Also featured in various television comic specials, television series, and talk shows, including *Today Show, To Tell the Truth, Cybill,* and the *Paula Poundstone Show.*

AWARDS, HONORS: Emmy Award, for her work on the PBS series *Life & Times;* Cable ACE Award, 1992, for *Cats, Cops, and Stuff,* and 1992, for Best Program Interviewer; American Comedy Award, for Best Female Stand-Up.

WRITINGS:

(With Faye Nisonoff Ruopp) *The Sticky Problem of Parallelogram Pancakes & Other Skill-Building Math Activities, Grades 4-5* ("Math with a Laugh" series), Heinemann (Portsmouth, NH), 2006.

(With Faye Nisonoff Ruopp) *Venn Can We Be Friends? & Other Skill-Building Math Activities, Grades 6-7* ("Math with a Laugh" series), Heinemann (Portsmouth, NH), 2006.

(With Faye Nisonoff Ruopp) *You Can't Keep Slope Down: & Other Skill-Building Math Activities, Grades 8-9* ("Math with a Laugh" series), Heinemann (Portsmouth, NH), 2006.

There's Nothing in This Book That I Meant to Say, foreword by Mary Tyler Moore, Harmony Books (New York, NY), 2006.

Wrote for her television specials, *Cats, Cops, and Stuff,* 1990, and *Look What the Cat Dragged In,* 2006. Contributor to *Mother Jones.*

SIDELIGHTS: Paula Poundstone is a stand-up comedian who has appeared on television, and in comedy clubs across the country. Poundstone's most notable television appearances have been on the *Today Show, To Tell the Truth, Cybill,* and the short-running *Paula Poundstone Show.* Poundstone has also had her stand-up routines aired on Home Box Office (HBO) and contributes as a panelist on National Public Radio (NPR). Poundstone gained unwanted attention in 2001 when she was arrested for driving under the influence of alcohol with her children in the car going to an ice cream shop. This subsequently led her to check into a rehabilitation center and serve five years probation. Although she lost the right to take care of her foster children, her three adopted children were returned to her full custody in late 2002. Despite these life-changing circumstances, Poundstone is able to use these hardships and incorporate them into her comedy routines and writing.

There's Nothing in This Book That I Meant to Say is part-memoir, part-history lesson comparing notable events in her life (such as her legal proceedings, alcoholism, and her children) to those of Abraham Lincoln, Joan of Arc, Helen Keller, and the Wright Brothers. Reviews of Poundstone's debut book were mostly positive. Susan McClellan, writing in *Library Journal,* noted that "readers will love the book's offbeat humor and interesting monolog." *Booklist* reviewer Whitney Scott called it a "sad but ultimately triumphal story." A critic writing in *Kirkus Reviews* noted that Poundstone's "descriptions of the bureaucratic nightmare of court dates and mandated therapy sessions, and of her love for her adopted children . . . are in fact the most compelling aspects of the book."

BIOGRAPHICAL AND CRITICAL SOURCES:

BOOKS

Poundstone, Paula, *There's Nothing in This Book That I Meant to Say,* Harmony Books (New York, NY), 2006.

PERIODICALS

Booklist, September 1, 2006, Whitney Scott, review of *There's Nothing in This Book That I Meant to Say,* p. 35.
Broadcasting & Cable, July 2, 2001, "Poundstone Busted for 'Lewd Acts'," p. 10.

Curve, February, 2002, Georgia Sand, "Free Paula!," p. 33.
Detroit News, November 7, 2006, Mekeisha Madden Toby, "Mekeisha's Pick."
Entertainment Weekly, February 7, 1992, Ken Tucker, "The Paula Poundstone Show," p. 46; August 17, 2001, "Star Treatment," p. 8; September 28, 2001, Nicholas Fonseca, "Monitor," p. 37; November 10, 2006, Paul Katz, review of *There's Nothing in This Book That I Meant to Say,* p. 89.
Good Housekeeping, March, 1998, Carrie St. Michel, review of *This Stand-up Stands Up for Children in Need,* p. 23.
Kirkus Reviews, August 15, 2006, review of *There's Nothing in This Book That I Meant to Say,* p. 828.
Library Journal, October 1, 2006, Susan McClellan, review of *There's Nothing in This Book That I Meant to Say,* p. 72.
Los Angeles Business Journal, August 13, 2001, "Promise Keeping," p. 4.
Mediaweek, November 8, 1993, Mark Hudis, "Paula Breaks the Mold," p. 16; May 29, 2000, Anne Torpey-Kemph, "Pearson Picks Up Poundstone," p. 43.
Mother Jones, March-April, 1993, Paula Poundstone, "Hey Paula!"
People, July 16, 2001, "Losing Her Children," p. 57; September 10, 2001, "Matter of Trust," p. 77; October 8, 2001, "Olivia Abel," p. 145; December 23, 2002, Michael A. Lipton, "Comic's Relief," p. 77.
Publishers Weekly, April 3, 2006, "Newhart, Poundstone at BEA," p. 8; August 7, 2006, review of *There's Nothing in This Book That I Meant to Say,* p. 41.
Time, fall, 1990, Stefan Kanfer, "Sauce, Satire, and Shtick," p. 62; November 16, 1998, Joel Stein, "Paula Poundstone," p. 124; September 13, 2004, Michele Orecklin, "Standing Back Up," p. 88.
Variety, October 27, 1997, Jenny Hontz, "Deals Put Lane, Poundstone on Small Screen," p. 25; May 29, 2000, Melissa Grego, "Poundstone and Taylor Find 'Truth'," p. 59.

ONLINE

Enigma, http://www.enigmaonline.com/ (May 12, 2004), Dave Weinthal, author interview.
Internet Movie Database, http://www.imdb.com/ (December 29, 2006), author profile.

Paula Poundstone Home Page, http://www.paula poundstone.com (December 30, 2006), author biography.

Rotten dot com, http://www.rotten.com/ (December 29, 2006), Poundstone life timeline.*

* * *

POWELL, Jim 1944-

PERSONAL: Born 1944. *Education:* Graduated from University of Chicago.

CAREER: Cato Institute, Washington, DC, R.C. Hoiles Senior Fellow, 1988—; Laissez Faire Books, Little Rock, AR, editor, 1992—. Has worked for the Manhattan Institute, Institute for Humane Studies, Citizens for a Sound Economy, National Right to Work Committee, and Americans for Free Choice in Medicine. Lecturer.

WRITINGS:

NONFICTION

The Triumph of Liberty: A 2,000-Year History, Told through the Lives of Freedom's Greatest Champions, Free Press (New York, NY), 2000.

FDR's Folly: How Roosevelt and His New Deal Prolonged the Great Depression, Crown Forum (New York, NY), 2003.

Wilson's War: How Woodrow Wilson's Great Blunder Led to Hitler, Lenin, Stalin, and World War II, Crown Forum (New York, NY), 2005.

Bully Boy: The Truth about Theodore Roosevelt's Legacy, Crown Forum (New York, NY), 2006.

Former editor, *New Individualist Review.* Contributor to periodicals, including *Wall Street Journal, New York Times, Esquire, Architectural Digest, Science Digest, Family Circle,* and *Connoisseur.*

SIDELIGHTS: Jim Powell is a historian, editor, lecturer, and author of several history books with a libertarian outlook. His first, *The Triumph of Liberty: A 2,000-Year History, Told through the Lives of Freedom's Greatest Champions,* presents stories of sixty-four people who fought against war, slavery, and oppression. The subjects in the book represent a wide range of heroes of all sorts: writers, philosophers, civil rights workers and many others, including Susan B. Anthony, Thomas Jefferson, Martin Luther King, Jr., Mark Twain, John Locke, and Victor Hugo. "On some books you feast. On others you nibble. Jim Powell's *The Triumph of Liberty* is one of the latter," reported John Hood in a review for the *Freeman: Ideas on Liberty* Web site. "A fascinating collection of brief biographical sketches of those who have championed human freedom throughout history, Powell's work is a seemingly inexhaustible source of information, insight, and inspiration. To sit down and read it cover to cover would be not to give Powell his due. His stories deserve to be savored, re-read, and retold," stated Hood. A *Publishers Weekly* writer called the profiles in the book "pithy" and "vivid."

In *Wilson's War: How Woodrow Wilson's Great Blunder Led to Hitler, Lenin, Stalin and World War II,* Powell reexamines the legacy of U.S. president Woodrow Wilson. Ranking him as the worst president in American history, Powell states that Wilson was responsible for involving the United States in World War I, and that Wilson was motivated by his desire leave a legacy as a peacemaker. In Powell's view, Wilson's actions paved the way for the Holocaust, the Cold War, and numerous other modern disasters. A *Kirkus Reviews* writer found that "none of it is convincing," however, and a *Publishers Weekly* writer called it "a tendentious and heavy-handed distortion of history."

Bully Boy: The Truth about Theodore Roosevelt's Legacy, also seeks to upend a popular president's reputation. According to Powell, Theodore Roosevelt was a reckless and destructive leader. Though Roosevelt is often praised for breaking up monopolies, promoting the sale of pure food, and advancing the cause of conservation, Powell believes that he really promoted big business, helped special interests who were often responsible for adulterated food, and did immeasurable harm to the environment by permitting harmful policies on dam-building and forestry. A *Kirkus Reviews* writer noted that those "who share Powell's enthusiasm for limited government and free markets will doubtless enjoy this skewering of a widely admired president," but added that other readers might be surprised to learn that Roosevelt's "stated good intentions always led to dark deeds."

Theodore Roosevelt's cousin, Franklin Delano Roosevelt, was taken to task by Powell in his book *FDR's Folly: How Roosevelt and His New Deal Prolonged the Great Depression.* Although Franklin Delano Roosevelt is usually at or near the top of lists of great presidents, Powell "argues that [New Deal] economic and regulatory policies were bad for many Americans, especially poor blacks." His case is at least somewhat "convincing and damning," noted Damon W. Root in *Reason.*

BIOGRAPHICAL AND CRITICAL SOURCES:

PERIODICALS

Booklist, August, 2000, Mary Carroll, review of *The Triumph of Liberty: A 2,000-Year History, Told through the Lives of Freedom's Greatest Champions,* p. 2085; August 1, 2006, Gilbert Taylor, review of *Bully Boy: The Truth about Theodore Roosevelt's Legacy,* p. 34.

Campaigns & Elections, July, 2005, Ron Faucheux, review of *Wilson's War: How Woodrow Wilson's Great Blunder Led to Hitler, Lenin, Stalin, and World War II,* p. 38.

Kirkus Reviews, January 15, 2005, review of *Wilson's War,* p. 109; June 15, 2006, review of *Bully Boy,* p. 623.

Library Journal, May 1, 2005, Thomas A. Karel, review of *Wilson's War,* p. 102; August 1, 2006, William D. Pederson, review of *Bully Boy,* p. 101.

Publishers Weekly, June 19, 2000, review of *The Triumph of Liberty,* p. 69; March 14, 2005, review of *Wilson's War,* p. 58; May 22, 2006, review of *Bully Boy,* p. 44.

Reason, November, 2000, Brian Doherty, interview with Jim Powell, p. 13; October, 2004, Damon W. Root, review of *FDR's Folly: How Roosevelt and His New Deal Prolonged the Great Depression,* p. 59.

ONLINE

Cato Institute Web site, http://www.cato.org/ (January 16, 2007), biographical information about Jim Powell.

Freeman: Ideas on Liberty, http://www.fee.org/ (February 9, 2007), John Hood, review of *The Triumph of Liberty.*

Liberty Story, http://www.libertystory.net (January 16, 2007), author's home page.*

*   *   *

POWER, Jo-Ann
(Ann Crowleigh, a joint pseudonym)

PERSONAL: Born in Baltimore, MD; married; children: three. *Education:* Attended University of Maryland.

ADDRESSES: Home—TX. *E-mail*—jo-annpower@ powerontheweb.com.

CAREER: Writer. Power Promotions (public relations and marketing firm), TX, founder, president, and chief executive officer, 1998—. Media director, Virgin Books. Former executive and lobbyist in Washington, DC; former teacher of English, and of Chinese and Japanese history.

AWARDS, HONORS: Eight KISS awards for romantic heroes, *Romantic Times* magazine; Best Debut Novel and Best Contemporary Novel Awards, *Romantic Times* magazine, 1992, for *Prime Time.*

WRITINGS:

NOVELS

The Mark of the Chadwicks, Zebra Books (New York, NY), 1993.

The Last Duchess of Wolff's Lair, Zebra Books (New York, NY), 1993.

You and No Other, Pocket Books (New York, NY), 1994.

Angel of Midnight, Pocket Books (New York, NY), 1995.

Remembrance, Pinnacle (New York, NY), 1995.

Treasures, Pocket Books (New York, NY), 1996.

Gifts, Pocket Books (New York, NY), 1996.

The Nightingale's Song, Pocket Books (New York, NY), 1997.

Never Before, Pocket Books (New York, NY), 1998.

Never Again, Pocket Books (New York, NY), 1998.

Allure, Sonnet Books (New York, NY), 1999.

Never Say Never, Sonnet Books (New York, NY), 1999.

Missing Member, Thomas Dunne Books (New York, NY), 2006.

MYSTERIES; WITH BARBARA CUMMINGS

Prime Time, Pinnacle (New York, NY), 1992.

Risks, Pinnacle (New York, NY), 1993.

(Under joint pseudonym Ann Crowleigh) *Clively Close, Dead as Dead Can Be,* Zebra Books (New York, NY), 1993.

(Under joint pseudonym Ann Crowleigh) *Clively Close, Wait for the Dark,* Zebra Books (New York, NY), 1993.

Contributor, with Barbara Cummings under pseudonym Ann Crowleigh, of short story "The Ghost of Christmas Past," in *Murder under the Tree,* Zebra Books (New York, NY), 1993. Contributor to periodicals, including *Washington Post, New York Times,* and *Wall Street Journal.* Author of weekly syndicated newspaper column, "Power in Marketing!"

SIDELIGHTS: Jo-Ann Power began writing novels after establishing herself as a corporate executive and public-relations expert. Her work in those fields required a great deal of nonfiction writing, "about such dry and uninteresting things, most people think, as insurance, securities, and banking," as she stated in an interview for *All about Romance.* When Power's children were young, she stayed home with them and began reading romance novels in her free time. Feeling that she could certainly write a book of equal quality to those she was reading, Power joined the Washington Romance Writers group. Recalling her early days as a fiction writer, she said in the *All about Romance* interview: "I would get on the subway and I'd get in the back where I could spread out, and I would write long-hand, fiction, on my way to work. When I got on the subway to come home, I would take out my yellow pad and I'd continue. And on the weekends I'd type it into my computer. And that's how I wrote maybe five manuscripts." Power's landed her first book contract in 1990, and within one year, she had sold several more books. She showed her versatility, selling mainstream novels, contemporary romances, a mystery series, and some gothic novels.

Power's books *Never Before, Never Again,* and *Never Say Never* are set in the Victorian era, and concern nineteenth-century American heiresses who travel to England, in search of husbands from the British aristocracy. Reviewing the first installment in this trilogy, Meredith Moore wrote on the *Romance Reader* Web site: "Power is deft at handling scenes showing the growing relationship between her hero and heroine. Her elegant use of language, which at times can be exquisitely delicate, is some of the most original I've read in years."

Missing Member is a contemporary mystery by Power, featuring Carly Wagner, a five-term congresswoman from Texas. Carly finds a fellow congressman murdered and mutilated in her office. Although Carly is not actually considered a suspect, she is eager to clear up the scandal. Helping her in this effort is Mr. Jones, a handsome, efficient private investigator who previously worked as a bodyguard. "Humor, politics, and likable characters distinguish this first in a series," stated Sue O'Brien in *Booklist.*

Power told the interviewer for *All about Romance:* "A romance novel is the exploration of how two people who have the potential to love fully, find each other, conquer whatever problems stand between them, and make a decision to continue with each other. By the fact that they have conquered their conflict or solved their conflict, they can then go on hand in hand through the rest of life continuing with that success to conquer the many other problems that are going to come their way." Power added: "In a society in which women still bear the brunt of broken marriages and children who need nurturing, romance gives hope that there may just be some happy ending."

BIOGRAPHICAL AND CRITICAL SOURCES:

PERIODICALS

Booklist, September 1, 2006, Sue O'Brien, review of *Missing Member,* p. 64.

Kirkus Reviews, July 15, 2006, review of *Missing Member,* p. 705.

Publishers Weekly, May 5, 1997, review of *The Nightingale's Song,* p. 206; October 5, 1998, review of *Never Again,* p. 87; April 26, 1999, review of *Never Say Never,* p. 79; July 24, 2006, review of *Missing Member,* p. 39.

ONLINE

All about Romance, http://www.likesbooks.com/ (January 8, 1998), interview with Jo-Ann Power.

Jo-Ann Power Home Page, http://www.jo-annpower. com (January 17, 2007).

Mystery Reader, http://www.newmysteryreader.com/ (February 9, 2007), Susan Illis, review of *Missing Member.*

Power Promotions, http://www.powerontheweb.com (January 17, 2007), company Web site; biographical information about Jo-Ann Power.

Romance Reader, http://www.theromancereader.com/ (January 17, 2007), Meredith Moore, review of *Never Before;* Bev Hill, review of *Never Again;* Jean Mason, review of *Never Say Never.*

Romantic Times, http://www.romantictimes.com/ (January 17, 2007), Kathe Robin, reviews of *Allure, Gifts, Never Again, Never Before, Never Say Never, Treasures, You and No Other,* and *Angel of Midnight.**

*   *   *

POWERS, Kim

PERSONAL: Born in TX; partner to Jess Goldstein (a costume designer). *Education:* Graduated from Yale School of Drama.

ADDRESSES: Home—New York, NY; Asbury Park, NJ. *E-mail*—kphistswimming@aol.com.

CAREER: Writer. Worked on ABC-TV programs *Good Morning America* and *Primetime;* staff writer for AMC series, *The Lot.* Executive developer of projects for various film and television companies; producer for PBS program *Great Performances.*

AWARDS, HONORS: Winner of an Emmy Award and a Peabody Award, for his coverage of 9/11.

WRITINGS:

The History of Swimming: A Memoir, Carroll & Graf (New York, NY), 2006.

Author of screenplay *Finding North.*

SIDELIGHTS: Kim Powers's first book, *The History of Swimming: A Memoir,* is both an examination of the unique relationship shared by twins, and a coming-of-age story of a gay man in the era of AIDS. Powers and his fraternal twin, Tim, were close as young children, grew apart as adolescents, and were in conflict as adults. Both identified themselves as homosexual, but they chose very different lifestyles. Kim made choices that brought him success, while Tim drifted into heavy drinking and eventually reached the point of making suicide attempts. When, at the age of twenty-eight, Tim suddenly drops out of sight altogether, Kim begins a search that leads him to various lovers, friends, and others who had encountered his brother. Fearing that Tim has been on a drinking binge, Kim fully expects to find him dead. The key to finding Tim turns out to be in a series of detailed letters the missing man has written to his brother over the years.

The author "writes with insight and intelligence about his brother's flaws and fears and the telepathic tendencies of souls separated by a few breaths," noted Allison Block in a *Booklist* review. *The History of Swimming* is "a powerful nod to familial bonding, written with verve and genuine affection," according to a *Kirkus Reviews* writer. *Library Journal* contributor Elizabeth Brinkley found Tim's letters "brilliant," and one of the best features of the book, making it "an often humorous, moving look at one man's complicated relationship with his brother."

BIOGRAPHICAL AND CRITICAL SOURCES:

BOOKS

Powers, Kim, *The History of Swimming: A Memoir,* Carroll & Graf (New York, NY), 2006.

PERIODICALS

Advocate, October 24, 2006, David Ehrenstein, review of *The History of Swimming,* p. 58.

Booklist, August 1, 2006, Allison Block, review of *The History of Swimming,* p. 25.

Dallas Morning News, December 4, 2006, Chris Vognar, review of *The History of Swimming.*

Kirkus Reviews, June 15, 2006, review of *The History of Swimming,* p. 623.

Library Journal, August 1, 2006, Elizabeth Brinkley, review of *The History of Swimming,* p. 109.

New York Times, September 17, 2006, Eve Conant, review of *The History of Swimming,*
Publishers Weekly, July 10, 2006, review of *The History of Swimming,* p. 68.
San Francisco Bay Times, November 16, 2006, Richard Labonte, review of *The History of Swimming.*
Washington Post, December 17, 2006, Juliet Wittman, review of *The History of Swimming,* p. BW10.

ONLINE

The History of Swimming Web site, http://www.thehistoryofswimming.com (January 12, 2007).*

* * *

PRIAL, Dunstan 1970(?)-

PERSONAL: Born c. 1970 (some sources say 1963), in NJ.

ADDRESSES: Home—Bristol, RI.

CAREER: Journalist and writer. Worked as a reporter for the Associated Press.

WRITINGS:

The Producer: John Hammond and the Soul of American Music, Farrar, Straus & Giroux (New York, NY), 2006.

SIDELIGHTS: Dunstan Prial is a journalist who became interested in music producer John Hammond because he produced records for one of Prial's favorite artists, Bruce Springsteen. In *The Producer: John Hammond and the Soul of American Music,* the author recounts Hammond's life and career producing records for some of the top recording artists of his time, who, in addition to Springsteen, included such wide-ranging talents as Billie Holiday and Bob Dylan. Prial reveals Hammond's upper-class roots as part of the noted Vanderbilt family and explores his career as Hammond drops out of Yale University to follow his love of jazz music. The author also delves into Hammond's leftist political beliefs and his fair treatment of

the artists he produced. A *Kirkus Reviews* contributor referred to *The Producer* as a "sympathetic, admiring biography" and as being "informative, compelling and gleefully, unapologetically tendentious." John Clarke, Jr., writing in *Variety,* commented that the biography "has a pitch-perfect story arc: rich boy discovers music and Harlem, gets job in record business, serves up historic talent to unreceptive, stone-faced record label brass, is mocked and ridiculed and later vindicated, if not canonized." In his review in the *Library Journal,* James E. Perone wrote: "He brings Hammond to life in clear, insightful prose." David Itzkoff, writing in the *New York Times Book Review,* noted: "The . . . triumph of *The Producer* is illustrating how . . . seemingly disparate phases of Hammond's career are actually points on a single line, defined by his lifelong passion for social justice."

BIOGRAPHICAL AND CRITICAL SOURCES:

PERIODICALS

Booklist, June 1, 2006, Ray Olson, review of *The Producer: John Hammond and the Soul of American Music,* p. 29.
Christian Science Monitor, October 3, 2006, John Kehe, review of *The Producer.*
Entertainment Weekly, June 30, 2006, Raymond Fiore, review of *The Producer,* p. 167.
Kirkus Reviews, May 15, 2006, review of *The Producer,* p. 510.
Library Journal, June 15, 2006, James E. Perone, review of *The Producer,* p. 73.
New York Times, August 11, 2006, Peter Keepnews, review of *The Producer.*
New York Times Book Review, October 1, 2006, Dave Itzkoff, review of *The Producer.*
Publishers Weekly, May 29, 2006, review of *The Producer,* p. 52.
Taipei Times, August 13, 2006, Peter Keepnews, review of *The Producer,* p. 19.
Twin Cities Reader Summer Books Issue, July 19, 2006, Jesse Berrett, review of *The Producer.*
Variety, August 21, 2006, John Clarke, Jr., review of *The Producer,* p. 30.

ONLINE

Forbes.com, http://www.forbes.com/ (July 14, 2006), Richard Hyfler, review of *The Producer.**

PRICE, Arnold H. 1912-2006
(Arnold Hereward Price)

OBITUARY NOTICE— See index for *CA* sketch: Born July 1, 1912, in Bonn, Germany; died of a stroke, December 10, 2006, in Springfield, VA. Historian and author. Price was a specialist in German history who worked for the Library of Congress. A graduate of the University of Michigan, where he earned a Ph.D. in German economic history in 1942, he served in the U.S. Army during World War II in the Office of Strategic Services. After the war, he was a specialist in German area studies with the U.S. Department of State until 1960. He joined the Library of Congress as a Central Europe specialist, retiring nineteen years later. One of his major accomplishments during his career was helping to recover a lost fragment of the German epic poem "Hildebrandslied." Price was an author and editor, as well, publishing such works as *The Evolution of the Zollverein* (1949), *East Germany: A Selected Bibliography* (1967), and *Germanic Warrior Clubs: An Inquiry into the Dynamics of the Era of Migrations and into the Antecedents of Medieval Society* (1994; 2nd edition, 1996). He released his memoirs, *My Twentieth Century: Recollections of a Public Historian*, in 2003.

OBITUARIES AND OTHER SOURCES:

BOOKS

Price, Arnold H., *My Twentieth Century: Recollections of a Public Historian*, Universitas Verlag Tübingen (Tübingen, Germany), 2003.

PERIODICALS

Washington Post, December 22, 2006, p. B9.

*   *   *

PRICE, Arnold Hereward
See PRICE, Arnold H.

PROFFITT, Nicholas 1943-2006
(Nicholas Charles Proffitt)

OBITUARY NOTICE— See index for *CA* sketch: Born February 23, 1943, in Sault Ste. Marie, MI; died of kidney cancer, November 10, 2006, in Naples, FL. Journalist and author. Proffitt was an award-winning journalist and novelist best known for his 1983 work, *Gardens of Stone*. The son of a sergeant, the young Proffitt joined the army after high school. He struggled at the U.S. Military Academy, however, and dropped out after a semester. Assigned to duty at Arlington National Cemetery, his experiences there became the basis for his novel *Gardens of Stone*, which was made into a 1987 Francis Ford Coppola movie. Leaving the military in 1964 with the rank of sergeant E-5, Proffitt attended the University of Arizona and earned a B.A. in 1968. Hired by *Newsweek*, he became a war correspondent in such locations as Saigon, South Vietnam; Beirut, Lebanon; and Nairobi, Kenya. He retired from journalism in 1981 to write full time, producing the novels *The Embassy House* (1986) and *Edge of Eden* (1990).

OBITUARIES AND OTHER SOURCES:

PERIODICALS

Chicago Tribune, November 19, 2006, Section 4, p. 6.
Los Angeles Times, November 27, 2006, p. B7.
New York Times, November 17, 2006, p. A29; November 18, 2006, p. A2.
Times (London, England), December 1, 2006, p. 85.
Washington Post, November 23, 2006, p. B5.

*   *   *

PROFFITT, Nicholas Charles
See PROFFITT, Nicholas

Q-R

QUAN, Andy 1969-

PERSONAL: Born July 7, 1969, in Vancouver, British Columbia, Canada; son of Joe (a notary public) and Hilda (a scientist) Quan. *Ethnicity:* "Asian-Canadian (Cantonese origins)." *Education:* Attended Lester B. Pearson College of the Pacific, 1986-88; Trent University, B.I.S., 1993; York University, M.A., 1994. *Hobbies and other interests:* Singing and writing songs, cycling.

ADDRESSES: Home—New South Wales, Australia. *Office*—Australian Federation of AIDS Organisations, P.O. Box 51, Newtown, New South Wales 2042, Australia. *E-mail*—andy@andyquan.com.

CAREER: International Lesbian Gay Association, Brussels, Belgium, coordinator, 1994-96; R.S. Health Ltd., London, England, project manager, 1997-98; Australian Federation of AIDS Organisations, Newtown, New South Wales, Australia, international policy officer, 1999—. Sydney Gay and Lesbian Mardi Gras, board member, 2001-05; Sydney Gay and Lesbian Community Publishing, board member, 2002-2005.

AWARDS, HONORS: Named writer of the year, Charity Erotic Awards and Sydney Gay and Lesbian Business Association, both 2005, for *Six Positions: Sex Writing by Andy Quan.*

WRITINGS:

(Editor, with Jim Wong Chu, and contributor) *Swallowing Clouds: An Anthology of Chinese-Canadian Poetry,* Arsenal Pulp Press (Vancouver, British Columbia, Canada), 1999.

Slant (poetry), Nightwood Editions (Roberts Creek, British Columbia, Canada), 2001.

Calendar Boy (short stories), New Star Books (Vancouver, British Columbia, Canada), 2001.

Six Positions: Sex Writing by Andy Quan, Green Candy Press (San Francisco, CA), 2005.

Work represented in numerous anthologies, including *Best Gay Erotica,* Cleis Press, annually, 1999-2000, 2002-05; *Striking the Wok: Anthology of Contemporary Chinese Canadian Fiction,* TSAR Publications; *Big Night Out,* Penguin Australia; *Seminal: Anthology of Gay Male Canadian Poetry,* Arsenal Pulp Press; and *Boyfriends from Hell,* Green Candy Press. Contributor of articles, short stories, essays, and poetry to magazines, including *Absinthe, Lustre, Positive Nation, Meanjin, Queer Words, Prism International, Canadian Literature, Modern Words, Freeze-Dried,* and *Asian Pacific American Journal.*

SIDELIGHTS: Andy Quan told *CA:* "I started writing simply because I loved doing it. As my writing developed, I found pleasure in working toward publication in magazines. I was motivated in my early years of writing to see myself reflected in gay literature. As much as I admired the books I'd read, they were mostly about gay, white, older men in major urban centers in the United States. Why not write about young gay men? About gay men who weren't white? My early stories were received with some success, which led to the publication of my first short fiction collection, *Calendar Boy,* which explores the themes of identity, community, coming out, and the intersection between race and sexuality. My latest collection is writings about sex, with many of the stories previously published in anthologies of gay erotica. These stories aim to go beyond simply bringing pleasure to a reader, but to write about, celebrate, and capture sex in its exciting, mundane, charged, and beautiful forms."

*　　　*　　　*

RAE, John Malcolm 1931-2006

OBITUARY NOTICE— See index for *CA* sketch: Born March 20, 1931, in London, England; died of cancer, December 16, 2006. School administrator and author. A controversial headmaster of the Westminster School in London, England, Rae was also a novelist known for such endearing tales as *The Custard Boys* (1961). He earned his master's degree at Cambridge University in 1955, taking the post of assistant master at Harrow School for the next eleven years. Serving as master of Taunton School in Somerset in the late 1960s, Rae began to aspire to more prominent posts. In particular, he hoped one day to be headmaster of Eton. This ambition inspired him to go back to university, and so he earned a Ph.D. at the University of London in 1965. During the 1960s, Rae became known for his outspoken, often negative opinions about public schools, and he drew criticism for publicly complaining in 1969 that parents were failing their children. His policies at Taunton were sometimes seen as heavy-handed, as well, and so Rae decided to accept a job at Westminster School in 1970. He led the school until 1986, never achieving his dream of going to Eton. However, Rae found himself much liked by students and parents at Westminster, though he continued to be criticized by those on the outside. Rae enjoyed making controversial appointments to jobs at the school, and his book *The Public School Revolution,* which criticized the school system, was not appreciated by many in the profession. Nevertheless, his accomplishments included opening up enrollment to girls at the formerly all-boys school and increasing enrollment significantly. When he left Westminster, he characteristically ruffled feathers by hiring a non-Caucasian woman to replace him. After his retirement from school administration, Rae volunteered at a leper colony in India for a time, then served as director of the London *Observer* from 1986 to 1993. Beginning in 1989, he directed the Portman Group, a trade group advocating responsible alcohol use, and he was a member of the National Board for Crime Prevention from 1993 to 1995. Among his

other fiction works are *The Golden Crucifix* (1974), *Christmas Is Coming* (1977), and *The Third Twin* (1980). Also the author of many nonfiction titles, his more recent works include *Letters from School* (1987), *Too Little Too Late?: The Challenges That Still Face British Education* (1989), *Sketch Book of the World* (1994), *Letters to Parents: How to Get the Best Available Education for Your Child* (1998), and the biography *Sister Genevieve* (2001).

OBITUARIES AND OTHER SOURCES:

BOOKS

Rae, John, *Delusions of Grandeur,* HarperCollins (New York, NY), 1993.

PERIODICALS

Times (London, England), December 19, 2006, p. 48.

*　　　*　　　*

RAICHEV, Raiko T.
　　See RAICHEV, R.T.

*　　　*　　　*

RAICHEV, R.T. 1968(?)-
　　(Raiko T. Raichev)

PERSONAL: Born c. 1968. *Ethnicity:* Bulgarian *Education:* Attended college.

ADDRESSES: Home—London, England.

CAREER: Writer.

WRITINGS:

The Hunt for Sonya Dufrette (mystery novel), Carroll & Graf (New York, NY), 2006.

SIDELIGHTS: Bulgarian writer R.T. Raichev lives in London, England, where she works as a researcher. Her first book, *The Hunt for Sonya Dufrette,* follows librarian and mystery writer Antonia Darcy as she sets out to solve a twenty-five-year old mystery with the assistance of handsome widower, Major Hugh Payne. On the morning of the royal wedding in 1981, an autistic child went missing at a house party that Antonia was attending and is presumed dead. More than two decades later, however, Antonia suspects that something else really occurred. Ilene Cooper, in a review for *Booklist,* remarked: "Antonia Darcy is a terrific sleuth, and Raichev is a very clever writer, indeed." A contributor to *Kirkus Reviews* wrote that "fans of cozies will love the light touch of Raichev's debut, right down to the charmingly titled chapters," while a reviewer for *Publishers Weekly* called the book an "auspicious first in a new mystery series from Raichev." Raichev plans to develop more adventures featuring Antonia Darcy and Hugh Payne. The majority of the stories will revolve around English country houses, a setting Raichev finds endlessly intriguing. She considers her work to be an homage to what she calls the "Golden Age of English detective fiction."

BIOGRAPHICAL AND CRITICAL SOURCES:

PERIODICALS

Booklist, July 1, 2006, Ilene Cooper, review of *The Hunt for Sonya Dufrette,* p. 38.
Kirkus Reviews, June 1, 2006, review of *The Hunt for Sonya Dufrette,* p. 552.
Library Journal, June 1, 2006, Jo Ann Vicarel, review of *The Hunt for Sonya Dufrette,* p. 92.
Publishers Weekly, June 5, 2006, review of *The Hunt for Sonya Dufrette,* p. 40.

ONLINE

R.T. Raichev Home Page, http://www.authortrek.com/r_t_raichev_page.html (January 30, 2007).*

*   *   *

RAIDER, Mark A.

PERSONAL: Married Miriam B. Roth (a scholar and educator); children: three. *Education:* University of California, Santa Cruz, B.A.; Brandeis University, Ph.D.

ADDRESSES: Office—Department of Judaic Studies, University of Cincinnati, 50 McMicken, Cincinnati, OH 45221-0169.

CAREER: Historian, scholar, educator, writer, and editor. University at Albany, State University of New York, faculty member, c. 1995-2005; University of Cincinnati, McMicken College of Arts and Sciences, Cincinnati, OH, Jewish Foundation Endowed Chair of the Department of Judaic Studies, c. 2006—.

WRITINGS:

(Editor, with Jonathan D. Sarna and Ronald W. Zweig) *Abba Hillel Silver and American Zionism,* Frank Cass (Portland, OR), 1997.
The Emergence of American Zionism, New York University Press (New York, NY), 1998.
(And annotator, with wife, Miriam B. Raider-Roth) *The Plough Woman: Records of the Pioneer Women of Palestine: A Critical Edition,* Brandeis University Press (Waltham, MA), 2002.
(Editor, with Shulamit Reinharz) *American Jewish Women and the Zionist Enterprise,* Brandeis University Press (Waltham, MA), 2005.

SIDELIGHTS: Mark A. Raider is a scholar of Judaic history and author of *The Emergence of American Zionism,* which focuses on the early twentieth-century labor Zionism movement in America. "Utilizing previously untapped archival sources, Raider describes how a handful of East European socialist-Zionist ideologues, transplanted to America's shores by Czarist oppression, sought to import their version of Zionism to their new homeland," wrote Rafael Medoff in *American Jewish History.* In his book, Raider focuses on the rise of the Zionist labor movement and its eventual waning in the late 1920s and on through the 1930s. Medoff noted: "Mark Raider has authored an engaging and provocative history of the emergence of Labor Zionism in the United States."

Raider is also editor with Shulamit Reinharz of *American Jewish Women and the Zionist Enterprise,* a collection of essays culled from the proceedings of a 1999 conference at Brandeis University called "Untold Stories: American Jewish Women in the Yishuv and Early State of Israel." The various essays, written by a variety of Jewish scholars and political activists, focuses on Zionism, American Jewish women, and the Yishuv, a term that used to refer to the Zionist movement and the Jewish residents of Palestine before the state of Israel was established. Sonja P. Wentling, writing in *American Jewish History,* commented that the book "provides a multifaceted account of American Jewish women's understanding of the Zionist idea, and how they advanced as well as sustained the Zionist agenda." In her review in *Nashim: A Journal of Jewish Women's Studies and Gender Issues,* Pamela S. Nadell wrote: "By bringing all these [essays] together in a single volume, [the editors] dramatically convey the range and depth of American women's Zionist involvements, commitments, and activities."

BIOGRAPHICAL AND CRITICAL SOURCES:

PERIODICALS

American Jewish History, September, 1998, Rafael Medoff, review of *The Emergence of American Zionism,* p. 367; September, 2004, Sonja P. Wentling, review of *American Jewish Women and the Zionist Enterprise,* p. 386.
Israel Studies, spring, 2006, Donna Robinson Divine, review of *American Jewish Women and the Zionist Enterprise,* p. 204.
Nashim: A Journal of Jewish Women's Studies and Gender Issues, fall, 2005, Pamela S. Nadell, review of *American Jewish Women and the Zionist Enterprise,* p. 250.

ONLINE

McMicken College of Arts and Sciences University of Cincinnati Web site, http://www.artsci.uc.edu/ (September 18, 2006), profile of author.*

*   *   *

RAND, Jonathan 1947-

PERSONAL: Born 1947. *Education:* University of Missouri, master's degree.

CAREER: Journalist and writer. Former sportswriter and columnist in Kansas City, MO, and at the *Miami News,* Miami, FL; also former staff member of the *Columbian Missouri.*

WRITINGS:

So Ditka Says to Buddy—: The Greatest Football Stories Ever Told, Chamberlain Bros. (New York, NY), 2005.
300 Pounds of Attitude: The Wildest Stories and Craziest Characters the NFL Has Ever Seen, Lyons Press (Guilford, CT), 2006.

SIDELIGHTS: A longtime sports writer and columnist, Jonathan Rand has also written books about the National Football League and its players and coaches. In *300 Pounds of Attitude: The Wildest Stories and Craziest Characters the NFL Has Ever Seen,* Rand relates numerous anecdotes about some of the National Football League's most well-known and, in some cases, most outrageous players and personalities. For example, he relates the exploits of Tim Rossovich, a 1960s' NFL player who was known to eat almost everything, from glass to cigarettes, and tells of the many pranks that former NFL quarterback Steve De-Berg liked to play on his teammates and coaches. The author also includes stories about more recent players, such as the trash talking that goes on between quarterback Bret Favre and defensive lineman Warren Sapp whenever their teams play each other. In addition to the NFL, the author includes anecdotes from other leagues past and present, such as the XFL and World Football League. In his review of *300 Pounds of Attitude,* John Maxymuk wrote in the *Library Journal* that "profiled characters fall into several categories, including the mouthy and obnoxious . . . the overly intense . . . and the fun-loving flakes." A *Kirkus Reviews* contributor noted that Rand "does present a number of amusing and interesting tales." A reviewer writing in the *Herald Standard* commented: "Reading this book is like having a series of replays on paper, and it's fantastic for football fans."

BIOGRAPHICAL AND CRITICAL SOURCES:

PERIODICALS

Booklist, July 1, 2006, Wes Lukowsky, review of *300 Pounds of Attitude: The Wildest Stories and Craziest Characters the NFL Has Ever Seen,* p. 20.
Herald Standard (PA), January 4, 2007, review of *300 Pounds of Attitude.*

Kirkus Reviews, June 15, 2006, review of *300 Pounds of Attitude,* p. 624.

Library Journal, July 1, 2006, John Maxymuk, review of *300 Pounds of Attitude,* p. 86.

ONLINE

Kansas City Chiefs News Web site, http://www.kcchiefs.com/news/ (January 20, 2004), "Jonathan Rand FAQ," interview with author.*

* * *

RASHKOW, Ilona N. 1947-
(Ilona Nemesnyik Rashkow)

PERSONAL: Born April 26, 1947, in New York, NY; married, 1975. *Education:* Catholic University, B.Mus., 1971; University of Maryland, M.A., 1984; Ph.D., 1988.

ADDRESSES: Office—Department of Comparative Studies, SUNY, Stony Brook, Stony Brook, NY, 11794-3355. *E-mail*—inr@worldnet.att.net.

CAREER: Educator, scholar, and writer. Speechwriter for Congressman Richard C. White, 1971-72; Education & Public Welfare Division: Congressional Research Service, Library of Congress, Washington, DC, specialist in social legislation and section head, 1972-82; University of Georgia, lecturer in English, 1988-89; State University of New York at Stony Brook, assistant professor of comparative literature, Judaic studies, and women's studies, 1989-95, professor of comparative literature, Judaic studies, and women's studies and director of graduate studies, 1995—. Also University of Maryland, teaching fellow, 1984-85, university fellow, 1985-88; University of Maryland Meyerhoff Center for Jewish Studies, visiting research scholar, 1992-93; Jewish Theological Seminary of America, visiting research scholar, 1997; and University of Alabama at Tuscaloosa, visiting Aaron Aronov Chair of Judaic Studies, 2000.

MEMBER: Society of Biblical Literature, American Academy of Religion, Modern Language Association, American Comparative Literature Association, World Union Jewish Studies, Association of Jewish Studies; Association for the Psychoanalysis of Culture and Society.

AWARDS, HONORS: New York State/United University Professions New Faculty Development Award, 1990; Faculty Development Grant, State University of New York at Stony Brook, 1990; American Council of Learned Societies Travel Grant, 1990.

WRITINGS:

Upon the Dark Places: Anti-Semitism and Sexism in English Renaissance Biblical Translation, Sheffield Academic Press (Sheffield, England), 1990.

The Phallacy of Genesis: A Feminist-Psychoanalytic Approach, Westminster/J. Knox (Louisville, KY), 1993.

Taboo or Not Taboo: Sexuality and Family in the Hebrew Bible, Fortress Press (Minneapolis, MN), 2000.

Contributor to books, including *Reading between Texts,* edited by Danna Nolan Fewell, Westminister/John Knox Press (Louisville, KY), 1992; *Reading Bibles, Writing Bodies,* edited by David Gunn and Timothy Beal, Routledge Press (London, England), 1996; *Feminist Readings of the Book of Genesis,* edited by Athalya Brenner Sheffield Academic Press (Sheffield, England), 1998; *Dictionary of Biblical Interpretation,* Abingdon Press (Nashville, TN), 1999; *Feminist Companion to Exodus through Deuteronomy,* edited by Athalya Brenner, Sheffield Academic Press (Sheffield, England), 2000; *A Handbook for Postmodern Biblical Interpretation,* Chalice Press (St. Louis, MO), 2000; and *Eerdman's Dictionary of the Bible,* Eerdman's Publishing (Grand Rapids, MI). Contributor to journals, including *Pastoral Psychology, Semeia, Sixteenth Century Journal,* and *Mid-Hudson Language Studies.* Contributor of book reviews to periodicals, including *Journal of the American Academy of Religion, Bible Review,* and *Hebrew Studies.*

SIDELIGHTS: Ilona N. Rashkow is a Judaic scholar whose interests include the Hebrew *Bible,* feminist literary criticism, psychoanalytic literary theory, women's studies, and career history. In her book *Upon the Dark Places: Anti-Semitism and Sexism in English Renaissance Biblical Translation,* the author writes about the various agendas, some of them covert, that resulted in specific translations of the English *Bible* during the "classical period." Covering the sixteenth and early seventeenth centuries, the author focuses on the poetic differences in various translations and how the text can be changed in content and meaning by the translator. Writing in *Interpretation,* William P. Brown commented: "Rashkow's primary agenda is to demonstrate the pervasive extent to which the ideologies of anti-Semitism and misogyny permeate English translations."

Rashkow interprets some of the most famous Biblical stories that feature dysfunctional families—such as the story of Lot and his daughters—in her book *Taboo or Not Taboo: Sexuality and Family in the Hebrew Bible.* She draws from the field of psychoanalysis for her interpretations of the Biblical stories and delves into various types of sexual conduct prohibited by the *Bible.* "The book's main target audience is interested *Bible* scholars, but Rashkow's clear style ensures that the book is not beyond the grasp of any curious, open mind," wrote Anthony Heacock in *Interpretation.* Rhonda Burnette-Bletsch, writing in the *Journal of Religion,* commented that the author "challenges a number of widely-held assumptions about the nature of texts and the act of reading." *Theological Studies* contributor Ronald A. Simkins wrote that the author's "interpretations are creative and original."

BIOGRAPHICAL AND CRITICAL SOURCES:

PERIODICALS

Interpretation, January, 1993, William P. Brown, review of *Upon the Dark Places: Anti-Semitism and Sexism in English Renaissance Biblical Translation,* p. 96; July, 2001, Anthony Heacock, review of *Taboo or Not Taboo: Sexuality and Family in the Hebrew Bible,* p. 318.
Journal of Religion, October, 2001, Rhonda Burnette-Bletsch, review of *Taboo or Not Taboo,* p. 633.
Theological Studies, September, 2001, Ronald A. Simkins, review of *Taboo or Not Taboo,* p. 649.

ONLINE

State University of New York at Stony Brook Web site, http://www.sunysb.edu/ (January 26, 2007), faculty profile and author curriculum vitae.*

RASHKOW, Ilona Nemesnyik
　　See RASHKOW, Ilona N.

*　　*　　*

RAUCHWAY, Eric

PERSONAL: Education: Cornell University, A.B. (cum laude), 1991; Stanford University, Ph.D., 1996.

ADDRESSES: Home—CA. *Office*—Department of History, University of California at Davis, Davis, CA 95616. *E-mail*—earauchway@ucdavis.edu.

CAREER: University of Nevada, Reno, visiting assistant professor, 1996-98; University of Oxford, Oxford, England, university lecturer, 1998-2001; University of California at Davis, associate professor, 2001-05, professor of history, 2005—.

AWARDS, HONORS: Named one of Top Young Historians by the History News Network at George Mason University, 2007.

WRITINGS:

The Refuge of Affections: Family and American Reform Politics, 1900-1920, Columbia University Press (New York, NY), 2001.
Murdering McKinley: The Making of Theodore Roosevelt's America, Hill & Wang (New York, NY), 2003.
Blessed among Nations: How the World Made America, Hill & Wang (New York, NY), 2006.

SIDELIGHTS: Eric Rauchway serves as a professor of history at the University of California at Davis. In his *Murdering McKinley: The Making of Theodore Roosevelt's America,* Rauchway suggests that McKinley was actually killed by two assassins, at least metaphorically. After the fatal shots were fired by Leon Czolgosz, it was then-vice president Theodore Roosevelt who caused both the public and historians to discount McKinley's legacy. Furthermore, Rauchway argues, Roosevelt approached social policy with Czolgosz in mind, attempting to create a new social system that would not create such violent men. A contributor for *Kirkus Reviews* wrote that the book was marked by "occasionally sluggish prose, but serviceable enough to convey ideas of great consequence." A reviewer for *Publishers Weekly* remarked: "This ambitious book paints a fresh picture of American culture a century ago and finds there the confused stirrings of our own age." A contributor in *Library Journal* called the book a "thought-provoking work." Scott McLemee, writing for *Inside Higher Education,* found Rauchway's book to be "very smart and well-written."

In *Blessed among Nations: How the World Made America,* Rauchway takes a fresh look at American exceptionalism, suggesting that the United States came to be considered a unique nation due to activities following the Civil War, when foreign investment was high and unskilled labor provided a diverse work force. He traces the dramatic rise of the nation, but also looks at why few countries attempted to emulate the United States' social or economic structure. A contributor to *Kirkus Reviews* wrote: "Given the current reliance on foreign capital and immigrant labor, Rauchway's book is right on time and right on target." Joshua Zeitz, in a review for *American Heritage Online,* commented: "Professional historians have made a habit of lamenting the disappearance of this kind of engaging public scholarship. With his new book, Eric Rauchway has reintroduced it to a new generation of Americans." In a contribution to the *California Literary Review,* Bradley Kreit noted that "it is clear from this book that [Rauchway] has the ability—as both a researcher and writer—to one day speak to an audience beyond historians. But he has not done that here. Eric Rauchway has written a very good half of a book." Rauchway told Scott McLemee, in an interview for *Inside Higher Education:* "I'm not persuaded that the persistence of exceptionalism points, all by itself, to a rock-bottom American distinctiveness—other countries, maybe all other countries, have their own similar senses of exceptionalism—but I would say that it's easier for Americans to indulge our exceptionalism, because recent history, and the rest of the world's people, have conspired with us in maintaining it."

BIOGRAPHICAL AND CRITICAL SOURCES:

PERIODICALS

American Historical Review, December, 2002, Elizabeth J. Clapp, review of *The Refuge of Affections: Family and American Reform Politics,* 1900-1920, p. 1568; December, 2005, Matthew Pratt Guterl, review of *Murdering McKinley: The Making of Theodore Roosevelt's America,* p. 1547.

Booklist, August, 2003, Gilbert Taylor, review of *Murdering McKinley,* p. 1949.

Choice, April, 2004, P.F. Field, review of *Murdering McKinley,* p. 1537; December, 2006, S.M. McDonald, review of *Blessed among Nations: How the World Made America,* p. 705.

Journal of American History, December, 2002, K. Walter Hickel, review of *The Refuge of Affections,* pp. 1086-1087; September, 2004, John Milton Cooper, Jr., review of *Murdering McKinley,* p. 657.

Kirkus Reviews, July 15, 2003, review of *Murdering McKinley,* p. 957; May 15, 2006, review of *Blessed among Nations,* p. 510.

Library Journal, June 15, 2003, "Murders of Consequence," p. 86; June 15, 2006, Peter R. Latusek, review of *Blessed among Nations,* p. 84.

Publishers Weekly, June 2, 2003, review of *Murdering McKinley,* p. 42.

Reviews in American History, September, 2004, Leslie Butler, review of *Murdering McKinley,* pp. 399-406.

Tribune Books (Chicago, IL), August 24, 2003, review of *Murdering McKinley,* p. 7.

Reference & Research Book News, August, 2001, review of *The Refuge of Affections,* p. 124.

ONLINE

American Heritage Online, http://www.american heritage.com/ (July 22, 2006), Joshua Zeitz, "Is America Really so Unique?" review of *Blessed among Nations.*

California Literary Review Online, http://www. calitreview.com/ (August 29, 2006), Bradley Kreit, review of *Blessed among Nations.*

Foreign Affairs Online, http://www.foreignaffairs.org/ (November-December, 2006), Walter Russell Mead, review of *Blessed among Nations.*

H-Net: Humanities and Social Sciences Online, http:// www.h-net.org/ (July, 2002), review of *The Refuge of Affections.*

Inside Higher Ed Online, http://insidehighered.com/ (August 23, 2006), Scott McLemee, "The Global Exception."

University of California at Davis Web site, http:// history.ucdavis.edu/ (February 5, 2007), faculty biography.

REHM, Rush 1949-

PERSONAL: Born September 9, 1949; son of Maurice Pate and June Rehm. *Education:* Princeton University, B.A. (summa cum laude), 1973; Melbourne University, M.A., 1975; Stanford University, Ph.D., 1985.

ADDRESSES: Home—Redwood City, CA. *Office*—Department of Drama, Stanford University, 551 Serra Mall, Stanford, CA 94305-5010. *E-mail*—mrehm@stanford.edu.

CAREER: Emory University, Atlanta, GA, assistant professor of drama and classics, 1985-89; Stanford University, Stanford, CA, assistant professor, 1990-95, associate professor of drama and classics, 1995-2002, professor of drama and classics, 2002—. Director of plays, including *The Homecoming, Emperor Jones,* and *The Curse of the Starving Class*; actor in plays, including *Twelfth Night, Tales from the Vienna Woods,* and *King Lear.*

MEMBER: American Philological Association, Phi Beta Kappa.

AWARDS, HONORS: National Merit Scholar, 1968-72; Fulbright-Hays fellow, 1973-75; Felix Mayer scholar, 1978-79; Whiting fellow, 1984-85; NEH summer stipend, 1986; grant from American Council of Learned Societies, 1987-88; Lila Wallace-Readers' Digest Arts Partners grantee, 1993.

WRITINGS:

(Adapter) Aeschylus, *The Oresteian Trilogy: A Theatre Vision,* Hawthorn Press (Melbourne, Australia), 1978.
Greek Tragic Theater, Routledge (New York, NY), 1994.
Marriage to Death: The Conflation of Wedding and Funeral Rituals in Greek Tragedy, Princeton University Press (Princeton, NJ), 1994.
The Play of Space: Spatial Transformation in Greek Tragedy, Princeton University Press (Princeton, NJ), 2002.
Radical Theatre: Greek Tragedy and the Modern World, Duckworth (London, England), 2003.

Contributor of articles to professional journals.

SIDELIGHTS: Rush Rehm is a drama and classics professor, actor, and theater director whose books illuminate various aspects of Greek tragedy. In *Marriage to Death: The Conflation of Wedding and Funeral Rituals in Greek Tragedy,* Rehm examines the correlation between Athenian weddings and funerals from the fifth century B.C.E., and what their similarities symbolized. His theory is that the juxtaposition and manipulation of these events on stage was a way of challenging the prevailing morals of the day and pushing for social change. Though it is a work of academic analysis, the author "writes accessibly enough for performers of ancient tragedy on the modern stage," noted Edith Hall in her *Times Literary Supplement* review. Discussing the book in the *Classical Journal,* Nanci DeBloois found that "Rehm's conclusions and interpretations are persuasive, even though they are not unique." She considered the book's greatest value to be in the way that it discusses several plays in which this topic is prominent. *Choice* contributor M. Damen termed it "concise and well-written."

Rehm's next book, *Greek Tragic Theater,* is "ambitious in its aims, businesslike in construction, thought-provoking in assertions," praised Everard Flintoff in the *Classical Review,* adding that it "addresses an awesomely wide range of issues." These include details on performance techniques, such as the use of masks and choruses, and a discussion of four seminal Greek plays. Rehm explains how religious and artistic festivals were a crucial part of life in ancient Athens, and shows "very clearly how much Greek tragedy owes to the nature of the city which gave it birth," claimed Michael Anderson in *Theatre Research International.*

Rehm analyzes a more specific aspect of Greek theater in his next book, *The Play of Space: Spatial Transformation in Greek Tragedy.* In it, he reminds readers that while the Greek tragedies are often regarded in the modern age as textual matter, to be read and analyzed, they were really meant to be performed. "He has a fascinating and persuasive account of the physical geography of the theater of Dionysus in the fifth century," reported Emily Wilson in the *Times Literary Supplement.* She added: "Rehm's readings of individual scenes are frequently stimulating and original."

Rehm followed up this book with *Radical Theatre: Greek Tragedy and the Modern World* in 2003. It consists of five interconnected essays. The book covers a range of topics, including the theater of Dionysus' physical space and religious significance, a discussion of the word 'fear' in tragedy, a comparison of current day world events with ancient Greek drama, and an evaluation on Greek tragedy to look beyond past hardships and disasters and into the future. Writing in the *Scholia Reviews*, Betine van Zyl Smit called Rehm's descriptions and comparisons "sensitive and provocative" while overall dubbing it "a passionately argued, yet always scholarly, work." She went on to say that "it is clear that Rush Rehm has a thorough knowledge of and deep love of Greek tragedy." Charles E. Jenkins, writing in the *Bryn Mawr Classical Review*, labeled the book "an intensely personal, deeply felt meditation on the power of Greek tragedy to expose and confront contemporary and modern social ills."

BIOGRAPHICAL AND CRITICAL SOURCES:

PERIODICALS

Bryn Mawr Classical Review, March 28, 2004, Thomas E. Jenkins, review of *Radical Theatre: Greek Tragedy and the Modern World*.

Choice, March, 1993, M. Damen, review of *Greek Tragic Theater*, p. 1158; February, 1995, M. Damen, review of *Marriage to Death: The Conflation of Wedding and Fundamental Rituals in Greek Tragedy*, p. 931.

Classical Journal, October-November, 1995, Nanci DeBloois, review of *Marriage to Death*, p. 80.

Classical Review, February, 1993, Everard Flintoff, review of *Greek Tragic Theater*, pp. 434-435.

Classical World, January, 1996, Richard Jones, review of *Greek Tragic Theater*, p. 229.

Comparative Drama, fall, 1995, David Konstan, review of *Marriage to Death*, p. 382.

Greece & Rome, April, 2003, Stephen Halliwell, review of *The Play of Space: Spatial Transformation in Greek Tragedy*, p. 102.

Journal of Hellenic Studies, 2004, Barbara Goff, review of *Radical Theatre*, p. 223.

Reference & Research Book News, February, 1993, review of *Greek Tragic Theatre*, p. 30; August, 2005, review of *Radical Theatre*, p. 241.

Religious Studies Review, July, 1995, review of *Marriage to Death*, p. 228.

Scholia Reviews, 1996, Margaret R. Mezzabotta, review of *Marriage to Death*, p. 13; 2004, Betine van Zyl Smit, review of *Radical Theatre*, p. 30; 2005, Stanley Ireland, review of *The Play of Space*, p. 20.

Theatre Research International, spring, 1996, Michael Anderson, review of *Greek Tragic Theater*, p. 79.

Theatre Survey, May, 1994, Clifford Ashby, review of *Greek Tragic Theater*, p. 163; November, 2005, Edmund P. Cueva, review of *Radical Theatre*, p. 324.

Times Literary Supplement, December 25, 1992, Malcolm Heath, review of *Greek Tragic Theater*, p. 21; May 12, 1995, Edith Hall, review of *Marriage to Death*, p. 26; January 17, 2003, Emily Wilson, review of *The Play of Space*, p. 11.

ONLINE

Stanford University Department of Classics Web site, http://www.stanford.edu/dept/classics/home/ (January 3, 2007), author profile.

*   *   *

RICHARDSON, Evelyn 1950-
[A pseudonym]
(Cynthia Johnson)

PERSONAL: Born October 20, 1950, in Rochester, MN; daughter of Hugh A. (a surgeon) and Madeleine Johnson; married Brian Susnock (an executive). *Education:* Wellesley College, B.A., 1972; Simmons College, M.L.S., 1973; Northwestern University, M.A., 1977.

ADDRESSES: Home—Lexington, MA. *Office*—Cary Memorial Library, 1874 Massachusetts Ave., Lexington, MA 02420.

CAREER: Environmental Impact Center, Cambridge, MA, consulting librarian, 1973; Time Museum, Rockford, IL, consulting librarian, 1973; Memorial Hall Library, Andover, MA, reference and young adult librarian, 1973-77; Emmanuel College, Boston, MA, reference librarian, 1980-82, senior assistant director of admissions, 1982-83; Cary Memorial Library, Lexington, MA, reference and young adult librarian, 1983-88, supervisor of reference services, 1989-97, acting assistant director, 1996, head of adult services, 1997-99, assistant director, 1999-2004, head of reference, 2004—. Writer. Member of steering committee, Friends of Wellesley College.

MEMBER: American Library Association, American Society for Eighteenth Century Studies, Romance Writers of America, Lexington Historical Society, Boston Athenaeum.

AWARDS, HONORS: Reviewers' Choice Award, *Romantic Times,* 1997, for *My Wayward Lady.*

WRITINGS:

ROMANCE NOVELS

The Education of Lady Frances (also see below), New American Library (New York, NY), 1989.

Miss Cresswell's London Triumph (also see below), New American Library (New York, NY), 1990.

The Nabob's Ward, New American Library (New York, NY), 1991.

The Bluestocking's Dilemma, New American Library (New York, NY), 1992.

The Willful Widow, New American Library (New York, NY), 1994.

Lady Alex's Gamble, New American Library (New York, NY), 1995.

The Reluctant Heiress, New American Library (New York, NY), 1996.

My Wayward Lady, New American Library (New York, NY), 1997.

The Gallant Guardian, New American Library (New York, NY), 1998.

My Lady Nightingale, New American Library (New York, NY), 1999.

Lord Harry's Daughter, New American Library (New York, NY), 2001.

Fortune's Lady, New American Library (New York, NY), 2002.

A Foreign Affair, New American Library (New York, NY), 2003.

The Scandalous Widow, New American Library (New York, NY), 2004.

A Lady of Talent, Signet Books (New York, NY), 2005.

The Education of Lady Frances and *Miss Cresswell's London Triumph,* Penguin Group (New York, NY), 2006.

Historical fiction reviewer, *Library Journal,* 1981—.

SIDELIGHTS: Regency historical romance writer Evelyn Richardson is a pseudonym for Cynthia Johnson, a professional librarian. Richardson told *CA:* "I literally began my writing career in 1983 when I was looking for the job that led to the one I now have. In an effort to distract myself from the frustration and insecurity that naturally beset someone who is between jobs, I did what I have always done to amuse, distract, and comfort myself. I told myself a story—my usual type of story—about an independent, hardworking, and intelligent heroine who eventually succeeds in achieving her dreams regardless of what society thinks of her. But this time, instead of keeping the story locked inside my head, I wrote it down, and it grew into my first book, *The Education of Lady Frances.* But in truth, my writing career began the first time I was able to read books by myself and I discovered that other people, other places, and other times were only a page turn away. I spent my summers haunting the public library and bringing home stacks of books . . . .

"Then, when I was fifteen and stranded at home on a snow day with nothing from the library to read, I discovered *Pride and Prejudice* on our very own bookshelves. Elizabeth Bennett, clever and independent, was the perfect heroine for a girl who was more interested in schoolwork than social activities, and then and there I fell in love with Jane Austen and the Regency period. When I had exhausted Jane Austen, I was lucky enough to discover Georgette Heyer and went on from there to read Claire Darcy and all the others who created that wonderful world of witty dialogue, and heroines who thought for themselves.

"I enjoyed this world to such a degree that I studied late-eighteenth- and early- nineteenth-century literature in college and graduate school and wrote my honors thesis on Fanny Burney whose *Evelina* gave me my pseudonymous first name, and whose diaries gave such a wonderful picture of the times. I have been living and breathing this period ever since. Writing gives me a wonderful excuse to seek out the details of my characters' daily lives in the newspapers, periodicals, books, and diaries of the time and to bury myself in the research that, as a librarian, I live for.

"My first brush with historical fiction as a fourth grader made me grateful to those authors who could entertain and inform at the same time. If I could choose to do anything in the world, it would be to do that for my readers as well."

Richardson's historical romances have been consistently praised for their wealth of period detail and their rich characterizations. In *Library Journal*, Kristin Ramsdell called the author a "veteran writer of intelligent, well-received Regencies." Elsewhere in *Library Journal*, Ramsdell noted that Richardson's novels are "filled with complex, fully developed relationships and rich, uncommon historical detail." John Charles, who has reviewed several of Richardson's Regencies for *Booklist*, remarked on the author's "gift for subtle character development and deliciously dry wit."

BIOGRAPHICAL AND CRITICAL SOURCES:

BOOKS

Charles, John, and Shelley Mosley, *Romance Today: An A to Z Guide to Contemporary American Romance Writers*, Greenwood Publishers (Westport, CT), 2006, pp. 326-328.

PERIODICALS

American Libraries, November, 1991, "In Pursuit of the Muse: Librarians Who Write."
Booklist, March 1, 2003, John Charles, review of *A Foreign Affair*, p. 1151; April 1, 2004, John Charles, review of *The Scandalous Widow*, p. 1356; February 15, 2005, John Charles, review of *A Lady of Talent*, p. 1068.
Library Journal, March 15, 1990, "Reviewer's File"; November 15, 1999, Kristin Ramsdell, review of *My Lady Nightingale*, p. 57; February 15, 2001, Kristin Ramsdell, review of *Lord Harry's Daughter*, p. 155; February 15, 2003, Kristin Ramsdell, review of *A Foreign Affair*, p. 123; February 15, 2004, Kristin Ramsdell, review of *The Scandalous Widow*, p. 113.

Publishers Weekly, February 4, 2002, review of *Fortune's Lady*, p. 59.

ONLINE

Romance Reader, http://theromancereader.com/ (December 27, 2006), Jean Mason, review of *The Gallant Guardian*; review of *Lord Harry's Daughter*; Cathy Sova, review of *My Lady Nightingale*.

* * *

RICHTER, Duncan 1966-
(Duncan John Richter)

PERSONAL: Born December 26, 1966, in Chester, England. *Education:* Oxford University, B.A. (with honors), 1988; University of Wales, University College of Swansea, M.Phil., 1989; University of Virginia, Ph.D., 1995.

ADDRESSES: Office—Department of Psychology and Philosophy, Virginia Military Institute, Lexington, VA 24450. *E-mail*—eichterdj@vmi.edu.

CAREER: Virginia Military Institute, Lexington, professor of philosophy, 1995—. University of Virginia, instructor, between 1992 and 1994; University of Richmond, replacement instructor, 1995; conference and seminar participant.

MEMBER: Phi Kappa Phi.

WRITINGS:

Ethics after Anscombe: Post "Modern Moral Philosophy," Kluwer Academic Publishers (Boston, MA), 2000.
Historical Dictionary of Wittgenstein's Philosophy, Scarecrow Press (Lanham, MD), 2004.
Wittgenstein at His Word, Thoemmes Continuum (Bristol, England), 2004.

Contributor to books, including *Ethical Issues in the New Genetics: Are Genes Us?*, edited by Brenda Almond and Michael Parker, Ashgate Publishing (Burlington, VT), 2003. Contributor to periodicals, including *Philosophical Papers, Erkenntnis, Religious Studies, Essays in Philosophy, Review Journal of Philosophy and Social Science, Southern Journal of Philosophy,* and *Journal of Value Inquiry.*

* * *

RICHTER, Duncan John
    See RICHTER, Duncan

* * *

RIMLAND, Bernard 1928-2006

OBITUARY NOTICE— See index for *CA* sketch: Born November 15, 1928, in Cleveland, OH; died of prostate cancer, November 21, 2006, in El Cajon, CA. Psychologist, researcher, and author. Rimland is widely regarded as the man who modernized the study and treatment of childhood autism. He was a graduate of San Diego State University, where he earned a B.A. in 1950 and an M.A. in 1952. He then completed his Ph.D. at Pennsylvania State University in 1954, quickly returning to his favorite home city. Here he was a director at the U.S. Navy Personnel Research Laboratory until 1973. Named director of the Applied Psychobiology Program that year, he continued to work for the Navy until 1983, when he would focus on his own research. Rimland first became interested in autism after the birth of his son, Mark, who was diagnosed with the illness. At the time, psychologists believed in the conclusions of Bruno Bettelheim, the psychologist who blamed autism on mothers who had lacked emotional attachment to their children. Rimland knew his wife was a loving, attentive mother, and dismissed the conventional wisdom as ridiculous. He set out to research the little-understood illness for the next five years, publishing his conclusions in the landmark book *Infantile Autism: The Syndrome and Its Implications for a Neural Theory of Behavior* (1964). The psychologist saw autism as being caused by neurological birth defects, which he attributed to mercury poisoning that was the result of vaccines being used at the time. He campaigned to have the heavy metal removed from such drugs, but met with resistance from the government and medical community. Now on a mission to make autism better understood by parents and physicians, he founded the

Autism Research Institute in 1967, as well as the Autism Society of America. Rimland's work showed that autism was a much more common mental illness than previously believed, and it is now believed to affect one in every 175 children in America. The psychologist saw this as a growing epidemic related to environmental pollution. He developed behavioral therapies, first advocated by psychologist O. Ivar Lovaas, to treat the disease that many saw as very effective. Also coeditor of the book *Modern Therapies* (1976), Rimland will be remembered as the father of modern autism research.

OBITUARIES AND OTHER SOURCES:

PERIODICALS

Chicago Tribune, November 29, 2006, Section 3, p. 9.
Los Angeles Times, November 26, 2006, p. B14.
New York Times, November 28, 2006, p. C20.
Times (London, England), January 9, 2007, p. 48.

* * *

ROBERTS, Jason 1962-

PERSONAL: Born May 16, 1962 in Arcadia, CA; son of Anthony K. Roberts (a photojournalist) and Gloria Jean Neil (an actress); married Patricia Mixon; children: two. *Education:* University of California, Santa Cruz, B.A.

ADDRESSES: Home—Marin County, CA. *Office*—The Writers' Grotto, 490 2nd St., Ste. 200, San Francisco, CA 94107. *E-mail*—jason@jasonroberts.net.

CAREER: Freelance writer. *Learn2.com* Web site, creator and CEO, 1994-99. Guest lecturer at Stanford University, San Francisco State University, and California College of the Arts.

AWARDS, HONORS: Van Zorn Prize for fiction, 2004; finalist, National Book Critics Circle Award for Biography, 2006.

WRITINGS:

Director Demystified: Creating Interactive Multimedia with Macromedia Director, Peachpit Press (Berkeley, CA), 1995.

Director 5 Demystified: Creating Interactive Multimedia with Macromedia Director, Peachpit Press (Berkeley, CA), 1996.

Director 6 Demystified: The Official Guide to Macromedia Director, Lingo, and Shockwave, Peachpit Press (Berkeley, CA), 1998.

(With Phil Gross) *Director 7 Demystified: The Official Guide to Macromedia Director, Lingo, and Shockwave,* Peachpit Press (Berkeley, CA), 1999.

(Editor) *The Learn2 Guide: Burp a Baby, Carve a Turkey, and 108 Other Things You Should Know How to Do,* illustrated by Scott Hartley and Ethan Hay, Villard (New York, NY), 1999.

(With Phil Gross) *Director 8 Demystified: The Official Guide to Macromedia Director, Lingo, and Shockwave,* Peachpit Press (Berkeley, CA), 2000.

A Sense of the World: How a Blind Man Became History's Greatest Traveler, HarperCollins (New York, NY), 2006.

Contributor to *Village Voice, McSweeney's, The Believer,* the *San Francisco Chronicle,* and *Washington Post.*

SIDELIGHTS: Jason Roberts is a freelance writer who has written for numerous periodicals, including *McSweeney's, The Believer, San Francisco Chronicle,* and *Village Voice.* In 1994 Roberts founded the *Learn2.com* Web site, considered among the first uses of the Internet as an education outlet to the general public. The company grew and ultimately was listed on the NASDAQ. Five years after its start, *Yahoo.com* Web site named the site "one of the twelve most important Web sites of the 20th century," according to the profile on the *Jason Roberts Home Page.* It is around this time that Roberts decided to leave the company to continue writing. In 2004, he was awarded the Van Zorn Prize, an award established and bestowed by author Michael Chabon, for fiction by an emerging writer "in the tradition of Edgar Allan Poe."

Although Roberts had several books already published, his first publication to receive wide critical success was *A Sense of the World: How a Blind Man Became History's Greatest Traveler* in 2006. This book is a biography of James Holman (1786-1857), a blind man who garnered some international acclaim for traveling around the world on his own. Holman's travels and even specific conversations were documented well enough for Roberts to reconstruct his life travels and

bring him out of obscurity. Many critics were pleased with the amount of research that went into the book. Gilbert Taylor, in his review for *Booklist,* commented that "Roberts reveals thorough research through a perceptive, expressive narrative." A reviewer in the *Economist* noted that Roberts "paints a convincing and well-researched picture." Alan Turner, reviewing the book in *Publishers Weekly,* found the book to be "a fascinating, compelling, and very entertaining combination of travelogue and character study."

BIOGRAPHICAL AND CRITICAL SOURCES:

PERIODICALS

Biography, summer, 2006, Florence Williams, review of *A Sense of the World: How a Blind Man Became History's Greatest Traveler,* p. 523.

Booklist, June 1, 2006, Gilbert Taylor, review of *A Sense of the World,* p. 29.

California Bookwatch, October, 2006, review of *A Sense of the World.*

Chicago Tribune, August 13, 2006, Danielle Chapman, review of *A Sense of the World,* p. 8.

Economist, August 26, 2006, review of *A Sense of the World,* p. 70.

Kirkus Reviews, May 1, 2006, review of *A Sense of the World,* p. 449.

Library Journal, December, 1996, review of *Director 5 Demystified: Creating Interactive Multimedia with Macromedia Director,* p. 138; March 1, 1998, Thom Gillespie, review of *Director 6 Demystified: The Official Guide to Macromedia Director, Lingo, and Shockwave,* p. 121; November 1, 1999, Thom Gillespie, review of *Director 7 Demystified: The Official Guide to Macromedia Director, Lingo, and Shockwave,* p. 120; May 1, 2006, Robert J. Andrews, review of *A Sense of the World,* p. 94.

London Review of Books, September 7, 2006, Jenny Diski, review of *A Sense of the World,* p. 23.

Publishers Weekly, April 3, 2006, review of *A Sense of the World,* p. 49; April 10, 2006, Alan Turner, review of *A Sense of the World,* p. 6; May 1, 2006, Chris Barsanti, "The Blind Traveler: PW talks with Jason Roberts," p. 46.

School Library Journal, September, 2006, Dori DeSpain, review of *A Sense of the World,* p. 250.

SciTech Book News, December, 1999, review of *Director 7 Demystified,* p. 19.

Seattle Times, July 5, 2006, Mary Ann Gwinn, review of *A Sense of the World.*

Spectator, July 29, 2006, Sandy Balfour, review of *A Sense of the World.*

Time, June 12, 2006, Lev Grossman, review of *A Sense of the World,* p. 102.

Washington Post Book World, July 9, 2006, review of *A Sense of the World,* p. 9.

ONLINE

Jason Roberts Home Page, http://www.jasonroberts. net (January 2, 2007), author biography.

*   *   *

ROBERTS, Siobhan

PERSONAL: Female.

ADDRESSES: Home—Toronto, Ontario, Canada. *E-mail*—siobhan.roberts@sympatico.ca.

CAREER: Writer and journalist. *National Post,* Canada, national reporter and feature writer, 1999-2001.

AWARDS, HONORS: National Magazine Award (two), Canada, for articles "Figure Head" in *Toronto Life* and "Broken Records" in *Saturday Night.*

WRITINGS:

King of Infinite Space: Donald Coxeter, the Man Who Saved Geometry, Anansi (Toronto, Ontario, Canada), 2006.

Contributor to periodicals, including *SEED, Walrus, Toronto Life, Saturday Night, Canadian Geographic, Mathematical Intelligencer, Globe and Mail,* and the *National Post. King of Infinite Space* has also been published in Italy, Japan, and Korea.

SIDELIGHTS: Siobhan Roberts is a freelance journalist who wrote an article about mathematician Donald Coxeter that won Canada's National Magazine Award and led her to write the book *King of Infinite Space: Donald Coxeter, the Man Who Saved Geometry.* The biography combines the life story of Coxeter and, in the process, reveals the progress of twentieth-century mathematics. In her story of the late mathematician at Toronto University, Roberts examines how, in her opinion, Coxeter kept the field of classical geometry from falling into oblivion during the many advances of modern mathematics. Although some were decrying geometry as irrelevant by the 1940s and 1950s, Roberts writes that Coxeter's work on group theory and the principles of symmetry reestablished geometry's validity and influenced noted mathematicians and inventors such as Buckminster Fuller. She also describes Coexter's relationship with graphic artist M.C. Escher. Ian D. Gordon, writing in the *Library Journal,* called *King of Infinite Space* "a significant work for mathematicians at all levels." Toronto *Globe and Mail* reviewer Jeffrey S. Rosenthal referred to the biography as "part biography, part scientific history and part epic," adding that "the book also occasionally offers poignant looks into Coxeter's soul." In a review in *Booklist,* Gilbert Taylor noted that the "biography bears inclusion in the popular mathematics collection." A *Publishers Weekly* contributor wrote: "Roberts . . . puts most of the technical material in appendixes, so the text is readily accessible to a general audience."

BIOGRAPHICAL AND CRITICAL SOURCES:

PERIODICALS

Booklist, September 15, 2006, Gilbert Taylor, review of *King of Infinite Space: Donald Coxeter, the Man Who Saved Geometry,* p. 12.

Chicago Tribune, December 3, 2006, Nathan L. Harshman, review of *King of Infinite Space.*

Globe and Mail (Toronto, Ontario, Canada), October 14, 2006, Jeffrey S. Rosenthal, review of *King of Infinite Space.*

Library Journal, August 1, 2006, Ian D. Gordon, review of *King of Infinite Space,* p. 118.

Publishers Weekly, June 26, 2006, review of *King of Infinite Space,* p. 43.

Science News, October 14, 2006, review of *King of Infinite Space,* p. 255.

ONLINE

Agony Column Book Reviews and Commentary, http:// trashotron.com/agony/ (September 8, 2006), review of *King of Infinite Space.*

American Scientist Online, http://www. americanscientist.org/ (January 25, 2007), Greg Ross, "The Bookshelf Talks with Siobhan Roberts."

Not Even Wrong, http://www.math.columbia.edu/~woit/ wordpress/ (October 19, 2006), review of *King of Infinite Space.*

Siobhan Roberts Home Page, http://www.siobhan roberts.com (January 25, 2007).

Walker Books Web site, http://www.walkerbooks.com/ (January 25, 2007), profile of author.*

* * *

ROBINS, Jane

PERSONAL: Female.

ADDRESSES: Home—London, England.

CAREER: Journalist and writer. Has worked as a reporter for the British Broadcasting Corporation's (BBC) *On the Record* and editor of Radio 4's *The Week in Westminster.*

WRITINGS:

The Trial of Queen Caroline: The Scandalous Affair That Nearly Ended a Monarchy (nonfiction), Free Press (New York, NY), 2006, published as *Rebel Queen: The Trial of Queen Caroline,* Simon & Schuster Ltd. (London, England), 2006.

Contributor to periodicals, including the *Economist, Independent, Spectator* and the *New Statesman.*

SIDELIGHTS: In her book *The Trial of Queen Caroline: The Scandalous Affair That Nearly Ended a Monarchy,* published in England as *Rebel Queen: The Trial of Queen Caroline,* Jane Robins tells the story of Caroline of Brunswick, who married the British Prince of Wales in 1795. When the Prince became King George IV in 1820, he set out to divorce Caroline. Robins begins her tale with the engagement of Caroline to the Prince, who never saw her before and found her unattractive. She then follows the couple's tumultuous relationship, which included a long separation. As she delves into the resulting divorce trial before the House of Lords, where the very popular Queen was accused of adultery, the author ultimately reveals how Caroline was acquitted of infidelity charges and the unpopular King was forbidden to divorce her. A *Kirkus Reviews* contributor referred to *The Trial of Queen Caroline* as "a lucid account of one of the messiest, sleaziest and most dangerous times in British history." Brad Hooper, writing in *Booklist,* commented that "George and Caroline . . . were colorful in their own fashion and make engaging reading for the history buff." A contributor to the *Economist* called Robins's book "fascinating," adding: "The English, it was said, were an 'inquisitive, prying, doubting, reading people' and Ms. Robins brings them richly to life—especially the women who, for the first time in English history, came out collectively and publicly as a sisterhood."

BIOGRAPHICAL AND CRITICAL SOURCES:

PERIODICALS

Booklist, July 1, 2006, Brad Hooper, review of *The Trial of Queen Caroline: The Scandalous Affair That Nearly Ended a Monarchy,* p. 25.

Economist (U.S.), August 5, 2006, review of *The Trial of Queen Caroline,* p. 76.

Guardian (London, England), September 30, 2006, David McKie, review of *The Trial of Queen Caroline.*

Kirkus Reviews, June 1, 2006, review of *The Trial of Queen Caroline,* p. 564.

Library Journal, July 1, 2006, Matthew Todd, review of *The Trial of Queen Caroline,* p. 90.

Publishers Weekly, June 5, 2006, review of *The Trial of Queen Caroline,* p. 51.

Reference & Research Book News, November, 2006, review of *The Trial of Queen Caroline.*

ONLINE

Simon & Schuster Web site, http://www.simonsays. com/ (January 25, 2007), brief profile of author.

Telegraph.co.uk, http://www.telegraph.co.uk/ (June 18, 2006), review of *Rebel Queen.**

RODGER, Katharine A. 1974-

PERSONAL: Born November 17, 1974, in Lawrence, MA; daughter of David (a bookseller and educator) and Katharine (an educator) Rodger; married Jonathan Feagle (an educator), August 12, 2006. *Ethnicity:* "White." *Education:* University of California, San Diego, B.A., 1998; San Jose State University, M.A., 2001; University of California, Davis, Ph.D. studies.

ADDRESSES: Home—Berkeley, CA. *E-mail*—ktrodger@yahoo.com.

CAREER: Writer.

WRITINGS:

(Editor) *Renaissance Man of Cannery Row: The Life and Letters of Edward F. Ricketts,* University of Alabama Press (Tuscaloosa, AL), 2002.
(Editor) *Breaking Through: Essays, Journals, and Travelogues of Edward F. Ricketts,* University of California Press (Berkeley, CA), 2006.

*   *   *

ROSENBLUM, Robert H. 1927-2006

OBITUARY NOTICE— See index for *CA* sketch: Born July 24, 1927, in New York, NY; died of complications from colon cancer, December 6, 2006, in New York, NY. Historian, educator, and author. A New York University professor of fine arts, Rosenblum was noted for helping redefine Modernism and was remembered for organizing sometimes quirky art exhibitions. A 1948 graduate of Queens College, he attended Yale for his master's degree in 1948 and completed a Ph.D. at New York University in 1956. He was an associate professor of art and archeology at Princeton University from 1956 until 1966. After a year at Yale, he joined the New York University faculty in 1967. That year, Rosenblum published what is considered to be his most important work, *Transformations in Late Eighteenth-Century Art* (1967). Here he argued that the roots of Modernism could be traced back well before the turn of the twentieth century, which had been the benchmark previously espoused by art historians. Rosenblum thought that the stirrings of Modernism could be found as far back as eighteenth-century France, and he also broadened the movement's scope to include artists from such countries as Denmark and Germany. Having eclectic tastes for an art historian, Rosenblum was just as interested in minor artists as he was in the masters; at times, this caused him to be criticized for low-brow tastes, especially when he included such artists as Norman Rockwell in his organized exhibitions. Also a dog lover, Rosenblum published a book all about canines featured in art titled *The Dog in Art from Rococo to Post-Modernism* (1988). Among his other notable works are *Modern Painting and the Romantic Tradition: Friedrich to Rothko* (1975), which was nominated for the National Book Award, and *On Modern American Art: Selected Essays* (1999), which received a PEN Award nomination. His last book was *Introducing Gilbert & George* (2004). Rosenblum was named a Commander of the French Order of Arts and Letters and was inducted into the Legion of Honor in 2003 for his contributions to French art history. Learning of his cancer in 2004, he continued to write and teach until a few weeks before his passing. He had been a favorite professor at New York University, where he was presented with the Distinguished Teaching Award in 2005.

OBITUARIES AND OTHER SOURCES:

PERIODICALS

New York Times, December 9, 2006, p. A16.
Times (London, England), December 29, 2006, p. 57.

*   *   *

ROUSH, Robert A. 1962-

PERSONAL: Born January 6, 1962, in Buffalo, NY; son of Richard (in sales) and Ruth (in travel business) Roush; companion of Steven Olofson (in information technology). *Ethnicity:* "German American." *Education:* State University of New York at Buffalo, B.F.A., 1986, M.A.H., 1988; Westbrook University, Ph.D., 2001. *Politics:* Democrat. *Religion:* Untiarian-Universalist.

ADDRESSES: Office—Geisinger Health System Foundation, 100 N. Academy Ave., Danville, PA 17822. *E-mail*—rroush@ptd.net.

CAREER: Geisinger Health System Foundation, Danville, PA, senior development officer, 2005—.

WRITINGS:

Complementary and Alternative Medicine: Clinic Design, Haworth Press (New York, NY), 2003.

Contributor to periodicals, including *Valley Gay Press.*

SIDELIGHTS: Robert A. Roush told *CA:* "I am interested in varying cultural interpretations of the aspects of humanity we all share. I believe that we can synthesize these different approaches (especially in health care) to create a more perfect understanding of our universe."

* * *

RUSSELL, Karen 1981-

PERSONAL: Born 1981. *Education:* Columbia University, M.F.A.

ADDRESSES: Home—New York, NY.

CAREER: Writer. Worked previously in the publicity department of Perseus Books, New York, NY.

AWARDS, HONORS: Transatlantic Review/Henfield Foundation Award, 2005.

WRITINGS:

St. Lucy's Home for Girls Raised by Wolves (short stories), Knopf Publishing (New York, NY), 2006.

Contributor of short stories to numerous publications, including *Conjunctions, Granta, Zoetrope, Oxford American,* and the *New Yorker.*

SIDELIGHTS: Karen Russell was an avid reader as a child, drawn to both typical young adult fare and to classic literature, and began writing at an early age.

Ultimately earning a master of fine arts degree from Columbia University, Russell made a name for herself in 2005 when she was selected by *New York* magazine as one of twenty-five New Yorkers to watch under the age of twenty-five. Her story "Haunting Olivia" was published in the *New Yorker*'s debut fiction issue. That story was included along with nine others in Russell's first published collection, *St. Lucy's Home for Girls Raised by Wolves.* Her work has been lauded by critics as being wholly original and powerful in its fantastical imagery. In an interview with *New Yorker* contributor Carin Besser, Russell explained what she believes to be her creative inspiration: "Probably some mental Bermuda Triangle formed by diet Coke, cartoons, and insomnia. . . . I'm also from South Florida, where the lines between fantasy and reality have all melted together. Things like the goggles seem a lot less fantastical when you grow up in the shadow of a giant fibreglass dolphin."

Gillian Engberg wrote in a review for *Booklist:* "Original and astonishing, joyful and unsettling, these are stories that will stay with readers." A *Publishers Weekly* reviewer commended Russell's "powers of description and mimicry," further noting: "Her macabre fantasies structurally evoke great Southern writers like Flannery O'Connor." In a *People* feature, Lauren Gallo called Russell "a storyteller with a voice like no other." *Library Journal* contributor Amy Ford described the collection as a "startlingly original set of stories," remarking that Russell is "poised to become a literary powerhouse."

BIOGRAPHICAL AND CRITICAL SOURCES:

PERIODICALS

Booklist, September 15, 2006, Gillian Engberg, review of *St. Lucy's Home for Girls Raised by Wolves,* p. 29.
Library Journal, October 1, 2006, Amy Ford, review of *St. Lucy's Home for Girls Raised by Wolves,* p. 64.
People, September 18, 2006, Lauren Gallo, review of *St. Lucy's Home for Girls Raised by Wolves,* p. 51.
Publishers Weekly, July 24, 2006, review of *St. Lucy's Home for Girls Raised by Wolves,* p. 33.

ONLINE

New Yorker Online, http://www.newyorker.com/ (June 13, 2005), Carin Besser, author interview.*

RYAN, Darlene 1958-

PERSONAL: Born 1958, in Fredricton, New Brunswick, Canada; daughter of John W. Arsenault and Elsie Dorothy Stairs; married J. Patrick Ryan; children: one daughter. *Education:* University of New Brunswick, B.Sc., 1980; St. Thomas University, B.Ed., 1982.

ADDRESSES: Home—New Brunswick, Canada. *E-mail*—darlene@darleneryan.com.

CAREER: Writer. Has worked as a lab instructor, chambermaid, fitness teacher, lifeguard, and disk jockey.

MEMBER: Sisters in Crime (Guppy chapter).

AWARDS, HONORS: New Brunswick Arts Board creation grant, 2000; University of New Brunswick Childhood Centre Writing-for-Babies Contest winner, 2003, for *Kisses, Kisses, Kisses;* YALSA Teen Top-Ten List nomination, 2005, American Library Association Best Books for Young Adults list nomination, Canadian Children's Book Centre Our Choice listee, 2005, and Stellar Book Award nomination, 2006-07, all for *Rules for Life.*

WRITINGS:

FOR CHILDREN

Kisses, Kisses, Kisses, illustrated by Peter Manchester, University of New Brunswick Early Childhood Centre (Fredricton, New Brunswick, Canada), 2003.
Rules for Life (young-adult novel), Orca Book Publishers (Victoria, British Columbia, Canada), 2004.
Saving Grace (young-adult novel), Orca Book Publishers (Custer, WA), 2006.

OTHER

A Mother's Adoption Journey, Second Story Press (Toronto, Ontario, Canada), 2001.

SIDELIGHTS: Darlene Ryan once commented: "One of my favorite movies is the Billy Crystal/Danny De-Vito comedy, *Throw Momma from the Train.* In it, Crystal's character, a creative writing teacher, gives what I still consider is the best piece of writing advice: 'A writer writes.' I know it seems sort of obvious, but think about it. Writes. Not watches *Friends* re-runs. Not plays solitaire on the computer. Not sleeps late on Saturday morning.

"A writer writes.

"Not talks about writing. Not spends three months fixing up an office to write in.

"A writer writes.

"I spent a lot of years working in radio, something I loved. I've been a late-night disk jockey, a producer, an entertainment columnist, a consumer reporter, a news reader, and a copywriter. One way or another, I was always writing. I actually learned a lot from writing commercial, which some people say isn't very different from writing fiction. I learned how to write when I was bored, when I was tired, and when I had nothing to say. I learned how to write fast. My spelling got a little better. My handwriting got worse. I learned that criticism didn't always mean something I'd written was awful. And praise didn't always mean it was good.

"And then one day I went to China to adopt a baby girl and everything in my life changed. I kept a journal during the adoption process—twenty-two long months. I thought that maybe our baby would want to know how she ended up as ours and I wanted her to know what I was thinking and feeling when it was all happening.

"In November of 2001 my first book, *A Mother's Adoption Journey,* was published. That happened because for months and months before, I was writing. I didn't really have any time to write. I was a first-time mother to a beautiful thirteen-month-old daughter. And after my husband's short parental leave expired, I was a single mom five days out of every nine.

"The book was the story of the journey—literally and figuratively—that had brought me to my child. I wanted someday to be able to hand my daughter her story. I wanted to write that book more than anything. More than I wanted to soak in a tub steaming with the scent of eucalyptus. More than I wanted to talk to someone with a vocabulary beyond 'bye' and 'up.' More than I wanted to sleep.

"A writer writes.

"My second book, *Kisses, Kisses, Kisses,* happened because of a contest. I hadn't planned to write a children's picture book although I'd always made up stories for my daughter. As part of the "Born to Read" program, *Kisses, Kisses, Kisses* is now in the home of close to 12,000 babies. (Wow.)

"I wrote the first chapter of *Rules for Life* as a writing sample for a workshop with Kevin Major at the Maritime Writers' Workshop. It began from a very simple premise: What if you had an evil stepmother, except she was nice? In our one-on-one meeting, Kevin said, 'This is good.' When Kevin later asked if there were any more pages, I lied and said there were—and then raced home to write them.

"A writer writes.

"When *Rules for Life* was published, I realized that I seemed to have a career as a writer going. My second book, *Saving Grace,* begins with another what if. What if you had a baby and put it up for adoption . . . and then stole it back?

Now I have four books published, two more I'm working on, and a file full of ideas. And I still don't have enough time to write. But I do.

"A writer writes."

BIOGRAPHICAL AND CRITICAL SOURCES:

PERIODICALS

Bulletin of the Center for Children's Books, February, 2005, Deborah Stevenson, review of *Rules for Life,* p. 264.
Canadian Book Review Annual, 2001, review of *A Mother's Adoption Journey,* p. 72.
Kliatt, March, 2005, Olivia Durant, review of *Rules for Life,* p. 23; January, 2007, Lisa Carlson, review of *Saving Grace,* p. 25.
Resource Links, April, 2006, Elisabeth Hegerat, review of *Rules for Life,* p. 38.
School Library Journal, March, 2005, Elizabeth Fernandez, review of *Rules for Life,* p. 218.
Voice of Youth Advocates, June, 2005, Jennifer McIntosh, review of *Rules for Life,* p. 138.

ONLINE

Darlene Ryan Home Page, http://www.darleneryan. com (February 7, 2007).*

S

SACHS, Aaron
(Aaron Jacob Sachs)

PERSONAL: Education: Harvard University, A.B., 1992; Yale University, Ph.D., 2004.

ADDRESSES: Office—Cornell University, 450 McGraw Hall, Ithaca, NY 14853-4601; fax: 607-255-0469. *E-mail*—as475@cornell.edu.

CAREER: Historian, educator, and writer. Cornell University, Ithaca, NY, professor of intellectual history. Formerly worked as an environmental journalist.

AWARDS, HONORS: Project Censored Award in U.S. journalism, 1998, for an article on Nigerian playwright and environmentalist Ken Saro-Wiwa; Honorary Mellon fellowship, 1998-99; Jacob K. Javits fellowship, U.S. Department of Education, 1998-2002; Bienecke Library Research fellowship, 2001; Huntington Library Research fellowship, 2001-20; John F. Enders Research fellowship, Yale University, 2002; Graduate Affiliate fellowship, Whitney Humanities Center, Yale University, 2003-04; Prize Teaching fellowship, Yale University, 2003-04; Mrs. Giles Whiting Dissertation Fellowship, 2003-04; John Addison Porter Prize, Yale University and Washington Egleston Historical Prize, both 2005, both for dissertation; George Washington Egleston Historical Prize (for dissertation), Yale University, 2005; Andrew W. Mellon Short-Term fellowship, Massachusetts Historical Society, 2006-07. Also recipient of research grants.

WRITINGS:

(With John E. Young) *The Next Efficiency Revolution: Creating a Sustainable Materials Economy,* edited by Ed Ayers, Worldwatch Institute (Washington, DC), 1994.

Eco-Justice: Linking Human Rights and the Environment, edited by Jane A. Peterson, Worldwatch Institute (Washington, DC), 1995.

The Humboldt Current: Nineteenth-Century Exploration and the Roots of American Environmentalism, Viking (New York, NY), 2006.

Contributor to journals, including *Pacific Historical Review, History and Theory, Palimpsest,* and *World Watch.*

SIDELIGHTS: In his book *The Humboldt Current: Nineteenth-Century Exploration and the Roots of American Environmentalism,* Aaron Sachs tells how Prussian naturalist and explorer Alexander von Humboldt, who was world-famous in late eighteenth and early nineteenth centuries, profoundly influenced the development of ecology and environmentalism. Considered by many to be the first ecologist, Humboldt developed many areas of expertise, according to Sachs, including inventor, explorer, climatologist, botanist, cosmic theorist, and philanthropist. The author begins by outlining Humboldt's life and career and then incorporates Humboldt's extensive philosophy on interconnectedness of nature as he tells the story of four American explorers who were influenced by Humboldt's thoughts and philosophies. The explorers are Clarence King, first director of the

U.S. Geological Survey; George Melville, an Arctic expedition survivor; John Muir, famous environmentalist and founder of the Sierra Club, and J.N. Reynolds, who helped push for an expedition that discovered Antarctica.

Writing in *Audubon,* Kathleen McGowan noted that "the portraits of these early environmentalists are compelling, particularly the surprising depiction of John Muir." A *Kirkus Reviews* contributor wrote: "The book's greatest achievement lies in its deeply impressive scope, its integration not just of science and exploration, but also of the art, literature and politics of the 19th century." Referring to Humboldt's influence on the growth of environmentalism in America, a *Publishers Weekly* contributor commented: "This ambitious subject is admirably tackled in this complexly argued book by Sachs." Donald Worster wrote in the *American Scholar* that "as a history of exploration, it is brilliant, imaginative, and bold."

BIOGRAPHICAL AND CRITICAL SOURCES:

PERIODICALS

American Scholar, autumn, 2006, Donald Worster, review of *The Humboldt Current: Nineteenth-Century Exploration and the Roots of American Environmentalism,* p. 130.
Audubon, November-December, 2006, Kathleen McGowan, review of *The Humboldt Current,* p. 84.
Booklist, August 1, 2006, Gilbert Taylor, review of *The Humboldt Current,* p. 21.
Harper's, August, 2006, John Leonard, review of *The Humboldt Current,* p. 83.
Kirkus Reviews, June 1, 2006, review of *The Humboldt Current,* p. 564.
Library Journal, July 1, 2006, Patricia Ann Owens, review of *The Humboldt Current,* p. 105.
Publishers Weekly, June 26, 2006, review of *The Humboldt Current,* p. 47.

ONLINE

Cornell University ChronicleOnline, http://www.news. cornell.edu/ (October 10, 2006), Franklin Crawford, "Aaron Sachs Follows 'The Humboldt Current' in New Book."

Cornell University College of Arts and Sciences Web site, http://www.arts.cornell.edu/ (January 28, 2007), faculty profile of author.*

*   *   *

SACHS, Aaron Jacob
    See SACHS, Aaron

*   *   *

SACHS, Dana

PERSONAL: Born in Memphis, TN; married; children: two sons. *Education:* Wesleyan University, graduated; University of North Carolina, M.F.A.

ADDRESSES: Home—Wilmington, NC. *Agent*—Douglas Stewart, Sterling Lord Literistic, 65 Bleecker St., New York, NY 10012. *E-mail*—dana@ vietnamuniverse.com.

CAREER: Freelance journalist, educator, and novelist. University of North Carolina, Wilmington, journalism and Vietnamese literature teacher. Codirector of the documentary *Which Way Is East,* Canyon Cinema, 1994.

WRITINGS:

The House on Dream Street: Memoir of an American Woman in Vietnam, Algonquin Books of Chapel Hill (Chapel Hill, NC), 2000.
(Editor, with Nguyen Nguyet Cam) Nguyen Huy Thiep, *Crossing the River: Short Fiction,* Curbstone Press (Willimantic, CT), 2003.
(Compiler, with Nguyen Nguyet Cam) *Two Cakes Fit for a King,* University of Hawaii Press (Honolulu, HI), 2003.
If You Lived Here (novel), William Morrow (New York, NY), 2007.

Contributor to publications including *Mother Jones, San Francisco Chronicle, Far East Economic Review, Sierra,* and *Philadelphia Inquirer.* Translator of Vietnamese short fiction into English.

SIDELIGHTS: On a backpacking trip through Asia, Dana Sachs made a stop in Vietnam, not knowing that the experience would lead to several extended stays and ultimately a life-long fascination with the country and its people. In an interview with Allison Martin, owner of the *Adopt Vietnam* Web site, Sachs explained what it was about the country that kept drawing her back: "People are so much more interconnected in Vietnam than they are in the States. People watch out for each other, they keep an eye on each other's children, they even want to know if you remembered to eat lunch or not! Even though it's invasive, I loved feeling that I was a part of a household, a neighborhood, a city, this great complicated web of lives that make up Vietnamese society." In addition to writing several books that incorporate her experiences in the country, she has lent her expertise as editor and translator of several works written by Vietnamese authors.

The House on Dream Street: Memoir of an American Woman in Vietnam is Sachs's account of her experiences living in Hanoi, beginning with her first year as a resident as her life becomes enmeshed with that of her host family and she struggles with the typical fish-out-of-water sentiments as a foreigner. Over the course of her various stays in Hanoi, Sachs begins to the see Vietnam as a home and fully immerses herself in the culture. A *Publishers Weekly* reviewer commented about the book: "The real joy in her work is the engaging street-level view of Hanoi that she provides. . . . Sachs bravely renders Vietnam through fresh eyes." Kitty Chen Dean described Sachs in a *Library Journal* review as "an engaging and sensitive writer who tells her story ably." In a review of the book at *Things Asian.com,* a contributor wrote: "In a voice that feels less like an autobiography and more like a tête-à-tête, Sachs weaves her tale like a fine silk brocade, with the fabric of Hanoi in the background, overlaid with the intricate patterns of everyday life and the comings and goings of the people around her; the whole of which is delicately embroidered with her detailed observations and keen philosophical asides."

In 2007 Sachs published her first novel, the story of a woman who adopts a child from Vietnam. *If You Lived Here* follows Shelley as she travels to pick up her child, accompanied by her Vietnamese friend Mai who had immigrated to the United States to forget a troubled past. A *Kirkus Reviews* contributor regarded the novel as "very earnest, and it weaves together [the]

plots very carefully." Robin Nesbitt described the novel in a *Library Journal* review as "an interesting look at international adoption and the emotional toll it takes on people."

BIOGRAPHICAL AND CRITICAL SOURCES:

BOOKS

Sachs, Dana, *The House on Dream Street: Memoir of an American Woman in Vietnam,* Algonquin Books of Chapel Hill (Chapel Hill, NC), 2000.

PERIODICALS

Kirkus Reviews, October 15, 2006, review of *If You Lived Here,* p. 1042.
Library Journal, September 15, 2000, Kitty Chen Dean, review of *The House on Dream Street,* p. 102; October 1, 2006, Robin Nesbitt, review of *If You Lived Here,* p. 61.
Publishers Weekly, August 14, 2000, review of *The House on Dream Street,* p. 336.

ONLINE

Adopt Vietnam, http://www.adoptvietnam.org/ (January 11, 2007), Allison Martin, "Enamored of Vietnam" (author interview).
ThingsAsian, http://www.thingsasian.com/ (March 30, 2002), review of *The House on Dream Street.*

*   *   *

SAGE, Steven F. 1947-

PERSONAL: Born 1947.

ADDRESSES: Home—Rockville, MD. *E-mail*—SFSage@aol.com.

CAREER: Writer and historian. University of Massachusetts, senior research fellow; United States Holocaust Memorial Museum, research fellow, 2005; former officer in the U.S. foreign service.

WRITINGS:

Ancient Sichuan and the Unification of China, State University of New York Press (Albany, NY), 1992.

Ibsen and Hitler: The Playwright, the Plagiarist, and the Plot for the Third Reich, Carroll & Graf (New York, NY), 2006.

SIDELIGHTS: Steven F. Sage is a writer and historian who serves as a senior research fellow at the University of Massachusetts and was a research fellow at the United States Holocaust Memorial Museum in 2005. In *Ancient Sichuan and the Unification of China,* Sage offers a "fine study of the archaeology, history, and culture of one of China's most pivotal regions, Sichuan Province," noted Chun-Shu Chan in the *Journal of Asian Studies.* Sage looks at the prehistory of the province and at the two ancient subregions that once made up Sichuan: Ba in the east and Shu in the west. He describes the influential Kingdom of Qin and how the Qin made the best use of the region's human resources and material wealth to thrive, expand, and conquer neighboring states. Sage also asserts that it was the Qin who helped unify the ancient Chinese world, a position that Chan called "challenging." Sage also describes in detail recent, significant archaeological finds in Sanxingdui and elsewhere in the region, then "exploits the welter of recent findings by Chinese archaeologists to reconstruct the origins of civilization in Sichuan and the process whereby Sichuan was eventually integrated into a unified Sinitic polity under the Qin empire," stated Richard von Glahn in the *American Historical Review.*

Sage engages in another controversial reconsideration of history in *Ibsen and Hitler: The Playwright, the Plagiarist, and the Plot for the Third Reich.* In this book Sage suggests a strong connection between the works of playwright Henrik Ibsen and the life and behavior of Nazi leader Adolf Hitler. Sage asserts that "Hitler's life followed a 'script' based on his reading of three Ibsen plays": *The Master Builder, An Enemy of the People,* and *Emperor and Galilean,* commented a *Publishers Weekly* reviewer. In Sage's interpretation, Hitler was so profoundly influenced by Ibsen's plays that "these works not only scripted Hitler's self-image but also guided his political and military strategy," noted *Booklist* reviewer Brendan Driscoll. In his research Sage found direct reference to Ibsen's plays in Hitler's writings and papers. More importantly to Sage, he also detects parallels between Ibsen's works and the events that marked Hitler's rise to power. A *Kirkus Reviews* critic called Sage's position "a thesis that will provoke deliberation, debate, outrage and probably a little laughter." However, *Library Journal* reviewer Dan Forrest concluded that even readers who disagree with Sage's "sense of import about his discovery and conclusions will still find much of interest here."

Sage told *CA:* "The findings in *Ibsen and Hitler* came inadvertently, and as a surprise. I didn't make this stuff up; I merely happened to stumble on it. You look for one thing, you find another; that's the process of discovery. *Ibsen and Hitler* isn't conjecture, not what-iffing, not speculation, not the sort of thing anyone could invent no matter what they smoke. The facts ma'am, just the facts. Empirical facts.

"Documenting *Ibsen and Hitler* showed me that there are real secrets still hidden out there, of tremendous consequence, ready to be found if you seize upon a lead and follow it come what may. Even if they flout the received wisdom, just keep going where the clues take you."

BIOGRAPHICAL AND CRITICAL SOURCES:

PERIODICALS

American Historical Review, December, 1993, Richard Van Glahn, review of *Ancient Sichuan and the Unification of China,* p. 1661.

Booklist, June 1, 2006, Brendan Driscoll, review of *Ibsen and Hitler: The Playwright, the Plagiarist, and the Plot for the Third Reich,* p. 30.

Journal of Asian Studies, August, 1994, Chun-shu Chang, review of *Ancient Sichuan and the Unification of China,* p. 928.

Kirkus Reviews, April 15, 2006, review of *Ibsen and Hitler,* p. 398.

Library Journal, May 1, 2006, Dan Forrest, review of *Ibsen and Hitler,* p. 99.

Publishers Weekly, April 3, 2006, review of *Ibsen and Hitler,* p. 54.

ONLINE

Avalon Publishing Group Web site, http://www.avalonpub.com/ (December 10, 2006), biography of Steven Sage.

Library of Congress Web site, http://www.loc.gov/ (December 10, 2006), biography of Steven Sage.

* * *

SALTZ, Gail

PERSONAL: Married; children: three daughters.

ADDRESSES: Home—New York, NY.

CAREER: Writer, psychiatrist, psychoanalyst, commentator, columnist, relationship expert, and educator. New York Presbyterian Hospital Weill-Cornell School of Medicine, associate professor of psychiatry. New York Psychoanalytic Institute, psychoanalyst; psychoanalyst in private practice, New York, NY. Guest on television programs and networks, including *Today* (National Broadcasting Company), *Lifetime Live,* (Lifetime), *Biography* (Arts and Entertainment), the *Oprah Winfrey Show, Dateline,* the *Early Show,* Columbia Broadcasting System News, Fox News, and the Cable News Network and American Broadcasting Companies networks.

WRITINGS:

Becoming Real: Defeating the Stories We Tell Ourselves That Hold Us Back, Riverhead Books (New York, NY), 2004.
Amazing You!: Getting Smart about Your Private Parts, illustrated by Lynne Cravath, Dutton Children's Books (New York, NY), 2005.
Anatomy of a Secret Life: The Psychology of Living a Lie, Morgan Road Books (New York, NY), 2006.
Changing You: A Guide to Body Changes and Sexuality, illustrated by Lynne Cravath, Dutton Children's Books (New York, NY), 2007.

Author of weekly relationship column, *MSNBC.com.*

Contributor to periodicals, including *Good Housekeeping* and *Parade.*

Glamour, former contributing editor.

SIDELIGHTS: Psychiatrist, psychoanalyst, columnist, and commentator Gail Saltz is the author of books for both children and adults. In *Amazing You!: Getting Smart about Your Private Parts,* Saltz and illustrator Lynne Cravath offer an upbeat, straightforward introduction to human reproductive anatomy and childbirth aimed at preschool and early-grade readers. The book is "designed as much to allay parental anxiety as to provide answers to younger children's questions," observed a *Kirkus Reviews* contributor. Saltz describes the male and female anatomy using specific anatomical terms, avoiding euphemisms, and details the development of the human body from childhood to adulthood. Simplified explanations of conception and development help children understand what, to many, is one of the world's most perplexing questions: where do babies come from? Saltz "presents the information clearly in a cheerful, positive tone," encouraging children to learn about the human body, noted Gillian Engberg in *Booklist.* Saltz also provides authoritative guidance for parents facing the daunting task of explaining such issues to their children. Saltz and Cravath offer youngsters and preschoolers a "comfortable and positive jumping-off point for frank discussions of bodies and birth," commented reviewer Lauren Adams in *Horn Book Magazine.*

Saltz's books for adults concentrate on issues such as overcoming self-imposed obstacles to personal growth and reworking lives that have fallen into the constraints of too many secrets and lies. *Becoming Real: Defeating the Stories We Tell Ourselves That Hold Us Back* explores how most people live according to stories they devise about themselves and others during childhood, and how the deeply ingrained beliefs reinforced by those stories can be severely limiting to adults. Saltz notes that people craft stories of self that ascribe one of five major traits to themselves: dependent, superachiever, self-defeater, competitor, or perfectionist. These descriptions become unconscious motivators of behavior, Saltz asserts, and can lead to nonproductive, sometimes even self-destructive acts in adults whose experiences with themselves and the world are often in conflict with the stories and descriptions that they use to define themselves. Saltz suggests that persons hindered by these descriptors identify how their self-told stories are limiting them in their current lives and then literally rewrite the stories to bring them into conformity with desires and reality. Saltz provides "specific and clear" instructions for change "based on psychoanalytic technique that will take time and commitment," observed a *Publishers Weekly* reviewer.

In *Anatomy of a Secret Life: The Psychology of Living a Lie,* Saltz reveals the tremendous psychological costs of keeping secrets and shows how lives confined by too many secrets and lies can become intolerable and destructive. She notes that having and keeping some secrets can be a healthy part of psychological development, especially for children. However, she cautions that excessive reliance on secrets can lead to pathological conditions, including living what are essentially multiple lives that do not, and cannot, intersect. She looks at famous individuals who led such lives, including T.E. Lawrence (Lawrence of Arabia), Charles Lindbergh, and Peter Tchaikovsky, as well as serial killers such as Dennis Rader, the "BTK Killer." She profiles a variety of addicts, cheaters, and killers that kept secrets from themselves and others, developing alter egos and clearly defined boundaries between one life and the other. Lynn Harris, writing in the *New York Times Book Review,* commented that Saltz is "detailed and thoughtful in her inquiry" and that she "writes with eloquence and sophistication." A *Publishers Weekly* reviewer concluded: "This book serves as a cautionary tale of how a secret is formed, lived, justified—and eventually exposed."

BIOGRAPHICAL AND CRITICAL SOURCES:

PERIODICALS

Booklist, June 1, 2005, Gillian Engberg, review of *Amazing You!: Getting Smart about Your Private Parts,* p. 1817; March 15, 2006, Donna Chavez, review of *Anatomy of a Secret Life: The Psychology of Living a Lie,* p. 13.

Horn Book Magazine July-August, 2005, Lauren Adams, review of *Amazing You!,* p. 491.

Kirkus Reviews, May 1, 2005, review of *Amazing You!,* p. 546.

New York Times Book Review, April 16, 2006, Lynn Harris, "Don't Tell—The Psychiatrist Gail Saltz Says Secrets Can Be Good for You (and Not So Good)," review of *Anatomy of a Secret Life.*

Publishers Weekly, April 19, 2004, review of *Becoming Real: Defeating the Stories We Tell Ourselves That Hold Us Back,* p. 53; February 27, 2006, review of *Anatomy of a Secret Life,* p. 52.

School Library Journal, May, 2005, Kathleen Kelly MacMillan, review of *Amazing You!,* p. 116.

ONLINE

Gail Saltz Home Page, http://www.drgailsaltz.com (December 13, 2006).

Huffington Post, http://www.huffingtonpost.com/ (December 13, 2006), biography of Gail Saltz.

* * *

SALWAY, Sarah

PERSONAL: Married; children: two. *Education:* Attended London College of Fashion; University of Glamorgan, master's degree.

ADDRESSES: Home—Kent, England. *E-mail*—sarah@sarahsalway.com.

CAREER: Writer and educator. Teacher at University of Kent, University of Sussex, and Queen Margaret University College. Worked previously as an account director at a London public relations firm and as a freelance journalist.

WRITINGS:

Something Beginning With (novel), Bloomsbury Publishing (London, England), 2004, also published as *The ABCs of Love,* Ballantine Books (New York, NY), 2004.

Leading the Dance (short stories), Bluechrome Publishing (Bristol, England), 2006.

(With Lynne Reese) *Messages* (novel), Bluechrome Publishing (Bristol, England), 2006.

Tell Me Everything (novel), Ballantine Books (New York, NY), 2006.

Contributor of poems and short stories to periodicals.

SIDELIGHTS: Sarah Salway took writing seriously at an early age, creating a club for would-be novel writers at her school. Ultimately pursuing a career in journalism, she kept writing fiction as a hobby until enrollment in a creative writing workshop rekindled her desire to get published. Salway returned to school, earning master's and Ph.D. degrees in creative writing, and teaching English at several universities in her native England. Her first published works were short stories, which she discovered gave her the literary freedom to experiment with different writing processes and techniques. Even after becoming a published novelist, Salway explained on her home page: "It is the form I always come back to because I love the elegance of the form and the opportunity you have to play within it. . . . I get frustrated when people think it is an easy option because it is 'short' as in many ways it's technically difficult to get everything across in such a short space of time without confusing and getting too involved." A collection of Salway's short stories was published in 2006 and titled *Leading the Dance*.

Salway's first novel incorporates many short-story elements in its structure and style. *Something Beginning With* (published as *The ABCs of Love* in the United States) is set up as a series of vignettes written from the perspective of a young woman struggling with her love life, her career, and her self worth. There are twenty-six mini-chapters, each beginning with a letter of the alphabet ranging from "Ambition" to "Zzzz." A *Publishers Weekly* contributor commented in a review of the book: "Salway wraps her bright, comic writing in bite-sized chunks that make this first novel an easy-reading pleasure." Susie Boyt wrote in a review for the London *Independent*: "There is a deftness to Sarah Salway's writing, which is never clumsy or inelegant." A *Trashionista* writer remarked that "the fact that each entry can be taken as a work in itself means that the quality of writing is excellent. . . . Salway is an extremely skilled stylist."

In Salway's next novel, a young woman realizes the power of words and the havoc that can be wreaked by a single conversation. The central character of *Tell Me Everything* embellishes a description of her frustrating home life to a teacher, and she finds herself on her own after the social services department is called in. The novel follows the young woman as she sets herself up with a new job, a new love, and new friends and struggles to come to terms with her past. *Library Journal* reviewer Jan Blodgett described the novel as a "haunting tale about the power and danger of stories."

BIOGRAPHICAL AND CRITICAL SOURCES:

PERIODICALS

Library Journal, September 1, 2006, Jan Blodgett, review of *Tell Me Everything*, p. 138.

Publishers Weekly, April 5, 2004, review of *The ABCs of Love*, p. 40.

ONLINE

Independent Online, http://www.independent.co.uk/ (May 14, 2004), Susie Boyt, review of *Something Beginning With*.
Sarah Salway Home Page, http://www.sarahsalway.com (January 11, 2007).
Trashionista, http://www.trashionista.com/ (January 18, 2007), review of *Something Beginning With*.

*   *   *

SAMUEL, Wolfgang W.E. 1935-

PERSONAL: Born 1935, in Sagan, Germany (now Zagan, Poland); immigrated to the United States in 1951. *Education:* Attended National War College.

ADDRESSES: Home—Fairfax Station, VA.

CAREER: Retired colonel in the U.S. Air Force; writer.

AWARDS, HONORS: Three-time recipient of the Distinguished Flying Cross.

WRITINGS:

HISTORY

German Boy: A Refugee's Story (memoir), University Press of Mississippi (Jackson, MS), 2000.
I Always Wanted to Fly: America's Cold War Airmen, University Press of Mississippi (Jackson, MS), 2001.
The War of Our Childhood: Memories of World War II, University Press of Mississippi (Jackson, MS), 2002.
American Raiders: The Race to Capture the Luftwaffe's Secrets, University Press of Mississippi (Jackson, MS), 2004.

Coming to Colorado: A Young Immigrant's Journey to Become an American Flyer (memoir), University Press of Mississippi (Jackson, MS), 2006.

SIDELIGHTS: Born in Sagan, Germany, in 1935, Wolfgang W.E. Samuel was forced to flee his home at the age of ten, accompanied by his mother and younger sister, when the Red Army entered the country at the end of World War II. In the years following, he and his family suffered many hardships; his mother was raped, and his grandfather was murdered by German Communists. His mother, who had divorced Samuel's father, married an American serviceman, and in 1951 the family moved to the United States. Samuel was able to complete his education and go on to the National War College, eventually joining the U.S. Air Force. He served with the Air Force for thirty years, earned three Distinguished Flying Crosses during his tenure, and retired a colonel. In addition to his military career, Samuel devoted his time to writing, producing several volumes of history, some of which recount the story of his escape from occupied Germany and his experiences once he moved to the United States.

German Boy: A Refugee's Story chronicles Samuel's experiences as a child and young adult, covering not just the events that occurred, but his own emotional reactions to the traumatic events. Jay Freeman, writing for *Booklist,* called the book "an absorbing story of survival and redemption." A critic for *Publishers Weekly* remarked of Samuel that "he has produced an engrossing and powerful narrative." In a review for *Library Journal,* John E. Hodgkins dubbed the book a "deeply emotional and moving memoir."

In *I Always Wanted to Fly: America's Cold War Airmen,* Samuel gathers the stories of various airmen who inspired him to join the Air Force after he came to America, as well as those who participated in the air corps during World War II, Korea, and Vietnam. Many of the oral histories that Samuel collects have never been published before. Roland Green, in a review for *Booklist,* called the book "a valuable addition to any collection serving students of post-World War II military aviation." In a review for *Air Power History,* William Nardo noted: "The text was very well written and edited, making it easy for the non-flying civilian to understand."

The War of Our Childhood: Memories of World War II looks at the plight of German children during World War II through the eyes of twenty-seven survivors.

These individuals were between the ages of three and twelve during the war, and share their powerful memories of their lives at that time, including the bouts of hunger, the devastating air raids, and their fear of the invading armed forces. A contributor to *Kirkus Reviews* found the volume to be "of modest interest to historians and readers interested in having the German view of the war."

With *American Raiders: The Race to Capture the Luftwaffe's Secrets,* Samuel looks at the way the United States Army Air Force determined to obtain German technology at the end of World War II. Writing in the *Air & Space Power Journal,* Gilles VanNederveen found the book to be "a useful contribution to airpower history."

BIOGRAPHICAL AND CRITICAL SOURCES:

BOOKS

Samuel, Wolfgang W.E., *German Boy: A Refugee's Story,* University Press of Mississippi (Jackson, MS), 2000.

Samuel, Wolfgang W.E., *Coming to Colorado: A Young Immigrant's Journey to Become an American Flyer,* University Press of Mississippi (Jackson, MS), 2006.

PERIODICALS

Air & Space Power Journal, spring, 2006, Gilles VanNederveen, review of *American Raiders: The Race to Capture the Luftwaffe's Secrets,* p. 113.

Air Power History, winter, 2002, William A. Nardo, review of *I Always Wanted to Fly: America's Cold War Airmen,* p. 62.

Booklist, August, 2000, Jay Freeman, review of *German Boy,* p. 2107; August, 2001, Roland Green, review of *I Always Wanted to Fly,* p. 2062; September 1, 2002, George Cohen, review of *The War of Our Childhood: Memories of World War II,* p. 51.

Book World, May 30, 2004, Mark Lewis, "Air Raids" review of *American Raiders,* p. 3.

Kirkus Reviews, July 15, 2002, review of *The War of Our Childhood,* p. 1016.

Library Journal, July, 2000, John E. Hodgkins, review of *German Boy,* p. 108.

Publishers Weekly, July 17, 2000, review of *German Boy,* p. 183.

School Library Journal, June, 2001, Cynthia J. Rieben, review of *German Boy,* p. 188; December, 2001, review of *German Boy,* p. 51.*

* * *

SANTIAGO, Eduardo 1967-

PERSONAL: Born 1967, in Manzanillo, Cuba. *Education:* California Institute of the Arts, B.F.A.

ADDRESSES: Home—Los Angeles, CA. *E-mail*—eduardo@eduardosantiago.com.

CAREER: Writer and creative writing teacher. Writer for CBS2 News, Los Angeles, CA. Worked previously as an event organizer at independent bookstores.

AWARDS, HONORS: PEN Emerging Voices Rosenthal fellow, 2004.

WRITINGS:

Tomorrow They Will Kiss (novel), Back Bay Books (New York, NY), 2006.

Contributor to periodicals, including *Advocate, Zyzzyva, Caribbean Writer, Slow Trains Literary Journal, Los Angeles Times, Square Peg Magazine,* and *Infected Faggot Perspectives.*

SIDELIGHTS: Cuban-born writer Eduardo Santiago has had his work represented in literary magazines and newspapers, spoken on television, and taught in the classroom. Based in Los Angeles, California, he went to work for several television networks as a writer after graduating with a fine arts degree in film and television. In his twenties Santiago began exploring his Cuban roots in his writing, and went on to publish short stories in various publications. Santiago's first novel, *Tomorrow They Will Kiss,* incorporates many elements of Cuban immigrant life, including the struggles faced after Fidel Castro's revolution, the fascination with telenovelas (Spanish soap operas), and the cultural and language barriers that are exacerbated by poverty and class divisions. The novel is set in Union City, New Jersey, and follows several female Cuban American characters who work at a doll factory and struggle to make a life for themselves in their new home. Santiago felt a special kinship with his characters, he mentioned on the *PEN Center USA* Web site: "I set out to write something really dark and spiteful, but ended up with a very funny, and touching story. Even during countless rewrites I was repeatedly moved to tears and laughter. At a certain point the characters took over and told me what to write. I can't imagine how else this could have happened."

In an article for the *Advocate,* Regina Marler wrote: "Santiago's characters are distinctly drawn and larger-than-life, their colors bright against the winter backdrop of Union City." Marler went on to call the novel "a funny book about loss with a hard, satisfying kick at the end." *School Library Journal* contributor Ellen Bell maintained that "teens will relate to the immigrant experience as it is portrayed" in the novel. A reviewer for *Publishers Weekly* remarked that "the detailed immigrant community is vital and entertaining."

BIOGRAPHICAL AND CRITICAL SOURCES:

PERIODICALS

Advocate, October 24, 2006, Regina Marler, "Doll Factory Divas: *Tomorrow They Will Kiss,*" p. 58.
Publishers Weekly, April 24, 2006, review of *Tomorrow They Will Kiss,* p. 34.
School Library Journal, September, 2006, Ellen Bell, review of *Tomorrow They Will Kiss,* p. 248.

ONLINE

Eduardo Santiago Home Page, http://www.eduardosantiago.com (December 28, 2006).
PEN Center USA, http://www.penusa.org/ (May 10, 2005).*

* * *

SANTNER, Eric L. 1955-

PERSONAL: Born 1955. *Education:* Oberlin College, B.A., 1977; University of Texas at Austin, M.A., 1982, Ph.D., 1984.

ADDRESSES: Home—Chicago, IL. *Office*—Department of Germanic Studies, University of Chicago, Classics Building, Room 25F, 1050 E. 59th St., Chicago, IL 60637. *E-mail*—esantner@uchicago.edu.

CAREER: University of Texas at Austin, assistant instructor, 1978-84; Princeton University, Princeton, NJ, assistant professor, 1984-90, associate professor, 1990-94, professor of German, 1994-96; University of Chicago, Chicago, IL, Harriet and Ulrich E. Meyer Professor of Modern European History, 1996-2003, Philip and Ida Romberg Professor of Modern Germanic Studies, 2003—, chair of Department of Germanic Studies, 2000—. Charles H. McIlwain Preceptorship, Princeton University, 1988-90.

AWARDS, HONORS: American Council of Learned Societies research fellow, fall, 1986; John Simon Guggenheim fellow, 1997-98.

WRITINGS:

Friedrich Hölderlin: Narrative Vigilance and the Poetic Imagination, Rutgers University Press (New Brunswick, NJ), 1986.

(Editor) Friedrich Hölderlin, *Hyperion and Selected Poems,* Continuum (New York, NY), 1990.

Stranded Objects: Mourning, Memory, and Film in Postwar Germany, Cornell University Press (Ithaca, NY), 1990.

My Own Private Germany: Daniel Paul Schreber's Secret History of Modernity, Princeton University Press (Princeton, NJ), 1996.

On the Psychotheology of Everyday Life: Reflections on Freud and Rosenzweig, University of Chicago Press (Chicago, IL), 2001.

(Editor, with Moishe Postone) *Catastrophe and Meaning: The Holocaust and the Twentieth Century,* University of Chicago Press (Chicago, IL), 2003.

(With others) *The Neighbor: Three Inquiries in Political Theology,* University of Chicago Press (Chicago, IL), 2005.

On Creaturely Life: Rilke, Benjamin, Sebald, University of Chicago Press (Chicago, IL), 2006.

Contributor to numerous anthologies and journals, including *International Journal of Psychoanalytical Self Psychology, Qui Parle,* and the *German Quarterly.*

SIDELIGHTS: Eric L. Santner serves as chair of the Department of Germanic Studies at the University of Chicago. Santner's primary areas of research study include German culture—specifically German literature, history, and cinema—Modern European Jewish history, and the Holocaust. He is also interested in issues of memory and mourning in postwar Germany, and the use of psychoanalysis. His *On the Psychotheology of Everyday Life: Reflections on Freud and Rosenzweig* addresses the sociopolitical effects of theology and psychology, particularly as pertains to the works of Freud and Rosenzweig. Santner notes that religion, and monotheism in particular, has been linked to the majority of violent conflicts of the twentieth century and before. Michael Mack, in a review for the *Journal of Religion,* remarked: "No doubt, this philosophical essay will be highly influential in reconceptions of theology and its 'mundane' implications." Writing for *Theological Studies,* Michael L. Morgan commented: "Santner presents an important drama about modern life by mapping the vocabularies of a number of thinkers, one onto the other."

In *My Own Private Germany: Daniel Paul Schreber's Secret History of Modernity,* Santner looks at the life and writings of Daniel Paul Schreber, and analyzes Schreber's social theories regarding subjectivity as a cultural construction. Santner addresses the paradoxical nature of modernity, which encourages strong individualism, yet does not take into account the fact that such behavior results in a weakened and disconnected community. Schreber was a prime example of such behavior, the result of his own father's strict and particular upbringing according to his ideas of what constituted the perfect body—an ideal that Schreber's eventual descent into mental illness and paranoia shattered. Paul Bishop, writing for the *Journal of European Studies,* found the book offers "little which is new in terms of scholarship apart from its main argument."

Catastrophe and Meaning: The Holocaust and the Twentieth Century, which Santner edited with Moishe Postone, collects a series of essays pertaining to German history and the Holocaust. The volume stems from a conference held at the University of Chicago in 1998 which dealt with the four areas that make up the four sections of the book: history, anti-Semitism and the Holocaust; the Holocaust and the twentieth century; annihilation, victimhood, identity; and trauma and the limits of representation. Stephen Feinstein, in a review for *Shofar,* called the book "an exceptionally important and useful compilation," that "provides much food for thought about interpretation of the Holocaust from the perspective of the twenty-first century, especially as genocide continues without intervention." Brad Prager, in a review for the *German Quarterly,* remarked that "the high quality of this book and its contributions makes it clear that the dimensions of the field's various literary, philosophical, and historical debates have only broadened and generated more compelling scholarship over time."

BIOGRAPHICAL AND CRITICAL SOURCES:

PERIODICALS

American Journal of Sociology, November, 1997, Michael Steinberg, review of *My Own Private Germany: Daniel Paul Schreber's Secret History of Modernity,* p. 798.
German Quarterly, fall, 1998, Nina Zimnik, review of *My Own Private Germany,* p. 403; summer, 2004, Brad Prager, review of *Catastrophe and Meaning: The Holocaust and the Twentieth Century,* pp. 383-384.
Journal of European Studies, December, 1996, Paul Bishop, review of *My Own Private Germany,* p. 498.
Journal of Religion, July, 2002, Michael Mack, review of *On the Psychotheology of Everyday Life: Reflections on Freud and Rosenzweig,* p. 517.
Shofar, fall, 2005, Stephen Feinstein, review of *Catastrophe and Meaning,* p. 185.
Theological Studies, March, 2003, Michael L. Morgan, review of *On the Psychotheology of Everyday Life,* p. 206.
Times Literary Supplement, October 4, 1996, Ritchie Robertson, review of *My Own Private Germany,* p. 16.

ONLINE

H-Net: Humanities and Social Sciences Online, http://www.h-net.org/ (January 23, 2007), Timothy E. Pytell, review of *Catastrophe and Meaning.*

University of Chicago Department of Germanic Studies Web site, http://humanities.uchicago.edu/depts/german/index.html/ (February 5, 2007), faculty biography.*

* * *

SANTO PIETRO, Mary Jo 1945-

PERSONAL: Born 1945. *Education:* Attended the Catholic University of America (graduated); Columbia University, Ph.D.

CAREER: Writer, educator, and speech-language pathologist. Kean University, Union, NJ, professor of speech-language pathology. Jewish Home and Hospital, Bronx, NY, research consultant. Taught at Rutgers University and the City University of New York. Robert Wood Johnson University Hospital Stroke Club, founder and moderator. American Speech-Language-Hearing Association (ASHA), fellow.

MEMBER: American Speech-Language-Hearing Association (four-term legislative councilor); New Jersey Speech-Language-Hearing Association (former president).

WRITINGS:

(With Elizabeth Ostuni) *Getting Through: Communicating When Someone You Care for Has Alzheimer's Disease,* foreword by Jeffrey L. Cummings, Speech Bin (Vero Beach, FL), 1986.
(With R. Goldfarb) *TARGET: Techniques in Aphasia Rehabilitation: Generating Effective Treatment,* Speech Bin (Vero Beach, FL), 1995.
(With Elizabeth Ostuni) *Successful Communication with Alzheimer's Disease Patients: An In-Service Training Manual,* Butterworth-Heinemann (Boston, MA), 1997, 2nd edition, Butterworth-Heinemann (St. Louis, MO), 2003.
(With F. Boczko) *The Breakfast Club: Enhancing the Communication Ability of Alzheimer's Patients,* Speech Bin (Vero Beach, FL), 1997.

What Is Dementia?, Speech Bin (Vero Beach, FL), 1999.

Father Hartke: His Life and Legacy to the American Theater (biography), Catholic University of America Press (Washington, DC), 2002.

Contributor to periodicals, including *American Journal of Alzheimer Disease, Journal of Speech and Hearing Research,* and *Brain & Language.*

SIDELIGHTS: Mary Jo Santo Pietro is an author, biographer, educator, and speech pathologist who teaches at Kean University in Union, New Jersey. She is the author of numerous books on communication issues facing patients with degenerative conditions such as Alzheimer's disease and is a researcher on speech and language issues. In *Father Hartke: His Life and Legacy to the American Theater,* Santo Pietro offers a biography of a prominent figure in American theater who had a significant effect on her life and on the lives of countless others within and associated with the performing arts. Father Gilbert Vincent Hartke was a Dominican priest who in the 1940s founded the prestigious Department of Speech and Drama at the Catholic University of America in Washington, DC, which Santo Pietro attended as an undergraduate. An energetic, charismatic figure dedicated to his department, his religion, and his students, Hartke shaped his academic program into one of the best known and most respected in the country. His program attracted some of the brightest young talent in the performing arts and boasts such noted graduates as actors Jon Voight and Susan Sarandon; playwrights Jean Kerr and Jason Miller; and popular celebrities such as *Tonight Show* sidekick Ed McMahon. Santo Pietro "depicts her hero as a high-energy entrepreneur whose priestly character and personal charm provided easy access to the powerful and famous in the worlds of theater and politics," remarked Michael Tueth in *America: The National Catholic Weekly.* Though Hartke sometimes had conflicts with the administration of Catholic University, his persistence and unswerving commitment carried him through. Hartke "thrived on people, and people thrived on him—most especially the numerous students whose careers he launched, but also screen stars, politicians, and presidents, to whom he gave encouragement, sound advice, and religious counsel," noted Donn B. Murphy in the *Catholic Historical Review.* Among his other achievements, Hartke helped to promote theatrical performances at the White House and was instrumental, with others, in creating the Kennedy Center for the Performing Arts.

Santo Pietro's book is an "unabashedly affectionate account of Hartke's life and accomplishments," commented Tueth. Santo Pietro "has captured a life lived vigorously—and self-examined at its finale with deserved satisfaction," Murphy observed. Her work, Murphy continued, is a "testament to the virtues of trust in God, self-reliance, robust confidence and infectious camaraderie. It documents achievement, and the joy of seeing others achieve."

BIOGRAPHICAL AND CRITICAL SOURCES:

PERIODICALS

America: The National Catholic Weekly, July 1, 2002, Michael Tueth, "Dramatic Dominican," review of *Father Hartke: His Life and Legacy to the American Theater.*

Catholic Historical Review, April, 2003, Donn B. Murphy, review of *Father Hartke,* p. 349.

Library Journal, February 15, 2002, J. Sara Paulk, review of *Father Hartke,* p. 147.

ONLINE

Kean University Web site, http://www.kean.edu/ (December 13, 2006), biography of Mary Jo Santo Pietro.

*   *   *

SANTOPIETRO, Tom

PERSONAL: Born in Waterbury, CT. *Education:* University of Connecticut School of Law (graduated).

CAREER: Writer, biographer, lawyer, and Broadway stage manager. Manager of Broadway shows and performances, including *A Few Good Men, A Doll's House, Master Class, The Iceman Cometh, Tru,* and *Noises Off.*

WRITINGS:

The Importance of Being Barbra, Thomas Dunne Books (New York, NY), 2006.
Considering Doris Day, Thomas Dunne Books (New York, NY), 2007.

SIDELIGHTS: A writer, biographer, and non-practicing lawyer, Tom Santopietro is a stage manager on Broadway in New York, where he has worked for more than twenty years. In his first book, *The Importance of Being Barbra,* Santopietro takes a careful, critical look at the career and music of diva Barbra Streisand. Santopietro "evaluates Streisand's professional, not personal, life," noted a *Kirkus Reviews* critic, and added that private particulars are noted "only as they may have shaped her work." The author divides Streisand's work into distinct categories, including musical recordings, films, television specials, and concerts, and offers background information, accounts of contemporary events, and critiques of the material under survey. The book emerges as an "opinionated analysis of the Streisand canon, with distinctive views on her many career highs and those more-than-a-few career missteps," noted Phil Hall on the Web site *EDGE Boston.* In addition, "Santopietro astutely embeds his subject in cultural context to underscore her zeitgeist appeal," observed a *Publishers Weekly* critic, exploring her brash personality, her unabashed ethnicity, and her strong appeal to alternative audiences, including feminists and gays. Rob Lester, on *EDGE Boston,* commented that for Streisand's many and varied fans, Santopietro's work is "a treasure of information and does go through her many achievements without being distracted very much by her personal life. This is not the book for dish and gossip, but it's chatty and informal at times, while taking the work quite seriously."

Santopietro "holds strong opinions on all things Streisand that are usually right on," observed Rosellen Brewer in *Library Journal.* The *Kirkus Reviews* writer noted that Santopietro's "individual critiques are vivid and perceptive," while the *Publishers Weekly* contributor commented favorably on the author's "discerning, nuanced critiques of Streisand's works."

BIOGRAPHICAL AND CRITICAL SOURCES:

PERIODICALS

California Bookwatch, September, 2006, review of *The Importance of Being Barbra.*
Kirkus Reviews, April 1, 2006, review of *The Importance of Being Barbra,* p. 339.
Library Journal, May 15, 2006, Rosellen Brewer, review of *The Importance of Being Barbra,* p. 103.
Publishers Weekly, March 20, 2006, review of *The Importance of Being Barbra,* p. 46.
San Diego Union-Tribune, July 14, 2006, Howard Cohen, "A High Road, a Low Road on Streisand," review of *The Importance of Being Barbra.*

ONLINE

EDGE Boston, http://www.edgeboston.com/ (July 1, 2006), Rob Lester, review of *The Importance of Being Barbra;* (July 12, 2006), Phil Hall, review of *The Importance of Being Barbra.*
WTNH.com, http://www.wtnh.com/ (August 31, 2006), biography of Tom Santopietro.

*   *   *

SAUNDERS, Barbara R. 1967-
   (Barbara Ruth Saunders)

PERSONAL: Born February 20, 1967, in Bronx, NY; daughter of William A. (an educator and nonprofit director) and Anne (a teacher and minister) Saunders. *Education:* Stanford University, A.B., 1988.

ADDRESSES: *Home*—San Francisco, CA. *E-mail*—info@barbararuthsaunders.com.

CAREER: Writer.

WRITINGS:

Ivan Pavlov: Exploring the Mysteries of Behavior, Enslow Publishers (Berkeley Heights, NJ), 2006.

SIDELIGHTS: Barbara R. Saunders once told *CA:* "I started reading at age three and don't remember life before I could read. As a child, reading was a way for me to enter into conversations I couldn't find in daily life—conversations about places I'd never seen, and with a variety of people unlike the people who surrounded me.

"My dream is to expose people to ideas and stories that inspire them to expand their lives."

* * *

**SAUNDERS, Barbara Ruth
See SAUNDERS, Barbara R.**

* * *

**SCALZI, John 1969-
(John Michael Scalzi)**

PERSONAL: Born May 10, 1969, in CA; married; wife's name Kristine; children: Athena. *Education:* University of Chicago, graduated, 1991.

ADDRESSES: Home—Bradford, OH. *E-mail*—john@scalzi.com.

CAREER: Freelance writer. *Official U.S. Playstation Magazine,* chief entertainment media critic, 2000-06. Worked previously as a film critic for the *Fresno Bee.*

AWARDS, HONORS: Hugo Award nominee, 2006, for *Old Man's War;* Campbell Award for best new science fiction author, 2006, for *Old Man's War;* SCI FI Essential book, from *SciFi.com,* 2006, for *The Ghost Brigades.*

WRITINGS:

FICTION

Agent to the Stars, Subterranean Press (Burton, MI), 2005.

Old Man's War, Tom Doherty Associates (New York, NY), 2005.
Questions for a Soldier, Subterranean Press (Burton, MI), 2005.
The Android's Dream, Tor (New York, NY), 2006.
The Ghost Brigades, Tor (New York, NY), 2006.
The Last Colony, Tor (New York, NY), 2007.
The Sagan Diary, illustrated by Bob Eggleton, Subterranean Press (Burton, MI), 2007.

NONFICTION

The Rough Guide to Money Online, Rough Guides (New York, NY), 2000.
The Rough Guide to the Universe, Rough Guides (New York, NY), 2003.
Uncle John's Presents Book of the Dumb, Portable Press (San Diego, CA), 2003.
Uncle John's Presents Book of the Dumb 2, Portable Press (San Diego, CA), 2004.
The Rough Guide to Sci-Fi Movies, Rough Guides (New York, NY), 2005.
You're Not Fooling Anyone When You Take Your Laptop to a Coffee Shop: Scalzi on Writing, Subterranean Press (Burton, MI), 2007.

Contributor to the "Uncle John's Bathroom Reader" series, Portable Press (San Diego, CA). Regular contributor to *Dayton Daily News.* Author of the blogs *Whatever* and *By the Way.*

SIDELIGHTS: A prolific nonfiction author, John Scalzi has lent his wide-ranging expertise to countless magazine articles, newspaper columns, online web logs, corporate brochures, and books. He began his writing career as a film critic for the *Fresno Bee* in his native California. In the late 1990s Scalzi transitioned to full-time freelance writing and started a daily blog titled *Whatever* that gained a wide readership. He also began work on his first novel, *Agent to the Stars,* with no real intention of ever professionally publishing it. Instead he posted the story on his Web site and welcomed readers to send him a dollar if they enjoyed it.

Scalzi subsequently debuted a second novel online with an unexpected result: He was contacted by an editor who wished to see the military science fiction story published. *Old Man's War* earned Scalzi a 2006 Hugo Award nomination, critical acclaim, and a solid fan base. In a review for the *Magazine of Fantasy and Science Fiction,* Michelle West shared her opinion of the novel: "There's definitely Scalzi humor laced throughout it, which is to be expected; less expected, a genuine sense of regret, loss, and almost veneration for things that are taken for granted in our daily lives." Another *Magazine of Fantasy and Science Fiction* reviewer, Robert K.J. Killheffer, remarked: "Scalzi's straightforward, muscular prose and tightly focused pacing yield an undeniable page-turner." Noting similarities in prose to the works of science fiction great Robert A. Heinlein, a *Publishers Weekly* contributor described *Old Man's War* as a "virtuoso debut [that] pays tribute to SF's past while showing that well-worn tropes still can have real zip when they're approached with ingenuity."

The sequel to *Old Man's War,* titled *The Ghost Brigades,* is set in the same universe but picks up the story of a secondary character. The novel was selected by *SciFi.com* as a SCI FI Essential book for 2006. "Scalzi skillfully weaves together action, memorable characterizations, and a touch of philosophy," remarked Carl Hays in a *Booklist* review. *Bookslut* reviewer Stephen Granade noted that the book "delivers on its promise of solid science fiction entertainment with a leavening of serious issues." *The Android's Dream* is Scalzi's third novel of military science fiction that also incorporates political suspense and social commentary. Granade also reviewed the book and called it "a galloping caper that is very funny and very satisfying." He further commented: "By combining a tight ending with sympathetic characters and sharp, funny writing, *The Android's Dream* delivers top-notch entertainment."

Scalzi has written or contributed to a number of nonfiction books, including several in the "Rough Guide" and "Uncle John's Bathroom Reader" series. In 2007 selections from his popular blog were compiled into *You're Not Fooling Anyone When You Take Your Laptop to a Coffee Shop: Scalzi on Writing.*

BIOGRAPHICAL AND CRITICAL SOURCES:

PERIODICALS

Booklist, March 1, 2006, Carl Hays, review of *The Ghost Brigades,* p. 77.

Magazine of Fantasy and Science Fiction, June, 2005, Michelle West, review of *Old Man's War,* p. 33; September, 2005, Robert K.J. Killheffer, review of *Old Man's War,* p. 25.
Publishers Weekly, December 6, 2004, review of *Old Man's War,* 47.

ONLINE

Bookslut, http://www.bookslut.com/ (January 18, 2007), Stephen Granade, reviews of *The Ghost Brigades* and *The Android's Dream.*
John Scalzi Home Page, http://www.johnscalzi.com (January 11, 2007).*

* * *

SCALZI, John Michael
    See SCALZI, John

* * *

SCHALLER, Thomas F.

PERSONAL: Male.

ADDRESSES: Office—Department of Political Science, University of Maryland, Baltimore County, 1000 Hilltop Circle, Baltimore, MD 21250. *E-mail*—schaller@umbc.edu.

CAREER: University of Maryland, Baltimore County, Baltimore, MD, associate professor of political science, 1998—. Has appeared on C-SPAN, National Public Radio, and various other television and radio networks.

WRITINGS:

(With Tyson King-Meadows) *Devolution and Black State Legislators: Challenges and Choices in the Twenty-first Century,* State University of New York Press (Albany, NY), 2006.

Whistling Past Dixie: How Democrats Can Win without the South, Simon & Schuster (New York, NY), 2006.

Contributor of articles to *Constitutional Political Economy, Presidential Studies Quarterly, Wilson Quarterly, Public Choice,* and *Publius.* Contributor to the *Washington Post, Los Angeles Times, Baltimore Sun, Boston Globe, Pittsburgh Post-Gazette, Salon.com,* and *American Prospect* online; political writer for *Baltimore* magazine.

SIDELIGHTS: Thomas F. Schaller is the author of *Whistling Past Dixie: How Democrats Can Win without the South.* Schaller argues that Democrats, in order to win elections on a national scale, do not need the support of an increasingly conservative Southern electorate. Instead, he says, the party needs to abandon its attempts to win Southern votes in favor of cultivating liberal voters in other areas, particularly in the West. Through a policy like this, a *Kirkus Reviews* contributor explained, "the Democrats would prosper by branding the Republican Party as the instrument of Southern theocracy and reproductive tyranny."

Whistling Past Dixie points Democrats toward a strategy of breaking with the mainstream South. Schaller "stated that the situation for Democrats was bad in the south," reported Ammad Khan and Mia Brown in a *Retriever Weekly* article summarizing a presentation Schaller gave based on his book at the University of Maryland, "and that Republicans survived the 2006 cycle almost entirely unscathed in the area. Schaller went on to say that under Clinton-Gore, Democrats lost ground in relative terms in the south during the 1990s, and that Clinton was the first non-southern, southern Democrat in history." A "high population of blacks in the South," Vanessa Bush stated in *Booklist,* "will continue to provide the party with a toehold there." The book, declared a *Publishers Weekly* reviewer, will provide "a much-needed shot of realpolitik in the arm of the modern Democratic Party."

BIOGRAPHICAL AND CRITICAL SOURCES:

PERIODICALS

American Prospect, October, 2006, E.J. Dionne, Jr., "After the Fall of the Right," p. 52.

Booklist, October 1, 2006, Vanessa Bush, review of *Whistling Past Dixie: How Democrats Can Win without the South,* p. 10.
Kirkus Reviews, August 1, 2006, review of *Whistling Past Dixie,* p. 773.
New York Times Book Review, October 1, 2006, Andrew Hacker, "What's the Matter with Democrats?"
Publishers Weekly, August 21, 2006, review of *Whistling Past Dixie,* p. 60.

ONLINE

Retriever Weekly, http://trw.umbc.edu/ (January 1, 2007), Ammad Khan and Mia Brown, "Thomas Schaller Talks about Newest Book."
UMBC, http://www.umbc.edu/ (January 1, 2007), "Bringing Politics Close to Home."*

*   *   *

SCHEMBECHLER, Bo 1929-2006
(Glenn Edward Schembechler, Jr.)

OBITUARY NOTICE— See index for *CA* sketch: Born April 1, 1929, in Barberton, OH; died of heart failure, November 17, 2006, in Southfield, MI. Coach and author. Schembechler will long be remembered for his impressive winning record as football coach for the University of Michigan Wolverines from 1969 until 1990. Graduating from Ohio's Miami University in 1951, he was an assistant under Ohio State coach Woody Hayes in 1952 as Schembechler studied for his master's degree. Completing his graduate work in 1952, he served in the U.S. Army for a year and then coached football and baseball at Presbyterian College in South Carolina. Returning to the Midwest, he was an assistant football coach at Bowling Green for a year and then at Northwestern for the next season. Hayes hired Schembechler to be his assistant again in 1958, and then he accepted a job as head coach at Miami University in 1963. All of this, however, was preamble to the highlight of his career as head coach of the University of Michigan. Hired in 1969, Schembechler was put in charge of a Wolverine team with only a mediocre record. That year, he turned the team around completely, coaching a winning 7-2 season and beating arch rivals Ohio State 24-12 to win the Big Ten championship. Although he would never win a national championship, that fact never bothered Schembechler, who was more interested in the Big Ten, defeating Ohio State, and going to the Rose Bowl. His overall record against the Buckeyes would be 5-4-1, and his coaching years at Michigan ended with a 194-48-5 record, the best of any coach in the university's history. He also won or tied thirteen Big Ten championships, though he only had a 2-8 record at the Rose Bowl. Chronic heart problems over the years encouraged Schembechler to retire as head coach in 1990 after also spending two years as athletic director. He remained active in sports, however, as president and chief executive officer of the Detroit Tigers. Baseball and Schembechler were not well suited to each other, and the former football coach drew harsh criticism when he fired beloved Tigers broadcaster Ernie Harwell in 1990. Harwell was rehired in 1992, and Schembechler was fired in turn. He continued to work in sports as a football commentator. Ironically, Schembechler died the day before his favorite football game was to be played: the annual meeting between Ohio State and the Wolverines. The coach related his life experiences in two books: *Bo* (1989), written with sports columnist Mitch Albom, and *Michigan Memories: Inside Bo Schembechler's Football Scrapbook* (1998), written with Dan Ewald.

OBITUARIES AND OTHER SOURCES:

BOOKS

Schembechler, Bo, and Mitch Albom, *Bo,* Warner (New York, NY), 1989.
Schembechler, Bo, and Dan Ewald, *Michigan Memories: Inside Bo Schembechler's Football Scrapbook,* Sleeping Bear Press (Chelsea, MI), 1998.

PERIODICALS

Chicago Tribune, November 18, 2006, Section 1, pp. 1-2.
Los Angeles Times, November 18, 2006, p. B12.
New York Times, November 18, 2006, p. B9; November 22, 2006, p. A2.

Washington Post, November 18, 2006, p. B6.

*   *   *

SCHEMBECHLER, Glenn Edward, Jr.
See SCHEMBECHLER, Bo

*   *   *

SCHRADER, Leonard 1943-2006

OBITUARY NOTICE— See index for *CA* sketch: Born 1943, in Grand Rapids, MI; died of heart failure, November 2, 2006, in Los Angeles, CA. Film director, educator, and author. Schrader was best known as the critically acclaimed screenwriter of the movie *Kiss of the Spider Woman.* Growing up the son of strict Calvinist parents, he knew little about American movies and television until he left home for college. Still, he proved himself a natural storyteller, and after attending Calvin College he earned an M.F.A. at the University of Iowa Writers' Workshop. Schrader avoided the draft during the Vietnam War by moving to Japan. Here he taught American literature at Kyoto and Doshisha universities through the early 1970s and became fascinated with Japanese culture. This interest is evident in two films he wrote with his brother, Paul: *The Yakuza* (1975) and *Mishima: A Life in Four Chapters* (1985). *Kiss of the Spider Woman,* also released in 1985, was Schrader's adaptation of the Manuel Puig novel; it earned him an Oscar nomination for best screenplay based on material from another medium. His other films include *Blue Collar* (1978), which was another collaboration with his brother, *Old Boyfriends* (1979), and *Naked Tango* (1990), which he also directed. Although not a prolific screenwriter, Schrader had a great love of the medium, which he expressed as a popular faculty member at the University of Southern California and then at Chapman University. In 1999 he joined the American Film Institute as head of the graduate screenwriting program, and he was named senior filmmaker-in-residence and chair of the department in 2003.

OBITUARIES AND OTHER SOURCES:

PERIODICALS

Los Angeles Times, November 5, 2006, p. B15.
New York Times, November 7, 2006, p. C19.

SCHROEDER, Alan 1954-

PERSONAL: Born 1954. *Education:* Graduated from Wichita State University and Harvard University.

ADDRESSES: Office—School of Journalism, Northeastern University, 102 Lake Hall, Boston, MA 02115. *E-mail*—a.schroeder@neu.edu

CAREER: Northeastern University School of Journalism, Boston, MA, associate professor. Has also worked as a newspaper reporter, and as a television producer in Denver, CO, Wichita, KS, and Boston, MA. Guest commentator on television news shows.

WRITINGS:

Presidential Debates: Forty Years of High-Risk TV, Columbia University Press (New York, NY), 2000.
Celebrity-in-Chief: How Show Business Took Over the White House, Westview Press (Boulder, CO), 2004.

SIDELIGHTS: Alan Schroeder worked as a newspaper reporter and television producer before accepting a professorship at Northeastern University teaching general and television journalism. He is particularly interested in how television and the entertainment industry commingle with and impact politics. In *Presidential Debates: Forty Years of High-Risk TV,* Schroeder traces the history of the presidential debate from the first televised debate in 1960 to the highly choreographed events of the 1990s. In an article for *Variety,* Paula Bernstein wrote: "Presidential contenders . . . would be wise to study this comprehensive history of televised presidential debates before facing off in front of the American public." Bernstein further described the book as "thoroughly researched and concisely reported." A *Publishers Weekly* contributor commented: "Schroeder's 'tour' is a good one, sparked by lively writing and an eye for telling details." And *Library Journal* reviewer Michael A. Genovese concluded that the "very readable and highly informative work should be widely read."

Celebrity-in-Chief: How Show Business Took Over the White House is a study of the relationship between politicians and entertainers, and how each has both benefited and negatively impacted the other. Rich Martin described *Celebrity-in-Chief* in *Variety* as "a fun ride, full of great anecdotes." *Hollywood Reporter* contributor Gregory McNamee wrote that the book is "entertaining and thoughtful" and "makes for provocative reading," while a *Publishers Weekly* reviewer commended the book's "insightful analyses." The critic added that "Schroeder collects the most telling anecdotes from a century's worth of cultural cross-pollination."

BIOGRAPHICAL AND CRITICAL SOURCES:

PERIODICALS

Hollywood Reporter, March 31, 2004, Gregory Mc-Namee, review of *Celebrity-in-Chief: How Show Business Took Over the White House,* p. 10.
Kirkus Reviews, January 15, 2004, review of *Celebrity-in-Chief,* p. 75.
Library Journal, July, 2000, Michael A. Genovese, review of *Presidential Debates: Forty Years of High-Risk TV,* p. 111.
Publishers Weekly, August 7, 2000, review of *Presidential Debates,* p. 84; January 19, 2004, review of *Celebrity-in-Chief,* p. 62.
Variety, September 25, 2000, Paula Bernstein, review of *Presidential Debates,* p. 76; April 26, 2004, Rich Martin, review of *Celebrity-in-Chief,* p. 58.

ONLINE

Northeastern University School of Journalism Web site, http://www.journalism.neu.edu/ (December 2, 2006), faculty profile on Alan Schroeder.

*   *   *

SCHWARTZ, Toby D.
See DeVENS, Toby

*   *   *

SCOTT, Nathan A., Jr. 1925-2006
(Nathan Alexander Scott, Jr.)

OBITUARY NOTICE— See index for *CA* sketch: Born April 24, 1925, in Cleveland, OH; died of lung cancer, December 20, 2006, in Charlottesville, VA. Priest, educator, and author. An Episcopalian priest and university professor, Scott combined humanities and theology to teach students about religious expression through literature. A 1944 graduate of the University of Michigan, he earned his master's in divinity from Union Theological Seminary in 1946 and a Ph.D. from Columbia in 1949. Ordained in 1960, Scott combined church and university duties over his long career. He was an instructor at Howard University in the early 1950s, during which time he directed the general education program in the humanities for two years, and was on the Divinity School faculty at the University of Chicago from 1955 until 1976. The last part of his career was spent at the University of Virginia, where Scott chaired the department of religious studies. He retired in 1990. While at Chicago, Scott held the unique post of professor of theology and literature, leading an interdisciplinary program in which he taught students how spirituality can be fostered not only through the Bible but also by reading other literature. Conversely, as a canon theologian at Chicago's Cathedral of St. James from 1966 to 1976, he frequently alluded to great works of literature in sermons he presented. The combination of interests was apparent in his publications. Scott wrote and edited over two dozen books, including *Modern Literature and the Religious Frontier* (1958), *The Broken Center: Studies in the Theological Horizon of Modern Literature* (1966), *Mirrors of Man in Existentialism* (1978), and *Visions of Presence in Modern American Poetry* (1993).

OBITUARIES AND OTHER SOURCES:

PERIODICALS

Chicago Tribune, December 27, 2006, Section 3, p. 7.

*   *   *

SCOTT, Nathan Alexander, Jr.
   See SCOTT, Nathan A., Jr.

*   *   *

SCROOP, Daniel 1973-

PERSONAL: Born 1973 in Nuneaton, Warwickshire, England. *Education:* St. Anne's College, Oxford, B.A., D.Phil.; Lancaster University, M.A.

ADDRESSES: E-mail—Daniel.Scroop@liverpool.ac.uk.

CAREER: University of Liverpool School of History, Liverpool, England, lecturer in American history, 2003—. Visiting scholar, Columbia University, 1998; lecturer in American history, University of Wales Bangor, 2001-02; University Lecturer in American politics, Cambridge University 2002-03; visiting fellow, Rothermere American Institute, 2007.

MEMBER: American Political Science Association, American Historical Association, Organization of American Historians, British Association of American Studies.

AWARDS, HONORS: Beeke-Levy Award, Franklin and Eleanor Roosevelt Institute, 1998, for research in the history of the New Deal; Moody Grant, Lyndon Baines Johnson Library, 2002, for research in the LBJ Library Collections; Rivkin Research Fellowship, Franklin and Eleanor Roosevelt Institute, 2004; Herbert Hoover Association Travel Grant, 2006, for research in the collections of the Herbert Hoover Presidential Library.

WRITINGS:

Mr. Democrat: Jim Farley, the New Deal, and the Making of Modern American Politics, University of Michigan Press (Ann Arbor, MI), 2006.

Contributed to *Dictionary of Liberal Thought,* edited by J. Reynolds, Methuen/Politico (London, England), 2007. Contributor to the *Cambridge Review of International Affairs.*

SIDELIGHTS: Daniel Scroop is a scholar of American history who has specialized in how liberal politics evolved over the twentieth century. His 2001 doctoral thesis focused on 1930s political figure Jim Farley, who was a campaign manager for President Franklin D. Roosevelt and chair of the Democratic Party. Scroop further developed the biography into his first book, *Mr. Democrat: Jim Farley, the New Deal, and the Making of Modern American Politics.* In addition to providing background information regarding Farley's childhood and early years in politics, Scroop asserts that Farley played a key role in the development of modern-day liberalism as one of Roosevelt's closest political advisors and a proponent of the New Deal. *Library Journal* reviewer Michael LaMagna noted that the book "challenges the current historical understanding of Jim Farley" and is "more than a biography of achievement." A contributor to *Publishers Weekly* described *Mr. Democrat* as a "workmanlike study of Farley's role in forging the New Deal coalition and ushering in a new type of politics."

Scroop has also written articles on the anti-chain store movement of the 1920s and 1930s, the history of liberal sentiment against corporate monopolies, and the life of former U.S. senator Gerald Nye, as well as contributing a chapter on journalist Walter Lippmann in the *Dictionary of Liberal Thought.*

BIOGRAPHICAL AND CRITICAL SOURCES:

PERIODICALS

Library Journal, May 1, 2006, Michael LaMagna, review of *Mr. Democrat: Jim Farley, the New Deal, and the Making of Modern American Politics,* p. 94.
Publishers Weekly, March 6, 2006, review of *Mr. Democrat,* p. 57.

ONLINE

University of Liverpool School of History Web site, http://www.liv.ac.uk/history/ (December 2, 2006), faculty profile of Daniel Scroop.

*   *   *

SCUDAMORE, James 1976-

PERSONAL: *Education:* University of Oxford, B.A. (with honors); University of East Anglia, M.A.

CAREER: Freelance writer, 2006—. Worked in advertising for four years.

AWARDS, HONORS: Costa First Novel Award (short-list), 2006, for *The Amnesia Clinic.*

WRITINGS:

The Amnesia Clinic (novel), Harvill Secker (London, England), 2006, Harcourt (Orlando, FL), 2007.

SIDELIGHTS: James Scudamore's debut novel *The Amnesia Clinic* traces the journey of two fifteen-year-old boys, Fabian, scion of an ancient Quito family, and Anti, a British schoolboy, through Anti's last days in Ecuador before he is to return to England to continue his education. The two live a rich fantasy life, played out as "a game filled with shrunken heads, buried treasure and imagined seductions," according to Sam Alexandroni in the *New Statesman.* Fabian, having lost both his parents in a fatal car crash, is obsessed with the idea that his mother, whose body was never recovered, might still survive somewhere—perhaps as a patient in an amnesia clinic (an institution invented by Anti). "Scudamore," declared a reviewer for *Publishers Weekly,* "admirably portrays the braggadocio, sexual fantasies and obsessions of 15-year-old boys." The novel takes a darker turn as Fabian sinks deeper into his fantasy that his mother is alive somewhere in the hills of Ecuador. Eventually the conflict between their fantasies and reality bring the two boys into conflict with each another. Laurence Phelan, writing for the *Independent on Sunday* called *The Amnesia Clinic* "an exuberant first novel," adding that "Scudamore has fun blurring the edges of truth and fiction, creating fantastic and colourful stories within stories." In a review for *Time Out London,* Katie Dailey described the book as "a nostalgic, compelling adventure laced with black humour."

BIOGRAPHICAL AND CRITICAL SOURCES:

PERIODICALS

Guardian (London, England), April 29, 2006, review of *The Amnesia Clinic,* p. 8.
Independent on Sunday (London, England), May 7, 2006, Laurence Phelan, review of *The Amnesia Clinic.*
Kirkus Reviews, September 1, 2006, review of *The Amnesia Clinic,* p. 872.
Literary Review, June, 2006, "A Choice of First Novels," p. 57.
New Statesman, May 29, 2006, Sam Alexandroni, "American Dreams," p. 57.

Publishers Weekly, September 11, 2006, review of *The Amnesia Clinic,* p. 33.

Scotsman, August 12, 2006, review of *The Amnesia Clinic.*

Sunday Telegraph (London, England), June 11, 2006, review of *The Amnesia Clinic,* p. 55.

Time Out London, May 10, 2006, review of *The Amnesia Clinic.*

* * *

SEIGEL, Andrea 1979-

PERSONAL: Born October 28, 1979, in Anaheim, CA. *Education:* Graduated from Brown University; Bennington College, M.F.A., 2007.

ADDRESSES: Home—Los Angeles, CA. *Agent*—Doug Stewart, Sterling Lord Literary Agency, 65 Bleecker St., New York, NY 10012. *E-mail*—andrea@andreaseigel.com.

CAREER: Writer.

AWARDS, HONORS: Top Ten Debut Novels, Amazon.com, 2004, *Booklist* Best Adult Books for Young Adults citation, 2005, both for *Like the Red Panda.*

WRITINGS:

Like the Red Panda (novel), Harcourt (Orlando, FL), 2004.
To Feel Stuff (novel), Harcourt (Orlando, FL), 2006.

ADAPTATIONS: Like the Red Panda has been optioned for film by Reason Pictures.

SIDELIGHTS: Andrea Seigel's debut novel *Like the Red Panda* tells the story of a seventeen-year-old girl named Stella Parrish, whose life has made her cynical beyond her years. Stella's parents both died from drug overdoses six years before, leaving her in the hands of confused foster parents. Saddled with a soured view of life and a skeptical outlook, she "offers a Holdenesque view of her upper-middle-class Orange County, Calif., town and all its hypocrisy," stated a *Publishers Weekly* contributor, "the stupidities faced in classrooms and the absurdity of senior year rituals." "Two weeks before graduation, she decides to kill herself—but first, she explains her decision in a journal," wrote Lori Gottlieb in *People.* Stella's tale, explained Prudence Peiffer in her *Library Journal* review, demonstrates that she is an "inquisitive, funny, alienated young woman who is unsure whether a future at Princeton . . . or life itself means anything." But Stella, as Seigel depicts her, is a more complicated character than the disaffected outsider she pretends to be. "At heart," declared *Salon.com* contributor Christopher Farah, "she's an idealist, someone who still cares very deeply for the people in her life, even those who've treated her badly. Like a recovering Catholic, she wants to believe there's a purpose for everything, an underlying goodness that drives life."

Seigel followed *Like the Red Panda* with *To Feel Stuff,* a very different type of novel. The story centers on Brown University student Elodie Harrington, who suffers from such a variety of diseases (ranging from tuberculosis to epileptic-like seizures) that she moves into the campus infirmary in an attempt to take back her health. "The fever of love joins her physical afflictions," Jennifer Mattson wrote in *Booklist,* "when Chester [Hunter III, a fellow student,] moves into the ward, his sense of invincibility [is] as shattered as his crowbar-smashed kneecaps." Elodie is also the subject of the fascinated scrutiny of her doctor, Mark Kirschling, who believes the many diseases that afflict her may be a sign of emerging psychic powers. Kirschling's belief is reinforced when Elodie begins to see apparitions in the infirmary itself. "Does this mean the girl is out of her mind," asked a *Publishers Weekly* reviewer, "or could she actually be experiencing a kind of 'psychic puberty,' or physical awakening to her extraordinary abilities?" The author, another *Publishers Weekly* contributor explained, has "crafted believable characters to anchor the fantastical circumstances, and [the book is] a testament to her ability to captivate." "What makes '*To Feel Stuff*' a strong read," wrote *Seattle Times* contributor Betsy Aoki, "is the vivid precision with which 26-year-old Seigel . . . shapes her characters through their explanations of how they are feeling." "Readers under 25," Angie Kritenbrink declared in the *Seattle Weekly,* "will enjoy *Stuff*'s quirky characters, exploration of the paranormal, PG-13 sex scenes, [and] maybe even Andrea Seigel's ambitious narrative technique of using three different first-person points of view."

BIOGRAPHICAL AND CRITICAL SOURCES:

PERIODICALS

Booklist, January 1, 2004, Jennifer Mattson, review of *Like the Red Panda,* p. 828; May 1, 2006, Jennifer Mattson, review of *To Feel Stuff,* p. 73.
Entertainment Weekly, July 28, 2006, Hannah Tucker, review of *To Feel Stuff,* p. 71.
Kirkus Reviews, June 1, 2006, review of *To Feel Stuff,* p. 542.
Library Journal, February 1, 2004, Prudence Peiffer, review of *Like the Red Panda,* p. 125; May 15, 2006, Prudence Peiffer, review of *To Feel Stuff,* p. 91.
People, April 12, 2004, Lori Gottlieb, review of *Like the Red Panda,* p. 63.
Publishers Weekly, March 22, 2004, review of *Like the Red Panda,* p. 61; April 3, 2006, review of *To Feel Stuff,* p. 34; April 3, 2006, review of *To Feel Stuff,* p. 34 (second review).
Seattle Times, August 25, 2006, Betsy Aoki, "Love, Physical and Metaphysical, in the College Infirmary."
Seattle Weekly, August 30, 2006, Angie Kritenbrink, review of *To Feel Stuff.*

ONLINE

Absolute Write, http://www.AbsoluteWrite.com/ (January 28, 2007), Amy Brozio-Andrews, interview with Andrea Seigel.
Andrea Seigel Web site, http://www.andreaseigel.com (January 28, 2007), author biography.
Eugene Weekly, http://www.eugeneweekly.com/ (January 28, 2007), Suzi Steffen, "The Absurdities of Love."
Luke Ford.com, http://www.lukeford.net/ (January 28, 2007), author interview.
Salon.com, http://www.salon.com/ (January 28, 2007), Christopher Farah, review of *Like the Red Panda.*

*   *   *

SERVAN-SCHREIBER, Jean-Jacques 1924-2006

OBITUARY NOTICE— See index for *CA* sketch: Born February 13, 1924, in Paris, France; died of complications from bronchitis, November 7, 2006, in Fécamp, France. Publisher, editor, politician, journalist, and author. The cofounding editor of the periodical *L'Express,* Servan-Schreiber was a leftist intellectual and former politician best known for his views on American-European economic relations as expressed in his *The American Challenge.* Coming from an interesting family background, Servan-Schreiber was the grandson of Prussian chancellor Otto von Bismarck's Jewish political secretary, Joseph Schreiber. Schreiber fled to Paris when Bismarck decided to declare war on France, and the family would come to raise their children as Catholics. Servan-Schreiber and his family were nevertheless in danger when the Nazis invaded France, and so they moved to Spain. The young Servan-Schreiber immigrated to the United States and trained to be a fighter pilot with the Free French during World War II. He never had a chance to fly in combat, however, before the war ended. He returned to France and graduated with a degree in engineering from the Ecole Polytechnique in 1947. Servan-Schreiber was a reporter for *Le Monde* from 1947 to 1953, while also serving occasionally as a correspondent for *Reporter* and as a foreign affairs writer for *ParisPress.* Together with Françoise Giroud, he founded *L'Express* in 1953; later, in 1964, he also founded *L'Expansion.* Initially a strongly leftist publication, the paper eventually evolved to appeal to general audiences. At one point, it was said to so closely resemble the *New York Times* that the American newspaper tried to sue *L'Express.* Servan-Schreiber unexpectedly returned to active military duty from 1956 to 1957 during the war in Algeria, and here he earned a military cross of valor for his service. The year he returned home he published the controversial *Lieutenant en Algerie,* which was translated as *Lieutenant in Algeria* (1957). The work criticized the behavior of the French military in Algeria, including acts of torture that Servan-Schreiber said he witnessed. The author was subsequently charged with subverting troop morale, but he was cleared of any criminal wrongdoing. His next book, *Le Défi americain* (1967; translated as *The American Challenge* in 1968) was a best seller that warned Europe of American economic dominance. In it, he also came out in support of open markets and free trade, telling Europeans they needed to be more aggressive in the market. Long before the formation of the European Economic Union, Servan-Schreiber, who actually greatly admired the United States, declared that the best defense against American dominance was for European nations to combine their financial muscle. Continuing his left-leaning views, Servan-Schreiber was active in the Radical Socialist Party as a security general and then president. After Charles de Gaulle left office in 1969, he successfully ran for office in France's National Assembly in 1970. Under pressure from the public, Servan-Schreiber stepped down as editor of *L'Express* because it was felt his strong political views were influencing the newspaper too much. He still owned a stake in the newspaper until 1977, however, when he sold it to financier Jimmy Goldsmith. Remaining politically active, he helped Valery-Giscard d'Estaing win the presidency in 1974, and he briefly served as minister of reforms that year. In 1976 he was elected president of the regional council of Lorraine. Continuing his involvement in politics, he served as advisor to Home Secretary Gaston Defferre in 1981, as well as to President Francois Mitterrand in 1983. By the early 1980s Servan-Schreiber was developing a new interest in technology. Fascinated by the potential of computer technology, he ran the World Center for Informatics and Human Resources in Paris until 1985. His second best seller, *Le Défi mondial* (1981) expressed his ideas about Japan's economic dominance through its focus on the electronics industry. He then moved to Pittsburgh to chair the international committee at Carnegie-Mellon University, returning to France in the late 1980s. Servan-Schreiber spent several years on his memoirs, publishing *Passions* (1991) and *Les Fossoyeurs* (1993) before becoming incapacitated by a degenerative brain disease. Among his other publications available in English translation are *The Spirit of May* (1969) and *The Radical Alternative* (1970).

OBITUARIES AND OTHER SOURCES:

BOOKS

Servan-Schreiber, Jean-Jacques, *Passions,* Fixot (Paris, France), 1991.
Servan-Schreiber, Jean-Jacques, *Les Fossoyeurs,* Fixot (Paris, France), 1993.

PERIODICALS

Los Angeles Times, November 9, 2006, p. B11.
New York Times, November 8, 2006, p. A23.
Times (London, England), November 8, 2006, p. 69.
Washington Post, November 8, 2006, p. B5.

*   *   *

SETTERFIELD, Diane 1964(?)-

PERSONAL: Born c. 1964, in Reading, England; married Peter Whittall (an accountant). *Education:* Attended Bristol University.

ADDRESSES: Home—Harrowgate, Yorkshire, England.

CAREER: Writer. Worked variously as an English teacher in France, a French professor, and as a private French teacher for people moving to France.

WRITINGS:

The Thirteenth Tale (novel), Atria Books (New York, NY), 2006.

SIDELIGHTS: Diane Setterfield's best-selling literary mystery novel, *The Thirteenth Tale,* transformed her from a teacher into a professional writer. The book tells the story of Vida Winter, a famous author best known for her volume of thirteen stories, of which the last is missing. Winter hires Margaret Lea, a biographer and bookseller, to write about her life, but nothing about the situation is as straightforward as it might seem, and the result is a gothic tale of adultery, arson, and identity swapping. Setterfield admits that the most difficult thing about devoting her time to writing the book was the precariousness of a writer's life. She told *Publishers Weekly* contributor Dick Donahue: "There were no guarantees that my writing would be any good, that I would be able to finish the novel satisfactorily, or that anyone would want to read it." Setterfield's gamble to try her hand at writing paid off. Her novel sold in a ten-day auction, earning large advances for both the British and American rights. Rights to the novel were sold in more than thirty countries. The book also landed on the top of American best-seller lists the first week after it was published. Regarding her sudden popularity, Setterfield told *BookBrowse.com:* "I'm used to living a really quiet life with lots of space to think. I'm not used to being so busy and social and meeting all these people. It's not that I'm anti-social, just that I like my own company, and I've been living with people who aren't real for the past few years—I find real people a lot more demanding."

The Thirteenth Tale has garnered strong critical praise as well as commercial success. Kaite Mediatore Stover, in a review for *Booklist,* called the book "a wholly original work told in the vein of all the best gothic classics." A contributor to *Kirkus Reviews* noted that "this is no postmodern revision of the genre. It is a contemporary gothic tale whose excesses and occasional implausibility . . . can be forgiven for the thrill of the storytelling." In a review for *Entertainment Weekly,* Tina Jordan remarked: "Setterfield's spooky, gloom-infused work lovingly invokes both *Jane Eyre* and *Rebecca* . . . , but the mystery is very much her own." Frank Wilson, in the *Philadelphia Inquirer,* concluded that "those who buy and read this complex, compelling and, in the end, deeply moving novel are unlikely to feel they've been shortchanged." *Library Journal* contributor Jenne Bergstrom dubbed the novel "equally suited to a rainy afternoon on the couch or a summer day on the beach."

BIOGRAPHICAL AND CRITICAL SOURCES:

PERIODICALS

Booklist, May 15, 2006, author biography, p. S10; September 1, 2006, Kaite Mediatore Stover, review of *The Thirteenth Tale,* p. 58.

Bulletin with Newsweek, November 14, 2006, Anne Susskind, review of *The Thirteenth Tale,* p. 77.

Entertainment Weekly, September 15, 2006, Tina Jordan, "Winter's Tale" review of *The Thirteenth Tale,* p. 80.

Globe and Mail (Toronto, Ontario, Canada), September 30, 2006, Michelle Orange, review of *The Thirteenth Tale,* p. D8.

Kirkus Reviews, July 15, 2006, review of *The Thirteenth Tale,* p. 697.

Library Journal, August 1, 2006, Jenne Bergstrom, review of *The Thirteenth Tale,* p. 73.

People, October 2, 2006, Sue Corbett, review of *The Thirteenth Tale,* p. 61.

Philadelphia Inquirer, October 4, 2006, Frank Wilson, review of *The Thirteenth Tale.*

Publishers Weekly, June 26, 2006, review of *The Thirteenth Tale,* p. 27; August 14, 2006, Dick Donahue, author biography, p. 89.

Spectator, September 30, 2006, Miranda France, review of *The Thirteenth Tale.*

ONLINE

BookBrowse.com, http://www.bookbrowse.com/ (October, 12, 2006), author biography and interview.

Independent Online, http://enjoyment.independent.co.uk/ (September 25, 2006), Louise Jury, "British Teacher Becomes a Literary Sensation in the US."

Internet Writing Journal, http://www.internetwritingjournal.com/ (September 25, 2006), author biography and interview.

Scrinanbbles Blog, http://scrinanbbles.blogspot.com/ (October 16, 2006), Nancy Fontaine, review of *The Thirteenth Tale.**

*   *   *

SEWELL, Joan

PERSONAL: Married; husband's name Kip. *Education:* Earned master's degree.

ADDRESSES: Home—Seattle, WA. *E-mail*—joan@joansewell.com.

CAREER: Writer.

WRITINGS:

I'd Rather Eat Chocolate: Learning to Love My Low Libido (memoir), Broadway Books (New York, NY), 2007.

SIDELIGHTS: Joan Sewell not only felt out of place in an oversexed society but also found that her husband's sex drive, which was much higher than hers, was placing a strain on their marriage. Thinking something was wrong with her, Sewell set out to find a way to increase her desire to have sex. *I'd Rather Eat Chocolate: Learning to Love My Low Libido* is, as the author describes on her Internet home page, "the chronicle of my adventures through Sexpert Wonderland to cure my 'dysfunction.'" The author describes her meetings and studies with numerous experts in the field of human sexuality, from counselors and "sexperts" to writers in women's magazines. Sewell eventually comes to view most sex therapies and advice to be much too focused on men's desires and needs and ultimately decides that the difference in the sexual drives of her and her husband are natural and that their marriage can thrive despite the difference. A reviewer writing in *Publishers Weekly* called the book "honest and accessible," adding that it also makes good reading for those interested in taking "a closer look at one subject that continues to gap the genders." A *Kirkus Reviews* contributor referred to *I'd Rather Eat Chocolate* as "astonishingly frank and often funny disclosures about the author's sex life, with a serious underlying message about the actual differences between the libidos of women and men."

BIOGRAPHICAL AND CRITICAL SOURCES:

BOOKS

Sewell, Joan, *I'd Rather Eat Chocolate: Learning to Love My Low Libido,* Broadway Books (New York, NY), 2007.

PERIODICALS

Kirkus Reviews, October 15, 2006, review of *I'd Rather Eat Chocolate,* p. 1060.
Publishers Weekly, October 16, 2006, review of *I'd Rather Eat Chocolate,* p. 43.

ONLINE

Joan Sewell Home Page, http://www.joansewell.com (January 29, 2007).*

*   *   *

SGRENA, Giuliana 1948-

PERSONAL: Born December 20, 1948, in Masera, province of Verbano-Cusio-Ossola, Italy; daughter of Franco Sgrena (an activist). *Education:* Studied in Milan. *Politics:* Pacifist.

ADDRESSES: Home—Italy.

CAREER: Journalist. *Guerra e Pace,* Italy, reporter, 1980-88; *Il Manifesto,* Rome, Italy, reporter, 1988—; *Die Zeit* (German weekly), Germany, reporter.

WRITINGS:

Alla scuola dei Taleban, Manifestolibri (Rome, Italy), 2002.
Il fronte Iraq: diario di una guerra permanente, Manifestolibri (Rome, Italy), 2004.
Fuoco amico, Feltrinelli (Milan, Italy), 2005, translation published as *Friendly Fire: The Remarkable Story of a Journalist Kidnapped in Iraq, Rescued by an Italian Secret Service Agent, and Shot by U.S. Forces,* Haymarket Books (Chicago, IL), 2006.

ADAPTATIONS: Fuoco Amico is being adapted for film by La Lumiere production company, cowritten by director Enzo Monteleone and Sgrena.

SIDELIGHTS: Italian journalist Giuliana Sgrena first became interested in leftist politics when she was studying in Milan. Beginning in 1980, she was a reporter for *Guerra e Pace,* a weekly newspaper, and then in 1988 she went on to become a war correspondent for the communist newspaper, *Il Manifesto.* It was while working for that publication that she went to Baghdad in 2003 to cover the Iraqi war, and in February, 2005, she was kidnapped by armed gunmen from in front of the university. Sgrena was held for one month before she was released, due to negotiations. However, on her way to the airport following her rescue, Sgrena and the agents with her were fired upon by U.S. soldiers who were part of the security detail for American diplomat John Negroponte. Nicola Calipari, one of the agents protecting Sgrena, was killed, and Sgrena was injured when shrapnel entered her shoulder. The incident led to strained relations between Italy and the United States. Sgrena writes about her experiences in her book *Friendly Fire: The Remarkable Story of a Journalist Kidnapped in Iraq, Rescued by an Italian Secret Service Agent, and Shot by U.S. Forces,* detailing her capture, her imprisonment, and the aftermath of her release. She also calls into question the safety of journalists working abroad and in war zones. Vanessa Bush, writing for *Booklist,* called the book an "absorbing account." Ron Jacobs, in a review for *Dissident Voice Online,* wrote that the book "is more than the tale of one hostage's ordeal and it is more than just another tract on the US-created debacle that is Iraq. It is not a cry for revenge, but a tempered statement on a nation's shattered psyche and an individual attempt to share a perspective influenced by her unforeseen role in that nation's history."

BIOGRAPHICAL AND CRITICAL SOURCES:

BOOKS

Sgrena, Giuliana, *Fuoco amico,* Feltrinelli (Milan, Italy), 2005, translation published as *Friendly Fire: The Remarkable Story of a Journalist Kidnapped in Iraq, Rescued by an Italian Secret Service Agent, and Shot by U.S. Forces,* Haymarket Books (Chicago, IL), 2006.

PERIODICALS

Booklist, September 15, 2006, Vanessa Bush, review of *Friendly Fire,* p. 19.

Hollywood Reporter, June 24, 2005, Peter Kiefer, "Sgrena Saga Set for Film," p. 5.

Nation, April 4, 2005, Lucia Annunziata, "Anger in Italy," p. 5.

New York Times, March 5, 2005, Edward Wong, Jason Horowitz, "Italian Hostage, Released in Iraq, Is Shot by G.I.s," p. A1; March 7, 2005, Ian Fisher, "U.S. Killing of Italian Officer Stokes Anger against War," p. A11; March 9, 2005, Edward Wong, "Italian Disputes U.S. Version of Fatal Shots Fired at Journalist's Car," pp. A10, A14; March 16, 2005, Ian Fisher, "Italy Starting to Plan Pullout of Iraq Troops," p. A1; March 16, 2005, James Glanz, "Iraqis Say Italians Aren't Cooperating in Kidnapping Investigation," p. A10; May 1, 2005, Richard A. Oppel, Jr., and Robert F. Worth, "Ex-hostage's Italian Driver Ignored Warning, U.S. Says," p. A22.

Quill, April, 2005, "Italian Journalist Rejects U.S. Account of Shooting," p. 44.

Time, March 14, 2005, Melissa August and others, "Milestones," p. 19.

U.S. World & News Report, March 14, 2005, Lisa Stein, "Hostage Nightmare," p. 14; May 9, 2005, John Leo, "Full Disclosure," p. 74.

ONLINE

BBC News Online, http://news.bbc.co.uk/ (January 31, 2007), Giuliana Sgrena interview transcript.

Democracy Now Online, http://www.democracynow.org/ (November 22, 2006), "Giuliana Sgrena on the Ousting of Italy's Intelligence Chief for Involvement in CIA Kidnapping of Sheikh."

Dissident Voice Online, http://www.dissidentvoice.org/ (September 28, 2006), Ron Jacobs, "With Friends Like These," review of *Friendly Fire.*

Il Manifesto Online, http://www.ilmanifesto.it/ (January 31, 2007), Giuliana Sgrena on her kidnapping.

*   *   *

SHAARA, Lila 1958-

PERSONAL: Born August 21, 1958, in Tallahassee, FL; daughter of Michael Joseph (a novelist) and Helen Shaara; married Robert Edward Rayshich, April 24, 1993; children: Frederick, Maxwell. *Education:* University of Pittsburgh, M.A., 1988, Ph.D., 1994.

CAREER: Novelist, 2006—. University of Pittsburgh, Pittsburgh, PA, research associate, 1996; Indiana University of Pennsylvania, Indiana, PA, adjunct professor of anthropology, 1997—.

WRITINGS:

Every Secret Thing: A Novel, Ballantine (New York, NY), 2006.

SIDELIGHTS: Lila Shaara, daughter of novelist Michael Shaara, is both a cultural anthropologist and a novelist like her father—and her brother Jeff Shaara, also a very successful writer. Growing up with her father, she saw the bitter side of fiction writing and publishing: her father received little recognition for his writing during his lifetime, even though he received the Pulitzer Prize for *The Killer Angels* in 1975. "I grew up seeing writing as something that gripped you in poisoned talons," Lila Shaara recalled in an interview with Ron Hogan published on the *Beatrice* Web site, "gave you little or nothing back, drove you to addiction and depression, and killed you young. And so I avoided writing fiction for as long as I possibly could. When I couldn't hold it back any longer, it came out in great gushes. And so I've become, for better or worse, a writer."

Shaara's first published work, *Every Secret Thing: A Novel,* is "a complex, first-person tale of Gina Paletta, a Victoria's Secret model-turned-professor who is also a widowed mother of two sons," wrote *Pittsburgh Post-Gazette* contributor John Young. "Three major plot strands are launched when two of Paletta's students are suspected of murder and harboring unhealthy fixations about her." The two, "whom the police suspect of murdering a friend," explained a *Publishers Weekly* reviewer, "enter photos from her lingerie-modeling days onto an Internet site, then stalk her." "This is a dense, wonderful, lavish novel," concluded *Flint Journal* critic Helen S. Bas, "that draws in and engages the reader to the extent that it's not only hard to put down, it's hard to admit that when the last page has been read, there is no more Lila Shaara to read."

BIOGRAPHICAL AND CRITICAL SOURCES:

PERIODICALS

Flint Journal (Flint, MI), November 19, 2006, Helen S. Bas, "Literary Family Has Another Shining Star."

Kirkus Reviews, May 1, 2006, review of *Every Secret Thing: A Novel*, pp. 11-12.

Pittsburgh Post-Gazette, August 13, 2006, John Young, "A Literary Legacy: Lila Shaara Emerges as Novelist in Her Own Right."

Publishers Weekly, May 15, 2006, review of *Every Secret Thing*, p. 50.

ONLINE

Beatrice, http://www.beatrice.com/ (January 3, 2007), Ron Hogan, "Lila Shaara Considers Her 'Heavy Name.'"

BookLoons, http://www.bookloons.com/ (January 3, 2007), Hilary Williamson, interview with Lila Shaara.

Harriet Klausner's Review Archive, http://harrietklausner.wwwi.com/ (January 10, 2007), Harriet Klausner, review of *Every Secret Thing*.*

*   *   *

SHAPIRO, Anna

PERSONAL: Born in Italy. *Education:* Bennington College, B.A.; Columbia University School of the Arts, M.F.A.

ADDRESSES: Agent—Tina Bennett, Janklow Nesbit Associates, 445 Park Ave., New York, NY 10022.

CAREER: Writer and critic.

WRITINGS:

The Right Bitch (novel), Grove Weidenfeld (New York, NY), 1992.

Life and Love, Such as They Are (novel), Simon & Schuster (New York, NY), 1994.

A Feast of Words: For Lovers of Food and Fiction (essays), with drawings by the author, W.W. Norton (New York, NY), 1996.

The Scourge (e-book), USA Today, 2001.

Living on Air (novel), Soho Press (New York, NY), 2006.

Contributor to periodicals, including *New Yorker, New York Times Book Review, Nation, New York Observer, Washington Post, Los Angeles Times, Newsday,* and the London *Observer.*

SIDELIGHTS: Anna Shapiro is a novelist, nonfiction writer, and reviewer whose work has appeared in the *New Yorker.* In *A Feast of Words: For Lovers of Food and Fiction,* Shapiro offers a collection of essays that explore how food is used to tell stories. Drawing on the work of twenty prominent writers, Shapiro extracts from their stories the kernel of truth represented by food, highlighting "celebrations of food, memorably awful meals, plots that turn and fates that hinge on breakfast, lunch, and dinner," noted Francine Prose in *People.* She covers important food-related scenes and plot developments in a number of well-known stories, including important feasts in *Anna Karenina,* fish chowder in *Moby Dick,* revolution-spawning strawberries in *Emma,* and the frozen leg of lamb that served as a murder weapon in Roald Dahl's "Lamb to the Slaughter." Shapiro also includes a selection of straightforward recipes based on these references to literary foodstuffs. Shapiro "melds the art of literature with the craft of cuisine," observed *Booklist* reviewer Alice Joyce.

Life and Love, Such as They Are tells the story of six romantically entangled persons as they break up, fall in love, flirt, connect, and try to make sense of it all.

When aspiring painter Ella Vaporsky falls in love with Frank, a married photographer, she decides that she must make a break from her trustworthy but dull lover Steven, whom she has been with for more than ten years. Burton, a neurotic conductor, tries to romance quiet and talented violinist Cynthia, who loves him, but she is a woman who lacks self-confidence and who submits herself to being hurt because she doesn't believe she deserves anything better. Ave manipulates men to her advantage, but she has no illusions about what she does—and as Burton's lover, her hold on him is solid. "The interactions between these characters are both comical and tragic," commented *Booklist* critic Lindsay Throm. "For sharp characterization and wry, generally acerbic comments on relationships, Shapiro outclasses most of her peers," commented a reviewer in *Publishers Weekly*.

Maude Pugh, the teenage protagonist of *Living on Air*, is dissatisfied with her life as an artist's daughter. Her father, Milt, a struggling modernist painter, is an arrogant, domineering sort, involved with his own interests to the exclusion of most everyone else. To better display his brightly colored canvases, he paints every room in the house black. Maude's mother, Nina, is not merely socially conscious but socially terrified, worried that her neighbors may well be her social superiors. Maude's disaffected sixteen-year-old brother Seth, his parents' darling, has had enough of the foolishness at home and disappears, leaving his parents to blame Maude and to pummel her with emotional broadsides. Harboring a desire to be an artist, and covetous of the trappings of wealth she sees in her father's clients, Maude manages to get a short-lived scholarship to prep school Bay Farm. There, she befriends wealthy Weezie, who has mistaken romantic notions about the nobility of poverty. Meanwhile, a rocky romance with a boy named Danny threatens to devastate her emotionally. "Shapiro's portrait of Maude is knife-sharp; she completely inhabits the consuming inner world of a painfully intelligent adolescent girl, showing Maude's every mood, thought, and desire with piercing clarity," commented a *Kirkus Reviews* critic. The novel is "crowded with the closely observed details that describe both the lives of her characters and the culture they inhabit," observed Michael Cart in *Booklist*. A *Publishers Weekly* reviewer called Shapiro a "shrewd anthropologist well versed in the cultures of adolescence, the '60s, and class strife."

BIOGRAPHICAL AND CRITICAL SOURCES:

PERIODICALS

Booklist, December 15, 1993, Lindsay Throm, review of *Life and Love, Such as They Are,* p. 739; October 15, 1996, Alice Joyce, review of *A Feast of Words: For Lovers of Food and Fiction,* p. 399; April 1, 2006, Michael Cart, review of *Living on Air,* p. 21.
Entertainment Weekly, January 28, 1994, Kate Wilson, review of *Life and Love, Such as They Are,* p. 50.
Kirkus Reviews, March 1, 2006, review of *Living on Air,* p. 204.
New York Times, January 16, 1994, Elizabeth Gleick, review of *Life and Love, Such as They Are.*
People, September 23, 2006, Francine Prose, review of *A Feast of Words,* p. 36.
Publishers Weekly, April 27, 1992, review of *The Right Bitch,* p. 251; November 15, 1993, review of *Life and Love, Such as They Are,* p. 70; March 13, 2006, review of *Living on Air,* p. 40.

* * *

SHARP, Lesley A.
(Lesley Alexandra Sharp)

PERSONAL: Education: University of California, Berkeley, Ph.D., 1990.

ADDRESSES: Home—NY. *Office*—Department of Anthropology, Barnard College, 3009 Broadway, New York, NY 10027. *E-mail*—lsharp@barnard.edu; ls304@columbia.edu.

CAREER: Worked as a researcher, in Madagascar, 1988-95; Barnard College, New York, NY, professor of anthropology and chair of department; Columbia University, Mailman School of Public Health, New York, NY, associate professor of sociomedical sciences and anthropology.

WRITINGS:

The Possessed and the Dispossessed: Spirits, Identity, and Power in a Madagascar Migrant Town, University of California Press (Berkeley, CA), 1993.

The Sacrificed Generation: Youth, History, and the Colonized Mind in Madagascar, University of California Press (Berkeley, CA), 2002.

Strange Harvest: Organ Transplants, Denatured Bodies, and the Transformed Self, University of California Press (Berkeley, CA), 2006.

Bodies, Commodities, and Biotechnologies: Death, Mourning, and Scientific Desire in the Realm of Human Organ Transfer, Columbia University Press (New York, NY), 2007.

SIDELIGHTS: Lesley A. Sharp trained as a medical anthropologist and works as both an educator and a researcher. She spent an extensive period of time in Madagascar, where she studied a multicultural plantation community where the possession of spirits is considered an indication of the right to rule. She presented the results of her research in *The Possessed and the Dispossessed: Spirits, Identity, and Power in a Madagascar Migrant Town.* In a review for the *Journal of the Royal Anthropological Institute,* Karen Middleton remarked of Sharp's effort: "The data are fascinating, and the analysis is good. This is a very interesting book." Sharp followed up with a second volume on the same region, *The Sacrificed Generation: Youth, History, and the Colonized Mind in Madagascar,* which she wrote after a second visit to Madagascar in the mid- 1990s. In this book, Sharp looked at the educational system in the area, and the effects of the policies instituted by Didier Ratsiraka, then-president of Madagascar. Michael Lambek, also writing for the *Journal of the Royal Anthropological Institute,* commented: "This is a notable attempt to address the colonial legacy through the historical consciousness and political agency of those who have inherited it, but in the end this pioneering book is most welcome as an account of earnest, hard-working, capable young people struggling to acquire a decent education."

BIOGRAPHICAL AND CRITICAL SOURCES:

PERIODICALS

American Anthropologist, September, 1995, Linda L. Giles, review of *The Possessed and the Dispossessed: Spirits, Identity, and Power in a Madagascar Migrant Town,* p. 577.
American Ethnologist, May, 1995, Erika Bourguignon, review of *The Possessed and the Dispossessed,* p. 425.

Booklist, September 15, 2006, Donna Chavez, review of *Bodies, Commodities, and Biotechnologies: Death, Mourning, and Scientific Desire in the Realm of Human Organ Transfer,* p. 11.
Choice, April, 2003, W. Arens, review of *The Sacrificed Generation: Youth, History, and the Colonized Mind in Madagascar,* p. 1407; May, 1994, W. Arens, review of *The Possessed and the Dispossessed,* p. 1475.
Chronicle of Higher Education, December 1, 2000, Peter Monaghan, "Book Aims to Give a Voice to Relatives of Organ Donors."
International Journal of African Historical Studies, winter, 2003, Janice Harper, review of *The Sacrificed Generation,* pp. 208-210.
Journal of African History, January, 2004, Gerald M. Berg, "Youth, History, and Social Criticism," review of *The Sacrificed Generation,* p. 170.
Journal of the Royal Anthropological Institute, June, 1995, Karen Middleton, review of *The Possessed and the Dispossessed,* p. 452; December, 2003, Michael Lambek, "Anthropology and History," review of *The Sacrificed Generation,* p. 801.
Social Science & Medicine, August, 1998, Malcolm P. Cutchin, review of *The Possessed and the Dispossessed,* p. 549.

ONLINE

Barnard College Anthropology Department Web site, http://www.barnard.edu/anthro/index.html/ (February 12, 2007), faculty biography.
Columbia University Faculty Page, http://www.barnard.columbia.edu/ (January 31, 2007), faculty biography.*

*   *   *

SHARP, Lesley Alexandra
See SHARP, Lesley A.

*   *   *

SHELL, Barry 1951-

PERSONAL: Born May 1, 1951, in Winnipeg, Manitoba, Canada. *Education:* Reed College (Portland, OR), B.Sc., 1973; University of British Columbia, M.Sc., 1983. *Hobbies and other interests:* Bicycling.

ADDRESSES: Office—Faculty of Applied Sciences, Simon Fraser University, 8888 University Dr., Burnaby, British Columbia V5A 1S6, Canada.

CAREER: Educator, writer, researcher, and editor. University of Victoria, Victoria, British Columbia, Canada, instructor in general chemistry lab techniques, 1977-80; University of British Columbia, instructor in bioresource engineering, 1982-84; Simon Fraser University, Burnaby, British Columbia, research communications manager in Faculty of Applied Science. GCS Research Society, chair.

AWARDS, HONORS: Science in Society Book Award, Canadian Science Writers Association, for *Sensational Scientists*, 2006.

WRITINGS:

NONFICTION

Concise Guide to Hypertalk, Management Information Source (Portland, OR), 1988.
Running HyperCard with HyperTalk, Management Information Source (Portland, OR), 1988.
Great Canadian Scientists, Polestar Book Publishers (Custer, WA), 1997.
Sensational Scientists: The Journeys and Discoveries of 24 Men and Women of Science, Raincoast Books (Berkeley, CA), 2005.

Contributor of articles to periodicals, including: *New York Times, Mail West, Equinox, Adbusters, Nibble Mac, Hands-On,* and *Berkeley Macintosh Newsletter.*

SIDELIGHTS: A research communications manager at western Canada's Simon Fraser University, Barry Shell is the creator of *Science Canada,* a Web site through which researchers can access information on some of Canada's most prestigious scientists, as well as information about Canadian science in general. One outgrowth of this Web site has been *Sensational Scientists: The Journeys and Discoveries of 24 Men and Women of Science,* a book in which Shell profiles two dozen of his country's most respected scientists. Biographies include information about upbringing and areas of study, as well as Shell's discussion of each person's area of scientific expertise. Although its text

is geared for readers possessing some understanding of science, by including detailed diagrams, photographs, and interesting quotes Shell creates a resource that Philip Mills called "easy to read" in his *Resource Links* review. A *Kirkus Reviews* critic viewed the work as inspiring, particularly for Canadian students, because "the experiences, activities and advice" included in the book are valuable for "students considering scientific careers." In her *Kliatt* review of *Sensational Scientists,* Mary Ellen Snodgrass "highly recommended" the book, calling it a "intriguingly illustrated survey of scientific inquiry."

BIOGRAPHICAL AND CRITICAL SOURCES:

PERIODICALS

Booklist, February 15, 2006, Hazel Rochman, review of *Sensational Scientists: The Journeys and Discoveries of 24 Men and Women of Science,* p. 88.
Canadian Book Review Annual, 1997, review of *Great Canadian Scientists,* p. 553; 2005, Alice Kidd, review of *Sensational Scientists,* p. 551.
Canadian Chemical News, September, 2006, "Price-winning Book Promotes Canadian Science," p. 6.
Kirkus Reviews, February 1, 2006, review of *Sensational Scientists,* p. 136.
Kliatt, March, 2006, Mary Ellen Snodgrass, review of *Sensational Scientists,* p. 42.
Quill & Quire, March, 1998, review of *Great Canadian Scientists,* p. 1998.
Resource Links, December, 2005, Philip Mills, review of *Sensational Scientists,* p. 44.
School Library Journal, September, 1998, Miriam Driss, review of *Great Canadian Scientists,* p. 226.

ONLINE

Barry Shell Home Page, http://fas.sfu.ca/Members/shell (February 1, 2007).
Center for Systems Science Web site, http://www.css.sfu.ca/ (February 1, 2007), "Barry Shell."
Science Canada, http://www.science.ca/ (February 1, 2007).*

SHELLY, Adrienne 1966-2006

OBITUARY NOTICE— See index for *CA* sketch: Born June 16, 1966, in New York, NY; died November 1, 2006, in New York, NY. Actor, director, and author. Shelly was a successful actress and director known for her independent film work. She dropped out of Boston University as a junior in order to try to make it as an actress. Her first break came with 1990's *The Unbelievable Truth.* This was followed by other films through the 1990s, mostly independent features that eventually led to her reputation as a "quirky" actress who tended to appeared in dark comedies. Among her acting credits are *Hold Me, Thrill Me, Kiss Me* (1992), *Sleeping with Strangers* (1994), *Grind* (1997), *Revolution #9* (2001), and *Factotum* (2005). Also appearing Off-Broadway, especially at Manhattan's Workhouse Theater, as well as on television, Shelly became a writer and director. She wrote and directed *Sudden Manhattan* (1997), which won the Best Independent Feature Film Award at Portugal's Trola Film Festival, and *I'll Take You There* (1999), for which she won a Film Showcase Jury Award for best director at the U.S. Comedy Arts Festival. She was also the author of the play *Francis Ford Coppola and the Dream of Spring* (1997), a television special titled *Lois Lives a Little* (1997), and the screenplay *Urban Legend* (1994). Shelly had just completed a new film, *Waitress,* when she was found dead in her Greenwich Village office. As of November 7, 2006, a construction worker was in police custody for Shelly's murder.

OBITUARIES AND OTHER SOURCES:

BOOKS

Contemporary Theatre, Film, and Television, Volume 32, Thomson Gale (Detroit, MI), 2000.

PERIODICALS

New York Times, November 4, 2006, p. B15.

*   *   *

SHIRANE, Haruo 1951-

PERSONAL: Born 1951. *Education:* Columbia College, B.A., 1974; Columbia University, Ph.D., 1983.

ADDRESSES: Office—Department of East Asian Languages and Cultures, Graduate School of Arts and Sciences, Columbia University, 2960 Broadway, New York, NY 10027-6902. *E-mail*—hs14@columbia.edu.

CAREER: Columbia University, New York, NY, 1987—, began as assistant professor, became Department of East Asian Languages and Cultures director of graduate studies, Shincho Professor of Japanese Literature and Culture, 1996—.

AWARDS, HONORS: The Bridge of Dreams: A Poetics of the Tale of Genji was named a *Choice* outstanding book, the Japanese-language version was awarded the Kadokawa Gen'yoshi Prize, for the best study on Japanese literature; Haiku Society of America award, 1998, for *Traces of Dreams: Landscape, Cultural Memory, and the Poetry of Bashô,* the Japanese-language version was awarded the Ishida Hakyu Prize, 2002; grants from the Fulbright Foundation, National Endowment for the Humanities, American Council of Learned Societies, Social Science Research Council, and Japan Foundation.

WRITINGS:

The Bridge of Dreams: A Poetics of the Tale of Genji, Stanford University Press (Stanford, CA), 1987.
Traces of Dreams: Landscape, Cultural Memory, and the Poetry of Bashô, Stanford University Press (Stanford, CA), 1998.
(Editor, with Tomi Suzuki) *Inventing the Classics: Modernity, National Identity, and Japanese Literature,* Stanford University Press (Stanford, CA), 2000.
(Editor) *Early Modern Japanese Literature: An Anthology, 1600-1900,* Columbia University Press (New York, NY), 2002.
Classical Japanese: A Grammar, Columbia University Press (New York, NY), 2005.
(Editor) *The Tales of the Heike,* translated by Burton Watson, Columbia University Press (New York, NY), 2006.
(Editor) *Traditional Japanese Literature: An Anthology, Beginnings to 1600,* Columbia University Press (New York, NY), 2006.
Classical Japanese Reader and Essential Dictionary, Columbia University Press (New York, NY), 2007.

SIDELIGHTS: Haruo Shirane is a scholar of Japanese culture and literature who has written articles and books on premodern and postmodern fiction, poetry, literary theory, and history. His *Traces of Dreams: Landscape, Cultural Memory, and the Poetry of Bashô* is a study of the seventeenth-century Zen-influenced haiku poet. *Pacific Affairs* contributor Sonja Arntzen considered it "the most comprehensive study to date." She wrote: "What distinguishes Shirane's approach in this work is that he always interprets Basho's writing and thought from within the full complexity of his historical and discursive context. . . . Within that context, Basho's haiku and other writings are revealed as extraordinarily rich in meaning."

Julie Iezzi reviewed *Early Modern Japanese Literature: An Anthology, 1600-1900* in *Asian Theatre Journal,* writing: "This comprehensive anthology of early modern literature offers an extensive range of prose fiction, poetry, drama, essays, treatises, and literary criticism. More than two hundred woodblock prints and photographs illustrate the text, giving a sense of how the material looked on the page in the original Japanese, as well as how it appears on stage." The highlights of the volume include kabuki and puppet plays, contemporary and period plays, picture books, readers, satiric sermons, and books of humor.

A *Kirkus Reviews* contributor reviewed *The Tales of the Heike,* describing it as: "Intriguing, mini-sagas of samurai derring-do and nimble wit, with a distinctly Buddhist flavor." The warrior tales are spun by blind lute minstrels, the traditional method employed by Kabuki and No drama. Shirane provides an introduction and glossary of characters that make the stories more available for the scholar or student. The *Kirkus Reviews* critic concluded: "Terrifically exciting and spiritually rich."

BIOGRAPHICAL AND CRITICAL SOURCES:

PERIODICALS

Asian Theatre Journal, spring, 2006, Julie Iezzi, review of *Early Modern Japanese Literature: An Anthology, 1600-1900,* p. 207.
Kirkus Reviews, June 1, 2006, review of *The Tales of the Heike,* p. 542.

Pacific Affairs, fall, 2000, Sonja Arntzen, review of *Traces of Dreams: Landscape, Cultural Memory, and the Poetry of Bashô,* p. 458.

ONLINE

Columbia University Web site, http://www.columbia. edu/ (February 3, 2007), biography.
Haiku-heute, http://www.haiku-heute.de/ (December 15, 2006), Udo Wenzel, "Traces of Bashô" (interview).*

* * *

SHREEVE, Elizabeth 1956-

PERSONAL: Born January 17, 1956, in Riverhead, NY; daughter of Walton W. (a research physician) and Phyllis (Heidenreich) Shreeve; married Kenneth Robinson (a merchant), March 16, 1991; children: James, Sam. *Ethnicity:* "Caucasian." *Education:* Harvard University, B.A., 1978, M.A., 1983. *Politics:* Democrat.

ADDRESSES: Home—Mill Valley, CA. *Agent*—Andrea Brown, Andrea Brown Literary Agency, 1076 Eagle Dr., Salinas, CA 93905. *E-mail*—elizabethshreeve@comcast.net.

CAREER: SWA Group, Sausalito, CA, principal and environmental designer, 1984—.

MEMBER: Society of Children's Book Writers and Illustrators, Audubon Society, NCCBA.

WRITINGS:

CHILDREN'S BOOKS; "THE ADVENTURES OF HECTOR FULLER" SERIES

Hector Springs Loose, illustrated by Pamela Levy, Simon & Schuster (New York, NY), 2004.
Hector Finds a Fortune, illustrated by Pamela R. Levy, Simon & Schuster (New York, NY), 2004.
Hector Afloat, Simon & Schuster (New York, NY), 2004.

Hector on Thin Ice, Simon & Schuster (New York, NY), 2004.

SIDELIGHTS: Elizabeth Shreeve told *CA:* "I write to learn about life. My kids and my love of nature influence my work. I am interested in how kids grow, learn and become part of the world."

BIOGRAPHICAL AND CRITICAL SOURCES:

PERIODICALS

School Library Journal, March, 2004, Shelley B. Sutherland, review of *Hector Springs Loose,* p. 181; May, 2004, James K. Irwin, review of *Hector Finds a Fortune,* p. 124.

ONLINE

Elizabeth Shreeve Home Page, http://www.elizabeth shreeve.com (October 23, 2006).

*   *   *

SIMIS, Konstantin 1919-2006

OBITUARY NOTICE— See index for *CA* sketch: Born August 4, 1919, in Odessa, U.S.S.R. (now Ukraine); died December 14, 2006, in Falls Church, VA. Attorney, educator, and author. Simis was best known as a Soviet dissident who lived in exile in the United States because of his criticisms of Soviet Russia. Physical disability caused him to be discharged from military service as a young man, and so he attended law school during World War II. He studied in Tashkent, Uzbekistan, before completing a master's degree at the Moscow Legal Institute. In 1944 he earned a Ph.D. at the Institute of Soviet Law at the academy of Science of the U.S.S.R. The Moscow State Institute of International Relations hired him to its faculty after he graduated, but he was later fired because of his Jewish background. Simis continued to experience prejudice at Rostov State University, where he also lost his teaching job because of anti-Semitism. He then practiced law in Moscow as a defense attorney before becoming a researcher for the Institute of Soviet Law at the Ministry of Justice, where he worked until

1977. Here, Simis helped to write the language for the revised Soviet constitution. Along with his wife, attorney Dina Kaminskaya, he often traveled the countryside, where he was shocked by widespread evidence of political corruption. Simis came to conclude that the Soviet Union's corrupt government was also making its citizenry corrupt, and he began writing his thoughts down in book form. The KGB, the Soviet secret police, became suspicious of Simis and searched his home, discovering the manuscript and giving him two choices: remain in Russia and face trial, or leave the country. Simis and his wife decided to leave. Moving to the United States, in 1982 he released his book, *USSR: The Corrupt Society; The Secret World of Soviet Capitalism.*

OBITUARIES AND OTHER SOURCES:

PERIODICALS

Chicago Tribune, December 18, 2006, Section 1, p. 15.
Washington Post, December 17, 2006, p. C6.

*   *   *

SINBAD 1956-
(David Adkins)

PERSONAL: Original name, David Adkins; born November 10, 1956, in Benton Harbor, MI; son of Donald (a Baptist minister) and Louise Adkins; married, 1985; wife's name Meredith (divorced, 1992); children: Paige, Royce. *Education:* Attended University of Denver.

ADDRESSES: Agent—Agency for the Performing Arts, 405 S. Beverly Dr., Beverly Hills, CA 90212.

CAREER: Actor and comedian; David and Goliath Production Co., Studio City, CA, founder. Appeared in television series, including role of Byron Lightfoot, *The Redd Foxx Show,* Columbia Broadcasting System (CBS), 1986; as cohost, *Keep On Cruisin',* CBS, 1987; as Coach Walter Oakes, *A Different World,* National Broadcasting Company (NBC), 1987-91; as host, *It's Showtime at the Apollo,* syndicated, 1989-91;

as David Bryan, *The Sinbad Show* (also known as *Sinbad*), Fox, 1993-94; as host, *Vibe*, syndicated, 1997-98; in *Hollywood Squares*, syndicated, 1998; in *The Remarkable Journey*, 2000; and in *Just for Laughs* 2006. Appeared in television movies, including *Club Med*, American Broadcasting Companies (ABC), 1986; as Isaiah Turner in the title role, *The Cherokee Kid*, Home Box Office (HBO), 1996; as voice of "Hollywood Shuffle," *Ready to Run*, 2000; and as Myron Larabee, *Jingle All the Way*, 2001. Guest star in episodes of numerous television series, including *The Cosby Show; The Late Show; and Today;* voice of Simpleton, "The Golden Goose," and voice of the Frog Prince, "The Frog Prince," both *Happily Ever After: Fairy Tales for Every Child*, HBO, 1995; as Del, a recurring role, *Cosby*, 1998-99; as Professor LeCount, *Moesha*, 2000; as Odell Mason, *Resurrection Blvd.*, 2002; and in *Girlfriends*. Also appeared in *Star Search*, syndicated; *Comic Strip: Live*, Fox; *Comic Justice;* and *Instant Comedy with the Groundlings*, FX Network. Appeared in numerous television specials, including "Take No Prisoners: Robert Townsend and His Partners in Crime II," *HBO Comedy Hour*, HBO, 1988; *Stand-up Comics Take a Stand!*, syndicated, 1989; *Motown Thirty: What's Goin' On!*, CBS, 1990; *A Laugh, a Tear*, syndicated, 1990; *America's All-Star Tribute to Oprah Winfrey*, ABC, 1990; *Sinbad and Friends All the Way Live . . . Almost*, ABC, 1991; "Sinbad: Brain Damaged," *HBO Comedy Hour*, HBO, 1991; *Muhammad Ali's Fiftieth Birthday Celebration*, ABC, 1992; *The 10th Annual Montreal Comedy Festival*, 1992; (as host) *Back to School '92*, 1992; *Comic Relief V*, HBO, 1992; *Family Night*, 1992; *Free to Laugh: A Comedy and Music Special for Amnesty International*, 1992; *The All New Circus of the Stars and Side Show XVII*, 1992; *Disney's Countdown to Kid's Day* (also known as *Countdown to Kid's Day*), The Disney Channel, 1993; *New Year's Eve '94*, 1993; "Sinbad Live from the Paramount—Afros and Bellbottoms," *HBO Comedy Hour*, HBO, 1993; *The Winans' Real Meaning of Christmas*, syndicated, 1993; (in archive footage) *Mo' Funny: Black Comedy in America*, 1993; *Comic Relief VI*, HBO, 1994; *Fantasies of the Stars*, NBC, 1994; *A Comedy Salute to Andy Kaufman*, NBC, 1995; (as Aric) "Aliens for Breakfast," *McDonald's Family Theatre*, ABC, 1995; *Planet Hollywood Comes Home*, ABC, 1995; (as host) *Sinbad's Summer Jam: '70s Soul Music Festival*, HBO, 1995; *Celebrate the Dream: 50 Years of Ebony*, ABC, 1996; *CityKids All Star Club*, ABC, 1996; *Nissan Presents a Celebration of America's Music*, ABC, 1996; "Sinbad—Son of a Preacher Man," *HBO Comedy*

Hour, HBO, 1996; (as host) *Sinbad's Dynamite New Year's Eve 1997* (also known as *New Year's Eve Live in Las Vegas* and *Fox's New Year's Eve Live*), Fox, 1996; (as host) *Sinbad's Summer Jam II: '70s Soul Music Festival*, HBO, 1996; *The HBO Comedy Arts Weekend Highlight Show*, HBO, 1997; (as host) *Sinbad's Summer Jam 4: '70's Soul Music Festival*, HBO, 1998; *Redd Foxx: The E! True Hollywood Story*, 1999; (as master of ceremonies) *Miss Universe Pageant*, 2000; *Heroes of Black Comedy* (miniseries), 2002; and *Inside TV Land: African Americans in Television*, 2002. Appeared in televised award presentations, including *The 3rd Annual Soul Train Music Awards*, syndicated, 1989; *The 16th Annual Black Filmmakers Hall of Fame*, syndicated, 1989; *The 22nd Annual NAACP Image Awards*, NBC, 1990; *The 17th Annual People's Choice Awards*, CBS, 1991; *The 24th Annual NAACP Image Awards*, NBC, 1992; (as host) *The 19th Annual Black Filmmakers Hall of Fame*, 1992; *The 6th Annual Soul Train Music Awards*, 1992; *The Essence Awards*, 1992; (as presenter) *The 45th Annual Primetime Emmy Awards*, 1993; (as host) *Soul Train Comedy Awards*, 1993; *The 1993 Billboard Music Awards*, 1993; *The 7th Annual American Comedy Awards*, 1993; (as presenter) *The Walt Disney Company Presents the American Teacher Awards*, The Disney Channel, 1993; (as host) *The 15th Annual CableACE Awards*, 1994; *The 26th Annual NAACP Image Awards*, 1994; (as host) *The Essence Awards*, 1994; *The Soul Train 25th Anniversary Hall of Fame Special*, 1995; (as presenter) *Screen Actors Guild Awards*, 1995; (as cohost) *The 25th Anniversary Essence Awards*, 1995; *The 10th Annual Soul Train Music Awards*, 1996; (as host) *The 1996 Essence Awards*, 1996; (as host) *The 23rd Annual American Music Awards*, 1996; *The 27th Annual NAACP Image Awards*, 1996; (as presenter) *The Blockbuster Entertainment Awards*, 1996; (as presenter) *The 28th NAACP Image Awards*, 1997; (as host) *The 10th Essence Awards*, 1997; (as host, *The 24th Annual American Music Awards*, 1997; (as host) *The ShoWest Awards*, Turner Network Television (TNT), 1997; and (as himself) *26th Annual American Music Awards*, 1998. Creator and executive producer of the television series *The Sinbad Show*, Fox, 1993-94; executive producer of the television movie *The Cherokee Kid*, HBO, 1996; executive producer of television specials, including *Sinbad and Friends All the Way Live . . . Almost*, ABC, 1991; "Sinbad: Brain Damaged," *HBO Comedy Hour*, HBO, 1991; "Sinbad Live from the Paramount—Afros and Bellbottoms," *HBO Comedy Hour*, HBO, 1993; *Sinbad's Summer Jam: '70s Soul Music Festival*, HBO, 1995; "Sinbad—Son of a

Preacher Man," *HBO Comedy Hour,* HBO, 1996; and *Sinbad's Summer Jam II: '70s Soul Music Festival,* HBO, 1996. Actor in films, including *That's Adequate,* 1989; as Andre Krimm, *Necessary Roughness,* Paramount, 1991; *Time Out: The Truth about HIV, AIDS, and You,* 1992; as Otto, *Coneheads* (also known as *Coneheads: The Movie*), Paramount, 1993; as Malik, *The Meteor Man,* Metro-Goldwyn-Mayer, 1993; as Kevin Franklin/Derek Bond, *Houseguest,* Buena Vista, 1995; as Sam Simms (and executive producer), *First Kid,* Buena Vista, 1996; as voice of Riley, *Homeward Bound II: Lost in San Francisco* (also known as *Incredible Journey*), Buena Vista, 1996; as Myron Larabee, *Jingle All the Way,* Twentieth Century-Fox, 1996; as Mr. Wheat, *Good Burger,* Paramount, 1997; as orderly, *Crazy as Hell,* 2001; as voice of Raven, *Hansel & Gretel,* 2002; as security guard, *Treading Water,* 2002; and as Leila's uncle, *Leila,* 2006. Executive producer of the films *Leila* and *Coda,* both 2006. Appeared in the video game *I Was a Network Star,* 2006. Host of a morning radio show for KHHT-FM, Los Angeles, CA, beginning 2002. *Military service:* U.S. Air Force, c. 1978-1982.

AWARDS, HONORS: Candle Award, Morehouse College, 1994; named artist of the year, Harvard University, 1997; two Image Awards, National Association for the Advancement of Colored People, for Summer Jam Weekend shows.

WRITINGS:

Brain Damaged (comedy album), Polygram, 1990.
Sinbad and Friends All the Way Live . . . Almost (television special), American Broadcasting Companies (ABC), 1991.
(With David Ritz) *Sinbad's Guide to Life: Because I Know Everything,* Bantam Books (New York, NY), 1997.

Also creator and writer for the television series *The Sinbad Show,* 1993.

SIDELIGHTS: Sinbad is a popular mainstream comedian in American culture. The son of a Midwestern minister, Sinbad has always emphasized being funny rather than being profane in his comedy routines. His starring roles in films have often been in such family-friendly fare as *First Kid* and *Jingle All the Way,* and when he created his own sitcom, *The Sinbad Show,* it featured a single black man acting as a father and role model to two foster children. Sinbad consciously plotted the show this way to counteract the usual stereotypes of African-American men in the American media. "If I were a non-Black person and I watch what you see about us on TV and I watch constantly what you see in movies and I constantly watch the news, I would be scared of us also," he told an interviewer from *Jet.* "What's happening now in America is that this myth that African Americans do not take care of their children is perceived as reality—and that's not true."

The six-foot-five-inch Sinbad originally wanted to be a basketball player, but a knee injury suffered while playing for the University of Denver ended that plan. He dropped out four weeks before graduation ("I was still going through my militant, 'make a statement' phase and didn't want a degree from the White man," he told Aldore Collier of *Ebony*) and joined the Air Force, hoping to be sent overseas to live somewhere exotic. Instead he was assigned to a base in Wichita, Kansas. Sinbad has since declared joining the Air Force to have been a "cosmic mistake. The Air Force was three and a half years of torture, me going [absent without leave] and impersonating officers and finally getting kicked out—check this out—for parking my car in the wrong position," he told David Ritz of *Essence* in 1992. But the Air Force did give Sinbad his start in comedy, in base talent shows. After leaving the Air Force he opened for musicians in the Wichita area, then went on what he has dubbed his "Poverty Tour," taking buses to clubs across the country and talking his way into gigs. In 1984 Sinbad got his big break with an appearance on the television show *Star Search.* After making it to the finals there, Sinbad came to the attention of another family-oriented African-American comic, Bill Cosby, who helped to get him a role on the *Cosby Show* spin-off *A Different World.* That role propelled Sinbad into a high-profile gig hosting the series *Showtime at the Apollo,* and soon he was able to go on a real comedy tour and to launch his own series.

In 1997, Sinbad published his first book, *Sinbad's Guide to Life: Because I Know Everything.* The book is a spoof of the ever-popular self-help genre, and in the course of the book Sinbad makes clear that as an awkward preacher's kid and now as someone who has been divorced, he doesn't really know everything after all.

BIOGRAPHICAL AND CRITICAL SOURCES:

BOOKS

Contemporary Black Biography, Volume 16, Thomson Gale (Detroit, MI), 1997.

St. James Encyclopedia of Popular Culture, five volumes, St. James Press (Detroit, MI), 2000.

PERIODICALS

Atlanta Journal-Constitution, April 2, 1999, Sonia Murray, interview with Sinbad, p. Q4.

Arizona Daily Star (Tucson, AZ), November 14, 2001, Cathalena E. Burch, interview with Sinbad, p. E1.

Arizona Republic (Phoenix, AZ), May 6, 1999, Seth Landau, interview with Sinbad, p. 6; November 15, 2001, Sean L. McCarthy, profile of Sinbad, p. 24.

Billboard, August 16, 1990, Janine McAdams, "Sinbad Anchors Comedy with Music on New Disk," p. 23.

Black Collegian, October, 1999, Janette M. Millin, "Sinbad Keeping the Funk Alive," p. 26.

Broadcasting & Cable, October 27, 1997, Joe Schlosser, review of *Vibe,* p. 24; January 19, 1998, Joe Schlosser, "The Big Guys Battle in Late Night: The Tall Talents of Sinbad, Keenen and Now Magic Square Off in Syndication," pp. 25-26.

Current Biography, February, 1997, "Sinbad," pp. 39-42.

Detroit News, October 5, 2001, interview with Sinbad, p. 1.

Ebony, April, 1990, Aldore Collier, interview with Sinbad, pp. 104-105; June, 1997, Aldore Collier, interview with Sinbad, pp. 84-88.

Entertainment Weekly, September 24, 1993, review of *The Sinbad Show,* pp. 78-79; May 23, 1997, Megan Harlan, review of *Sinbad's Guide to Life: Because I Know Everything,* p. 60; May 30, 1997, Chris Nashaway, "Go Figure," p. 17.

Essence, November, 1992, David Ritz, interview with Sinbad, pp. 78-82.

Florida Times Union, October 18, 2002, Ivette M. Yee, interview with Sinbad, p. WE-15.

Grand Rapids Press (Grand Rapids, MI), December 15, 2002, interview with Sinbad, p. F11.

Jet, February 12, 1990, Aldore Collier, "Sinbad Tells Why He Keeps His Comedy Clean," pp. 60-61; November 22, 1993, interview with Sinbad, pp.

56-58; July 13, 1998, "HBO Debuts the Annual *Sinbad's Summer Jam 4: '70's Soul Music Festival,"* pp. 58-62.

Knight Ridder/Tribune News Service, September 15, 1993, Bob Curtright, interview with Sinbad, p. 0915K3568; August 28, 1996, Terry Lawson, interview with Sinbad, p. 828K5165.

Lansing State Journal (Lansing, MI), July 13, 2001, Jack Ebling, "Sinbad's Local Stop Wasn't for Laughs," p. D1.

Los Angeles Times, April 23, 1997, Candace A. Wedlan, interview with Sinbad, p. E2.

Mediaweek, November 3, 1997, review of *Vibe,* p. 9; February 4, 2002, Jeremy Murphy and Katy Bachman, "L.A.'s Latest Pirate Radio," p. 10.

Parade, September 11, 1994, Wallace Terry, interview with Sinbad, pp. 28-29.

People, October 18, 1993, David Hiltbrand, review of *The Sinbad Show,* p. 13; December 8, 1997, Terry Kelleher, review of *Vibe,* p. 18.

Sarasota Herald Tribune, January 21, 2000, Helena Finnegan, "Sinbad Promotes Hilarious Family Values," p. 6.

Seattle Times, October 15, 1998, profile of Sinbad, p. G12.

Top 40 Airplay Monitor, February 1, 2002, Marc Schiffman and Dana Hall, "Sinbad's New Voyage," p. 3.

Travel Weekly, March 20, 1997, Kristin O'Meara, "Island Officials Anticipate a Throng for Sinbad Soul Festival," pp. C13-C14.

TV Guide, September 25, 1993, Jeff Jarvis, review of *The Sinbad Show,* p. 47; November 27, 1993, Claudia Dreifus, "Original Sinbad," pp. 34-35.

Variety, January 6, 1992, Carole Kucharewicz, review of *Sinbad and Friends: All the Way Live . . . Almost,* p. 58; October 27, 1997, Cynthia Littleton, "Sinbad Feels Good 'Vibe' from Latenight Jones," p. 27; January 19, 1998, Cynthia Littleton, "Col Strikes Chord with Sinbad for *Vibe* Redux," p. 69.*

*   *   *

SLATER, Wayne

PERSONAL: Education: West Virginia University, B.A.; Ohio University, master's degree.

ADDRESSES: Home—Austin, TX. *Office*—Dallas Morning News, 606 Young St., Dallas, TX 75202.

CAREER: Journalist. *Parkersburg Sentinel,* Parkersburg, WV, reporter; Associated Press, West Virginia, Kansas, Illinois, Colorado, reporter; *Dallas Morning News,* Austin, TX, bureau chief for fifteen years, currently senior political writer and reporter; University of Texas at Austin, adjunct professor of public affairs, 2006.

WRITINGS:

(With James Moore) *Bush's Brain: How Karl Rove Made George W. Bush Presidential,* Wiley (New York, NY), 2003.
(With James Moore) *The Architect: Karl Rove and the Master Plan for Absolute Power,* Crown Publishers (New York, NY), 2006.
(With James Moore) *Rove Exposed: How Bush's Brain Fooled America,* Wiley (New York, NY), 2006.

Contributor to newspapers, including the *Dallas Morning Herald.*

SIDELIGHTS: Wayne Slater is a senior political writer and reporter for the *Dallas Morning News,* where he also served for fifteen years as the Austin bureau chief. Slater is known for his sharp commentary on current U.S. politics, and has written several books that take a close look at the administration of George W. Bush and the involvement of Bush's advisor Karl Rove in Bush's achievements and political agenda. Slater has followed Bush's career from its earliest days, and spoken with the president about how his religious faith has influenced his conservative political outlook. In an interview posted on the *PBS Web site,* Slater explained: "Bush believes very much in the core ideas of Christianity—the belief that you must believe in Jesus in order to go to heaven, that there is no other way to salvation. . . . That's a fundamental Christian belief, and he embraces it. He believes in the absolute nature of God. Fundamentally, he believes in the existence of evil, not as an abstract idea, a philosophy, but as something that's real and tangible. It's something we've seen really most recently when he talks about the terrorists." In *Bush's Brain: How Karl Rove Made George W. Bush Presidential,* Slater and coauthor James Moore discuss how political strategist Rove is credited with assisting Bush in his various campaigns and helping to turn him into a

candidate capable of winning elections. Rove also helped to orchestrate an attack on the Democratic Party that made Bush look the better choice because his opposition appeared weak and ineffectual in comparison. Gerald F. Kreyche, in a review for *USA Today,* remarked: "This book provides a hearty welcome to realpolitik."

In *The Architect: Karl Rove and the Master Plan for Absolute Power,* Slater provides a follow up to his earlier book on Karl Rove and his relationship to George W. Bush in which he and coauthor James Moore suggest that Rove carefully targeted the religious right in his attempt to make Bush a marketable candidate, and in the process Rove professed beliefs that were not in actuality his own. Vanessa Bush, in a review for *Booklist,* called *The Architect* a "probing look at the personality and political strategizing of Karl Rove," and concluded that the result was "riveting investigative journalism." A contributor for *Publishers Weekly* called the book "a compulsive page-turner that's bound to be divisive."

BIOGRAPHICAL AND CRITICAL SOURCES:

PERIODICALS

American Prospect, April, 2003, E.J. Dionne, Jr., "The Co-Presidency," p. 52.
Booklist, July 1, 2006, Vanessa Bush, review of *The Architect: Karl Rove and the Master Plan for Absolute Power,* p. 5.
Campaigns & Elections, June, 2003, review of *Bush's Brain: How Karl Rove Made George W. Bush Presidential,* p. 14.
Economist, February 22, 2003, "The Limits of Spin: American Politics."
Kirkus Reviews, July 1, 2006, review of *The Architect,* p. 667.
Library Journal, August 1, 2006, Jill Ortner, review of *The Architect,* p. 107.
New Statesman, May 12, 2003, Mick Hume, review of *Bush's Brain,* p. 52.
New York Review of Books, May 1, 2003, Elizabeth Drew, review of *Bush's Brain,* p. 14.
Publishers Weekly, July 24, 2006, review of *The Architect,* p. 52.
Reason, October, 2003, John F. Pitney, Jr., "Accidental Genius: Is Karl Rove Really Bush's Brain?," p. 58.

Reference & Research Book News, February, 2006, review of *Rove Exposed: How Bush's Brain Fooled America.*

Spectator, May 24, 2003, George Osborne, "This Month's Rasputin," p. 39.

USA Today (magazine), July, 2003, Gerald F. Kreyche, review of *Bush's Brain,* p. 81.

Wall Street Journal, March 19, 2003, Daniel Casse, "The Power behind the Throne, Supposedly," p. D14.

ONLINE

Free Republic Online, http://www.freerepublic.com/ (September 2, 2006), James Heston, review of *The Architect.*

New York Times Online, http://www.nytimes.com/ (October 15, 2006), Nicholas Confessore, "Strategist in Chief."

PBS Web site, http://www.pbs.org/ (January 24, 2007), author interview.

Random House Web site, http://www.randomhouse. com/ (January 24, 2007), author biography.

University of Texas at Austin Web site, http://www. utexas.edu/ (January 24, 2007), faculty biography.*

*   *   *

SMITH, Bill 1949-

PERSONAL: Born in 1949.

CAREER: Chef and author. Cofounder, Cat's Cradle (restaurant), NC, 1970s; established La Residence (restaurant), with Moreton Neal, NC; chef, Crook's Corner Cafe and Bar, Chapel Hill, NC, 1992—.

WRITINGS:

Seasoned in the South: Recipes from Crook's Corner and from Home, Algonquin Books of Chapel Hill (Chapel Hill, NC), 2005.

SIDELIGHTS: In *Seasoned in the South: Recipes from Crook's Corner and from Home,* chef Bill Smith explains the ins and outs of the spectacular North Carolinian cuisine that he has produced at the Chapel Hill restaurant since 1992. "A chef for more than two decades," declared a contributor to the Crook's Corner Web site, "Smith has cooked his signature dishes for most everyone who lives, works, farms and visits the good life we have in Chapel Hill, NC."

Perhaps because Chapel Hill is a college town, its busy season starting with the opening of classes at the University of North Carolina, Smith's cookbook begins with fall-themed dishes. No matter the season, however, his recipes offer Continental fare with a southern twist, and vice versa. For example, in one of only a "few instances where liquor benefits a liver," declared a *Publishers Weekly* critic, "duck and chicken organs are flavored with a jigger of Wild Turkey" bourbon whiskey instead of the traditional cognac. The chef's works also reinvent southern cuisine, blending local ingredients and traditions with techniques borrowed from classic French cooking. The result, said Mark Knoblauch, writing in a *Booklist* review of the cookbook, is "a new version of southern cooking that owes a great deal to classic French cuisine." "Recipes," concluded *Library Journal* reviewer Rosemarie Lewis, range "from appetizers and entrees to side dishes and desserts and provide nouvelle flair to familiar Southern favorites."

BIOGRAPHICAL AND CRITICAL SOURCES:

PERIODICALS

Booklist, October 1, 2005, Mark Knoblauch, review of *Seasoned in the South: Recipes from Crook's Corner and from Home,* p. 13.

Library Journal, September 15, 2005, Rosemarie Lewis, review of *Seasoned in the South,* p. 86.

Publishers Weekly, August 8, 2005, review of *Seasoned in the South,* p. 230.

ONLINE

Crook's Corner Web site, http://www.crookscorner. com/ (December 17, 2006), biography of Bill Smith.

SOLSTAD, Dag 1941-

PERSONAL: Born July 16, 1941, in Sandefjord, Norway. *Politics:* "Marxist-Leninist."

ADDRESSES: Home—Norway.

CAREER: Writer.

AWARDS, HONORS: Norwegian Critics Award, 1969, 1992, and 1999; Nordic Literary Prize, 1989, for *Roman, 1987;* Dagen's Literature Prize, 1990; Dobloug Prize, 1996; Gyldendal Prize, 1997; Brage Award, 1998.

WRITINGS:

Spiraler (short stories; title means "Spirals"), Aschehoug (Oslo, Norway), 1965.

Svingstol (short prose collection; title means "Swivel Chair"), Aschehoug (Oslo, Norway), 1967.

(With Georg Johannesen and Jan Erik Vold) *Gruppe 68, Ny norsk diktning,* Cappelen (Oslo, Norway), 1968.

(With Einar Økland) *Georg: Sit du godt?* (play; title means "George, Are You Sitting Comfortably?"), Norsk samlaget (Oslo, Norway), 1968.

Irr! Grønt! (novel; title means "Patina! Green!"), Aschehoug (Oslo, Norway), 1969.

Arild Asnes, 1970 (novel), Aschehoug (Oslo, Norway), 1971.

25. september-plassen (novel; title means "The 25th of September Square"), Aschehoug (Oslo, Norway), 1974.

Kamerat Stalin eller familien Nordby: et skuespill om en norsk kommunistfamilie i åra 1945-56, Oktober (Oslo, Norway), 1975.

Svik. Førkrigsàr (novel; title means "Betrayal: Prewar Years"), Oktober (Oslo, Norway), 1977.

Tilbake til Pelle Erobreren? artikler og intervjuer om arbeiderlitteratur, Oktober (Oslo, Norway), 1977.

Krig. 1940 (novel; title means "War: 1940"), Oktober (Oslo, Norway), 1978.

Brød vog våpen (novel; title means "Bread and Weapons"), Oktober (Oslo, Norway), 1980.

Artikler om litteratur, Oktober (Oslo, Norway), 1981.

Gymnaslaerer Pedersens beretning om den store politiske vekkelsen som har hjemsøkt vårt land (title means "High School Teacher Pedersen's Account of the Great Political Revival That Has Visited Our Country"), Oktober (Oslo, Norway), 1982.

Sleng på byen, Oktober (Oslo, Norway), 1983.

Forsøk på å beskrive det ugjennonntrengelige (novel; title means "An Attempt to Describe the Impenetrable"), Oktober (Oslo, Norway), 1984.

Roman 1987 (novel; title means "Novel 1987"), Oktober (Oslo, Norway), 1987.

Medaljens forside: en roman om Aker (novel), Cappelen (Oslo, Norway), 1990.

Three Essays, Oktober (Oslo, Norway), 1991.

Ellevte roman, (novel), Oktober (Oslo, Norway), 1992.

14 artikler på 12 år, Oktober (Oslo, Norway), 1993.

Svingstol og andre tekster (prose and poetry), Oktober (Oslo, Norway), 1994.

Genanse og verdighet (novel; title means "Shyness and Dignity"), Oktober (Oslo, Norway), 1994.

Professor Andersens natt (novel; title means "Professor Andersen's Night"), Oktober (Oslo, Norway), 1996.

T. Singer (novel), Oktober (Oslo, Norway), 1999.

Artikler, 1993-2004, Oktober (Oslo, Norway), 2004.

Shyness and Dignity, Graywolf Press (St. Paul, MN), 2006.

SIDELIGHTS: Considered one of the leading writers of prose fiction in mid-twentieth-century Norway, Dag Solstad began his career as a rebel against established literary tastes and conventions. His first book, *Spiraler,* a collection of Kafkaesque short fiction, was, in the opinion of Janet Garton in *Facets of European Modernism,* "one of the opening chords in what was very quickly to grow into a crescendo of literary and critical activity." With other young writers of his generation, Solstad associated himself with the progressive journal *Profil.* In its pages, he published several articles that identified two essential criteria for Norwegian Modernist fiction: the rejection of realism and probability in favor of a search for significance, or "essentialness," and the importance of myth and dream. Embodying these criteria, the stories in *Spiraler* focus on alienated individuals who, like many of Kafka's protagonists, seem to be caught up in a game with unknown rules. As Garton puts it, a *Spiraler* protagonist "has lost control of what happens, and fears that indeed anything may happen—silent women may suddenly explode, chandeliers may crash down and bury him. The people he meets are not real, but lifeless objects or figments of his own desires and fears." In one story, a comfortable hotel becomes a menacing prison; in another, the shards of a broken mirror become "bodies" and symbolize a man's loss of identity.

In his first novel, *Irr! Grønt!*, Solstad presents a more developed exploration of the individual's search for autonomy. The book reveals the unmistakable influence of Polish writer Witold Gombrowitz, whose theory of "Form," or the way in which human behavior is controlled by outside forces, particularly intrigued Solstad. In a critical article, Solstad explained Gombrowitz's theory: "Those who really identify completely with what they are doing are living a life without insight and in consequence a life of lies. Our only possibility of living a life which is relatively human and dignified lies in maintaining a distance to the way we behave." The protagonist of *Irr! Grønt!*, like that in Gombrowitz's satirical tour-de-force *Ferdydurke*, strives unsuccessfully to maintain such a distance, to become both observer and controller of his social behavior.

With *Arild Asnes, 1970*, Solstad began to move away from foreign influences and experimental styles, and toward a more direct political approach. The novel's central character is a young writer who returns to Oslo after living abroad. Feeling alienated in Norwegian society, he attempts to correct the problems of his culture through participation in Marxist politics. "An important aspect of the story," observed Jan I. Sjåvik in the *Encyclopedia of World Literature*, "is how Asnes overcomes his distaste for the simple and direct language of the Marxists and, in the end, becomes able to make it his own." The novel attracted considerable attention, as did Solstad's following novel, *25. september-plassen*, which explores the betrayal of working class values by Norwegian Labor Party leaders after World War II. This theme received even more extensive development in Solstad's trilogy, *Svik. Førkrigsàr, Krig. 1940*, and *Brød vog våpen*. The trilogy offers a Marxist version of twentieth-century Norwegian history, beginning with the years leading up to World War II and ending with the postwar collapse of socialist ideals. The novels suggest complicity between the Norwegian bourgeoisie and the Nazis, but also, in Sjåvik's view, offer "a highly readable [story] that contains skillfully drawn portraits of members of the working class and their lives during trying times."

When it became evident in the 1970s that Norway did not want a Marxist society, many committed socialist writers were prompted to re-think their philosophies. Solstad wrote two books exploring his politics: *Gymnaslaerer Pedersens beretning om den store politiske vekkelsen som har hjemsøkt vårt land*, which discusses—and appears to retract—his past political engagement, and *Forsøk på å beskrive det ugjennonntrengelige*, about the impossibility of a decent life under Labor Party policies.

Roman 1987, for which Solstad won the Nordic Literary Prize, is also a political novel. It recounts the experiences of a talented teacher who gives up his career to join the working class. Though this attempt to live as a factory worker ultimately fails, the protagonist insists that his effort still had value. In his later novels, including *Genanse og verdighet, Professor Andersens natt*, and *T. Singer*, Solstad continues to probe the problem of individual versus society.

Shyness and Dignity explores themes of identity. A reviewer for *Publishers Weekly* said of the book: "With sublime restraint and subtle modulation, Solstad conveys an entire age of sorrow and loss."

BIOGRAPHICAL AND CRITICAL SOURCES:

BOOKS

Encyclopedia of World Literature in the Twentieth Century, 3rd edition, St. James Press (Detroit, MI), 1999.
Garton, Janet, editor, *Facets of European Modernism: Essays in Honour of James McFarland Presented to Him on His 65th Birthday 12 December 1985*, University of East Anglia (Norwich, England), 1985.
Landro, Jan H., *Jeg er ikke ironisk: samtaler med Dag Solstad*, Pax (Oslo, Norway), 2001.

PERIODICALS

Kirkus Reviews, June 1, 2006, review of *Shyness and Dignity*, p. 543.
Library Journal, September 15, 2006, Maureen Neville, review of *Shyness and Dignity*, p. 51.
Pacific Coast Philology, November, 1983, Jan Sjåvik, "Language and Myth in Dag Solstad's *Arild Ashes, 1970*," pp. 30-36.
Publishers Weekly, June 26, 2006, review of *Shyness and Dignity*, p. 30.

Scandinavian Studies, summer, 2000, Monika Zagar, "Modernism and Aesthetic Dictatorship," p. 199.

Scandinavica, November, 1975, Janet Mawby, "The Norwegian Novel Today," pp. 101-113.

ONLINE

Bookslut.com, http://www.bookslut.com/ (November, 2006), Jessica A. Tierney, review of *Shyness and Dignity.*

Independent Online, http://enjoyment.independent.co.uk/ (January 5, 2007), Boyd Tonkin, review of *Shyness and Dignity.**

* * *

SOMERVILLE, Patrick 1979-

PERSONAL: Born 1979. *Education:* University of Wisconsin-Madison, B.A.; Cornell University, M.F.A.

ADDRESSES: Home—Chicago, IL. *Agent*—Brettne Bloom, Kneerim & Williams, 45 Rockefeller Plaza, Ste. 2800, New York, NY 10111. *E-mail*—deathblow@patricksomerville.com.

CAREER: Writer and educator. Has taught creative writing at Cornell University, Auburn SCF, and the University of Chicago.

WRITINGS:

Trouble (stories), Vintage Contemporaries (New York, NY), 2006.

Contributor to literary journals, including *One Story.*

SIDELIGHTS: Born in 1979, writer Patrick Somerville grew up in Green Bay, Wisconsin. He went on to earn his undergraduate degree at the University of Wisconsin in Madison, and an M.F.A. in creative writing from Cornell University. Somerville has taught creative writing at a number of schools, including Cornell and the University of Chicago. He also has written a number of short stories, a selection of which

were published in his first collection, *Trouble.* One of the stories in the book, "Trouble and the Shadow Deathblow," which was in part responsible for the title of the book, also appeared in *One Story* magazine. In an interview for that journal's Web site, Somerville discussed his inspiration for the work. Somerville explained: "All I had to go on was a friend of mine from college who went away for a summer internship at a big food company and came back talking about secret recipes and robots that sprayed an orange cheese liquid onto various snack products." Other stories in the collection look at different aspects of boyhood, and how they affect the way a man matures. A contributor for *Kirkus Reviews* noted that "the most powerful stories here are more quietly observed." He called Somerville "a new talent in need of some honing." A *Publishers Weekly* reviewer concluded: "At his best, Somerville crafts stories that . . . highlight mordant absurdity and revel in darkly comic moments."

BIOGRAPHICAL AND CRITICAL SOURCES:

PERIODICALS

Kirkus Reviews, June 15, 2006, review of *Trouble,* p. 600.

Publishers Weekly, May 22, 2006, review of *Trouble,* p. 27.

ONLINE

Chicago Reader Online, http://www.chicagoreader.com/ (November 3, 2006), Martha Bayne, review of *Trouble.*

Chicago Tribune Online, http://www.chicagotribune.com/ (February 1, 2007), Sharon Pomerantz, "Debut Collection Focuses on Men Behaving Oddly."

I Read a Short Story Today Blog, http://ireadashortstorytoday.com/ (February 1, 2007), review of "Trouble and the Shadowy Deathblow."

One Story Web site, http://www.onestory.com/ (February 1, 2007), author interview.

Patrick Somerville Home Page, http://www.patricksomerville.com (February 1, 2007).*

SOMOZA, José Carlos 1959-

PERSONAL: Born November 13, 1959, in Havana, Cuba; brought to Spain in 1960. *Education:* Studied medicine and psychiatry in Cordoba, Spain; earned a B.S. in psychiatry.

ADDRESSES: Home—Spain. *E-mail*—jcsomoza@ clubcultura.com.

CAREER: Worked in psychiatry, then became a full-time writer in 1994.

AWARDS, HONORS: Prize Vertical Smile, 1996, for *Blanca's Silence;* Prize Coffee Gijón, 1998, for *The Painted Window;* Fernando Lara, 2001, and Sahiell Hammett International, 2002, both for *The Art of Murder;* Macallan Gold Dagger, 2002, for *The Athenian Murders.*

WRITINGS:

Cartas de un asesino insignificante, Debate Editorial (Madrid, Spain), 1999.
La ventana pintada (title means: "The Painted Window"), Algaida (Seville, Spain), 1999.
La caverna de las ideas, Alfaguara (Madrid, Spain), 2000, translation by Sonia Soto published as *The Athenian Murders,* Farrar, Straus, & Giroux (New York, NY), 2002.
Dafne desvanecida, Destiny Editions (Barcelona, Spain), 2000.
Clara y la penumbra, Planeta (Barcelona, Spain), 2001, translation by Nick Caistor published as *The Art of Murder,* Abacus (London, England), 2004.
La dama nuemero trece, Random House Mondadori (Barcelona, Spain), 2003.
La caja de marfil, Areté (Barcelona, Spain), 2004.
El detalle: tres novelas breves (novellas), Mondadori (Barcelona, Spain), 2005.
Zigzag, Plaza & Janés (Barcelona, Spain), 2006, Rayo (New York, NY), 2007.

SIDELIGHTS: Born in Havana, Cuba, José Carlos Somoza immigrated to Spain with his family when he was less than a year old. They lived with friends for a period of time, as Somoza's parents had been forced to flee Fidel Castro's dictatorship without their money and belongings. As an adult, Somoza has lived in Madrid and Cordoba, where he went to school to study medicine and psychiatry. Although he did practice medicine for a time, he also discovered a love and talent for writing, and in 1994, began submitting his work to publishers and to writing contests. His first novel was soon published, and Somoza turned all of his attention to writing. He was awarded the Prize Vertical Smile in 1996 for *Blanca's Silence,* and the Prize Coffee Gijón, in 1998 for *The Painted Window.*

The Athenian Murders, a thriller, is the first of Somoza's novels that has been released in the United States. The book combines snippets of a Greek text with the life of the translator, who is translating an ancient Greek murder mystery. Ultimately, the translator finds himself to be the target of a murder plot in the present day. A reviewer for *Publishers Weekly* called the book "a highly original and literary approach to crime fiction." A contributor to *Kirkus Reviews* remarked: "Though the plot's deliberate obscurities both intrigue and annoy, the rich, elegant writing will please all comers." Pedro Ponce, writing for the *Review of Contemporary Fiction,* commented: "The thrill of this novel comes from both its ingeniously structured mystery plot and the larger questions it raises about what constitutes knowledge and experience." In a review for *World Literature Today,* David Ross Gerling noted that Somoza's effort "rewards the persistent reader with intellectual pleasure tinged with humor and a rarefied emotional experience." W.R. Greer, in a review for the *Review of Books Online,* wrote: "As with all good mysteries, all the pieces fall into place in hindsight once the book comes to an end. Unpredictable, intelligent, and a tour guide through ancient Greece, 'The Athenian Murders' is different from anything else you might read, and in the end, you'll be glad it is."

In *The Art of Murder,* Somoza has created an intriguing universe where posed people are considered works of art, and a young girl in this posed state can be sold for a great deal of money—as art. When one of these posed girls is killed, two detectives attempt to solve the crime and stop the killer before anyone else is hurt. David Pitt, reviewing the novel for *Booklist,* wrote: "It's a fascinating and certainly disquieting underworld, and readers are drawn deep into it." A contributor for *Kirkus Reviews* remarked: "Murder and the threat of more provides a pulse of underlying tension, but Somoza . . . elegantly explores larger metaphysical and artistic issues."

BIOGRAPHICAL AND CRITICAL SOURCES:

PERIODICALS

Booklist, June 1, 2006, David Pitt, review of *The Art of Murder*, p. 45.

Kirkus Reviews, April 1, 2002, review of *The Athenian Murders*, p. 459; May 15, 2006, review of *The Art of Murder*, p. 501.

Publishers Weekly, May 6, 2002, review of *The Athenian Murders*, p. 33.

Review of Contemporary Fiction, spring, 2003, Pedro Ponce, review of *The Athenian Murders*, p. 150.

World Literature Today, October-December, 2003, David Ross Gerling, review of *The Athenian Murders*, p. 148.

ONLINE

Bookbag Online, http://www.thebookbag.co.uk/ (January 2, 2007), Sue Magee, review of *The Athenian Murders*.

IT Web, http://www.itweb.co.za/ (August 25, 2006), Laura Franz, review of *The Art of Murder*.

Jim Mann's Reviews and Comments Online, http://dpsinfo.com/jblog/ (January 29, 2006), Jim Mann, review of *The Athenian Murders*.

Review of Books Online, http://www.reviewofbooks.com/ (January 2, 2007), W.R. Greer, review of *The Athenian Murders*.

Salon.com, http://www.salon.com/ (June 20, 2002), Laura Miller, review of *The Athenian Murders*.

San Francisco Chronicle Online, http://www.sfgate.com/ (June 16, 2002), Christine Thomas, review of *The Athenian Murders*.

TiraMillas Online, http://www.tiramillas.net/ (January 2, 2007), review of *Zigzag*.

Washington Post Online, http://www.washingtonpost.com/ (June 30, 2002), Sanford Pinsker, review of *The Athenian Murders*.

*   *   *

SOSNIK, Douglas B.

PERSONAL: Male.

ADDRESSES: E-mail—authors@applebeesamerica.com.

CAREER: Former political advisor to President Bill Clinton; consultant to clients that include Democratic governors and senators, the National Basketball Association, and Fortune 100 companies. *HotSoup.com*, editor-in-chief.

WRITINGS:

(With Ron Fournier and Matthew J. Dowd) *Applebee's America: How Successful Political, Business, and Religious Leaders Connect with the New American Community*, Simon & Schuster (New York, NY), 2006.

SIDELIGHTS: For Sidelights, see *CA* entry on Matthew J. Dowd.

BIOGRAPHICAL AND CRITICAL SOURCES:

PERIODICALS

American Prospect, October, 2006, E.J. Dionne, Jr., review of *Applebee's America: How Successful Political, Business, and Religious Leaders Connect with the New American Community*, p. 52.

Booklist, September 15, 2006, Vanessa Bush, review of *Applebee's America*, p. 13.

Library Journal, September 1, 2006, Carol J. Elsen, review of *Applebee's America*, p. 158.

Publishers Weekly, July 24, 2006, review of *Applebee's America*, p. 52.

San Francisco Chronicle, September 18, 2006, Austin Considine, review of *Applebee's America*.

Washington Post, September 12, 2006, Amy Goldstein, review of *Applebee's America*, p. A21.

ONLINE

Applebee's America Web site, http://www.applebeesamerica.com (January 11, 2007).

Think and Ask, http://www.thinkandask.com/ (September 3, 2006), review of *Applebee's America*.*

SOTIROPOULOS, Ersi 1953-

PERSONAL: Born 1953, in Patras, Greece. *Education:* University of Florence, B.A., M.A.

ADDRESSES: Home—Greece.

CAREER: Writer, poet. Greek Embassy, Rome, Italy, counsellor of cultural affairs, 1983-1991; Greek Film Centre, Athens, Greece, head of press office, 1994-1996; *Elefterotypia* (newspaper), Greece, columnist, 1998-2002.

AWARDS, HONORS: National Literature Prize and the Book Critics' Award, both for *Zigzag through the Bitter Orange Trees,* 2000. Fellowships from University of Iowa International Writing Program, 1981, Princeton University, 1996-97, Kunstlerhaus Schloss Wiepersdorf, 2004, and Sacatar Foundation, 2006; decorated Commendatore dell'Ordine by the president of the Italian Republic, 1992.

WRITINGS:

Vacation without a Corpse, Akmon, 1980, Kastaniotis, 1997.
Apple+Death+ . . . + . . . (poems), Plethron, 1980.
Holiday Weekend in Yannina, Nefeli, 1982, Kedros 2001.
He Pharsa: Mythistorema, Kedros (Athens, Greece), 1982.
Mexico, Kedros (Athens, Greece), 1988.
Camelpig (short stories), Kedros (Athens, Greece), 1992.
The Flipperking (short stories), Kastaniotis, 1998.
Zigzag through the Bitter Orange Trees, Kedros (Athens, Greece), 1999, translation by Peter Green, Interlink Publishing Group (Northampton, MA), 2006.
The Warm Circle (short stories and poems), Ellinika Grammata, 2000.
Taming the Beast, Kedros (Athens, Greece), 2003.
Achtida sto Skotadi, Kedros (Athens, Greece), 2005.

Has written television and film scripts, including *Cavafy,* 1998.

SIDELIGHTS: Ersi Sotiropoulos was born in 1958, in Patras, Greece. She studied philosophy and cultural anthropology in Florence, Italy, before going on to become a writer, poet, and screenwriter. She is the author of several books, as well as scripts for film and television. In 2000 her novel *Zigzag through the Bitter Orange Trees* won both the National Literature Prize of Greece and the Book Critics' Award. The novel tells the stories of four young modern-day Greeks whose lives intersect. There is Sid, an Athenian who whiles away his days and spends his nights in a local tavern. There he meets Julia, a Goth-like girl with whom he has an affair. Sid has a sister, Lia, who is in a hospital with a rare, fatal ailment, and who fights with her nurse, Sotiris. Sotiris spends his free time following a young girl named Nina, who is living with her aunt and who, as an aspiring writer, spends most of her time watching her surroundings and therefore becomes aware that Sotiris is following her. A contributor to *Kirkus Reviews* remarked: "Some memorable detail and wry observations, but capricious character behavior and too many anticlimaxes will frustrate readers." However, a reviewer for *Publishers Weekly* wrote: "Sotiropoulos describes shame and alienation so effectively that the narration feels voyeuristic—in a good way."

BIOGRAPHICAL AND CRITICAL SOURCES:

PERIODICALS

Kirkus Reviews, September 15, 2006, review of *Zigzag through the Bitter Orange Trees,* p. 928.
Publishers Weekly, September 25, 2006, review of *Zigzag through the Bitter Orange Trees,* p. 44.

ONLINE

Circumference Online, http://www.circumferencemag.com/ (February 1, 2007), author biography.
Griechische-Kulture Web site, http://www.griechische-kulture.de/ (February 1, 2007), author biography.
Interlink Books Web site, http://www.interlinkbooks.com/ (February 1, 2007), author biography.

[Sketch reviewed by Interlink Publishing Group publicity director, Moira Megargee.]

SPEED, John 1952(?)-

PERSONAL: Born c. 1952, in NC.

ADDRESSES: Home—Cardiff-by-the-Sea, CA.

CAREER: Freelance political consultant and journalist; owner of a software company.

WRITINGS:

The Temple Dancer: A Novel of India, St. Martin's Press (New York, NY), 2006.

SIDELIGHTS: John Speed first became interested in Indian culture when he was in high school, and began to study the art, history, and religion of the region, growing particularly interested in tales of the fall of the Mogul Empire and of the rise of the rebel prince Shivaji. He visited the country on many occasions, traveling through cities and remote areas as well. His book, *The Temple Dancer: A Novel of India,* is the result of more than thirty years of interest and study. Set in seventeenth-century India, the novel is intended to be the first in a series, and Speed thinks of them as an introduction to India in the way that James Clavell's *Shogun* opened up Japan to so many readers. In an interview with the *North County Times,* Speed described the book as "like a road trip . . . a highly romantic Hope and Crosby road movie. It is a sweeping adventure with a huge amount of characters, and it's a travel story where everybody's changed by the journey." A contributor for *Kirkus Reviews* called the book "a richly atmospheric debut," adding: "The author's fondness for his material keeps this convoluted romantic epic afloat." A reviewer for *Publishers Weekly* dubbed Speed's effort "an enjoyable adventure that still has respect for its characters." Margaret Flanagan, writing for *Booklist,* called the book "lavish and lush," as well as a "high-voltage adventure yarn."

BIOGRAPHICAL AND CRITICAL SOURCES:

PERIODICALS

Booklist, May 1, 2006, Margaret Flanagan, review of *The Temple Dancer: A Novel of India,* p. 74.

Kirkus Reviews, June 1, 2006, review of *The Temple Dancer,* p. 543.
Publishers Weekly, July 23, 2006, review of *The Temple Dancer,* p. 38.

ONLINE

North County Times Online, http://www.nctimes.com/ (October 1, 2006), Gary Warth, review of *The Temple Dancer.*
The Temple Dancer Web site, http://www.templedancer.com (December 31, 2006).*

*   *   *

SPRINGER, Gerald
   See SPRINGER, Jerry

*   *   *

SPRINGER, Jerry 1944-
   (Gerald Springer)

PERSONAL: Full name, Gerald Springer; born February 13, 1944, in London, England; immigrated to the United States, 1949; son of Richard (a stuffed animal maker) and Margot (a bank clerk) Springer; married Micki Velten (an administrative aide), 1973 (divorced, 1994); children: Katie. *Education:* Tulane University, B.A.; Northwestern University, J.D., 1968.

ADDRESSES: Office—The Jerry Springer Show, NBC Tower, 454 N. Columbus Dr., Ste. 200, Chicago, IL 60611. *Agent*—William Morris Agency, 1 William Morris Pl., Beverly Hills, CA 90212.

CAREER: Worked as campaign aide to presidential candidate Robert F. Kennedy, 1968; City of Cincinnati, Cincinnati, OH, council member at large, 1971-76, mayor, 1977-81; WLWT-TV, Cincinnati, political reporter, 1982-84, anchor and managing editor, 1984-93; *The Jerry Springer Show* (syndicated television series), host and executive producer, 1991—. *Cincinnati Reaches Out,* worked as on-site reporter; appearances in other television series include guest presenter, *This Morning* (also known as *This Morning with Rich-*

ard and Judy), 1999; host of *Jerry Springer UK*, 1999, *Late Night with Jerry Springer*, 2000, and *Now or Never: Face Your Fear*, Fox, 2000; appeared in *Greed*, 10 Network (Australia), 2001; and as guest host, *The Wright Stuff*. Appeared as the class photographer in the television movie *Since You've Been Gone* (also known as *Dog Water*, *Stepping in Dog Water*, and *Stepping in the Dog Water*), American Broadcasting Companies (ABC), 1998. Appeared in many television specials, including *Donahue: The 25th Anniversary*, syndicated, 1992; *The 1998 Billboard Music Awards*, Fox, 1998; *The Daily Show Year-End Spectacular '98*, Comedy Central, 1998; *Jerry Springer: In the Center Ring*, Arts and Entertainment, 1998; *Sex with Cindy Crawford*, 1998; *Barbara Walters Presents the 10 Most Fascinating People of 1998*, ABC, 1998; *My Favourite Frasier*, 1999; *Jerry Springer on Sunday*, 1999; *It's Only Talk: The Real Story of America's Talk Show*, Arts and Entertainment, 1999; *The Great American History Quiz: Pursuit of Happiness*, History Channel, 2000; as host, *Miss World 2000*, 2000; in *Talking to Americans* (also known as *Rick Mercer's Talking to Americans*), 2001; also appeared as cohost, *Jerry Lewis's Stars across America Muscular Dystrophy Labor Day Telethon*. Contestant on *Dancing with the Stars*, 2006; guest in episodes of other television shows, including *Married . . . with Children; Roseanne; The X-Files; The Tonight Show with Jay Leno; The Steve Harvey Show; The Wayans Bros.; Sabrina, the Teenage Witch; Malcolm & Eddie; Mad TV; Space Ghost Coast to Coast; Suddenly Susan; The Cindy Margolis Show; The Weakest Link; Rendez-Vous; Celebrity Deathmatch; Larry King Live; Who's Line is it Anyway?, The Late Late Show with Craig Kilborn, On Air with Ryan Seacrest*, and *The Chris Rock Show*. Appeared in films (usually as himself), including *Meet Wally Sparks*, Trimark Pictures, 1997; (in archive footage) *The Big One*, 1997; *Kissing a Fool*, Universal, 1998; as Jerry Farrelly (and producer), *Jerry Springer: Ringmaster* (also known as *Springers* and *Ringmaster*), Artisan Entertainment, 1998; *A Fare to Remember*, Artisan Entertainment, 1999; *The 24 Hour Woman*, 1999; *Kismet*, 1999; *Austin Powers: The Spy Who Shagged Me* (also known as *Austin Powers 2: The Spy Who Shagged Me*), New Line Cinema, 1999; *Sex: The Annabel Chong Story*, 2000; *Sugar & Spice*, New Line Cinema, 2001; *You'll Never Wiez in This Town Again*, Dimension Films, 2003; as Marty Rockman, *Citizen Verdict*, 2003; and as the president, *The Defender*, 2004. Appeared as himself in videos, including *The Best of Ed's Night Party*, 1996; *Jerry Springer: Too*

Hot for TV, Real Entertainment, 1998; *Killer Sex Queens from Cyperspace* (also known as *Killer Queens from Another World* and *V.I.C.T.I.M.*), 1998; *The Best of Jerry Springer*, Real Entertainment, 1998; *Secrets and Surprises*, Real Entertainment, 1998; *Springer: Bad Boys and Naughty Girls*, Real Entertainment, 1998; and *I Refuse to Wear Clothes!*, Real Entertainment, 1998. Air America Radio, host of *Springer on the Radio*, 2005-06. Recorded a country music album, *Dr. Talk*, 1995. Audrey Hepburn Hollywood for Children Fund, member of advisory board; National Muscular Dystrophy Association, vice president and board member; Kellman School, Chicago, IL, founder of scholarship fund.

AWARDS, HONORS: Emmy Award, for investigative journalism at WLWT-TV; Gates of Righteousness Award, Midwest Region, American Committee for Shaare Zadek Medical Center, Jerusalem, Israel, 2004.

WRITINGS:

(With others) *The Jerry Springer Show* (television series), syndicated, beginning 1991.
(With Laura Morton) *Jerry Springer: Ringmaster* (memoir), St. Martin's Press (New York, NY), 1998.
Jerry Springer: Too Hot for TV (video), Real Entertainment, 1998.
(With others) *Jerry Springer UK* (television series), 1999.
(With others) *Late Night with Jerry Springer* (television series), 2000.

Author of the country music single *Dr. Talk*.

ADAPTATIONS: A stage play titled *Jerry Springer: The Opera*, written by Stewart Lee and Richard Thomas, was produced at the National Theater, London, England, 2003-c. 2005, toured British cities thereafter, and was televised by the British Broadcasting Corp. in 2005.

SIDELIGHTS: Talk-show host Jerry Springer has become an American institution and a touchstone in debates about morality in modern pop culture. Whether or not his prominence in that culture is evidence of the downfall of Western civilization is in the eye of the beholder. To his critics, *The Jerry Springer Show*'s endless parade of voyeuristic topics and chair-throwing, hair-pulling brawls prove that it is "a perverse circus" and "a freak show," in the words of one of the shows more powerful critics, Connecticut senator Joseph Lieberman. But to Springer, the show is merely "chewing gum" for the mind. In an interview with Chris Nashawaty of *Entertainment Weekly*, Springer declared, "Look, if I'm Satan, then we're all okay—because then Satan ain't that bad."

Nothing in Springer's early life, as catalogued in his memoir, *Jerry Springer: Ringmaster*, would suggest that his greatest claim to fame would be as the host of a rowdy talk show. The son of German-Jewish refugees who fled from the Nazis, first to London, England (where Springer was born) and later to Brooklyn, New York, Springer headed first for a career in politics. Armed with a degree from Tulane University in political science and a law degree from Northwestern University, Springer joined the presidential campaign of Senator Robert F. Kennedy before taking a job with a law firm in Cincinnati, Ohio, and becoming involved in local politics there. He won a seat on the city council in 1971, resigned after it was discovered that he had patronized a prostitute, and then three years later was elected mayor. As the "boy mayor," as the early-thirties Springer was dubbed, he made a point of serving the interest of average citizens. With a van dubbed "Jerry Springer's Mobile City Hall," he worked on Cincinnati's streets; he spent a night in a city jail to bring publicity to the poor conditions there. It was only after losing his bid to become governor of Ohio that Springer turned to television. He became a journalist for a Cincinnati television station, where he won an Emmy for his investigative reporting. When he first launched his talk show, it was an extension of his "serious" journalism, featuring panel discussions about the issues of the day. But after three years of low ratings, in 1994 *The Jerry Springer Show* revamped itself into the carnival of camp that it is today.

To some television critics, *The Jerry Springer Show* is an extension of Springer's work as mayor in bringing disenfranchised people into the spotlight and the political debate. Buried under the hoopla that surrounds the show, Joshua Gamson wrote in *Tikkun*, "is a serious, class-tinged battle over who gets to do what in public, who gets to speak and how." On other shows, guests are required to conform to the "self-appointed gate-keepers of public space and the chaperones of middle-class public propriety"; on Springer's show, they are free to act as they wish. In an interview with Rebecca Johnson and Kathleen Powers for *Good Housekeeping*, Springer seemed to confirm this interpretation of what he does. "Virtually all of television is a canned, restricted, vanilla view of life," he said, "and the people on television are always white, upper-middle-class people wearing jackets and ties. We are showing a non-power group. They're not powerful because of their education or their age, and they're not the people we're used to seeing on TV. I like the people on our show because they don't put on airs. They are real."

BIOGRAPHICAL AND CRITICAL SOURCES:

BOOKS

Newsmakers 1998, Issue 4, Thomson Gale (Detroit, MI), 1998.
St. James Encyclopedia of Popular Culture, five volumes, St. James Press (Detroit, MI), 2000.

PERIODICALS

Broadcasting & Cable, December 15, 1997, Joe Schlosser, "Jerry Springer: Punching the Envelope," pp. 32-35; April 27, 1998, Joe Schlosser, "*Jerry Springer:* Scraps or Scripts? Talk Show under Fire for Allegations of Staging," p. 10; July 31, 2000, Susanne Ault, "Another Talk Show on Trial?," p. 10; November 12, 2001, Joe Schlosser, "Springer Staying Put—For Now," p. 39.
Crain's Chicago Business, March 16, 1998, Jeff Borden, "Jerry's Talking Trash, Counting Cash," pp. 1-2.
Entertainment Weekly, October 20, 1995, Ken Tucker, review of *Dr. Talk,* p. 66; January 23, 1998, Kristen Baldwin, profile of Springer, pp. 16-17; November 20, 1998, Chris Nashawaty, review of *Jerry Springer: Ringmaster,* p. 80.
Esquire, January, 1999, Mim Udovitch, interview with Springer, p. 89.
Good Housekeeping, September, 1998, Rebecca Johnson and Kathleen Powers, "Jerry Springer under Siege," pp. 114-119.

National Review, June 2, 1998, Richard Brookhiser, review of *The Jerry Springer Show,* pp. 56-57.

New Orleans, November, 1997, interview with Springer, p. 11.

Newsweek, August 16, 1999, Martha Brant, "Senator Springer? TV's Smutmeister Toys with a Bid from Ohio," p. 27.

New York Post, December 13, 2006, Don Kaplan, "Jerry Rigged: Reality Series Shocker."

People, November 27, 1995, Bryan Alexander, review of *Dr. Talk,* p. 26; August 14, 2000, "Talk Show Triangle: A Guest on Jerry Springer Winds Up Dead—with Her Ex-Husband Accused of Murder," p. 143.

PR Newswire, May 21, 2004, "Jerry Springer to be Given Gates of Righteousness Award by the Midwest Region of the American Committee for Shaare Zadek Medical Center in Jerusalem."

Sarasota, January, 2006, Kay Kipling, "If You Knew Jerry: There's Much More to Sarasota's Most Famous Resident, Trash-Talk TV Icon Jerry Springer, Than Most of Us Would Ever Imagine," p. 112.

Television Week, July 28, 2003, Chris Pursell, "Springer Senate Bid Dims," p. 1; May 8, 2006, Allison J. Waldman, "American Pie: The In-Your-Face Success of 'The Jerry Springer Show,'" p. 31.

Tikkun, November-December, 1998, Joshua Gamson, "Why They Love Jerry Springer," pp. 25-27.

U.S. News & World Report, January 8, 1996, Jim Impoco, interview with Springer, pp. 50-51.

Vanity Fair, February, 2006, interview by George Wayne, p. 118.

Variety, November 23, 1998, Dennis Harvey, review of *Jerry Springer: Ringmaster,* p. 48; May 31, 1999, Cynthia Littleton, "Stations, Solons Wrestle over Jerry," p. 19.

ONLINE

Jerry Springer Show Web site, http://www.jerryspringertv.com (February 5, 2007).*

*   *   *

STEWART, Will
  See WILLIAMSON, John Stewart

STOLZ, Mary 1920-2006
  (Mary Slattery Stolz)

OBITUARY NOTICE— See index for *CA* sketch: Born March 24, 1920, in Boston, MA; died December 15, 2006, in Longboat Key, FL. Author. Stolz was an award-winning author of books for children and young adults. Educated at Columbia University Teacher's College and the Katharine Gibbs School in the 1930s, she first worked as a secretary at Columbia University. Stolz, unfortunately, suffered from arthritis at an early age. During one severe bout with the ailment, she decided to work on her first book. This was released in 1950 as *To Tell Your Love.* Many more works of fiction would follow, and Stolz developed a reputation for writing novels that appealed to young girls. Her stories were frequently on American Library Association notable book lists, and several titles were award winners. Her *In a Mirror* (1953), for example, won the Children's Book Award from Bank Street College; she was a National Book Award finalist for *The Edge of Next Year* (1974), and her *Belling the Tiger* (1961) and *The Noonday Friends* (1965) were both Newbery Honor books. Praised for her strong characterizations of teenagers facing troubles in love and with family, Stolz penned such other memorable young adult titles as *Leap before You Look* (1972), *Go and Catch a Flying Fish* (1979), and *Coco Grimes* (1994). Her titles for younger children include favorites like *Emmett's Pig* (1959), *The Bully of Barkham Street* (1963), and *Bartholomew Fair* (1990).

OBITUARIES AND OTHER SOURCES:

PERIODICALS

Chicago Tribune, January 23, 2007, Section 2, p. 10.
New York Times, January 22, 2007, p. A18.

*   *   *

STOLZ, Mary Slattery
  See STOLZ, Mary

*   *   *

STONE, Peter H. 1946-

PERSONAL: Born 1946.

*ADDRESSES: E-mail—*pstone@nationaljournal.com.

CAREER: Journalist. *National Journal,* Washington, DC, staff member, 1992—.

WRITINGS:

Heist: Superlobbyist Jack Abramoff, His Republican Allies, and the Buying of Washington, Farrar, Straus, & Giroux (New York, NY), 2006.

Contributor to periodicals, including the *Washington Post, New York Times, American Prospect, Atlantic Monthly, Mother Jones,* and the *Paris Review.*

SIDELIGHTS: Peter H. Stone is a politics and finance writer, serving on the staff of the *National Journal* since 1992, where he covers lobbying and campaign finance issues. *Heist: Superlobbyist Jack Abramoff, His Republican Allies, and the Buying of Washington,* Stone's first book, is an exposé of the Washington scandal involving lobbyists seeking deals on behalf of the gaming casinos run by various Native American tribes. The book focuses on heavy-hitting lobbyist Jack Abramoff, known for his strong ties to both then-House Majority Leader Tom DeLay and Christian Coalition leader Ralph Reed. According to Stone, Abramoff is responsible for siphoning millions of dollars from the casinos. In a review for *Publishers Weekly,* one contributor called the book "a troubling but colorful portrait of business as usual in Washington." Chris Lehmann, writing for the *New York Observer,* opined: "Mr. Stone's Abramoff chronology is just that—a tour of the horizon already charted in great detail by Senator John McCain's Committee on Indian Affairs inquiry, together with background interviews with disillusioned former clients and colleagues of the high-riding Mr. Abramoff." However, a contributor for *Kirkus Reviews* found the book more intriguing, and remarked: "With luck, this lively little study will help inspire reforms."

BIOGRAPHICAL AND CRITICAL SOURCES:

PERIODICALS

Kirkus Reviews, August 15, 2006, review of *Heist: Superlobbyist Jack Abramoff, His Republican Allies, and the Buying of Washington,* p. 831.

Publishers Weekly, May 2, 2005, John F. Baker, "Lid Off Casino Scandal," p. 14; August 7, 2006, review of *Heist,* p. 46.

ONLINE

Mother Jones Online, http://www.motherjones.com/ (November 12, 2006), author biography.
New York Observer Online, http://www.observer.com/ (October 2, 2006), Chris Lehmann, "The Gaud That Failed: A Tour of New Jack City," review of *Heist.**

*   *   *

STOVER, Leon E. 1929-2006
   (Leon Eugene Stover)

OBITUARY NOTICE— See index for *CA* sketch: Born April 9, 1929, in Lewistown, PA; died of complications from diabetes, November 25, 2006, in Chicago, IL. Anthropologist, educator, and author. A former professor of anthropology at the Illinois Institute of Technology, Stover was often best remembered for his extensive knowledge of science fiction. He was a 1950 graduate of Western Maryland College and attended Columbia University's graduate school, earning a Ph.D. in 1962. His academic career started in the 1950s, when he was an instructor at the American Museum of Natural History. An associate professor at Hobart and William Smith Colleges until 1965, he joined the Illinois Institute of Technology faculty in 1966. Here he was made a tenured professor of anthropology in 1974, retiring in 1994. More interesting than his academic career, perhaps, was Stover's love of science fiction and his friendship with some of the genre's greatest writers, including Harry Harrison. He also came to personally know Isaac Asimov, L. Sprague de Camp, and Robert Sheckley, a fact that no doubt came in handy when he taught a science fiction course at IIT. Stover had eclectic interests ranging from Chinese history to Stonehenge to the writings of H.G. Wells. He wrote on all of these subjects, and even collaborated with Harrison on a couple of books, including as coeditor of *Apeman, Spaceman: Anthropological Science Fiction* (1968) and coauthor of the novel *Stonehenge* (1972). Fascinated by Wells,

Stover edited the six-volume *The Annotated H.G. Wells* (1995-98) and also published *Things to Come: The Annotated H.G. Wells* (2006). Among his other books are *Stonehenge and the Origins of Western Culture* (1978), *Harry Harrison* (1990), *Science Fiction from Wells to Heinlein* (2002), and *Imperial China and the State Cult of Confucius* (2004). A book he had just completed editing at the time of his passing was scheduled for publication in 2007.

OBITUARIES AND OTHER SOURCES:

PERIODICALS

Chicago Tribune, November 27, 2006, Section 1, p. 13.

* * *

STOVER, Leon Eugene
 See STOVER, Leon E.

* * *

STRAUS, Scott 1970-

PERSONAL: Born 1970.

ADDRESSES: Office—Department of Political Science, University of Wisconsin—Madison, 110 North Hall, 1050 Bascom Mall, Madison, WI 53706. *E-mail*—sstraus@wisc.edu.

CAREER: University of Wisconsin—Madison, assistant professor of political science and international studies. Former freelance journalist based in Nairobi, Kenya.

WRITINGS:

(With David K. Leonard) *Africa's Stalled Development: International Causes and Cures,* Lynne Rienner Publishers (Boulder, CO), 2003.

(Author of introduction and interviewer) Robert Lyons, *Intimate Enemy: Images and Voices of the Rwandan Genocide,* photographs by Robert Lyons, MIT Press (Cambridge, MA), 2006.
The Order of Genocide: Race, Power, and War in Rwanda, Cornell University Press (Ithaca, NY), 2006.

Also translator of *The Great Lakes of Africa,* MIT Press. Contributor of articles to academic journals, including *Foreign Affairs.*

SIDELIGHTS: As a former journalist, political science professor Scott Straus became familiar with modern African conflicts, particularly with the war and genocide in the southeastern nation of Rwanda. His first work, *Africa's Stalled Development: International Causes and Cures,* written with David K. Leonard, looks at the more general problem of underdevelopment in Africa, however. Acknowledging that the continent's problems arise from its colonial history, the two authors suggest that a lasting answer to Africa's widespread poverty and violence can only be found through systemic change fostered by the rest of the world. "The authors," concluded Andrew Francis Clark in *Africa Today,* "argue that the lack of development, caused largely by Africa's relationship with the international system and the weak states it has fostered, can be solved only with international cooperation and profound structural change within the continent and in the international community's understanding and approach to African problems. Based on an extensive review of the literature and a series of original proposals, this book is essential reading for Africanists concerned with issues related to economic and political development."

In *Intimate Enemy: Images and Voices of the Rwandan Genocide,* a photographic depiction of the conflict there by Robert Lyons for which Straus wrote the introduction, Straus "brings a more intimate dimension to attempts to understand the personal and cultural issues surrounding the genocide" in 1994—the largest mass killing of one group by another in the twentieth century, reported Vanessa Bush in *Booklist.* "Teachers, businessmen, a plumber, farmers, an accountant, etc. . . . committed horrific crimes," observed *Library Journal* contributor James Thorsen. "Most confessed to killing, and few will be allowed to leave prison."

Straus's book places perpetrators and victims in close proximity, trying to demonstrate that, as a *Publishers Weekly* critic explained, we all have a "generalized potential for evil."

BIOGRAPHICAL AND CRITICAL SOURCES:

PERIODICALS

Africa Today, Volume 51, number 1, 2004, Andrew Francis Clark, review of *Africa's Stalled Development: International Causes and Cures,* pp. 129-130.

Booklist, March 15, 2006, Vanessa Bush, review of *Intimate Enemy: Images and Voices of the Rwandan Genocide,* p. 21.

Library Journal, May 15, 2006, James Thorsen, review of *Intimate Enemy,* p. 115.

Publishers Weekly, February 13, 2006, review of *Intimate Enemy,* p. 79.

ONLINE

University of Wisconsin Department of Political Science Web site, http://www.polisci.wisc.edu/ (December 5, 2006), faculty profile of Scott Straus.

*   *   *

STREET, Libby
See MORRIS, Emily S.

*   *   *

STREET, Libby
See BUSHWELLER, Sarah

*   *   *

STYRON, William 1925-2006
(William Clark Styron, Jr.)

OBITUARY NOTICE— See index for *CA* sketch: Born June 11, 1925, in Newport News, VA; died of pneumonia, November 1, 2006, in Martha's Vineyard, MA. Author. Styron was a Pulitzer Prize-winning author best known for his novels *The Confessions of Nat Turner* and *Sophie's Choice.* After attending Davidson College for a year, he served in the U.S. Marine Corps from 1944 to 1945, achieving the rank of first lieutenant. Styron completed his bachelor's degree at Duke University in 1947 and studied writing briefly at the New School. After graduation, he took a job as an associate editor at the publishing house McGraw-Hill, but soon found success with his first novel, *Lie Down in Darkness* (1951). The work won him the American Academy of Arts and Letters Prix de Rome. Styron, however, was a slow and methodical writer and did not produce another novel until 1957's *The Long March.* This was followed three years later by *Set This House on Fire.* It was 1967's *The Confessions of Nat Turner* that earned him the Pulitzer, as well as the Howells Medal from the American Academy of Arts and Letters. Though the book was critically acclaimed as a literary masterpiece, some complained that Styron did not have the right to assume the narration of the novel from the perspective of the African American Turner, whom Styron fictionalized based on the famous leader of the American slave revolt. The author, in turn, replied that artists should be allowed the freedom to express themselves as they saw fit. *Sophie's Choice* (1979) earned him the American Book Award and a National Book Critics Circle Award nomination and was adapted as a 1982 movie. It also drew some protests because Styron wrote about the Holocaust from the viewpoint of a woman who was Catholic, not Jewish. Despite such complaints, Styron was more often praised than criticized, and his rich writing style was sometimes compared to that of William Faulkner. *Sophie's Choice* would prove to be the author's last major work, however, and by the mid-1980s he was struggling with severe depression aggravated by his attempts to treat the illness with the drug Halcion. In 1984 he checked himself into the Yale-New Haven Hospital for treatment, which he would credit with saving his life. He would write about this chapter in his life in *Darkness Visible: A Memoir of Madness* (1990).

OBITUARIES AND OTHER SOURCES:

BOOKS

Styron, William, *Darkness Visible: A Memoir of Madness,* Random House (New York, NY), 1990.

Styron, William, and James L.W. West III, *William Styron: A Life,* Random House (New York, NY), 1998.

PERIODICALS

Chicago Tribune, November 2, 2006, Section 3, p. 7.
Los Angeles Times, November 2, 2006, pp. A1, A17.
New York Times, November 2, 2006, p. C17; November 4, 2006, p. A2.
Times (London, England), November 3, 2006, p. 78.

*   *   *

STYRON, William Clark, Jr.
    See STYRON, William

*   *   *

SULLIVAN, James 1965-

PERSONAL: Born 1965; married; wife's name Thuy; children: Cullen, Vivian. *Education:* Graduated from Colby College, 1987; University of Iowa Writers' Workshop, M.F.A., 1992.

ADDRESSES: Home—ME.

CAREER: Journalist.

WRITINGS:

Over the Moat: Love among the Ruins of Imperial Vietnam (memoir), Picador (New York, NY), 2004.

Contributor to magazines, including *Bicycling.*

SIDELIGHTS: James Sullivan went to Vietnam on assignment for *Bicycling* magazine, but what he found when he reached that country changed his entire life. The site of this profound change was the Vietnamese fortress of Hue, which is located between Hanoi and Ho Chi Minh City. It is where he met Thuy, a Vietnamese woman whom he would marry and take home with him to Quincy, Massachusetts. Sullivan was biking the arduous 700-mile route between the two cities with college friend David Relin, and writing about the experience for the magazine, but his encounter with Thuy set the groundwork for what would become his book, *Over the Moat: Love among the Ruins of Imperial Vietnam.* While still in Vietnam, Sullivan needed to cross a moat each time he visited Thuy, providing the title for his book. Although Sullivan chronicles the relationship, he also observes and details his experiences in Vietnam. A contributor for *Kirkus Reviews* wrote: "Cultures clash, but love conquers, with some fascinating twists and plenty of intimate details." Harold M. Otness, writing for the *Library Journal,* commented that Sullivan's effort offers up "a narrow if revealing account of Vietnam just before diplomatic relations with the United States were restored."

BIOGRAPHICAL AND CRITICAL SOURCES:

BOOKS

Sullivan, James, *Over the Moat: Love among the Ruins of Imperial Vietnam,* Picador (New York, NY), 2004.

PERIODICALS

Book World, February 22, 2004, Amy Kroin, review of *Over the Moat,* p. 13.
Boston, January, 2004, Bill Beuttler, review of *Over the Moat,* p. 154.
Kirkus Reviews, November 1, 2003, review of *Over the Moat,* p. 1307.
Library Journal, January, 2004, Harold M. Otness, review of *Over the Moat,* p. 143.
Publishers Weekly, October 20, 2003, review of *Over the Moat,* p. 41.

ONLINE

Colby College Web site, http://www.colby.edu/ (December 31, 2006), alumnus listing.

University of Iowa News Releases Online, http://news-releases.uiowa.edu/ (February 12, 2004), "UI Alumni Return to Read 'Live from Prairie Lights' Week of Feb. 23-27."

Vietnam Veterans Association Online, http://www.vva.org/ (December 31, 2006), review of *Over the Moat.**

*   *   *

SULLIVAN, Robert 1963-

PERSONAL: Born 1963; married; father. *Hobbies and other interests:* Accordion, tin whistle, old music, travel, hiking.

ADDRESSES: Home—Brooklyn, NY.

CAREER: Writer. *Vogue,* New York, NY, contributing editor.

AWARDS, HONORS: Alex Award, 2005, for *Rats: Observations on the History and Habitat of the City's Most Unwanted Inhabitants; New York Times* Notable Books of the Year citations, for *The Meadowlands: Wilderness Adventures at the Edge of a City, A Whale Hunt,* and *Rats.*

WRITINGS:

The Meadowlands: Wilderness Adventures at the Edge of a City, Anchor Books (New York, NY), 1998.
A Whale Hunt, Scribner (New York, NY), 2000.
Rats: Observations on the History and Habitat of the City's Most Unwanted Inhabitants (children's book), Bloomsbury (New York, NY), 2004.
How Not to Get Rich; or, Why Being Bad Off Isn't So Bad, illustrations by Scott Menchin, Bloomsbury (New York, NY), 2005.
Cross Country: Fifteen Years and Ninety Thousand Miles on the Roads and Interstates of America with Lewis and Clark, a Lot of Bad Motels, a Moving Van, Emily Post, Jack Kerouac, My Wife, My Mother-in-Law, Two Kids, and Enough Coffee to Kill an Elephant, Bloomsbury (New York, NY), 2006.

Contributor to periodicals, including *Vogue, Condé Nast Traveler, New York Times Magazine,* and the *New Yorker.*

SIDELIGHTS: Robert Sullivan does not consider himself to be a nature writer, although his books are frequently shelved in the nature section of the bookstore or local library. Instead of writing about nature as it is most commonly considered—far removed from the cities, still untouched by man-made structures or industry—he writes about the ways in which nature coexists with technology and urban sprawl. In his book *The Meadowlands: Wilderness Adventures at the Edge of a City,* Sullivan explores the swamp area that lies within view of the Manhattan skyline. Considered an eyesore by most, and often used as a dumping ground, the swampy area still manages to hold Sullivan's interest, and the book chronicles his explorations of the area by foot, car, and even by boat. Sullivan provides a history of the Meadowlands as well, both factual and rumored. Donna Seaman, in a review for *Booklist,* remarked that the author was "irrepressible and irresistible as he captures the Meadowlands' anomalous beauty and revels in its colorful lore." A reviewer for *Publishers Weekly* called Sullivan's effort a "sad if intriguing tale of industrial carnage." Writing in the *Library Journal,* Lonnie Weatherby labeled the book as "finely wrought and imaginatively styled."

In *A Whale Hunt,* Sullivan explores the glorious Olympic Peninsula in Washington, a region inhabited by the Makah Native Americans. This tribe was once known for its whale hunting skill, but when commercial whaling endangered the gray whale common in the local waters, the Makah were forced to cease whaling. Once the whale's numbers increased sufficiently, the Makah began a legal battle to regain their whaling rights. However, so many years had passed since the tribe had gone whaling, many of their whaling techniques had been lost. The tribe was forced to create new methods of whaling, and Sullivan spent two years observing them as they went through the process of building a whaling canoe, training a crew, and setting out to capture a whale. Nancy Bent, in a review for *Booklist,* observed: "No matter where one stands on the subject of aboriginal whaling rights, this book will be fascinating reading."

Sullivan was inspired to write *Rats: Observations on the History and Habitat of the City's Most Unwanted*

Inhabitants in part due to his experiences watching the Makah. After seeing the spectacle of whaling, he found himself wondering what sort of animal was at the opposite end of the spectrum—something no one would make a grand effort to chase and capture. His answer was the rat. So he set out to determine why most people consider rats to be disgusting, and why they hold so little interest. He spent time talking to experts on the species, and also observing them in the alleyways of New York City. A contributor for *Kirkus Reviews* called the book a "skittering, scurrying, terrific natural history." Michael D. Cramer, writing for the *Library Journal,* noted: "Well written and fun to read, this book has only one drawback: a lack of more detailed information on rat biology." However, writing for the *School Library Journal,* Jamie Watson remarked: "This creative writer has taken on a seemingly unappealing subject and turned it into a topnotch page-turner." A contributor for *Publishers Weekly* wrote: "This book is a must pickup for every city dweller, even if you'll feel like you need to wash your hands when you put it down."

With *Cross Country: Fifteen Years and Ninety Thousand Miles on the Roads and Interstates of America with Lewis and Clark, a Lot of Bad Motels, a Moving Van, Emily Post, Jack Kerouac, My Wife, My Mother-in-Law, Two Kids, and Enough Coffee to Kill an Elephant,* Sullivan takes a step away from pure nature writing and takes a look at his own traveling history with his family. Sullivan determined that he had made approximately twenty-seven trips from coast to coast across the United States over the fifteen years that he and his wife had been taking driving vacations with the family. He explains that this is due to the fact that he is from the New York/New Jersey area, while his wife is originally from Oregon, providing them with extended families on both sides of the country and ample excuses to drive back and forth to visit. Sullivan does not escape nature writing entirely, of course, as he chronicles many of the sites visited during his cross country vacations, along with a history of road trips, starting with Lewis and Clark's expedition, and provides amusing and colorful family anecdotes. Finn-Olaf Jones, writing for the *New York Times Book Review,* commented: "There are moments of brilliance along the way." A contributor for *Kirkus Reviews* called the book "a dazzling account of America's most archetypal odyssey, with much social history slyly and wryly inserted."

BIOGRAPHICAL AND CRITICAL SOURCES:

BOOKS

Sullivan, Robert *Cross Country: Fifteen Years and Ninety Thousand Miles on the Roads and Interstates of America with Lewis and Clark, a Lot of Bad Motels, a Moving Van, Emily Post, Jack Kerouac, My Wife, My Mother-in-Law, Two Kids, and Enough Coffee to Kill an Elephant,* Bloomsbury (New York, NY), 2006.

PERIODICALS

Booklist, March 1, 1998, Donna Seaman, review of *The Meadowlands: Wilderness Adventures at the Edge of a City,* p. 1088; September 15, 1998, Brad Hooper, review of *The Meadowlands,* p. 189; October 1, 2000, Nancy Bent, review of *A Whale Hunt,* p. 309; December 1, 2000, Donna Seaman, review of *A Whale Hunt,* p. 686; April 1, 2004, Ray Olson, review of *Rats: Observations on the History and Habitat of the City's Most Unwanted Inhabitants,* p. 1338; April 1, 2005, Gillian Engberg, "The Alex Awards, 2005," p. 1355.
Bookwatch, July, 2005, review of *Rats.*
Commonweal, June 19, 1998, George W. Hunt, review of *The Meadowlands,* p. 25; April 7, 2006, Peter Quinn, "Don't Worry, Be Happy," review of *How Not to Get Rich; or, Why Being Bad Off Isn't So Bad,* p. 26.
Entertainment Weekly, March 26, 2004, Gregory Kirschling, "The Rat Packer," p. 77; June 30, 2006, Gilbert Cruz, review of *Cross Country,* p. 165.
Forbes FYI, March 29, 2004, review of *Rats,* p. 84.
Kirkus Reviews, January 15, 2004, review of *Rats,* p. 77; May 1, 2006, review of *Cross Country,* p. 450.
Library Journal, July, 1998, Lonnie Weatherby, review of *The Meadowlands,* p. 120; March 1, 2004, Michael D. Cramer, review of *Rats,* p. 100; Library Journal, June 1, 2006, Mari Flynn, review of *Cross Country,* p. 140.
Mother Jones, September-October, 2006, Jon Mooallem, "Running on Empty: Looking for America in the Wild Red Yonder," review of *Cross Country,* p. 97.
Natural History, May, 2004, Laurence A. Marschall, review of *Rats,* p. 54.

People, July 17, 2006, Natalie Danford and Emily Chenoweth, review of *Cross Country,* p. 49.

Publishers Weekly, February 16, 1998, review of *The Meadowlands,* p. 194; October 2, 2000, review of *A Whale Hunt,* p. 66; February 2, 2004, review of *Rats,* p. 65; May 1, 2006, review of *Cross Country,* p. 50; May 22, 2006, A. Boaz, "PW Talks with Robert Sullivan," p. 40.

School Library Journal, September, 2004, Jamie Watson, review of *Rats,* p. 237; April, 2005, review of *Rats,* p. S67.

Spectator, January 22, 2005, Sara Wheeler, "The Year of the Rat," p. 34.

U.S. News & World Report, July 3, 2006, Christopher Elliott, interview with Robert Sullivan, p. 49.

ONLINE

BookBrowse.com, http://www.bookbrowse.com/ (January 2, 2007), author biography.

New York Times Book Review Online, http://www.nytimes.com/ (October 15, 2000), Nathaniel Philbrick, "In a Gray Area"; (April 4, 2004), William Grimes, "Pack Journalism"; (December 18, 2005), Tara McKelvey, "Nonfiction Chronicle"; (July 2, 2006), Bruce Barcott, "Are We There Yet?"; (July 14, 2006), Finn-Olaf Jones, "An Impala's-Eye View of Highway History."

Powell's Online, http://www.powells.com/ (April 21, 2004) David Weich, "Walled in with Robert Sullivan."

*   *   *

SUMMERS, Andrew James
    See SUMMERS, Andy

*   *   *

SUMMERS, Andy 1942-
    (Andrew James Summers)

PERSONAL: Born December 31, 1942, in Poulton-Fylde, England; married Robin Lane, 1968 (divorced, 1970), married Kate Unter, 1973 (divorced, 1981; remarried, 1985); children (with second wife): Layla Z. Summers, Anton Y. Summers and Maurice X. Summers (twins); Andrew (from another relationship). *Education:* Studied classical composition and guitar at the University of California, Los Angeles, 1969-73.

ADDRESSES: *Home*—Los Angeles, CA. *Agent*—Susan Schulman, A Literary Agency, 454 W. 44th St., New York, NY 10036.

CAREER: Guitarist, songwriter. Worked variously as a musician, playing with Big Roll Band, on their album *The All Happening Zoot Money's Big Roll Band at Klook's Kleek,* Dantalion's Chariot, Soft Machine, the Animals, on their album *Love Is,* and as back up for performers Neil Sedaka, Kevin Coyne, and Kevin Ayers; The Police, guitarist, 1977-1984, on their albums *Outlandos D'Amour,* 1978, *Reggatta De Blanc,* 1979, *Zenyatta Mondatta,* 1980, *Ghosts in the Machine,* 1981, and *Synchronicity,* 1983; collaborated with Robert Fripp on two albums; performed as a solo artist and on film scores. Has appeared as an actor and/or musician in several films and television programs.

AWARDS, HONORS: *Guitar Player* Readers Poll, best pop guitarist, 1984-89; Orville H. Gibson Lifetime Achievement Award, 2000.

WRITINGS:

SOUND RECORDINGS

(With Robert Fripp) *I Advance Masked,* A&M (Los Angeles, CA), 1982.

Throb, Quill (New York, NY), 1983.

(With Robert Fripp) *Bewitched,* A&M (Los Angeles, CA), 1984.

(Contributor) *Down and Out in Beverly Hills* (soundtrack), MCA (Universal City, CA), 1986.

XYZ, MCA (Universal City, CA), 1987.

Mysterious Barricades, Private Music (New York, NY), 1988.

(Contributor) *Out of Time* (soundtrack), MCA (Universal City, CA), 1988.

(Contributor) *End of the Line* (soundtrack), MCA (Universal City, CA), 1988.

The Golden Wire, Private Music (New York, NY), 1989.

(Contributor) *A Weekend at Bernie's* (soundtrack), MCA (Universal City, CA), 1989.

Charming Snakes, Private Music (New York, NY), 1990.

World Gone Strange, Private Music (New York, NY), 1991.

Andy Summers, MCA (Universal City, CA), 1991.

Invisible Threads, Private Music (New York, NY), 1993.

Synaesthesia, CMP (Minneapolis, MN), 1995.

The Last Dance of Mr. X, Private Music (New York, NY), 1997.

A Windham Hill Retrospective, Windham Hill Records, 1998.

Green Chimneys: The Music of Thelonious Monk, RCA (New York, NY), 1999.

Peggy's Blue Skylight, BMG International, 2000.

Earth & Sky, Basement Music, 2004.

The X Tracks: Best of Andy Summers, Random Music UK, 2005.

OTHER

Light Strings: Impressions of the Guitar (photographs by Ralph Gibson), Chronicle (San Francisco, CA), 2004.

One Train Later: A Memoir, Thomas Dunne Books (New York, NY), 2006.

I'll Be Watching You: Inside The Police, 1980-83 (photography), Taschen (New York, NY), 2007.

SIDELIGHTS: Guitarist and songwriter Andy Summers grew up in Bournemouth, England, where his father owned a restaurant. He was first exposed to music through his brother's jazz record collection, the local jazz scene, and his own childhood piano lessons. Summers loved music and soon moved on to playing the guitar, becoming truly serious about music when he was fourteen years old. His first regular gig was at a local jazz club with a hotel band when he was just sixteen. He then met George "Zoot" Money, and the two went to London to form the rhythm-and-blues band, the Big Roll Band jazz ensemble, and record the album, *The All Happening Zoot Money's Big Roll Band at Klook's Kleek.* From there, Summers went on to play with a number of groups, including Dantalion's Chariot, Soft Machine, and the Animals. Then in the spring of 1977, he met rockers Stewart Copeland

and Sting of the newly formed band The Police at an event in London. Summers went on to join the band, becoming their primary guitar player when their previous guitarist Henri Padovani left the group. The Police experienced a rapid rise in popularity, and Summers contributed to that success, playing on the group's most famous albums, including *Outlandos D'Amour,* in 1978, *Reggatta De Blanc,* in 1979, *Zenyatta Mondatta,* in 1980, *Ghosts in the Machine,* in 1981, and *Synchronicity,* in 1983. Although the group eventually disbanded, Summers continued to produce music, in conjunction with guitarist Robert Fripp, and as a solo artist. On his own, he returned to his jazz roots, producing a number of jazz albums, including *The Last Dance of Mr. X.*

In addition to his music, Summers has written a book on playing the guitar, *Light Strings: Impressions of the Guitar,* which includes photographs by Ralph Gibson, and an autobiographical work, *One Train Later: A Memoir.* Summer's memoir deals both with his meteoric rise with The Police and with his earlier career as part of the British rock scene in the 1960s, and what it was like to grow up in England in the 1950s. Todd Spires, in a review for the *Library Journal,* remarked: "This terrific book should be in demand in public libraries." Dave Itzkoff, writing for the *New York Times,* noted that Summers remained "sufficiently impartial to recognize that The Police were beneficiaries of both talent and good timing." A reviewer for *Publishers Weekly* called the book "an honest travelogue of a British kid who, . . . traversed the most coveted landscapes of pop culture and lived to write about it." Summers himself remarked of his experience with The Police: "I wish I could put my finger on why we we're so successful. I think everyone wants to understand that secret. I think because the reggae/ska sound was relatively new to the States, and had not been worked into the pop/punk hybrid coming out of the UK, people were just completely turned on by it. We loved the freedom of working in a number of forms, and creating a signature sound that took years for others to duplicate."

BIOGRAPHICAL AND CRITICAL SOURCES:

BOOKS

Summers, Andy, *One Train Later: A Memoir,* Thomas Dunne Books (New York, NY), 2006.

PERIODICALS

Amusement Business, March 6, 2000, "Andy Summers," p. 8.

Booklist, September 15, 2006, June Sawyers, review of *One Train Later,* p. 15.

Entertainment Weekly, September 29, 2006, Michael Endelman, Lisa Greenblatt, "Rock of Pages," p. 86.

Guitar Player, January, 1998, Jas Obrecht, "Andy Summers: Out of the Jazz Closet," p. 29; January, 2001, Adam Levy, "Harmonic Divergence," p. 84; March, 2005, Julia Crowe, "Dynamic Duo: Andy Summers and Ben Verdery Collaborate on a Classical Concerto and an Ambient Jamfest," p. 66.

Kirkus Reviews, August 1, 2006, review of *One Train Later,* p. 775.

Library Journal, December 15, 1983, GraceAnne A. DeCandido, review of *Throb,* p. 2327; August 1, 2006, Todd Spires, review of *One Train Later,* p. 89.

Los Angeles Times, November 20, 1983, Kristine McKenna, review of *Throb,* p. 90.

New York Times Book Review, December 4, 1983, Janet Maslin, review of *Throb,* p. 73.

People, December 19, 1983, review of *Throb,* p. 20.

Publishers Weekly, July 31, 2006, review of *One Train Later,* p. 63.

Studio Photography & Design, November, 2004, review of *Light Strings: Impressions of the Guitar,* p. 49.

Teen, November, 1983, "The Police: Music's Most Arresting Superstars," p. 47.

WWD, November 10, 2004, Rose Apodaca, review of *Light Strings,* p. 24.

ONLINE

Andy Summers Home Page, http://www.andysummers.com (January 25, 2007).

Internet Movie Database, http://www.imdb.com/ (January 25, 2007), author biography.

Joyzine, http://www.artistwd.com/joyzine/ (January 25, 2007), Joy Williams, author interview.

Larry Sakin Blog, http://mytown.ca/sakin/ (October 27, 2006), author interview.

New York Times Book Review Online, http://www.nytimes.com/ (December 3, 2006), Dave Itzkoff, review of *One Train Later.*

VH-1 Web site, http://www.vh1.com/ (January 25, 2007), artist biography.

* * *

SUTHERLAND, Amy

PERSONAL: Married. *Education:* University of Paris, certificate, 1980; University of Cincinnati, B.A., 1982; Northwestern University, M.S.J., 1987.

ADDRESSES: Home—Boston, MA. *Agent*—Jane Chelius Literary Agency, 548 2nd St., Brooklyn, NY 11215; fax: 718-499-0714. *E-mail*—info@amysutherland.com.

CAREER: Reporter and author. *Burlington Free Press,* Burlington, VT, arts and entertainment reporter, 1988-92; *Portland Press Herald,* Portland, ME, arts and features reporter, 1993-2001; Boston University Department of Journalism, Boston, MA, lecturer, 2006—.

AWARDS, HONORS: Thomas A. Gallagher Award for Outstanding Achievement in Article Writing, Iota Sigma Epsilon Writing Contest, 1988; John D. Donoghue Award for Arts Criticism, Vermont Press Association, 1991; Barnes and Noble Discover Great New Writer, fall, 2003.

WRITINGS:

Cookoff: Recipe Fever in America, Viking (New York, NY), 2003.

Kicked, Bitten, and Scratched: Life and Lessons at the World's Premier School for Exotic Animal Trainers, Viking (New York, NY), 2006.

Contributor to numerous newspapers, including *Portland Press Herald,* Portland, ME; *Los Angeles Times, Boston Globe, Art New England, Artist's Magazine, Cincinnati Magazine, Cincinnati Post, Cooking Light, DownEast, Family Fun, Ohio Magazine, Restaurant Business News, UVM Quarterly, Vermont Magazine, Christian Science Monitor,* and *Disney Magazine.*

SIDELIGHTS: After graduating from Northwestern University with a graduate degree in journalism, Amy Sutherland worked as a features reporter for a number of New England newspapers. It was while working at the *Portland Free Press* in Maine that Sutherland first became enamored of cooking, a passion that ultimately translated into a regular column about food. An assignment on the Pillsbury Bake-Off piqued Sutherland's interest, and eventually lured her into the world of competitive cooking. She commented to *Salon.com* contributor Rebecca Traister: "I was intrigued that the Bake-Off was still around and still very vibrant in a day and age when more women were working and American cooking was getting so much respect. It was a strange anachronism, this thing that was still kicking." After a year traveling the cookoff circuit, Sutherland wrote a book on the topic, *Cookoff: Recipe Fever in America.* A reviewer for *Publishers Weekly* called the book a "wonderful portrait of a true slice of Americana." *Library Journal* contributor Peter Hepburn commented: "The reader will enjoy what amounts to a series of short epics. . . . An engrossing read."

Sutherland's next book focuses on a unique degree-granting program in which students learn to handle, train, and manage animals. She spent a year working with both the trainers and trainees as part of Moorpark College's Exotic Animal Training Management Program, an experience culminating in 2006's *Kicked, Bitten, and Scratched: Life and Lessons at the World's Premier School for Exotic Animal Trainers.* *Moorpark Acorn Online* reporter Sylvie Belmond wrote: "The book reads like a novel, but the story is real and Sutherland sheds light on the unassuming zoo nestled above Moorpark College." A *Publishers Weekly* contributor described *Kicked, Bitten, and Scratched* as "a fascinating study in human as well as animal behavior."

BIOGRAPHICAL AND CRITICAL SOURCES:

PERIODICALS

Library Journal, September 15, 2003, Peter Hepburn, review of *Cookoff: Recipe Fever in America,* p. 83.
Publishers Weekly, September 15, 2003, review of *Cookoff,* p. 55; March 13, 2006, review of *Kicked,*

Bitten, and Scratched: Life and Lessons at the World's Premier School for Exotic Animal Trainers, p. 51.

ONLINE

Amy Sutherland Home Page, http://www.amysutherland.com (November 11, 2006).
Moorpark Acorn Online, http://www.mpacorn.com/ (June 9, 2006), Sylvie Belmond, "Author Explores Magic of Moorpark Training Zoo."
Salon.com, http://www.salon.com/ (November 13, 2003), Rebecca Traister, "Classic American Food Fights."

*   *   *

SWEENEY, Michael S. 1958(?)-

PERSONAL: Born c. 1958; married; wife's name Carolyn (a technical writer and editor); children: David. *Education:* University of Nebraska, B.A., 1980; University of North Texas, M.J., 1991; University of Ohio, Ph.D., 1996.

ADDRESSES: Home—Logan, UT. *Office*—Journalism & Communication, Utah State University, Room 310-B, Animal Science Building, Logan, UT 84322-4605. *E-mail*—mike.sweeney@usu.edu.

CAREER: Nebraska Press Association, photographer, 1978-80; *Springfield Daily News,* education reporter, 1980-81, general assignment reporter, 1981; *Star-Telegram,* Fort Worth, TX, copy editor, 1981-87, copy desk chief, 1987-89, deputy features editor, 1989-93; Texas Christian University, Fort Worth, adjunct professor, 1992; Ohio University, Athens, teaching associate, 1993-96; Utah State University, Logan, assistant professor, 1996-2002, associate professor, 2002-06, professor of journalism, 2006—.

MEMBER: Association of Educational Journalism and Mass Communication, American Journalism Historians Association (chair of research committee, 2006).

AWARDS, HONORS: Book of the Year award, American Journalism Historians Association, and outstanding academic title citation, *Choice,* both 2001, both for *Secrets of Victory: The Office of Censorship and the American Press and Radio in World War II.*

WRITINGS:

Secrets of Victory: The Office of Censorship and the American Press and Radio in World War II, University of North Carolina Press (Chapel Hill, NC), 2001.
(Author of text) *From the Front: The Story of War,* National Geographic (New York, NY), 2002.
(With Janet F. Davidson) *On the Move: Transportation and the American Story,* National Geographic (New York, NY), 2003.
(With Robert D. Ballard) *Return to Titanic: A New Look at the World's Most Famous Lost Ship,* National Geographic (Washington, DC), 2004.
The Military and the Press: An Uneasy Truce, Northwestern University Press (Evanston, IL), 2006.
Last Unspoiled Place: Utah's Logan Canyon, National Geographic (Washington, DC), 2007.
(With John Bul Dau) *God Grew Tired of Us,* National Geographic (Washington, DC), 2007.

Contributor to numerous periodicals and scholarly journals, including *Journalism and Mass Communication Quarterly, Journalism History,* and *American Journalism.*

SIDELIGHTS: Michael S. Sweeney is a writer and educator who wanted to be a journalist from the time he was fourteen, when he worked delivering copies of the *Washington Evening Star* to the University of Maryland's student housing. He went on to study journalism at the University of Nebraska at Lincoln, earning his B.A., and then earned his master's degree at the University of North Texas. Sweeney cites his college reporting professor, Jim Patten, as having a profound effect on his development through his insistence on accuracy, and also Gale Baldwin, his first city editor, who allowed Sweeney to watch him correct his stories so he could understand why he made the changes that he did. Sweeney went on to

work as a journalist for over a decade before turning his attention to teaching, and the opportunity to share his experience with young journalism students.

Since beginning his academic career, Sweeney has written a number of books. His *Secrets of Victory: The Office of Censorship and the American Press and Radio in World War II* is a study of wartime censorship of print and electronic media in the United States during World War II, conducted primarily in the interests of national security. Sweeney describes the creation of a national Office of Censorship in the period immediately after the Japanese attack on Pearl Harbor, and examines how that office was able to work effectively throughout the war to stifle, among other stories, reporting on the development of atomic weapons and on President Roosevelt's travels. Sweeney shows how the director of the Office of Censorship, Byron Price, was able to control most reporters by persuasion rather than threat, because Price himself was a respected Associated Press journalist. A *Publishers Weekly* contributor called *Secrets of Victory* "an even-paced, exhaustively researched" book, and Gerald R. Costa, in a review for the *Library Journal,* deemed it "timely and important." *Secrets of Victory* won the 2001 Book of the Year award from the American Journalism Historians Association.

Sweeney is also author of the text for *From the Front: The Story of War,* an illustrated volume of photographs and dispatches from American war correspondents. With Janet F. Davidson, he also released *On the Move: Transportation and the American Story,* a companion volume to a Smithsonian Institution exhibit on travel patterns in America. Jim Ross, in a review for *American Road,* found the book to be "tightly packed with a wealth of historical facts and anecdotes that make reading it a trip worthwhile." Gilbert Taylor, writing for *Booklist,* found that "the crowd-pleasing authors hit on all cylinders."

The Military and the Press: An Uneasy Truce looks at the relationship between the military and the press through the decades, particularly during times of war when freedom of speech can work against the military's need to protect their objectives. In a review for *Journalism History,* contributors David Copeland and Karen Miller Russell noted: "Even though Sweeney is a former journalist, this history is not written solely from the point of view of the press, and this may be the most valuable element of this book."

BIOGRAPHICAL AND CRITICAL SOURCES:

PERIODICALS

American Historical Review, February, 2002, David F. Krugler, review of *Secrets of Victory: The Office of Censorship and the American Press and Radio in World War II,* p. 237.

American Road, autumn, 2004, Jim Ross, *On the Move: Transportation and the American Story,* p. 61.

Booklist, November 15, 2002, Gilbert Taylor, review of *From the Front: The Story of War,* p. 550; December 1, 2003, Gilbert Taylor, review of *On the Move,* p. 638.

Book World, May 27, 2001, review of *Secrets of Victory,* p. 8.

Choice, July-August, 2001, R.J. Goldstein, review of *Secrets of Victory,* p. 2025.

Columbia Journalism Review, March, 2001, James Boylan, review of *Secrets of Victory,* p. 70.

Globe and Mail (Toronto, Ontario, Canada), November 23, 2003, review of *From the Front.*

Historian, winter, 2002, Frank Warren, review of *Secrets of Victory,* p. 477.

International History Review, March, 2002, Lawrence C. Soley, review of *Secrets of War,* p. 186.

Journal of American History, March, 2002, Holly C. Shulman, review of *Secrets of Victory,* p. 1590.

Journal of Military History, July, 2001, William M. Hammond, review of *Secrets of Victory,* p. 840.

Journalism History, fall, 2006, David Copeland, Karen Miller Russell, review of *The Military and the Press.*

Library Journal, February 15, 2001, Gerald R. Costa, review of *Secrets of Victory,* p. 184.

Political Communication, January-March, 2004, Doris A. Graber, review of *Secrets of Victory,* pp. 133-136.

Publishers Weekly, February 26, 2001, review of *Secrets of Victory,* p. 76.

Washington Post, May 27, 2001, "Allied Confidential," p. T08.

ONLINE

Utah State University Web site, http://www.usu.edu/ (January 2, 2007), faculty biography.

SYKES, Tom 1974(?)-

PERSONAL: Born c. 1974; married; children: one son. *Education:* Attended Eton College.

ADDRESSES: Home—Ireland.

CAREER: Evening Standard, London, England, former writer; *British GQ,* London, England, former writer; *New York Post,* New York, NY, former night-life columnist.

WRITINGS:

What Did I Do Last Night? A Drunkard's Tale (memoir), Rodale (Emmaus, PA), 2006.

Contributor to various periodicals, including *Men's Vogue, British GQ,* and the *Evening Standard.*

SIDELIGHTS: Writer and journalist Tom Sykes got his start living the high life as a student at Eton in England, where his drinking and partying eventually got him expelled. However, coming from an established family—his sisters are Lucy, Plum, and Alice Sykes, all known for their appearances in the society pages and Plum for her own writing efforts, while his grandfather wrote Eveyln Waugh's biography—Sykes found himself afforded numerous second chances. He went on to write for a series of publications, first in London and then in New York, continuing his active nightlife as the years went on, though his behavior resulted in several lost jobs. However, his glittering personality aided him in continually landing on his feet. Finally, while working as the nightlife columnist for the *New York Post,* Sykes hit bottom, and was forced to address his growing addiction to alcohol and narcotics. *What Did I Do Last Night? A Drunkard's Tale* is Sykes's account of his experiences, from his childhood encounters with alcohol to his raucous days as a reporter on the town who never needed to pay for his meals or liquor. Ian Chipman, writing for *Booklist,* remarked: "Sykes's reflective humor . . . and his rapid, easy pacing keep this telling crisp, riotous, and not entirely unrepentant." A contributor for *Publishers Weekly* called the book "a raw, dizzying testimony," and concluded: "Throughout, Sykes's voice is candid and the details gritty." Once out of rehab, Sykes moved to Ireland, where he lives with his wife and son.

BIOGRAPHICAL AND CRITICAL SOURCES:

BOOKS

Sykes, Tom, *What Did I Do Last Night? A Drunkard's Tale,* Rodale (Emmaus, PA), 2006.

PERIODICALS

Booklist, September 1, 2006, Ian Chipman, review of *What Did I Do Last Night?,* p. 32.

People, November 13, 2006, Josh Emmons, review of *What Did I Do Last Night?,* p. 51.

Publishers Weekly, September 18, 2006, review of *What Did I Do Last Night?,* p. 51.

ONLINE

Bookseller.com, http://www.thebookseller.com/ (October 27, 2006), "Tom Sykes: Legless in Manhattan."

Get Underground Web site, http://www.getunderground.com/ (December 1, 2006), Q & A with Tom Sykes.

New York Times Book Review Online, November 19, 2006, Campbell Robertson, "Drinking on the Job."

PR Web Direct Web site, http://www.prwebdirect.com/ (October 5, 2006), "Eton College: Breeding Ground for Teenage Alcoholics?"*

T

TAL, Eve 1947-

PERSONAL: Born 1947, in Rockville Centre, NY; children: Erez (son). *Education:* Oberlin College, B.A.; Hollins University, M.A., 2006.

ADDRESSES: Home and office—Kibbutz Hatzor, Israel. *E-mail*—contact@eve-tal.com.

CAREER: Educator and author. Kibbutz Cabri, Israel, English teacher; has worked as a secretary, copywriter, events planner, and fund raiser.

MEMBER: Society of Children's Book Writers and Illustrators.

AWARDS, HONORS: Israeli Museum Honor Award for illustrations by Ora Swartz, for *I Want to Go Home;* National Jewish Book Award runner-up, 2005, and Paterson Prize for Books for Young People, *Skipping Stone* Honor Award, International Reading Association Notable Book for a Global Society designation, and Association of Jewish Libraries Notable Children's Book of Jewish Content, all 2006, all for *Double Crossing.*

WRITINGS:

HaAgalah borahat, illustrated by Ora Swartz, Sifriyat (Tel-Aviv, Israel), 1985, translation published as *A New Boy* (bilingual English/Hebrew), Milk and Honey Press (Denver, CO), 2006.

Double Crossing: A Jewish Immigration Story for Young Adults, Cinco Puntos Press (El Paso, TX), 2005.

Also author of Hebrew-language picture books with titles translated as *The Runaway Carriage, New Kid in the Class, I Want to Go Home,* and *Not Afraid of Dogs.*

SIDELIGHTS: Growing up in the United States, Eve Tal enjoyed writing and reading. However, as she got older and began working, traveling, and raising her family, Tal's writing was relegated to hobby status. Eventually moving to Israel, Tal began teaching English at Kibbutz Cabri, a collective farm, and her interest in writing was rekindled. In addition to creating picture-book texts in Hebrew, Tal also draws on her family history in a longer work of fiction, the award-winning children's novel *Double Crossing: A Jewish Immigration Story for Young Adults.*

Double Crossing opens in 1905 as eleven-year-old Raizel Balaban and her sickly father emigrate from Ukraine to the United States in search of a better life. At the turn of the twentieth century, Eastern Europe was plagued by hard times, and the region's Jewish population suffered immensely. Forced undercover because of laws against Jewish emigration, the two make it to the Russian coast and across the ocean to Ellis Island only after a long journey. While father and daughter are initially refused entry by U.S. immigration authorities due to concerns about Papa's poor health, Papa's willingness to forgo his traditional Orthodox Jewish customs and Americanize ultimately gains them entry. With the help of his daughter,

Binyumin Balaban becomes Benjamin Altman, an American. "Tal's fictionalized account of her grandfather's journey to America is fast paced, full of suspense, and highly readable," remarked Rachel Kamin in a review for *School Library Journal,* while *Kliatt* contributor Janis Flint-Ferguson praised the book's "haunting images" of the immigrant experience. Hazel Rochman, writing in *Booklist,* cited Tal's surprise ending for providing readers with a version "of the immigration story [that has been] left too long untold."

On her home page Tal provided advice for aspiring writers: "Write. Don't talk about it. Do it. And then rewrite. Find people who can provide insightful criticism. Rewrite. And then submit. But most important, don't give up. Stubbornness is a writer's most important trait. Or, if you want to be fancy, call it dedication."

BIOGRAPHICAL AND CRITICAL SOURCES:

PERIODICALS

Booklist, August, 2005, Hazel Rochman, review of *Double Crossing: A Jewish Immigration Story for Young Adults,* p. 1967.
Bulletin of the Center for Children's Books, February, 2006, Hope Morrison, review of *Double Crossing,* p. 288.
Kirkus Reviews, October 1, 2005, review of *Double Crossing,* p. 1091.
Kliatt, January, 2006, Janis Flint-Ferguson, review of *Double Crossing,* p. 13.
School Library Journal, October, 2005, Rachel Kamin, review of *Double Crossing,* p. 175.
Voice of Youth Advocates, April, 2006, Beth Karpas, review of *Double Crossing,* p. 52.

ONLINE

Eve Tal Home Page, http://www.eve-tal.com (February 3, 2007).*

*   *   *

THACKER, Brian 1962-

PERSONAL: Born 1962, in England; immigrated to Australia; married; wife's name Natalie; children: Jasmine.

ADDRESSES: Home—East St. Kilda, Victoria, Australia. *E-mail*—brian@brianthacker.tv.

CAREER: Worked as an advertising agency art director in London England; tour guide and ski guide in Europe; writer, 2003—.

WRITINGS:

Rule No. 5—No Sex on the Bus: Confessions of a Tour Leader (memoir), Allen & Unwin (Crows Nest, New South Wales, Australia), 2001.
Planes, Trains & Elephants, Allen & Unwin (Crows Nest, New South Wales, Australia), 2002.
The Naked Man Festival: And Other Excuses to Fly around the World (memoir), Allen & Unwin (Crows Nest, New South Wales, Australia), 2004.
I'm Not Eating Any of That Foreign Muck: Travels with Me Dad (memoir), Allen & Unwin (Crows Nest, New South Wales, Australia), 2005.

SIDELIGHTS: Brian Thacker was born in England and moved to Australia with his family when he was six. As a student, he took an advertising course, then hitchhiked around Europe before returning to London and working for two years at an advertising agency. Travel was in Thacker's blood, however, and he returned to Europe to work as a tour and ski guide. Three years later, he went back to his advertising career, which lasted until 2003, at which time Thacker turned his full attention to writing. According to his Web site, Thacker has visited seventy-two countries, seventy-three, he notes, if you count Tasmania.

Thacker's first book, *Rule No. 5—No Sex on the Bus: Confessions of a Tour Leader,* includes many anecdotes about the consumption of both sex and beer. Thacker writes amusingly of both the good and bad experiences of twenty tour trips he conducted.

Thacker was inspired to write *The Naked Man Festival: And Other Excuses to Fly around the World* because during his backpacking days, he often had his best experiences at festivals that were being held in various locations he visited, ranging from a beer festival in Germany, to the Snow Festival in Japan, to a voodoo ceremony in Haiti. In an interview with *Bant* contributor James Hakan Dedeoglu, Thacker said that the most unusual festivals are held in Japan and the United States. "Only in Japan could you attend (and participate in) a Penis Festival, a Used Pins and Needles Festival, a Crying Baby Festival, a Staring Festival, a Quarreling Festival and a Knickers Festival. The King of Kook crown, however, belongs to the good ol' U.S. of A., where you can party on at the Testicle Festival, the Snowman Burning Festival, the Barbed Wire Festival, the Big Whopper Liar's Festival, the Roadkill Festival and the Rotten Sneaker Festival."

Thacker's father, Harry, lived in many places, including Gibraltar, Malta, Sri Lanka, and Singapore, before settling in Australia with his family. Thacker revisited these places with him in order to better understand the man, who had retained his conservative values, love of beer, and preference for heavy English foods. *Booklist* reviewer Mark Knoblauch described Thacker's memoir, *I'm Not Eating Any of That Foreign Muck: Travels with Me Dad* as "an amusing portrait of a prickly but affectionate father-son relationship."

BIOGRAPHICAL AND CRITICAL SOURCES:

BOOKS

Rule No. 5—No Sex on the Bus: Confessions of a Tour Leader (memoir), Allen & Unwin (Crows Nest, New South Wales, Australia), 2001.
The Naked Man Festival: And Other Excuses to Fly around the World (memoir), Allen & Unwin (Crows Nest, New South Wales, Australia), 2004.
I'm Not Eating Any of That Foreign Muck: Travels with Me Dad (memoir), Allen & Unwin (Crows Nest, New South Wales, Australia), 2005.

PERIODICALS

Booklist, September 15, 2006, Mark Knoblauch, review of I'm Not Eating Any of That Foreign Muck, p. 23.

ONLINE

Aussiereviews.com, http://www.aussiereviews.com/ (February 3, 2007), Sally Murphy, review of The Naked Man Festival.

Bant Online (Turkey), http://www.bantdergi.com/ (February 3, 2007), James Hakan Dedeoglu, "Brian Thacker" (interview).
Brian Thacker Home Page, http://www.brianthacker.tv (February 3, 2007).
Northern Rivers Echo Online, http://www.echonews.com/ (February 3, 2007), Evelyn Gough, review of Rule No. 5—No Sex on the Bus.*

*   *   *

THEISEN, Gordon

PERSONAL: Born in Queens, NY; married; children: one son. *Education:* State University of New York at Binghamton, Ph.D.

ADDRESSES: Home—Carrboro, NC.

CAREER: Writer. Worked variously as a landscaper, dishwasher, barback, cashier, library clerk, construction worker, telemarketer, taxi driver, teacher, and proofreader.

WRITINGS:

(With John Craddock) *The Buzz on Golf*, Lebhar-Friedman Books (New York, NY), 2001.
The Buzz on Gambling, Lebhar-Friedman Books (New York, NY), 2001.
Staying Up Much Too Late: Edward Hopper's "Nighthawks" and the Dark Side of the American Psyche, T. Dunne Books (New York, NY), 2006.

Writer of single-sheet guides for the History Channel.

SIDELIGHTS: Gordon Theisen's *Staying Up Much Too Late: Edward Hopper's "Nighthawks" and the Dark Side of the American Psyche* is a study of the early 1940s Hopper painting of a New York diner, late at night and nearly empty but for a couple, a single man sitting alone, and the worker behind the counter. Hopper (1882-1967), whose themes most often represent urban isolation, has said that he feels the painting represents the loneliness of a big city. The painting hangs in the Art Institute of Chicago.

Theisen sees more, however, including his suggestion that the customers may be planning to rob the diner. A *Publishers Weekly* reviewer noted that he refers to the wide-screen proportions of the painting, although that film technology had yet to be invented. The reviewer felt that "some readers may conclude that Nighthawks is better off letting its powerful imagery speak for itself." A *Kirkus Reviews* contributor noted that Theisen provides histories of not only diners, but of coffee, cigars, and cigarettes, which he feels are relevant to the painting. He also alludes to the plots of films, such as *The Asphalt Jungle* and *Taxi Driver.* The reviewer wrote that Theisen "makes some worthwhile points when discussing Hopper and film noir, a genre the artist apparently admired," but concluded by describing the book as being "an overreaching microanalysis."

In reviewing *Staying Up Much Too Late* for *Seven Oaks Online,* George Fetherling commented that Theisen uses the painting to explore biblical thinking, "the reckless optimism of the New Testament and the depressive apocalyptic vision of the Old." He notes that Hopper, who was a descendant of the Puritans, "was torn between these extremes and his work was to some extent a means for him to negotiate a middle path."

BIOGRAPHICAL AND CRITICAL SOURCES:

PERIODICALS

Kirkus Reviews, May 15, 2006, review of *Staying Up Much Too Late: Edward Hopper's "Nighthawks" and the Dark Side of the American Psyche,* p. 512.
Publishers Weekly, May 22, 2006, review of *Staying Up Much Too Late,* p. 46.

ONLINE

Seven Oaks Online, http://www.sevenoaksmag.com/ (December 26, 2006), George Fetherling, review of *Staying Up Much Too Late.**

*   *   *

THOMPSON, Diane P. 1940-

PERSONAL: Born October 3, 1940, in Los Angeles, CA; daughter of Solomon (in sales) and Blanche (a homemaker) Eisenbach; married H. Paul Thompson (a systems analyst), July 12, 1960; children: Bryan, Eric.

Ethnicity: "Jewish." *Education:* University of California, Los Angeles, B.A., 1961, M.A., 1963; City University of New York, Ph.D., 1981. *Politics:* Independent. *Religion:* "Independent." *Hobbies and other interests:* Yoga, cooking, gardening.

ADDRESSES: Home—Reston, VA. *Office*—Department of English, Northern Virginia Community College, Neabsco Mills Rd., Woodbridge, VA 22191. *E-mail*—dthompson@nvcc.edu.

CAREER: Northern Virginia Community College, Woodbridge, professor of English, 1982—.

WRITINGS:

The Trojan War: Literature and Legends from the Bronze Age to the Present, McFarland (Jefferson, NC), 2003.

Contributor to books, including *Network-Based Classrooms: Promises and Realities,* edited by Bertram C. Bruce, Joy Kreeft Peyton, and Trent Batson, Oxford University Press (Cambridge, MA), 1993. Contributor to periodicals, including *Northern Virginia Review, Computers and Composition, Journal of Computer-Based Instruction, Journal of Teaching Writing, Teaching English in the Two-Year College, Collegiate Microcomputer,* and *Journal of the Open University Shakespeare Society.*

SIDELIGHTS: Diane P. Thompson told *CA:* "My primary interest as a scholar is in the past 3,000 years of stories about the Trojan War. Why the Trojan War? Because, aside from the Bible, there is no other set of written stories that have been retold for such a long period of time. Not only are there many great stories about this ancient war (such as Homer's *Iliad,* Euripides's *Iphigenia,* Virgil's *Aeneid,* and Chaucer's *Troilus and Criseyde*) but, strangely enough, stories of that war continue to be retold, right up to the present. The Trojan War came at the end of the long, wealthy, stable Mediterranean Bronze Age. Troy and the other great cities of that time were destroyed by war, and many were never rebuilt. The time was an end of civilization; everyone lost, the winners as well as the losers.

"My interest in Troy began in graduate school, and I wrote my dissertation on Troy stories from Homer to Shakespeare. My question at that time was whether any of the great writers who had told stories about the fall of Troy had any useful answers about why and how great civilizations can destroy themselves and who was responsible. I really found no answers, except the sad acknowledgement that Troy fell because rulers and their advisors made rather small mistakes that grew into major disasters. It took me years to realize that I was asking the wrong question, one to which there will never be any good answers.

"I no longer look for truth in Troy, but for a record of how many different writers, over a very long period of time, have used the event to tell their own stories of love and war, loss and death. It's a fascinating story, and the continuity of the Troy traditions helps readers to see what has remained the same and what has changed. For example, Virgil used the destruction of Troy to represent a kind of 'fortunate fall.' The small band of Trojan survivors, led by Aeneas, struggled from Troy to Italy, where they became the founders of the Roman people. A very different use of Trojan material is Goethe's idealistic use of the story of Iphigenia. Goethe transforms the daughter of Agamemnon, leader of the Greek armies against Troy, into a perfect being who can lead less perfect human beings into enlightenment, peace, and freedom.

"My book, *The Trojan War: Literature and Legends from the Bronze Age to the Present,* starts with the archaeological 'reality' of the Mediterranean Bronze Age and the actual (or probable) Trojan War and follows the path of stories about Troy from Homer through the Greek tragedies, Virgil, the Middle Ages, into Renaissance and Enlightenment Europe and to America in the twentieth century. The final chapter looks at uses of Trojan legends in current popular culture. The book is aimed at general readers, not specialized scholars. I hope to communicate my interest and pleasure in these stories to people who will enjoy the history of 3,000 years retold through great stories.

"I have developed a course about these stories, which I first taught at the Woodbridge campus of Northern Virginia Community College in the spring of 1997. The students enjoyed the reading material and found it surprisingly relevant to their own experiences and concerns. I now offer this as an Internet course through the Extended Learning Institute of the college."

THOMPSON, Neal 1965-

PERSONAL: Born 1965, in NJ; married, 1994; wife's name Mary; children: Sean, Leo. *Education:* University of Scranton, B.A., 1987.

ADDRESSES: Home—Ashville, NC. *E-mail*—neal@ nealthompson.com.

CAREER: Journalist. Worked for newspapers, including the *Philadelphia Inquirer, Roanoke Times & World-News, St. Petersburg Times,* and the *Bergen Record; Baltimore Sun,* Baltimore, MD, reporter for five years; University of North Carolina-Ashville, Great Smokies Writing Program, teacher; freelance journalist.

WRITINGS:

Light This Candle: The Life and Times of Alan Shepard, America's First Spaceman, Crown Publishers (New York, NY), 2004.
Driving with the Devil: Southern Moonshine, Detroit Wheels, and the Birth of NASCAR, Crown Publishers (New York, NY), 2006.

Contributor to periodicals including the *Outside, Esquire, Men's Health, Backpacker,* and the *Washington Post* magazine.

SIDELIGHTS: Journalist Neal Thompson wrote for a number of newspapers over a fifteen year period, focusing on investigative reporting and profiles, before settling at the *Baltimore Sun* for five years, covering the military. It was during this time that he began research on the book that would become *Light This Candle: The Life and Times of Alan Shepard, America's First Spaceman.* In the book, Thompson delves into the life of the man who was the first American in space, looking not just at his career and marriage, but at his penchant for pretty girls and his erratic temper. A reviewer for *Publishers Weekly* dubbed the book "a snappily written, factual counterbalance to Tom Wolfe's [*The Right Stuff*] sometimes poetic renderings of the heroes of the early space program." Sam Jack, in a review on his Blog, *Lowether,* noted: "Thompson does not lack for information or interesting events. Shepard was a trouble-maker for most of his life, and the book is peppered with accounts of his exploits." A contributor to *Kirkus Reviews* wrote of Thompson's effort: "Just what a biography should be: sharp, evocative, and brisk." In a review for the *Library Journal,* contributor Nancy R. Curtis noted that Thompson's book "does much to illuminate the life and personality of perhaps the most private, mad, complex member of the Mercury Seven."

In *Driving with the Devil: Southern Moonshine, Detroit Wheels, and the Birth of NASCAR,* Thompson looks at an entirely different type of adventurer, delving into the roots of stock-car racing, which go back to the days of Prohibition. Although NASCAR has developed into a family-style form of entertainment, with clean cut drivers and sponsors such as Tide, Nextel, and the U.S. Army, it used to have a far more seedy reputation. Thompson tracks the sport's progress while including entertaining stories from the its origins. A contributor to *Kirkus Reviews* said of the book: "It's a provocative premise." He went on to praise Thompson's pacing and storytelling skills, but remarked that "his awestruck worship of his subjects, voiced in purplish prose, betrays a 'homer' mindset." A reviewer for *Publishers Weekly* wrote that "the enthusiasm of this breathless, nostalgic account will be contagious to Southern history buffs and historically minded NASCAR fans." Gilbert Taylor, in a review for *Booklist,* called Thompson's effort "a colorful, multifaceted history of the hell-raising origins of stock-car racing." Writing for the *Library Journal,* Eric C. Shoaf noted that Thompson succeeded in "capturing not only the regional appeal of the sport, but also the tenor of the times."

BIOGRAPHICAL AND CRITICAL SOURCES:

PERIODICALS

Booklist, January 1, 2004, Roland Green, review of *Light This Candle: The Life and Times of Alan Shepard, America's First Spaceman,* p. 800; September 1, 2006, Gilbert Taylor, review of *Driving with the Devil: Southern Moonshine, Detroit Wheels, and the Birth of NASCAR,* p. 49.

Kirkus Reviews, January 1, 2004, review of *Light This Candle,* p. 30; August 1, 2006, review of *Driving with the Devil,* p. 775.

Library Journal, February 15, 2004, Nancy R. Curtis, review of *Light This Candle,* p. 158; August 1, 2006, Eric C. Shoaf, review of *Driving with the Devil,* p. 97.

Publishers Weekly, January 12, 2004, review of *Light This Candle,* p. 44; July 24, 2006, review of *Driving with the Devil,* p. 45.

Time, November 20, 2006, Sean Gregory, "5 Sports Books That Deserve Big Cheers," review of *Driving with the Devil,* p. 76.

ONLINE

Lowether Blog, http://www.lowether.blogspot.com/ (April 12, 2005), Sam Jack, review of *Light This Candle.*

Neal Thompson Home Page, http://www.neal thompson.com (January 25, 2007).

Neal Thompson MySpace Page, http://www.myspace. com/neal_thompson (January 25, 2007).

*   *   *

TIMBERLAKE, Amy

PERSONAL: Married. *Education:* Mount Holyoke College, graduated; University of Illinois, Chicago, M.A.

ADDRESSES: Home—Chicago, IL. *E-mail*—amy@ amytimberlake.com.

CAREER: Worked as a book reviewer, columnist, bookseller, and book event coordinator; Virginia Commission for the Arts, public information officer; writing instructor at the Hand Workshop Art Center, Richmond, VA, and at the University of Illinois, Chicago.

AWARDS, HONORS: Judy Delton scholarship, 2001; Anderson Center for Interdisciplinary Studies fellowship, 2002; Golden Kite Award, Society of Children's Book Writers and Illustrators, Parents' Choice Gold Medal, International Reading Association notable book citation, Bulletin Blue Ribbon, and Marion Vannett Ridgway Award, all for *The Dirty Cowboy.*

WRITINGS:

The Dirty Cowboy (juvenile), illustrated by Adam Rex, Farrar, Straus (New York, NY), 2003.
That Girl Lucy Moon (juvenile), Hyperion Books for Children (New York, NY), 2006.

SIDELIGHTS: Amy Timberlake's debut book for children is the multiaward-winning *The Dirty Cowboy*, a picture book illustrated by Adam Rex. Timberlake notes that the story has been handed down through generations of her family. The nameless cowboy of the title has fleas in his hair and tumbleweed in his chaps, but when he pulls a doodlebug out of his eyebrow, he decides that he has become sufficiently dirty and needs to take a bath. He goes with his dog to a New Mexico river where he tells the dog, "Dawg! No one touches these clothes but me. Hear?" He then takes a bar of lye soap and jumps into the river to scrub the smell of animals and sweat from his body. Reviewers commented on Rex's illustrations, which conceal the cowboy's private parts with a bird, a dust cloud stirred up by a rabbit, bubbles, and a frog. *New York Times Book Review* contributor Aaron Latham wrote: "I loved this artwork, I laughed at it, I didn't find it at all troubling."

When the cowboy emerges clean and odorless, his dog does not recognize his scent and refuses to let him near his master's clothes. They struggle over the clothes, the cowboy ends up as dirty as he had been before his bath, and the clothes are shredded. Ultimately, the cowboy has to walk home wearing only his hat and boots. A *Publishers Weekly* contributor wrote: "Transcending the cowboy-tale genre, this raucous romp should tickle bath-averse children everywhere." *School Library Journal* reviewer Joy Fleishhacker concluded her review by saying: "The hangdog expression on the pooch's face when he realizes his mistake is priceless. A fun look at life on the range."

Timberlake followed with *That Girl Lucy Moon*, a story for middle-grade readers. Lucy is an activist for all sorts of causes, including worker and animal rights, and is finding it difficult to adapt to junior high, where the students are primarily concerned with their hormonal development. Lucy's mother, a photographer and her closest ally, has gone on an extended trip, leaving her with her somewhat detached father. Lucy's dif-

ficulties intensify after two classmates are arrested for sledding on property owned by the wealthy Miss Ilene Viola Wiggins, who then fences off the sledding hill. Lucy retaliates by launching a "Free Wiggins Hill" campaign, but has trouble convincing the town and her friends that her actions are valid. Lee Bock wrote in the *School Library Journal:* "Ultimately, all the plot threads pull together to create a satisfying conclusion." "Lucy's a winning character, whose native fierceness and sudden uncertainty will resonate with readers," commented a *Kirkus Reviews* contributor. Jennifer Wardrip reviewed the novel for *TeensReadToo.com*, commenting: "The true gem, the delight that makes *That Girl Lucy Moon* such a wonderful novel is the very real feelings of hope and discouragement that mingle inside of the free spirit that is Lucy."

BIOGRAPHICAL AND CRITICAL SOURCES:

PERIODICALS

Booklist, September 1, 2003, Todd Morning, review of *The Dirty Cowboy,* p. 131.
Bulletin of the Center for Children's Books, October 2006, Loretta Gaffney, review of *That Girl Lucy Moon,* p. 97.
Kirkus Reviews, June 15, 2003, review of *The Dirty Cowboy,* p. 865; August 1, 2006, review of *That Girl Lucy Moon,* p. 796.
New York Times Book Review, December 7, 2003, Aaron Latham, review of *The Dirty Cowboy,* p. 78.
Publishers Weekly, July 14, 2003, review of *The Dirty Cowboy,* p. 75.
School Library Journal, September, 2003, Joy Fleishhacker, review of *The Dirty Cowboy,* p. 192; September, 2006, Glenn Bock, review of *That Girl Lucy Moon,* p. 220.

ONLINE

Amy Timberlake Home Page, http://www.amy timberlake.com (December 19, 2006).
TeensReadToo.com, http://www.teensreadtoo.com/ (December 19, 2006), Jennifer Wardrip, review of *That Girl Lucy Moon.*

TINDALL, George Brown 1921-2006

OBITUARY NOTICE— See index for *CA* sketch: Born February 26, 1921, in Greenville, SC; died of complications from diabetes, December 3, 2006, in Chapel Hill, NC. Historian, educator, and author. A retired University of North Carolina professor, Tindall was noted for his books about the modern history of the American South. Graduating from Furman University in 1942, he served in the U.S. Army Air Force during World War II and saw action in the Pacific theater. Returning to his studies after the war, he attended the University of North Carolina, earning a master's degree in 1948 and a Ph.D. in 1951. He taught briefly at Eastern Kentucky State University, the University of Mississippi, and the Women's College of the University of North Carolina in the early 1950s, and was an assistant professor at Louisiana State University from 1953 to 1958. Joining the University of North Carolina faculty, he became a full professor of history in 1964 and was named Kenan Professor in 1969. Tindall retired in 1990 as professor emeritus. As a scholar, Tindall was known for his books about the evolution of the South after the Civil War. Among his most praised works are *South Carolina Negroes, 1877-1900* (1952) and *The Emergence of the New South, 1913-1945* (1967). Other publications by Tindall include *The Persistent Tradition in New South Politics* (1975), *America: A Narrative History* (1984), and *Natives & Newcomers* (1995).

OBITUARIES AND OTHER SOURCES:

PERIODICALS

New York Times, December 8, 2006, p. C11.

*   *   *

TODD, Kim 1970-

PERSONAL: Born 1970; married; husband's name Jay; children: two (twins). *Education:* Yale University, B.A., University of Montana, M.S., M.F.A.

ADDRESSES: Home—Missoula, MT. *E-mail*—email@kimtodd.net.

CAREER: Environmental Leadership Program, senior fellow. Sierra Club national headquarters, editor, writer, and designer; taught environmental and nature writing at the University of Montana, University of California, Santa Cruz, and the Environmental Writers Institute.

AWARDS, HONORS: PEN/Jerard Award, Sigurd Olson Nature Writing Award, and *Booklist's* Top Ten Science/Technical Books designation, all for *Tinkering with Eden: A Natural History of Exotics in America.*

WRITINGS:

Tinkering with Eden: A Natural History of Exotics in America, illustrated by Claire Emery, W.W. Norton (New York, NY), 2001.
Chrysalis: Maria Sibylla Merian and the Secrets of Metamorphosis, Harcourt (Orlando, FL), 2007.

Contributor to periodicals, including *Grist, Orion, Backpacker, Northern Lights, Sierra,* and *California Wild.*

SIDELIGHTS: Kim Todd frequently writes about environmental issues and has taught environmental and nature writing at a number of colleges. In a *Grist* article she writes of her childhood as the daughter of a Bay Area Rapid Transit electrical engineer whose preferred method of getting from place to place was either public transportation or walking. Each family trip included an inspection of the local rail systems— the T in Boston, the Metro in Washington, the subway in New York. He never said that their long walks to distant destinations that included parks and playgrounds saved fuel, instead he used the walks to talk about things that interested him and about which he wanted to teach his children. Todd wrote that "nothing that I've read since I was a child, no late-night discussions, no lecture by an eminent biologist or activist has had the same effect. A book or article laying out a graceful argument for avoiding meat from factory farms or creating a compost bin might spur a week-long transformation. But at root, my sole environmental virtue springs not from logic or good intentions. It comes from him."

Todd's first book, *Tinkering with Eden: A Natural History of Exotics in America,* is a history of the introduction of nonnative species in America, some of which proved to be positive, while others were disastrous. The ladybug that was brought to California to combat the cottony cushion scale destroying orange groves continues to benefit farms and gardens, and the brown trout is a favorite of fly fishermen. Introductions such as the English sparrow, pigeon, and starling became nuisances, while others, like the gypsy moth, which was imported to attempt to breed a better silkworm, devastated half of the country after a small number escaped and spread. Some animals destroyed vegetation, such as the mountain goats that were released on Washington's Olympic Peninsula. In a review of *Tinkering with Eden*, *Library Journal* contributor Nancy Moeckel wrote that because of the debate over the release of genetically modified organisms, "there may be renewed interest in the impact of exotics."

Chrysalis: Maria Sibylla Merian and the Secrets of Metamorphosis, Todd's biography of and tribute to German naturalist Merian (1647-1717), was described by a *Kirkus Reviews* contributor as "a breathtaking example of scholarship and storytelling." Merian, daughter of a publisher, learned to draw and engrave while studying silkworm metamorphosis and painted butterfly and moth larvae as she studied a range of insects, life forms that were neglected by her male contemporaries. She considered their relationship to the environment and became a friend of naturalists and scientists, left her husband to live in the Netherlands, and sold her art to support her daughters. She published four books about caterpillars, and at the age of fifty-two, she traveled to the Amazon to study and document species and bring many home. In order to finance the trip, Merian sold everything she owned, and she faced many dangers and obstacles in accomplishing her objectives for the expedition. After she died, Peter the Great bought her field notes and paintings, which were underappreciated until well beyond the Russian revolution. A *Publishers Weekly* reviewer concluded that Todd's biography "should do much to further the renewed interest in this unusual woman and her pioneering approach to insect illustration."

BIOGRAPHICAL AND CRITICAL SOURCES:

PERIODICALS

American Scholar, spring, 2001, Chris Mooney, review of *Tinkering with Eden: A Natural History of Exotics in America,* p. 148.

Booklist, January 1, 2001, Nancy Bent, review of *Tinkering with Eden,* p. 893.
Grist, June 15, 2006, Kim Todd, "Dad Reckoning: How My Father Taught Me to Leave Cars Behind."
Kirkus Reviews, November 1, 2006, review of *Chrysalis: Maria Sibylla Merian and the Secrets of Metamorphosis,* p. 1119.
Kliatt, November, 2002, Katherine E. Gillen, review of *Tinkering with Eden,* p. 38.
Library Journal, March 1, 2001, Nancy Moeckel, review of *Tinkering with Eden,* p. 124.
New York Times Book Review, May 20, 2001, Carol Peace Robins, review of *Tinkering with Eden.*
OnEarth, winter, 2002, Anthony Jaffe, review of *Tinkering with Eden,* p. 39.
Publishers Weekly, October 2, 2006, review of *Chrysalis,* p. 47.
Science News, June 15, 2002, review of *Tinkering with Eden,* p. 383.

ONLINE

Kim Todd Home Page, http://www.kimtodd.net (January 10, 2007).

* * *

TOLL, Ian W.

PERSONAL: Married; wife's name Kathryn; children: Henry. *Education:* Georgetown University, B.A., 1989; Harvard University, M.P.P., 2005. *Hobbies and other interests:* Sailing.

ADDRESSES: Home—San Francisco, CA, and Chatham, NY. *Agent*—Elizabeth Shreve Public Relations, LLC, 6208 32nd Pl., N.W., Washington, DC 20015.

CAREER: Financial analyst, political aide, and speechwriter. Credit Suisse First, Boston, MA, worked in enterprise software and e-commerce; Alex Brown and Thomas Weisel Partners, worked in wireless communications, e-commerce, and software; Federal Reserve Bank of New York, financial analyst. Also served as a legislative staff assistant to U.S. Senator Paul Sarbanes and a policy analyst for New York Lieutenant Governor Stan Lundine.

WRITINGS:

Six Frigates: The Epic History of the Founding of the U.S. Navy, W.W. Norton (New York, NY), 2006.

Contributor to periodicals, including *Current Issues.*

SIDELIGHTS: Ian W. Toll has worked in state and national politics, in the technology industry, and on Wall Street. His varied career is complemented after hours by his love of sailing. It is this avocation, rather than his work experience, and his admiration of Patrick O'Brian's novels that provided Toll with the background and inspiration to write his first book, *Six Frigates: The Epic History of the Founding of the U.S. Navy.* The book outlines the commissioning of the fledgling United States' navy, consisting of six American-made and designed frigates and the political fighting surrounding their creation.

Evan Thomas, writing in the *New York Times Book Review,* called Toll's *Six Frigates* "a fluent, intelligent history of American military policy from the early 1790s" paired with a strong "grasp of the human dimension of his subject." In a *Philadelphia Inquirer* review, Brother Edward Sheehy called it "not only a scholarly effort, but also an exceptionally readable one." Gilbert Taylor's review in *Booklist* mirrored these sentiments, labeling the "fluent account" as "vibrant and comprehensive." Concluding a review in the *Houston Chronicle,* Chris Patsilelis described the book as "comprehensive, beautifully written, and exciting to read," adding that "every naval aficionado will want it."

BIOGRAPHICAL AND CRITICAL SOURCES:

PERIODICALS

Booklist, September 15, 2006, Gilbert Taylor, review of *Six Frigates: The Epic History of the Founding of the U.S. Navy,* p. 11.
Boston Globe, December 19, 2006, Michael Kenney, review of *Six Frigates.*
Economist, November 4, 2006, review of *Six Frigates,* p. 94.
Houston Chronicle, November 24, 2006, Chris Patsilelis, review of *Six Frigates.*

Kirkus Reviews, August 15, 2006, review of *Six Frigates,* p. 831.
Library Journal, September 15, 2006, David Lee Poremba, review of *Six Frigates,* p. 73.
Los Angeles Times, December 3, 2006, Nicholas A. Basbanes, review of *Six Frigates.*
New York Times Book Review, December 17, 2006, Evan Thomas, review of *Six Frigates.*
Observer (London, England), December 17, 2006, Tim Gardam, review of *Six Frigates.*
Philadelphia Inquirer, December 26, 2006, Brother Edward Sheehy, review of *Six Frigates.*
Publishers Weekly, August 21, 2006, review of *Six Frigates,* p. 60.

ONLINE

Ian W. Toll Home Page, http://www.iantoll.com (January 27, 2007), author biography.
Subsim.com, http://www.subsim.com/ (January 27, 2007), Daryl Carpenter, review of *Six Frigates.**

*   *   *

TRIGGER, Bruce G. 1937-2006
(Bruce Graham Trigger)

OBITUARY NOTICE— See index for *CA* sketch: Born June 18, 1937, in Preston (now Cambridge), Ontario, Canada; died of cancer, December 1, 2006. Anthropologist, educator, and author. Trigger was a leading archeologist in Canada who was best known for his work on Canadian prehistory and in Egyptology. After completing undergraduate work in 1959 at the University of Toronto, he participated in expeditions to Egypt and the Sudan and earned a doctorate at Yale University in 1964. He taught at Northwestern University for a year before settling in at McGill University in Montreal. Here he would spend the rest of his academic career, chairing the department of archeology in the early 1970s. The author of numerous scholarly works, ranging from studies of the Nubian region of Egypt to native Canadian tribes and general theoretical works on archeology, Trigger has been credited with contributing greatly to the understanding of archeological methods, theories, and antiquarian studies in general. Among his many publishing contributions are *History and Settlement in Lower Nubia* (1965), *Gordon Childe*

(1980), *Natives and Newcomers: Canada's "Heroic Age" Reconsidered* (1985), *History of Archeological Thought* (1989; revised edition, 2006), and *Understanding Early Civilizations: A Comparative Study* (2003). Trigger received many honors and prizes for his work, including the Queen's Silver Jubilee Medal in 1977, the Cornplanter Medal in 1979, the Innis-Gerin Medal in 1985, and the John Porter Prize from the Canadian Sociology and Anthropology Association in 1989. He was named an Officer of the National Order of Quebec in 2001 and an Officer of the Order of Canada in 2005.

OBITUARIES AND OTHER SOURCES:

PERIODICALS

Times (London, England), December 7, 2006, p. 78.

*   *   *

TRIGGER, Bruce Graham
    See TRIGGER, Bruce G.

*   *   *

TRIMBORN, Jürgen 1971-

PERSONAL: Born 1971, in Cologne, Germany. *Education:* Graduate of the University of Cologne, 1995; Ph.D.

ADDRESSES: Home—Cologne, Germany. *Office*—Institut for Theatre, Film, and Television Science, University of Cologne, Albertus-Magnus Plaza, Cologne 50923, Germany.

CAREER: Institut for Theatre, Film, and Television Science, University of Cologne, Cologne, Germany, professor.

WRITINGS:

Die Pose als Inszenierungsmittel der Sexbombe im amerikanischen Film der fünfziger und sechziger Jahre, Leppin (Cologne, Germany), 1997.

Denkmale als Inszenierungen im öffentlichen Raum: Blick auf die gegenwärtige Denkmalproblematik in der Bundesrupublik Deutschland aus denkmalpflegerischer und medienwissenschaftlicher Sicht, Leppin (Cologne, Germany), 1997.

Sammlung Max Skladanowsky: aus dem Nachlass eines Filmpioniers, Leppin (Cologne, Germany), 1997.

Fernsehen der Neunziger: die deutsche Fernsehlandschaft seit der Etablierung des Privatfernsehens, Teiresias (Cologne, Germany), 1999.

Riefenstahl: eine deutsche Karriere (biography), Aufbau (Berlin, Germany), 2002, translation by Edna McCown published as *Leni Riefenstahl: A Life,* Faber & Faber (New York, NY), 2007.

Der Herr im Frack, Johannes Heesters (biography), Aufbau (Berlin, Germany), 2003.

Hildegard Knef: das Glück kennt nur Minuten (biography), 2005.

Rudi Carrell: ein Leben für die Show (biography), Bertelsmann (Munich, Germany), 2006.

SIDELIGHTS: Jürgen Trimborn, who has taught film and theater courses at the University of Cologne, is also the author of books, including several biographies. His *Riefenstahl: eine deutsche Karriere* was the first to be translated for English-speaking readers as *Leni Riefenstahl: A Life.* Leni Riefenstahl, who died in 2003 at the age of 101, spoke with Trimborn six years before her death. A filmmaker of note, at that time she had yet to make her final film, *Underwater Impressions.*

Riefenstahl was known to fabricate pieces of her history, and Trimborn's most difficult task was to separate fact from fiction. What is known is that Riefenstahl was forced to give up dancing because of a bad knee, then became a sexy film star. Her ambition, however, was to become a film director in a field that was dominated by men, and she directed and acted in the "mountain film" subgenre. She admired Adolph Hitler, who became her patron, and she made films for him, including the notorious propaganda film *The Triumph of the Will* and *Olympia.* When *The Triumph of the Will* premiered in 1938, Riefenstahl became a celebrity, but her fame did not last. She claimed that she was late in understanding the Nazi plan and took no responsibility for the Holocaust. Following World War II, she took on a number of film projects, almost none of which were successful, but she did achieve financial security from the beautiful photographs she took of the Nuba people of Africa.

A *Kirkus Reviews* contributor concluded by writing that Trimborn's biography "casts a bright light on the dark past of a superb artist who cozied up to killers, got what she wanted and spent the ensuing decades as the queen of denial."

BIOGRAPHICAL AND CRITICAL SOURCES:

PERIODICALS

Kirkus Reviews, October 15, 2006, review of *Leni Riefenstahl: A Life,* p. 1062.
Library Journal, November 15, 2006, Roy Liebman, review of *Leni Riefenstahl,* p. 73.
Publishers Weekly, October 16, 2006, review of *Leni Riefenstahl,* pp. 44-45.

ONLINE

Teiresias Publishing Online, http://www.teiresias.de/ (February 3, 2006), brief biography.
Turner Classic Movies Web site, http://www.tcm.com/ (February 3, 2007), review of *Leni Riefenstahl.**

*   *   *

TROW, George William Swift, Jr.
  See TROW, George W.S.

*   *   *

TROW, George W.S. 1943-2006
  (George William Swift Trow, Jr.)

OBITUARY NOTICE— See index for *CA* sketch: Born September 28, 1943, in Greenwich, CT; died November 24, 2006, in Naples, Italy. Critic and author. Trow was a former *New Yorker* critic who lamented what he considered the demise of American culture at the hands of television. The son of a prominent *New York Post* editor, he graduated from Harvard University with a B.A. in English in 1965. His career as a society critic had already begun at Harvard, where he was the editor of the *Harvard Lampoon.* After university, he also contributed to the *National Lampoon* for some time. Hired by the New

Yorker in 1966, Trow contributed short fiction and "Talk of the Town" articles. He gained particular attention in 1980 when he published his essay "Within the Context of No Context" in his magazine. Here he complained that substantive, intellectual discourse in America had died to be replaced by celebrity worship and bombast engendered by the rise of television. His arguments were expanded and published in book form in 1981. Although his title became a catch phrase among intellectual circles, Trow was also criticized for frequently offering unsubstantiated arguments and advising readers merely to "trust me on this one." Becoming increasingly discontented by the state of the media, he quit the *New Yorker* in 1994 after Tina Brown took over as editor and hired comedienne Roseanne Barr to edit one of the issues. Trow left New York and took to wandering the countryside; at one point he underwent treatment at a psychiatric hospital. Eventually, he forsook his country completely for an expatriate life in Italy. Found dead in his Naples apartment from what local authorities described as natural causes, Trow left behind several works of fiction and nonfiction, including two coauthored movie screenplays: *Savages* (1972) and *The Proprietor* (1996). Among his other works are the plays *Prairie Avenue* (1979) and *Elizabeth Dead* (1980), the short-story collection *Bullies* (1980), the novel *The City in the Mist* (1984), and the nonfiction *My Pilgrim's Progress: Media Studies, 1950-1998* (1999) and *The Harvard Black Rock Forest* (2004).

OBITUARIES AND OTHER SOURCES:

PERIODICALS

Chicago Tribune, December 3, 2006, Section 4, p. 6.
New York Times, December 1, 2006, p. C11.

*   *   *

TRYTHALL, Anthony John 1927-2006

OBITUARY NOTICE— See index for *CA* sketch: Born March 30, 1927, in Rugby, England; died of cancer, December 2, 2006. Military officer, educator, and author. A retired general in the British Army, Trythall was a former director of army education who also headed Brassey's Defence Publishers. Educated at St.

Edmund Hall, Oxford, where he completed a history degree in 1947, he did his compulsory National Service the next year. Trythall earned a diploma in education in 1951 and embarked on a career as a secondary-school teacher, but found it did not pay well. He therefore returned to the military in 1953. Specializing as an educationist, he pursued a long career in officer education. He served in Malaya for three years, then joined the War Office in 1956 and commanded the Royal Army Education Corps in Germany. Receiving a master's degree in education from the University of London in 1969, from that year until 1971 he was education advisor to the Regular Commissions Board. This was followed by assignments as chief inspector of army education, a post in the Ministry of Defense, and work as chief education officer for the United Kingdom Land Forces from 1976 to 1980. That year, Trythall was named director of army education. He retired from this job in 1984 and was going to leave the military completely. However, Trythall had the opportunity to head the military's publishing house, Brassey's. Taking over the reins in 1984, he was credited with turning the publisher around, spurring it on to release many respected publications. At Brassey's he was managing director from 1984 to 1987, executive department chair from 1988 to 1995, director of Brassey's (U.K.)

from 1984 to 1997 and of Brassey's (U.S.) from 1987 to 1995, also serving as vice chair of the latter from 1994 to 1997. With the Cold War over, interest in military publications declined, and Trythall decided to leave Brassey's. He accepted a job as governor of the Selwyn School for girls in 1996, and was named its chair in 1997. Trythall, who retired as a major-general, was also named Companion of the Bath. He was the author of *Boney Fuller: The Intellectual General, 1878-1966* (1977), *The Downfall of Leslie Hore-Belisha in the Second World War* (1982), and *J.P.C. Fuller: Staff Officer Extraordinary in the British General Staff* (2002).

OBITUARIES AND OTHER SOURCES:

PERIODICALS

Times (London, England), January 23, 2007, p. 55.

*   *   *

TÜROQUE, Björn
    See CRANE, Dan

V

VAN BALEN, John A. 1947-

PERSONAL: Born March 19, 1947, in Utrecht, Netherlands; naturalized U.S. citizen; son of Jan (an artist and woodworker) and Belia (a homemaker) Van Balen; married Jeanne M. Fuerstenberg (a health administrator); children: Killian Cocco, Jessica, Kathryn. *Ethnicity:* "White." *Education:* University of Utah, M.S., 1973; State University of New York College at Geneseo, M.L.S., 1974.

ADDRESSES: Home—Custer, SD. *E-mail*—vanbalen@goldenwest.net.

CAREER: Bridgewater State University, Bridgewater, MA, librarian, 1974-75; University of South Dakota, Vermillion, professor and head of public services at Weeks Library, 1976-2005. *Military service:* U.S. Army, 1966-68; served in Vietnam.

WRITINGS:

Geography and Earth Science Publications, Pierian (Ann Arbor, MI), 1978.
Index to Earth Science Publications, Greenwood Press (Westport, CT), 1985.
A Contribution to Andreas' Atlas of Dakota-1884, and G.K. Warren's Military Map of Nebraska and Dakota-1858, University of South Dakota (Vermillion, SD), 1997.
Dakota Place Names: Geographical Names on 18th and 19th Century Maps, University of South Dakota (Vermillion, SD),1998.

South Dakota Chronology from Prehistoric Times to 1899, University of South Dakota (Vermillion, SD), 1998.
Great Plains Indian Illustration Index, McFarland (Jefferson, NC), 2004.

SIDELIGHTS: John A. Van Balen told *CA:* "My publications are in the form of finding-aids and guides—reference works that are designed for researchers, students, genealogists, and individuals interested in regional history and geography. My primary research focus has been the Northern Great Plains, the study of place names, and Native American biography. I noted gaps in reference materials particularly related to the Northern Plains region."

*   *   *

VANDERBILT, May

PERSONAL: Education: Baylor University, B.A.; Johns Hopkins University, M.A.

ADDRESSES: Home—San Francisco, CA. *E-mail*—may.vanderbilt@gmail.com.

CAREER: Writer, editor, and novelist. Has worked as an editor for Random House and Broadway Books.

WRITINGS:

(With Anne Dayton) *Emily Ever After,* Broadway Books (New York, NY), 2005.

(With Anne Dayton) *Consider Lily,* Broadway Books (New York, NY), 2006.

SIDELIGHTS: For Sidelights, see DAYTON, Anne.

BIOGRAPHICAL AND CRITICAL SOURCES:

PERIODICALS

Booklist, May 1, 2005, Kristine Huntley, review of *Emily Ever After,* p. 1568.
Kirkus Reviews, April 15, 2005, review of *Emily Ever After,* p. 436; May 1, 2006, review of *Consider Lily,* p. 425.
Publishers Weekly, May 9, 2005, review of *Emily Ever After,* p. 47.
School Library Journal, November, 2005, Molly Connally, review of *Emily Ever After,* p. 181.
Today's Christian Woman, July-August, 2005, review of *Emily Ever After,* p. 59.

ONLINE

Columbia News Service Web site, http://jscms.jrn.columbia.edu/cns/ (November 15, 2005), Jessica Heasley, "They Love Jesus (and Cute Boys Too!)," profile of Anne Dayton and May Vanderbilt.
Daystar eStore, http://www.daystarestore.com/ (November 25, 2006), brief biography of Anne Dayton.
GoodGirlLit.com, http://www.goodgirllit.com/ (November 25, 2006), brief biography of Anne Dayton.*

*　　*　　*

van GELDEREN, C.J. 1960-
　(Cornelis Johannes van Gelderen)

PERSONAL: Born 1960.

ADDRESSES: Office—Firma C. Esveld, Rijneveld 72, 2771 XS Boskoop, Netherlands.

CAREER: Firma C. Esveld (plant nursery), Boskoop, Netherlands, co-owner.

WRITINGS:

(With D.M. van Gelderen) *Maples for Gardens: A Color Encyclopedia,* Timber Press (Portland, OR), 1999.
(With D.M. van Gelderen) *Encyclopedia of Hydrangeas,* Timber Press (Portland, OR), 2004.

BIOGRAPHICAL AND CRITICAL SOURCES:

PERIODICALS

Library Journal, August 1, 1999, William H. Wiese, review of *Maples for Gardens: A Color Encyclopedia.*
Reference & Research Book News, November, 2004, Charles W.G. Smith, review of *Encyclopedia of Hydrangeas,* p. 246.

[Sketch reviewed by brother, Dirk van Gelderen.]

*　　*　　*

VAN GELDEREN, Cornelis Johannes
　See VAN GELDEREN, C.J.

*　　*　　*

van HARTESVELDT, Fred

PERSONAL: Education: Maryville College, B.A., 1967; Auburn University, M.A., 1969, Ph.D., 1975.

ADDRESSES: Office—Fort Valley State University, 135 Horace Mann Bond Bldg., 1005 State University Dr., Fort Valley, GA 31030-4313. *E-mail*—hartesvf@fvsu.edu.

CAREER: Educator, writer. Fort Valley State University, Fort Valley, GA, professor of history.

MEMBER: North American Conference on British Studies, Southern Historical Association, Victorian Military Society, Nineteenth Century Studies Association, Southern Conference on British Studies (secretary-treasurer, 1986—), Georgia Association of Historians.

AWARDS, HONORS: Governor's Teaching Fellow, 1999-2000.

WRITINGS:

NONFICTION

(Editor) *The 1918-1919 Pandemic of Influenza: The Urban Impact in the Western World,* E. Mellen Press (Lewiston, NY), 1992.

(Compiler) *The Battles of the Somme, 1916: Historiography and Annotated Bibliography,* Greenwood Press (Westport, CT), 1996.

(Compiler) *The Dardanelles Campaign, 1915: Historiography and Annotated Bibliography,* Greenwood Press (Westport, CT), 1997.

The Boer War: Historiography and Annotated Bibliography, Greenwood Press (Westport, CT), 2000.

The Battles of the British Expeditionary Forces, 1914-1915: Historiography and Annotated Bibliography, Praeger (Westport, CT), 2005.

Contributor of articles to professional journals and periodicals, including *Maryland Historian, Teaching History,* and *Proceedings and Papers of the Georgia Association of Historians.* Editor, *British Studies Mercury,* 1986—.

SIDELIGHTS: Professor Fred van Hartesveldt focuses his work on studying the history of the early twentieth century, concentrating particularly on the wars. Works such as *The Battles of the Somme, 1916: Historiography and Annotated Bibliography, The Dardanelles Campaign, 1915: Historiography and Annotated Bibliography,* and *The Battles of the British Expeditionary Forces, 1914-1915: Historiography and Annotated Bibliography* catalogue and describe, not the events themselves, but the ways in which historians have written about British military campaigns in World War I. *The Dardanelles Campaign,* for instance, looks at one of the great early fiascoes of the war: the attempted invasion of Turkey (an ally of Austro-Hungary and Germany) at the straits between Asia Minor and Europe. British, New Zealand, and Australian forces tried for months to seize control of the strategic waterway, but failed and were forced to withdraw, humiliated. *The Battles of the Somme*—a series of Allied attacks against the German lines in France lasting for four and a half months—explores the historiography of one of the bloodiest struggles in military history. "A turning point in the war," explained Antulio J. Echevarria II on *H-Net Reviews Online,* "the Somme battles marked the beginning of greater British influence in Entente strategy, saw the introduction of new technologies, especially the tank, and tipped the strategic initiative away from the Central Powers." "Overall, this annotated bibliography is a welcome and useful addition to any personal and institutional library," Echevarria concluded. "Undergraduate and graduate students alike will find that it saves them a great deal of time. Even experienced professors will be grateful for the convenient way that it compiles over 700 books and articles."

Van Hartesveldt is also the author of *The Boer War: Historiography and Annotated Bibliography,* an examination of the writings about the twentieth century's first colonial war. One of the most controversial conflicts of the era, the Boer War pitted a great colonial power (Great Britain) against a much smaller group of Africans descended from Dutch settlers (the Afrikaaners or Boers). Following the discovery of gold in the Boer-controlled Transvaal in 1885, large numbers of British citizens streamed out of South Africa into the Boers' territory. The war began in 1899, supposedly because the rights of the British emigrants were being abused. For the Boers, however, the war was a fight for their political independence. The Boer War prefigured in many ways some of the characteristics of later twentieth-century wars; for instance, during the war the British introduced "concentration camps" to hold Boer women and children. Conditions in the camps were horrendous, rivaling those in the concentration camps of World War II. "To anyone who already knows the significance of the war," wrote Bill Nasson on *H-Net Reviews Online,* "this volume is renewed confirmation; to anyone who has never happened to give the conflict much thought, it may well come as some sort of literary revelation." "Van Hartesveldt's book is an indispensable guide to works on the war," Dylan Craig concluded in the *Journal of African History,* "particularly with respect of those—such as the writings of many Afrikaans authors—which exist outside the international main stream."

BIOGRAPHICAL AND CRITICAL SOURCES:

PERIODICALS

Journal of African History, July, 2002, Dylan Craig, review of *The Boer War: Historiography and Annotated Bibliography,* p. 371.

Reference & Research Book News, February, 2006, review of *The Battles of the British Expeditionary Forces, 1914-1915: Historiography and Annotated Bibliography.*

ONLINE

H-Net Reviews Online, http://www.h-net.msu.edu/ (January 28, 2007), Bill Nasson, review of *The Boer War,* Antulio J. Echevarria II, review of *The Battles of the Somme: Historiography and Annotated Bibliography.*

*   *   *

VANLIERE, Donna 1966-

PERSONAL: Born 1966, in OH; married; husband's name Troy; children: Grace, Kate.

ADDRESSES: Home—Franklin, TN.

CAREER: Writer.

AWARDS, HONORS: Retailers's Choice Award; Dove Award; Silver Angel Award, for *Sheltering Trees: The Power, Promise, and Refuge of Friendship.*

WRITINGS:

"CHRISTMAS" SERIES

The Christmas Shoes, St. Martin's Press (New York, NY), 2001.
The Christmas Blessing, St. Martin's Press (New York, NY), 2003.
The Christmas Hope, St. Martin's Press (New York, NY), 2005.

OTHER

They Walked with Him: Stories of Those Who Knew Him Best, Howard Publishing (West Monroe, LA), 2001.

(With Eddie Carswell) *Sheltering Trees: The Power, Promise, and Refuge of Friendship,* Howard Publishing (West Monroe, LA), 2001.
(With Evelyn Husband) *High Calling: The Courageous Life and Faith of Space Shuttle Columbia Commander Rick Husband,* Thomas Nelson (Nashville, TN), 2003.
The Angels of Morgan Hill, St. Martin's Press (New York, NY), 2006.

ADAPTATIONS: The Christmas Shoes and *The Christmas Blessing* were adapted for television by Columbia Broadcasting System (CBS).

SIDELIGHTS: Donna VanLiere's first book, *They Walked with Him: Stories of Those Who Knew Him Best,* contains stories about the apostles. Her second, written with Eddie Carswell, is *Sheltering Trees: The Power, Promise, and Refuge of Friendship.* It is a collection of contributions on friendship by a variety of people who include singer Randy Travis and motivational speaker and writer Zig Ziglar.

VanLiere began a series of Christmas-themed books with her debut novel, *The Christmas Shoes,* a story of two families. Bankruptcy lawyer Robert Layton and his wife, Kate, are about to divorce because of his absence from their family life. Mechanic Jack Andrews will soon lose his wife, Maggie, to ovarian cancer. The attorney comes to the rescue of Nathan, the boy who is about to lose his mother, when the child is unable to pay for the shoes he wants to buy her. A *Publishers Weekly* contributor wrote that the author "writes some affecting family scenes that contrast the material poverty of the Andrewses with the spiritual poverty of the Laytons." The book was made into a television movie featuring Rob Lowe and Kimberly Williams. The idea of the story came from the author's friend Carswell of the group NewSong, which recorded the hit song.

The Christmas Blessing finds Nathan in medical school and torn about whether or not he wants to become a doctor. He is also distressed because the young woman he loves is ill. The story includes a reunion between Nathan and Robert Layton. In *The Christmas Hope,* Nathan is a minor character, now a doctor and expecting his first child. The plot centers on the Addisons, Patti and Mark, whose son, Sean, died in a car accident and whose marriage is troubled because Patti, a social worker, finds it impossible to be close to her husband or happy about anything in her life. This changes when five-year-old Emily, an orphan in foster care, is left without a place to stay when her foster parents face an emergency. "VanLiere serves up another heart-tugging holiday tale," concluded a *Publishers Weekly* contributor.

VanLiere wrote, with Evelyn Husband, *High Calling: The Courageous Life and Faith of Space Shuttle Columbia Commander Rick Husband*. The book contains entries from Rick's journal, interviews with people who knew him, and Evelyn's memories of their life before his death in 2003. A *Publishers Weekly* reviewer wrote that "scenes of Evelyn and her children . . . learning of Rick's death, and relying on God to help them cope with it, radiate honesty, and power."

The narrator of *The Angels of Morgan Hill* is Jane Gable, who lives in Morgan Hill, Tennessee. She tells of seeing black people for the first time when she was nine, on the day of the funeral of her alcoholic father. The Turners, who work on a tobacco farm, are treated badly, and when their house is burned down, Jane's pregnant mother, Fran, who had becomes friends with Mrs. Turner, takes in their surviving son, Milo. *School Library Journal* contributor Teri Titus wrote: "Teens looking for a warm, gentle story that also provides food for thought will find it here."

BIOGRAPHICAL AND CRITICAL SOURCES:

PERIODICALS

Kirkus Reviews, August 1, 2005, review of *The Christmas Hope,* p. 814.

Publishers Weekly, October 8, 2001, review of *The Christmas Shoes,* p. 43; September 22, 2003, review of *The Christmas Blessing,* p. 77; December 22, 2003, review of *High Calling: The Courageous Life and Faith of Space Shuttle Columbia Commander Rick Husband,* p. 58; September 19, 2005, review of *The Christmas Hope,* p. 45; September 18, 2006, review of *The Angels of Morgan Hill,* p. 35.

School Library Journal, October, 2006, Teri Titus, review of *The Angels of Morgan Hill,* p. 188.

ONLINE

The Angels of Morgan Hill Home Page, http://www.angelsofmorganhill.com (February 12, 2007).

Donna VanLiere Home Page, http://www.donnavanliere.com (January 10, 2007).

*   *   *

VAN STOCKUM, Hilda 1908-2006

OBITUARY NOTICE— See index for *CA* sketch: Born February 9, 1908, in Rotterdam, Netherlands; died of a stroke, November 1, 2006, in Berkhamsted, England. Author. Van Stockum was a popular author and illustrator of children's books. Born in the Netherlands, she would also spend some of her childhood years in Ireland, and in adulthood she lived in the United States, Canada, and England. All of these settings would eventually work their way into her children's stories. Her first book, *A Day on Skates: The Story of a Dutch Picnic* (1934), included a foreword by her aunt, the noted author Edna St. Vincent Millay. After attending the Corcoran School of Art in Washington, DC, in the mid-1930s, she continued to release more self-illustrated children's titles. Among these are *Francie on the Run* (1939), *Pegeen* (1941), and *The Mitchells* (1945). Van Stockum's books were typically gentle stories of family life, but in some cases, as with *The Winged Watchman* (1962) and *The Borrowed House* (1975), she would write on serious topics, such as World War II and the Holocaust. Also a translator and illustrator of other authors' works, such as Catherine C. Coblentz and Louisa May Alcott, Van Stockum published over twenty of her own titles. Among her other works are *Canadian Summer* (1948), *Little Old Bear* (1962), *Rufus Round and Round* (1973), and *The Mitchells: Five for Victory* (1995). Van Stockum was an accomplished still-life painter, too, and she was honored in 1993 when one of her artworks was featured on an Irish postage stamp.

OBITUARIES AND OTHER SOURCES:

BOOKS

Twentieth-Century Children's Writers, 3rd edition, St. James Press (Detroit, MI), 1989.

PERIODICALS

New York Times, November 4, 2006, p. B15.

VAUGHAN, Hal 1928-

PERSONAL: Born 1928; married.

ADDRESSES: Home—Paris, France. *E-mail*—halvaughan@noos.fr.

CAREER: Writer, diplomat, and journalist. Has worked as an officer in the U.S. Foreign Service, as a journalist for ABC News, *New York Daily News,* and Voice of America, and as a documentary film producer.

WRITINGS:

Doctor to the Resistance: The Heroic True Story of an American Surgeon and His Family in Occupied Paris, Brassey's (Washington, DC), 2004.
FDR's Twelve Apostles: The Spies Who Paved the Way for the Invasion of North Africa, Lyons Press (Guilford, CT), 2006.

SIDELIGHTS: Hal Vaughan, a journalist and a former officer in the U.S. Foreign Service, is the author of *Doctor to the Resistance: The Heroic True Story of an American Surgeon and His Family in Occupied Paris,* a biography of Sumner Jackson. Jackson, who volunteered as a physician for the British Army during World War I, later settled in Paris, becoming the medical director of the American Hospital. During World War II, the hospital served as Jackson's base of operations for Resistance activities, which including secretly treating Allied soldiers. According to *Library Journal* critic Marie Marmo Mullaney, *Doctor to the Resistance* "is both an important chronicle of Parisian life under the Vichy regime and an exposé of Resistance operations."

In *FDR's Twelve Apostles: The Spies Who Paved the Way for the Invasion of North Africa,* Vaughan "uses newly available sources to describe a triumph of amateur diplomacy," remarked a *Publishers Weekly* reviewer. The work describes the efforts of North Africa Minister Robert Murphy and twelve vice consuls, specially appointed by U.S. President Franklin D. Roosevelt, to plan and prepare for Operation Torch, an Allied invasion of North Africa in October of 1942. Ed Goedeken, reviewing *FDR's Twelve Apostles* in the *Library Journal,* called it a "valuable addition to the literature on World War II espionage."

Vaughan told *CA:* "I hope that young people will catch the history 'bug,' visit their libraries and delve into how the past influences the future."

BIOGRAPHICAL AND CRITICAL SOURCES:

PERIODICALS

Library Journal, July, 2004, Marie Marmo Mullaney, review of *Doctor to the Resistance: The Heroic True Story of an American Surgeon and His Family in Occupied Paris,* p. 100; October 15, 2006, Ed Goedeken, review of *FDR's Twelve Apostles: The Spies Who Paved the Way for the Invasion of North Africa,* p. 75.
Publishers Weekly, August 7, 2006, review of *FDR's Twelve Apostles,* p. 46.

ONLINE

Hal Vaughn's Home Page, http://www.halvaughan.com (January 15, 2007).

*   *   *

VOAKE, Steve 1961-

PERSONAL: Born December 26, 1961, in Midsomer Norton, England; son of Norman (a schoolteacher) and Betty (a nurse) Voake; married; wife's name Tory (a schoolteacher); children: Tim, Daisy. *Education:* University of Liverpool, B.A. (hons.); University of Exeter, postgraduate certificate in education. *Religion:* Methodist.

ADDRESSES: Home—Somerset, England. *Agent*—Clare Conville, Conville & Walsh, 2 Ganton St., London W1F 7QL, England.

CAREER: Schoolteacher in Somerset, England, 1983-97; Kilmersdon School, Somerset, headmaster, 1997-2005; writer, 2005—. Hornet Productions Ltd., director.

WRITINGS:

NOVELS

The Dreamwalker's Child, Faber & Faber (London, England), 2005.

The Web of Fire, Faber & Faber (London, England), 2006.

Daisy Dawson, Walker Books (London, England), 2007.

The Starlight Conspiracy, Faber & Faber (London, England), 2007.

Voake's books have been published in Japan, Greece, Russia, Portugal, Italy, and Germany.

SIDELIGHTS: Steve Voake told *CA:* "In order to find the time to write my first novel, *The Dreamwalker's Child,* I used to get up at three o'clock in the morning and work for several hours before anyone else was awake. Now that I am writing full-time, I try to set myself a minimum target of 1,000 words a day to keep me from wandering off and playing the guitar too often."

*   *   *

VONNEGUT, Laureen
   (Laureen G. Vonnegut)

PERSONAL: *Hobbies and other interests:* Traveling, running.

ADDRESSES: *Home*—Bucharest, Romania. *E-mail*—lgvonnegut@gmail.com.

CAREER: Writer and screenwriter.

WRITINGS:

Oasis (novel), Counterpoint (New York, NY), 2006.

Contributor of short stories to various publications, including *The Nerve, Book of Writing Women,* and *EM3* magazine. Screenwriter (and coproducer) for short film, *Stuff That Bear!,* and feature-length film *Anybody Love.* Screenwriter (and director) for short film, *Cuckoo and Ice Cream*

SIDELIGHTS: Laureen Vonnegut is an American with a penchant for traveling. Prior to living in Bucharest, Romania, Vonnegut lived in England, California,

Mexico, Bulgaria, and Hungary. She has written several screenplays, one of which, *Stuff That Bear!,* won fifteen awards and played at various film festivals around the world, including the Cannes Film Festival. Vonnegut, a cousin of celebrated author Kurt Vonnegut, is also active publishing short stories in various publications. Her first book, however, was not published until 2006. *Oasis* presents Lili, a young Russian girl sold into sexual slavery to a Moroccan, and her attempts to free herself while encountering a cast of characters in the Sahara.

Donna Seaman, writing in *Booklist,* called the "harrowing and farcical" tale "archly theatrical, sometimes poetic, [and] always enigmatic." A contributor to *Kirkus Reviews* labeled it "a novel as dry and empty as the desert in which it is set." A reviewer writing in *Publishers Weekly* worried that "readers not versed in the region's political conflicts will find the motivations difficult to track." Lamia Doumato's review in *Library Journal,* however, noted that the story "is skillfully woven together" and that the style and scenes "reflect Vonnegut's experiences as a screenwriter."

BIOGRAPHICAL AND CRITICAL SOURCES:

PERIODICALS

Booklist, September 1, 2006, Donna Seaman, review of *Oasis,* p. 59.

Kirkus Reviews, June 15, 2006, review of *Oasis,* p. 600.

Library Journal, October 1, 2006, Lamia Doumato, review of *Oasis,* p. 62.

Publishers Weekly, July 10, 2006, review of *Oasis,* p. 48.

ONLINE

Laureen Vonnegut Home Page, http://www.lvonnegut.com (January 28, 2007), author biography.

*   *   *

VONNEGUT, Laureen G.
   See VONNEGUT, Laureen

W

WALKER, Blair S.

PERSONAL: Male.

ADDRESSES: Home—MD.

CAREER: Former journalist; freelance writer.

WRITINGS:

"DARRYL BILLUPS" MYSTERY SERIES

Up Jumped the Devil, Avon Books (New York, NY),
1997.
Hidden in Plain View, Avon Twilight (New York, NY),
1999.
Don't Believe Your Lying Eyes, Ballantine Books
(New York, NY), 2002.

OTHER

Inner City Miracle, Ballantine Books (New York,
NY), 2002.
(With Reginald F. Lewis) *Why Should White Guys
Have All the Fun? How Reginald Lewis Created a
Billion-Dollar Empire,* Wiley (New York, NY),
2005.

SIDELIGHTS: Blair S. Walker is a former journalist
who now works as a freelance writer. Walker is the
coauthor, with Reginald F. Lewis, of the best-selling
volume *Why Should White Guys Have All the Fun?
How Reginald Lewis Created a Billion-Dollar Empire.*
The book is based on Lewis's uncompleted
autobiography, which was left behind when Lewis
passed away in 1993 at the age of fifty from a brain
tumor. Walker stepped in to finish Lewis's book,
interviewing his friends, family, and numerous business associates to gain a thorough understanding and
complete picture of the billionaire businessman. Lewis
began as an African American growing up in
segregated Baltimore, but he worked hard, gaining an
education at parochial schools, and eventually attending Harvard University Law School. Lewis became a
successful lawyer and businessman. At the height of
his success, Lewis performed a leveraged buyout of
Beatrice International Foods in 1987, and his personal
wealth swelled to four hundred million dollars. Alfred
Edmond, Jr., in a review for *Black Enterprise,*
remarked that the book was "a requisite addition to an
American business library that includes far too few
books about accomplished African-American
entrepreneurs."

In addition to writing nonfiction, Walker is known for
his mystery novels featuring black reporter Darryl Billups. The first book in the series, *Up Jumped the Devil,*
introduces Billups, whose job is to cover the police
beat while working for a white-owned Baltimore
newspaper. Billups begins to receive phone calls warning of a neo-Nazi plot to bomb the NAACP headquarters, and he finds himself pitted against white suprema-
cists as he attempts to thwart their plans. A reviewer
in *Publishers Weekly* considered the book to be "a
debut marred by awkward writing and sloppy characterization." However, Emily Melton, in a review for
Booklist, wrote: "Walker's debut mystery makes fine
entertainment."

Hidden in Plain View continues Darryl Billups's adventures. A serial killer in Baltimore is targeting young African American professionals, and Billups finds himself the killer's next target. Jenny McLarin, in a review for *Booklist,* wrote: "This suspenseful, rich mystery will have readers impatient for the next installment." Thea Davis, writing for the *Mystery Reader Online,* remarked that the book was "sufficiently interesting to overcome the occasional disjointed feelings one has from the author's attempt to cram too much data into too small a space." The series continues with *Don't Believe Your Lying Eyes,* in which Billups finds himself teamed up with homicide detective Scott Donatelli to investigate what appears to be a cover up. A contributor for *Kirkus Reviews* remarked: "Walker's at his best when wandering the mean streets with Billups, or riffing on race, or just talking trash, with the mystery a real but secondary interest." Rex E. Klett, writing for the *Library Journal,* called the book an "engaging addition to the increasingly popular genre of African American mysteries."

BIOGRAPHICAL AND CRITICAL SOURCES:

PERIODICALS

Black Enterprise, February, 1995, Alfred Edmond, Jr., review of *Why Should White Guys Have All the Fun? How Reginald Lewis Created a Billion-Dollar Empire,* p. 224.
Booklist, November 1, 1994, David Rouse, review of *Why Should White Guys Have All the Fun?,* p. 465; February 15, 1996, Brad Hooper, review of *Why Should White Guys Have All the Fun?,* p. 973; October 1, 1997, Emily Melton, review of *Up Jumped the Devil,* p. 311; April 15, 1999, Jenny McLarin, review of *Hidden in Plain View,* p. 1486; February 15, 2000, Deborah Taylor, review of *Hidden in Plain View,* p. 1097.
Kirkus Reviews, May 1, 2002, review of *Don't Believe Your Lying Eyes,* p. 623.
Library Journal, October 1, 1997, Rex E. Klett, review of *Up Jumped the Devil,* p. 130; September 15, 1998, Denise A. Garafolo, review of *Up Jumped the Devil,* p. 130; April 1, 1999, Rex E. Klett, review of *Hidden in Plan View,* p. 133; June 1, 2002, Rex E. Klett, review of *Don't Believe Your Lying Eyes,* p. 200.
Publishers Weekly, October 3, 1994, review of *Why Should White Guys Have All the Fun?,* p. 60; August 11, 1997, review of *Up Jumped the Devil,* p. 388; May 27, 2002, review of *Don't Believe Your Lying Eyes,* p. 40; August 26, 2002, review of *Inner City Miracle,* p. 55.

ONLINE

Mystery Reader Online, http://www.themysteryreader.com/ (January 25, 2007), Thea Davis, review of *Hidden in Plain View.*
New York Times Online, http://www.nytimes.com/ (January 25, 2007), review of *Don't Believe Your Lying Eyes.**

*　　*　*　*

WALKER, J. Samuel

PERSONAL: Male.

CAREER: U.S. Nuclear Regulatory Commission, Washington, DC, historian, 1979—.

WRITINGS:

The Perils of Patriotism: John Joseph Henry and the American Attack on Quebec, 1775, illustrated by Joann W. Hensel, Lancaster County Bicentennial Committee (Lancaster, PA), 1975.
Henry A. Wallace and American Foreign Policy, Greenwood Press (Westport, CT), 1976.
(Editor, with Gerald K. Haines) *American Foreign Relations, a Historiographical Review,* Greenwood Press (Westport, CT), 1981.
(With George T. Mazuzan) *Controlling the Atom: The Beginnings of Nuclear Regulation, 1946-1962,* University of California Press (Berkeley, CA), 1985.
Containing the Atom: Nuclear Regulation in a Changing Environment, 1963-1971, University of California Press (Berkeley, CA), 1992.
A Short History of Nuclear Regulation, 1946-1990, U.S. Nuclear Regulatory Commission (Washington, DC), 1993.
Prompt and Utter Destruction: Truman and the Use of Atomic Bombs against Japan, University of North Carolina Press (Chapel Hill, NC), 1997, revised 2nd edition, 2005.

Permissible Dose: A History of Radiation Protection in the Twentieth Century, University of California Press (Berkeley, CA), 2000.

Three Mile Island: A Nuclear Crisis in Historical Perspective, University of California Press (Berkeley, CA), 2004.

SIDELIGHTS: J. Samuel Walker, a longtime historian for the U.S. Nuclear Regulatory Commission, is the author of a number of volumes focusing on the development of nuclear energy and the safety regulations that have been enacted over the years. In his book, *Three Mile Island: A Nuclear Crisis in Historical Perspective,* Walker addresses the concerns that arose at the time of the Three Mile Island nuclear accident, finding that the public uproar over the incident was partly fueled by the simultaneous release of the film *The China Syndrome,* which happened to deal with similar issues in dramatic fashion. Walker explains the precautions taken in the use of nuclear energy and argues that only very small amounts of the most dangerous forms of radiation were released at Three Mile Island. He concludes that while the events at Three Mile Island did amount to a crisis, they did not make for a public health disaster. Bernard L. Cohen, writing for *Physics Today,* observed that "the book contains little technical information, and many of the technical explanations that do appear range from inadequate to misleading to incorrect." However, Jack M. Holl, in a review for the *Journal of American History,* remarked: "Perhaps Walker's is not the last word on the Three Mile Island accident, but his broad-gauged history of the NRC and TMI whets one's appetite to read his subsequent official histories of his agency." In a review for *Science,* Gene I. Rochlin wrote: "Presented as clearly, expertly, and gracefully as Walker has done here, Three Mile Island is more than just an interesting historical story."

BIOGRAPHICAL AND CRITICAL SOURCES:

PERIODICALS

Isis, September, 2006, Robert W. Seidel, review of *Three Mile Island: A Nuclear Crisis in Historical Perspective,* p. 591.

Journal of American History, June, 2005, Jack M. Holl, review of *Three Mile Island,* pp. 312-313.

Physics Today, February, 2005, Bernard L. Cohen, review of *Three Mile Island,* p. 63.

Science, July 9, 2004, Gene I. Rochlin, review of *Three Mile Island,* p. 181.

ONLINE

History Cooperative Online, http://www.history cooperative.org/ (December 5, 2006), author biography.

*   *   *

WALKER, Julia M. 1951-

PERSONAL: Born 1951.

ADDRESSES: *Office*—Department of English, State University of New York, College at Geneseo, Welles 226, 1 College Cir., Geneseo, NY 14454; fax: 716-245-5181. *E-mail*—walker@geneseo.edu.

CAREER: State University of New York, College of Geneseo, professor of English.

WRITINGS:

NONFICTION

(Editor) *Milton and the Idea of Woman,* University of Illinois Press (Urbana, IL), 1998.

(Editor) *Dissing Elizabeth: Negative Representations of Gloriana,* Duke University Press (Durham, NC), 1998.

Medusa's Mirrors: Spenser, Shakespeare, Milton, and the Metamorphosis of the Female Self, University of Delaware Press (Newark, DE), 1998.

The Elizabeth Icon, 1603-2003, Palgrave Macmillan (New York, NY), 2003.

SIDELIGHTS: Julia M. Walker is a professor of English who specializes in the studies of seventeenth-century English author John Milton, representations of Queen Elizabeth I, the poetry of seventeenth-century English metaphysical poet John Donne, the writings of medieval rhetorician Christine de Pizan, and women's studies in general.

In 1998 Walker wrote *Medusa's Mirrors: Spenser, Shakespeare, Milton, and the Metamorphosis of the Female Self.* The book outlines how certain male writers, in this case Spenser, Shakespeare, and Milton, played off the significance of female characters in literature and history, including Medusa and Cleopatra. Also published in 1998 was Walker's editing of *Dissing Elizabeth: Negative Representations of Gloriana.* Here a collection of eleven essays unmask Elizabeth I in a way that shows what she did to make enemies and what they did as a response. The book includes less familiar and canonical sources, such as sermons, popular verse, and visual representations. Anne Shaver, praising the book in the *Journal of English and Germanic Philology,* called it an "extremely valuable collection of essays." On the other hand, Christopher Haigh, writing in the *English Historical Review* commented: "It is just a pity the editor did not write a longer, braver introduction." Mary Hill Cole noted poor proofreading in *Dissing Elizabeth* in her article in *History: Review of New Books.* Cole mentioned, however, that "the collection contains some incisive, subtle essays on the queen and her monarchy."

BIOGRAPHICAL AND CRITICAL SOURCES:

PERIODICALS

Contemporary Review, December, 2004, review of *The Elizabeth Icon, 1603-2003,* p. 377.

English Historical Review, September, 1999, Christopher Haigh, review of *Dissing Elizabeth: Negative Representations of Gloriana,* p. 977.

History: Review of New Books, winter, 1999, Mary Hill Cole, review of *Dissing Elizabeth,* p. 69.

History Today, July, 1999, Simon Adams, review of *Dissing Elizabeth,* p. 59.

Journal of English and Germanic Philology, October, 1999, Anne Shaver, review of *Dissing Elizabeth,* p. 560.

Modern Language Review, October, 2000, Elizabeth Heale, review of *Medusa's Mirrors: Spenser, Shakespeare, Milton, and the Metamorphosis of the Female Self,* p. 1066.

Shakespeare Oxford Newsletter, summer, 2000, Alex McNeil, review of *Dissing Elizabeth,* p. 18.

ONLINE

State University of New York, College of Geneseo Web site, http://www.geneseo.edu/ (January 28, 2007), author profile.*

WALTERS, Mark Jerome 1952-

PERSONAL: Born December 24, 1952, in Melbourne, FL. *Education:* McGill University, B.A., 1976; Columbia University, M.S.J., 1977; Tufts University, D.V.M., 1993.

ADDRESSES: Office—University of South Florida, 140 7th Ave. S., St. Petersburg, FL 33701. *E-mail*—mjw@stpt.usf.edu.

CAREER: Veterinarian. University of South Florida, St. Petersburg, affiliate.

AWARDS, HONORS: Independent Publisher Book Award, 2004, for *Six Modern Plagues and How We Are Causing Them.*

WRITINGS:

The Dance of Life: Courtship in the Animal Kingdom, Arbor House (New York, NY), 1988, published as *Courtship in the Animal Kingdom,* Doubleday (New York, NY), 1989.

A Shadow and a Song: The Struggle to Save an Endangered Species, Chelsea Green Publishing (Post Mills, VT), 1992.

Six Modern Plagues and How We Are Causing Them, Island Press (Washington, DC), 2003.

Seeking the Sacred Raven: Politics and Extinction on a Hawaiian Island, Island Press (Washington, DC), 2006.

BIOGRAPHICAL AND CRITICAL SOURCES:

PERIODICALS

Booklist, September 15, 2003, Ray Olson, review of *Six Modern Plagues and How We Are Causing Them,* p. 191.

Boston Globe, February 7, 1988, review of *The Dance of Life: Courtship in the Animal Kingdom.*

Environmental Health Perspectives, January, 2004, Donald S. Burke, review of *Six Modern Plagues and How We Are Causing Them,* p. A66.

Library Journal, September 15, 2003, Tina Neville, review of *Six Modern Plagues and How We Are Causing Them,* p. 83.

Los Angeles Times, November 29, 1993, review of *A Shadow and a Song: The Struggle to Save an Endangered Species.*

New York Times, November 4, 2003, review of *Six Modern Plagues and How We Are Causing Them.*

OnEarth, fall, 2003, Martin Downs, review of *Six Modern Plagues and How We Are Causing Them,* p. 39.

Publishers Weekly, August 11, 2003, review of *Six Modern Plagues and How We Are Causing Them,* p. 271.

Regulation, summer, 2004, Angela Logomasini, review of *Six Modern Plagues and How We Are Causing Them,* p. 69.

Science News, November 15, 2003, review of *Six Modern Plagues and How We Are Causing Them,* p. 319; August 5, 2006, review of *Seeking the Sacred Raven: Politics and Extinction on a Hawaiian Island.*

World Watch, January-February, 2004, Clayton Adams, review of *Six Modern Plagues and How We Are Causing Them,* p. 31.

*   *   *

WANSINK, Brian 1960(?)-

PERSONAL: Born c. 1960, in Sioux City, IA; married; wife's name Jennifer. *Education:* Wayne State College, B.A., 1982; Drake University, M.S., 1984; Stanford University, Ph.D., 1990. *Hobbies and other interests:* Playing tenor saxophone in a jazz quartet called Shaken Not Stirred, and in an eight-piece rhythm and blues dance band called The Usual Suspects.

ADDRESSES: Home—Urbana, IL. *Office*—Cornell Food and Brand Lab, Cornell University, 109-111 Warren Hall, Ithaca, NY 14853-7801.

CAREER: Dartmouth College, Hanover, NH, professor of marketing, 1990-94; Vrije University, Amsterdam, Netherlands, professor of marketing, 1994-95; University of Pennsylvania, Philadelphia, Wharton School of Business, professor of marketing, 1995-97; University of Illinois at Urbana-Champaign, Cham-

paign, established Food and Brand Lab, 1997-2005; INSEAD, Fountainbleu, France, member of staff, 2004-05; U.S. Army Research Labs, Natick, MA, member of staff, 2005; Cornell University, Ithaca, NY, John S. Dyson Professor of Marketing, Director of Cornell Food and Brand Lab, 2005—.

AWARDS, HONORS: United Negro College Fund, distinguished leadership award, 1991; Army ROTC faculty advisor award, 1999 and 2001; University of Illinois, MBA core professor of the year, 1999 and 2001, graduate professor of the year, 2001, and Dean's senior researcher award for excellence in research, 2003; Wayne State College, outstanding alumni award, 2005.

WRITINGS:

WWHP 98.3 FM: Interactive Case Study, Southwestern Publishing (Cincinnati, OH), 2001.

(With Seymour Sudman) *Consumer Panels,* American Marketing Association (Chicago, IL), 2002.

(With others) *Asking Questions: The Definitive Guide to Questionnaire Design—For Market Research, Political Polls, and Social and Health Questionnaires,* Jossey-Bass (San Francisco, CA), 2004.

Marketing Nutrition: Soy, Functional Foods, Biotechnology, and Obesity, University of Illinois Press (Urbana, IL), 2005.

Mindless Eating: Why We Eat More Than We Think, Bantam Books (New York, NY), 2006.

Contributor to journals, including *Journal of Marketing Research, Journal of Marketing, Cornell Hotel and Restaurant Administrative Quarterly, American Journal of Preventive Medicine, Annals of Internal Medicine, Journal of Food Science, International Journal of Obesity, Journal of the American Dietetic Association, Military Medicine, Nutrition, Food Policy,* and *Food Quality and Preference.*

SIDELIGHTS: Brian Wansink is a professor of marketing with a particular interest in food, nutrition, and the ways in which marketing campaigns affect how Americans address meals and food choices. He is an expert in nutritional science, food psychology, consumer behavior, food marketing, and grocery shopping behavior, and teaches at Cornell University. In addition, he is the director of the Cornell Food and

Brand Lab, and has written extensively on food marketing and behavior regarding nutrition. Wansink's book *Mindless Eating: Why We Eat More Than We Think* addresses the psychological reasons behind the tendency to overeat, looking at what factors make it difficult to restrict oneself to a limited nutritional regime and eliminate poor food choices from one's diet. Mark Knoblauch, in a review for *Booklist,* wrote that Wansink's book offers an "unpretentious blend of psychology and nutrition science."

BIOGRAPHICAL AND CRITICAL SOURCES:

PERIODICALS

Booklist, September 15, 2006, Mark Knoblauch, review of *Mindless Eating: Why We Eat More Than We Think,* p. 13.
New York Times, October 11, 2006, Kim Severson, "Seduced by Snacks? No, Not You."
Publishers Weekly, September 4, 2006, review of *Mindless Eating,* p. 58.

ONLINE

Cornell University Web site, http://aem.cornell.edu/faculty/ (January 25, 2007), faculty biography.
Crimson Online, http://www.thecrimson.com/ (October 25, 2006), Madeleine K. Ross, "Why Do I Keep Super Sizing Me? Brian Wansink Explains Why We Eat Too Much and Offers Tips on How to Stop."
University of Illinois at Urbana-Champaign Web site, http://www.business.uiuc.edu/faculty/ (January 25, 2007), faculty biography.*

*   *   *

WARD, Kyle 1969-

PERSONAL: Born 1969.

ADDRESSES: Home—Terre Haute, IN. *Office*—Department of History, Vincennes University, 1002 N. 1st St., Vincennes, IN 47591.

CAREER: Vincennes University, Vincennes, IN, assistant professor of history and political science.

WRITINGS:

In the Shadow of Glory: The Thirteenth Minnesota in the Spanish-American and Philippine-American Wars, 1898-1899, North Star Press of St. Cloud (St. Cloud, MN), 2000.
(With Dana Lindaman) *History Lessons: How Textbooks from around the World Portray U.S. History,* New Press (New York, NY), 2004.
History in the Making: An Absorbing Look at How American History Has Changed in the Telling over the Last 200 Years, New Press (New York, NY), 2006.

SIDELIGHTS: Kyle Ward, who teaches history and political science, is the author of a number of books, including, with Dana Lindaman, *History Lessons: How Textbooks from around the World Portray U.S. History.* The book notes that American history is seen from a different perspective by other participants in its creation. For example, the Monroe Doctrine and the Great Depression are viewed by textbooks in the Caribbean as being notable for their impact on sugar prices. Canadian textbooks note the importance of that country's participation in World War II and in the development of the atom bomb.

Daniel Swift wrote in a *New York Times Book Review* article: "Much entertainment is to be found in what's excluded and included. An excerpt from a British textbook on the American Revolution snootily refers to 'the colonies' . . . and notes that Tom Paine, the author of *Common Sense* and godfather of America, 'earned a living first as a maker of ladies' underwear.'"

Swift felt that in certain instances, the authors are dismissive of entries found in history books, including one in a Cuban book that states that the Americans, not the Spanish, blew up the U.S.S. *Maine,* leading to American participation in the Spanish-Cuban War and eventual invasion of Cuba, an idea that Ward and Lindaman call a "conspiracy theory." "In treating the Cuban argument so offhand[ed]ly," wrote Swift, "Lindaman and Ward diminish the valuable lessons of their own shocking and fascinating book." Other opposing versions of history include a Saudi Arabian entry that claims that all American intervention in the Middle East is part of a war on Islam.

History in the Making: An Absorbing Look at How American History Has Changed in the Telling over the Last 200 Years shows, in but one example, how the historical treatment of Native Americans changed over time. In writing the chapter "Slavery in America," Ward takes passages from nine textbooks that were published from 1851 to 1995. He studies the treatment of such well-known events as the battle for the Alamo and the Boston Tea Party, and notable people from the past, including Presidents Washington and Lincoln. *Library Journal* contributor Frederick J. Augustyn, Jr. wrote: "This thought-provoking study is ideal for history buffs and the general public."

BIOGRAPHICAL AND CRITICAL SOURCES:

PERIODICALS

Booklist, Jay Freeman, review of *History in the Making: An Absorbing Look at How American History Has Changed in the Telling over the Last 200 Years,* p. 19.

Foreign Affairs, January-February, 2005, Walter Russell Mead, review of *History Lessons: How Textbooks from around the World Portray U.S. History,* p. 187.

Kirkus Reviews, July 15, 2006, review of *History in the Making,* p. 718.

Library Journal, June 1, 2004, Frederick J. Augustyn, Jr., review of *History Lessons,* p. 153; September 1, 2006, Frederick J. Augustyn, Jr., review of *History in the Making,* p. 160.

New York Times Book Review, July 4, 2004, Daniel Swift, review of *History Lessons..**

*　　*　　*

WEBER, Caroline 1969-

PERSONAL: Born 1969; married. *Education:* Harvard University, B.A., 1991; Yale University, Ph.D., 1998.

ADDRESSES: Home—New York, NY. *Office*—Barnard College, Columbia University, 305 Milbank Hall, 1150 Amsterdam Ave., New York, NY 10027. *E-mail*—ceweber@barnard.edu.

CAREER: Writer, historian, and educator. Barnard College, Columbia University, associate professor of French. Taught for seven years at the University of Pennsylvania.

WRITINGS:

Terror and Its Discontents: Suspect Words in Revolutionary France, University of Minnesota Press (Minneapolis, MN), 2003.
Queen of Fashion: What Marie Antoinette Wore to the Revolution, Henry Holt (New York, NY), 2006.

Contributor to books, including *French Popular Culture: An Introduction,* edited by Hugh Dauncey, Hodder Arnold (London, England), 2003; *Gender and Utopianism in the Eighteenth Century,* edited by Nicole Pohl and Brenda Tooley, Routledge (New York, NY), 2004; and *Columbia Dictionary of Twentieth-Century French Thought,* edited by Lawrence D. Kritzman, Columbia University Press (New York, NY), 2005.

Contributor to journals and periodicals, including *Studies in Eighteenth-Century Culture, South Central Review, Philosophy and Literature, Yale French Studies, Lacanian Ink,* and *Utah Foreign Language Review.*

SIDELIGHTS: Author and historian Caroline Weber is an associate professor French at Columbia University's Barnard College. A specialist in French literature, history, and culture, Weber frequently writes on issues related to aspects of life in Revolutionary France. In *Queen of Fashion: What Marie Antoinette Wore to the Revolution,* Weber explores the very real impact of clothing and fashion on the politics and culture of France in the late eighteenth century. Fashion during the days of Marie Antoinette cannot be dismissed as the whims of royalty and dalliances of the rich, whose towering hairdos, elaborate cosmetics, and frilly outfits were just another way to pass the time at the top of the socioeconomic ladder. Weber explains that in pre-republican France, power was precisely reflected in appearances and behavior. The wealthy and powerful of France, therefore, displayed their status conspicuously by their luxurious garments, fanciful hair styles, and affected deportment. Power was defined by fashion, and fashion as created and encouraged by Marie Antoinette was a political game played with real and sometimes deadly results. This ostentatious display of wealth, Weber notes, was generally resented by the poor and lower classes of French society, which helped fuel the hatred that led to the overthrow of the monarchy during the French Revolution. The queen herself refused to obey accepted fashion codes in France, declining to wear constricting whalebone corsets, reintroducing her most opulent jewelry, and asserting her own personality and identity in her clothing choices. To her last, Marie Antoinette understood the strength of character and potency of statement that well-selected clothing could relate to onlookers. Weber's "account of the queen's final appearance—all in glorious white—on the ride to the guillotine carries enormous poignancy," remarked a *Kirkus Reviews* critic. "This thoroughly researched, intelligently presented and supported portrait will best serve scholars of history and culture," noted James F. DeRoche in the *Library Journal*. Though "the book is rigorously researched, Weber's narrative style is energetic and alive with her own feminine pleasure at a beautiful dress or an outrageous pouf," observed Lisa Schwarzbaum in *Entertainment Weekly*. A *Publishers Weekly* contributor called Weber's work a "prodigiously researched, deliciously detailed study" of the unlikely combination of politics and fashion. "Using bold and engaging prose, the author has created a whole new appreciation for academic writings," commented *Booklist* reviewer Barbara Jacobs.

BIOGRAPHICAL AND CRITICAL SOURCES:

PERIODICALS

Booklist, September 15, 2006, Barbara Jacobs, review of *Queen of Fashion: What Marie Antoinette Wore to the Revolution,* p. 11.

Entertainment Weekly, September 22, 2006, Lisa Schwarzbaum, "Classic Frock," review of *Queen of Fashion,* p. 96.

Kirkus Reviews, August 1, 2006, review of *Queen of Fashion,* p. 776.

Library Journal, October 1, 2006, James F. DeRoche, review of *Queen of Fashion,* p. 70.

Publishers Weekly, July 31, 2006, review of *Queen of Fashion,* p. 66.

ONLINE

Columbia University Web site, http://www.columbia.edu/ (January 22, 2007), biography of Caroline Weber.*

WEISSMAN, Steven 1968-
(Steven Knight Weissman)

PERSONAL: Born June 4, 1968, in CA; married; wife's name Charissa; children: Charles. *Education:* Attended California State University and the Academy of Art.

ADDRESSES: Home—Los Angeles, CA. *E-mail*—tinstars@sbcglobal.net.

CAREER: Graphic novelist and comic book writer and artist, 1993—.

AWARDS, HONORS: Harvey Award, for best new talent, 1998.

WRITINGS:

Yikes (minicomic), self-published, 1993.

Yikes, Volume 1 (minicomic), five issues, self-published, 1994–96.

Tykes, Alternative Comics Press (Gainesville, FL), 1997.

Yikes, Volume 2, two issues, Alternative Comics Press (Gainesville, FL), 1997–98.

The Lemon Kids, Alternative Comics Press (Gainesville, FL), 1999.

Champs, Fantagraphics (Seattle, WA), 1999.

Fichtre!, Editions Amok (France), 2000.

White Flower Day, Editions Amok (France), 2001, Fantagraphics (Seattle, WA), 2002.

Les Choupin Sherifs, 9eme Monde (France), 2001.

Don't Call Me Stupid!, Fantagraphics (Seattle, WA), 2001.

The Kid Firechief, Fantagraphics (Seattle, WA), 2004.

Chewing Gum in Church, Fantagraphics (Seattle, WA), 2006.

Contributor to numerous comic anthologies, including *The Big Book of Grimm;* contributor to periodicals, including *Bizarro Comics, Pulse!, Buzzard, Dark Horse Presents, Marvel Vision, Triple Dare, Dirty Stories, Chicago New City, Nickelodeon, Legal Action Comics, Non, Present: The Comics Journal, Shout,* and *Swell.* Contributor to foreign periodicals, including *Quadrado* (Portugal), *Mammoth* (Japan), *Stereoscomic* (France), and *Le Phaco* (France).

SIDELIGHTS: Steven Weissman is a comic book and graphic novel writer and artist best known for his "Yikes" children. With their pudgy faces and oversized heads, Weissman's tykes are mildly reminiscent of Charles M. Schulz's *Peanuts* kids, but Weissman's cast includes characters with a darker, satirical edge, more like the kids in *South Park.* They include Li'l Bloody, a vampire; Pullapart Boy, who is stitched together in the Frankenstein manner; X-Ray Spence, who possesses special glasses; Kid Medusa, who will turn you to stone if you look at her; Dead Boy, a zombie; Chubby Cheeks; and Li'l Tin Stars.

White Flower Day consists of three stories, "White Flower Day," "Look Out for Big Della," and "I Saw You," the last of which introduces a new character, College Boy, Pullapart Boy's cousin. The recurring theme in these stories is revenge.

Don't Call Me Stupid! collects Alternative Press releases from 1997 to 1998. In reviewing this book for *Locus Online,* Claude Lalumière commented that the seven-page story "Back in the Day," in which the dog Elzie Crisler recalls the circumstances of her death and her resurrection by Professor Boy, is the "most heart-wrenching tale," adding that it "evocatively contrasts brutality and tenderness while painting with great empathy a picture of heartless disregard."

A reviewer for *Comics Reporter* online said of *The Kid Firechief:* Much of what works best . . . are those moments in which the narratives loosen up and flow with an almost giddy, bouncy sense of timing, like the moments of sublime action that sometimes took over the "Our Gang" films.

Weissman employs a four-panel structure and bright colors for *Chewing Gum in Church,* while keeping his kids violent and cruel. A *Publishers Weekly* contributor wrote that "these bizarre explorations of childhood friendships (not to mention competitiveness and mutual enmity) are hilarious."

BIOGRAPHICAL AND CRITICAL SOURCES:

PERIODICALS

Booklist, February 1, 2003, Ray Olson, review of *White Flower Day,* p. 970; August 1, 2006, Ray Olson, review of *Chewing Gum in Church,* p. 62.

Publishers Weekly, July 31, 2006, review of *Chewing Gum in Church,* p. 61.

ONLINE

Comics Reporter, http://www.comicsreporter.com/ (October 29, 2004), review of *The Kid Firechief.*
Comic World News, http://www.comicworldnews.com/ (January 13, 2007), review of *Chewing Gum in Church.*
Fantagraphics Books Web site, http://www.fantagraphics.com/ (January 13, 2007), brief biography.
Locus Online, http://www.locusmag.com/ (November 30, 2001), Claude Lalumière, review of *Don't Call Me Stupid!*

* * *

WEISSMAN, Steven Knight
   See WEISSMAN, Steven

* * *

WELLS, C.M.
   See WELLS, Colin

* * *

WELLS, Colin 1960-
   (C.M. Wells, Colin Michael Wells)

PERSONAL: Born 1960; married; wife's name Kate. *Education:* Attended University of California, Los Angeles; Oxford University, B.A., M.A., D.Phil.

ADDRESSES: Home—NY.

CAREER: Taught at University of Ottawa; Trinity University, San Antonio, TX, 1987-2004, became professor of history and Frank Murchison Distinguished Professor of Classical Studies; member of faculty of Oxford University and Brasenose College. Director of excavations at Carthage, Tunisia,

1976—, and at the United Nations Educational, Scientific, and Cultural Organization (UNESCO) "Save Carthage" project.

MEMBER: Archaeological Institute of America, German Archaeological Institute, Society of Antiquaries of London (fellow).

WRITINGS:

(As C.M. Wells) *The German Policy of Augustus: An Examination of the Archaeological Evidence,* Clarendon Press (Oxford, England), 1972.

(Editor, as C.M. Wells) *Roman Africa/L'Afrique romaine: The 1980 Governor-General Vanier Lectures,* University of Ottawa Press (Ottawa, Ontario, Canada), 1982.

The Roman Empire, Stanford University Press (Palo Alto, CA), 1984, 2nd edition, Harvard University Press (Cambridge, MA), 1995.

Sailing from Byzantium: How a Lost Empire Shaped the World, Delacorte (New York, NY), 2006.

Contributor of articles to professional journals.

SIDELIGHTS: Colin Wells, a specialist in Roman history and archaeology in the Mediterranean, is the author of *Sailing from Byzantium: How a Lost Empire Shaped the World,* an examination of Byzantium's influence on Western Europe, Islam, and the Slavic world. Wells divides his work into three parts. In the first, he describes how Byzantine scholars preserved the works of ancient Greek civilization and introduced this learning to fifteenth-century Italy. According to a critic in *Kirkus Reviews,* "If Byzantine scholars had not preserved ancient Greek culture, Wells establishes, Western Europe might well never have recovered the pillars of literature, philosophy and science upon which to build the Renaissance." Next, the author explores how Arab Muslims absorbed Byzantium's teachings on philosophy, medicine, and science. Finally, he looks at the effects of the Byzantine empire on the eastern Slavic world, particularly its religious legacy. *Sailing from Byzantium* earned strong reviews. "In this deft synthesis of scholarship," remarked a critic in *Publishers Weekly,* "classicist Wells shows how the Byzantines exerted a profound influence on all neighboring civilizations." In *Booklist,* George Cohen wrote that the author "brings vividly to life this history of a long-lost era and its opulent heritage," and Robert J. Andrews, writing in the *Library Journal,* noted: "This history is a needed reminder of the debt that three of our major civilizations owe to Byzantium."

BIOGRAPHICAL AND CRITICAL SOURCES:

PERIODICALS

Booklist, July 1, 2006, George Cohen, review of *Sailing from Byzantium: How a Lost Empire Shaped the World,* p. 26.

Kirkus Reviews, June 15, 2006, review of *Sailing from Byzantium,* p. 629.

Library Journal, June 15, 2006, Robert J. Andrews, review of *Sailing from Byzantium,* p. 86.

Publishers Weekly, May 29, 2006, review of *Sailing from Byzantium,* p. 52.*

*   *   *

WELLS, Colin Michael
See WELLS, Colin

*   *   *

WESTFIELD, Robert 1972-

PERSONAL: Born 1972, in MD. *Education:* Columbia University, B.A., 1994.

ADDRESSES: Home—New York, NY. *E-mail*—robert@robertwestfield.com.

CAREER: Novelist and playwright. Writer-in-residence for The Working Group. Has also worked as a caterer and a tour guide.

AWARDS, HONORS: Received playwriting prize, fiction award, and Henry Evans traveling fellowship, all from Columbia University.

WRITINGS:

Suspension (novel), HarperPerennial (New York, NY), 2006.

Also author of plays, including *A Wedding Album, The Pennington Plot, A Tulip Economy,* and *A Home Without.*

SIDELIGHTS: Robert Westfield, a playwright and novelist based in New York City, is the author of *Suspension,* a work set in the months just before and after the terrorist attacks of September 11, 2001. The novel concerns Andy Green, a resident of Hell's Kitchen, who earns a living by penning multiple-choice questions for educational tests. While attending a cabaret performance by his exotic Russian friend, Sonia Obolensky, Green falls for her mentor, a handsome philanthropist named Brad Willet. Green's life comes apart at the seams, however, after he becomes the victim of a hate crime, Willet abruptly breaks off contact with him, and the Twin Towers fall. A fearful and paranoid Green refuses to leave his apartment for months and sees few visitors. He finally musters the courage to reenter society after he receives a mysterious package from Willet. *Suspension* received strong reviews. "Westfield wryly paints a series of seemingly unrelated events" against the backdrop of the terrorist attacks, noted *Entertainment Weekly* contributor J.P. Mangalindan, and a critic in *Publishers Weekly* called the work "a striking portrait of life in the Big Apple." "Gay-bashing, 9/11, free-floating paranoia and fanaticism make pretty grim ingredients for a comedy, however dark," observed a contributor to *Kirkus Reviews,* "but this ambitious debut ably wrests smart laughs from terror."

BIOGRAPHICAL AND CRITICAL SOURCES:

PERIODICALS

Entertainment Weekly, August 4, 2006, J.P. Mangalindan, review of *Suspension,* p. 73.
Kirkus Reviews, June 1, 2006, review of *Suspension,* p. 545.
Publishers Weekly, May 1, 2006, review of *Suspension,* p. 32.

ONLINE

Pulp Noir.com, http://www.pulpnoir.com/?p=74 (September 11, 2006), Charlie Huston, "Unsolicited Work of the Young," interview with Robert Westfield.

Robert Westfield's Home Page, http://www.robert westfield.com (January 15, 2007).
Southern Maryland Online, http://somd.com/ (November 3, 2006), "Interview: Bryans Road Author, Robert Westfield Returns to Maryland."

*   *   *

WHITMAN, Amber A. 1969-

PERSONAL: Born March 13, 1969, in Toronto, Ontario, Canada; daughter of Gerald and Alice (Gallagher) Whitman; married David Currier (a tile setter); children: Mathew. *Education:* Attended Canadian collegiate schools. *Religion:* Christian.

ADDRESSES: *Home*—Ontario, Canada. *E-mail*—restless80@hotmail.com.

CAREER: Writer, poet and freelancer.

AWARDS, HONORS: Writing award from *Today's Woman.*

WRITINGS:

Dreams of Grandeur (poetry), L&R Hartley Publishers (Murwillumbah, New South Wales, Australia), 2005.

Also author of short stories, poetry, and articles.

SIDELIGHTS: Amber A. Whitman told *CA:* "I have been writing since my youth when I attended a private school. I won awards for my writing. I have taken it up again and have been writing for several years now. Writing has become a passion, and I hope my work is read and enjoyed."

Later, she added: "The most surprising thing I have learned as a writer is that it is a process. You have to be alone much of the time. I learned that it is competitive and can be overwhelming at times. It is surprising the number of people who have asked me certain questions about writing. The funny thing is that I learned basically everything on my own, without help. I designed my own Web site. I published without knowing much about it. I wrote my own press release, bio and resume. I am still going through the process, but I hope at the end it will all be worth it."

BIOGRAPHICAL AND CRITICAL SOURCES:

ONLINE

Passion for Writing, http://homebody2001-ivil.tripod.com (October 23, 2006).

*   *   *

WILLIAMS, Lance

PERSONAL: Male.

ADDRESSES: E-mail—lwilliams@sfchronicle.com.

CAREER: Writer, journalist, and investigative reporter, 1973—. *San Francisco Chronicle,* reporter.

AWARDS, HONORS: George Polk Award, Long Island University, 2004, for sports reporting involving investigation into use of steroids in major sports; Dick Schaap Excellence in Sports Journalism Award, 2004; Journalist of the Year, Northern California Pro Chapter, Society of Professional Journalists, 2006.

WRITINGS:

(With Mark Fainaru-Wada) *Game of Shadows: Barry Bonds, BALCO, and the Steroids Scandal That Rocked Professional Sports,* Gotham Books (New York, NY), 2006.

SIDELIGHTS: See Fainaru-Wada, Mark, for Sidelights.

BIOGRAPHICAL AND CRITICAL SOURCES:

PERIODICALS

Booklist, September 1, 2006, Mike Tribby, review of *Game of Shadows: Barry Bonds, BALCO, and the Steroids Scandal That Rocked Professional Sports,* p. 150.

Chicago Sun Times, March 9, 2006, Roman Modrowski, "Author Knows All about This Giant Controversy," profile of Mark Fainaru-Wada.

Entertainment Weekly, April 21, 2006, Melissa Rose Bernardo, Jeff Labrecque, and Bob Cannon, review of *Game of Shadows,* p. 77.

Hollywood Reporter, August 16, 2006, "Talk, Judges Rule," p. 3; September 22, 2006, "Facing Jail," p. 5.

New York Times Book Review, March 23, 2006, Michiko Kakutani, "Barry Bonds and Baseball's Steroids Scandal," review of *Game of Shadows;* May 7, 2006, Michael Sokolove, review of *Game of Shadows,* p. 12.

Newsweek, March 20, 2006, Mark Starr, "Bonds Gets Blasted: A Scorching New Book Boosts the Case That the Slugger's Records Were Drug-Assisted," review of *Game of Shadows,* p. 49.

Quill, October-November, 2006, "NorCal Chapter to Honor Bay Area Journalists," p. 11.

San Francisco Chronicle, February 22, 2005, Stacy Finz, "*Chronicle* Reporters Honored for Sports Steroids Coverage; Polk Award among Journalism's Highest," p. A-2; August 30, 2006, Debra J. Saunders, "Justice Department of Steroids," p. E-7; September 21, 2006, "Statement by *Chronicle* reporter Mark Fainaru-Wada"; September 21, 2006, "Statement by *Chronicle* reporter Lance Williams."

ONLINE

ABC News Web site, http://abcnews.go.com/ (September 22, 2006), Wright Thompson, "Jail for Barry Bonds Reporters: We All Lose."

Bookreporter.com, http://www.bookreporter.com/ (December 20, 2006), Ron Kaplan, review of *Game of Shadows.*

CJR Daily, http://www.cjrdaily.org/ (December 17, 2004), Susan Q. Stranahan, "Mark Fainaru-Wada on the Sports Doping Probe and Protecting Sources," interview with Mark Fainaru-Wada.

San Francisco Magazine, http://www.sanfranciscomagazine.com/ (December 20, 2006), Steve Kettmann, "Who Put the *Chron* on Steroids?," profile of Mark Fainaru-Wada and Lance Williams.

Scriptorium, http://illuminate.redline6.net/ (June 20, 2006), Matthew Davis, review of *Game of Shadows.*

Truthdig.com, http://www.truthdig.com/ (June 13, 2006), James Harris, interview with Mark Fainaru-Wada.

*   *   *

WILLIAMS, Polly 1971-

PERSONAL: Born 1971; children: Oscar.

CAREER: Writer and journalist. *Scene* magazine (now defunct), creator and editor; worked at *Frank, Punch, You,* and *In Style* magazines.

WRITINGS:

NOVELS

The Yummy Mummy, Hyperion (New York, NY), 2006.
The Egg Race, Sphere (Great Britain), 2007.

Contributor to periodicals.

SIDELIGHTS: Polly Williams was inspired to write her first novel, *The Yummy Mummy,* by the birth of her son, Oscar. "Because he was tiny and slept a lot, I wrote, mostly rubbish," the author reveals on her official home page. "My light bulb moment came when I realised I couldn't find the novel I wanted to read, a novel about the contradictory and messy business of being a new mum in the twenty-first century. And so I started *The Yummy Mummy.*" The novel tells the story of Amy Crane, who, six months after the birth of her first child, finds herself rejecting her fellow dowdy mommies and turning to the "chic" mommy set as she diets, buys clothes, exercises, and even has Botox injections. In the process she seems to be alienating Joe, her boyfriend and the father of her child, who may be having an affair. In a review of *The Yummy Mummy* in *Publishers Weekly,* a contributor noted that the author's "wit and Amy's appealing foibles will make readers stick around." A *Kirkus Reviews* contributor wrote that "there are some clever and endearing moments between mother and child." Amy Brozio-Andrews, writing in the *Library Journal,* commented that the "narrative is flush with self-deprecating humor, label namedropping, and characters embodying all manner of modern motherhood."

BIOGRAPHICAL AND CRITICAL SOURCES:

PERIODICALS

Kirkus Reviews, October 15, 2006, review of *The Yummy Mummy,* p. 1045.
Library Journal, November 15, 2006, Amy Brozio-Andrews, review of *The Yummy Mummy,* p. 60.
Publishers Weekly, October 16, 2006, review of *The Yummy Mummy,* p. 32.

ONLINE

Polly Williams Home Page, http://www.pollywilliams. com (January 30, 2007).*

*   *   *

WILLIAMSON, Debrah

PERSONAL: Born in Claremore, OK; married; children: three.

ADDRESSES: Home—OK. *Agent*—Pamela Harty, The Knight Agency, 570 East Ave., Madison, GA 30650. *E-mail*—debrah@debrahwilliamson.com.

CAREER: Novelist.

WRITINGS:

Singing with the Top Down, New American Library (New York, NY), 2006.
Paper Hearts, NAL Trade, 2007.

Also author of more than twenty romance novels under a variety of pseudonyms.

SIDELIGHTS: Debrah Williamson, who has more than twenty romance novels to her credit, is the author of the coming-of-age tale *Singing with the Top Down.* Set in 1955, the work follows thirteen-year-old Pauly Mahoney and her eight-year-old brother, Buddy, a frail polio survivor. When their young, irresponsible parents are killed in a roller-coaster accident at a traveling carnival in Oklahoma, the pair are taken in by their eccentric Aunt Nora, who claims to be an aspiring Hollywood actress. During their road trip to California, which Nora dubs "The Daring Adventure of Us," the trio pick up a nursing-home runaway and his dog, rescue a mummified Indian baby from a museum, and join forces with an ex-fighter pilot. Along the way, the spirited Pauly, "often made to shoulder adult responsibilities, finds that her aunt is a good listener with a generous heart," noted Joanne Wilkinson in *Booklist*. "Pauly is a true parental child, the calm head in chaos," Williamson told Kelley Hartsell in an interview on the *CK2S Kwips and Kritiques* Web site. "She coped with the lack of security her parents provided by making herself indispensable, at least in her mind. When she had to start over with Aunt Nora, she realized she didn't have to be the grown-up. That she could be a child and let someone else shoulder responsibility. Her life with Nora in California represents the life she always wanted, but didn't think she could have." "Graceful and witty, Pauly's courageous voice is this bighearted novel's greatest strength," wrote a critic in *Publishers Weekly*.

Williamson told *CA:* "I've been writing stories ever since I learned to put words on paper, probably as an extension of my love of reading. I think my writing today is most influenced by the wonderful novels I read as a child and young adult. I grew up in a rural small town and reading about interesting characters doing exciting things in intriguing settings made me feel part of the bigger world. In a way, I think I write in order to recreate the sense of discovery that reading great books gave me then.

"It would be impossible to describe my writing process because it is not static. Creating stories is an organic process that changes with each novel I write. I almost always start with characters and go from there. For me, characters are everything. Plot and setting and all the rest grow out of the characters once I make them come alive on the page.

"I suppose the most surprising thing I've learned is that I can actually write professionally. As a youngster devouring the words of others, it never occurred to me that someday people would read the stories I made up. I just knew I had stories to tell and would write them regardless of whether or not they were published.

"Asking a novelist to name her favorite book is a bit like asking a mother which child she loves best. I like them all, for different reasons. If I didn't love a story—at least for as long as it takes to write it—I don't believe I would ever make it to The End.

"That said, there will always be a special place in my heart for *Singing with the Top Down* because it was the story that made me stretch and grow as a writer. It taught me perseverance and the ultimate truth in the advice 'write what you love and the rest will follow.'

"The effect of my books on readers informs my writing from conception of an idea to conclusion of the novel. When readers finish my book, I want them to be a little sad that the story is over because now they must say good-bye to the characters. I want my stories to remind them of the goodness in ordinary people and renew their belief that each of us has the strength to overcome whatever obstacles life places in our paths."

BIOGRAPHICAL AND CRITICAL SOURCES:

PERIODICALS

Booklist, July 1, 2006, Joanne Wilkinson, review of *Singing with the Top Down*, p. 35.
Kirkus Reviews, June 1, 2006, review of *Singing with the Top Down*, p. 545.
Publishers Weekly, May 29, 2006, review of *Singing with the Top Down*, p. 34.

ONLINE

Cindy Procter-King Web site, http://www.cindyprocter-king.com/yadda.html/ (May 29, 2007), "Chatting with . . . Debrah Williamson."
CK2S Kwips and Kritiques Web site, http://www.ck2skwipsandkritiques.com/ (May 29, 2007), Kelley Hartsell, "An Interview with Debrah Williamson."
Deanna Carlyle Web site, http://www.deannacarlyle.com/ (May 29, 2007), "Debrah Williamson: How She Creates Character Sympathy."
Debrah Williamson's Home Page, http://www.debrahwilliamson.com (January 15, 2007).

*   *   *

WILLIAMSON, Jack
See WILLIAMSON, John Stewart

WILLIAMSON, John Stewart 1908-2006
(Will Stewart, Jack Williamson)

OBITUARY NOTICE— See index for *CA* sketch: Born April 29, 1908, in Bisbee, Arizona Territory (now AZ); died November 10, 2006, in Portales, NM. Author. Williamson was a pioneering, award-winning science-fiction author whose career spanned the pulp era through the twenty-first century. Born in Arizona before it became a state, he was witness to the radical transformations of the United States in the twentieth century. His own early life on the farm was fairly isolated from human contact, and so he developed a vivid imagination to pass the time. When he came across his first science-fiction pulp magazine, *Amazing Stories,* in 1926, the world of planetary and time travel was a revelation for him. Williamson was immediately inspired to write, and he had his first success just two years later when "The Metal Man" appeared in that same pulp magazine. Over the next years, he regularly contributed to the pulps, and many of his stories were cover features. His first novel, *The Girl from Mars,* written with Miles J. Breuer, was released in 1929. Continuing to write, he attended what is now West Texas State University and the University of New Mexico, though he did not complete a degree. When the United States entered World War II, Williamson joined the U.S. Army Air Forces; he served as a weatherman and was promoted to staff sergeant. After the war, he worked briefly as a wire editor for the Portales, New Mexico, *News Tribune* and released one of his best-remembered science-fiction novels, *The Legion of Space* (1947), as well as the classic *The Humanoids* (1949). With the publication of the latter, Williamson was beginning to prove himself to be a writer of considerable depth. Much of the science fiction being written at the time was about space travel heroics and ugly alien monsters. Williamson, on the other hand, was one of the first authors in the genre to focus more on characterization and to address serious themes, such as the potential hazards to humanity of advanced technology. Occasionally collaborating with other writers, he partnered most successfully with Frederik Pohl, with whom he would write the "Jim Eden," "Starchild," and "Cuckoo's Saga" series, among other works. Also the creator of the "Beyond Mars" comic strip, which ran in the New York *Sunday News* from 1953 to 1956, Williamson would publish over sixty science-fiction novels and short-story collections, as well as several works of nonfiction. He returned to university studies to complete a master's degree at

Eastern New Mexico University in 1957, and a doctorate from the University of Colorado at Boulder in 1964. Not only did his own gifts as a writer contribute to the legitimacy of his favorite genre, but the author sought to make science fiction and fantasy literature legitimate works to study at the college level. He therefore enjoyed being a faculty member at Eastern New Mexico University, teaching courses in creative writing and genre fiction. He was an associate professor there in the 1960s and a professor from 1969 until his 1977 retirement. Williamson continued to publish into the twenty-first century, with his last novel being *The Stonehenge Gate* (2005). His contributions to science fiction were recognized with just about every major award in the field. Among his honors were the 1976 Grand Master Award for lifetime achievement from the Science Fiction Writers of America, the 1994 World Fantasy Award for lifetime achievement from the World Fantasy Convention, the 1998 Bram Stoker Award for superior achievement from the Horror Writers Association, the 2001 Hugo and Nebula Awards for his novella *The Ultimate Earth,* and the 2001 John W. Campbell Memorial Award for *Transforming Earth.* A former president of the Science Fiction Writers of America, he also won the prestigious Hugo for his autobiography, *Wonder's Child: My Life in Science Fiction* (1985).

OBITUARIES AND OTHER SOURCES:

BOOKS

Williamson, Jack, *Wonder's Child: My Life in Science Fiction,* Bluejay (New York, NY), 1985.

PERIODICALS

Chicago Tribune, November 15, 2006, Section 2, p. 13.
Los Angeles Times, November 14, 2006, p. B10.
New York Times, November 14, 2006, p. C21.
Washington Post, November 17, 2006, p. B7.

*   *   *

WILLIS, Ellen Jane 1941-2006

OBITUARY NOTICE— See index for *CA* sketch: Born December 14, 1941, in New York, NY; died of lung cancer, November 9, 2006, in New York, NY. Critic, editor, and author. A former critic for the *New Yorker,*

Willis was a noted leftist intellectual who also wrote for *Rolling Stone, Village Voice,* and *Ms.* An alumna of Barnard College, where she graduated in 1962, she attended graduate school at the University of California at Berkeley for a year. During the turbulent 1960s, she cofounded the feminist Redstockings group, which regularly campaigned for abortion laws. Later, in the 1980s, she also was a founder of the street theater protest group called the No More Nice Girls, which similarly advocated abortion rights. During her early career, Willis was a freelance writer and briefly worked for *Cheetah* magazine. The *New Yorker* hired her in 1967 to be its pop music critic. She remained there until 1975, simultaneously working as an associate editor for *Us* in 1969 and as a contributing editor to *Ms.* in the early 1970s. From 1976 to 1978 she was a contributing editor to *Rolling Stone,* and then she joined the *Village Voice* writing staff. At the time of her death, she was a journalism professor at New York University, where she had founded the cultural reporting and criticism program in 1995. Willis not only wrote about music but was also a social critic with strong leftist leanings. Despite such political tendencies, she sometimes came out against groups such as feminists and antiwar demonstrators. For example, she was skeptical of the feminist goal of banning pornography, and she interpreted the anti-Israel position some leftists took as a form of anti-Semitism. Willis more recently came out in favor of the war against Iraq, having a distaste for the authoritarian rule of Saddam Hussein. In general, Willis viewed herself as a resister to authority; as a journalism teacher, she encouraged her students to think critically of both leftist and rightist biases, neither one of which were to be fully trusted at face value. Willis published her essays in several collections over the years, including *Beginning to See the Light: Pieces of a Decade* (1981), *No More Nice Girls: Countercultural Essays* (1992), and *Don't Think, Smile!: Notes on a Decade of Denial* (1999).

OBITUARIES AND OTHER SOURCES:

PERIODICALS

Chicago Tribune, November 12, 2006, Section 4, p. 10.
Los Angeles Times, November 15, 2006, p. B8.
New York Times, November 10, 2006, p. A29.
Washington Post, November 17, 2006, p. B7.

WINGET, Larry

PERSONAL: Married; wife's name Rose Mary; children: Tyler, Patrick.

ADDRESSES: Home—Paradise Valley, AZ. *Agent*—Jay Mandel, William Morris Agency, 1325 Avenue of the Americas, New York, NY 10019.

CAREER: Writer. Venture Industries, founder and former associate; Arts and Entertainment (cable television network), host of the series *Big Spender.*

WRITINGS:

Money Stuff: How to Increase Prosperity, Attract Riches, Experience Abundance, and Have More Money, Win Publications (Tulsa, OK), 1993.
Stuff That Works Every Single Day, Win Publications (Tulsa, OK), 1994.
(With Pamela S. Carter) *The Enlightened Business Directory: Redesigning the Language of Business,* Win Publications (Tulsa, OK), 1995.
Just Do This Stuff: The Practical Application of Success; Steps and Guidelines on How to Really Do It, Win Publications (Tulsa, OK), 1995.
(Compiler) *Profound Stuff,* Win Publications (Tulsa, OK), 1995.
Only the Best on Customer Service, Win Publications (Tulsa, OK), 1996.
Only the Best on Leadership, Win Publications (Tulsa, OK), 1996.
Shut Up, Stop Whining, and Get a Life: A Kick-Butt Approach to a Better Life, Wiley (Hoboken, NJ), 2004.
It's Called Work for a Reason! Your Success Is Your Own Damn Fault, Gotham Books (New York, NY), 2007.

BIOGRAPHICAL AND CRITICAL SOURCES:

PERIODICALS

Incentive, September, 2005, Suzie Amer, review of *Shut Up, Stop Whining, and Get a Life: A Kick-Butt Approach to a Better Life,* p. 114.

Publishers Weekly, October 16, 2006, review of *It's Called Work for a Reason! Your Success Is Your Own Damn Fault,* p. 46.

ONLINE

Larry Winget Home Page, http://www.larrywinget.com (February 4, 2007).*

*　　*　　*

WISHART, Adam 1968-

PERSONAL: Born 1968. *Education:* University of Manchester, B.A. (first-class honors), 1990.

ADDRESSES: *Home*—London, England. *E-mail*—adam@adamwishart.info.

CAREER: Writer. Director of films for BBC science department.

AWARDS, HONORS: Best Feature, Royal Television Society, 1998, for "Back to the Floor."

WRITINGS:

NONFICTION

(With Regula Bochsler) *Leaving Reality Behind: The Battle for the Soul of the Internet,* Fourth Estate (London, England), 2002, published as *Leaving Reality Behind: Etoy vs. eToys.com & Other Battles to Control Cyberspace,* Ecco (New York, NY), 2003.

One in Three: A Son's Journey into the History and Science of Cancer, Grove Press (New York, NY), 2006.

Contributor to periodicals, including the *Guardian, Times Literary Supplement,* and the London *Times.*

SIDELIGHTS: In *Leaving Reality Behind: The Battle for the Soul of the Internet,* British writer and director Adam Wishart tells the story of a conflict between a radical group of artists and a rising star of the new Internet economy. The tale, as Wishart and his coauthor Regula Bochsler tell it, is (on the surface) a classic David-and-Goliath story, pitting a retail giant against a group of independent artists. The online store eToys.com wanted to sell toys online; the artists wanted to spoof capitalist culture through "an online gallery and virtual workspace," according to a *Publishers Weekly* reviewer, taking advantage of the freedom of the new medium of the Internet. The name the artists chose for their satirical Web site was etoy.com. "In September 1999," explained Michael Stern in *American Lawyer,* "online toy retailer eToys.com sued the Swiss art collective etoy Corporation over the group's use of the etoy.com domain name, alleging trademark infringement, unfair competition, and interference with prospective economic advantage." "The authors track the story of both sites as they explore the seamy world of domain-name control," wrote a *Kirkus Reviews* contributor, and "deliver an astute history of search engines."

Although the public perceived the conflict between eToys.com and etoy.com as a good-versus-evil story, Wishart and Bochsler point out that the real story is much more complicated. "Wishart and Bochsler," wrote the *Publishers Weekly* contributor, "reveal how the dot-com boom warped the perceptions of artist and corporate executive alike." The artists of etoy.com were willing to use pornography, drug abuse, and violence on their Web site to express their critique of middle-class values. The internet toy retailer, on the other hand, was anxious to protect its family-friendly reputation, fearing that children and their parents might mistake the artists' site for its own. The struggle over the domain identity, however, ruined both Web identities. Today, Stern concluded, "eToys is long gone. It disappeared after the bubble burst in the spring of 2000. The company lost 189 million dollars on revenues of 151 million dollars in 1999; the coup de grace was a poor Christmas quarter in 2000." For its part, the etoy.com group "sold out"—members of the group could not resist the chance to win easy money by prolonging the lawsuit in hopes of a huge settlement. Over time, "the etoy website (www.etoy.com) [sank] into obscurity," Tristan Quinn wrote in the *New Statesman.*

The title of Wishart's second book, *One in Three: A Son's Journey into the History and Science of Cancer,* is derived from statistics: over thirty percent of people alive today "will be diagnosed with cancer at some point in their lives," explained *Guardian* contributor P.D. Smith. One of them was the author's own father, whose prostate cancer metastasized throughout his body, killing him within a year of his initial diagnosis. "Wishart seamlessly weaves together the personal, the historical and the scientific threads of his narrative to tell the story of cancer from the perspective of his father's illness," Smith continued. "The result is both moving and informative, a book that tries to answer the questions Wishart's father asked when he was first diagnosed." "Although one in three of us will develop cancer," declared a reviewer for the *Telegraph*, "Wishart explains how science is gradually developing a deeper understanding of its causes, and thus offers hope for the future. The complex interaction of chemicals, genetics, ageing and diet is slowly making sense, and this book helps elucidate that scientific story." The book, concluded a *Kirkus Reviews* contributor, is "a loving portrait of one man and an accessible account of what cancer is, where research and treatment are now and how they got there."

BIOGRAPHICAL AND CRITICAL SOURCES:

BOOKS

Wishart, Adam, *One in Three: A Son's Journey into the History and Science of Cancer*, Grove Press (New York, NY), 2006.

PERIODICALS

American Lawyer, March, 2003, Michael Stern, review of *Leaving Reality Behind: Etoy vs. eToys.com & Other Battles to Control Cyberspace*, p. 57.
Booklist, January 1, 2003, Mary Whaley, review of *Leaving Reality Behind*, p. 819.
Guardian, September 9, 2006, P.D. Smith, "The Hidden Assassin."
Kirkus Reviews, December 1, 2002, review of *Leaving Reality Behind*, p. 1759; November 15, 2006, review of *One in Three*, p. 1169.
New Statesman, July 1, 2002, Tristan Quinn, "Toy Story," p. 53.
Publishers Weekly, January 13, 2003, review of *Leaving Reality Behind*, p. 49; October 16, 2006, review of *One in Three*, p. 42.

Sunday Times, June 25, 2006, John Cornwell, "A Voyage through the Topic of Cancer."
Telegraph, July 9, 2006, "A History of Cancer and a Touching Personal Memoir."*

*   *   *

WOLF, Diane L.
(Diane Lauren Wolf)

PERSONAL: Education: Cornell University, Ph.D.

ADDRESSES: Office—Department of Sociology, University of California, 1282 Social Sciences and Humanities, 1 Shields Ave., Davis, CA 95616. *E-mail*—dlwolf@ucdavis.edu.

CAREER: University of California, Davis, professor of sociology.

WRITINGS:

(Under name Diane Lauren Wolf) *Factory Daughters: Gender, Household Dynamics, and Rural Industrialization in Java*, University of California Press (Berkeley, CA), 1992.
(Editor and contributor) *Feminist Dilemmas in Fieldwork*, Westview Press (Boulder, CO), 1996.
(Editor, with Judith M. Gerson) *Sociology Confronts the Holocaust: Memories and Identities in Jewish Diasporas*, Duke University Press (Durham, NC), 2007.
Beyond Anne Frank: Hidden Children and Postwar Families in Holland, University of California Press (Berkeley, CA), 2007.

Contributor to periodicals, including *Sociological Perspectives* and *Signs*.

BIOGRAPHICAL AND CRITICAL SOURCES:

PERIODICALS

Gender, Place, and Culture: Journal of Feminist Geography, July, 1997, Pamela Moss, review of *Feminist Dilemmas in Fieldwork*.

Publishers Weekly, October 16, 2006, review of *Beyond Anne Frank: Hidden Children and Postwar Families in Holland,* p. 43.

*   *   *

WOLF, Diane Lauren
   See WOLF, Diane L.

*   *   *

WOLF, Markus 1923-2006

OBITUARY NOTICE— See index for *CA* sketch: Born January 19, 1923, in Hechingen, Germany; died November 9, 2006, in Berlin, Germany. Spy, government official, and author. Wolf was the former head of East Germany's spy agency, die Hauptverwaltung Aufklärung (H.V.A.), part of the Ministry for State Security, or Stasi. Born to a Jewish family, he was the son of a physician who was a member of the Communist Party. Thus, when the Nazis rose to power in 1933, his family immigrated to Moscow. Here, Wolf attended the Soviet Comintern, where he was trained in propaganda and weapons use and nurtured to become a radio broadcaster for the Communist Party. While covering the Nuremburg trials after World War II, Wolf decided to join the Stasi, and by 1956 he was put in charge of the H.V.A. He proved to be a highly effective espionage chief for the East Germans during the Cold War. His operatives worked their way deep inside West German government offices, obtaining classified documents on a regular basis. One of Wolf's most successful spies, Günter Guillaume, was credited with bringing down the Willy Brandt government. Wolf would later joke that the original plan had only been to discredit one of West Germany's labor leaders, but Guillaume far exceeded the goal. One of his most effective tools, Wolf would come to explain, was the use of sex to obtain information. He would have operatives romance key officials and office personnel who had access to information, or he would lure Western officials to brothels or even arrange potential spouses for them in order to get their cooperation. When Mikhail Gorbechev took power in the Soviet Union and ushered in the era of glasnost and perestroika, Wolf saw changes coming and resigned his post in 1986. He had come out in support of the new Soviet policies of tolerance and freedom, but eventu-

ally realized it was time to leave. Before East and West Germany unified in 1990, he immigrated to Russia and then to Austria. He tried to find amnesty through the U.S. government, but because he refused to cooperate with the C.I.A. he was denied a visa. In his later years, he turned increasingly to writing. He released a novel, *Die Troika,* in 1989, as well as several nonfiction works. His autobiography, *The Man without a Face* (1997), got its title from the fact that Wolf remained little photographed throughout his years with the Stasi.

OBITUARIES AND OTHER SOURCES:

BOOKS

Wolf, Markus, *The Man without a Face,* Times Books (New York, NY), 1997.

PERIODICALS

Chicago Tribune, November 10, 2006, Section 3, p. 8.
Los Angeles Times, November 10, 2006, p. B9.
New York Times, November 10, 2006, p. A28.
Times (London, England), November 10, 2006, p. 69.
Washington Post, November 10, 2006, p. B6.

*   *   *

WYATT, David K. 1937-2006
   (David Kent Wyatt)

OBITUARY NOTICE— See index for *CA* sketch: Born September 21, 1937, in Fitchburg, MA; died of emphysema and congestive heart failure, November 14, 2006, in Ithaca, NY. Historian, educator, and author. A Cornell University professor, Wyatt was a renowned authority on the history and culture of Thailand. His educational background included a B.A. from Harvard in 1959, an M.A. from Boston University in 1960, and a Ph.D. from Cornell University in 1966. He lectured in history at the School of Oriental and African Studies at the University of London for two years, then taught briefly at the University of Michigan. In 1969, Wyatt joined the Cornell University faculty as an associate professor, and he made full professor in 1975. The director of the university's Southeast Asia program from 1976 to 1979, he chaired the department of history from 1983 to 1987, and again from 1988 to 1989. Wyatt was named John Stambaugh Professor of Southeast Asian History in 1984. The author of *Thailand: A Short History* (1984), which became a standard in history classes, Wyatt revised the work substantially in 2003 and was widely praised for making the nation and its people understandable to the general reader. Among his other publications are *The Politics of Reform in Thailand: Education in the Reign of King Chulalongkorn* (1969), *The Crystal Sands: The Chronicles of Nagara Sri Dharmaraja* (1975), and *Studies in Thai History: Collected Articles* (1994).

OBITUARIES AND OTHER SOURCES:

PERIODICALS

Los Angeles Times, November 17, 2006, p. B9.
New York Times, November 17, 2006, p. A29.

*   *   *

WYATT, David Kent
    See WYATT, David K.

Y-Z

YOO, David 1974-

PERSONAL: Born 1974, in Manchester, CT. *Ethnicity:* "Asian American." *Education:* Skidmore College, B.A., 1996; University of Colorado-Boulder, M.A., 1998. *Hobbies and other interests:* "Soccer, tennis, Crock-Pot cooking, napping in the afternoon and waking up extremely angry, and backgammon."

ADDRESSES: Home—MA. *Agent*—Steve Malk, Writer's House, 3368 Governor Dr., #224F, San Diego, CA 92122; smalkwritershouse.com. *E-mail*—contact@daveyoo.com.

CAREER: Writer.

AWARDS, HONORS: Books for the Teen Age selection, New York Public Library, 2006, for *Girls for Breakfast.*

WRITINGS:

Girls for Breakfast (novel), Delacorte (New York, NY), 2005.
Guys Write for Guys Read, edited by Jon Scieszka, Viking (New York, NY) 2005.

Contributor to books, including *Rush Hour: Face: A Journal of Contemporary Voices,* edited by Michael Cart, Delacorte (New York, NY), 2005.

SIDELIGHTS: David Yoo is the author of the coming-of-age novel *Girls for Breakfast.* The work concerns Nick Park, a frustrated Korean-American high school student in suburban Connecticut. While his classmates rehearse for graduation, Nick looks back at his childhood and adolescence, hoping to discover what led to his disastrous experience at senior prom. "Some of Nick's predicaments are amusing," noted a critic in *Kirkus Reviews,* such as Nick's attempt to gain friends by offering martial arts lessons despite his absolute lack of knowledge and training. Recalling how friends would mock his father's heavy accent and how girls would ignore him, Nick mistakenly concludes that his problems are tied to his ethnicity, rather than to his insecurities. Through his recollections, "readers get to know a confused and lonely young man who is trying to know himself by any means necessary," remarked Jessi Platt in the *School Library Journal.*

"I suppose there are any number of ways to write," Yoo observed on the Random House Web site, "but in my case I simply can't do it unless I have total isolation. So much so that on the rare occasion when I do venture outside, my voice sounds funny to me, and I walk weird, as if I'm fourteen again and paranoid that everyone's watching me. Actually, this hermit-lifestyle has helped me write about teens, because in regressing I get to re-experience how I used to function back then."

BIOGRAPHICAL AND CRITICAL SOURCES:

PERIODICALS

Horn Book, May-June, 2005, Lauren Adams, review of *Rush Hour: Face: A Journal of Contemporary Voices,* p. 321.

Kirkus Reviews, May 1, 2005, review of *Girls for Breakfast,* p. 549.

School Library Journal, May, 2005, Jessi Platt, review of *Girls for Breakfast,* p. 142.

ONLINE

David Yoo's Home Page, http://www.daveyoo.com/html/index.html (January 15, 2007).

Random House Web site, http://www.randomhouse.com/ (January 15, 2007), "Author Spotlight: David Yoo."

*   *   *

YOUNGSON, R.M. 1926-
(Robert M. Youngson, Robert Murdoch Youngson)

PERSONAL: Born November 13, 1926, in Falkirk, Scotland; son of James Youngson (a Presbyterian minister); children: Carol, Robin, France, Annabel, Neil. *Education:* University of Aberdeen, M.B., Ch.B.; Royal College of Surgeons, D.T.M.&H. (Diploma in Tropical Medicine and Hygiene). *Politics:* Conservative. *Religion:* "Rationalist." *Hobbies and other interests:* Music, playing piano, writing poetry.

ADDRESSES: Home—Dorset, England. *E-mail*—robert_youngson26@btinternet.com.

CAREER: British Army, career officer as ophthalmologist, 1951-86, retiring as colonel; writer, 1986—.

MEMBER: Royal Society of Medicine (fellow), Royal College of Ophthalmologists (fellow), Order of St. John of Jerusalem (officer).

AWARDS, HONORS: Montefiore Prize for Surgery.

WRITINGS:

Everything You Need to Know about Contact Lenses, Sheldon (London, England), 1984.

Everything You Need to Know about Your Eyes, Sheldon (London, England), 1985.

Everything You Need to Know about Shingles, Sheldon (London, England), 1986.

How to Cope with Tinnitus and Hearing Loss, Sheldon (London, England), 1986.

Learning to Live with Diabetes, Corgi (London, England), 1987.

Stroke! A Self-Help Manual for Stroke Sufferers and Their Relatives, David & Charles (Newton Abbot, England), 1987.

The Healthy Executive, Telegraph (London, England), 1988.

Grief: Rebuilding Your Life after Bereavement, David & Charles (Newton Abbot, England), 1989.

Collins Dictionary of Medicine, HarperCollins (Glasgow, Scotland), 1992, 3rd edition, 2004, published as *Medicine,* 1999.

(Coauthor) *The Surgery Book,* St. Martin's Press (New York, NY), 1993.

(Coauthor) *Collins Gem First Aid,* HarperCollins (London, England), 1993, abridged edition published as *Collins First Aid,* 1994.

The Antioxident Health Plan, Thorsons (London, England), 1994.

The Guinness Encyclopedia of Science, Guinness Publishing (Enfield, England), 1994.

The Guinness Encyclopedia of the Human Being, Guinness Publishing (Enfield, England), 1994.

Prescription Drugs, HarperCollins (Glasgow, Scotland), 1994.

Women's Health, HarperCollins (Glasgow, Scotland, 1994.

(Coauthor) *Collins Gem Holiday Health,* HarperCollins (Glasgow, Scotland), 1995.

Living with Asthma, Sheldon (London, England), 1995, new edition, 2002.

Coping Successfully with Hay Fever, Sheldon (London, England), 1995.

Coping with Eczema, Sheldon (London, England), 1995.

The Royal Society of Medicine Encyclopedia of Family Health: The Complete Medical Reference Library in One Volume Bloomsbury (London, England), 1995, revised edition published as *The Royal Society of Medicine Health Encyclopedia: The Complete Medical Reference Library in One A-Z Volume,* 2001.

The Royal Society of Medicine Dictionary of Symptoms: A Complete A-Z of Thousands of Symptoms and Signs, Bloomsbury (London, England), 1996.

The Royal Society of Medicine Encyclopedia of Children's Health, Bloomsbury (London, England), 1996, published as *The Royal Society of Medicine Encyclopedia of Child Health,* 1997.

(With Ian Schott) *Medical Blunders,* New York University Press (New York, NY), 1996.

Royal Society of Medicine Guide to Health in Later Life: Health and Vitality for Everyone in Their Later Years, Bloomsbury (London, England), 1997.

(Compiler) *Medical Curiosities: A Miscellany of Medical Oddities, Horrors, and Humours,* Carroll & Graf (New York, NY), 1997, published as *Medical Curiosities and Mistakes: A Miscellany of Medical Oddities, Horrors, and Humours,* Parragon (Bath, England), 1999.

(Coauthor) *First Aid,* HarperCollins (Glasgow, Scotland), 1997.

Scientific Blunders: A Brief History of How Wrong Scientists Can Sometimes Be, Carroll & Graf (New York, NY), 1998.

Coping with Rheumatism and Arthritis, Sheldon (London, England), 1998.

The Madness of Prince Hamlet and Other Extraordinary States of Mind, Carroll & Graf (New York, NY), 1999.

(With David B. Jacoby) *Encyclopedia of Family Health,* 3rd edition, Marshall Cavendish (Tarrytown, NY), 2004.

Author of the free Internet medical encyclopedia *NHS Direct Medical Encyclopedia;* other writings include *Coping with Rheumatism and Arthritis,* Sheldon (London, England); *Cellular Biology and Genetics,* Facts on File; *Antioxident Vitamins for Health,* Sheldon (London, England); and *Collins Dictionary of Human Biology.* Also author of nearly twenty unpublished novels.

Youngson's books have been translated into French, German, Spanish, Portuguese, Italian, Dutch, Danish, Hungarian, Polish, Bulgarian, Romanian, Russian, Indonesian, Chinese, Japanese, Czech, and Greek.

SIDELIGHTS: R.M. Youngson told *CA:* "I am a doctor who, after a varied career as a general medical practitioner, medical administrator, lecturer, and clinical consultant, retired from clinical practice to become a full-time writer. I am now an established author with many published books to my credit, including the *NHS Direct Medical Encyclopedia,* an Internet medical encyclopedia written in simple language and accessible to the public free of charge from the NHS Direct Home Page. It receives thousands of hits every month.

"My work as an army doctor took me to many parts of the world, and about half my medical career was spent abroad, especially in Singapore, Malaysia, and Hong Kong. I also worked in Germany, Nepal, Jerusalem, and Cyprus. When I retired from clinical work I was a consultant ophthalmic surgeon and head of army ophthalmology.

"Having made my contribution to popular medicine, science, and technology, I have now moved on to more creative and artistic levels as a writer. My fiction titles represent a continuous learning experience, and I recognize that some of the earlier novels must be regarded as apprentice work. I am now devoting my time to the revision and improvement of the more recent titles."

*   *   *

YOUNGSON, Robert M.
See YOUNGSON, R.M.

*   *   *

YOUNGSON, Robert Murdoch
See YOUNGSON, R.M.

*   *   *

YU, Charles 1976-

PERSONAL: Born 1976. *Education:* Graduated from University of California at Berkeley and Columbia Law School.

ADDRESSES: Home—Los Angeles, CA. *Agent*—Imprint Agency, 5 W. 101st St., Ste. 8B, New York, NY 10025.

CAREER: Attorney and writer. Practices law in Los Angeles, CA.

AWARDS, HONORS: Sherwood Anderson Fiction Award, 2004, for "Class Three Superhero."

WRITINGS:

Third Class Superhero, Harcourt (Orlando, FL), 2006.

Contributor to *The Robert Olen Butler Prize Stories, 2004,* del sol Press, 2005. Contributor to periodicals, including *Oxford Magazine, Gettysburg Review, Harvard Review, Mid-American Review, Mississippi Review,* and *Alaska Quarterly Review.*

SIDELIGHTS: Writer and attorney Charles Yu published *Third Class Superhero,* his debut story collection, in 2006. According to *Library Journal* contributor David A. Berona, the author "uses an inventive style to probe fundamental questions about modern life from a variety of distinct perspectives." In the title story, a hapless superhero named Moisture Man makes a deal with evildoers after his fellow superheroes deny his application for higher status. In "My Last Days as Me," the star of the hit television series "Me and My Mother" rejects his new on-screen mom for being too clingy. Set one million years in the future, "Florence" posits a universe in which each human lives alone on his own planet and efforts at communicating with other people seem futile. A few of Yu's tales experiment with form; "Problems for Self-Study," for example, unfolds as a series of multiple-choice questions.

Reviewers offered generous praise for the collection. A *Publishers Weekly* contributor called *Third Class Superhero* "an imaginative excursion into the burrow Kafka built," and Robert Ito, writing in *Los Angeles Magazine,* similarly noted that the work "reminds one of Kafka, if Kafka had had a geekish passion for science fiction and TV." In his stories, Yu "uses language to suggest what language cannot express, as he deals with themes such as the nature of distance, the essence of time and the illusion of self," observed a critic in *Kirkus Reviews.*

BIOGRAPHICAL AND CRITICAL SOURCES:

PERIODICALS

Kirkus Reviews, June 15, 2006, review of *Third Class Superhero,* p. 601.
Library Journal, September 1, 2006, David A. Berona, review of *Third Class Superhero,* p. 140.
Los Angeles Magazine, October, 2006, Robert Ito, review of *Third Class Superhero,* p. 190.
New York Times, December 31, 2006, Todd Pruzan, "Fiction Chronicle," review of *Third Class Superhero.*
Publishers Weekly, June 12, 2006, review of *Third Class Superhero,* p. 27.

*   *   *

ZEMACH, Eddy M. 1935-

PERSONAL: Born 1935, in Jerusalem, Palestine (now Israel). *Education:* Yale University, Ph.D., 1965.

ADDRESSES: Office—c/o Institute of Languages, Literature, and Art, Hebrew University of Jerusalem, Mount Scopus, Jerusalem 91905, Israel. *E-mail*—emzem@huji.ac.il.

CAREER: Hebrew University of Jerusalem, Jerusalem, Israel, former professor of philosophy, now professor emeritus.

WRITINGS:

Estetikah analitit (nonfiction), Daga Books (Tel-Aviv, Israel), 1970.
(With Tovah Rozen-Moked) *Yetsirah mehukmah: iyun be-shire Shemu'el ha-Nagid,* Keter (Jerusalem, Israel), 1983.
(With Menahem Brinker and Meir Pail) *Iyunim ba-tarbut ha-politit be-Yiśreal,* ha-Bamah le-vikoret ha-hevrah yeha-tarbut be-Yisra'el le-zikhro shel Tsevikah Doitsh. Mifgash (Jerusalem, Israel), 1985.

Keri'ah ah tamah: be-sifrut Ivrit bat ha-me'ah ha-esrim, Mosad Byalik (Jerusalem, Israel), 1990.

The Reality of Meaning and the Meaning of "Reality," University Press of New England (Hanover, NH), 1992.

Types: Essays in Metaphysics, E.J. Brill (New York, NY), 1992.

Sipurim lo neimim, ha-Kibuts ha-meuchad (Tel-Aviv, Israel), 1993.

Real Beauty, Pennsylvania State University Press (University Park, PA), 1997.

Kolot zarim: sipurim, ha-Kibuts ha-meuchad (Tel-Aviv, Israel), 2000.

Al ha-guf, al ha-ruah, al mah she-yesh ye-al mah she-ra'ui li-heyot, Hostaet sefarim (Jerusalem, Israel), 2001.

BIOGRAPHICAL AND CRITICAL SOURCES:

PERIODICALS

Philosophical Quarterly, July, 1999, Robert Stecker, review of *Real Beauty.**

*   *   *

ZEVIN, Gabrielle 1977-

PERSONAL: Born October 24, 1977, in New York, NY; partner of Hans Canosa (a director). *Education:* Harvard University, B.A., 2000.

ADDRESSES: Home and office—New York, NY.

CAREER: Author and screenwriter.

WRITINGS:

NOVELS

Margarettown (for adults), Miramax Books (New York, NY), 2005.

Elsewhere (for young adults), Farrar, Straus & Giroux (New York, NY), 2005.

Memories of a Teenage Amnesiac, Farrar, Straus & Giroux (New York, NY), 2007.

SCREENPLAYS

(And producer and designer) *Alma Mater,* produced, 2002.

Conversations with Other Women (screenplay), produced 2005.

After Dark, produced 2008.

SIDELIGHTS: A screenwriter who has seen several of her films produced, Gabrielle Zevin became a published novelist in 2005 with the publication of *Elsewhere.* In fact, Zevin's young-adult novel started out as a potential play or screenplay, but it morphed into prose fiction as writing progressed. As *Elsewhere* opens, fifteen-year-old Lizzie is tragically killed in a car accident while on her way to meet a friend at the mall. The recently deceased teen now finds herself in the afterlife, "Elsewhere," living with her grandmother. In this place, Lizzie can look back on the world of the living from a special Observation Deck. As *Elsewhere* unfolds, Lizzie reflects on her life, particularly on those things she did not get to experience, and in her afterlife existence she eventually manages to come to terms with those lost opportunities. Charles de Lint, reviewing the novel in the *Magazine of Fantasy and Science Fiction,* commented that Zevin's fiction debut "makes for a most absorbing and fascinating read" because the author "peoples her book with such an interesting cast of characters." A *Publishers Weekly* critic also enjoyed the novel, predicting that "even readers who have strong views on what happens after death may find themselves intrigued by the fascinating world of *Elsewhere.*

In addition to *Elsewhere,* Zevin also wrote the adult novel *Margarettown,* "an original look at love and how you never really know your beloved," according to *Library Journal* contributor Robin Nesbitt. Told from the point of view of a professor identified only as N., the work begins as Zevin's narrator falls in love with Maggie, a student who takes him to visit her family in Margarettown. The story takes a surreal turn, however, when N. discovers that only women named Margaret, or some variant, live within the town's limits, and

Maggie eventually confides that she lives under a curse. The entire tale turns out to be a long letter from N. to his daughter, Jane, describing the bizarre twists in his courtship and marriage to Margaret as well as their subsequent separation.

Discussing her career as a writer, Zevin once commented: "I've never been the type of person who sat around waiting for ideas to come to her or to 'be inspired' or what have you. I think, as a writer, that sort of wait-and-see mentality leaves too much to chance and can end up being pretty destructive. And writing is 'wait-and-see' enough as it is. So, I've always sat around and thought as hard as I could and just let my brain free-associate and wander until I come up with something that strikes my fancy."

BIOGRAPHICAL AND CRITICAL SOURCES:

PERIODICALS

Booklist, April 1, 2005, Joanne Wilkinson, review of *Margarettown,* p. 1346; August, 2005, Jennifer Mattson, "A Death Well Lived," p. 2017; April 15, 2006, Traci Todd, review of *Elsewhere,* p. 70.

Bookseller, August 12, 2005, Becky Stradwick, review of *Elsewhere,* p. 28.

Bookwatch, January, 2006, review of *Elsewhere.*

Bulletin of the Center for Children's Books, September, 2005, Deborah Stevenson, review of *Elsewhere,* p. 58.

Horn Book, September-October, 2005, Kitty Flynn, review of *Elsewhere,* p. 591; January-February, 2006, review of *Elsewhere,* p. 12.

Kirkus Reviews, August 15, 2005, review of *Elsewhere,* p. 925.

Kliatt, May, 2006, Janet Julian, review of *Elsewhere,* p. 43.

Library Journal, May 1, 2005, Robin Nesbitt, review of *Margarettown,* p. 78; September, 2005, Janis Flint-Ferguson, review of *Elsewhere,* p. 16.

Magazine of Fantasy and Science Fiction, April, 2006, Charles de Lint, review of *Elsewhere,* p. 32.

Publishers Weekly, March 28, 2005, review of *Margarettown,* p. 55; August 29, 2005, review of *Elsewhere,* p. 57.

School Library Journal, October, 2005, Sharon Grover, review of *Elsewhere,* p. 180.

Times Educational Supplement, December 9, 2005, Geraldine Brennan, review of *Elsewhere,* p. 18.

Voice of Youth Advocates, April, 2006, Pam Spencer Holley, review of *Elsewhere,* p. 31.

ONLINE

Bloomsbury Web site, http://bloomsbury.com/ (February 4, 2007), "Gabrielle Zevin."

Farrar, Straus Giroux Web site, http://www.fsgkidsbooks.com/ (February 4, 2007), "Gabrielle Zevin."

TeenReads.com, http://www.teenreads.com/ (September 20, 2006), interview with Zevin.*

*   *   *

ZNAMENSKI, Andrei A. 1960-

PERSONAL: Born 1960.

CAREER: Alabama State University, Montgomery, began as assistant professor, became associate professor of history. Library of Congress, resident scholar at John W. Kluge Center.

WRITINGS:

Shamanism and Christianity: Native Encounters with Russian Orthodox Missions in Siberia and Alaska, 1820-1917, Greenwood Press (Westport, CT), 1999.

Shamanism in Siberia: Russian Records of Indigenous Spirituality, Kluwer Academic Publishers (Boston, MA), 2003.

(Translator and author of introduction) *Through Orthodox Eyes: Russian Missionary Narratives of Travels to the Denaína and Ahtna, 1850s-1930s,* University of Alaska Press (Fairbanks, AK), 2003.

(Editor) *Shamanism: Critical Concepts in Sociology,* three volumes, Routledge (New York, NY), 2004.

The Beauty of the Primitive: Shamanism and Western Imagination, Oxford University Press (New York, NY), 2007.

BIOGRAPHICAL AND CRITICAL SOURCES:

BOOKS

.

PERIODICALS

American Historical Review, December, 2001, Marjorie Mandelstam Balzer, review of *Shamanism and Christianity: Native Encounters with Russian Orthodox Missions in Siberia and Alaska, 1820-1917,* p. 1759.

Pacific Northwest Quarterly, fall, 2001, Gunther Barth, review of *Shamanism and Christianity,* p. 205.

Reference & Research Book News, August, 2003, review of *Through Orthodox Eyes: Russian Missionary Narratives of Travels to the Denaína and Ahtna, 1850s-1930s,* p. 57

Russian Review, April, 2001, Eva-Maria Stolberg, review of *Shamanism and Christianity,* p. 287.

Slavic Review, winter, 2000, John J. Stephan, review of *Shamanism and Christianity,* p. 907.

ONLINE

Shaman's Drum Journal Online, http://shamansdrum. org/ (February 4, 2007), Timothy White, review of *Shamanism in Siberia: Russian Records of Indigenous Spirituality.**

*   *   *

ZORRO VIEJO
   See LOPEZ DZUR, Carlos